D0138221

ADMINISTRATIVE OFFICE MANAGEMENT

Seventh Edition

ADMINISTRATIVE OFFICE MANAGEMENT
An Introduction

Zane K. Quible

Upper Saddle River, New Jersey 07458

Library of Congress Cataloging-in-Publication Data

Quible, Zane K.,
    Administrative office management : an introduction / Zane K. Quible—7th ed.
        p.   cm.
    Includes index.
    ISBN 0–13–085957–5
    1. Office management.   I. Title.
HF5547.Q49   2001
651.3—dc21
                                                                        00–039136

Acquisitions Editor: Elizabeth Sugg
Managing Editor: Mary Carnis
Director of Production and Manufacturing: Bruce Johnson
Editorial Assistant: Delia Uherec
Production Liaison: Eileen O'Sullivan
Editorial and Production Services: WordCrafters Editorial Services, Inc.
Manufacturing Buyer: Ed O'Dougherty
Marketing Manager: Shannon Simonsen
Senior Design Coordinator: Miguel Ortiz
Cover Director: Jayne Conte
Cover Designer: Bruce Kenselaar
Composition: Publishers' Design and Production Services, Inc.
Printer/Binder: Banta, Harrisonburg, VA

Prentice-Hall International (UK), Limited, *London*
Prentice-Hall of Australia Pty., Limited, *Sydney*
Prentice-Hall Canada, Inc., *Toronto*
Prentice-Hall Hispanoamericana, S.A., *Mexico*
Prentice-Hall of India Private Limited, *New Delhi*
Prentice-Hall of Japan, *Tokyo*
Pearson Education Asia, *Singapore*
Editora Prentice-Hall do Brasil, Ltda., *Rio de Janeiro*

Copyright © 2001 by Prentice-Hall, Inc., Upper Saddle River, New Jersey 07458.
All rights reserved. Printed in the United States of America. This publication is protected by Copyright and permission should be obtained from the publisher prior to any prohibited reproduction, storage in a retrieval system, or transmission in any form or by any means, electronic, mechanical, photocopying, recording, or likewise. For information regarding permission(s), write to: Rights and Permissions Department.

10 9 8 7 6 5 4 3 2 1
ISBN 0-13-085957-5

To Patricia and Chris

CONTENTS

Chapter 21
RECORDS MANAGEMENT AND
MICROGRAPHICS   443

Part Five   **Management of Office Functions**

Chapter 22
FORMS DESIGN AND CONTROL   475

Chapter 23
OFFICE REPROGRAPHICS AND MAIL
SERVICES   494

Chapter 24
QUALITY AND QUANTITY CONTROL   517

PREFACE

Considerable change has taken place in the administrative office management field. Technology—especially the desktop computer and the Internet—were unknown concepts when the first edition of this text was published in 1977. Today, technological advances have had a significant impact on the topics presented in the seventh edition of this text. Although no one can definitively determine the future direction of administrative office management, we can be sure of one thing: *It will change.* The office will experience more change in the next decade than it has from 1977 until now.

Managers and executives in companies of all sizes are focusing an ever-increasing concern on "the bottom line" because it is the most effective means of assuring their survival. The administrative office management field affects how well companies perform financially. As companies maximize the efficiency with which they carry out their office operations, they will perform better financially. All managers and executives can maximize the effectiveness of their areas of responsibility by improving administrative office management.

STRUCTURE OF THE TEXT

As a field evolves, so must the materials used in the process of educating individuals about the field. Accordingly, several fundamental changes were made in the basic structure of the current edition. Perhaps the most drastic are the inclusion of a new chapter on applications software and the elimination of the chapters concerned with word processing and office automation. Some of the content of these two chapters has been incorporated into other chapters.

The configuration of the five basic text units includes chapters dealing with these topics:

> **Unit I: Principles of Administrative Office Management** includes chapters dealing with these topics: the managerial process, the organizing process, and the communication process.
>
> **Unit II: Management of the Office Environment** includes chapters dealing with office layout, office environment, and office equipment and furniture.
>
> **Unit III: Management of Office Employees** contains chapters dealing with the following topics: selecting office employees, developing office employees, supervising office employees, motivating, performance appraisal, job analysis, job evaluation, salary administration, work measurement, and productivity.

Unit IV: Management of Office Systems includes chapters pertaining to systems analysis, computer technology, telecommunications technology, applications software, and records management and micrographics.

Unit V: Management of Office Functions includes chapters on forms design and control, office reprographics and mail services, quality and quantity control, and budgetary and cost control.

Among the topics new to this edition include globalization, employee empowerment, work teams, focus groups, telecommuting, hoteling, computer vision syndrome, electroic résumé banks, Web-based employment services, job instruction training, mission and vision statements, technostress, computerized performance appraisal, 360-degree appraisal feedback, PPOs, knowledge management, palmtop computers, recordable CDs, DVDs, mirroring software, MANs, ISDN, ADSL, fax on demand, Internet fax, Internet, WWW, FTP, Usenet, Listserv, IRC, spreadsheet software, database software, scheduling software, digital stamps, and ISO 9000 certification.

Because most chapters are not dependent on either the preceding or following chapter, instructors have considerable flexibility in changing the order of coverage. Doing so will not impede learner understanding because chapter content is not interdependent.

CHAPTER FEATURES

Several features are found in each chapter, including these opening features: chapter outline, chapter aim, and chapter terms. Marginal notations are found throughout each chapter. Features found at the end of each chapter include review questions, discussion questions, projects and activities, a minicase, and a case.

The **chapter outline** lists the primary and secondary headings found in the chapter. The **chapter terms** section gives the important terms found within the chapter. Each of these terms is shown in bold type at the point of first reference in the chapter. The **chapter aim** identifies the knowledge the student should possess after studying the chapter. The **marginal notations** ask a question about the material presented.

The **review questions** at the end of each chapter provide questions that can be used to determine how well the material has been mastered. The **discussion questions** are also designed to help the learner more quickly grasp the important concepts presented in the chapter and to become more knowledgeable about the topic of the chapter. The **projects and activities** are designed to provide an enrichment and/or growth opportunity, including one activity in each chapter that involves using the Internet. The **minicase** in each chapter presents a situation, followed by two or three items requiring learner response. The **case** presents details about a situation, along with a list of items to which the learner is to respond. Each minicase and case is designed to give the learner an opportunity to apply important chapter concepts.

SUPPLEMENTARY MATERIALS

The supplementary materials that accompany this text include a CD-ROM-based instructor's manual and a Web site, accessible using the following URL: **www.prenhall.com/business_studies.**

The instructor's manual contains a variety of information, including suggested time schedules for a two-term course, a semester course, or a term course, as well as sample course objectives and suggested teaching procedures. Other content includes supplementary teaching material, identification of helpful software programs, answers to review questions and discussion questions, examination questions, solutions to the minicases and cases, and lecture notes with examination questions. Also included is an electronic test bank for instructor use in creating course examinations.

The Web site includes several types of information, including interactive examination review questions for each chapter and the text comprising the PowerPoint slides. PowerPoint slides for the instructor are also available on the CD-ROM.

DISTINCTIVE FEATURES OF THIS TEXT

Among the distinctive features of this text is presentation of technical material in an easy-to-understand manner.

1. Inclusion of up-to-the-minute material as the book went into production.
2. Focus on the learning process and student mastery of important course concepts.
3. Emphasis on and recognition of the human element, the critical link in any office.

A NOTE OF THANKS

A project of this magnitude is never successfully completed without the help, love, and understanding of the author's family. To my wife, Patricia, words are inadequate to express my appreciation for your support during this undertaking.

For their technical expertise, I also wish to thank Elizabeth Sugg, senior editor at Prentice Hall, and Laura Cleveland of WordCrafters (Sterling, VA), production editor. Also acknowledged is the assistance provided by Delia Uherec, an administrative assistant at Prentice Hall. The assistance of Su Zhang, my graduate assistant, and Linda Wheeler, my secretary, is also acknowledged and greatly appreciated.

Zane K. Quible
Stillwater, OK

ADMINISTRATIVE OFFICE MANAGEMENT

*C*hapter 1

THE MANAGERIAL PROCESS

*C*hapter *A*ims

After studying this chapter, you should be able to develop an appropriate management strategy for use by an administrative office manager, taking into consideration the evolutionary nature of the broader field of management.

*C*hapter *O*utline

Current Thrust
Administrative Office Management Function
    Objectives
A Career in Administrative Office Management
The Administrative Office Manager
    Responsibilities
    Challenges
    Qualifications
    Professionalism
    Educational Background
    Profile
    Roles and Skills
Evolution of Management Theory
    Scientific Management Movement
    Administrative Movement
    Human Relations Movement
    Modern Movement
Implications for the Administrative Office
    Manager

*C*hapter *T*erms

Administrative movement
Behavioral sciences approach
Certified Administrative Manager (C.A.M.)
Contingency management
Enterprise-wide systems
Globalization
Hawthorne Studies
Human relations movement
Information management
Knowledge management
Management functions
Modern movement
Motion study
Office technology
Operations approach
Roles
Scientific management movement
Skills
Systems approach
Theory Z
Time study
Total Quality Management (TQM)

How is today's administrative office management function different from yesterday's office management area?

*T*oday's administrative office management function permeates the entire organization more than ever. With its ever-increasing dependence on technology and technologically oriented applications and processes, today's administrative office management function is quite different from what it was as recently as ten years ago. Regardless of the position an employee holds within the modern organization, a variety of tasks that comprise his or her position are apt to be directly related to the administrative office management function.

Today's widespread use of technology and related applications and processes is making available a vast accumulation of information. In the past, a lack of information often stymied employees as they attempted to carry out their job tasks. Today, the information they may find useful likely exists; a more common stumbling block involves how to find the desired information. One response to this dilemma has been the development of software-based **enterprise-wide systems,** which allow an organization to integrate a diverse array of functions. These systems provide a powerful tool for managerial decision making and control.

CURRENT THRUST

What is the most significant new thrust in administrative office management?

The most significant thrust in administrative office management continues to be its involvement in creating, processing, storing, and retrieving organizational information. The **information management** thrust makes the administrative office management area more crucial to organizational success now than ever before. Increasingly, the systems being installed to manage organizational information are technologically oriented and result in greater levels of automation. In the future, the information management thrust will likely evolve into a new thrust for the administrative office management field. **Knowledge management** involves managing the organization's intellectual capital, human resources, and strategic relationships.

Regardless of their field of specialization, managers often consider information to be their most important managerial tool as well as a fundamental and precious organizational resource. Never before have managers had so much information available to support their decision-making efforts. Administrative office management makes a significant contribution to organizational success by providing specialized support in the management of information.

The efficiency with which an organization manages its information is affected by several factors directly related to the administrative office management functions, including office environment, office employees, office systems, and a variety of office functions. The important role the administrative office manager plays in each of the areas is thoroughly covered in this text.

ADMINISTRATIVE OFFICE MANAGEMENT FUNCTION

The nature of the background and role of administrative office management makes it the most logical of all organizational areas to have responsibility for the management of the organization's information. Increasingly, the administrative office management function and administrative office managers are being recognized and credited for their contribution to organizational success.

In what ways does administrative office management impact on office employees?

Administrative office management has a significant impact on employees throughout the organization, perhaps most significantly by enabling them to enhance their productivity. In addition to relieving employees of responsibility

Figure 1-1 Objectives of administrative office management

1. To ensure that relevant organizational activities are designed to minimize individual and unit productivity.
2. To provide effective management of the organization's information.
3. To maintain reasonable quantity and quality standards.
4. To develop effective work processes and procedures.
5. To provide a satisfactory physical and mental working environment for the organization's employees.
6. To help define duties and responsibilities of employees assigned within the administrative office management functional area.
7. To develop satisfactory lines of communication among employees within the administrative office management functional area and between these employees and employees in other areas within the organization.
8. To help employees maintain a high level of work effectiveness.
9. To enhance the effective supervision of office personnel.
10. To assure the efficient and proper use of specialized office equipment.

for certain tasks, this position helps them maximize the efficiency of other designated tasks. Also, administrative office management helps provide employees with the information they need, when they need it, and in the format they desire. This partially explains why the administrative office management function in most organizations transcends all units, functions, and departments.

The current practice of centralizing many of the office functions and services found in the modern organization has added a new perspective to the administrative office management function. In the early days of office management, only a few functions and services were centralized. Today, administrative office management has a significant impact on virtually every white-collar worker in the organization.

The increased use of **office technology** has considerably broadened the scope of administrative office management. Various elements of office technology, which contributes significantly to organizational productivity, are discussed in several chapters in this text.

In the future, office functions and services will become even more systems oriented and will use even greater amounts of technology. As a result, today's administrative office management function likely will evolve as tomorrow's information systems function.

Objectives

Administrative office management, like any other managerial area, has a common core of objectives. Some of the more common ones are illustrated in Figure 1–1.

A CAREER IN ADMINISTRATIVE OFFICE MANAGEMENT

Paralleling the rapid growth in organizational information is the increased number of career opportunities in administrative office management. Managers are readily discovering that an effective way for their organizations to become more profitable is to scrutinize closely the cost of their office operations and to develop efficient work methods and procedures. Accordingly, the number of career opportunities in administrative office management increases proportionately to the ever-growing contribution this field makes to organizational success.

Administrative office management is generally considered to be within the middle-management level of the organizational hierarchy. In some organizations, especially in larger ones, administrative office management typically is an important component of one of the functional areas, such as the administrative services area. A vice president of administrative services (or a vice president with some other similar title) is likely to be responsible for the area, and several middle-level managers are likely to report to this individual.

The structure shown in Figure 1–2 identifies the nature of a new career opportunity for middle-level managers: the vice presidency of the functional area. In the illustration, this individual's title is vice president of administrative services. Increasingly, individuals who started in a low-level office job can now become a vice president of administrative services. Such opportunities make a career in administrative office management challenging and rewarding.

Another new career opportunity found attractive by individuals who have training and/or a background in administrative office management is in facility management. Individuals who serve their organization as a facility manager are concerned with efficient utilization of facilities and control of operating costs associated with the organization's facilities. Another important responsibility involves various aspects of the work environment, especially compliance with federal, state, and local environmental regulations. Another area with which facility managers are concerned is efficient utilization of work space, especially when the workforce expands or contracts. With the increasing use of facility managers, administrative office managers have expanded career opportunities.

An ever-increasing number of organizations are creating a new position, that of chief information officer. This individual is likely a member of the senior management team and has as a primary role the management of organizational information. In many of these organizations, the individual who has

What is the nature of the new career opportunity for middle-level managers?

What is the primary role of an organization's chief information officer?

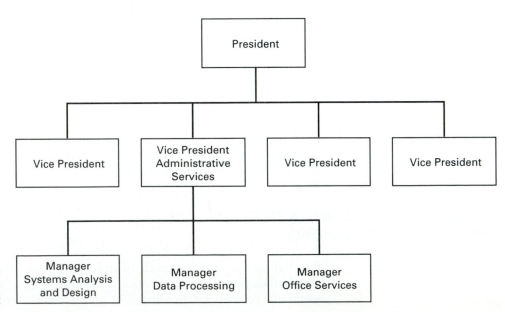

Figure 1–2 Hierarchical structure of administrative office management

served as administration office manager is in a prime position to assume the role of the organization's chief information officer.

THE ADMINISTRATIVE OFFICE MANAGER

The broad nature of the responsibilities of administrative office managers creates considerable diversity in their positions. In fact, finding two administrative office managers with identical job responsibilities is virtually impossible.

The job responsibilities of administrative office managers, as well as the titles of their jobs, are diverse. Among the job titles found are the following: administrative office manager, administrative manager, office manager, office administrator, manager of office support, and director of administrative services. Although the title administrative office manager will be used throughout the remainder of this text when referring to a person with these job responsibilities, other job titles would have been just as appropriate.

Responsibilities

Administrative office managers have several important job responsibilities within each of the five basic **management functions** of planning, organizing, staffing, directing, and controlling. Some of the more common responsibilities are presented in Figure 1–3.

Challenges

What is the nature of the challenges affecting administrative office managers?

Administrative office managers are performing an important new role as change agents. Among their important responsibilities are implementing a variety of new systems and helping employees overcome their resistance to these systems. Ability to cope with change and to help others accept change will continue to create a challenge for administrative office managers.

Another significant challenge will be brought about by a vast increase in new technology used in offices, most of which will be found in such areas as data processing, information processing, word processing, reprographics, and telecommunications. Although some of the new technology will result in more sophisticated versions of existing equipment, much of the technology that will likely be common in a few years is currently in the developmental stage.

A variety of government regulations will continue to create a challenge for administrative office managers. In many organizations, this manager is responsible for creating the data needed to complete a variety of required compliance reports as well as for maintaining the data banks in which this information is stored.

Organizational productivity is another area in which administrative office managers will continue to be challenged. Managers will be responsible for continually developing efficient systems that enable employees to maximize their productivity and for designing strategies that motivate office employees to want to be productive.

Another challenge confronting an increasing number of administrative office managers results from the discovery that some of the newly implemented office systems have not performed according to expectations. Increasingly, a variety of different brands of equipment and technology constitute these systems, with some of the hybrid systems not performing as anticipated. When this happens, the administrative office manager has either primary or secondary responsibility for making systems modifications.

Planning Function

1. Developing goals and objectives for each of the office functions and services, including layout, environment, telecommunications, word processing, automation, electronic data processing, records management, forms design, reprographics, mail services, and control.
2. Keeping abreast of new developments in the field and determining what changes should be made in existing functions and services to maintain a state-of-the-art position.
3. Assessing the need for designing and implementing totally new functions and services.
4. Developing policies that will help assure the attainment of goals and objectives.
5. Determining the most effective means of implementing desired changes.
6. Developing the unit's budget.
7. Determining personnel requirements.
8. Determining space and equipment needs.
9. Designing new operating systems.

Organizing Function

1. Determining the most effective means of organizing resources to achieve goals and objectives.
2. Determining the most effective way for employees to perform specific tasks.
3. Designing efficient work methods and procedures.
4. Assuring the maximum utilization of the organization's office equipment.
5. Developing techniques for maximizing organizational and individual productivity.
6. Developing effective methods and techniques when implementing changes.
7. Developing effective procedures for evaluating equipment being considered for acquisition.

Staffing Function

1. Assuring the use of efficient employee selection procedures including placement and orientation.
2. Providing sufficient growth opportunities and experiences for employees.
3. Providing appropriate training experiences.
4. Assuring effective appraisal of employee performance.
5. Assuring the realistic description of employees' jobs.

Directing Function

1. Using effective techniques to supervise employees.
2. Using effective techniques to motivate employees.
3. Designing effective lines of communication within the unit.
4. Assuring employee compliance with organizational policies and procedures.
5. Assuring that employee performance meets expectations.
6. Helping employees solve work-related problems.
7. Using a fair, objective approach for adjusting employees' salaries.

Controlling Function

1. Developing efficient procedures for controlling the quantity and quality of work processed in areas for which the administrative office manager is responsible.
2. Developing efficient procedures for scheduling work.
3. Developing efficient procedures for use in readily determining the status of unfinished work.
4. Maintaining the unit's budget.
5. Assuring that methods and procedures are cost-effective.
6. Motivating employees to be cost-conscious.
7. Developing effective assessment procedures for use in determining why actual results fail to conform with anticipated results.
8. Developing effective procedures for dealing with employees who fail to comply with organization's rules and policies.
9. Developing effective strategies for taking corrective action when and where necessary.

Figure 1-3 Responsibilities of the administrative office manager

As the workforce becomes more culturally diverse, administrative office managers will also be challenged by having to become familiar with ways to accommodate the diversity. The customs, beliefs, habits, and attitudes of culturally diverse individuals make managerial acceptance—and subsequent accommodation—of the diversity more important than ever before.

Finally, the **globalization** taking place in many organizations is presenting another challenge for the administrative office manager. Making sure that operating systems and technology in all locations mesh well is critical, as is assuring compliance with governmental regulations in the remote site. Too, assimilating diverse cultures into the organization's workforce can present another set of challenges for the administrative office manager.

Qualifications

What are the important qualifications of administrative office managers?

Administrative office managers must possess a thorough understanding of various business fundamentals. Because administrative office management is primarily supportive in nature and is designed to help others achieve personal or organizational goals, a solid background in such areas as accounting, marketing, management, statistics, economics, and psychology is desirable. Administrative office managers responsible for systems analysis and design will find helpful a thorough understanding of such functional areas as production, marketing, and finance.

A specialized knowledge of the following areas is also important: work simplification, work measurement, work standards, records management, forms design, data processing, job analysis, job evaluation, office layout, office equipment, cost control, performance appraisal, employee selection, productivity improvement, word processing, and office automation.

Leadership is another important qualification. As supervision responsibilities increase, so does the need for well-developed leadership skills. Effective leadership skills enable one to inspire and motivate employees and to instill in subordinates the desire to act in the best interests of the organization, to be loyal to the organization, and to be cooperative. In addition, interpersonal behavior and human relations skills are crucial for the administrative office manager.

A commitment to ethical behavior is another qualification administrative office managers must possess. Increasingly, organizations are becoming concerned about ethics and the display of ethical behavior among employees. Over the past decade, lack of ethical behavior among employees has been quite costly—both in dollars and reputation—to a number of organizations.

The ability to delegate responsibility is another important qualification of the administrative office manager; effective decision-making and communication also are essential skills. The administrative office manager must also be able to accept the viewpoint of others and to exercise good judgment. Furthermore, the administrative office manager must have the initiative and desire to continue to learn and develop professionally.

Professionalism

How can administrative office managers become professional?

An excellent way for administrative office managers to increase their professionalism is to participate in professional organizations and associations and to earn a certification. For example, the **Certified Administrative Manager (C.A.M.)** is a certification program for administrative managers. Certification requires two years of administrative managerial experience, passing the Certified Manager exams, and subsequently passing a second set of exams that covers principles of office systems management, information systems management, and financial management. The program is sponsored by the Institute of Certified Professional Managers.

Professional organizations of interest to administrative office managers are the American Records Management Association, Association for Systems Management, Data Processing Management Association, National Microfilm Association, Office Automation Management Association, Society of Office Automation Professionals, Association for Information Systems Professionals, Society for Advancement of Management, International Facility Management Association, Office Systems Research Association, and the Business Forms Management Association.

An abundance of professional literature of interest to administrative office managers also exists. Some of the more useful periodicals include *Managing Office Technology, Words, Office Systems, Office Solutions, Office Technology Management, Records Management Quarterly, The Office, OSRA Journal,* and *Supervisory Management.*

Educational Background

What educational background do administrative office managers need?

To be successful as an administrative office manager, certain minimal educational requirements are needed, coupled with appropriate work experience. Traditionally, a position in administrative office management has not been an entry-level position. Although an individual may have the needed educational requirements for becoming an administrative office manager, most organizations require a certain amount of related work experience. For this reason, many administrative office managers have "come up through the ranks," having served previously as a supervisor of employees in one of the functional areas of administrative office management, such as data processing.

Some of the college-level courses that administrative office managers find helpful are accounting, economics, business law, finance, statistics, office systems, telecommunications, and oral and written communication, as well as administrative office management. Also helpful are courses in psychology, sociology, and human relations.

Profile

The profile of the typical administrative office manager includes the following characteristics: male, although the number of female managers is rapidly increasing; between forty and fifty years of age; salary ranging between $60,000 and $70,000; a bachelor's degree; supervisor of three to fourteen employees; ten to fifteen years of prior work experience; and employment as an administrative office manager for five or fewer years.

An increasing number of educational institutions are offering office systems and administrative office management curricula, resulting in the opportunity for students to major in this important specialized area. Therefore, younger and less experienced individuals will be able to begin a career as an administrative office manager. Individuals who wish a career in this area will find that specializing enables them to perform more efficiently and with greater effectiveness than has been the case with some of their predecessors.

Roles and Skills

How do roles and skills differ from each other?

Administrative office managers assume a number of roles and skills within the organizations in which they work. **Roles** are defined as the set of behaviors and job tasks they are expected to perform. **Skills,** on the other hand, are defined as those abilities individuals possess that enable them to carry out well their specified roles.

Among the important roles for which administrative office managers have responsibility are decision-making roles, information-management roles, and interpersonal roles. An effective administrative office manager is able to make effective decisions regarding employees, operations, and resources. The nature of the administrative office manager's position makes him or her responsible for maintaining and using effectively the information needed to carry out important job functions, as well as for effectively managing information on an organization-wide basis. Finally, the effective administrative office manager will also deal effectively with his or her subordinates, peers, and superiors.

Among the important skills that administrative office managers must possess are technical skills, conceptual skills, and human skills. The ever-increasing amount of new technology that is currently available or will be available in the future requires that the administrative office manager be able to use it himself or herself but also help others use it to its maximum potential. Conceptual skills enable the administrative office manager to analyze a wide variety of situations, both technical and nontechnical, as a prelude to solving problems. Human skills enable the administrative office manager to work through and with others, including subordinates, peers, and superiors.

EVOLUTION OF MANAGEMENT THEORY

An understanding of the evolution of management theory is essential for a complete appreciation of the managerial process. The administrative office management area is firmly grounded in the theory of management that has evolved during the last 100 years. This evolution has progressed through four rather distinct phases, beginning with the **scientific management movement** in the early 1900s, and continuing with the **administrative movement** of the 1930s, the **human relations movement** of the 1940s and 1950s, and the current **modern movement.**

Scientific Management Movement

What are the characteristics of the scientific management movement?

Generally regarded as the founder of scientific management, Frederick W. Taylor was greatly concerned during the late 1800s and early 1900s with the emphasis that organizations placed on production. Taylor, an engineer for Bethlehem Steel, believed that any major problem confronting an organization could be resolved if management would scientifically determine and communicate to employees their expected output levels. Scientific management, as conceived by Taylor, was designed to increase the output of the employees and to improve the operating efficiency of management.

Taylor viewed workers as an economic entity whose motivation to work stemmed from their financial needs. He also believed that workers had to produce more at a lower cost and that they should be paid on a piecework basis, which would enable them to increase their earnings.

The cornerstone of scientific management was the use of time and motion study for increasing workers' efficiency in using machines. Frank and Lillian Gilbreth, also pioneers of the scientific-management era, were responsible for developing the time and motion studies that Taylor subsequently implemented. **Time study** is concerned with the amount of time it takes to complete a task, while **motion study** is concerned with the efficiency of the motion involved in performing a task.

Taylor believed in the need to identify one best way to do a job and to select and train employees carefully and thoroughly to perform their tasks. He also stressed the need for management and employees to cooperate with one another as a means of maximizing production. Because the mechanical and physiological aspects of work were emphasized during the scientific management era, the workers' psychological and social needs were often neglected. In spite of its criticism, the presence of scientific management continues to be felt today in such areas as employee training and job design.

Administrative Movement

Popular during the 1930s, the administrative movement focused on the firm as a whole or total entity rather than on specific isolated functions. During this movement, the following specific management functions were identified: planning, organizing, commanding, coordinating, and controlling. While scientific management focused on employee productivity and efficiency, administrative management focused on coordinating and managing various organizational endeavors.

Henri Fayol, a French geologist and engineer, was one of the more important proponents of the administrative philosophy. Fayol and his followers believed that management, regardless of the specialized area, was comprised of the following universal principles:

What principles constituted the administrative movement?

1. Division of labor
2. Authority
3. Discipline
4. Unity of command
5. Unity of direction
6. Subordination of the individual interest to the general interest
7. Remuneration
8. Centralization
9. Scalar chain (line of authority)
10. Order
11. Equity
12. Stability of tenure of personnel
13. Initiative
14. Esprit de corps[1]

Another important proponent of administrative management was Max Weber, a German sociologist. Weber's beliefs, which resulted in the development of the bureaucracy concept, were centered around having well-defined hierarchies, employee task specialization, written policies and procedures, technical competence among employees, and separation of ownership and management.

Human Relations Movement

Emerging during the 1940s and 1950s, the human relations movement was largely a response to the failure of organizations to treat their employees in a humane manner. Rather than focusing on the whole organization, which was the philosophy of the administrative movement, the human relations era was primarily concerned with individuals and groups and providing employees with growth opportunities and challenge. The human relations movement focused on the human and social dimensions of work and on the relationship between the superior and subordinate, particularly in terms of interpersonal relations and communication. Much of the work that evolved out of the human relations movement was concerned primarily with the lower levels of management.

One of the main proponents of the human relations movement was Elton Mayo. The well-known **Hawthorne Studies,** conducted in the late 1920s and early 1930s by Mayo and other researchers from Harvard University, provided the primary impetus for the development of the human relations movement. Undertaken at Western Electric's plant in Hawthorne, Illinois, the Hawthorne Studies were concerned with determining the effects that such factors as lighting, heating, fatigue, and layout had on productivity.

One phase of the study determined the relationship between the illumination level of the employees' work area and their output. As the illumination level was increased, the output also predictably increased. Unexpectedly, however, the output continued to increase even when the illumination level was decreased. The researchers concluded that the human element had greater impact on determining output and reaction to change than did the technical factor. Those advocating human relations strongly believed, therefore, treating employees in a humane manner had a greater effect on operating efficiency and output than did any of the technical factors.

During this era, three individuals gained prominence for their research on the relationship between employees and their jobs. These individuals are Abraham Maslow (Hierarchy of Needs), Douglas McGregor (Theory X–Theory Y), and Frederick Herzberg (Motivation-Hygiene Theory).

Modern Movement

The fourth phase in the evolution of management theory, the modern movement, began in the early 1950s and continues today. The modern movement consists of two approaches: the quantitative approach and the nonquantitative approach. The quantitative approach is also known as the **operations approach,** while the nonquantitative approach is frequently called the **behavioral sciences approach.**

The operations approach is concerned primarily with the making of decisions, especially decisions about which operations should be undertaken and about how they should be carried out.

The behavioral sciences approach is the scientific study of observable and verifiable human behavior. The effects of behavioral sciences can be observed at the individual, group, and organizational levels. The individual level is concerned with such factors as motivation, attitudes, and personality. The group level is concerned with interactions, interrelationships, group norms, and group leadership. The organizational level is concerned with such areas as bureaucracy and the effect of the system's design on employee behavior.

Other comparisons can be made between the behavioral sciences approach and the operations approach. The behavioral sciences approach is concerned with the manner in which decisions are made, whereas the operations approach is concerned with the way they ought to be made. This approach uses psychology, sociology, and anthropology as its base, whereas the operations

What was the major finding of the Hawthorne Studies?

How does the operations approach differ from the behavioral approach?

approach is more concerned with mathematics, computer science, and statistical applications.

Increasingly, the modern movement is heading toward a **systems approach** to management in which the organization is thought to be comprised of a number of systems with interdependent parts. A change in one part can affect other parts. **Contingency management,** a concept of fairly recent origin, recognizes that no one best way exists in all situations. Rather, managers need to examine the facts of a given situation and choose a tool, method, or process that will best handle the situation. Therefore, effective management depends on correctly assessing a number of contingency variables.

What is TQM?

Although not a new management concept—but one that is currently receiving increased attention—**Total Quality Management (TQM)** has important implications for administrative office management. Rather than emphasizing hierarchical structures and managerial control of employees and work processes, TQM puts emphasis on teamwork, empowerment of employees, and organization-wide recognition and acceptance of the critical need to serve its customers.

Adherence to the TQM philosophy effectively diminishes the adversity common in many organizations, replacing it with a spirit of cooperation. Instead of wasting their energies dealing with subversive and divergent behaviors, employees' energies are expended toward better serving the organization's customers. TQM results in a 100 percent commitment of 100 percent of the employees to 100 percent quality 100 percent of the time.

Although TQM programs found in organizations vary in their approach, sometimes quite extensively, they possess the following common elements:

1. Focus on customer satisfaction.
2. Ongoing improvement of the organization's products and/or services.
3. Work teams based on trust and cooperation.
4. Statistical measurement techniques designed to identify causes of production problems.

What are the major concepts of Theory Z?

The most recent management theory to evolve is **Theory Z,** which was developed by William G. Ouchi. This theory is based heavily on the Japanese style of management. Among the important Theory Z concepts are those shown in Figure 1–4.

Figure 1–4 Theory Z concepts

1. Employees are assumed to have lifetime employment. They need not be concerned about layoffs.
2. Employees are hired for their specific talents. The nature of an employee's job will be determined by his or her specific talents rather than by using a job to determine what talents an employee should have.
3. Decision making uses a consensus process that eventually results in widespread agreement on all decisions.
4. Managers and workers trust one another and are loyal to one another.
5. Managers are genuinely concerned about their subordinates' well-being.

IMPLICATIONS FOR THE ADMINISTRATIVE OFFICE MANAGER

Many administrative office management elements impact both directly and indirectly on the organization's ability to operate in a cost-effective manner. A failure by organizations to enhance the efficiency of their office operations results in operating costs that are higher than they otherwise would be.

The administrative office management function permeates the entire organization. For this reason, administrative office managers need to have a broad understanding of the various business functions as well as an excellent grasp of the various areas that comprise the administrative office management function.

Developments in the administrative office management area closely parallel the evolution of management theory. In the 1930s and 1940s, office managers readily adopted various principles that emerged from the human relations movement. As the modern movement surfaced in the 1950s, the administrative office management area again responded quickly to new beliefs, philosophies, and developments.

NOTE

1. Henri Fayol, *General and Industrial Management* (London: Sir Isaac Pitman and Sons Ltd., 1949), pp. 19–42.

REVIEW QUESTIONS

1. What is the current thrust of administrative office management?

2. What factor is primarily responsible for the increasing number of career opportunities in administrative office management?

3. What kind of challenges will administrative office managers likely confront in the future?

4. What educational qualifications do administrative office managers need?

5. What opportunities are available to help administrative office managers further their professional development?

6. During the scientific management movement, what technique or process was used to help increase workers' efficiency in using machines?

7. In what ways does the scientific management movement differ from the administrative movement?

8. What impact have the Hawthorne Studies had on the development of management theory?

9. What is the primary belief about the systems approach to management?

10. What organizational elements does TQM emphasize?

11. What are some of the basic elements of Theory Z?

DISCUSSION QUESTIONS

1. Why is administrative office management considered to be a service function in most organizations?

2. Assume that you are an administrative office manager in an insurance company. The professor who teaches the administrative office management course at the local college recently asked you to make a presentation before her students. She would like the presentation to be career oriented. One area you want to include in your presentation is that of "professionalism." What do you plan to tell these students about

the "professionalism" of those who choose a career in administrative office management?

3. Assume that you are an administrative office manager in the year 2050. Of the four schools of management theory discussed in this chapter, which one is most consistent with your present philosophy? Why?

STUDENT PROJECTS AND ACTIVITIES

1. Interview an administrative office manager to determine his or her specific job duties and the nature of his or her educational preparation.

2. Talk with the individual responsible for the management information system within an organization. What specific organizational functions are included in the management information system?

3. Going Online: Using the Internet, conduct an online search based on one of the concepts presented in this chapter or based on one of the chapter terms. Identify four or five things you learned from the material that you did not know prior to your online search.

Minicase

The board of directors of the Allied Paper Company has recently approved a policy supporting the professionalization of its managers. The company will pay half of any costs incurred by employees, will enact higher salary increases, and will publicly recognize the professional activities of employees. The directors on the company's board believe that any costs incurred will be more than offset by the managers' ability to perform more capably in their jobs.

David Von Braun, the administrative office manager at Allied, is interested in the professionalization program.

1. In what ways might Mr. Von Braun increase his professionalization as an administrative office manager?

2. What benefits does the company gain by assisting employees to increase their professionalization?

Case

The Jackson Manufacturing Company, which is located in Casper, Ohio, was founded in the 1940s by two brothers, Art and John Jackson. The company has manufactured several different products during its existence but has experienced its greatest success in the manufacture of automobile axles. The growth of the organization has been slow but steady. The managerial philosophy of the company has always been rather traditional. Neither of the Jackson brothers believed in implementing any of the newer managerial or personnel concepts.

David Jackson, the son of one of the founders, recently became president of the company when his father, who had been president for the last twenty years, retired. The new president's managerial philosophy is more progressive. He believes in implementing new personnel programs and managerial concepts, all of which have been quite successful.

David Jackson is concerned about the overall lack of coordination of office activities. At the present time, each office supervisor (the organization now has twenty) is totally responsible for all office activities under his or her jurisdiction. Although some of the units are efficiently administered, others are not. Mr. Jackson believes that a new employee with the title of administrative office manager is needed. A primary function of this individual would be the overall coordination of all office activities throughout the organization.

1. What benefits would likely emerge from employing an administrative office manager whose

responsibility would be the overall coordination of office activities?

2. What would likely be the most serious disadvantages that would result from making an administrative office manager responsible for the coordination of office activities?

3. What qualifications would likely be required of the individual hired as administrative office manager?

4. Identify five areas for which the administrative office manager would likely be responsible.

$\mathcal{C}$hapter 2

THE ORGANIZING PROCESS

$\mathcal{C}$hapter $\mathcal{A}$ims

After studying this chapter, you should be able to develop an appropriate philosophy regarding the organizing function of administrative office management.

$\mathcal{C}$hapter $\mathcal{O}$utline

Organizational Principles
  Definition of Objectives
  Span of Control
  Interrelated Functions
  Chain of Command
  Unity of Command
  Commensurate Authority and Responsibility
  Work Assignment
  Employee Empowerment
Organizational Structures
  Line Structure
  Line and Staff Structure
  Functional Structure
  Product Structure
  Committee Structure
  Matrix Structure
Centralization versus Decentralization
  Factors that Determine the Feasibility of
    Centralization
  Advantages of Centralization
  Disadvantages of Centralization
Organization Chart
Informal Organization
Implications for the Administrative Office
  Manager

$\mathcal{C}$hapter $\mathcal{T}$erms

Authority
Centralization
Chain of command
Committee structure
Decentralization
Empowerment
Functional areas
Functional structure
Informal organization
Line and staff structure
Line structure
Matrix structure
Organization chart
Organizational principles
Product structure
Responsibility
Span of control
Systems approach
Teams
Unity of command

*T*he organizing function, one of the five managerial functions introduced in Chapter 1, is vital to the operational effectiveness and efficiency of all organizations. The organizing function is a significant determinant of whether organizations maximize the efficient use of their resources, both human and nonhuman.

Among the ways the organizing function is helpful to organizations are that it: (1) assures more efficient use of the organization's resources; (2) improves employee understanding of job duties and responsibilities; (3) improves employee morale; and (4) provides a sense of direction for each of the organization's functional areas.

The **organizational principles** managers use today originated in the various management theories that have evolved during the last one hundred years. These principles provide basic guidelines that are useful when designing and structuring various organizational activities. Furthermore, these principles play an important role in guiding organizations toward the successful achievement of their goals.

In what ways is the organizing function helpful?

ORGANIZATIONAL PRINCIPLES

The organizational principles discussed in this chapter apply to any type of firm and to nearly every activity found within a firm. Adherence to the principles results in more efficient use of the firm's resources, especially human and financial resources.

Definition of Objectives

For objectives to be meaningful, they must be clearly defined, understood, and accepted by each individual concerned with their attainment. Objectives devoid of these characteristics hinder the managerial process. Determining whether objectives have been attained is accomplished more easily when they are stated in numerical terms involving quantity or time elements. For example, an objective of the word processing center may be to increase its output 5 percent between January 1 and June 30. The numerical elements found in this objective are helpful in determining whether and when the desired level was attained. Objectives can be either short or long range; and some will involve only a few of the organization's employees whereas others concern virtually the entire workforce.

Span of Control

What is meant by span of control?

The number of subordinates an individual is able to supervise effectively is known as **span of control.** Although no formula exists for determining an appropriate span, several factors should be considered. For example, the nature of the work being performed is important. Some office activities require a greater amount of supervision than others. Another factor is the capability of supervisors and subordinates. Skilled supervisors generally are more able to work with a greater number of subordinates than are supervisors whose skills are less well developed. Likewise, if subordinates are well trained, supervisors may be able to increase their span of control because less time will be consumed helping employees. Other factors affecting span of control are leadership style, the latitude extended to the subordinates in decision making, and the nature of interpersonal relationships inherent in each situation.

The nature of the supervisor's responsibilities can be significant in determining an appropriate span of control. If the individual has numerous responsibilities in addition to supervising subordinates, the span of control will likely have to be smaller. The supervisor's level in the organizational hierarchy is also an important determinant. Generally, higher level supervisors tend to supervise fewer employees than lower level supervisors.

Implementing Total Quality Management, which was introduced in Chapter 1, is responsible for increasing the span of control in a growing number of organizations. For example, self-directed **teams** and the **empowerment** of employees lessen the amount of direct control supervisors have over their subordinates. Thus, supervisors can deal effectively with a larger number of subordinates than is possible when they exercise a greater amount of direct control over their subordinates.

Interrelated Functions

Most organizations are no longer composed of mutually exclusive **functional areas.** Rather, such areas as sales, production, finance, marketing, and personnel are becoming more interrelated—and sometimes intricately so, a common element of the **systems approach** that is characteristic of today's management-theory thinking. Consequently, problems that emerge in one functional area will often expand to or influence other areas. For example, if the marketing function is experiencing difficulties, the sales function will likely experience problems as well.

The interrelated nature of these areas requires that the objectives of one area be consistent with those of other areas. Furthermore, related activities should be grouped together in one functional area. Otherwise, coordination of activities cannot be maximized.

Chain of Command

What is the essence of chain of command?

The formal identification of who reports to whom within the organization is known as **chain of command.** The chain is a series of superior-subordinate relationships (from the highest position in the organization to the lowest position in the organization). Each employee within an organization should be familiar with the chain as it affects him or her. Lack of adherence to the chain may cause the communication process to break down. Generally, simple chains are more effective than complex ones because they are more readily understood and because communication moves through a simple chain more rapidly than through a complex one. Furthermore, simple chains provide the benefit of being more clear-cut and definitive than their complex counterparts.

Unity of Command

What is the essence of unity of command?

The chain of command principle is closely related to the **unity of command** principle which states that an employee should be directly responsible to only one supervisor. An employee who has more than one supervisor is likely to be put into a precarious situation, especially when receiving conflicting orders or directions from each supervisor. Difficulties arise when both supervisors give the employee work to do at the same time, and one supervisor expects the employee to fulfill his or her request first. The absence of unity of command produces job-related frustration, job dissatisfaction, and loss of morale.

Commensurate Authority and Responsibility

Why do authority and responsibility have to be commensurate?

Another organizational principle states that individuals who are given the **responsibility** to undertake a task must also be given an appropriate amount of **authority** to assure task completion. Otherwise, they cannot be held accountable for the ultimate outcome. The inability to delegate authority—a common problem for some supervisors—results in their performing many duties that could be effectively assigned to their subordinates. The failure of supervisors to delegate often prevents their performing at an optimum level. Subordinates, therefore, experience a loss of morale because they are unable to exercise full authority over those situations for which they are responsible.

Among the reasons supervisors avoid delegating authority are that they: (1) lack confidence in their subordinates; (2) lack understanding of the nature of the supervisory role; (3) believe that unless they do the work, they cannot "stay on top" of the situation; and (4) lack technical competence.

Occasionally, subordinates assume too much authority, resulting in their taking excessive liberties or control. Although this does not occur as frequently as the failure of supervisors to delegate authority, the results may be just as disastrous. Usually, when a subordinate is allowed to assume too much authority, the cohesion of the work group deteriorates, and the cooperation among the group members diminishes.

Work Assignment

When making work assignments, each individual's special strengths and talents should be considered. This helps assure that each person's work assignment is consistent with his or her ability and interest. The absence of clearly defined job duties and responsibilities makes it more difficult to hold an employee accountable for unsatisfactory performance.

An individual's work assignment should be determined before he or she is hired. Defining a new employee's job duties and responsibilities once he or she is on the job is not recommended.

Employee Empowerment

Why should employees be encouraged to participate in decision-making processes?

When employees are empowered, they are encouraged to participate as much as possible in making decisions that affect all aspects of their job tasks. Thus, they are given the ability and authority—without their supervisor's approval—to take actions that will lead to high-quality work and performance.

Many administrative office managers have recognized the advantages of employee empowerment. Because employees are often more familiar with a given situation than a manager or supervisor, their insight and suggestions are invaluable in the decision-making process. The recognition employees receive from their empowerment has a positive impact on their motivation. Older management practices attempted to motivate employees with such extrinsic rewards as money; empowerment is an intrinsic system that is more effective because it instills in employees pride in their workmanship.

ORGANIZATIONAL STRUCTURES

The organization's internal structure determines the authority relationships among its employees. Common structures are line structure, line and staff structure, functional structure, product structure, committee structure, and matrix structure. The typical organization uses a combination of two or more of these structures.

Line Structure

In **line structure**—the oldest and simplest of the structures—direct authority flows vertically from the top hierarchical levels, through the middle levels, and on to the bottom levels. The activities characteristic of line structure are directly associated with the organization's attainment of its primary objectives. Line organization is sometimes called military or scalar organization.

Because of the growing complexity of most organizations, the line structure is generally found only in small organizations or in those recently founded. Typically, owners or managers in small or new organizations have time to perform duties directly related to the organization's primary objectives as well as those not directly related. As the organization increases in size and managerial duties become more complex and diverse, however, the hiring of additional support staff becomes necessary. When this happens, the line structure is no longer "pure." In some large organizations today, a line structure is used for certain activities even though one of the other structures is predominant.

The direct authority characteristic of the line structure makes each employee directly responsible for the performance of designated duties. Although direct line authority gives the supervisor the right to take disciplinary action against subordinates who fail to carry out reasonable orders and directions, supervisors do not have direct authority over individuals in other units or departments.

Advantages of Line Structure. Use of the line structure results in several advantages. Because of direct authority and clearly defined areas of responsibility, employees are fully aware of the boundaries of their jobs. Decision making is expedited because bureaucratic buck passing is virtually eliminated. Also, employees readily understand the simplicity of line structure. Finally, because employees are familiar with their duties and responsibilities, they can be held directly accountable when their performance is less than expected.

Disadvantages of Line Structure. The most serious disadvantage of line structure is its failure to provide the specialization needed by organizations when they become larger and more complex. Line managers have to perform certain specialized activities themselves because staff assistance is unavailable. As a manager's line duties expand, other duties will eventually have to be slighted. The line structure occasionally fails to provide for the adequate replacement of key managerial personnel because, in some cases, the limited nature of employees' duties prevents their getting the broad experiences they need for moving into managerial positions.

Line and Staff Structure

The **line and staff structure** is similar to the line structure, with one added dimension. The direct authority characteristic of line structure is still present, as are those line activities concerned with the attainment of the organization's primary objectives. The new dimension is the addition of specialized staff activities that support line activities. Staff employees assist the line function by facilitating the attainment of the organization's primary objectives.

Line activities in one organization may be staff activities in another organization. The appropriate classification of each type of activity can be deter-

Why is line structure not found in large organizations?

How does line structure differ from line and staff structure?

mined by answering the following question: Does the activity contribute directly to the attainment of the organization's primary objectives? Line activities make a direct contribution; staff activities do not.

Managers or supervisors of staff units possess line authority (or direct authority) over their subordinates. For example, the office services area of most organizations is considered to be a staff unit; when administrative office managers are given line authority to issue orders, however, they have line authority over their subordinates. Typically, they have only an advisory relationship with all other employees. Giving administrative office managers line authority over the employees in their units enhances the operational effectiveness of the office services area.

A partial organization chart depicting line and staff organizational relationships is illustrated in Figure 2–1. The shaded boxes are line positions; the unshaded boxes are staff positions.

In the illustration, the vice presidents for production and sales are line managers because their activities contribute directly to the attainment of the organizations's primary objective: to make a profit on the products it manufactures and sells. The vice presidents for finance and corporate affairs perform support staff activities.

Advantages of Line and Staff Structure. The most distinct advantage of line and staff structure is the freeing of line employees from having to perform specialized activities that can be assigned to staff employees. Consequently, line managers have more time to perform activities that contribute directly to the attainment of the organization's primary objectives. Also beneficial is the use of the specialized assistance of staff personnel. The flexibility of most staff units enables them to undertake and successfully complete new projects within a minimum amount of time. Rarely is this flexibility possible in pure line structures. Many individuals use their staff experience as preparation for moving into a line position.

Disadvantages of Line and Staff Structure. Conflict between line and staff employees may become troublesome. For example, because staff employees perform primarily in supportive or advisory capacities, line employees may ignore their input. In other instances, staff employees have added to line-staff conflict by usurping line authority. In addition, some line managers continually suppress the talents of capable staff employees, which hampers the development of an effective line-staff working relationship.

Functional Structure

Organizations that use **functional structure** are built around specialized areas that tend to parallel the departments in many organizations. For example, in a manufacturing organization, the specialized areas might be production, sales, marketing, finance, corporate relations, and so forth. A specialist, perhaps with the title of vice president, manages each functional area. These managers have both line authority and functional authority: line authority over the subordinates in their own unit and functional authority over activities in other departments that relate to their own specialized areas.

The functional structure is most commonly found in small- and medium-sized organizations. It tends to centralize decision making at the top levels of the organization. The functional structure is illustrated in Figure 2–2.

For example, in the partial organization chart illustrated in Figure 2–2, the manager of office services has line authority over the office workers in the

What are the advantages of line and staff structure?

What are the disadvantages of line and staff structure?

What rights does functional authority provide?

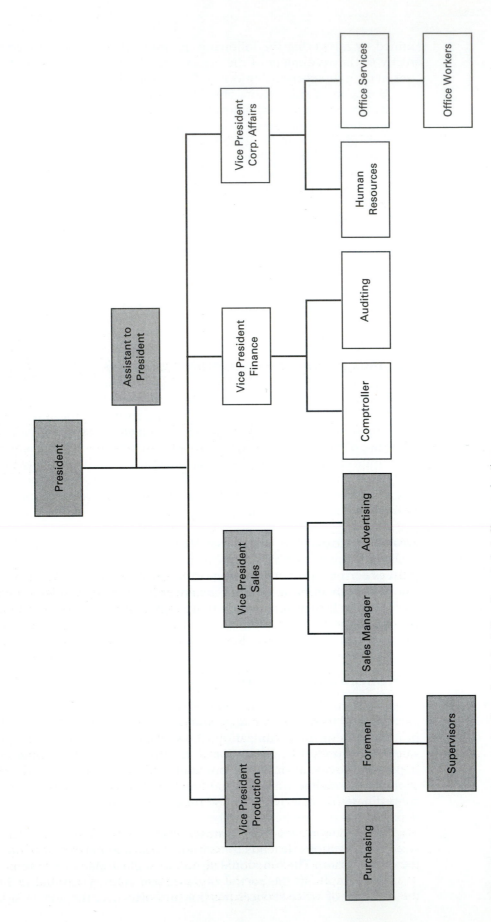

Figure 2-1 Partial organization chart depicting line and staff organization

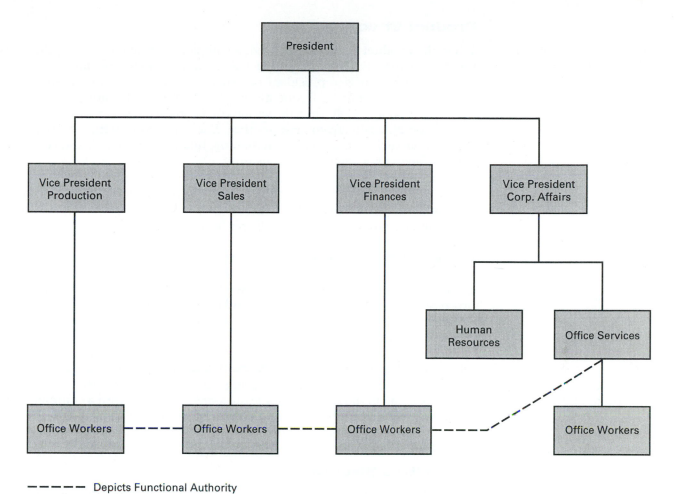

─ ─ ─ ─ ─ Depicts Functional Authority

Figure 2-2 Partial organization chart depicting functional organization

office services unit and functional authority over the office workers found in the other functional areas. The manager has the right to issue orders and to take disciplinary action against those over whom he or she has line authority. Although the manager cannot take disciplinary action against individuals for whom he or she has only functional authority, he or she generally has the right to issue orders and to make suggestions. With the functional structure, an employee may have two or more supervisors, a potential violation of the unity of command principle discussed earlier in this chapter.

Advantages of Functional Structure. The most distinct advantage of using the functional organizational structure is the expertise provided by the functional specialists. Their expertise enables them to contribute significantly to solving complex problems that arise within their specialized areas. Unlike some of the others, the functional structure prevents employees from slighting certain specialized areas within the organization.

Disadvantages of Functional Structure. The confusion that arises when an employee has two or more supervisors is a weakness of the functional structure. Another potential disadvantage is the tendency for some managers to evade areas in which they have functional authority, a situation that may impact negatively on the coordination of activities.

Product Structure

What is the essence of product structure?

When the **product structure** is used, a company's products provide the basis for its structure. Each major product is given division status, and a top-level official—perhaps a vice president or general manager—heads the unit. Line and staff organization is frequently used within each division. The product structure functions well when the various divisions of an organization are separated geographically from one another. Each division—with its own functional areas such as production, marketing, finance, personnel, and corporate affairs—operates as an autonomous unit.

The concept of product organization is presented in the partial chart in Figure 2–3. In the illustration, each of the major products is placed in separate divisions, with a vice president heading each unit. The vice presidents for finance and corporate affairs basically perform staff activities.

Advantages of Product Structure. The product structure enables the various divisions to develop processes and procedures that best meet their needs. When an alternative structure is used—line and staff, for example—the processes and procedures are likely standardized throughout the organization. Furthermore, each division is able to coordinate its activities without undue constraint from headquarters.

Disadvantages of Product Structure. The product structure allows each division to "go its own way" more so than some of the other structures. This may result in the failure of some divisions to work toward a common goal. Furthermore, the problems experienced by certain divisions may be felt throughout the entire organization.

Committee Structure

Although not everyone agrees that the **committee structure** should be viewed as an organizational structure, its use provides an important function in most organizations. Some committees perform important managerial functions, whereas others are simply advisory in nature. The purpose for which a particular committee is formed has a significant bearing on its perceived importance. This type of organizational structure is appropriately used in conjunction with any of the three types of organizational structures previously discussed. Although some committees within organizations have perpetual existence, others are dissolved after they fulfill their designated functions.

What are the advantages of committee structure?

Advantages of Committee Structure. Recommendations made by a committee are often accepted more readily than are those made by one individual. In addition, the widely varying views of the committee members broaden the nature of their recommendations and increase their acceptance by others, seeming to increase the validity of the recommendations. The use of the committee structure also reduces the risk of making a wrong decision.

Disadvantages of Committee Structure. Committees are often criticized for requiring considerable time to function properly. Not all committees are equally productive, especially those dominated by certain individuals.

Matrix Structure

The **matrix structure,** which is the newest of those presented in this chapter, is most frequently used by organizations undertaking a complex project. This

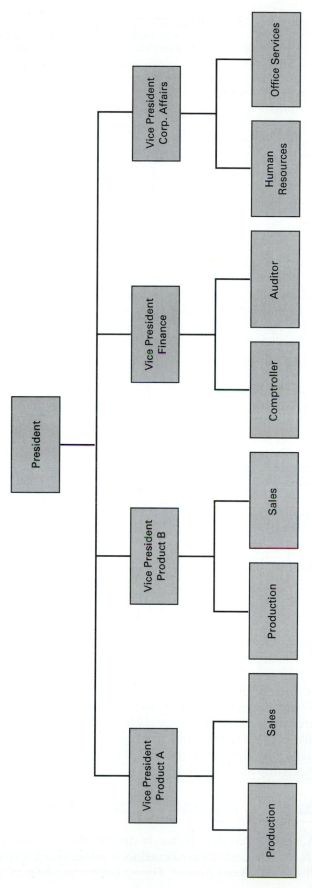

Figure 2-3 Partial organization chart depicting product organization

Figure 2-4 Matrix structure

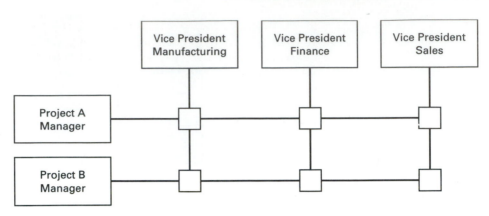

structure integrates both vertical and horizontal relationships into a temporary new unit called a *project*. Figure 2–4 illustrates the matrix concept.

What are the characteristics of matrix structure?

Matrix structure involves temporarily borrowing employees from various functional areas—such as manufacturing, finance, and sales—and reassigning them to work part time or full time on a project. Those who are borrowed are likely to have expertise in various phases of the project. For example, if Project A involves developing, manufacturing, and marketing a new product, employees in those functional areas who have relevant expertise are likely to be assigned to the project. Perhaps five employees from manufacturing, three from sales, and one from finance are temporarily reassigned. In the matrix structure, an employee can have his or her job split several ways—among several projects and the permanent position. Once the project is completed, employees generally return full time to their respective permanent units.

Advantages of Matrix Structure. The use of the matrix structure enables organizations to assign employees with expertise in certain areas to work on complex projects, resulting in more efficient use of human resources. The alternative to this may result in the organization's having to hire employees with expertise in specialized areas to work on the project. But once the project is completed, employees either have to be terminated or integrated into a functional area, which may not be an easy task. The use of the matrix structure also facilitates involvement of employees from several functional areas. Its use facilitates the organization's adapting quickly to a given situation because employees with expertise in specialized areas can be readily reassigned to a project.

Disadvantages of Matrix Structure. In an organization using the matrix structure, employees may have two supervisors: the manager of their functional area and the project manager. This situation violates the unity of command principle discussed earlier. Unity problems are more likely to occur when an employee works part time on the project and part time in a functional area. Also, some employees believe that the matrix structure creates job-related pressure. Managers may find greater difficulty coordinating employee activities when they are temporarily assigned to a project than when they are permanently assigned to a functional area.

CENTRALIZATION VERSUS DECENTRALIZATION

What factors determine the feasibility of centralization?

Activities that were formerly decentralized in many organizations are now being centralized. **Centralization** involves placing related activities under the jurisdiction of one person. The activities may be performed centrally, or they may be performed in several locations. The former arrangement is known as centralized control over centralized operations; the latter is known as centralized control over decentralized operations. With **decentralization,** several individuals located throughout the organization have control or jurisdiction over related activities.

As an example, consider a centralized records management program. One individual within the organization is responsible for the program, and the records of the various functional areas are most likely stored in one central location. Conversely, if records management is decentralized, the managers of each unit are totally responsible for the maintenance of the records in their respective departments. In addition to records management, other office activities that may be centralized are mail services, reprographics, word processing, data processing, employee selection, and so forth.

Several degrees of centralization are found within the administrative office management area. The highest degree of centralization is the placement of all office activities under the jurisdiction of the administrative office manager, with the unit supervisors responsible for the day-to-day supervision of the employees who perform these activities.

Also quite widely used is the alternative that centralizes certain office activities, while other activities remain decentralized and under the jurisdiction of individual units or departments. The administrative office manager is responsible for the centralized office activities, whereas unit or department managers maintain responsibility for the decentralized office activities within their respective areas. In many cases, the managers of the other units or departments make use of the expertise of the administrative office manager in solving office-related problems found within their departments.

Computer technology facilitates the centralization of a variety of activities within the organization. One such example is data processing. On the other hand, some office activities, such as the organization's mail service, can be centralized without using computer facilities.

Factors that Determine the Feasibility of Centralization

Following is a discussion of several of the factors that determine the extent to which centralization of office activities is feasible or desirable.

Nature of Organization. The greater the volume of office work and paper-processing activities found in the organization, the more desirable the centralization of office activities becomes. Two types of organizations—financial institutions and insurance companies—have centralized most of their office activities because of the vast amount of paperwork they process. Organizations that are not as paper intensive may find centralization less crucial or desirable.

Size of Organization. As organizations become larger, the need for centralized control over certain operations increases. An example is the purchasing function. Without the coordination that results from centralized control, various activities may not be carried out efficiently.

Diversification of Organization. Organizations widely diversified in their products, processes, and personnel often find centralization to be somewhat awkward. Therefore, only a minimum number of office activities and perhaps even fewer other types of activities are likely to be centralized in widely diversified organizations.

Conformity to Standardized Processes. Standardized procedures tend to be used in centralized activities. The extent to which standardization is possible determines the feasibility of centralization.

Quality of Personnel. Many organizations find that higher quality employees are needed when office activities are decentralized. When operations are centralized, activities are usually overseen by a specialist who is able to direct the employees' activities more closely. In decentralized operations, however, the unit or department manager may know little about specialized office activities. The employees, therefore, will have to assume greater responsibility for determining the proper ways to do their work.

Distribution of Operations. When the operations of an organization are distributed over a wide geographical area, physical centralization may be less feasible. An organization, however, may be able to centralize control over the activities even though they are carried out at different locations. An example is an organization's computer network.

Attitude of Personnel. Regardless of the amount of time, effort, and planning expended in centralizing office activities, nothing likely will be gained as long as employees resist the change to centralization. In some instances, the process of overcoming employee resistance will consume more time than the actual planning of the change. Unless this resistance can be overcome, centralization may not be possible.

Advantages of Centralization

What are the advantages of centralization?

When compared with decentralization, centralization of office activities results in the following advantages:

1. Work methods and procedures are carried out more uniformly.
2. Duplication of effort and equipment occurs less frequently.
3. Duplicate copies of documents are not as likely to be stored.
4. Employees' skills are better used because workers can be assigned to their areas of specialization.
5. Work processes are standardized.
6. Peak workloads can be handled efficiently because all employees in the unit can be assigned to help with the peak work.
7. Absence of an employee does not disrupt the performance of a task or job.
8. Salaries are more equitable because management can easily determine which employees perform comparable jobs and therefore should receive comparable salaries.

Disadvantages of Centralization

What are the disadvantages of centralization?

The disadvantages of centralization include the following:

1. Centrally locating an activity may result in more employee time being consumed in transporting work to and from the unit.
2. Widely dispersed centralized activities may not be equally accessible to all personnel.

3. The technical nature of some work cannot be efficiently accommodated in a centralized unit.

4. The confidential status of materials cannot always be maintained when they are processed through a centralized unit.

5. Centralization does not always permit the assigning and completing of work according to its priority.

ORGANIZATION CHART

The formal relationships between various individuals and the organizational structure are illustrated on an **organization chart.** The chart identifies lines of authority and responsibility, flow of work between individuals, and span of control. Although the chart illustrates who reports to whom, it does not illustrate informal relationships between individuals.

The organization chart illustrates hierarchical relationships; therefore, it is most logically constructed by starting at the top and working downward in a vertical arrangement. The primary functions of the organization and the subfunctions within each primary function must be identified. An alternative to the vertical arrangement is the horizontal arrangement in which the highest ranking position is placed on the left and the lowest ranking ones on the right.

What guidelines are useful in preparing organization charts?

Figure 2–5 identifies several guidelines helpful when preparing organization charts.

By identifying lines of authority, the organization chart gives employees a better understanding of the formal structure of the organization. It also helps identify areas of overlapping responsibility that should be eliminated. Furthermore, the chart is used to identify promotional opportunities for job applicants and new employees as well as areas suitable for training and orientation.

The most significant disadvantage of the organization chart results from its failure to illustrate the informal interaction that is necessary between employees as they carry out their day-to-day activities. Another disadvantage is the impression the chart may give that all departments or units can be well defined and are distinguishable from one another, which may not always be the case.

INFORMAL ORGANIZATION

What is informal organization?

Formal organization—discussed earlier in this chapter—is planned organization established by formal authority. Many of the spontaneous personal and social relationships that exist in an organization, however, are more appropriately classified as **informal organization.**

Figure 2-5 Guidelines for use in preparing organization charts.

1. Hierarchical relationships should be determined to place individuals or departments of similar hierarchical importance on the same horizontal level.
2. Vertical and horizontal authority are identified by solid lines.
3. Functional authority is illustrated with dotted lines.
4. The titles illustrated on the chart should be complete.
5. The chart should include the name of the organization and the date of its preparation.

Informal groups and informal communication patterns are two important elements of informal organization. Informal groups tend to have a powerful influence on their members. Often, standards of conduct or performance are imposed on individuals by the work group to which employees belong. The behavior of the informal group can be either a help or a hindrance to the administrative office manager.

To illustrate how informal organization can be helpful, suppose a new procedure has been installed in a work unit. Also suppose the procedure, although efficient, is not popular among employees. If the manager can get the informal "leaders" in the work unit to accept the new procedure, they may also be able to convince others to accept the new procedure.

Informal organization can also be a hindrance to management. Suppose, for example, that an informal group loses confidence in the capability of the group's manager. The group can make life so miserable for the manager that he or she resigns. In some instances, the informal group may be able to pressure the manager's superior into replacing the manager.

IMPLICATIONS FOR THE ADMINISTRATIVE OFFICE MANAGER

The attention administrative office managers give to the organizing function contributes significantly to their success. Most managers agree that the more attention given to this function, the more readily able they are to stay abreast of activities for which they are responsible. Their management strategies can be more proactive and less reactive when they give the organizing function the attention it deserves and requires. When managers are in a proactive position, they are able to control their destinies; when they manage from a reactive position, the situation at hand essentially controls their destinies.

The organizing function helps administrative office managers in several ways, including the following: increases the efficiency with which they are able to carry out their job functions; promotes better working relations with subordinates and superiors; facilitates the development of effective work processes and procedures; enables them to maintain more effective control over their areas of responsibility; and helps in the coordination of various activities.

REVIEW QUESTIONS

1. What benefits result from giving adequate consideration to the organizing function?
2. Why should objectives be clearly defined?
3. What determines an adequate span of control for a supervisor?
4. Why should an employee be responsible to only one supervisor?
5. Why is the line structure not feasible in some organizations?
6. What are the basic differences between line structure and line and staff structure?
7. What basic concepts characterize functional structure?
8. What is meant by the terms *centralization* and *decentralization* as they relate to the organizational process?
9. What is informal organization? Why can't informal organization be depicted on an organization chart?
10. What guidelines are helpful when preparing organization charts?

DISCUSSION QUESTIONS

1. You are employed in the centralized records area of a large manufacturing company. Because you have had a course in administrative office management, you are aware of several ways that operations in this area could be improved. When making suggestions to your supervisor, she generally says, "If it isn't broken, don't fix it." You have an idea that was rejected by your supervisor that would likely save the company thousands of dollars a year. Because your supervisor is not open to your suggestions, you are considering "going over her head." Discuss the ramifications of taking this course of action.

2. Several operations in the company where you work were recently restructured in an attempt to streamline them as much as possible. In doing so, you now discover that you have two individuals to whom you are primarily responsible. What are the implications of this situation?

3. You fill a staff position in the company for which you work. Several of the other employees you talk with regularly are in line positions. Some of these individuals let you know from time to time that their line positions are more valuable than your staff position. Discuss how you might defend the value of your staff position the next time it is mentioned.

STUDENT PROJECTS AND ACTIVITIES

1. Interview a manager in an organization that uses line and staff structure. What does this individual consider to be the most significant advantage of line and staff structure? The most significant disadvantage?

2. Discuss with an administrative office manager the nature of employee participation he or she uses in carrying out his or her job responsibilities.

3. Going Online: Using the Internet, conduct an online search based on one of the concepts presented in this chapter or based on one of the chapter terms. Identify four or five things you learned from the material you read that you did not know before.

Minicase

The Chung Corporation, an organization that manufactures several different components used in automobile transmissions, has been plagued with increasing employee dissatisfaction. A frequent complaint of several employees is that they spend considerable time in committee meetings, most of which produce few positive results. Most of the committee meetings are devoted to making plans about various aspects of corporate activities or operations. From these planning sessions, operations and activities evolve rather haphazardly, apparently with very little attention given to organizing any of the operations or activities on a formal basis.

1. Discuss the implications of this situation.
2. Identify problems that are likely to result from this situation.

Case

The Levec Corporation, founded in 1971 by James and Richard Levec, manufactures a full line of camping trailers. For several years, the corporation experienced a very small net profit. About three years ago, however, the company made a substantial turnaround and now has a much-improved financial picture. The significant increase in the number of people who enjoy camping is responsible for the increased sales of the firm.

At the present time, the corporation has four employees in a managerial capacity: the two Levec brothers, Dick Anders, and Ronald Smith. The job titles of these four individuals are used only to satisfy government regulations.

The firm's limited financial resources at the time the corporation was founded resulted in the hiring of only four managers. Consequently, these four individuals have been performing a variety of tasks that are inconsistent with their job titles. Each of the four individuals performs tasks that are concerned with the production and marketing of the camping equipment.

Increasing evidence indicates that the firm's present organization structure is not working as well as it did when the firm's operations were less involved. Evidence also indicates the need for hiring additional managers to handle the increase in the volume of operations.

1. What organization structure is presently being used?

2. What clues are likely to emerge as evidence that the present structure is no longer feasible?

3. What organizational structure do you recommend as a replacement for the present structure? Why?

4. What are the characteristics of the structure you recommend?

5. What are the advantages and disadvantages of the structure you recommend?

*C*hapter 3

THE COMMUNICATION PROCESS

*C*hapter *A*ims

After studying this chapter, you should be able to develop an appropriate philosophy regarding the important role communication plays in administrative office management.

*C*hapter *O*utline

Elements of Communication Process
The Flow of Communication
    Downward Communication
    Upward Communication
    Horizontal Communication
Small-Group Communication
    Reasons People Belong to Small Groups
    Advantages and Disadvantages
Large-Group Communication
Nonverbal Communication
    Impact of Nonverbal Cues on Communication Process
    Elements of Nonverbal Communication
Barriers to Effective Communication
Development of Listening Skills
    Elements of the Listening Process
    Suggestions for Improving Listening
Application of Communication Process
    Decision-Making Process
    Conflict Resolution
    Implementation of Change
Implications for the Administrative Office Manager

*C*hapter *T*erms

Barriers
Body language
Communication process
Decision-making process
Downward communication
Focus groups
Gestures
Grapevine
Groupthink
Horizontal communication
Kinesics
Listening
Nominal grouping technique
Nonverbal communication
Occulesics
Paralanguage
Planned change
Proxemics
Reactive change
Small-group communication
Tactilics
Time
Upward communication
Work-team concept

A major part of each work day for administrative office managers is spent engaged in the common types of communication: reading, writing, speaking, and listening. In a typical work day, they will spend more time engaged in communicating than in any other activity. In fact, most of the tasks for which administrative office managers are responsible involve significant levels of communication. One of the key attributes of successful administrative office managers is their ability to communicate effectively.

The communication process is affected by a number of variables. First, the nature of the message affects the process as does the background of the sender and receiver. Other variables include the environment in which communication occurs, the relationship between the sender and receiver, the time of day, and unusual mannerisms of those communicating. Time and effort are well spent by administrative office managers who try to improve their communicating effectiveness by minimizing the negative influence of any of these variables.

ELEMENTS OF COMMUNICATION PROCESS

What elements constitute the communication process?

The **communication process** comprises the following elements: sender, receiver, message, channel, feedback, and noise. Figure 3–1 presents a graphic illustration of the process.

The communication process begins with the sender's decision to communicate with the receiver. At this point, the sender forms a message either by creating a thought that he or she wishes to communicate or by selecting a bit of information to transmit. Before the message can be sent, it first has to be encoded, a process that involves translating the thoughts or information into words, signs, or symbols. This step enables the message to be transmitted to the receiver by means of a channel that uses either oral or written media.

Using the message to express himself or herself, the sender typically uses one or more of the following formats: written words, electronic communica-

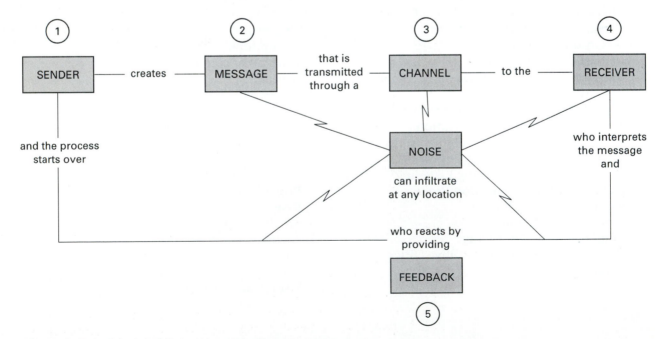

Figure 3-1 Model of the communication process

tion (such as e-mail), spoken words, facial expressions, gestures, pictures, and so forth. In a face-to-face conversation, the nonverbal elements of the message often convey as much or more meaning as the spoken words. In a written message, the way words are used often affects its outcome.

What media are used in the communication process?

The message is transmitted to the receiver by means of different media. The sender can use a variety of media, including face-to-face communication, written documents, electronic communication, telephone conversation, radio, television, and newspapers.

The receiver decodes the message upon receiving it. This process, which is essentially the opposite of encoding, occurs when the receiver interprets the message and gives it meaning from his or her own perspective.

Why is feedback important?

Feedback enables the sender to determine how much of the message was actually received and how accurately the receiver interpreted it. Only when the desired feedback is received can the sender be sure that he or she communicated accurately and effectively. Additional communication is likely to be needed when feedback indicates the receiver misinterpreted or misunderstood the message. Feedback can be in the form of a gesture or an expression that indicates understanding, a request for additional information, a request for clarification, a facial expression, or even failure of the receiver to comply with the sender's request.

Noise, which can enter the communication process at each step, is a distraction, disruption, or interference in the communication process. Examples include physical noise, an inconsistency between what the speaker says and his or her facial expressions, a garbled message, semantics, psychological elements, and mechanical concerns (such as errors in grammar and punctuation usage).

THE FLOW OF COMMUNICATION

In what directions does communication flow in an organization?

In an organization, communication flows in three directions. Administrative office managers communicate in an upward direction with their superiors, downward with their subordinates, and horizontally (or laterally) with other managers. Most find that talking and listening activities consume more of their time than do reading and writing. Much of the content of this chapter is concerned with what occurs in talking and listening processes.

Downward Communication

The success experienced by many administrative office managers is often determined by how well they communicate with their subordinates. Well-informed subordinates not only tend to be more productive, but also tend to derive greater satisfaction from their work. Administrative office managers use **downward communication** to keep their subordinates informed, give them job-related instructions, and provide them feedback regarding their performance.

What kinds of information are communicated through downward communication?

Among the factors administrative office managers consider when deciding which medium to use in transmitting downward communication are the following:

1. Permanency of record. If an official written record needs to be kept, written or electronic communication rather than oral communication is used.
2. Immediacy. If the information needs to be communicated immediately, oral or electronic communication may be more appropriate than written communication.

3. Need for evidence of understanding or feedback. When evidence of understanding or feedback is needed, an oral conversation (either face to face or by telephone) should be used.

4. Formality. If the communication situation is more formal than informal, then written communication rather than oral or electronic communication needs to be used.

Employees need to be kept informed about a variety of items, including new policies, procedures, goals, rules, benefits, and developments in the organization. The administrative office manager is responsible for keeping his or her subordinates informed unless someone above him or her does so. Oral, written, and electronic communication channels are used. Small-group meetings, manuals, e-mail messages, and memorandums are three common techniques for keeping employees informed.

The communication of job instructions to employees has a twofold purpose: to inform them of their specific duties and to instruct them about how these duties are to be performed. A variety of techniques are used, including verbal orders and directions, written job descriptions and procedures statements, manuals, e-mail messages, and handbooks. In situations involving complex duties, the use of two techniques (such as verbal directions and written procedures) may enhance subordinate understanding. In deciding which technique is appropriate for a given situation, the manager should consider the complexity of the task and the subordinate's background.

Employees interested in improving their work effectiveness as well as those who need reassurance that they are performing well desire feedback about their job performance. Performance appraisal, which is discussed in Chapter 11, is a formal procedure, whereas giving subordinates oral and written feedback about their performance is informal. Written feedback is considered to be more official than oral feedback.

What factors affect the success of downward communication?

Among the factors that affect the success of downward communication are the appropriateness of the communication channel, the timing and clarity of the message, and the attitudes of those involved in the communication process. When the desired outcome of downward communication is to produce either an attitudinal or behavioral change in a subordinate, the manager has to be even more concerned about the factors that affect communication success.

In addition to the media already mentioned, others include house organs, bulletin boards, pamphlets, posters, annual reports, conferences, interviews, the grapevine, public address, and speeches.

Upward Communication

The value of **upward communication** in organizations is more apparent today than ever before. Until the human relations movement emerged several decades ago, management solicited little if any input from subordinates, and minimal value was placed on the input it received.

Today, most employees have a strong desire to convey to supervisors and managers their feelings, ideas, aspirations, and attitudes, especially in organizations where such information is desired by those receiving it. Employees rightfully believe they know better than their superiors what is best for them. Employees also believe supervisors and managers can and should consider their input. However, in some organizations, managerial attitude stifles such upward communication, especially when senders fear reprisal.

What types of information are transmitted through upward communication?

Several types of information are transmitted upward from subordinates to the administrative office manager. Although some of these communication encounters with the manager are optional, others are required. Examples of upward communication include information about one's job and work-related problems, organizational policies and procedures, and suggestions for improving existing practices. In most instances, upward communication enables subordinates to relate more closely to and identify with their superiors.

The factors considered in deciding which downward communication channel to use are the same ones considered when deciding which upward channel to use. Upward channels involve oral, written, and electronic communication media.

Upward communication provides a useful feedback function, just as downward communication does. Management can use the input to assess the effectiveness of its practices. In addition, management often assesses the quality of subordinates' input in evaluating their promotability to higher level positions.

The effectiveness of upward communication is influenced by such variables as the nature of the relationship between the subordinate and the manager; the quality of the subordinate's presentation of the message; the extent to which the content of the message is positive or negative; the timeliness of the message; and the extent to which the substance of the message is useful.

Examples of upward communication include suggestion systems, grievance procedures, face-to-face conversations, written and oral reports, e-mail messages, and questionnaires.

Organizations use a number of methods to encourage upward communication. Many of the methods are designed to make employees more comfortable with the process of communicating in an upward direction. Among the methods used are social gatherings, publications (such as newsletters), meetings, performance appraisals, attitude surveys, suggestion systems, and a "true" open-door policy.

Horizontal Communication

What is the function of horizontal communication?

While upward and downward communication tend to have a more formal status, **horizontal communication** is more informal. Authority relationships that exist between senders and receivers in vertical communication do not exist in the horizontal communication that occurs between individuals of equal hierarchical rank.

Horizontal communication provides a useful function in the organization. In addition to allowing employees to fulfill certain socialization needs, it helps employees and departments coordinate their activities with one another. Horizontal communication enables others to better understand the nature of individual and departmental responsibilities. It is also used to help individuals solve their own problems before others have to become involved in these interpersonal entanglements.

The effectiveness of horizontal communication is influenced by the communication abilities and the interpersonal relations skills of the sender and the receiver. Common examples of horizontal communication are face-to-face conversation, small-group meetings (such as committee meetings), and electronic communication.

What is the grapevine?

As a type of informal communication, the **grapevine** is an unofficial communication tool employees of the same hierarchical level often use. Depending on the situation, the information may subsequently be shared with individuals in other hierarchical levels until it is transmitted throughout the entire organization. Sometimes the grapevine is activated because of the failure or absence of formal communication. The grapevine communication process, given its nature, is fast and surprisingly accurate. But in some cases, the information transmitted through the grapevine is nothing but an unfounded rumor.

Management can successfully use the grapevine to assess employee reaction to a proposed change. For example, suppose management is thinking about installing a cafeteria approach to fringe benefits. The grapevine can be used as a barometer to measure the level of employee acceptance of the cafeteria approach. If the level of acceptance is sufficiently high, the program can be installed; if not, the idea can be scrapped.

SMALL-GROUP COMMUNICATION

What three hierarchical levels do administrative office managers occupy in small groups?

For administrative office managers, **small-group communication** has important implications because much of their oral communication occurs within groups of ten or fewer persons. In small groups, administrative office managers occupy three hierarchical levels. They can be the highest ranking individual, be of equal rank with all the members, or be outranked by one or more of the members. Understanding the dynamics of small groups will help the manager more effectively maximize their use.

Small groups are more than just a mere assemblage of individuals who happen to be at the same place at the same time. Having a reason for existing, groups are structured so they can accomplish their tasks as efficiently as possible. They also typically operate according to guidelines or established procedures.

The administrative office manager's membership in some small groups is involuntary, especially within staff groups. A common example of such a group is one comprised of the administrative office manager and his or her subordinate supervisors. The administrative office manager usually presides over periodic group meetings in which problems are solved, decisions are made, and information is passed downward to the unit supervisors or upward to higher level managers.

Administrative office managers are also required to participate in staff groups comprised of their equals and presided over by their superior. Common functions of these groups are problem solving, decision making, and information sharing.

What is the nature of the work-team concept?

An increasing number of organizations are implementing the **work-team concept** in which a small team of employees is responsible for an entire process rather than having employees be responsible for the separate and distinct tasks that comprise the process. Within the work team, each employee typically knows how to perform each task that comprises the process, a concept known as *cross-training*. In organizations that continue to use more traditional work processes, any given employee may know how to perform several of the tasks that comprise a process but does not know how to perform all of the tasks. Much communication will take place among the members of the small group (the team). Too, the administrative office manager may be solicited to work with the team, especially when problems arise.

Reasons People Belong to Small Groups

Why do people belong to small groups?

People belong to groups for a variety of reasons. The extent to which group participation meets members' needs largely determines the amount of satisfaction they derive from their belonging.

Security, one of the reasons for which humans voluntarily join small groups, is one of the basic needs of humans. Employees who are either new to the organization or to their position often feel more secure when they belong to a small group relevant to their needs. In most cases, employees who join small groups are all of equal rank, and the membership of the group may change fairly often.

Another reason employees sometimes voluntarily join small groups is for the power or strength that numbers can exert. The ideas and suggestions promoted by a group tend to be listened to and implemented more often than when the same ideas and suggestions are provided or supported by one person. This is especially true if management needs to be persuaded to take a particular action. Such groups tend to form as issues arise, and the group membership changes as issues change.

Some employees—managers especially—join small groups to have ready access to advice that others can provide. When managers have a specific problem to solve or desire feedback, a small group comprised of their equals is helpful, especially when they do not believe consulting their superior or subordinates is appropriate. Often these group members can provide the needed moral support. Although groups of this type operate rather informally, they can greatly enhance managerial effectiveness.

Advantages and Disadvantages

The small-group process has several advantages and disadvantages. A significant advantage results from the increased breadth and depth of information available within a group. In addition, groups are generally able to identify a greater number of approaches to problem solving than an individual can generate. Managers also find that involving employees as a group is an excellent way to increase their commitment to the solution of a problem.

What is groupthink?

One of the potential disadvantages that results from the small-group technique is the tendency for the process to produce conformity among its members. **Groupthink** considerably reduces a group's creativity because all members begin to think alike. Also of significance is the tendency for one or more persons to dominate the group, which may also reduce its effectiveness. In most instances, the group process is slower than the individual process; a group may become counterproductive once it begins to stray from its original mission.

LARGE-GROUP COMMUNICATION

Large-group communication generally involves planning or participating in meetings and conferences. The leadership capabilities of many administrative office managers enable them to play a critical role in planning a variety of large-group communication situations, including meetings and conferences. Although some of the meetings or conferences that administrative office managers help plan are job related, other events involve the professional and civic organizations to which they belong.

When planning meetings and conferences, several elements need to be considered, including those presented in Figure 3–2.

Figure 3-2 Elements involved in planning meetings or conferences

1. Set date, time, and place of meeting or conference. If the meeting or conference is to be held off the premises, ample time will have to be allotted for locating a suitable facility where the event can be held. The greater the number of participants involved, the earlier the event will have to be scheduled.
2. Plan program or agenda. If the event is primarily designed to share information with the participants, the usual procedure is to plan a program with a variety of presenters or speakers. Ample time will have to be allotted to ensure their availability to make the presentation and for them to prepare their presentation. The printed program needs to be distributed with the announcement of the meeting. If the event primarily has a decision-making focus, an agenda will likely be used. Parliamentary procedures or customs typically determine the order of the items on the agenda. The agenda needs to be distributed with the announcement of the meeting.
3. Arrange for supplementary materials and needed equipment. The individuals responsible for planning the meeting or conference are often responsible for the duplication of materials distributed by the presenters or speakers. Arrangements also have to be made for audiovisual equipment needed by those making presentations.
4. Arrange for dissemination of postmeeting communication. A variety of types of postmeeting communication is distributed to participants and others. Examples of such communication are proceedings, minutes, abstracts, reports, and so on. Those responsible for planning the event may also be responsible for the preparation or distribution of postmeeting communication.

NONVERBAL COMMUNICATION

The nonverbal element of the communication process speaks just as loudly and powerfully as the verbal element—and at times even more so. Therefore, administrative office managers may learn just as much by assessing the nonverbal cues of those with whom they are communicating as they can by listening to the message being communicated. Managers not only should have an understanding of the significance of others' nonverbal cues but also should learn how to use these cues to maximize the effectiveness of their own communication.

Impact of Nonverbal Cues on Communication Process

In what ways do nonverbal cues impact on the communication process?

Nonverbal cues can impact the communication process by:

- *Confirming.* These cues confirm a verbal message, such as when a person points to an object while mentioning it in a conversation.
- *Replacing.* These cues replace spoken words. An example is a negative nod replacing a verbal negative response.
- *Contradicting.* These cues, which contradict the verbal message, add an element of confusion to the communication process. In most cases, the nonverbal cues tend to be more reliable than the verbal message. An example

is a person whose facial expressions indicate that he or she is in considerable pain but who says that he or she feels fine.

- *Emphasizing.* These cues support the verbal message by emphasizing certain aspects. For example, a speaker may emphasize an idea in a speech by slowing down and distinctly verbalizing key words as he or she pounds on the podium.

Elements of Nonverbal Communication

Nonverbal communication is expressed in several ways. The most common way is through **body language;** other ways are through **paralanguage, proxemics,** and **time.**

What are the elements of body language?

Body Language. In the communication process, the human body speaks a language of its own. Gestures, **kinesics** (posture), **occulesics** (facial expressions), eye contact, and **tactilics** (touch) comprise the elements of body language.

When communicating, the **gestures** people use often provide cues about their emotional state, especially when gesturing occurs simultaneously with certain facial expressions. As people become more excited, their gestures tend to become more expansive. Anger and hostility are often signaled through clenched fists, whereas finger tapping and foot tapping indicate nervousness. Folding one's arms across the chest signals uneasiness or disinterest, whereas opened arms and hands show openness and receptivity.

Another common gesture that can either enhance or impede the communication process is head nodding. An affirmative nod from the listener shows agreement with the speaker's message and signals for the speaker to continue speaking. A negative nod signals disagreement and often will cause the speaker to quit talking.

Posture often sends signals about an individual's mood. An upbeat, happy mood is generally signaled through an erect, upright posture, whereas a sad or unhappy mood often causes people to slouch.

Occulesics (facial expressions) play a large role in the communication process. Of all the parts of the human body involved in communicating, the face tends to be the most expressive. The muscular structure of the face enables several of its parts to communicate simultaneously. For example, certain simultaneous expressions of the jaw, lips, eyes, and forehead communicate anger. Happiness is communicated nonverbally through the lips and eyes, whereas disgust tends to be expressed through the lips, eyes, and forehead. Feelings of sadness and fear are communicated by the eyes and forehead.

People often use facial expressions to hide their true feelings in much the same way that individuals do not always verbalize their true feelings. Just as people learn to say the right things at the right time, they also learn to make the right facial expressions at the right time. Facial expressions inconsistent with the message add an element of confusion to the communication process. Therefore, the receiver does not know whether to believe the verbal message or the nonverbal message. In such instances, the reader will usually believe the nonverbal signs, however.

Communication between two people is also influenced by the nature of the eye contact between them. By maintaining direct eye contact with the speaker, the receiver signals that the communication channel is open and that he or she wishes to continue listening. Direct eye contact may also indicate solidarity, whereas a break in the contact may signal that the receiver desires to end the communication process. A break in eye contact may also indicate a feeling of tension, distrust, or uneasiness. Conversely, a cold stare signals a feeling of authority or domination. The nature of eye contact between two individuals is culture bound.

What is meant by the term *tactilics?*

Tactilics (touching) is often used in the communication process to support the verbal message that it accompanies. A handshake is a cordial nonverbal greeting that supports the verbal greeting. Even the firmness of the handshake is considered by many to carry a nonverbal message about one's assertiveness. A pat on the back during the verbal exchange indicates solidarity, approval, and support. The same feelings can be communicated by grabbing hold of someone's arm during the conversation.

What is paralanguage?

Paralanguage. The way people express themselves—known as paralanguage—often communicates more meaning than their verbal messages. When voice quality is inconsistent with the verbalized message, the speaker's sincerity or credibility may be questioned. To be believed, people have to sound as though they mean what they say.

Among the voice elements that affect the communication process are range, rate of speaking, pitch, volume, pauses, and intrusions. The more variable the range of one's voice, the less monotonous it will be. Consistently speaking in a monotone conveys the impression of disinterest, whereas a more variable range conveys an impression of commitment and enthusiasm. A change in the rate of speaking is effectively used to emphasize the importance of certain ideas or thoughts.

Emotional feelings are conveyed by the pitch of the speaker's voice. A high-pitched voice signals excitement and enthusiasm, but a low-pitched voice signals seriousness. Importance is attached to key items by verbalizing them more loudly or softly. Pauses in speaking, which may indicate contemplation, are also effectively used to help recapture the listener's attention. Such intrusions as "ah" or "um" tend to signal tension, a feeling of pressure, or lack of certainty.

What is proxemics?

Proxemics. The way people structure their territory and space—known as proxemics—also has an impact on communication. When their space is inhibited, employees tend to become less comfortable and more inhibited.

The nature of the situation should be considered in determining an appropriate location to hold a communication encounter. For example, a manager who wishes to have a cordial discussion with a subordinate will find that a neutral location may enhance their discussion. An informal conversational area in the manager's office is more neutral than the space around the manager's desk. If the situation requires that the manager defend his or her position or negotiate with another person, territorial strength can be enhanced by remaining behind the desk, even though doing so creates a natural communication barrier. The amount of control one has over the communication process is greatly affected by the location of the encounter.

Humans continuously maintain "protective custody" of the space around themselves. This space moves with people as they move about. A distance ranging from 18 inches to 4 feet is reserved for visual and social encounters, whereas an area closer than 18 inches is reserved for intimacy. An inappropriate violation of one's space—regardless of the range—often creates a barrier in the communication process.

In what ways does room ambience affect the communication process?

The ambience of the room in which the communication occurs affects the communication process. Rooms that are warm and cheerful tend to create a more cordial communicating atmosphere, whereas a cold, unfriendly ambience may detract from the communication process. The nature of the seating arrangement also affects communication. People seated beside each another will find communication more difficult than will those who are seated across from each another.

The artifacts and objects in one's work area also communicate. Office furniture is an indicator of status. Wooden office furniture tends to communicate more status than metal furniture; optional pieces, such as credenzas and upholstered furniture, also communicate status. By providing a conversational topic, artifacts often enhance the communication process. Membership and award certificates provide clues about one's professional involvements, leadership, and expertise. While they rarely stimulate the amount of conversation that artifacts do, certificates provide recognition for their beholder.

How does time communicate nonverbally?

Time. The time of day that people communicate may provide insight into the importance of the message. For example, you would likely attach more importance to a request by your superior to see her "first thing in the morning" than to a request that you see her "tomorrow whenever it fits into your schedule." When you receive an after-work telephone call from your superior, the message likely will be interpreted as having more importance than if you received the identical message while you were at work.

When a caller arrives late for an appointment, the negative nonverbal message that is conveyed can be interpreted in several ways. Arriving late may signal that the caller is undependable, unreliable, or unorganized. It may also signal that the caller believes the person with whom he or she is meeting does not have sufficient importance or status to merit arriving on time.

How well people manage their time in meeting deadlines conveys a message about their work habits and organizational skills. Those who are habitually late are viewed as being disorganized and unable to manage their time well. The situation may be further compounded when people accept more responsibilities than they can effectively handle in the allotted time, which conveys the impression that they are inefficient in their work habits.

Because nonverbal communication is culture bound, the implications of its various elements do not have universal meaning throughout the world. For example, some gestures commonly used in the United States are considered vulgar in other cultures. Americans believe in maintaining eye contact with those with whom they are speaking. But in other cultures, especially Asian cultures, younger people avoid eye contact with their elders as a way of showing them respect. Americans do less touching and like having more space between them than do people of some other cultures. While we believe in close adherence to a time schedule, less emphasis on being timely is found in other cultures. Because people of other cultures are being assimilated into American companies and there is a growing trend for companies to operate abroad, individuals who work closely with people from other cultures are wise to become aware of the nonverbal communication differences.

BARRIERS TO EFFECTIVE COMMUNICATION

Regardless of our position in life, we continually need to work at becoming more effective communicators. Being aware of the **barriers** to effective communication is one way of improving communication abilities. Skilled communicators are able to minimize or neutralize the impact these barriers have on their communication activities.

What are the barriers to effective communication?

A potential impediment to the communication process results from taking certain things or people for granted. For example, we may assume that a listener has the needed background information about a problem situation when in fact he or she has very little information. Or we may take for granted that the listener has almost no background information, and we provide several details about which he or she is already familiar.

In some instances, managers mistakenly believe that subordinates do not care to interact with their supervisor. In reality, subordinates often desire to have more opportunities to interact with management than are available. Incorrectly perceiving the amount of communication appropriate for a given situation can significantly hamper one's effectiveness.

Some of the characteristics of upward, downward, and horizontal communication also create barriers. For example, when downward communication makes no provision for feedback, management can never be certain how much of the message was received, understood, or interpreted correctly. In addition, management and subordinates often perceive downward communication differently. So what management believes is a reasonable rationale for a certain course of action, subordinates may interpret as an attempt to manipulate them. Because some subordinates are generally suspicious of their superiors, they question the validity of much of the downward communication they receive.

What are the barriers to upward communication?

Upward communication also is affected by certain barriers. When subordinates have an opportunity to communicate upward, they tend to transmit only the information that enhances their standing with their superiors. The message will likely become distorted if negative information is withheld. In other instances, subordinates provide the information they believe management wants to hear. A serious information void is created if subordinates misinterpret the type of information management desires or if they withhold information management badly needs.

Upward communication is also affected by management's reaction to the information it receives from subordinates. If management continually avoids making use of the information it solicits, subordinates will likely discontinue providing it. Unless management conveys the impression that it appreciates receiving information from employees in the lower levels of the organization, only minimum amounts of input are likely to be provided.

How can semantics affect the communication process?

Semantics can also create a communication barrier. Because words mean different things to people, the manner in which individuals interpret the words can create a communication barrier. Consequently, if the speaker uses a word to which the listener attaches a different meaning, the opportunity for miscommunication is present.

A communication barrier can also be created by perception. We all have perceptions, often largely affected or influenced by our experiences. Miscommunication can occur when individuals who actually see the same phenomenon or hear the same message believe they saw or heard something else. In some instances, our perceptions cause us to make decisions prematurely or to make quick judgments.

In addition, certain barriers affect horizontal communication, which is informal. Interpersonal rivalry between two individuals may cause one person to withhold information from another, primarily to put that person in a disadvantaged position. In other cases, a person may pass on preconceived notions as though they were true, which may cause some communication difficulties. As humans, we often tend to let our feelings about others affect our communication with them. Because actions tend to speak louder than words, disguising our true feelings may be difficult. Status differences between individuals can also become a powerful communication barrier. Finally, cultural differences among employees can produce a communication barrier.

DEVELOPMENT OF LISTENING SKILLS

Although **listening** is the weakest communication skill of many administrative office managers, most, ironically, spend more time each day listening to others than reading, writing, or speaking. To improve their listening skills, managers may have to undertake their own development efforts because minimal time in formal education is devoted to these critical skills.

Elements of the Listening Process

The listening process is affected by internal elements, contextual elements, and relationship elements.

Internal Elements. If the listening process is to be effective, the listener not only has to hear the message but also has to be able to attach proper meaning to the words that constitute the message. The listening process breaks down when the listener either does not hear, does not understand, or does not attach proper meaning to the message.

Another internal element is the individual's capacity for listening. The length of time individuals are able to listen and the amount of information they are able to absorb in a given time varies considerably from person to person. An individual's listening capacity also varies from hour to hour and from day to day.

What are the contextual elements of the listening process?

Contextual Elements. The listening process is also affected by the context or environment in which communication occurs. Among the contextual elements are the presence of noise, the constraints of time, the accessibility of the sender and receiver to one another, and the communication channel that is used.

As managers move upward in the organization hierarchy, time pressures become more significant. Special care has to be taken to prevent these pressures from having a negative impact on their ability to listen. In addition, access to managers diminishes as they move upward, which may eliminate some opportunities for them to interact with others.

Also affecting the listening process is the type of communication channel being used. In some instances, individuals may be able to listen more effectively in a face-to-face conversation than in a telephone conversation. In other instances, the opposite will be true.

Relationship Elements. The nature of a relationship that develops between a sender and receiver as they communicate affects the listening process. A cordial relationship enhances listening; a strained relationship destroys listening.

How do relationships between people affect listening?

When interacting with certain individuals, the desire to say the right thing at the right time may cause the listener to concentrate more on what he or she is going to say next rather than on listening to the message. Obviously, this destroys listening effectiveness.

For self-protection, the listener in other instances filters out the sender's negative comments. Adverse information is not allowed to penetrate the listener's mind and therefore will not be as "fully heard" as positive information.

Suggestions for Improving Listening

Managers who are effective listeners readily admit that these skills did not just happen; rather, they became better listeners as a result of conscientious development efforts. Figure 3–3 presents several suggestions designed to help individuals improve their listening skills.

Figure 3-3 Suggestions for improving the effectiveness of listening skills

1. Concentrate on what the sender says by clearing your mind of other thoughts and by giving the communication process your undivided attention.
2. Avoid doodling or playing with desk accessories or objects while interacting with others.
3. Accept senders for whom they are and not how they express themselves or how they appear.
4. Avoid "tuning out" senders whose conversation may not be intrinsically interesting to you because the content is dull, irrelevant, or difficult to understand.
5. Learn to "listen" to the nonverbal component of a message with your eyes as well as to the verbal component with your ears.
6. Keep your listening speed consistent with the sender's conversation rate.
7. Seek clarification of messages you do not understand.
8. Learn to listen more objectively by not allowing your preconceptions, biases, or prejudices to infiltrate the communication process.
9. Listen as intently to unimportant messages as you do to the important ones.
10. Avoid "listening between the lines" in oral communication in the same way that you avoid "reading between the lines" of a written message.

APPLICATION OF COMMUNICATION PROCESS

Administrative office managers extensively use the communication process as they make decisions, resolve conflicts, and implement changes. This section provides a discussion of these three important topics.

Decision-Making Process

Decision making is one of the most important responsibilities of administrative office managers. The communication process is likely to be used actively before a decision is made. This is because administrative office managers often solicit information from others prior to making a decision. After the decision is made, it has to be communicated to others. Managerial effectiveness is often influenced by how well a manager's decisions are communicated to those who are affected by them.

Steps. The **decision-making process** is comprised of the following steps:

What steps constitute the decision-making process?

1. Defining and limiting the problem (or situation).
2. Analyzing the problem (or situation).
3. Defining criteria to be used in evaluating various solutions.
4. Gathering the data/information.
5. Identifying and evaluating possible solutions.
6. Selecting the best solution.
7. Implementing the solution.

Within each step, various aspects of the participants' communication effectiveness can either enhance or impede the ultimate outcome of the decision. Too, the effort that is put into each step can affect the quality of the decision.

The accuracy with which a problem/situation is defined at the outset often affects the outcome of the decision. During the entire decision-making process, considerable time and effort can be saved by working with a problem/situation that has been accurately defined. This is the time to ask a variety of questions about the problem/situation. In addition to focusing directly on the problem/situation, an examination of the peripheral circumstances may also be helpful. The more precisely the individuals involved in the decision-making process differentiate between a problem/situation and its symptoms, the more accurately the problem/situation can be defined.

The second step—identifying the circumstances or underlying factors that created the problem/situation—is facilitated by accurately defining the problem/situation. Examples are financial conditions, interpersonal problems between individuals, and poor management. Once the decision makers are aware of the causes of the problem/situation, its solution will be easier.

Those involved in making decisions generally are not given free rein but rather must act within certain constraints in solving a problem/situation; therefore, they need to be aware of their limits. In turn, these limits help when defining the criteria that are used in evaluating various solutions. Examples of criteria are financial considerations, procedural restrictions, human factors, time constraints, and policy restrictions. In some instances, individuals who rank higher than those responsible for making the decision define a portion of the criteria.

Once the decision makers are aware of their constraints, they are able to begin identifying possible solutions. The solutions that clearly exceed the limits of the criteria established in step 3 can be quickly eliminated from further consideration. This step will consume less time if the criteria are realistically defined at an early stage.

An effective way to evaluate possible solutions is to determine the impact that each solution will have on the desired outcome. Unless extenuating circumstances exist, the solution believed to provide the maximum positive effect is the one likely to be chosen. Once selected, the acceptability of the solution may be affected by the way in which others are informed of the decision. The more effectively the administrative office manager communicates the decision, the more likely he or she will be able to sell others on its merits.

Typically, communication is extensively involved in the implementation of decisions. Those affected by the decision have to be informed of the decision and its impact on them. Implementation plans have to be developed and responsibilities for various tasks must be assigned. Depending on the nature of the decision, a fair amount of time and communication effort may have to be devoted to gaining its acceptance. Communication is a useful technique in diminishing individual resistance to the problem/situation.

The nature of some decisions will require the use of certain control measures to help assure that decisions are being properly implemented. These control devices may be in the form of progress reports, briefing sessions, or other types of follow-up techniques. When results show that corrective measures are needed, the administrative office manager will have to determine the appropriate measures.

Nominal Grouping Technique. Group decision-making processes are becoming increasingly attractive to administrative office managers. The **nominal grouping technique**—a useful group decision-making process—is highly structured and minimizes the amount of personal interaction among the group members. This technique is comprised of the following five steps:

What is the purpose of the nominal grouping technique?

1. *Listing.* Working alone, each member of the group prepares a written list of ideas or suggestions for solving a given problem.

2. *Recording.* On a one-by-one basis, each member offers an idea from his or her list; the group leader records each idea on a master list that everyone

can see. The members continue to contribute their ideas, one by one, until all ideas are presented.

3. *Voting.* Each member selects the five best ideas on the master list and presents on a ballot his or her ideas in priority preference. The ideas are weighted (for example, the highest priority idea receives five points).

4. *Discussing.* Each idea is discussed to help clarify any ambiguous points and to evaluate the worth of the various items.

5. *Final voting.* Each member votes a second time, again presenting the ideas in a priority order.

The nominal grouping technique is useful in situations in which members spend considerable time debating the worth of each other's suggestions. This technique enables individuals to spend more time in creative activity and less time in promoting their individual positions.

Conflict Resolution

Another task consuming an ever-increasing amount of managerial time is the resolution of conflict. Although conflict has always existed, managerial recognition of its presence is of rather recent origin. For many years, the prevailing belief seemed to be that if managers did not recognize conflict, then it did not exist; and, therefore, one did not have to deal with it.

A total absence of conflict within an organization is not necessarily a healthy situation. Properly managed conflict within a unit may increase its creativity. It may also increase the number of alternatives identified for solving a specific problem.

Sources of Conflict. Conflict between individuals and within groups arises for several reasons. Most organizations have limited resources that individuals and groups must share. Conflict arises when individual employees or groups of employees believe they are not getting their "fair share" or that others are getting more than their "fair share." Another source of conflict results from goal incompatibility. Although overall organizational goals are generally compatible with one another, conflict sometimes arises as a result of incompatibility between overall goals and individual and/or group goals.

Other sources of potential conflict are the various organizational reward systems. Examples of such reward systems are individual or unit incentive plans, merit salary increase plans, and so forth. When employees believe they have not been treated fairly in relation to others, conflict may result. Various changes in the organizational environment may also stimulate conflict. To illustrate, as the organization responds to a changing environment, the level of responsibility or importance of one unit may increase as the level of another unit decreases, giving rise to potential conflict between the two units.

Regardless of the nature of the conflict situation or the strategy selected for its resolution, the communication process is likely to be used extensively. A certain amount of conflict may have been avoidable had more extensive communication between individuals occurred. Therefore, communication is helpful in preventing a certain amount of conflict from arising and in forming resolution efforts should problems arise.

Resolution strategies significantly determine the effectiveness and efficiency with which conflict is resolved. Before selecting a strategy, the astute manager will assess a variety of factors, including the following:

1. *Background of the conflict situation.* Familiarity with the background of the situation helps the manager determine the amount of flexibility available

What are the sources of conflict?

What factors should be considered in selecting a conflict resolution strategy?

to resolve the conflict. In some instances, almost no flexibility is apparent. The number of people involved in the conflict should be determined. Various issues that must be dealt with before the situation can be resolved also need to be identified.

2. *Background of those involved in the conflict.* Some employees do not find conflict all that unpleasant and, therefore, are likely to become involved more frequently and to a greater extent than other employees. These are the employees who often have a "cause," which results in their becoming preoccupied with the conflict situation. How managers deal with these individuals may be quite different from how they deal with those who are rarely involved in a conflict situation. In assessing the backgrounds of individuals involved in the conflict situation, such factors as their values, attitudes, and beliefs should be considered. The more a manager knows about the backgrounds of the conflicting parties, the more likely he or she will be able to select a strategy that ends a conflict rather than simply puts the conflict into remission.

3. *Relationship between conflicting parties.* The conflict between individuals may be of rather long duration. Even though the severity of the conflict may increase or decrease over time, it is always present. The strategy used to resolve this type of conflict may be quite different from the strategy used to resolve conflict between individuals who have never had difficulties with each other before. In addition, the way individuals feel toward each other may be a consideration in selecting a strategy.

4. *Benefits to be derived from resolving conflict.* In some instances, the conflicting parties may see almost no benefit from their settling differences with one another. When this happens, the manager may have to be somewhat more creative in his or her resolution efforts and use different strategies. In other instances, the manager may have to use his or her communication skills to convince the conflicting parties that settling their differences is not only desirable for the individuals but also for the work unit.

Conflict Resolution Strategies. The strategies used to resolve conflict often enable some individuals to win and cause others to lose. Rarely will all of the parties involved in a conflict lose, and seldom can they all win.

The importance a person attaches to winning in a conflict situation is directly related to the importance he or she attaches to the issue. People naturally want to win in those situations they consider crucial; therefore, they exert more effort toward winning.

Employees will sometimes rationalize losing the "small ones." Because the odds are against their winning every conflict, they believe they can better their chances of winning the important situations if they lose the less important ones.

A person who has excellent persuasive communication skills tends to win more often than one whose skills are weak. Also, the power that a person can exert is a determinant as is the amount of support that can be mustered from others. The extent to which a person can compromise is also a factor. A small compromise may enable a person to win, perhaps to a lesser degree than he or she would like; however, the inability to make any compromise may result in total loss.

Implementation of Change

Increasingly, administrative office managers are finding themselves in the situation of having to respond to both internal and external forces that result in the need for change. Communication is one of the most effective managerial tools to implement change.

Administrative office managers are confronted with two types of change: planned change and reactive change. **Planned change,** which is proactive, occurs as a result of careful planning, developing, and implementing. This type of change precedes the occurrence of events that necessitate change. **Reactive change,** conversely, is generally forced change, resulting from the occurrence of events that make change necessary. Planned change is generally considered to be superior to reactive change, primarily because those involved in implementing the change may have more flexibility at their disposal than when change is forced upon them.

What steps are involved in implementing change?

Steps. Among the steps involved in implementing change are the following:

1. *Recognize need for change.* Generally, the need for change, planned or reactive, arises from internal and/or external forces. Communication is extensively involved in assessing the need for change.
2. *Plan the change.* Once the need for change arises, the planning process begins. During this step, several ideas are likely to be considered that have the potential for dealing with the various events necessitating the change. This step also involves extensive amounts of communication.
3. *Recommend a plan.* Generally, the recommendation of a plan for implementing the change is presented in a written proposal or report to the decision makers. The recommendation might be presented orally if the situation lacks complexity, however. The plan, whether it is presented in writing or orally, requires the effective use of communication skills.
4. *Decide about the plan.* After the decision makers have had an opportunity to consider the recommended plan, the next step involves making an implementation decision. The nature of the situation for which the plan is being proposed will likely determine who will make the final decision. Those charged with making a decision can range from the organization's board of directors to unit supervisors. Communication is used extensively in deciding whether or not to implement the plan.
5. *Implement the plan.* Once the plan has been approved, the next step involves making implementation plans, followed by the actual implementation. Included in this step is the commitment of various types of organization resources. This step makes extensive use of communication.

People have a natural tendency to resist change, resulting from such factors as fear of the unknown, self-interest, lack of trust in management, and lack of flexibility needed to adapt to change. Communication is one of the most effective tools management has at its disposal for overcoming resistance. Another effective tool is to allow those affected by the change to participate in the planning and implementing process. Supporting those affected by the change as they prepare for the change also helps reduce the amount of resistance.

What are focus groups?

Increasingly, organizations use **focus groups** when planning for change. These groups are likely comprised of a broad spectrum of employees who may be knowledgeable about the situation or phenomenon undergoing change. The leader of the group poses a series of questions to which the participants provide input. Generally, focus-group sessions do not involve assessing the worth of participants' input; rather, the goal is to obtain from the participants as much input as possible. One of the distinct advantages of the focus-group process is that the input of one participant will likely stimulate input of other participants.

IMPLICATIONS FOR THE ADMINISTRATIVE OFFICE MANAGER

The ability to communicate effectively is among the most crucial of the various background skills needed of the administrative office manager. No matter how well developed his or her decision-making skills are or how well he or she manages a unit, an individual with weak communication skills will be limited in his or her managerial effectiveness.

Managers are more readily able to disguise weak reading skills than to disguise weaknesses in speaking, listening, or writing. Communication has become such an important criterion for managerial success that every attempt should be made to overcome any deficiencies. Self-study, formal courses, and seminars are three means available for use by managers to improve their skills.

The more effectively one's communication skills are developed, the more meaningful, satisfying, and relevant one will find the communication process. For example, by learning to read nonverbal cues, the manager will find that the verbal message has much more meaning. By being aware of potential communication barriers, the manager can more readily make adjustments to counteract the negative influence of any impediments. The best way to avoid the frustration that frequently accompanies conflict is to develop effective resolution skills.

Unfortunately, in some instances a manager takes the communication process for granted. The fact that an individual has communicated in one form or another since the moment of birth does not necessarily mean that his or her skills are well developed. Communication is spontaneously used many times during each day, and one's skills should be developed to a level where they help rather than hinder managerial effectiveness.

REVIEW QUESTIONS

1. What are the elements of the communication process, and what occurs within each element?
2. Identify several specific differences between upward, downward, and horizontal communication.
3. Why do individuals join small groups?
4. In what ways do nonverbal cues affect the communication process?
5. What is paralanguage?
6. What is proxemics?
7. Identify several suggestions that will be helpful in improving one's listening skills.
8. What are the elements of the listening process?
9. What are the steps in the decision-making process?
10. What factors should a manager consider before he or she selects an appropriate strategy for resolving conflict?

DISCUSSION QUESTIONS

1. Assume you are one of five administrative office managers being interviewed for a feature article that will be printed in the local newspaper. The reporter conducting the interview asked several questions, one of which was: "What types of communication skills do you use during a typical day in your position as an administrative office manager?" How do you respond?

2. As a supervisor of seven subordinates, you have noticed that a relationship seems to exist between the quickness with which a new employee identifies with a small group and his or her acclimatization to the job. Why do you believe your observation is true? As a supervisor, what might you do to facilitate an employee's identifying with a small group?

3. Comparing the communication skills needed of today's administrative office manager with the skills that you perceive will be needed in ten years, do you believe the skills will become more or less important, or do you perceive they will be similar in their level of importance? Why?

STUDENT PROJECTS AND ACTIVITIES

1. Discuss with an administrative office manager the importance of effective communication skills to his or her job success.
2. Observe someone engaged in conversation. What nonverbal signals did you notice?
3. Going Online: Using the Internet, conduct an online search based on one of the concepts presented in this chapter or based on one of the chapter terms. Identify four or five things you learned from the material you read that you did not know before.

Minicases

You are the administrative office manager in XYZ Manufacturing Company. The philosophy of the company president is to appoint a committee to deal with problems or issues when they arise rather than to bring in consultants. Consistent with this philosophy, he recently appointed you to chair a communications committee that is charged with developing an in-house seminar for employees who wish to improve their communication skills.

1. Outline the methods you plan to use in determining the appropriate content for this seminar.
2. Identify topics or areas that you think should be included in the seminar.

Case

John Lezenski, the administrative office manager of the L-H Paper Company, which is located in Lincoln, Nebraska, recently attended a three-day management communication seminar. The brochure he received that publicized this seminar stated that it would present "practical, down-to-earth information" about ways managers can improve their communication skills. He was delighted to discover that the seminar did just that, because the following sessions were offered: improving listening skills, understanding the communication process, using nonverbal communication to one's benefit, overcoming communication barriers, and so forth.

Mr. Lezenski was also surprised to learn that communication was so important to job success. He was not aware, before attending the seminar, just how much he communicates on his job, nor was he aware of the extent that effective communication facilitates job performance.

Most of his thoughts on the flight home from the seminar focused on points that presenters made. He is troubled, however, about one question: How can he determine whether he has a communication problem. He believes that he learned enough to overcome many types of problems he might have, but he is not sure whether he has any of major significance.

1. Prepare for Mr. Lezenski a list of questions he could ask himself that would be useful in determining the nature of any communication problems he might have. (Prepare questions that can be answered with a "yes" or "no" response.)
2. From the list of questions you prepare, assume Mr. Lezenski discovers he has a problem with face-to-face communication encounters with his superior. What suggestions can you offer that will help him overcome this communication weakness?

*C*hapter 4

OFFICE LAYOUT

*C*hapter *A*ims

After studying this chapter, you should be able to design an efficient layout for a general office area.

*C*hapter *O*utline

The Preliminary Planning Stage
    Tasks
    Work Flow
    Organization Chart
    Projection of Employees Needed in the Future
    Communication Network
    Departmental Organization
    Private and General Offices
    Space Requirements
    Specialized Areas
    Safety Considerations
    Barrier-free Construction
    Expansion
    Environmental Conditions
    Equipment and Furniture
Costing of Office Space
Open Office Concept
    Modular Workstation Approach
    Cluster Workstation Approach
    Landscape Approach
Principles of Effective Layout
Preparing the Layout
    Templates
    Cutouts
    Plastic Models
    Magnetic Board
    Computer-Aided Design
Implications for the Administrative Office
    Manager

*C*hapter *T*erms

Barrier-free construction
Cluster workstation approach
Communication matrix
Communication network
Cybernetics
Ergonomics
Hoteling
Modular workstation approach
Office landscaping
Open plan concept
Shared office
Space analysis
Telecommuting
Work-based teams
Work flow

*T*he layout of an organization's work areas can significantly affect—both positively and negatively—its productivity. Designing efficient work areas is critically important from a cost-effectiveness standpoint. Layout design requires consideration of the interrelationships between the following three components: equipment, flow of work, and employees. Therefore, these interrelationships must be thoroughly studied and analyzed in the process of planning efficient employee work areas.

Office layout determines whether space is used in an efficient and cost-effective manner as well as affects how much satisfaction employees derive from their jobs. Furthermore, layout has an impact on the impression people get of the work areas.

Efficient layout results in the following significant operational and economic benefits:

What are the operational and economic benefits of layouts?

1. It provides effective allocation and use of floor space.
2. It creates a pleasant working environment for employees.
3. It has a positive impact on the organization's clients.
4. It facilitates efficient work flow.
5. It provides employees with efficient, productive work areas.
6. It facilitates future expansion when the need arises.
7. It facilitates employee supervision.

Extensive preliminary planning is essential when preparing the layout for a new facility or when making major renovations in an existing facility. Planning, the most important stage in the project, affects all other stages and will ultimately determine whether the final results are effective and efficient.

In addition to preliminary planning, which is discussed in detail in the next section, the undertaking of layout projects involves two other stages: preparing architectural and construction drawings followed by constructing or renovating of the premises.

Inadequate space planning is likely to result in reduced employee productivity, increased absenteeism, increased turnover, decreased physical comfort, and decreased employee morale. Among the most visible situations resulting from inadequate space planning are the following:

What results are likely to occur when inadequate attention is given to space planning?

1. Future growth that is not accurately anticipated.
2. Storage facilities and areas that are inadequate.
3. Office furniture that fails to meet the needs of its users.
4. Work flow patterns that are cumbersome and awkward.
5. Traffic patterns that are inefficient.

Organizations that have a facility manager will likely involve that person in workplace design, along with the administrative office manager. Although the facility manager and the administrative office manager have a differing set of responsibilities within the organization, they work cooperatively in a number of areas, including the design of each employee's workplace.

Three rather new work-arrangement concepts are impacting office layout and design and will likely impact this area even more so in the future. These include **telecommuting, work-based teams,** and **hoteling.**

Telecommuting is a work arrangement that allows employees to perform some or all of their work tasks off premises. From an office-layout standpoint, the more time the employee works off premises, the less he or she will need a full-fledged office on the organization's premises. From an office-design standpoint, a streamlined office area may be quite satisfactory. In some instances, several employees who frequently telecommute may share the same office.

Increasing numbers of organizations are performing an ever-greater amount of their functions using work-based teams whose members generally have frequent interaction with one another. Therefore, an open environment that facilitates ready communication and a greater number of small conference areas may need to be installed throughout the premises or at least in the locations, sometimes referred to as "neighborhoods," where work-based teams are commonly found. Depending on the nature of the tasks performed by these teams, verbal privacy may be essential. Consequently, some of the small conference areas may need to be enclosed to accommodate both work teams and individuals who need a quiet place to concentrate on certain of their tasks. Increasingly, the office furniture used by these work-based teams is mounted on casters to facilitate quick rearrangement of work areas to accommodate the task at hand.

What is hoteling?

Hoteling typically involves employees who spend a significant amount of their time off premises, such as outside sales representatives, and to a lesser extent, telecommuting employees. Rather than provide these employees with a costly, full-fledged office, a number of work carrels are provided that they can reserve when they need to work on the premises. These carrels are generally equipped with a phone and a computer network jack for use in connecting a laptop computer to the organization's network, although some may be permanently equipped with a desk-top computer or a docking station.

When a number of the organization's employees who work under the telecommuting or hoteling arrangements live in close proximity to one another, providing them with work space near where they live may be advantageous. Satellite offices are generally found to be quite effective from both a cost and employee morale standpoint.

THE PRELIMINARY PLANNING STAGE

Preliminary planning of office layout is one of the areas in which administrative office managers are often and significantly involved. But once the preliminary work is completed, their involvement may decrease somewhat. Many of the activities of the planning stage focus on assessing the nature of the organization's needs. This information is compiled from the assessment process and subsequently transformed into drawings and finally into the actual layout.

In some organizations, employees undertake the preliminary planning. Other organizations base their planning on the collaborative efforts of their employees and consultants.

The preliminary planning stage involves the consideration of several factors, including tasks, work flow, organization chart, projection of employees needed in the future, communication network, departmental organization, private and general offices, and space requirements. Other factors include specialized areas, safety considerations, barrier-free construction, expansion, environmental conditions, and equipment and furniture.

Tasks

Increasingly, the tasks performed by individuals have an important role in determining the type of office facilities they need to maximize their productivity. For example, employees who frequently work collaboratively have different office needs than those who rarely, if ever, work collaboratively. Because of the increased ability to provide employees with ergonomically designed offices based on their tasks, their productivity can be enhanced. Too, the tasks employees perform are changing more rapidly than ever, which mandates the flexibility of office design.

Work Flow

What is involved in the flow of work in most departments?

Work flow refers to the movement of information either vertically (between superiors and subordinates or vice versa) or horizontally (between employees of the same responsibility level). Accurate work flow analysis is critical in the designing of effective layout.

An efficient work flow places employees and equipment in a pattern that facilitates the straight-line flow of information, which helps eliminate backtracking and crisscrossing work patterns. To accomplish the straight-line flow, the duties, responsibilities, and activities of each employee must be thoroughly studied. Inadequate attention given to work flow often results in delays in processing information, excessive handling of documents, and the need for personnel to exert more effort than would otherwise be necessary.

The flow of work in most departments usually involves major source documents, typically forms. For example, in a credit department, the major source document may be the credit application; in an accounts payable department, the payment voucher; and in a purchasing department, the purchase order. An effective means of studying the work flow is to follow the movement of the major source documents through the department. The movement may be traced in either of two ways: (1) by preparing and analyzing a flow process chart (see Figure 17–7), or (2) by actually charting or diagraming the movement of the document through its work flow patterns (see Figure 17–8).

Because effective layout is based on the interrelationships among equipment, work flow, and employees, an analysis must be made of the effect the equipment component has on the flow of work between employees. More and more, the equipment component involves the use of computer or data processing devices or facilities.

Organization Chart

What does the organization chart depict?

Closely related to the study of work flow is the analysis of the organization chart. When the flow of work is primarily vertical (superior to subordinate or vice versa), the organization chart clearly depicts organizational lines of authority. The organization chart also identifies job relationships among employees of similar hierarchical rank, thus helping determine the appropriate location of employees and work units.

Projection of Employees Needed in the Future

Determining how much space will be needed in the years ahead requires a careful, accurate projection of employees needed in the future. The following should be considered in making the projection:

1. The likelihood of developing new products or services that will require large increases in the number of office employees.
2. The firm's expected yearly growth rate as measured by profit.
3. The expected yearly increase in the number of employees.
4. The possible changes in office operations that will require new employees.

The absence of careful consideration of these factors may result in inadequate space to meet the organization's future needs.

Communication Network

In addition to studying the flow of work between individuals and departments, an analysis of the nature of telephone, e-mail, and face-to-face contact between individuals and departments is essential. When the work flow, the organization chart, and the **communication network** indicate that certain individuals and departments have extensive contact and interaction, the individuals and departments are logically grouped near one another.

To summarize data about the frequency of telephone and face-to-face contacts, preparing a **communication matrix** similar to Figure 4–1 is useful. This is a summary of tally sheets kept by each employee over a representative period (perhaps a two-week period that is void of any unusual fluctuations, such as those created by seasonally busy times of the year). For example, the data in Figure 4–1 indicate that forty telephone and e-mail contacts were made between the president and assistant to the president, whereas sixty face-to-face contacts were made between these two individuals during the same time.

Departmental Organization

Most organizations continue to be organized by functions, specifically by departments or areas. Such technological developments as the computer, however, have brought about some changes in the structures found in many organizations. Deciding on the location of each department involves considering the flow of work between various departments.

Some departments, such as accounting and data processing, are closely related and should be placed near one another. Likewise, departments with frequent public contact, such as purchasing and personnel, should be located near the entrance or reception area of the building.

Noise-producing departments or areas—such as receiving or printing and duplicating, for example—should be located near one another and away from areas that require a noise-free environment. Areas that cut across all departments, such as central records and central word processing, should be located as centrally as possible for convenience and accessibility. Individuals or departments with minimal public contact, such as the president and other executive officers, should be located in a less heavily traveled, fairly secluded, quiet area of the building.

Private and General Offices

The use of more general offices and fewer private offices is emerging as a trend. In the past, private offices were used for reasons of prestige and status. They were also made available to employees who needed a quiet area for concentration and to those individuals whose jobs involved working with an abundance of confidential materials.

The following reasons are frequently cited for doing away with private offices: (1) the cost of building private offices is considerably greater than providing a comparable amount of space in a general office; (2) private offices complicate supervision of employees; (3) the permanent walls surrounding private offices make layout changes difficult; (4) the task of heating, cooling, and lighting private areas is more difficult than in open areas; and (5) private offices impede communication.

For what is a communication matrix used?

Why are private offices being eliminated?

	President	Assistant to President	Tax and Legal Advisor	V.P. Corporate Relations	V.P. Finances	V.P. Production	Administrative Officer Manager	Central Records Supervisor	Data Processing Supervisor	Sales Manager
President	■	40/60	10/17	18/10	20/7	10/12	3/0	0/0	3/0	1/0
Assistant to President		■	30/25	20/16	18/18	7/3	10/8	5/0	18/4	15/10
Tax and Legal Advisor			■	20/19	8/12	3/0	0/1	4/7	0/0	7/12
V.P. Corporate Relations				■	17/23	15/12	5/9	0/0	4/2	1/0
V.P. Finances					■	14/16	5/3	3/1	15/21	5/8
V.P. Production						■	5/3	4/1	10/5	18/23
Administrative Officer Manager							■	19/27	15/13	5/9
Central Records Supervisor								■	21/18	5/8
Data Processing Supervisor									■	15/18
Sales Manager										■

The intersection of the rows and columns is coded as follows:

upper number - number of phone and e-mail contacts between individuals

lower number - number of personal contacts between individuals

Figure 4–1 Communication matrix

Further reducing the need for private offices is the **open plan concept,** which is discussed in a subsequent section of this chapter.

Space Requirements

Several factors determine the minimum amount of space suitable for individual employees and various work areas. For example, employees who use equipment when performing their job functions will need more space than will employees whose jobs do not require the use of equipment. Other factors affecting space allocation are nature and type of furniture, location of structural pillars and columns, windows, and nature of each employee's job responsibilities. For example, when an employee spends a significant portion of the work day communicating with one or more individuals in his or her office, more space will have to be allocated to accommodate this responsibility.

Minimum space requirements for various individuals and work areas are identified in Figure 4–2. The figures given in the illustration are helpful in approximating the total amount of space an organization requires.

Specialized Areas

A variety of specialized areas should be considered in planning office layout. The nature of the organization is a basic determinant of the needed and/or useful areas.

What should be considered in planning the reception area?

Reception Area. The reception area affects one's first impression of the organization. Good first impressions impact positively on public relations; and over the long run, favorable first impressions may result in increased profit for the organization.

The maximum number of individuals expected in the reception area at any one time is considered in determining the approximate size of the reception area. Thirty to thirty-five square feet of space is allocated for each individual. Therefore, if the maximum number of people anticipated at one time is ten, a space allocation of 300 to 350 square feet will be needed.

The flow of traffic through the area is also considered. The layout should facilitate the movement of people through reception without disturbing those seated in the area. Other important considerations include the choice of furniture, color scheme, lighting, and location of other rooms in relation to the reception area. Blocking the view of office areas from the reception area helps eliminate the possibility that visitors will distract employees.

Some manufacturing organizations use the reception area to display company products, whereas others display a map identifying the location of branch offices. Still others provide short video presentations informing visitors about various organizational operations or activities.

Board or Conference Room. Because the cost of office space is increasing, many organizations cannot afford the luxury of an infrequently used but elaborately appointed board room. Consequently, multipurpose board or conference rooms are often viewed as a desirable alternative. Such rooms are sufficiently elaborate to serve as the board room, yet functional enough to serve as a conference room, helping maximize the use of expensive office space. Depending on the size of the organization and the nature of its layout, additional smaller conference rooms may be located throughout the premises.

Individual Room	Space Requirements
Top-level executives	425 square feet
Middle-level executives	350 square feet
Supervisors	200 square feet
Office employees	75–100 square feet
Modular workstation	100 square feet
Conference room	25 square feet per person
Reception room	35 square feet per person
Main corridor	6–8 feet wide
Secondary corridor	4–5 feet wide
Cross aisles (every 25–30 feet)	3–4 feet wide

Figure 4–2 Minimum space guidelines

Multipurpose board or conference rooms are typically designed with built-in soundproof dividers, which permit the area to be separated into two or three smaller rooms. This design makes possible the simultaneous use of these rooms.

The board or conference room is made more versatile by installing state-of-the-art audiovisual and communications equipment. In large board rooms, microphones for voice amplification are sometimes installed in the ceiling; many rooms are equipped with telephones for making and receiving important calls during meetings. These rooms may also be equipped with computer network jacks, which facilitate immediate access to data and information. In some instances, a teleconferencing system, which is discussed in Chapter 19, is installed in the board or conference room. Other commonly found devices are chalkboards, projector screens, and recording equipment. Limited kitchen facilities adjacent to the room are also common.

Computer Room. Per square foot of space, the computer room is the most costly of all rooms in many organizations. No other room within an office building has a more restrictive environment. Computer manufacturers stress the importance of considerable preplanning in designing the computer room. Because computer hardware changes so rapidly, space needs to be accurately projected for several years hence. The physical specifications of the computer equipment also must be thoroughly analyzed and taken into consideration before determining the size of the room. Furthermore, provisions have to be made for computer and auxiliary devices located throughout the building to be interconnected to the equipment in the computer room.

In planning the computer room, a fundamental consideration is its location in a fireproof, noncombustible area of the building. The walls, floors, and ceiling of the computer room need to be constructed of noncombustible materials. Because water can severely damage computer installations, the fire extinguishing systems used in these rooms are gas-vapor based rather than water based.

Strict maintenance of temperature and humidity levels enhances the operation of computer equipment. A temperature of 75 degrees Fahrenheit and a relative humidity level of 50 percent are recommended. Most equipment manufacturers also suggest that the computer installation have its own air conditioning system independent of the building's system.

Typically, computer equipment is installed on a raised platform above the regular floor, a feature that permits future layout changes with a minimum of structural changes. The raised floor protects cables interconnecting the various devices. To conserve energy, some organizations in warmer climates use the air warmed by the equipment as an auxiliary heating system for the building. During the cooling season, the warm air created by the computer equipment is often vented from the room to reduce cooling requirements.

Other factors to consider are providing suitable office space for the computer personnel (programmers, supervisors, and technicians) and suitable storage vaults for tapes, as well as space for the type and amount of auxiliary equipment needed.

Mailroom. As a communication center, the mailroom has a significant impact on the efficiency with which information moves in and out of the organization. To a great extent, proper layout can enhance mailroom efficiency. The room should be located near the receiving area of the building and also be

What special features might be found in the board or conference room?

What needs to be remembered in planning the layout of the computer room?

centrally located as much as possible. The following three areas are found in mailrooms:

What areas are typically found in the mailroom?

1. Incoming area—where incoming mail is received and placed in dumping bins.
2. Sorting area—where mail is sorted and readied for distribution throughout the organization.
3. Outgoing area—where outgoing mail is stamped, sealed, and readied for mailing.

The flow of mail through the mailroom should be considered when deciding on the appropriate location of the various pieces of equipment. A more thorough coverage of the mailroom is presented in Chapter 23.

Printing and Duplicating Room. The printing and duplicating room should be located where it is readily accessible to the majority of its users. This guideline often results in locating the duplicating room near the physical center of the building. Special acoustical construction materials can control the noise that equipment makes. The room should also be properly ventilated because some materials found in printing and duplicating processes produce unpleasant fumes and generate a sizeable amount of heat. Other desirable special features are a darkroom, washing and storage facilities, and adequate counter space.

Where should central records be located?

Central Records Area. For maximum convenience, the central records area needs to be located centrally within the organization. Special provision may also need to be made for fire protection, proper atmospheric conditions, and security to prevent unauthorized entry. Because of the extreme weight of materials stored in the central records area, structural requirements may have to be considered in the construction process.

Safety Considerations

The design and layout of the office should facilitate the movement of employees from one area to another. Layout should enable employees to move easily through the aisles rather than having to take shortcuts through work areas. Aisles and corridors should not be obstructed by equipment or furniture nor should doors swing open into aisles. Stairwells and exits should conform with the guidelines established by the National Fire Protection Association Code No. 101.

Barrier-Free Construction

In what buildings does barrier-free construction need to be provided?

Barrier-free construction is another important factor to consider in planning layout. In 1973, Congress passed the Rehabilitation Act, which requires all new federal buildings and buildings of private organizations in which more than $2,500 of federal funds are used to be accessible to individuals with disabilities. Several states have passed companion legislation. As increasing numbers of organizations employ individuals with disabilities, making the facilities convenient and comfortable for them is essential. Architectural services are able to provide valuable assistance in designing and planning barrier-free work areas.

The 1990 Americans with Disabilities Act also has implications for planning office work areas. This act guarantees equal opportunity for individuals with disabilities in employment, public accommodations, transportation, state and local government services, and telecommunications. Employers are required to provide "reasonable accommodation" to individuals with disabilities, including job restructuring and modifying of equipment. Specifically, a work area or equipment that an employee with disabilities uses in performing his or her duties cannot be an impediment to job performance.

Of concern in planning layout are sufficiently wide aisles, corridors, and doors that facilitate wheelchair passage. Workstations large enough to accommodate wheelchairs require at least a 60-by-60-inch area to make a 180- or 360-degree turn.

Expansion

The possibility for expansion must be considered each time the layout is changed. To maximize flexibility, many organizations prepare a yearly space analysis in much the same way that the yearly budget is prepared. A space analysis is usually made for each of the next five consecutive years, for the tenth year, and for the fifteenth year.

What categories of space are considered in undertaking a space analysis?

When undertaking a **space analysis,** the following categories of space are considered:

1. Space needed for employees at all hierarchical levels of the organization. Calculating the amount of space for this category is done in the following manner: Multiply the number of employees needed at various levels throughout the organization by the amount of space to be allocated each type of employee.

2. Space needed for special areas including conference rooms, the computer room, and the mailroom. These areas generally contain furniture or equipment that consumes greater amounts of space than typical employee workstations. Therefore, a greater amount of space per employee has to be allocated for these areas than for areas that contain typical employee workstations (category 1).

3. Space needed for corridors and aisles. To accommodate future growth, sufficient space needs to be allocated for corridors and aisles.

Figure 4–3 presents a space analysis chart.

Environmental Conditions

Environmental conditions, including color, lighting, air conditioning, and noise control, are also important factors to consider in planning layout. Each of these is covered in Chapter 5.

Equipment and Furniture

Equipment and furniture, which have an effect on space requirements, decor, and noise, must also be considered in planning layout. The trend is to use systems furniture, which is comprised of a variety of modules enabling each employee to have the furniture configuration that best meets his or her needs. The topic of equipment and furniture is discussed in Chapter 6.

	XYZ Company				
	Present needs		Future needs		
	No. of employees	Sq. feet per person	No. of employees	Sq. feet per person	Total
Corporate offices					
President	————	————	————	————	————
Vice-Presidents	————	————	————	————	————
Treasurer	————	————	————	————	————
Middle managers					
Administrative Office Manager	————	————	————	————	————
Systems and Procedures Manager	————	————	————	————	————
Human Resources Manager	————	————	————	————	————
Open office area					
Accounting Department	————	————	————	————	————
Sales Department	————	————	————	————	————
Special areas					
Conference Room	————	————	————	————	————
Computer Room	————	————	————	————	————
Reception Area	————	————	————	————	————
Word Processing Center	————	————	————	————	————
Mailroom	————	————	————	————	————
Copy Center	————	————	————	————	————
Central Records Area	————	————	————	————	————
Special purpose areas				Total (A)	————

	No. required	Sq. feet per item	No. required	Sq. feet per item	Total
Filing cabinets	————	————	————	————	————
Storage closets	————	————	————	————	————
Corridors/aisles	————	————	————	————	————
				Total (B)	————
				Grand Total (A + B)	————

Figure 4-3   Space analysis chart

COSTING OF OFFICE SPACE

With organizations becoming increasingly concerned about the "bottom line," the cost of their office space is being closely scrutinized. In terms of cost, organizations' investment in physical facilities is generally exceeded only by their investment in human resources. A positive cost/benefit relationship is not only needed but also required.

What factors are considered in costing office space?

When an organization calculates the cost of its office space, a number of factors must be considered. Included are such factors as rent or mortgage payments, utilities, maintenance, maintenance services, taxes, insurance, required environmental control equipment, special assessments, operating licenses and permits, and so forth.

Concern also has to be given to the potential cost of a variety of inefficiencies affecting layout. These include inefficient layout that impedes work flow, poor work space design that impedes maximizing employee productivity, and environmental elements that affect employee well-being. Adequate planning early on helps minimize the negative effect of these problems.

In some organizations, the nature of certain employees' duties keeps them away from their work areas for extended periods of time. Examples of such employees are those involved with sales, auditing, and recruiting, as well as those who telecommute (includes employees who are able to work from their homes most of the time). Allocating a separate work area for each of these employees, a work area that is underutilized a significant portion of the time, has a negative impact on the cost/benefit return. For that reason, some organizations are beginning to provide these employees with a **shared office,** which means they share their assigned work area with others. Other organizations respond to this situation by using the hoteling concept, which was discussed earlier in this chapter. Using the shared office and/or hoteling concept has enabled some organizations to delay for five to seven years the acquisition of additional office space.

OPEN OFFICE CONCEPT

A critical decision in designing office layout is whether to use a conventional walled office layout or the open office concept. If the latter is selected, then a decision will have to be made about which of various alternative approaches is best suited for the circumstances. Special care should be taken to select the approach best suited for the given situation.

Many of the disadvantages inherent in conventional walled layout are overcome by the open office concept. The conventional approach, which uses many private offices with permanent walls, is based on the hierarchical structure of the organization. The open office concept, conversely, is based on the nature of the relationship between the employee and his or her job duties, which is more consistent with office **ergonomics,** a concept discussed in detail in Chapter 5. Ergonomics helps ensure that the employees' tasks, tools and equipment, and physical environment closely match their individual needs.

Approximately two out of three offices are presently being constructed or renovated with the open concept. Its popularity is increasing because it provides a cost-effective method for making layout changes. The open office concept is especially attractive to organizations needing to make rapid layout changes. The most frequent criticisms of the open office concept are that there is a lack of privacy and greater noise, which employees find distracting.

On what is the open office concept based?

Open office planning is based on the **cybernetics** of the organization, which means that information flows or processes are considered when designing layout. The information flow of the organization typically consists of paper flow, telephone communications, and personal visits. Open office planning is based on the simultaneously interacting relationships of the following factors: communication, workplace design, and the physical environment. For this reason, systems and procedures analysts and communications consultants should work closely with the architects and interior/space designers when using the open office concept.

Among the special features of the open office concept are the following:

What factors need to be considered in planning employee work areas in the open concept?

1. Open offices use only a minimum number of permanent walls. Large open areas with approximately 10,000 square feet of space are most desirable for developing the open office concept. By using a floor grid system (5 feet by 5 feet, for example) for electrical and telephone connections, individual workstations can be conveniently placed at any location and at any angle.

2. The location of each workstation affects the efficiency of work flow and helps prevent work backlogs as well as crisscrossing and backtracking of work.

3. To provide a suitable work environment, special attention may have to be given to acoustics and noise control. The acoustical devices used in a conventional office may not be sufficient for large open office areas. Sound-absorbing walls, ceilings, panels, and carpeting may have to be used. Acoustical conditioning is sufficient when sounds are no longer disturbing at a distance of 15 feet from the source.

4. Uniform air conditioning and humidity control in large open areas is easily accomplished, although climatic systems appropriate for conventionally designed office areas may not be appropriate for large open areas.

5. Color schemes and furniture arrangements can provide a pleasant working environment for employees. The use of panels, modular furniture, and planters provides privacy while adding aesthetically to the area.

6. The furniture used in an open office facilitates worker efficiency. For example, if a portion of an individual's work is more easily performed in a standing position, the furniture can be designed to accommodate the employee in that position. The amount of storage space given each employee is determined by his or her storage needs. In most cases, conventional desks are replaced with function-oriented workstations comprised of a working surface, privacy panels, and materials storage components.

What are the benefits of the open office concept?

Several benefits result from the use of the open office concept, including the following:

1. The cost of changing layout in an open space office is much less than changing conventional layout. Moving a square foot of open space costs approximately $1.10 compared with an approximate cost of $20–25 for moving a square foot of conventionally designed space.

2. The initial cost of installing an open office may be as much as 10 to 25 percent less than the cost of installing conventional space.

3. The elimination of permanent walls and private offices increases the amount of usable floor space by as much as 15 to 20 percent.

4. The open office concept improves office productivity by increasing the efficiency of work flow, improving communications, improving worker

morale, increasing the feeling of worker involvement, and creating a more comfortable working environment.

5. Open offices help conserve energy because heating, ventilation, and air conditioning systems are not impeded by permanent walls.

Modular Workstation Approach

What are the characteristics of the modular workstation approach?

A characteristic of the **modular workstation approach** is the use of panel-hung furniture components to create individual work areas. Storage cabinets and files of adjustable height are placed adjacent to desks or tables. Modular units provide employees with a "total" office in terms of desk space, file space, storage space, and work-area lighting. These units, which can be specially designed to meet the specific needs of employees, are illustrated in Figure 4–4.

The modular approach, in certain circumstances, is preferred to either the cluster workstation approach or the landscape approach. The modular approach is especially suited for those situations that require considerable storage space. Also, when contrasted with conventional layout, the modular approach is highly advantageous because most permanent walls are eliminated, and the work area is designed around the specific needs of each user. Another distinct advantage is the ease and speed with which changes in layout can be made.

Figure 4–4   Modular work station unit. Courtesy: Steelcase, Inc.

Cluster Workstation Approach

What are the
characteristics of the
cluster workstation
approach?

The unique characteristic of the **cluster workstation approach** is the clustering of work areas around a common core, such as a set of panels that extends from hublike spokes in a wheel. Panels are used to define each employee's work area, which encompasses a writing surface, storage space, and filing space. Although exceptions exist, cluster workstations are not as elaborate as modular work stations or work areas provided employees using the landscape approach. The cluster approach is well suited for work situations in which employees spend a portion of their work day away from their work area. Figure 4–5 illustrates the cluster workstation approach.

The cluster workstation approach provides a distinct advantage of providing considerable flexibility in changing layout and in redesigning individual work areas. In addition, this approach is seen as being more economical than either the modular or the landscape approach.

Landscape Approach

What are the
characteristics of the
landscape approach?

Developed by the Quickboner Team in Germany, **office landscaping** was implemented in that country for the first time in 1960 and is now being used quite extensively in this country. To a certain extent, landscaping is a blend of the

Figure 4–5 Movable cluster workstation unit. Courtesy: Westinghouse Furniture Systems.

Figure 4-6 Office landscaping. Courtesy: Sheraton Worldwide Reservations, Raleigh, NC.

What are the special features of landscaping?

modular and cluster workstation approaches. In addition, it makes abundant use of plants and foliage in the decor. To partition work areas, furniture is arranged in clusters and at various angles instead of in traditional rows. The landscape approach is illustrated in Figure 4–6.

In its "pure" form, landscaping uses no private offices. Increasingly, however, a "hybrid" landscape rather than the "pure" landscape is found. A ratio of 80 percent open area to 20 percent nonopen area is common in offices in which the "hybrid" version is found.

In a conventional layout, having a private office is a status symbol. In landscaped offices, however, status is accorded employees through their work assignments, by the location and size of their work area, and from the type and amount of furniture they are given.

The panels used in modular, cluster, and landscape workstations are available in a variety of sizes and shapes and with several different types of outer surfaces including wood, metal, plastic, glass, and carpet. Traditional panels are 2 inches wide and can be prewired with telephone and electrical connections as well as constructed with special sound-absorbing materials. With the increased use of fiber optics and Category 5 networks, however, 2-inch panels may not accommodate the new technology. Accommodation can be achieved by using either transfer boxes or panel stacking systems. Some of the newer panels also incorporate heating, cooling, and air purification vents.

PRINCIPLES OF EFFECTIVE LAYOUT

Various principles of effective layout are useful in planning and designing office layout. Illustrated in Figure 4–7 are several principles that can be used effectively as evaluative criteria.

Figure 4-7 Principles of effective layout

1. Interrelationships among equipment, information, and personnel in the flow of work should be analyzed.
2. Work flow should move in as straight a line as possible. Crisscrossing and backtracking should be avoided.
3. Work flow should revolve around major source documents.
4. Hierarchical and communication relationships between individuals should be considered in planning layout.
5. Individuals or work groups performing similar or related duties should be located near one another.
6. Individuals or work groups with frequent public contact should be located near the entrance to the premises.
7. Individuals or work groups whose tasks require considerable concentration should be placed in a low-traffic, quiet area of the building.
8. Space allocation should be based on the position of the individual, the nature of the work being performed, and the amount of special equipment required.
9. Groups or individuals providing specialized services should be located near those who use the specialized services.
10. Furniture and equipment should meet user needs.
11. Aisles should be sufficiently wide to accommodate the rapid, efficient movement of employees.
12. Safety considerations should be given high priority in planning layout.
13. Large open areas are more efficient than are smaller enclosed areas.
14. Adequate provisions have to be made for lighting, decor, air conditioning, humidity control, and noise control.
15. Concern for future expansion is important.
16. Work should come to the employee, not vice versa.

PREPARING THE LAYOUT

The administrative office manager is likely to be largely responsible for planning and designing minor layout changes. In such instances, the following information will be helpful.

After completing the study and analyzing each of the important design and layout factors, a scaled model of the floor plan should be prepared. To facilitate its preparation, a construction blueprint that shows the location of support pillars, doors, windows, stairwells, and other structural features will be useful.

What tools are used in planning layout?

Once the floor area has been scaled, the exact location of each piece of furniture and equipment should be determined. Tools available for preparing the layout are templates, cutouts, plastic models, magnetic models, and computer-aided design. To assure accurate spatial relationships, the floor drawing and the furniture and equipment drawings must use the same scale.

Templates

Consisting of scaled versions of furniture and equipment, templates are typically constructed of cardboard or plastic. The template, which is used in tracing the various items on the layout, is illustrated in Figure 4–8.

Figure 4-8 Office layout template. Coutesy: Pickett Industries.

Cutouts

Cutouts are purchased in sheets. Individual furniture or equipment drawings are simply cut from the sheet. Two types of cutouts are available: paper and self-adhering Mylar. Figure 4–9 illustrates paper cutouts.

Plastic Models

Plastic models are scaled versions of various pieces of office furniture and equipment. The ease with which these models can be repositioned on the floor plan facilitates experimentation with various layout possibilities. Figure 4–10 illustrates plastic models positioned on a layout board.

Magnetic Board

Magnetized models of furniture and equipment are also frequently used for preparing office layouts. Although magnetism readily adheres the models to the board, they can be easily repositioned. A layout using a magnetic board is illustrated in Figure 4–11.

Computer-Aided Design

What is CAD?

Computer-aided design (CAD) uses computer technology and the appropriate software to assist in designing an effective layout. Several affordable computer software programs are now available that facilitate an easy and efficient layout design process.

Some CAD programs provide an optimum layout after such important variables as area dimensions, size and number of workstations, and aisles and corridors are input. Others require that the user "draw" the area dimensions and workstation configurations on the video display terminal (VDT) screen. Any

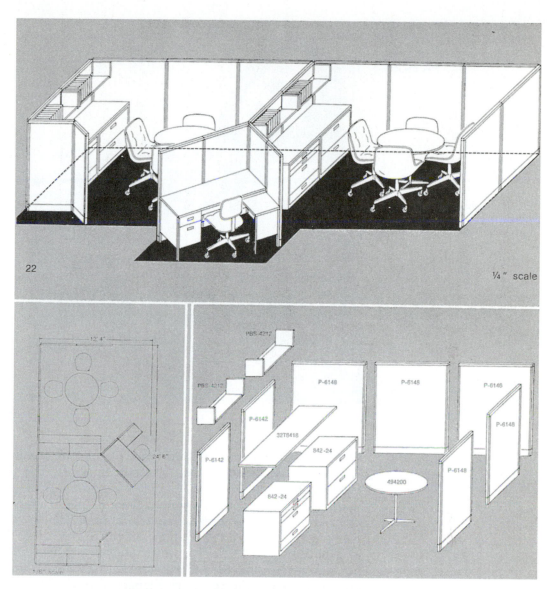

Figure 4-9 Paper cutouts. Courtesy: Steelcase, Inc., Grand Rapids, MI.

items on the screen, such as a wall or piece of equipment or furniture, can be easily relocated using a light pen or the "drag and drop" feature of the computer mouse. Most CAD systems also facilitate the preparation of a printed copy of any screen configuration.

IMPLICATIONS FOR THE ADMINISTRATIVE OFFICE MANAGER

In many organizations, the administrative office manager has the distinction of possessing greater expertise than any other employee in planning and designing layout. The reason for this distinction is apparent: He or she is more familiar with many of the factors that have to be considered in the planning and designing process. No other employee is likely to be as familiar with organizationwide work flow patterns or communication processes. Unless the

Figure 4-10 Plastic models. Courtesy: A.D.S. Company, Indianola, PA 15051.

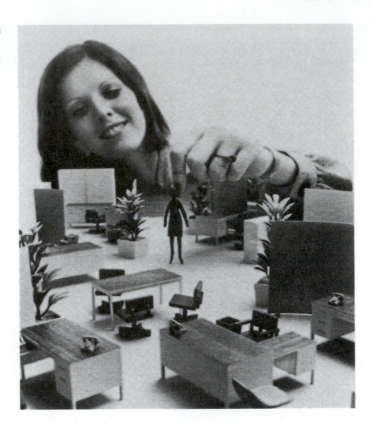

organization employs a full-time space planner, no one else is likely to be more knowledgeable about new developments in layout than the administrative office manager.

A layout project involves more than simply placing furniture and equipment in a given area. Organizations that undertake layout projects by merely rearranging furniture and equipment soon discover that the outcome is not as ideal as anticipated. The only way to salvage projects undertaken in this manner is to assess carefully other important factors that impact on office layout and then to make the necessary changes.

Unless the administrative office manager has had in-depth training in designing office layouts, he or she is well advised to consult individuals who have the needed expertise. The consulting costs will likely be offset many times by having an efficient, effective layout from the beginning, especially if the alternative is a layout developed through a hit-or-miss process.

REVIEW QUESTIONS

1. How does the layout of an office affect its efficiency and productivity?

2. What do you consider to be the five most important factors that have to be dealt with during the preliminary planning stage of a layout project? Be prepared to discuss the factors you identify.

3. When planning layout, why is the study of the work flow important? How might the work flow be studied?

4. What are the reasons for decreased use of private offices in office buildings?

Figure 4-11 Magnetic board. Courtesy: Magna Visual, Inc.

5. What factors determine the appropriate amount of space to allocate to each individual within the organization?

6. What factors should an organization consider in determining the cost of its office space?

7. What are the characteristics of open planning?

8. What are the characteristics of office landscaping, and what are its benefits?

9. Discuss five principles of effective layout and give or cite examples where you have seen these principles violated.

10. What tools are available for use in preparing office layout diagrams?

11. What is CAD?

DISCUSSION QUESTIONS

1. You are the administrative office manager in a company that is planning a new building. The architects and corporate management recently decided that the new facility will make extensive use of the open plan concept. On hearing about this decision, many employees are quite upset as the facility in which the company is presently located makes extensive use of private offices. As the administrative office manager, you have been asked to help those employees opposed to the open plan concept overcome their resistance. What do you plan to tell them about the merits of the open plan concept?

2. The members of a professional organization to which you belong recently had the opportunity to tour the new facilities in which another member of the organization works. The pretour publicity indicated that this new facility incorporated "all the latest developments in office design." Yet, when you toured the facility, you noticed that the four employees in the word processing center were in an open area with no privacy, that the personnel manager was located in the office farthest from the entrance to the building, and that the president was located near the reception area. When you asked questions about these three situations, the executive vice president, who was your tour guide, indicated that the company "went along" with the recommendations made by an interior designer. What are your reactions to these three situations?

3. You work as a consultant in an interior design firm. This morning you met for the first time with a new client whose company is relocating to another floor of the same building because it has outgrown its current space. Because none of the other occupants of the floor are moving in the foreseeable future, the company has no choice but to move. The client asked that you prepare a layout with several private offices and some open area in the middle. When you asked if he had considered open planning, he said that he had not given it much thought but that if you could convince him that it would work in his company, he would consider it. You believe that the nature of the company, its employees, and its functions make it ideally suited to the use of open planning. Outline what you plan to say to the client during your next meeting to convince him that he should consider open planning.

STUDENT PROJECTS AND ACTIVITIES

1. Talk with an office space designer regarding the specific tasks he or she must be concerned with in planning office space.

2. Talk with an architect about the specific requirements he or she must be concerned with in designing barrier-free office areas.

3. Going Online: Using the Internet, conduct an online search based on one of the concepts presented in this chapter or based on one of the chapter terms. Identify four or five things you learned from the material you read that you did not know before.

Minicase

The Christensen Manufacturing Company, which is located in Lansing, Michigan, is about to undertake a major renovation of its office building, which is now twenty years old. Although the original layout of the building used the latest concepts at the time it was designed, the premises are now considered to be out of date. Extensive use is made of private offices and large rooms where a row-after-row arrangement of desks is found. The vice president of administration, who is responsible for the renovation of the building, is intrigued with the office landscaping concept. Before she decides whether or not to study the concept further, she contacts you, an office design specialist, to learn more about the concept.

1. Outline what you plan to tell the vice president of administration about the office landscaping concept.

Case

James Coleman and Joe Carrick, partners in a law practice, are adding a third partner, Anne Levens, to their practice. This necessitates moving to a new location. They have purchased a building that contains approximately 2,000 square feet. Except for the restrooms, a small galley-type kitchen, and the mechanical room, the area is open.

You, an office designer, have been hired by the law firm to design the layout of its new facility. Except for the existing permanent walls, the attorneys have specified that no others are to be added except for their offices and the conference room. Movable partitions are to be used to achieve privacy in the other areas. The following personnel are to be planned for in designing the layout:

3 attorneys

2 legal secretaries

2 clerks

1 receptionist

1 law clerk (this individual compiles briefs for the attorneys and is responsible for the law library)

The equipment and furniture consists of the following items:

9 desks and desk chairs

16 four-drawer file cabinets

6 credenzas (one for each attorney, one for each legal secretary, and one for the law clerk)

10 four-shelf bookcases (one for each attorney and the remainder are to be placed in the law library)

4 sofas (one for each attorney and one in the reception area)

12 straight-back chairs (four for each attorney's office)

3 small, round conference tables (one for each attorney)

1 conference table

10 conference chairs

8 chairs (four each in the law library and reception area)

5 computers (for use by each legal secretary, the two clerks, and the receptionist)

Using an enlargement of the diagram, prepare a layout showing the location of permanent walls, each piece of furniture and equipment, and the movable partitions (Figure 4–12). (Note: Your instructor will provide you with paper cutouts of the various pieces of furniture and equipment that are to be placed on the layout.)

Figure 4-12 Layout.

Scale: 1/8" = 1'

$\mathcal{C}$hapter 5

OFFICE ENVIRONMENT

$\mathcal{C}$hapter $\mathcal{A}$ims

After studying this chapter, you should be able to design an effective environment for a general office area.

$\mathcal{C}$hapter $\mathcal{O}$utline

The Impact of the Office Environment on Employees
The Healthy Office Environment
Lighting
    Characteristics of Lighting Systems
    Types of Lighting Systems
    Task/Ambient Lighting
    Kinds of Lighting
    Automatic Light Control Systems
    Lighting Maintenance
    Lighting and Video Display Terminals
Color
    Color Considerations
    Guiding Principles
    Floor Coverings
    Wall Coverings
    Color of Furniture
Noise Control
    Control of Office Noise
    Control of Noise in Offices Using Open
        Space Planning
Conditioning the Air
    Temperature of Air
    Humidity Level of Air
    Circulation of Air
    Cleanliness of Air
Music
Conservation of Energy in Offices
    The Energy Conservation Program
    Techniques for Conserving Energy
Office Security
Implications for the Administrative Office Manager

$\mathcal{C}$hapter $\mathcal{T}$erms

Carpal tunnel syndrome
Computer Vision Syndrome (CVS)
Decibel
Direct lighting
Equivalent Spherical Illumination (ESI)
Ergonomics
General diffuse lighting
Green-office movement
Indirect lighting
Masking-sound system
Office environment
Primary colors
Secondary colors
Semidirect lighting
Semi-indirect lighting
Smart office
Task/ambient lighting
Task Illumination (TI)
Tertiary colors
Visual Comfort Probability (VCP)
White noise

*E*mployees' productivity and job satisfaction can be affected significantly by the physical environment in which they work. A number of the elements in the **office environment** can affect the financial well-being of the organization, especially when employees' dissatisfaction with their working environment has a negative impact on their productivity. Whenever making changes in the working environment, the potential financial impact of these changes on these elements should be calculated.

What is a smart office?

Several of the environmental elements, especially lighting, heating, cooling, and energy conservation, increasingly are becoming computerized. This practice results in what is often referred to as a **smart office.** Some technologies are likely to be either partially or fully integrated in the smart office, including data communications, data processing, environmental control, office automation, security, and fire/life protection systems. Among the more common features of a smart office are the following:

1. *Small-zone lighting, heating, and air conditioning.* These systems light, heat, and cool small areas rather than entire floors. Consequently, employees who work after hours or on weekends have a suitable working environment in their specific areas without having to light or heat/cool the entire floor. While the lights might be activated by motion or body heat sensors, the heating/cooling system is likely activated by means of a telephone or a computer.

2. *"Smart-wired" telecommunications systems.* Included in many new office buildings is a "smart-wired" telecommunication system in which a telephone is used to perform a number of functions, including voice and data communication, electronic mail and messaging, energy management, fire protection, and life/safety systems. The keypad on the telephone is typically used to activate and/or control several of the systems, while others, such as fire protection, operate automatically. A growing number of developers of office buildings are installing telecommunication systems for their tenants who simply lease the telephone system and needed phone lines from the developer. A shared system enables tenants to have a more sophisticated system at a lower cost than they might otherwise be able to afford.

The office environment is multifaceted. A number of factors, including lighting, color scheme, acoustics, and condition of the air, affect the environment. Each of these topics is discussed in this chapter. Layout, which was discussed in Chapter 4, and furniture and equipment, which are discussed in Chapter 6, also affect the environment. Some of the environmental elements impact significantly on an organization's energy consumption. A discussion of energy conservation programs is also included in this chapter.

An increasing number of organizations are becoming more environmentally conscious, resulting in the **green-office movement.** Although this movement began primarily with the recycling of paper, it has continued with the retrofitting of lighting, heating, and air conditioning systems. Another action that leads to a greener office is the recycling of toner cartridges for laser printers and photocopy equipment. Too, the remanufacturing of office furniture and equipment has resulted in salvaging a significant number of items that likely would have been deposited prematurely in a landfill.

THE IMPACT OF THE OFFICE ENVIRONMENT ON EMPLOYEES

What is ergonomics?

Each of the elements of the office environment can affect office employees physically and psychologically. **Ergonomics,** the study of the relationship of employees to their physical environment, is helpful in designing a suitable environment. Ergonomics helps ensure that the task, the tools and equipment used in task performance, and the environment in which the employee works match his or her needs. Special effort should be directed toward modifying any ergonomic factors or elements that impact negatively on employees.

By integrating several disciplines—including psychology, physiology, sociology, and communication theories—ergonomics provides useful guidelines for designing an effective environment. The integration of the various disciplines helps ensure the employees' well-being and the ability to maximize their productivity. The use of ergonomics means employees' work areas are based on their needs, and the methods they use to carry out their job tasks are based on their capabilities.

Evidence of the failure to consider the office environment may be noticed in several ways. An unsatisfactory environment often results in decreased levels of productivity and employee morale. Absenteeism and tardiness are apt to increase, as are the number of errors made by employees. In extreme cases, the employees' physical well-being may even be jeopardized.

THE HEALTHY OFFICE ENVIRONMENT

One of the office environment concerns receiving an increased amount of attention is how to provide a healthy workplace for employees. No longer can employers assume that a healthy environment "just happens." Rather, a healthful environment must be planned.

The sick-building syndrome that results from unfavorable environmental conditions is a phenomenon of the last two decades. This syndrome manifests itself among employees in the following ways: headaches, dizziness, abnormal tiredness, nausea, breathing difficulties, sore throats, upper-respiratory infections, coughing, skin rashes, and so forth. The syndrome is considered to exist in a particular building when at least 20 percent of the employees complain of similar symptoms that tend to disappear after they leave the premises.

Among the most common of the specific environmental conditions that cause the sick-building syndrome are indoor air pollution, noise pollution, and lighting glare. The syndrome is most commonly found in office buildings constructed after the late 1960s and early 1970s that have permanently sealed windows.

What conditions detract from a healthy environment?

Included in the growing list of concerns that detract from a healthy environment are the following:

1. Repetitive motion injuries are occurring among employees who, without interruption for long periods of time, perform repetitive tasks. For office employees, the most prevalent repetitive motion injury is called **carpal tunnel syndrome,** resulting from the long-term irritation of the tendons connecting one's hand and arm.

   How can the occurrence of CTS be reduced?

   Among the ways to overcome this situation is to place the employees' keyboards and screens at the appropriate height, require that they take frequent breaks away from their work areas (short, frequent breaks are more beneficial than longer, less-frequent breaks), and provide them with wrist rests and with adjustable chairs and moveable keyboards. Stretching exercises involving the back, arms, wrists, and fingers are also helpful. Taking the action necessary to reduce the incidence of repetitive motion injuries is not that costly, especially when compared with the benefits received. In the United States, medical costs and lost wages resulting from repetitive motion injuries consume between $20 and $30 billion a year.

2. Electromagnetic radiation emanating from video display terminals (VDTs) is the cause, according to some researchers, of higher than average rates of miscarriage, cancer, birth defects, and heart disease. Among the ways to diminish this concern are the following: install a radiation screen on the face of the display unit, use an MPR II-certified low-frequency monitor, or use a liquid-crystal-display (LCD) unit commonly found on laptop computers. Having employees distance themselves a minimum of 28 inches from their VDTs and 40 inches from other VDTs is also a viable recommendation.

   Another related concern is the impact that video display terminals have on employees' eyesight. Of recent origin is the **computer vision syndrome (CVS),** which occurs when the viewing requirements of the task being performed exceed the visual capabilities of the person performing the task. Symptoms of CVS include eyestrain, headaches, dry eyes, irritated eyes, blurred vision, delay in refocusing, light sensitivity, double vision, neck ache, and back ache.

3. Indoor air pollution is a result of improperly designed building ventilation systems; unclean ventilation systems; and outdated heating, ventilating, furnishings (especially carpeting and items made with pressed wood), cleaning solvents, tobacco smoke, and air conditioning systems. Some types of office equipment, most specifically electrostatic copiers and laser printers, produce an ozone that is also a source of indoor air pollution. Some ventilation problems occur when an organization remodels office areas without giving consideration to the ventilation needs of the new premises. The ventilation system appropriate for the original premises may not be appropriate for a remodeled area. Those responsible for equipment maintenance also need to make sure that the ozone produced by the equipment is properly filtered. In some instances, additional air purification and filtration devices may need to be installed.

4. Noise pollution is another contributor to the sick-building syndrome. This phenomenon results from the occurrence of high levels of unwanted sound originating from conversation, machines and equipment, telephones, and various noise-producing building systems. Several ways to diminish noise pollution are discussed in a subsequent section of this chapter.

5. Lighting systems can also diminish the healthiness of an office environment. The goal is to provide employees with the proper type of light for the tasks they perform. One of the most significant lighting problems in offices is glare, which is light reflected from the surface of an object. Of particular concern is the glare on video display terminals. Such glare is likely to manifest itself as eyestrain, fatigue, and headaches. Equipping video display terminals with an antiglare screen is an effective way to eliminate problems caused by screen glare, as is the prevention of light directly hitting the screen.

LIGHTING

How does the lighting system affect office employees?

Affecting employees both physically and psychologically, lighting is one of the most important aspects of the office environment. Physically, inadequate lighting increases employees' fatigue as a result of excessive eye strain. Psychologically, inadequate lighting results in loss of morale and eventually causes a decrease in the quantity and quality of employee performance. Effective lighting takes into consideration the quantity and quality of illumination best suited for the employees, their work styles, their tasks, and the space involved.

In addition to being concerned about providing employees with satisfactory lighting, organizations are increasingly concerned about another lighting dimension: its cost. In 1991, the Environmental Protection Agency (EPA) initiated the Green Light Program, which encourages organizations to use energy-efficient lighting. Because lighting accounts for approximately 25 percent of the nation's energy consumption, the Green Light Program helps organizations rid themselves of energy-inefficient lighting. To help organizations install energy-efficient lighting, the EPA provides low-cost loans and advice about designing new, efficient lighting systems.

Characteristics of Lighting Systems

Lighting systems should possess certain well-defined characteristics. Several changes in the way these characteristics are used have taken place in the last few years. To illustrate, for many years, the foot-candle[1] and the foot-lambert[2] were the two commonly used measures of lighting systems. Now, **Equivalent Spherical Illumination (ESI), Visual Comfort Probability (VCP),** and **Task Illumination (TI)** are also used to describe these characteristics.

Equivalent Spherical Illumination. ESI is used to measure the effectiveness of lighting systems. The task being performed at the work surface determines the appropriate ESI value for a given area. The value is influenced negatively by glares and reflections on the work surface and is affected by the degree of contrast between the work surface and the materials with which the employee works. An ESI value of 40 or higher is recommended for most work surfaces.

What is Equivalent Spherical Illumination?

ESI is also used to provide a measure of the uniformity of the lighting system. If the minimum ESI of the work surface is at least two-thirds of the maximum ESI, the lighting of the work area is considered adequately uniform. Thus, if the maximum ESI is 60, the minimum ESI will have to be at least 40.

Visual Comfort Probability. Visual Comfort Probability is a direct-brightness ratio and should be at least .70. A VCP of .80 means that 80 percent of the employees seated in the least desirable locations of an office are not bothered by glares created by the lighting system nor by veiling reflections when working on flat surfaces directly beneath the lighting fixture. While employees whose tasks are primarily paper oriented should work in areas in which the VCP is at least .70, those whose tasks involve frequent use of a terminal screen should be provided a VCP of .90.

What does Visual Comfort Probability measure?

Sources of bright light visible to the naked eye or visible reflectors that are bright can cause a poor VCP ratio. When fixtures are selected, their design should be evaluated to make sure neither of these conditions exists.

Task Illumination. Expressed in raw foot-candles, Task Illumination measures the quantity of light at the work surface. It does not measure quality or visibility. A high TI value does not necessarily ensure high visibility in a work area, especially if glares and reflections are present. Most office work areas require a TI of 100 to 150 foot-candles.

What is the unit of measure of Task Illumination?

Types of Lighting Systems

Lighting systems consist of the following types: **direct, semidirect, indirect, semi-indirect,** and **general diffuse.**

Direct. By directing approximately 90 to 100 percent of the illumination downward to the work surface, direct lighting systems are likely to create bothersome glares and reflections. Shadows are created because only a minimal amount of light is diffused. Unless the light fixtures are quite close together, the working areas most likely will not be uniformly lit.

Semidirect. With semidirect lighting, 60 to 90 percent of the light is directed downward. The remainder of the light is directed upward and then reflected back downward. Semidirect systems eliminate some of the shadows that are characteristic of the direct lighting system.

Indirect. Indirect lighting is the system recommended for most types of office tasks. With indirect lighting, 90 to 100 percent of the light is first directed upward. The light then becomes diffused and is reflected downward to the work area. The diffusion of the light eliminates most shadows and glares.

Semi-indirect. With semi-indirect lighting, 60 to 90 percent of the light is directed upward and then reflected downward. The remainder of the light is immediately directed downward. Although the semi-indirect lighting system may produce a greater amount of light for the same wattage level than the indirect system, shadows and glare are also likely to be a greater problem with semi-indirect lighting.

General Diffuse. This lighting system directs 40 to 60 percent of the light directly to the work surface, with the remainder of the light reflected downward. Although the general-diffuse system produces more light for the same wattage than the semi-indirect system, shadows and glare are also more noticeable than when using semi-indirect lighting.

Task/Ambient Lighting

The newest concept in office lighting is known as **task/ambient lighting,** which uses fixtures mounted in the furniture. Task lighting illuminates the work surface, while ambient lighting illuminates the area surrounding the work surface. Task lighting is frequently downward directed; ambient lighting is generally directed upward when it is part of the furniture components. Ambient lighting can also be provided by strategically placed ceiling fixtures that provide overall room lighting.

Task/ambient lighting results in an efficient, economical use of energy. Less wattage is required because light has to travel shorter distances (perhaps 3 feet) to the work surface. In some instances, task lighting uses 40 percent less wattage per square foot than ceiling-mounted fluorescent fixtures.

When using a task/ambient lighting system, balance is critical. Contrast between the task work area and the background needs to be provided. As a guideline, the task area should be two to three times brighter than the area surrounding it and as much as five times brighter than the general surroundings. The task area also needs to be as much as ten times brighter than remote surroundings.

An illustration of task lighting is presented in Figure 5–1.

Accent lighting is often incorporated into task/ambient systems. This type of lighting, which is directional, acts as a stimulant by drawing attention to a horizontal or vertical surface. Properly done, accent lighting also provides a sense of dimension.

How do direct and indirect lighting systems differ?

What are the differences between task lighting and ambient lighting?

Figure 5–1 Task/ambient lighting. Courtesy: Steelcase, Inc., Grand Rapids, MI.

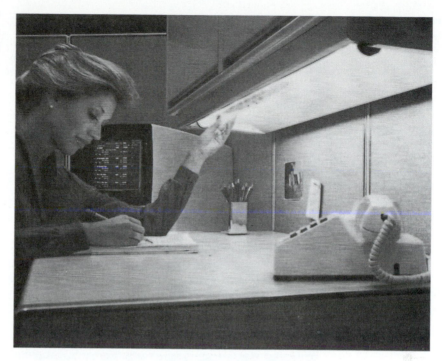

Figure 5–2 identifies the advantages of task/ambient lighting.

Kinds of Lighting

The four most commonly used kinds of office lighting are natural daylight, fluorescent, incandescent, and high-intensity discharge lighting.

Natural Light. Although natural light is an efficient lighting system, its lack of dependability requires the use of alternative lighting systems. In addition to its efficiency, natural light often provides psychological advantages for employees. However, natural light is not capable of penetrating very far into work areas. On extremely bright days, the intensity of natural light may result in its having to be controlled.

Many newer office buildings are constructed with a glass-enclosed courtyard at the center of the building, a feature that increases the number of working areas with windows. Consequently, a greater number of employees can take advantage of natural light.

When natural lighting is used as a lighting source, how should one be positioned in relation to the source?

Employees whose work areas utilize natural light should be situated so that light comes over their left shoulders if they are right-handed but over their right shoulders if they are left-handed. Under no circumstances should employees face windows in their normal working positions.

When an abundance of natural light is used to illuminate a work area, additional consideration will have to be given to the effect the light has on air temperature. Because natural light is heat-producing, additional air-cooling measures may have to be taken—especially during the summer months—to moderate the effect of the heat.

Fluorescent Lighting. Fluorescent lighting continues to be the most common type of light source in office buildings. The illumination fluorescent lighting produces closely resembles that of natural light. Although fluorescent

Figure 5-2 Advantages of task/ambient lighting.

1. Task lighting, unlike ceiling systems, is not permanent, which facilitates the rearrangement of workstations in an office area.
2. Areas are illuminated in a nonuniform pattern, which provides a greater sense of dimension than is possible with systems that provide uniform lighting.
3. The acoustical system is easier to develop because of the limited number of lighting fixtures that are used.
4. Task lighting eliminates glare and reflections.
5. Because task lighting requires less wattage, less energy is consumed.
6. Installation costs are significantly reduced.
7. Because fewer fixtures are used, fewer bulbs have to be replaced.
8. The amount of space needed between the ceiling and the floor above it is reduced, which increases the amount of usable vertical space in a building.
9. Because the fixtures are considered to be part of the furniture, a tax advantage may result.
10. Renovation of work areas is easily accomplished.
11. The absence of light fixtures in the ceiling helps improve the fire rating of the facility because of the unbroken nature of the ceiling.

What are the advantages of fluorescent lighting?

lighting is more expensive to install than incandescent lighting, fluorescent lighting offers the following advantages over incandescent lighting: (1) it produces less heat and glare, (2) fluorescent tubes last ten times longer than incandescent bulbs, (3) it consumes less electricity, (4) the illumination it provides is more evenly distributed, and (5) fluorescent lighting is approximately five times more efficient than incandescent lighting.

Many buildings have been constructed with luminous ceilings similar to the one illustrated in Figure 5–3. A significant advantage of this ceiling is the

Figure 5-3 Illuminated ceiling. Courtesy: Armstrong Cork Company.

extent to which shadows and glares on the work surfaces are eliminated. Because of the uniformity of light produced by the luminous ceiling, several techniques are used to produce lighting variation in office areas. One such device is the small, strategically placed spotlight.

Incandescent Lighting. Using filament bulbs, incandescent lighting is the type most commonly found in homes. It can also be used effectively in offices, although fluorescent lighting is generally regarded as more efficient. Incandescent lighting is often used to break up the monotony of lighting panels and to draw attention to certain areas. Compared with other kinds of lighting, incandescent lighting is the least cost effective in terms of the amount of light produced in relation to the energy consumed.

The cost of installing incandescent lighting is less than the cost of installing fluorescent lighting. Among the disadvantages of incandescent lighting when compared with fluorescent lighting are the following: An incandescent bulb does not last as long, colors appear less natural, it consumes more electricity, and it is apt to produce a greater amount of glare and shadowing.

In some instances, the heat generated by incandescent bulbs is used as an auxiliary heating source. This technique is discussed in the "Conditioning the Air" section of this chapter.

High-Intensity Discharge Lamps. The use of high-intensity discharge lamps for illuminating office areas is fairly new. These lamps, which were first used for street and stadium lighting, provide an extremely efficient lighting system. The greatest disadvantage of these bulbs is their effect on color as they sometimes make it more difficult to distinguish between various colors.

Automatic Light Control Systems

What types of automatic light control systems are used?

Automatic light control systems are now being installed in many office buildings. These systems have a positive impact on energy conservation, which enables the organization to recoup purchase outlay in a relatively short time.

One type of automatic light control system uses a photocell to measure the amount of illumination in a given area. With an electronic feedback mechanism, the control system is able to maintain the desired preset lighting level. As lamps age and accumulate dirt, they produce less light. To compensate, the control system increases the amount of light to maintain the desired preset illumination level. For areas near windows and skylights, the control system automatically adjusts the quantity of artificial light in relation to the amount of available natural light. The primary advantage of this type of control system is the lighting consistency it facilitates.

Another type of automatic light control system senses the presence of people in a given area. Automatic light control systems use two types of sensors: ultrasonic wave sensors that detect movement and infrared occupancy sensors that detect body heat. The sensors function by automatically activating the lighting system when people are detected. Automatic light control systems deactivate the lighting system a specified amount of time (perhaps 10 minutes) after the sensors no longer detect the presence of people. In addition to conserving energy, this system also has a residual benefit of providing security.

Some automatic light control systems utilize computer technology. At predetermined times, lights are automatically turned on and off. Certain devices, most commonly the telephone, are used to override the system should it be necessary to do so.

Lighting Maintenance

Over time, lamps used to produce artificial light begin to provide less output for the same amount of energy. The output depreciation begins after approximately 100 hours of usage. At some point during the life of each type of lamp, replacing old ones, even though they haven't burned out, is often cost effective. Increasingly, organizations are implementing lamp replacement programs that result in the regular replacement of all lamps in a given work area. Replacement schedules take into consideration the average rated life of the lamps being replaced. From a labor standpoint, total replacement is also more cost effective than waiting until lamps burn out to replace them.

A regular fixture cleaning program is another important aspect of lighting maintenance. As fixtures gather dust and grime, their light-reflection surfaces are not as effective, thus reducing illumination effectiveness. Dirt and grime buildup on fixtures, coupled with aging lamps, deplete output by as much as 50 percent during the life of the lamp.

Lighting and Video Display Terminals

Adding to the complexity of designing efficient lighting systems is the presence of video display terminals in many offices. Failure to give adequate attention to proper lighting in areas where the terminals are found may result in a significant number of employee concerns and/or vision problems.

What should be remembered in designing a lighting system in an area where VDTs are used?

Among the suggestions for helping design a lighting system for use in an area that contains terminals are the following:

1. Eliminate glare by reducing the amount of artificial or natural light hitting the terminals.
2. Use tiltable terminals to help reduce the amount of lighting glare.
3. Adjust either or both the contrast and brightness controls on the terminals to minimize the amount of glare.
4. Consider the use of screens to reduce the amount of glare on the terminals.
5. Minimize the amount of downward-directed light and maximize the amount of indirect lighting in the VDT work area.
6. Use a flat-screen monitor rather than a convex-screen monitor.

COLOR

Color is another element of the office environment that impacts significantly on humans. While most employees are aware of the physical impact of color, many are not aware of its psychological impact—both positive and negative—on their productivity, fatigue, morale, attitudes, and tension. Color in an office provides not only an aesthetic value, but also a functional value.

Color Considerations

What color considerations are important?

Among the important factors that should be considered in developing a desirable color scheme are color combination, effect of light on color, reflectance value of color, and impact of color. Each factor is discussed in the following sections.

Color Combination

What is the composition of tertiary colors?

Combining the **primary colors**—yellow, red, and blue—produces **secondary colors.** For example, mixing red and yellow makes orange, mixing yellow and blue makes green, and mixing blue and red makes violet. **Tertiary colors** are made by combining two parts of one primary color and one part of another primary color. This concept is illustrated in Figure 5–4. Tertiary colors are yellow-orange, yellow-green, blue-violet, and so forth. The twelve colors in Figure 5–4 provide the foundation for color coordination because the colors for a scheme are selected according to their position on the color chart. Some acceptable color coordination schemes are:

1. Complementary colors—opposite each other on the color chart. For example, red-green, violet-yellow, and blue-orange.

2. Split-complementary colors—the colors on either side of a complementary color. For example, blue-violet and blue-green are the split complementary colors of orange.

What are triad colors?

3. Triad colors—the three colors equally distant from one another on the color chart. Triad colors are orange, green, violet, or yellow-orange, blue-green, and red-violet.

Effect of Light on Color. Because various types of artificial light have different color spectrums, the lighting system used in an office may also have a significant effect on the color scheme. The light source will enhance only those colors that fall within its spectrum. To illustrate, fluorescent lighting generally does not enhance reds and oranges because most fluorescent tubes are void of these two colors. Incandescent lighting will not enhance purple-blue color schemes, although fluorescent systems may. When compared with either fluorescent or incandescent lights, high-intensity lamps have a rather insignificant impact on color enhancement.

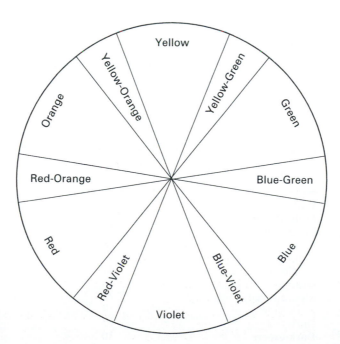

Figure 5–4   Color chart

Reflectance Value of Color.   Various colors possess different reflectance values. For example, lighter colors reflect a greater percentage of light than do darker colors. Certain areas of the office require colors with higher reflectance values than others. The ceiling, for example, requires a color with a higher reflectance value than does the floor. A light-colored ceiling helps reflect light downward, which reduces glare and shadows on work surfaces. In areas in which natural light is minimal, light-colored walls will help reduce the amount of artificial light that must be provided to achieve lighting adequacy, thus helping conserve energy consumption as well.

Figure 5–5 illustrates the reflectance value for various colors.

Impact of Colors.   Colors tend to create moods. Cool colors—blue, green, and violet—create calm and retiring moods. Warm colors—red, orange, and yellow—on the other hand, create warm and cheerful moods. The natural tints, including beige, buff, peach, and off-white, are mildly stimulating, while deep purple and pale violet often create depressing moods. Gray tends to have a sleep-inducing effect.

Guiding Principles

What principles must be considered when designing a color scheme?

Illustrated in Figure 5–6 are a number of guidelines useful in developing a color scheme. Those responsible for developing a color scheme in an office should be thoroughly familiar with the principles before beginning the planning process.

Floor Coverings

What advantages result from the use of carpeting as a floor covering?

The color of walls and ceilings is just one aspect of the color scheme in an office. The color of the floor covering is also important. Although tile and other floor finishes are still widely found, carpeted office work areas are more prevalent. Coordination is quite simple because of the almost infinite number of carpet colors that can be coordinated with other aspects of the color scheme.

Among the advantages of using carpet as the floor covering are:

1. Carpet is useful for noise control.
2. Carpet is often less costly to maintain than other types of floor coverings.
3. Carpet, when compared with other types of floor coverings, is more comfortable and less tiring for employees who stand for a substantial portion of each day.

Color	Reflectance value (percent)
White	86
Light green	67
Light yellow	64
Light blue	58
Light gray	54
Medium yellow	47
Orange	35
Medium red	23
Dark blue	17
Dark red	13
Dark green	10

Figure 5-5   Reflectance values of colors.

Figure 5-6 Color scheme guidelines

1. Color cannot be considered by itself; rather, its impact on the total office environment must be considered.
2. Black and white influence other colors. Black makes other colors appear lighter and more distinctive. White makes other colors appear darker.
3. Any color used against a darker color will appear lighter than it actually is, whereas any color used against a lighter one will appear darker.
4. Colors lose their brilliance and "wash out" in bright light, and darken and lose their intensity in dim light.
5. Warm colors are considered to advance, whereas cool colors recede.
6. The use of two sharply contrasting colors tends to tire the eyes rather quickly.
7. Small areas of bright, secondary colors that are balanced with the colors used in large areas are often attractive.
8. Light colors will make a small room look larger.
9. A narrow area can be made to appear wider by using a color on the end walls that is brighter than the color used on the side walls.
10. Of the deep colors appropriate for office use, brown is the most preferred.
11. A low ceiling can be made to appear higher by painting it a lighter color than the walls.
12. In working areas, floors should be darker than walls, and the walls should be darker than the ceiling.
13. Because of excessive contrast, dark colors should not be used on walls with windows.
14. When natural light enters a work area from the north or east, a warm color should be used on the wall opposite the window; however, when the natural light is from the south or west, a cool color should be used on the wall opposite the window.
15. Window coverings, such as drapes and other kinds of shades, should be functional as well as aesthetic.

When carpeting creates electrostatic charges, special provisions may have to be made to prevent these charges from interfering with the operation of sensitive electronic office equipment, such as computers. The fire-retardant rating of the carpet is also a concern that cannot be ignored, especially when local restrictions/regulations are in existence.

Wall Coverings

Carpeting has become a popular wall covering because of its aesthetic value and its ability to absorb noise. The carpeting used on walls must have a high fire-retardant value. Carpet with a foam backing is not recommended as a wall covering because of the dense smoke it creates when it burns.

A variety of other types of wall coverings are used frequently in offices, including vinyl, cloth, cork, and paper. Interior designers are helpful in selecting an appropriate covering for a given wall.

Color of Furniture. When planning an appropriate color coordination scheme for an office, consideration must also be given to furniture color. Because most furniture outlasts wall colors, alternative color schemes should be considered at the time the initial color scheme is planned. Flexibility is destroyed when floor and furniture colors allow the use of only one or two wall colors.

What is the trend in
selecting furniture colors?

An emerging trend is to select furniture colors that contrast with wall colors. This practice not only provides greater flexibility in designing a color scheme but also helps eliminate some of the monotony of having similar colors. An example is a scheme built around gray walls and upholstered furniture in deep blue, green, or mauve.

When selecting furniture, the contrast value and the reflectance value of the working surface should be considered. If these values are excessive, undue eye strain will occur. Shiny and highly polished surfaces on furniture should also be avoided if the lighting system produces an appreciable amount of either direct or reflected glare.

NOISE CONTROL

The noise level in an office is another of the environmental factors that must be considered. When noise reaches an undesirable level, various physical and psychological conditions occur. For example, continued high noise levels can result in either temporary or permanent hearing loss. High noise levels produce fatigue and hamper productivity, as well as cause nervous conditions, tension, and irritability. In addition, high noise levels can increase one's blood pressure and metabolic rate, both of which over time can create serious health problems.

What is a decibel?

The **decibel,** the unit measure of sound, is the smallest change in sound detectable by the human ear. The faintest sound that the human ear can detect is zero decibels. Therefore, other sounds with greater intensity have decibel values higher than the zero value. Figure 5–7 illustrates the decibel values for several common office sounds. Because the decibel scale is logarithmic, a small increase in a decibel value doubles the actual sound level. The maximum decibel level in an office should be 90, while a decibel level of 50 is preferred. Sustained decibel levels of 120 or higher may result in hearing loss.

The goal of a noise control system is to produce speech privacy. Confidential privacy is achieved when no more than 5 percent of the words are understood in an adjacent area. Normal privacy is achieved when no more than 20 percent of the words in a conversation can be understood in an adjacent area.

Today, noise control in many organizations is handled through a systems approach, integrating such components as a sound-absorbing ceiling; effective sound barriers, such as sound-absorbing panels, window coverings, floor coverings; and a noise-masking system. While none of the components by themselves is effective, when integrated into a system, they produce the desired results.

Control of Office Noise

Several techniques are available for controlling the noise in an office, including proper construction, use of sound-absorbing materials and devices, and

Office area	Decibels
Loud office machines room	90
Noisy office	70
Average office	50
Quiet office	30
Soundproof office	10

Figure 5-7 Decibel levels of office sounds.

installation of a **masking-sound system** designed to make noise levels less noticeable.

Proper Construction. Significant amounts of office noise can be controlled by using effective building construction techniques. Sound travels either through the air (called *airborne sounds*) or through structural facilities (*structural sound*) prior to its becoming airborne. Examples of airborne sound are conversation and the sound generated by various pieces of equipment. An example of structural sound is equipment vibration; before becoming airborne, vibration sounds travel through a structural device in the work area.

What is structural sound?

The following construction techniques are recommended as ways of eliminating undesirable structural sounds:

1. Attach a network of feeder ducts to the main ducts in the heating/cooling system. A system using only main ducts allows considerable noise to be carried through the ducts.

2. Use windows and doors that seal properly.

3. Build dead airspace into the structural features; this helps decrease the amount of noise that travels from one feature to another.

4. Use construction materials that prohibit vibration noises from occurring.

Sound-Absorbing Materials. Many types of sound-absorbing materials suitable for office use are available today. Most of the materials, which include wall-, window-, and floor-covering materials as well as ceiling products, have functional and aesthetic value.

Sound absorption is measured using a noise reduction coefficient (NRC). Most materials carry a rating of .50 to .95. A rating of .50 means that 50 percent of the sound is absorbed by the materials. For the purpose of controlling noise, materials with a NCR of less than .75 are ineffective.

Of the noise-controlling wall-covering materials that are available, soft, porous materials such as cork and carpeting are most desirable. In addition, a number of companies manufacture permanent, full-length sound-absorbing wall panels.

If the ceiling and floor coverings are adequate to control noise, special wall coverings probably are not needed. But in offices in which a high concentration of noise exists, special ceiling, wall, and floor materials may be needed.

The most efficient sound-absorbing floor covering is carpet. Because static can affect office equipment, static-free carpet may have to be installed. Static can also be controlled by placing a grid of copper grounding wires beneath the carpet.

What characteristics should sound-absorbing materials possess?

For maximum benefit, materials used for noise control should possess three characteristics or qualities:

1. Absorption—the degree to which noise is absorbed within the material. Absorption is measured by the Noise Reduction Coefficient discussed earlier.

2. Reflection—the degree to which sound is not absorbed by various materials but rather is reflected back into space.

3. Isolation—the degree to which materials prevent sounds from passing through them.

A proper balance between reflection and absorption is needed to help eliminate work areas with a "dead" sound. As noise levels increase, absorption needs to be increased and reflection decreased. Materials with hard surfaces—metal, glass, and plastic—reflect a greater amount of noise than do surfaces with soft finishes—draperies, porous ceiling tiles, and the like. Isolation of noise is affected by such characteristics as airtightness, weight, and stiffness of materials.

Sound-Absorbing Devices. Several sound-absorbing devices are frequently used as a means of controlling office noise. Sound-absorbing materials can be placed under certain kinds of office machines—for example, the typewriter or dot-matrix printer. Another device used in many offices is a sound-absorbing cover placed over a noise-generating machine, such as a typewriter or printer. Figure 5–8 displays a sound-absorbing cover.

In addition to being used for privacy, movable panels such as those illustrated in Figure 4–5 are also used to absorb sound.

Masking. Another noise-controlling method is the masking technique, which involves blending office noise with low-level, nondisturbing background sounds. Also known as **white noise,** masking noise is similar to the sound heard when air passes through a duct or tunnel. Public address systems are frequently used to transmit masking sound throughout the work areas.

Control of Noise in Offices Using Open Space Planning

Open space planning provides special challenges for noise control. Greater amounts of sound-absorbing materials may have to be used because most permanent walls are eliminated when open space planning is used. Noise-masking devices may also have to be used. If the office area continues to be too noisy after all the noise control techniques are used, greater space between workstations may have to be provided to achieve the desired level of speech privacy.

What is white noise?

Figure 5–8 Sound-absorbing cover. Courtesy: Gates Co., Santa Rosa, CA

CONDITIONING THE AIR

The air in which employees work also impacts on their physical and psychological well-being. In fact, with employees spending 90 percent of their waking hours indoors (approximately 2,000 hours per year), air quality is a major concern. In many of today's office buildings, the air contains more chemical irritants and biological matter than the outside air. Air-quality factors involve temperature, humidity, ventilation, and air cleanliness. Major contributors to the indoor air pollution found in many of today's buildings are excessive levels of moisture, inadequate mechanical ventilation, and to a lesser extent than previously, tobacco smoke.

Most new office buildings located in areas with varied climates are constructed with a year-round, integrated air conditioning system. Therefore, the atmospheric condition of the office is constant day after day.

In most instances, the benefits of installing systems designed to condition office air properly are more than worth their cost. For example, if employee comfort is improved, greater levels of productivity and efficiency can be expected. Absenteeism and tardiness are reduced, and in some cases employees' health is improved. Furthermore, cleaning and redecorating costs can be reduced by using an integrated air conditioning system.

What new devices help reduce heating costs?

Several technological advances are now available that help organizations reduce their heating costs. These new devices use reclaimed heat to warm work areas. For example, the heat created by lights, office equipment, and even humans is collected through special vents and redistributed throughout the premises. This reclaimed heat can also be used to heat water. During the summer, reclaimed heat is removed from the premises to reduce air cooling needs.

Several new computerized heat control systems are used in office buildings. Temperature sensors continually provide a computer with temperature data from each area of the building. The computer then makes needed temperature adjustments. During nonworking hours, temperatures are automatically adjusted to conserve energy.

Temperature of Air

When the humidity level is within the proper range, the ideal working temperature in an office is 68 degrees Fahrenheit. To conserve energy, the temperature should be lowered a few degrees in winter and raised a few degrees in summer.

In the future, solar energy will undoubtedly be a primary heating source in office buildings in certain parts of the world. Depending on the geographical location of the building, solar energy may be able to provide all the heat that is needed.

Two types of air-cooling units are available: central units similar to those found in most new office buildings and self-contained units that are often installed in buildings that were not designed to accommodate central systems. One way to determine whether or not installing an air-cooling system is cost-worthy is to determine its impact on increased worker efficiency. The use of professional consultants is recommended when the installation of an air-cooling system is being considered.

Humidity Level of Air

How does humidity affect the comfort of various temperature levels?

For maximum comfort, the humidity level of an office should range somewhere between 40 and 60 percent, with the optimum humidity level around 50 percent. A year-round air conditioning system humidifies the air in the winter and dehumidifies it in the summer.

The humidity level has an impact on the temperature level. If the humidity level is within the recommended range, the actual temperature of an office can be lowered in the winter and raised in the summer and still be comfortable. If the humidity level is less than the recommended range, the temperature will have to be either raised or lowered to achieve the same degree of comfort.

Circulation of Air

The air in working areas, especially those in which equipment produces heat buildup, must be properly circulated if its quality is to be maintained. Without air circulation, the temperature of the air that surrounds an individual tends to increase, which results in a certain amount of discomfort. An adequate air exchange rate is 25 cubic feet of air per minute per person. Therefore, a "block" of air measuring approximately 4 feet by 3 feet by 2 feet will have to be replaced each minute for each employee in a given area. An acceptable standard for air circulation is approximately 50 feet per minute. Hence, a "block" of air that moves 50 feet in one minute is acceptable. Air circulated at too fast a rate creates a draft. Greater air circulation will have to be provided if smoking is allowed in the work area.

Cleanliness of Air

Devices designed to cleanse the air are now being installed in many office buildings. These devices cleanse the air of germs, dust, and dirt. Air cleanliness is becoming a greater concern as buildings become more airtight and energy efficient, two features that entrap unclean, stagnate, stale air within the confines of work areas. While ultraviolet lights are useful for killing germ-laden bacteria, mechanical filters are used to remove dust and other foreign particles. Because of the sensitivity of computer equipment, a dust-free atmosphere is essential in the data processing center. Of significant concern are such air pollutants as cigarette/cigar/pipe smoke and toxic substances, including asbestos, carbon monoxide, and a variety of cleaning and furniture-restoration products. Eventually, the presence of tobacco smoke will not be a concern as organizations are rapidly moving toward a smoke-free work environment.

Increasingly, professional associations are developing standards that address the air cleanliness issue. For example, the American Society of Heating, Refrigeration, and Air Conditioning Engineers (ASHRAE) Standard 62, which is concerned with ventilation, clearly specifies the amount of outdoor air that must be brought into a work area as a way of diluting contaminants. The employee within the organization who has overall responsibility for the building's climate system should be familiar with recommended standards. A socially responsible organization will address these climate issues as a benefit to its employees but also to help avoid costly litigation that often results when a lack of concern is shown for air cleanliness.

MUSIC

A music system produces several beneficial results. Music in an office helps increase job satisfaction and productivity by eliminating boredom and monotony. Music also has the general effect of relieving mental and physical fatigue and reducing nervous tension and strain. The type of music being played affects the productivity of employees. In addition, music has a positive effect on employees' attitudes, often resulting in their making fewer errors and their being absent and tardy less often.

What are the sources of office music?

Several alternatives are possible for developing a music system. Music can be obtained from a service vendor that specializes in programming music for offices. One such vendor is Muzak. Service vendors typically charge according to the number of employees in the organization.

A local radio station can also be used as the music source. Special equipment is available that shuts the system down during the broadcast of commercials and news so that only music is heard. Some organizations provide their own music source, such as tapes and CDs. In most cases, conventional public address systems satisfactorily accommodate each of these alternatives. With CD-ROMs being commonly found today in desk-top computers, some organizations allow their employees whose primary job function is data entry or keyboarding to use headsets to listen to CDs or an Internet radio station as they work.

The success of a music system is significantly affected by the nature of the music programming. The kind of work being performed should be considered in determining the types of music—show tunes, classical numbers, semiclassical numbers, and popular tunes—that should be played. Employees whose work requires a high degree of concentration should be subjected to only the most subdued types of music.

The time of the work day that music is played in relation to its intended impact on the employees should also be considered in programming. Playing more stimulating music is psychologically advantageous when employees' efficiency is below par as a result of fatigue or boredom. Fatigue is generally most noticeable midway through the morning and afternoon work periods and just before the lunch hour and quitting time.

What impact does continuously played music have on employees?

Research has also shown that continuously played music loses its full impact because employees are no longer conscious of its presence. Therefore, short breaks in the music program create awareness. An on-for-fifteen-minutes, off-for-fifteen-minutes cycle provides the necessary breaks.

CONSERVATION OF ENERGY IN OFFICES

One of the realities of life is the growing need to conserve energy. An increasing portion of the administrative office manager's job is devoted to this important task. No longer can conservation be taken for granted; rather, it has to be a formally planned and coordinated activity. The development of a proper attitude toward energy conservation has to start at the top of the organizational management structure.

The Energy Conservation Program

An energy conservation program is comprised of several components, including an energy conservation committee, an energy efficiency study, and the development of goals for conserving energy.

What are the responsibilities of the energy conservation committee?

Energy Conservation Committee. Appointment to the energy conservation committee, also known in some organizations as the "green-office committee," is often made by the organization's president, which helps signal organizational commitment to this important activity. The members of the committee, who generally have expertise in energy conservation, oversee the total energy program. Important activities include undertaking the energy efficiency study and formulating goals. The committee can also provide a valuable public relations function. To perform effectively, the committee must have the authority to ensure compliance with its recommendations.

In some instances, the administrative office manager will chair the committee. In other instances, the committee will be chaired by a full-time energy advisor. In extremely large organizations, the energy advisor will likely be supported by a full-time staff.

Energy Efficiency Study. Before a conservation plan can be devised, an energy conservation study of the facility must be undertaken. The purpose of this study is to identify areas where excessive energy is being used, as well as to determine areas where energy conservation techniques might be implemented. Special emphasis should be placed on those areas where the greatest energy conservation can be realized. The results of the study provide the basis for the development of the conservation goals, another vital component of the energy conservation program.

Development of Energy Conservation Goals. Once the energy efficiency study has been completed, conservation goals are developed. After their approval, every effort should be made to assure their attainment. A periodic follow-up should be undertaken to determine the amount of progress toward reaching the goals. Those areas in which progress is not sufficient should be closely scrutinized. Successful goal attainment should be well publicized throughout the organization.

Techniques for Conserving Energy

With concerted effort, many organizations have been able to reduce their energy consumption by at least 10 to 15 percent. Because of its potential financial impact, energy conservation has to be a top-priority activity in most organizations.

Following is a discussion of several techniques for conserving energy.

Conserving Energy in the Lighting System. Because the lighting system may consume as much as 25 percent of the total energy outlay, special attention should be focused on it. The following suggestions outline energy conservation techniques in terms of the lighting system:

What techniques are used to conserve energy in an office lighting system?

1. Use the appropriate amount of light—but not more than is needed—for the task being performed. Lighting systems that provide the same amount of light in all areas of the premises tend to waste energy.

2. Provide sufficient light in a given area; providing more light than needed may require additional air cooling, which adds to energy consumption.

3. Develop the practice of turning off lights when not needed.

4. Use task lighting or the high-intensity discharge lamps where possible. Each of these uses less energy than alternative types of lighting.

5. Consider installing automatic light control systems to help conserve energy. The payback period for these systems is typically quite short.

6. Clean bulbs and tubes regularly. Dirty lightbulbs and tubes reduce the amount of light they provide.

7. Use light colors that reflect more light throughout the office. Dark colors tend to absorb light and therefore are more wasteful of energy.

8. Reduce outside lighting except where needed for safety and security.

9. Replace aging fluorescent tubes and lightbulbs that no longer provide lighting efficiency. Over the long run, their replacement may be more energy efficient that waiting until they actually burn out.

10. Engage the services (usually free) of the local utility company to conduct an energy audit, the purpose of which is to determine where additional savings from the lighting system can be attained.

Conserving Energy in the Heating/Cooling System. The energy used for heating/cooling also consumes a large part of the total energy allocation. Following are suggestions for conserving energy:

1. Reduce the temperature to 65 degrees Fahrenheit in the winter and increase the temperature to 78 degrees Fahrenheit in the summer.

2. Make sure windows and doors seal properly.

3. Use reclaimed heat where possible, such as that produced by office equipment.

4. Adjust the temperature of work areas when they are not being used.

5. Reduce ventilation during nonworking hours.

6. Consider the installation of an automatic control device that assures the efficient use of energy. The cost of the equipment is likely to be offset quickly by energy savings.

7. Make sure heating and cooling equipment is properly maintained to ensure proper functioning.

8. Maintain proper humidity levels as a means of enhancing human comfort.

Other Conservation Measures. Following is a list of other conservation measures:

1. Install an adequate amount of insulation.

2. Incorporate energy conservation devices and techniques, including solar devices, when designing and constructing new buildings.

3. Purchase equipment that has a high energy-efficiency level.

4. Use one temperature of water (around 95 degrees Fahrenheit) in the restroom lavatories to avoid having to mix hot and cold water to attain a comfortable hand-washing temperature.

5. Replace old faucet aerators with reduced-flow aerators and reduce water levels in toilet tanks.

6. Encourage employees to conserve energy whenever and wherever they can.

7. Encourage employees to adjust their attire to compensate for warmer work area temperatures in the summer and cooler work area temperatures in the winter.

OFFICE SECURITY

Office security is becoming an area of significant concern in many organizations. Security has two dimensions: protection of the organization's physical property (such as equipment, machines, and furniture) and protection of the organization's vital information (data and records) that if stolen or lost will have dire consequences on the organization's ability to continue to function. In some cases, vital information that becomes available to competitors, perhaps because of a lack of proper security, seriously erodes the organization's ability to remain competitive in the marketplace.

Among the factors that should be examined to determine the need for and extent of security are the following: office equipment and machines, computer terminals, data files (including both hard and soft copy), and office furniture. The more valuable an item is to the organization, the more securely it will need to be maintained.

What types of security devices are commonly used?

Limiting access to vital areas is a common means of providing a secure environment. Among the devices used to restrict access are photo IDs, push-button locks, card-lock systems, and physical attribute systems (most commonly fingerprint- and eye-oriented systems). A new type of security device is the proximity card that allows the card holder access to a secure area when his or her card is in close proximity to the card reader. Older card technology requires a "swipe" of the card through the reader.

Another level of security is provided by the automatic light control systems that are activated by either motion or body heat sensors. These systems, when activated, can be designed to summon police units automatically unless they are overridden by an employee with the proper authorization to do so. Also used are intrusion-alarm and sound-alarm systems that automatically summon police units. In addition to these devices, many organizations use closed-circuit television to provide security for an area. Security guards are also commonly used in many organizations.

A common means of securing vital data stored within a computer system is to require the use of passwords to access the data. To maximize security, passwords should be changed frequently. In some instances, a system is used that requires two or more employees to enter passwords before data can be accessed. The level of security provided for the organization's data/information is usually determined by the importance of the data/information. A system that uses a combination of passwords and the security devices discussed earlier provides maximum security.

IMPLICATIONS FOR THE ADMINISTRATIVE OFFICE MANAGER

The nature of his or her background and training makes the administrative office manager well qualified to guide organizational efforts in designing an effective office environment. No employee in the organization is likely to be more familiar with the basic components of an effective environment.

In most instances, the environment in which employees work will affect them more than the layout of their work area. Except for a few fundamental management practices, the office environment is likely to impact more extensively on employees than any other factor.

An effective environment is balanced in an integrative way. Improving one element of the environment while other elements are unsatisfactory is useless. Rather, a more logical approach is to improve all unsatisfactory elements as much as possible.

The administrative office manager will find an understanding of the physical and psychological needs of employees helpful in planning an effective environment. Each element of the environment affects employees physically and/or psychologically.

NOTES

1. The foot-candle, which describes the quantity of light, is the amount of light a distance of 1 foot from a standard candle. One watt of light per square foot produces approximately 15 foot-candles.

2. The foot-lambert measures the brightness of light and is approximately equal to 1 foot-candle of either directed or reflected light.

REVIEW QUESTIONS

1. How does the environment of an office impact on employees?

2. What causes the sick-building syndrome?

3. What do Equivalent Spherical Illumination, Visual Comfort Probability, and Task Illumination measure?

4. What are the advantages and disadvantages of each of the five kinds of ceiling lighting systems discussed in this chapter?

5. What advantages result from the use of task lighting?

6. In what ways do task lighting and ambient lighting differ from one another?

7. What suggestions are helpful in designing a lighting system in areas where terminals are used?

8. How are complementary colors, split-complementary colors, and triad colors used in developing a color scheme?

9. What is the average decibel noise level found in most offices?

10. What characteristics should sound-absorbing materials possess?

11. What temperature, humidity, and circulation standards should exist for most offices?

12. What is the principal factor used to determine the nature of the music that is most appropriate for different times of the day?

13. What are the components of an energy conservation program?

DISCUSSION QUESTIONS

1. Comment on the validity of the following statement that was recently heard during a conversation between two individuals who were discussing the topic of office environment:

   Why pay much attention to the office environment? Humans have an amazing capacity to be dissatisfied, so regardless of what is provided, some employees will never be satisfied. For example, some will find a work area too hot, while others will find it too cold. In the final analysis, ignoring the environment will result in approximately the same amount of satisfaction as will trying to maximize the environment.

2. Your old metal office desk was replaced several months ago with a new one that has a laminated top with a dark-tone simulated wood grain. After several weeks, you began to notice that your eyes were quite fatigued at the end of the day, al-

though the papers you work with are just like the ones you worked with before you got your new desk. To determine whether your eyes have changed since you last had them checked, you decided to have an eye exam. The eye doctor was pleased that your eyes have not changed. Why is your new desk likely to be causing the eye fatigue? How can the problem be resolved?

3. You recently heard a presentation on task lighting. The speaker indicated that task light is not new because years ago most office desks were equipped with a desk lamp. Although the speaker who made this statement is theoretically correct, you know that some important differences do exist. Discuss what you perceive these differences to be. How do you perceive today's task lighting concept to be more effective than the early 1900s concept?

STUDENT PROJECTS/ACTIVITIES

1. Tour the office area of an organization to learn what special kinds of noise control techniques are used.
2. Discuss with an organization's facility manager the special energy conservation techniques that are used.
3. Going Online: Using the Internet, conduct an online search based on one of the concepts presented in this chapter or based on one of the chapter terms. Identify four or five things you learned from this material that you did not know previously.

Minicase

The Midwest Insurance Company is in the process of designing a new building for its headquarters. At the time the company decided to construct the new building, the board of directors requested that energy conservation techniques be used throughout the facility. Because the firm plans to purchase all new office furniture, any kind of savings—no matter how large or small—is necessary. In carrying out the conservation mandate, the vice president who is working with the architect has requested that the most economical energy-efficient lighting system be installed, especially because lighting consumes the greatest portion of the energy budget.

1. What kind of lighting system do you recommend for installation in the new building? Why?
2. What are its advantages?

Case

The home office of the Adolph Food Company is located in Lincoln, Nebraska. Because of the company's fairly steady growth, the original building became too crowded. The company was considering moving to another building when the owners of an adjacent building decided to sell their business. The management of the Adolph Food Company was delighted to be able to purchase the property, which had 20 percent more space than they currently needed. At the company's present rate of growth, the space in the two buildings would be adequate for the next ten years.

However, very little attention was given to the environment of either building. When the personnel department discovered a rapid increase in the number of employees who quit, the decision was made to talk with each individual who terminated employment. The most frequently cited reasons why employees left was because of the rather drab, dreary, unpleasant areas in which they worked. Some employees even claimed that the dark, noisy environment gave them headaches and made them nervous.

The management of the organization has decided to investigate the possibility of improving the overall environment.

1. You are asked to provide the company with a list of criteria that are necessary for a desirable office environment. The list will subsequently be used by the company to evaluate its environment.
2. In what ways will a satisfactory working environment affect the employees?

Chapter 6

OFFICE EQUIPMENT AND FURNITURE

Chapter Aims

After studying this chapter, you should be able to select appropriate equipment and furniture for a general office area.

Chapter Outline

Office Equipment
  Planning Considerations
  Use of Comparative Analysis Form
  Obtaining Office Equipment
  Equipment Maintenance Considerations
  Replacement Considerations
  Inventory Control Considerations
Office Furniture
  New Developments in Office Furniture
  Use of Safety and Performance Standards
Implications for the Administrative Office
  Manager

Chapter Terms

Break-even analysis
Business and Institutional Furniture Manu-
  facturers Association (BIFMA)
Buyers Laboratory, Inc.
Carpal tunnel syndrome (CTS)
Ergonomics design
Functional design
Leases with option to purchase
Modular design
Payback period
Portable design
Sale-leaseback
Systems furniture
True leases

*I*ndividuals responsible for selecting office equipment and furniture devote considerable attention to the process. Generally, a positive correlation exists between the amount of care exercised and the satisfaction employees derive from equipment and furniture they use to carry out their job functions. Reasons for exercising considerable care include the following: (1) equipment and furniture represent a significant investment for the organization; (2) a greater number of equipment and furniture sources now exists than ever before, thus providing a far greater number of options; (3) the specialized nature of much of the equipment and furniture requires considerable care in the selection process; and (4) the increased need for employees to be as productive as possible requires use of equipment and furniture that enhance their productivity.

Among problems likely to result when the equipment and furniture selection process is not given the care it deserves are the following:

What problems are likely to arise when equipment and furniture are not carefully selected?

1. The equipment and furniture, although adequate at the present time, will not meet organizational needs very well or very far into the future.
2. The equipment and furniture are not sufficiently functional; thus, they have a detrimental effect on employee productivity.
3. The organization is unable to achieve a desirable return on its equipment and furniture investment, which is often a sizeable amount.

OFFICE EQUIPMENT

Often a time-consuming process, the selection of office equipment is especially involved when a large amount and a great variety of equipment are needed. The information in the following sections will be helpful to those undertaking this important task.

Planning Considerations

Several factors need to be considered when selecting new office equipment. The number of factors and their importance are likely to be determined by the type of equipment needed and the functions for which the equipment will be used. Although only a few factors have to be considered in selecting some types of equipment, all of the factors should be considered in selecting other types.

What is the purpose of the comparative analysis form?

A comparative analysis of the various brands of equipment being considered is often helpful in selecting office equipment. Each brand is evaluated on the basis of the functions it is capable of performing, its manufacturer, and its vendor.

Of growing concern to increasing numbers of office employees is **carpal tunnel syndrome (CTS),** which is thought to be caused by repetitive stress when using certain office equipment to perform repetitive motions over a long period of time. Physiologically, it occurs when the protective sheath around wrist tendons swell, putting pressure on nerves that results in numbness as well as pain and a tingling sensation in the fingers, wrists, and hands. CTS is best avoided by using one or more of the following techniques: (1) use correct posture when working with office equipment; (2) assure that workstations are comfortable, which means they will likely have to be adjustable; (3) redesign work processes, which helps employees avoid repetitive motions over a long time; and (4) have an adequate number of rest or break periods during the work day.

Following is a discussion of the factors that should be considered in selecting new office equipment. Each factor is classified as an equipment consideration, a vendor consideration, or a maintenance consideration.

Equipment Considerations

1. *Purpose of the equipment.* Before selecting new equipment, its purpose must be determined. This can be either partially or wholly determined by the work the equipment will be used to process. Too often, organizations either purchase or lease equipment that is more sophisticated than needed. Equipment functions that are never used increase the cost of the equipment and lower the organization's return on its investment. If an operating system requires the use of the proposed new equipment, someone familiar with the system should help determine equipment needs. Equipment that fails to meet the needs for which it was purchased or leased is often caused by an inaccurate assessment of how it will be used.

2. *Determination of appropriate equipment.* After the equipment needs have been assessed, determining which brands of equipment will most appropriately meet these needs is the next step. Because equipment needs often can be adequately met by several brands of equipment, a fairly comprehensive equipment search should be undertaken. One of the most commonly used means of identifying the appropriate equipment is to provide vendors with detailed descriptions of the way in which the equipment will be used. The vendors can then determine which equipment is appropriate. This step is generally less important with low-cost, nonspecialized equipment than it is with high-cost, specialized equipment.

How can equipment dependability be determined?

3. *Dependability of equipment.* Once the various brands of equipment appropriate for the situation have been identified, the dependability of the equipment is assessed. Although some equipment manufacturers have reputations for producing dependable office equipment, others do not enjoy the same reputation.

   Equipment dependability can be assessed in several ways. One way is to contact administrative office managers in other organizations that use the same type of equipment. Although most equipment vendors willingly provide the names of their most satisfied customers, other users of the same equipment should also be contacted when possible. The names of other equipment users can usually be obtained quite readily. In some instances, nonreferred users may provide a more realistic evaluation than will those users referred by equipment manufacturers or vendors.

   The dependability of the equipment can also be determined by reading equipment reports compiled by such independent organizations as **Buyers Laboratory, Inc.,** a New Jersey-based testing firm. A final way to assess equipment dependability, although not always totally reliable, is to assess the dependability of other equipment of the same brand used within the organization.

4. *Specifications of the equipment.* For certain types of equipment, specifications have to be determined; this refers to such factors as equipment size, electrical requirements, installation requirements, and special structural requirements. Some equipment, although suitable in all other respects, has to be eliminated from consideration because of inappropriate specifications. Now that devices are being interlinked, especially computer peripheral equipment, the compatibility of these devices is also important.

5. *Cost of the equipment.* The cost of equipment has a significant impact on the organization's return on its investment. Although cost is important, some organizations place too much emphasis on this factor. Consequently, less expensive equipment is selected. And if it fails to perform as well as other equipment or is less efficient than other equipment that was

considered, the organization will not be able to maximize the return on its investment.

6. *Operational processes of the equipment.* Some types of office equipment require the use of specialized supplies, especially certain photocopiers and printers. The necessity of such specialized supplies should be determined as well as the possibility of using these supplies on other brands of equipment.

7. *Safety features.* Also to be considered are the safety features of office equipment. Although most routine office equipment is not hazardous, certain types of equipment used in printing and duplicating processes can be, especially when employees misuse the equipment.

How is equipment flexibility determined?

8. *Flexibility of equipment.* Increasingly, equipment is becoming available that can be modified with additional components or attachments as the need arises. Although these attachments may not be needed at the time of purchase, consideration should be given to the possibility of future need. Another dimension of equipment flexibility is its possible use for a variety of work processes. Because some equipment is more suitable than other equipment for a wider variety of work processes, its flexibility should be thoroughly evaluated.

9. *Ease of equipment operation.* Also to be considered is the ease with which the equipment is operated, as office devices are not equally user friendly. One of the more efficient ways of determining operating ease is to seek input from individuals who will operate the equipment being considered. To make a comparative analysis, have the vendors outline in detail how the equipment can be used to perform several specific procedures.

10. *Speed of equipment operation.* In some instances, the operational speed of the equipment is an important consideration. If this is the case and if the speeds are quite variable, the operational speeds of the different pieces of equipment should be assessed.

11. *Cost of equipment operation.* The per unit cost of producing work is especially important when selecting equipment to be used in high-volume operations. Although operating costs may be quite similar for various devices being considered, differences in costs may be significant over time. Cost comparison is especially important when selecting printing, duplicating, and photocopying equipment. Because the various operating processes are quite variable, the per unit cost may vary considerably.

12. *Equipment operator input.* Employees who will be responsible for operating the equipment are often given an opportunity to provide input into deciding which piece of equipment to select. This practice not only improves the opportunity for selecting equipment that employees find suitable, but also gives them a feeling of involvement. Unless employees are satisfied with the operation of a particular piece of equipment, its efficient use cannot always be guaranteed.

What advantages result from standardizing equipment brands?

13. *Standardization of equipment.* The use of only a few different brands of equipment, resulting in standardization, is found desirable by most organizations. This practice may enable the organization to take advantage of quantity purchasing as well as reduce its service costs because fewer brands of equipment have to be maintained. Another advantage is the ease with which employees can learn to operate similar pieces of equipment.

Vendor Considerations

1. *Reputation of the equipment vendor.* An important consideration when selecting office equipment is the reputation of the vendor. Factors that affect

the vendor's reputation are age of the firm, size of the firm, services provided by the firm, financial stability of the firm, range of equipment sold by the firm, and the firm's reputation in the community. Most organizations are more concerned about the reputation of the vendor when purchasing specialized, costly equipment than when purchasing low-cost, nonspecialized equipment.

How should the nature of training provided by manufacturers or vendors be determined?

2. *Training provided by the manufacturer or equipment vendor.* Because of the specialized nature of some new types of office equipment, employees may need to be trained before they are able to use the equipment effectively. The quality of training experiences the various manufacturers or vendors provide is quite variable. Some vendors provide training only at the time the equipment is installed, whereas others provide training whenever a new operator uses the equipment. Thus, if the original equipment operator leaves the organization, the vendor will train the replacement operator. When specialized equipment is being considered, an investigation should be made of the nature of the training experiences provided by the manufacturer or vendor.

   Today, fewer manufacturers and vendors provide training. The trend is to provide the purchaser with quality training materials that enable users to self-train. In such cases, the quality of the training materials should be evaluated during the selection process.

3. *Purchasing option.* Some vendors only sell certain types of equipment, whereas others lease as well as sell equipment. If an organization is interested in only one of the two options, but not both, this factor needs to be considered early in the selection process. The advantages and disadvantages of purchasing and leasing are discussed in a subsequent section of this chapter.

4. *Delivery of the new equipment.* The timing of equipment purchase or replacement cannot always be planned. Because of circumstances beyond the organization's control, the immediate delivery of new equipment may be important. Vendors unable to guarantee a delivery date may have to be eliminated from consideration.

Maintenance Considerations

1. *Servicing the equipment.* The ability to obtain fast, reliable service on the equipment is another factor that should be considered. This is especially true in situations where no backup equipment is available to perform crucial work processes. Some equipment vendors do not provide the same quality of equipment servicing as others; therefore, this factor should be carefully weighed, especially when purchasing expensive, intricate, or specialized equipment. In addition, the geographical location of the vendor may be important. Vendors who are located a considerable distance from the organization may not be able to provide rapid service.

2. *Equipment maintenance.* Another factor to be considered is the nature of the routine maintenance required by the equipment. This factor is important because some brands of equipment require more routine maintenance than others. The nature of equipment maintenance is especially important when purchasing printing, duplicating, and photocopying equipment, because the amount of maintenance required varies considerably from brand to brand.

Use of Comparative Analysis Form

When several brands of equipment are being considered, the equipment has to be compared on a systematic, objective basis. As the number of brands under consideration increases, the task of comparing the equipment becomes more difficult. To facilitate the comparison, using a form such as the one illustrated in Figure 6–1 is helpful. The form assures the comparison of the equipment on a consistent, objective basis.

Obtaining Office Equipment

What two alternatives are available for obtaining office equipment?

Basically, organizations have two alternatives for obtaining office equipment: leasing and purchasing. Before making a final decision, the advantages and disadvantages of using both alternatives for the procurement of specific pieces of equipment should be considered.

Leasing Considerations. Some organizations find equipment leasing to be a more desirable alternative than purchasing. Of the various types of office equipment leased, computers are the most common, followed by office copiers.

What is the difference between true leases and leases with the option to purchase?

Two basic types of office equipment leases are available: **true leases** and **leases with the option to purchase.** A true lease, also known as a tax, operating, or fair market value lease, is one in which the lessee never intends to purchase the equipment. True leases may be obtained either for a short time or for a longer time with an option to renew. Short-term leases are frequently used for obtaining equipment when an organization has a short-term heavy workload or is concerned about the equipment's becoming technologically obsolete in a relatively short time. This enables the lessee to avoid having to pay on a lease for a long time, having to purchase additional equipment, or having to use obsolete equipment.

The long-term lease with an option to renew is used for leasing equipment that will be needed for several years. At the end of the initial lease period, some lessors lower the cost on renewal of the lease.

A lease with the option to purchase is also known as a capital lease, a conditional sale, or dollar buyout. At the end of the lease period, or at any time the lease is in effect, the lessee has the option of purchasing the equipment. These leases typically run for the length of the useful life of the equipment. The amount that the lessee has paid on the lease is usually applied toward the equipment's purchase price. Some organizations use this alternative to determine how well the equipment will meet its needs before making a purchasing decision.

What is sale-leaseback?

Another alternative, although one that is not too commonly used for obtaining office equipment, is **sale-leaseback.** The organization purchases the equipment, which is then sold to a lessor, who then gives the organization a lease on the equipment. This alternative is desirable for organizations that have to obtain capital rather quickly.

What are the advantages of leasing?

To help determine which of the various leasing alternatives to use, answering the following questions will be helpful:

1. What will the organization want to do with the equipment at the end of the lease period? (Exercising the right to purchase equipment likely to become technologically obsolete in a relatively short time is generally an unwise decision.)
2. What is the status of the organization's cash flow situation? (The longer a cash flow concern is likely to exist, the more desirable a longer term lease becomes.)
3. What is the organization's tax liability situation? (The greater the need to lease equipment for a tax advantage, the more desirable is a true lease rather than a lease with the option to purchase, which has no tax advantage.)
4. How long will the organization likely want to use the equipment? (True leases provide greater flexibility in terms of lease length.)

Name of Manufac- turer	Model No.	Pitch	Price	Correction Buffer Size (Characters)	Text Memory Size (in K)	Memory Protection	Visual Display Size (Characters)	Automatic Error Correction	Automatic Underlining	Automatic Word Wraparound	Automatic Centering	Automatic Relocate	Automatic Line Spacing	Playback Speed	Hyphenation	Column Layout	Search-Replace
1																	
2																	
3																	
4																	
5																	
6																	
7																	

Figure 6-1 Comparative analysis form

Advantages of Leasing Office Equipment

1. Leasing conserves working capital that may be needed for other purposes, such as expansion, market development, or construction.

2. The organization is able to obtain up-to-date equipment. The financial cost of exchanging obsolete leased equipment is less than the cost of purchasing new equipment and trying to sell or trade in old equipment. A related

advantage is the ease with which the organization can keep replacing currently used equipment with the technologically latest equipment.

3. True lease payments are tax deductible. A lease with an option to purchase is considered a conditional sales contract and, therefore, is not deductible.

4. Leasing equipment enables an organization to use its financial resources more efficiently. A short-term lease is advantageous for obtaining equipment needed for only a short time each year. An organization that purchases equipment for such purposes is unable to maximize the return on its investment.

Disadvantages of Leasing Office Equipment

What are the disadvantages of leasing?

1. Leased office equipment is frequently more costly than purchased equipment. The total lease payments frequently exceed the purchase price of the equipment.

2. The lease may stipulate that the lessee is responsible for equipment maintenance and repairs. Equipment leased under these terms can be quite costly if its service needs are higher than average.

3. Most leases stipulate that the lessee keep detailed records on the leased equipment. If this is the case and if the organization leases a considerable amount of equipment, the paperwork may become quite burdensome.

4. If the lease gives the lessee an opportunity to purchase the equipment, the lease payments are not tax deductible. Only payments made on true leases are deductible.

A fairly new development in office equipment leasing is the emergence of leasing companies. Rather than lease equipment from an equipment vendor or manufacturer, the equipment is obtained from a leasing company. The leasing company—by purchasing the desired equipment from the manufacturer and then leasing the equipment to the lessee—acts as a third party between the lessee and the manufacturer. One desirable characteristic of leasing companies is the flexibility of the leasing arrangements they provide.

Equipment leasing and rental differ from one another in the following ways: Leasing frequently involves a contract that clearly stipulates the length of time the lease is in effect. Rental, conversely, may not require that the lessee use the equipment for a specified period. At any time, the equipment can be returned with no further obligations to its owner.

When leasing office equipment, the formulation of the lease is critical to the program's success. Negotiation is a frequent tactic in obtaining a favorable equipment leasing arrangement. In many instances, organizations use three or four negotiation rounds to obtain acceptable lease terms. Among the factors to consider in formulating a lease are: cost of the equipment, projected length of the lease, and the organization's plans for purchasing the equipment toward the end of the lease.

Purchasing Considerations. Many organizations prefer to purchase their office equipment because it is considered an asset, and it can be used in whatever manner the organization wishes. Some leasing arrangements put restrictions on the use of leased equipment. Purchased equipment can also be disposed of by selling, which to some individuals makes purchasing preferable to leasing.

What are the advantages of purchasing?

Purchased equipment provides the organization with financial advantages that are not available when equipment is leased. To illustrate, purchased equipment can be depreciated, which helps reduce the organization's income tax obligation.

Some equipment manufacturers provide their customers with financial assistance. To illustrate, some manufacturers sell their equipment on an interest-free credit basis. For example, a six-months-same-as-cash arrangement is a common offer many manufacturers provide. In other instances, the organization is able to obtain a loan through a manufacturer that has a lower interest rate than a loan obtained from a commercial lending institution.

Making the Decision. Among the various factors that should be considered when deciding whether to lease or to purchase office equipment are the following:

1. *How rapidly are new technological developments occurring in the type of equipment being considered?* If the equipment is undergoing frequent technological change, leasing may be more desirable. Thus, the organization is able to update its equipment regularly.

2. *What is the purchase cost of the equipment?* Some of the more expensive equipment is leased rather than purchased. When equipment is obtained in this way, capital is available for more urgent needs.

3. *What leasing arrangements are equipment vendors willing to provide?* Although most equipment vendors in a given geographical area are quite competitive in terms of the leasing arrangements, some vendors may provide conditions that make leasing more desirable than purchasing. In such cases, leasing should be given serious consideration.

4. *What special provisions become available when leasing equipment?* In some instances, the lessor is responsible for equipment maintenance. Some organizations find this to be a significant reason for leasing rather than purchasing.

5. *How stable are the various work processes for which the equipment is needed?* If the work processes are expected to change significantly during the life of the equipment, leasing should be given serious consideration. Consequently, the organization is not forced to sell an unneeded piece of equipment or burdened with a device that does not adequately meet its work processing requirements.

6. *What is the per unit cost of work when leasing equipment and when purchasing equipment?* When the equipment is to be used for high-volume operations, the per unit cost of each of the two alternatives should be determined. If the leasing alternative is considerably less costly over time, leasing may be a more desirable option.

7. *What are the results of a break-even analysis?* Often helpful in making a decision about leasing or purchasing equipment is a **break-even analysis.** Such an analysis is calculated for both the leasing and the purchasing alternatives. The break-even point occurs when the income from the units produced by the equipment equals the aggregate expenses incurred in producing the units. Stated another way, the point occurs when the organization experiences neither income nor a loss in terms of the number of units produced. If the organization anticipates that it will use the equipment to produce more than the minimum number of units needed to achieve the break-even point, the procurement of the equipment is likely to be financially feasible. If the break-even point is not likely to be reached in terms of the volume produced, then the financial feasibility of the equipment is

What is break-even analysis?

questionable. To calculate the break-even point, the following data are needed: fixed costs, variable costs, and anticipated production volume.

8. *What is the length of the payback period?* Also helpful in making a decision about which procurement alternative to use is the calculation of the **payback period.** This calculation will enable the organization to determine how long it must use the equipment to recover an amount of cash equal to the procurement cost. Depending on the type of equipment, the payback period may be so long that the use of the equipment cannot be financially justified. In some cases, the payback period for purchasing and leasing is similar; in other instances, one of the two alternatives is clearly advantageous. If the purchase alternative has a long payback period and if the equipment has a chance of becoming obsolete within a short time, the leasing alternative becomes much more attractive.

What is meant by the payback period?

Equipment Maintenance Considerations

Maintenance of office equipment is important not only because of problems arising from improperly maintained equipment but also because of the cost of repairs resulting from inadequate maintenance. The life of office equipment can be affected by the quality of its maintenance. Day-to-day operator maintenance is also helpful in increasing the useful life of equipment and for decreasing the number of needed equipment repairs.

Equipment maintenance is typically provided by one or more of the following three methods: service contract with a representative of the equipment manufacturer or service agency; service provided on a call basis by a representative of the equipment manufacturer or service agency; and an in-house service department. Some organizations put a portion of their equipment on a service contract, and the remainder is maintained on a call basis. Each of the three methods is explained in the following paragraphs.

Service Contract. This method of equipment maintenance involves a service contract with a manufacturer's representative or with a service agency. Most contracts are valid for increments of one year. During the term of the contract, the manufacturer's representative or service agency generally is responsible not only for equipment repairs but also for routine maintenance, such as cleaning and oiling.

Some service contracts specify that equipment will receive a thorough cleaning and oiling once a year, in addition to a specified number of routine inspections during the year. Preventive maintenance is a distinct characteristic of this method. Depending on the nature of the contract, the cost of minor replacement parts may be covered, whereas the owner of the equipment may be responsible for the cost of major replacement parts.

What are the benefits of using the service contract method of equipment maintenance?

Service contracts provide several important benefits. Perhaps most important is the preventive maintenance benefit. Another advantage is the reduced amount of paperwork involved. If maintenance is provided on a call basis, the amount of paperwork involved in preparing vouchers and checks over time can be quite extensive. When a service contract is used, the paperwork is processed only once a year. Another advantage of the service contract is the fairly quick response time that it provides.

Perhaps the most significant disadvantage of service contracts is their cost. Depending on the provisions and the type of equipment covered, the cost may range from a hundred dollars to several hundred dollars a year per device. Therefore, equipment needing no repairs will cost as much to maintain as equipment needing frequent repairs. Although service contracts may be quite expensive, their cost can be partially offset in a variety of ways, making their use more feasible. Equipment may last longer, which helps offset the cost of the contract. The cost can also be partially offset by the reduced amount of paperwork. Before an organization purchases a service contract, the following provisions in the contract need to be carefully assessed:

What factors about a service contract need to be considered before signing the contract?

1. Nature of the coverage of service calls, parts, and labor.
2. Minimum number of inspections during contract period.
3. Provisions or restrictions for on-site and shop work.
4. Renewal conditions.
5. Availability of loaner equipment when needed.
6. Mileage for service technician.
7. Nature of exclusions.
8. Specific machines covered by the equipment.
9. Dates of coverage.
10. Cost of contract.

Call Basis. When equipment is maintained on a call basis, the representative of the equipment manufacturer or service agency is called each time the equipment needs to be repaired. Unless special provisions are made, the equipment does not receive the yearly cleaning and oiling customarily included with service contracts. The owner of the equipment, therefore, pays only for services performed.

In comparison to a service contract, this method of equipment maintenance appears on the surface to be less costly. But when the cost of preparing payment invoices and checks and the lack of preventive maintenance are considered, the call basis may be more expensive over the long run than having a service contract on the equipment. Furthermore, the call basis typically does not produce as fast a repair time as the service contract.

In what situation is in-house service typically used?

In-House Service. Large organizations sometimes have their own in-house service departments. The organization employs individuals trained to service the equipment. Because of frequent changes in equipment technology, these employees periodically have to undergo training to update their knowledge. In addition to the salaries of these individuals, the organization must also consider the cost of fringe benefits and retraining. For these reasons, this maintenance method is generally feasible only for larger organizations. When an organization has its own in-house service, the number of brands of equipment is frequently kept to a minimum. However, this may prevent the organization from achieving the flexibility that is possible when a greater number of brands of equipment is used.

The use of an in-house service department often results in more rapid repair of equipment than is possible with either of the other two methods. This has a significant impact on equipment downtime. When the service department is not busy with equipment repair, preventive maintenance on equipment can be performed. In addition to the cost of staffing the in-house service department, the cost of equipment parts and tools must be considered.

What factors should be considered in deciding which method of equipment maintenance to use?

Figure 6–2 identifies several factors to consider when deciding which of the three methods of equipment maintenance to use.

Figure 6-2 Factors to consider when deciding on equipment maintenance method.

1. Cost and provisions of a service contract.
2. Frequency of equipment repair.
3. Impact of preventive maintenance on increasing the life of equipment.
4. Availability of and expense incurred in employing trained service personnel.
5. Number of different brands of office equipment owned by the organization.
6. Type of equipment to be maintained.
7. Cost of paperwork associated with equipment maintenance.
8. Speed with which the equipment must be repaired.

Replacement Considerations

The administrative office manager also has to be concerned about equipment replacement. The useful life of office equipment is often determined by the nature of the equipment and by the amount of its usage. Equipment that receives considerable use or that tends to become obsolete quite rapidly may be depreciated over a shorter time than other types of equipment. For example, a computer used most of each work day may be depreciated over a three-year period, whereas an adding machine that is seldom used may be depreciated over a ten-year period. At the end of the depreciation period, the equipment is traded for new equipment.

Keeping office equipment for the length of time that it is being depreciated is not always financially feasible. Changes in technology or work processes may make the present equipment inefficient, or perhaps a particular piece of equipment requires frequent repair. In those instances, the organization may consider accelerating the trade-in time. Some equipment has a good repair record at the time it is to be traded in, however, and the decision may be made to keep the equipment longer.

Inventory Control Considerations

The administrative office manager is also frequently given the responsibility for equipment inventory. The absence of accurate inventory control records makes maintaining control over equipment more difficult. Inventory control involves keeping detailed records on each piece of equipment, including such information as:

What information about each piece of equipment needs to be kept for inventory control?

1. Serial number of each piece of equipment the organization owns, leases, or rents.
2. Date the organization purchased, leased, or rented the equipment.
3. Purchase cost of the equipment.
4. Life of the equipment (either actual life or lease life).
5. Yearly depreciation of the equipment.
6. Book value of the equipment.
7. Location of each piece of equipment.
8. Inventory control number assigned to each device.
9. Costs involved in servicing the equipment.

Keeping the inventory control records updated is critical. Otherwise, little will be gained by maintaining an inventory of the equipment. Most organizations undertake a detailed inventory on a yearly basis to determine whether or not equipment is located where the record indicates it is.

OFFICE FURNITURE

The selection of office furniture should receive the same careful attention the selection of office equipment receives. The effect of improperly selected office furniture may be felt for a long time because the disposal of pre-owned furniture, which is typically purchased rather than leased, is often quite difficult. Too, the useful life of office furniture is generally quite long, making its proper selection even more critical.

What factors need to be assessed in selecting office furniture?

Several factors guide the selection of office furniture. The impact of these factors should be thoroughly assessed before the furniture is selected.

1. *Intended use of the furniture.* Before furniture is selected, the tasks that will be performed using it, in addition to the equipment the employee uses to perform the tasks, must be thoroughly analyzed. Also to be considered is the possibility of multiple tasks performed simultaneously as well as the need for quickly accessible reference materials the employee needs as he or she performs assigned job tasks.

2. *Appropriateness of furniture in relation to decor of office.* The coordination of the office furniture with the decor is desirable. Because most offices are redecorated several times during the life of the furniture, its versatility for use in other color schemes should be considered. To select office furniture appropriate only for the present decor is a questionable practice.

Why should suitability of office furniture for its users be considered?

3. *Suitability of furniture for its users.* Much employee fatigue can be prevented by adjusting furniture to meet user requirements. Most chairs and some desks are adjustable to compensate for the variability of employees' physical characteristics. Floor-mounted furniture components, such as the desk, are easier to adjust than are panel-mounted furniture components.

Of special concern are furniture components suitable for long-term users of computer monitors and video display terminals (VDTs). The nature of their jobs typically puts them in a stationary position for longer periods than any other category of office employees. Consequently, these employees can experience considerable discomfort unless the furniture can be adjusted to meet their specific physical characteristics. The work area on which the monitor or terminal sits should be adjustable, making it possible for the employee to be able to look slightly downward at the display. The center of the terminal display should be 30 to 45 inches above the floor, and the keyboard should be at a height that enables the employee to keep his or her arms nearly level. The employee's chair should provide back support and promote upright posture, and the chair height should put the employee's knees slightly higher than his or her hips.

4. *Versatility of furniture.* Some types of office furniture have more than one function. An example is a desk that can also function as a drafting table. Therefore, investigating furniture versatility is advisable.

5. *Durability of furniture.* The durability of the furniture is determined by manufacturing techniques and the materials of which it is constructed. For example, metal furniture is generally more durable than wood furniture.

6. *Hierarchical level of furniture user.* Because certain types of office furniture have more prestigious characteristics than others, most organizations match the prestige of the furniture with the hierarchical level of the user.

Employees at higher levels are generally given more prestigious furniture than those at lower levels. Furniture characteristics that determine prestige are the materials used in the construction process, the size of the furniture, and the special design characteristics of the furniture.

7. *Size of furniture in relation to room or area size.* When selecting new office furniture, the size of the area or room in which the furniture is to be placed must be considered. Selecting furniture too large for its area causes a variety of problems and affects the aesthetics of the decor.

8. *Fire-retardant value of furniture.* Upholstered office furniture must be constructed of fire-retardant materials that will have a positive impact on eliminating some of the dense smoke created in a fire.

New Developments in Office Furniture

What are the characteristics of systems furniture?

New developments in office furniture use the systems approach. Comprised of a number of furniture components designed to accommodate the user and the tasks he or she performs, **systems furniture** is replacing traditional office furniture in many offices. Systems furniture possesses the following characteristics: **modular design, portable design, functional design,** and **ergonomics design.** Each of these characteristics is discussed in the following sections.

When compared with traditional office furniture, systems furniture enjoys several distinct advantages. Systems furniture requires less floor space. It also provides a wide range of finishes (both wood and nonwood); a variety of heights, shapes, and color; and a response to user needs. Systems furniture is also more adaptable to existing space than is traditional furniture, and it can be readily modified to accommodate changes in work flow, employees' tasks, and workforce needs.

In designing the work space for a given employee, the following factors should be considered: job tasks, including multiple job tasks performed simultaneously; equipment used to perform job tasks; type of computer work; and reference materials needed to carry out job tasks. In selecting the furniture components to create a work space, the ease with which the components can be adapted and adjusted is critical.

What are the characteristics of modular design?

Modular Design. Modular office furniture is designed to facilitate the use of different components and variations in the way the components are arranged. A modular unit may consist of such components as a desk or working space, storage space, file space, and shelf space.

The employee's job responsibilities are considered when determining the components needed in a modular unit. Employees whose jobs require greater amounts of working space and less storage space can be easily accommodated. In many cases, modular design results in a self-contained workstation, such as the one illustrated in Figure 6–3. These stations, in addition to containing the necessary working and storage space areas, also contain electrical and telephone connections.

What are the characteristics of portable design?

Portable Design. The increasing use of open space planning in office layout has increased the need for portable office furniture. One of the characteristics of open space planning is the ease with which office areas can be arranged. Movable panels and screens, such as those illustrated in Figure 6–4, are examples of portable office furniture. Movable panels, which serve the same purposes as permanent walls, are desirable because extensive remodeling is not required when rearranging office space.

Figure 6–3 Modularly designed work station. Courtesy: Flex-Y-Plan.

What are the characteristics of functional design?

Functional Design. Basing the design of office furniture on individual needs results in functional design. Much of the new office furniture has resulted from an analysis of work processes and employees' effort in the performance of their jobs. This information is subsequently used in designing furniture components and their appropriate configuration in the work area.

To illustrate, if an employee is able to perform job duties more effectively by standing rather than by sitting, the functionally designed furniture can readily accommodate him or her. In fact, a number of office furniture manufacturers have added to their product line an upscale desk, costing several thousands of dollars, that enables the user to adjust it easily to accommodate work in the normal sitting position, a standing position, or tilting the desk top for docu-

Figure 6–4 Portable furniture components. Courtesy: The Knoll Group.

ment display. Another feature of these desks is a regular beep to remind users to change their position, which helps relieve fatigue and boredom.

In addition, increasing numbers of manufacturers are becoming more sensitive to the needs of individuals with disabilities. Most people with disabilities find a 28-inch desk more comfortable than the standard 29-inch desk. Office chairs should be equipped with arms to enable people with disabilities to lift themselves more easily. The Americans with Disabilities Act passed in 1990 has important implications for workplace accommodation of individuals with disabilities.

Ergonomics Design. Growing numbers of furniture manufacturers are taking ergonomics into consideration when designing office furniture. Ergonomics is the scientific study of the relationship between employees and their physical environment.

The science of ergonomics can be applied most directly to the chairs employees use. An ergonomically designed chair is adjustable to accommodate variations in the sizes and shapes of human bodies. More chairs are becoming readily adjusted to accommodate the various work styles of the user. For example, if the user is working at his or her desk, a locked position to support the back is likely preferred. When the user is in conference, however, being able to lean back is desirable. A truly ergonomic chair readily accommodates the following adjustments: back height, seat height (a five-inch range is generally adequate), arm height, back tilt, seat tilt, and arm width. Ergonomic chairs are now available with such a variety of adjustments that each individual user needs a "fitting" when the chair is put into use, especially the height, the lumbar support, and backrest position.

Office chairs should meet the standards set by the American National Standards Institute/Human Factors and Ergonomics Society (ANSI/HFES), an independent group that develops product standards. Among the standards for office chairs set by this group include these:

1. The user should be able to sit flat on the chair with knees bent and feet flat on the floor.
2. The chair should support the user's back in an upright position.
3. The user should be able to hang his or her arms straight down from the shoulders with the elbows bent.

Ergonomically designed office furniture is more comfortable, less fatiguing, and less mentally exhausting and provides better support for the human body. Employees who use ergonomically designed furniture are often able to produce more work over a longer period and at a higher quality than are those who use standard furniture.

Figure 6–5 illustrates the design characteristics of new developments in office furniture.

Use of Safety and Performance Standards

The **Business and Institutional Furniture Manufacturers Association (BIFMA)** provides an important service to administrative office managers involved in selecting office furniture. The BIFMA, by being concerned with safety and performance standards in office furniture, benefits the purchaser. Any office product carrying a BIFMA rating has been subjected to certain testing and evaluation procedures that certify its safety and performance level.

What are the characteristics of ergonomics design?

What are the standards that office chairs should meet?

Figure 6-5 Drawing showing new developments in office furniture. Courtesy: School Arts Magazine, Davis Publications, Inc.

IMPLICATIONS FOR THE ADMINISTRATIVE OFFICE MANAGER

The administrative office manager plays a significant role in the process of selecting office equipment and furniture. The manager has expertise in determining equipment needs and evaluating how well various devices actually meet these needs. Often, the amount and variety of equipment now available enable the organization to maximize the match between needs and functions.

In most organizations, the administrative office manager determines which alternative—leasing or purchasing—should be exercised in obtaining office equipment. This may involve calculating per unit cost of work, which is affected by the volume of the work processed by the device. Generally, as volume increases, the per unit cost decreases.

The process of selecting furniture is often as involved as selecting equipment. The functionality of the furniture has to be evaluated, in addition to its appropriateness for the work areas in which it will be used. Its suitability for the overall decor also has to be assessed. Unless careful attention is paid to important details, some of the attractiveness of the environment can be destroyed once the furniture is in place. Now that furniture is available in so many exciting, vibrant colors, even greater care has to be exercised.

The background and training of the administrative office manager enables him or her to direct the process of selecting office equipment and furniture. No other individual is likely to have as broad an understanding of what is involved or as much knowledge about the process.

REVIEW QUESTIONS

1. In what ways can the dependability of equipment be determined?

2. When selecting new equipment, why should the ability to obtain fast, reliable service be considered?

3. When selecting new equipment, why is its flexibility an important consideration?

4. When a particular line of equipment is experiencing rapid technological advancements, is purchasing or leasing generally more desirable? Why?

5. What is the difference between equipment leasing and rental?

6. What are the advantages and disadvantages of equipment leasing?

7. What types of services are provided by equipment leasing companies?

8. When determining which alternative—service contracts, call basis, or in-house maintenance—would be most desirable, what factors should be considered?

9. In what ways do functional design and modular design of office furniture differ from one another?

10. What is meant by ergonomics design in office furniture?

DISCUSSION QUESTIONS

1. In a recent discussion with your superior, you indicated that some new office chairs were needed. Your superior indicated that a purchase was likely possible at this time and that "you should requisition the lowest priced ones possible so that we can get more." Discuss the implications of your superior's suggestion.

2. The company for which you worked suffered a net loss last year. Among the actions top management took was to defer all equipment purchases for one year. As the administrative office manager, you believe this was not a wise decision. What negative implications is this decision likely to have? What alternative recommendation can you offer?

3. Your company will soon be moving into its new building, the interior of which will be designed using open planning with traditional desks and chairs. You, the administrative office manager, have an appointment tomorrow morning with the vice president for corporate relations, who is coordinating the entire project. The purpose of your meeting is to discuss the new desks and chairs that are to be purchased. Your superior has asked that you provide her with a list of factors or guidelines that should be considered in making the purchasing decision. Identify the items that will be on your list.

STUDENT PROJECTS AND ACTIVITIES

1. Using a comparative analysis form, evaluate two comparable brands of a specific type of office equipment.

2. Discuss leasing versus purchasing a piece of office equipment with an office equipment sales representative.

3. Going Online: Using the Internet, conduct an online search based on one of the concepts presented in this chapter or based on one of the chapter terms. Identify four or five things you learned from the material that you did not know prior to your online search.

Minicases

Each department manager at the Christopher Corporation is currently responsible for maintaining the department's inventory of office equipment and furniture. Some of the managers do not consider this a crucial aspect of their job, so the inventory of equipment and furniture is either poorly handled or simply not done. The result has been the misplacement of considerable amounts of equipment and furniture. Although some of the misplaced items are eventually recovered, many are never found.

1. What recommendations can you make to overcome the present problem?

2. What advantages result from having an effective inventory process?

Case

Located in Cape Girardeau, Missouri, the Le Creux Lumber Company is one of the largest wholesale distributors of building supplies and materials in the Midwest. The building supply stores served by Le Creux Lumber Company are currently located in seven states, and plans are being made to expand into two more states within the next two years.

The Le Creux Lumber Company needs a considerable amount of office equipment to process its paperwork. Because the firm has grown quite rapidly, no attempt was ever made to determine whether the equipment should be rented, leased, or purchased. A recent informal study completed by the administrative office manager resulted in the conclusion that the firm does not always maximize its equipment investment. In some instances, it would be more appropriate to purchase equipment than to rent or lease it. In other instances, the rental or lease alternative would be more appropriate than the purchasing alternative.

The company believes that a set of guidelines is needed to help determine which alternative (purchasing or leasing) is more appropriate under the given circumstances.

1. Under what conditions would purchasing be the more appropriate of the two alternatives?

2. Under what conditions would leasing be the more appropriate of the two alternatives?

3. How might the accuracy and validity of your guidelines be determined?

Part Three **Management of Office Employees**

Chapter 7

SELECTING OFFICE EMPLOYEES

Chapter Aims

After studying this chapter, you should be able to design an effective program for selecting office employees for any type of organization.

Chapter Outline

*C*hapter *T*erms

Aptitude tests
Biodata tests
Biographical information blank
Bona fide occupational qualifications (BFOQ)
Career fairs
Construct validity
Content validity
Criterion-related validity
Differential validity
Direct interview
Electronic résumé banks
Employee leasing
Employee requisition blank
Functional interview
Indirect interview

Intelligence tests
Job descriptions
Job specifications
Offer-to-hire ratio
Outsourcing
Patterned interview
Performance (achievement) tests
Personality tests
Selection ratio
Test reliability
Test validity
United States Employment Service (USES)
Unsolicited application
Web-based employment service

*T*he quality of an organization's workforce is directly related to its employee selection process. Ultimately, workforce quality is a powerful determinant of organizational success. The organization's ability to achieve its goals is to a certain extent influenced either positively or negatively every time an employee is hired. An effective selection program helps reduce employee training time, absenteeism, and turnover and helps increase overall employee productivity.

The organization's workforce requirements have to be determined before the process of selecting employees begins. Selection is comprised of several steps, beginning with employee recruitment and ending with job placement.

The cost of hiring one office employee earning an average salary has steadily increased over the years, often reaching the $3,500 to $5,000 range. An effective selection process is advantageous for a number of reasons, one of which is the cost reduction attributable to effective hiring activities.

Another means of reducing the cost of hiring employees is to computerize as much as possible the human resources function, including employee selection. Computer software can be used to prepare a variety of letters for communicating with applicants, it can be used in keyword searching of applicant databases to locate the best candidates for a given position, and it can be used to keep records useful in assessing compliance with federal and state legislation.

An increasing number of organizations are now hiring individuals with disabilities, and the results are positive. A section on hiring people with disabilities is included later in this chapter.

SOURCES OF POTENTIAL OFFICE EMPLOYEES

What internal and external sources of potential office employees exist?

The recruitment of office employees can be done either internally or externally. Internal sources consist of employee referral, promotion from within, and data banks, whereas external sources are more varied and consist of the following: unsolicited applications, advertising, educational institution placement services, professional organizations, employee leasing, public employment agencies, private employment agencies, temporary help agencies, and electronic résumé data banks.

Employee recruiting can be enhanced in several ways. Among these are using a sufficient number of recruiting sources, using appropriate recruiting sources for the position being filled, and identifying clearly the requirements of the vacant position. Furthermore, recruiting from a sufficiently wide geographical area may also enhance the quality of the applicant pool.

Internal Sources

In some respects, using internal sources is more desirable than using external sources. If a new supervisor is needed in a certain department and one of the present employees meets the stated requirements, promoting that individual to the supervisory position may be a wiser move than hiring from outside. Hiring from within provides tangible evidence that employee competence is rewarded. Too, more is generally known about present employees than can be learned about employees new to the organization. Finally, present employees may require less orientation and training than new employees.

Among the disadvantages of hiring from within are the following: Those who apply for a position and who do not obtain it may become discontent, especially when this happens to them several times; always hiring from within, especially at the managerial level, prevents the organization from hiring new employees who can offer new approaches.

Employee Referral. When the referral method is used, employees recommend individuals for open positions within the organization. Although referral may give employees a feeling of recognition and importance, it may also create some problems. For instance, an employee may experience considerable embarrassment if the individual he or she recommended does not perform satisfactorily. However, some organizations consider this recruiting source to be so valuable that bonuses are given to employees if the individuals they recommend stay with the organization a specified length of time.

Employee Promotion. A second internal source is promoting employees to higher level positions. Promotion is desirable for several reasons. Employees are apt to perform better when they know promotions are available. Furthermore, morale is likely to increase and turnover decrease when employees can be promoted. Perhaps the greatest disadvantage of filling open positions through promotion is that new ideas are not brought in from the outside.

Data Banks. Numerous organizations, especially larger ones, are maintaining their employees' job qualifications in a computerized data bank. Thus, the entire workforce can be easily and quickly screened to determine which employees are presently qualified for an open position. Those who possess the qualifications are then further screened to determine suitability for the open position. The information stored in data banks is also helpful in preparing a variety of employment reports. To maintain a high level of validity, the information in data banks must be continually updated. On a recurring basis, employees should have the opportunity to verify the accuracy and completeness of their information in the data bank.

External Sources

Using an external source may be preferable to drawing from an internal source. An external source likely will be considered when present employees are neither qualified for nor interested in the open position.

Among the primary advantages of using external sources are that the potential applicant pool will be larger, and employees with new ideas are brought

---

Margin notes (handwritten):

Advantages
① reward competence
② know current environment
③ less orientation and training

Disadvantages
① discontent employees
② prevents new approaches from being add to company environment

What is the potential problem that arises from using employee referral?

Why is the use of employee promotion desirable?

into the organization. Disadvantages are the possibility of having a large number of applicants for just one opening and the ever-increasing difficulty of obtaining background information about job applicants, which may result in hiring mediocre to unsatisfactory employees. Thus, careful applicant screening is becoming ever more crucial.

Unsolicited Applications. An **unsolicited application** is used to apply for a position without knowing whether an opening actually exists. This type of application is more common among hourly than salaried positions. Individuals using this method may apply either in person or by mail.

What is an unsolicited application?

To a certain extent, unsolicited applications are viewed negatively in some organizations, although a percentage of the individuals who use unsolicited applications have excellent qualifications. An organization should not totally discount the value of all unsolicited applications simply because this recruiting source may not yield a high number of acceptable applicants. Unsolicited applications often create additional work for the human resources department, especially when very few if any openings exist.

Advertising. As a recruiting source, advertising includes classified newspaper advertisements, magazine and journal advertisements, and radio and television notices. The newest form of advertising open positions is on electronic bulletin boards found on the Internet. Because advertising reaches a wide audience in a short time, many individuals may apply for only a few openings. Using this source of recruiting may result in many marginally qualified or even unqualified applicants. Consequently, the screening process may be considerably more time consuming. The use of advertising may be desirable, however, when many employees are needed in a short time, such as when a new facility opens.

Educational Institution Placement Services. Use of the placement services of educational institutions to recruit potential employees is common in large organizations and a growing number of smaller organizations. Although many organizations see this type of recruiting as being fairly costly in terms of recruiter time and travel expenses, it is an important source of employees, especially those in salaried positions.

What services are provided by educational institution placement services?

Educational institution placement services provide important services to both the employer and the job seeker. For example, the placement service usually develops interview schedules and provides recruiters with copies of interviewees' résumés and references. A potential disadvantage is the tendency for some organizations to recruit only at a limited number of colleges or universities. In time, because of a lack of diversity in the backgrounds of employees, an organization may find that its managerial philosophy has narrowed.

Increasingly, educational institutions are holding periodic job or **career fairs** that are designed to bring together a number of potential employers and employees. Although the fairs are primarily designed for graduating students, persons who are a year or two from graduation are often invited to attend as a means of obtaining career- or employer-related information. Students actively seeking employment may either be interviewed at the fair or invited to interview at a later date.

Professional Organizations. As a benefit to their members, a growing number of professional organizations are developing and operating placement services. These professional organizations often provide job placement services at their conventions or meetings. In addition, many of these organizations also list openings in their journals and other publications. Because the members of professional organizations tend to be homogeneous, screening of applicants to identify those who are not qualified is not of much concern.

Employee Leasing. Another means of obtaining employees is through employee leasing, also known as contract staffing. In this arrangement, workers who are employees of the leasing company are "leased" to various employers in the community. The leasing company and the employer enter into a contract whereby the employer's permanent workers are provided by the leasing company. As with any contractual arrangement, organizations that lease employees need to be familiar with their rights and responsibilities as well as the rights and responsibilities of the leasing company.

In many cases, when an organization enters into an employee-leasing arrangement, its employees are terminated at the end of one work day. These employees return the next day as employees of the leasing company. Thus, operational continuity can be easily maintained. When the organization needs new employees, the leasing company screens applicants; but the organization generally has final approval over which applicants are hired.

The employee-leasing concept is similar in many respects to the temporary help agency concept that is discussed later. The main difference is in the length of employment. In the temporary arrangement, the employee works for a short time; in the leasing arrangement, the employee works for the employer on a permanent basis.

The leasing arrangement is particularly attractive to employers who have only a handful of employees. These employers may not be able to provide the same number or level of fringe benefits as larger employers and thus are not as competitive in terms of hiring top-quality employees. The leasing company is able to provide its leased employees a greater number of benefits because of economy of scale; this often results in improved morale and lessened turnover among employees.

Some employers enter into an employee-leasing arrangement because of its positive impact on reduction of personnel and associated administration costs, such as paperwork. Because the leasing company is responsible for all facets of personnel administration, the employer is able to eliminate a variety of related costs. Employee leasing also enables small companies to avoid having to comply with certain federal and state regulations that pertain to employers with ten to twenty-five employees.

Public Employment Agencies. Although the **United States Employment Service (USES)** has control over public employment agencies, each state is responsible for operating its own agencies. Public employment agencies are found in nearly all metropolitan areas and in several smaller cities in every state. These agencies help employers design testing programs, assist with wage surveys, and help with job analysis and evaluation.

By law, an individual who receives unemployment compensation must be registered with the state's public employment agency. The law also requires that an individual who receives unemployment compensation be willing to accept any suitable employment offer. Neither an employer nor the employee is charged for the use of services provided by public employment agencies.

USES eventually plans to provide a nationwide service that will enable individuals in one state to learn of job openings in another state. At present, USES distributes a monthly publication, *Occupations in Demand,* to help job seekers become more aware of employment opportunities in other regions.

What is employee leasing?

What does USES do for employee selection?

Private Employment Agencies. Unlike public employment agencies, private agencies charge for the services they provide. The fee charged largely depends on the nature of the open position (higher fees are usually charged for higher level positions), the location of the agency, and the reputation of the agency. Fees may range anywhere from a few days' salary to a percentage of the annual salary of the position being filled.

In many instances, the employer pays either a portion or all of the fee the employment agency charges. Generally, the higher the agency fee, the greater the likelihood that the employer will pay for most or all of it.

Certain factors should be considered when selecting a private employment agency. The reputation of a private agency can be determined to a certain extent if it is a subscribing member of the National Employment Association. Employees and individuals might also contact the agency's former clients to determine how well others were satisfied with its services. Another factor to consider is the agency's ability to provide the quality of employee sought by the organization.

Temporary Help Agencies. Numerous organizations use temporary help agencies to obtain office workers for a short time—from one day to as long as two months. Temporary help agencies are frequently used to obtain employees, known as contingent workers, during seasonally busy times as well as to obtain substitutes for ill or vacationing employees. Productivity conscious organizations find use of temporary employees desirable because they only work (and therefore are only paid) when they are needed.

The services of the temporary help agency are monetarily attractive, especially for short-term projects. The organization pays the temporary agency for the service rendered, and the agency pays the individual. Consequently, the organization is relieved of the responsibility of having to pay Social Security benefits, payroll taxes, unemployment compensation, insurance benefits, or any of the other fringe benefits the organization provides its full-time employees.

In many instances, an organization will find the cost of a temporary employee to be less than the cost incurred when hiring a full-time employee. Another advantage is the decrease in the amount of time consumed by recruiting applicants and filling the job. Furthermore, many organizations find that use of temporary employees is an excellent way to obtain employees with specialized skills, especially skills in data entry, word processing, and so forth. Finally, the use of temporary employees provides greater staffing flexibility than hiring permanent employees. Kelly Services and Manpower, Inc., are two of the better known temporary agencies for office employees.

Electronic Résumé Banks

A relatively new external source of job applicants is the **electronic résumé bank,** which is similar to the data banks discussed earlier, with one exception. A data bank is an internal source that maintains the job qualifications of only employees currently working within an organization. Electronic résumé banks, on the other hand, maintain the résumés of any individual, regardless of where he or she works, who wishes to pay the fee (if one is charged, it will likely be $50 or less) to have his or her résumé stored. Two types of electronic résumé bank services exist: Web-based and non-Web-based services.

During the past few years and especially since the Internet has become a popular tool, a large number of **Web-based employment services** have been founded: Monster Board, careerWEB, JobHunt, National Career Search, and

Who typically pays the fee for the use of the services of a private employment agency?

high fees for use

For what situations are temporary help agencies typically used?

What is an electronic résumé bank?

American's Job Bank. Using the Web, the job seeker registers with the employment service and electronically submits résumé-type information. Because employers can post information about their open positions, the job seeker can search and subsequently apply for a specific opening. An alternative is to wait until the employment service identifies the job seeker as a suitable potential applicant, at which time the seeker is invited to apply for the position. The use of Web-based career services is likely to increase rapidly for both employers and job seekers. Although the employer may have to pay a fee to use a Web-based career service, most are cost free to the job seeker.

Non-Web-based services typically accept résumés from their clients, and the résumés are then scanned using optical-character processes. The scanned results are stored electronically in a database, which facilitates the process of identifying suitable applicants. An example of such a non-Web-based service is Resumix.

In both the Web-based and non-Web-based services, the computerized search to identify suitable applicants is conducted using job-related terms and phrases. After the search is completed and potentially suitable applicants are identifed, the résumés of the identified individuals are likely to be screened manually. The purpose of manual screening is to help ensure a close match between an applicant's qualifications and an organization's needs.

OUTSOURCING

What is outsourcing?

Although **outsourcing** is not a new means of obtaining employees to staff various work units, it is currently receiving considerably more attention than ever before. When using outsourcing, the organization turns over certain of its functions to an outside agency that has the specialization necessary to perform those functions well. Thus, operating costs can be reduced. The outside agency is responsible for providing employees (including supervisors and management), supplies, and equipment to perform the function. Some of the more common functions performed by outsourcing include office services, food service, janitorial, security, payroll processing, mail room, records management, copying and duplicating, computer processing, and health and wellness services. Generally, any function is eligible for outsourcing except those central to the organization's primary operations.

What are the advantages of using outsourcing?

The use of outsourcing results in several advantages, perhaps most significant of which is cost reduction. Often outsourcing firms that specialize in certain functions are able to perform the functions less expensively (because of economy of scale). Because the outsourcing agency is responsible for its employees' salaries and fringe benefits as well as for the equipment it uses, the organization is able to reduce some of its recurring costs. Too, overstaffing is often less of a concern with outsourcing than when a work unit provides its own staff.

Another distinct advantage of outsourcing is the quality of work processes it provides. Because the outsourcing agency likely provides the same services in a number of other organizations, it is able to use quality work processes that it has refined over the years. The more efficient and cost effective the outsourcing agency is, the more profitable it will become, which provides the agency additional incentive to use effective operating procedures.

A third distinct advantage is the organization's elimination of the need to supervise or manage the outsourced functions. Because the outsourcing agency is responsible for supervising and managing its own functions, the organization is able to reduce its administrative overhead. While the organization has to be concerned about advancement opportunities and/or promotions and the periodic appraisal of the work performance of its own employees, it is not concerned about these personnel matters for the individuals who work on an outsourcing arrangement. Too, outsourcing enables an organization to have a smaller workforce that it otherwise would have when certain of its operations are performed by nonemployees.

HIRING PEOPLE WITH DISABILITIES

The impetus for hiring people with disabilities stems from the passage of the Vocational Rehabilitation Act in 1973 and its 1980 amendments. The law requires federal contractors or subcontractors that have a federal contract exceeding $2,500 to take positive action to hire, advance, and treat in a nondiscriminatory way qualified employees with disabilities. Contractors with federal contracts ranging from $2,500 to $500,000 must submit to the Department of Labor an affirmative action program that outlines their procedures for hiring people with disabilities. The Office of Federal Contract Compliance (OFCC) enforces the provisions of the law. The Vocational Rehabilitation Act is also concerned with training, promotion, transfer, and termination practices.

Also well known is the Americans with Disabilities Act that was passed in 1990. This act covers both private and public employers engaged in an industry affecting commerce and who have fifteen or more employees for each working day in each of twenty or more calendar weeks in the current or preceding calendar year. Employers cannot discriminate against an individual with a disability as long as the person is otherwise qualified for the job. During the hiring process, employers can ask about an applicant's ability to perform a job but cannot inquire whether he or she has a disability or subject him or her to tests designed to eliminate the applicant from further consideration. Furthermore, employers need to provide "reasonable accommodation" in the employment and placement of disabled individuals on the job, including—but not limited to—job structuring, restructuring, and equipment modification. Employers are not required to provide reasonable accommodation if doing so would create an undue financial hardship, however.

The two primary reasons that organizations have been reluctant to hire people with disabilities are (1) the fear that the employer's insurance costs will increase and (2) the belief that people with disabilities do not perform as well as those without disabilities. Research has proved the fallacy of these two claims.

Advantages of Employing People with Disabilities

What advantages result from the employment of people with disabilities?

1. Insurance costs do not increase.
2. Job performance of many persons with disabilities equals and often exceeds the performance of people without disabilities.
3. Absenteeism and tardiness rates of people with disabilities tend to be lower than those of people without disabilities.
4. The accident rates of persons with disabilities tend to be lower than those of persons without disabilities.
5. Tax incentives are available for organizations that employ disabled persons.

Several sources are available for use in locating persons with disabilities who are seeking employment, including Social Security divisions, hospitals, vocational rehabilitation agencies, and physicians. In addition, the President's Committee on the Employment of the Handicapped has published the *Directory of Organizations Interested in the Handicapped,* a document that identifies 225 organizations that assist employers in locating qualified persons with disabilities.

THE SELECTION PROCESS

The selection process begins when a position becomes vacant or a new position is created. The following is a detailed discussion of the various steps involved in a comprehensive selection program.

Employee Requisition Blank

For what is an employee requisition blank used?

In a well-developed employee selection process, the first step involves notifying the human resources department that an opening exists. In many instances, the manager or supervisor of the unit that has an opening completes an **employee requisition blank.** This authorizes the human resources department to begin recruiting potential employees to fill the open position. Some employee requisition blanks contain limited information including date, name of department, and the title of the open position. Other requisitions are more comprehensive and include a description of job duties and requirements of the job holder. The employee requisition blank lists a number of qualifications, each of which must have a direct, obvious relationship to successful job performance. The absence of such a relationship may violate federal legislation. The "Federal Legislation" section of this chapter provides a discussion of pertinent legislation.

The employee requisition blank is useful for organizations that maintain an applicant waiting list. By using the information contained on the requisition, an employer can quickly identify the individuals on the waiting list who are well qualified for the vacant position. Individuals who have the needed qualifications can then be contacted and invited to interview for the position if they are still available.

Job Descriptions and Job Specifications

How do job descriptions and job specifications differ?

Job descriptions and **job specifications,** which are discussed in detail in Chapter 12, should play an integral role in employee selection. Job descriptions identify the duties and responsibilities of a particular job, and job specifications outline the requirements of the job. Applicants who are shown the job description and specification for a particular job can readily determine whether they are both qualified for and interested in the position. This step can provide an important screening function because individuals who decide they lack either or both qualifications or interest in the job can terminate the application process at this point. Those who wish to continue do so by participating next in the screening interview.

Screening Interview

Although not a part of the selection process in all organizations, the screening interview is used to screen job applicants further. Skillful interviewers are frequently able to determine which applicants are unqualified. An effective screening interview process conserves time and effort for the interviewer and the applicant.

In some organizations, applicants fill out only a portion of the application blank before they participate in a screening interview. In other organizations, applicants will have completed the entire application blank before the interview. In still other organizations, applicants will be given the application blank to complete after the screening interview.

The screening interview is usually fairly short, and the interviewer should make every effort to develop good rapport with the applicant. Subsequent interviews will probably be more realistic, and the information provided by the applicants will be more specific. Most questions asked during a screening interview are of a direct nature and are designed to assess the applicant's suitability for a particular position.

In conducting a screening or selection interview, the interviewer has the potential for creating a legal liability for himself or herself and the employer when asking questions about inappropriate topics. Inappropriate topics include children, age, disabilities, physical characteristics, citizenship, maiden name, arrest record, smoking habits, AIDS and/or a positive HIV test, and sexual orientation.

Application Blank

An applicant who is qualified for a position typically is required to complete an application blank, which continues to be the most widely used form in the selection process.

For what is an application blank used?

The application blank is useful for collecting the same categories of information from all applicants. Therefore, the blank is helpful when comparing one applicant's background with another's. Some organizations also use the application to provide a record of each individual's employment history. Depending on the questions or items included on the blank, the psychological impact of certain applicant responses may also be determined. All the information found on the application blank is a potentially significant indicator of an applicant's interests, motivation, personality, and employment qualifications.

The content of application blanks must be closely scrutinized because federal legislation prohibits the inclusion of any items that might result in unfair discrimination against any job applicant. Content sections frequently found are personal data, educational background, employment history, and references. The information asked for on the blank has to be directly related to job performance.

Following is a partial list of topics or areas that cannot be included on the application blank:

1. Applicant's citizenship.
2. Applicant's arrest record.
3. Applicant's marital status or spouse's employment status.
4. Nature and number of dependents the applicant has.
5. Applicant's arrangements for child care.
6. Nature of the applicant's military discharge.
7. Applicant's race or color of hair, skin, or eyes.
8. Applicant's gender.
9. Applicant's religious preference including holidays observed.
10. Applicant's total club, organization, society, and lodge affiliation.
11. Applicant's height, weight, or nature of disabilities that do not have a bearing on the ability to perform the job for which he or she is applying.
12. Nature of the applicant's pregnancy record.
13. Nature of any changes in the applicant's name.

Figure 7–1 illustrates a typical application blank.

Application For Employment

Applicants are considered for all positions without regard to race, color, religion, sex, national origin, age, marital or veteran status, or the presence of a non-job-related medical condition or handicap.

(PLEASE PRINT)

Position(s) Applied For _____ Date of Application _____

Referral Source: ☐ Advertisement ☐ Friend ☐ Relative ☐ Walk-In
☐ Employment Agency ☐ Other _____

Name _____
    LAST   FIRST   MIDDLE

Address _____
    NUMBER   STREET   CITY   STATE   ZIP CODE

Telephone ( ) _____ Social Security Number _____
    AREA CODE

If employed and you are under 18, can you furnish a work permit? ☐ Yes ☐ No

Have you filed an application here before? ☐ Yes ☐ No   If Yes, give date _____

Have you ever been employed here before? ☐ Yes ☐ No   If Yes, give date _____

Are you employed now? ☐ Yes ☐ No   May we contact your present employer? ☐ Yes ☐ No

Are you prevented from lawfully becoming employed in this country because of Visa or Immigration Status? ☐ Yes ☐ No
(Proof of citizenship or immigration status may be required upon employment)

On what date would you be available for work? _____

Are you available to work ☐ Full Time ☐ Part-Time ☐ Shift Work ☐ Temporary

Are you on a lay-off and subject to recall? ☐ Yes ☐ No

Can you travel if a job requires it? ☐ Yes ☐ No

Have you been convicted of a felony within the last 7 years? ☐ Yes ☐ No

If Yes, please explain _____

AN EQUAL OPPORTUNITY EMPLOYER M/F/V/H

Veteran of the U.S. military service? ☐ Yes ☐ No   If Yes, Branch _____

Do you have any physical, mental or medical impairment or disability that would limit your job performance for the position for which you are applying? ☐ Yes ☐ No

If Yes, please explain _____

Are there workplace accommodations which would assure better job placement and/or enable you to perform your job to your maximum capability? ☐ Yes ☐ No

If Yes, please indicate: _____

Indicate what foreign lanuages you speak, read, and/or write.

	FLUENTLY	GOOD	FAIR
SPEAK			
READ			
WRITE			

List professional, trade, business or civic activities and offices held. (Exclude those which indicate race, color, religion, sex or national origin): _____

Give name, address and telephone number of three references who are not related to you and are not previous employers. _____

Special Employment Notice to Disabled Veterans, Vietnam Era Veterans, and Individuals with Physical or Mental Handicaps.

Government contractors are subject to Section 402 of the Vietnam Era Veterans Readjustment Act of 1974 which requires that they take affirmative action to employ and advance in employment qualified disabled veterans and veterans of the Vietnam Era, and Section 503 of the Rehabilitation Act of 1973, as amended, which requires government contractors to take affirmative action to employ and advance in employment qualified handicapped individuals.

If you are a disabled veteran, or have a physical or mental handicap, you are invited to volunteer this information. The purpose is to provide information regarding proper placement and appropriate accommodation to enable you to perform the job in a proper and safe manner. This information will be treated as confidential. Failure to provide this information will not jeopardize or adversely affect any consideration you may receive for employment.

If you wish to be indentified, please sign below.

☐ Handicapped Indiviudal ☐ Disabled Veteran ☐ Vietnam Era Veteran

Signed _____

Figure 7-1 Application blank. Courtesy: Amsterdam Printing and Litho Corporation.

Education

School Name	Elementary					High				College/University				Graduate/Professional			
Years Completed: (Circle)	4	5	6	7	8	9	10	11	12	1	2	3	4	1	2	3	4
Diploma/Degree																	
Describe Course of Study:																	
Describe Specialized Training, Apprenticeship, Skills and Extra-Curricular Activities																	

Honors Received:

State any additional information you feel may be helpful to us in considering your application.

Agreement

I certify that answers given herein are true and complete to the best of my knowledge.

I authorize investigation of all statements contained in this application for employment as may be necessary in arriving at an employment decision.

In the event of employment, I understand that false or misleading information given in my application or interview(s) may result in discharge. I understand, also, that I am required to abide by all rules and regulations of the Company.

Signature of Applicant _____ Date _____

For Personnel Department Use Only

Arrange Interview ☐ Yes ☐ No

Remarks _____

Employed ☐ Yes ☐ No   Date of Employment _____

Hourly Rate/Salary _____

Job Title _____   Department _____

By _____   INTERVIEWER _____ DATE _____

_____
NAME AND TITLE   DATE

This Application For Employment and Application Data Record is sold for general use throughout the United States. Amsterdam Printing and Litho Corp. assumes no responsibility for the inclusion in said form of any questions which, when asked by the employer of the job applicant, may violate State and/or Federal Law.

Employment Experience

Start with your present or last job. Include military service assignments and volunteer activities. Exclude organization names which indicate race, color, religion, sex or national origin.

1

Employer		Dates Employed		Work Performed
		From	To	
Address				
Job Title		Hourly Rate/Salary		
		Starting	Final	
Supervisor				
Reason for Leaving				

2

Employer		Dates Employed		Work Performed
		From	To	
Address				
Job Title		Hourly Rate/Salary		
		Starting	Final	
Supervisor				
Reason for Leaving				

3

Employer		Dates Employed		Work Performed
		From	To	
Address				
Job Title		Hourly Rate/Salary		
		Starting	Final	
Supervisor				
Reason for Leaving				

4

Employer		Dates Employed		Work Performed
		From	To	
Address				
Job Title		Hourly Rate/Salary		
		Starting	Final	
Supervisor				
Reason for Leaving				

If you need additional space, please continue on a separate sheet of paper.

Special Skills and Qualifications

Summarize special skills and qualifications acquired from employment or other experience _____

_____

Figure 7-1 (Continued)

Increasingly, organizations are designing application blanks that incorporate numerical scoring scales. A score can be obtained for each applicant, and those whose scores fall below a minimum cutoff point are automatically eliminated from further consideration.

The individuals who are still considered to be viable applicants at this point may be asked to take one or more of a variety of tests.

Biographical Information Blank

For what is the biographical information blank used?

As a supplement to the application blank, the **biographical information blank** is being used in an increasing number of organizations. The biographical information blank provides the applicant an opportunity to provide information about his or her preference for working alone, being transferred, being a member of a rotating pool, working overtime and on weekends as the need may arise, and so forth. The items included on the biographical information blank are determined by the nature of the job being filled. Essentially, the questions are tailored to the specific job. Biographical information blanks, over the long run, help reduce job turnover resulting from employee dissatisfaction with various employment conditions.

Employee Testing

In many organizations, the use of tests in selecting office employees is fairly common. Although numerous standardized tests are available, some organizations have developed their own.

The use of well-designed tests is desirable for the following reasons: (1) test results can be objectively obtained, which eliminates some of the effect of human bias that may develop during an interview; (2) depending on the nature of the test, unknown talents or skills of applicants may be uncovered.

A more detailed discussion of employee testing is presented in the "Testing Program" section later in this chapter. Care must be taken to assure that the testing program conforms with the Equal Employment Opportunity Act of 1972, which is discussed later in the "Federal Legislation" section.

Background and Reference Investigation

What are the uses of the background and reference investigation?

Individuals who remain viable candidates after test results have been analyzed may be subjected to a background and reference investigation. These investigations are used (1) to verify information provided by the applicants, (2) to obtain additional information about the applicants' backgrounds, and (3) to obtain information about the applicants' performance while employed elsewhere.

The provisions of several legislative acts restrict the type of information employers are able to obtain when checking applicants' background information. This legislation includes the Privacy Act, the Fair Credit Reporting Act, the Family Education Rights and Privacy Act, the Freedom of Information Act, and the Privacy Protection Act.

Among the guidelines that should be considered when requesting background information about applicants are the following:

1. Request only job-related information.
2. Obtain written releases from applicants before requesting information about them from their references.
3. Disregard the use of subjective information obtained from others when evaluating and assessing the applicants.

The validity of written letters of recommendation has been challenged recently by many organizations because applicants normally ask for letters of recommendation only from those individuals who are certain to provide positive information. Therefore, the information in letters of recommendation may be somewhat distorted. For this reason, many organizations place more emphasis on information obtained from former employers than on the information provided in letters of recommendation.

During the background check, increasing numbers of present or former employers are providing potential employers with minimal information about an applicant. Employers or former employers are reluctant to provide potential employers with information that could hurt the applicant's opportunity to be hired, primarily because of the fear of being sued for defamation. Consequently, some employers are providing information limited to the following areas: the applicant's last job title, his or her last salary, and dates of employment.

Selection Interview

Who typically conducts the selection interview?

At this point in the selection process, the two or more applicants thought to have the greatest potential for succeeding will have been identified. These applicants are usually interviewed by the manager or supervisor of the department in which the opening exists. The selection interview should provide information that enables the manager or supervisor to identify the candidate who is best qualified. Interviewing will be discussed in greater detail in a subsequent section of this chapter.

Medical Exam

With the passage of the Americans with Disabilities Act, requiring applicants to undergo a medical exam before a job is offered is prohibited. Therefore, no longer can an organization screen out an applicant who has an increased risk of an on-the-job injury or a medical condition that could be worsened by the demands of the job for which he or she applied. However, an organization can require that the applicant satisfactorily pass a medical exam as a condition of the employment offer. The exam results cannot be used to withdraw the offer unless they show the individual is not able to perform the tasks required by the position.

Payroll Change Notice

After the applicant who is offered the position accepts it, a payroll change notice is completed. This notice authorizes the payroll department to begin paying the new employee. A payroll change notice is illustrated in Figure 7–2.

Employee File

Although not an official part of the selection process, once an applicant has accepted a job offer, an employee file must be created. The file contains a variety of employment-related information, including an employment history form, a data sheet, record of absences, vacation days used, and salary increases. The information in the file is continuously updated.

For what are the contents of an employee file used?

The information in the employee file has a variety of functions including use in appraising employee performance, validating hiring procedures, and preparing various statistical reports, some of which may be required by government agencies.

Figure 7-2 Payroll change form. Courtesy: Amsterdam Printing and Litho Corporation.

TO: PAYROLL DEPARTMENT

Please Enter the Following Change(s) in Your Records to Take

Effect _____
                    (Date and Time)

Employee _____

Social Security No. _____ Clock No. _____

THE CHANGE(S)

✓ Check all Applicable Boxes	From	To
☐ Department		
☐ Job		
☐ Shift		
☐ Rate		
☐		

REASON FOR THE CHANGE(S)

☐ Hired   ☐ Probationary Period Completed

☐ Re-Hired   ☐ Length of Service Increase

☐ Promotion   ☐ Re-evaluation of Existing Job

☐ Demotion   ☐ Resignation

☐ Transfer   ☐ Retirement

☐ Merit Increase   ☐ Layoff

☐ Union Scale   ☐ Discharge

☐ Leave of Absence From _____ Until _____
                              (Date)   (Date)

☐ Other (Explain) _____

_____

_____

_____

Change Authorized by _____ Date _____

Change Approved by _____ Date _____

Form # 08320   Amsterdam Printing and Litho Corp. Amsterdam, N.Y. 12010

TESTING PROGRAM

The administration of selection tests and the interpretation of their results requires care on the part of those responsible for test administration. Some organizations now employ individuals who have specialized training in testing and evaluation procedures. Other organizations have eliminated completely the testing element of the selection process. Reasons attributed to this are the belief that testing is risky and that validation requirements are too laborious. Still other organizations contract with professional test designers to prepare valid and reliable selection tests.

Test Reliability and Validity

How do test reliability and validity differ?

Before using a test as a measurement or assessment tool, its **reliability** and **validity** must be determined. A test is considered reliable if it produces consistent results. If the same test is given to matched sets of people or if the same group of people takes a slightly different version of the test, it is reliable when approximately equal scores are obtained on several different test administrations.

Test validity refers to the predictive value of the test. To be valid, the test must predict the performance that it is intended to predict, which is the quality with which the potential employee will perform on the job. A valid selection test will identify those likely to succeed and those likely to fail in a particular job or in a particular skill or task.

Several types of test validation procedures are used. Included are criterion-related validity, construct validity, content validity, and differential validity.

Criterion-related validity is the process of statistically relating measures of job performance, such as training time and work proficiency, to test scores. A valid test predicts how well the applicant will be able to perform his or her job duties. These criteria must be critical to the job for which the test is designed. Criterion-related validity studies are carried out in two ways. Concurrent studies use present employees to gather data on both test scores and employee performance. Longitudinal studies compare the prehiring test scores of individuals with their performance data after they have been on the job for a period of time.

Construct validity provides a measure of specific theoretical constructs, such as aptitude and intelligence, that are crucial to job performance.

Content validity measures the relationship between test items and job tasks. Thus, it shows that the test constitutes a reasonable sample of the content of a job.

Differential validity provides test results for each cultural subgroup as a means of predicting job success for its members. If tests are properly used and if the results are properly interpreted, many available standardized tests are both reliable and valid. Reliability and validity cannot be guaranteed when tests are used improperly, however.

A commonly used test in the selection of office workers is a five-minute timed typing or keyboarding test. Although the test is reliable (applicants will be fairly consistent in their typing or keyboarding rates), the test lacks validity. A five-minute timed test does very little to predict a typist's performance when typing or keyboarding letters, statistical tables, reports, and so forth. A much more valid test could be developed to include typing or keyboarding tasks that applicants will actually experience on the job.

Legal Considerations

What legal aspects must be considered when developing the testing program?

To avoid discriminating against any ethnic or cultural group, special attention should be focused on the legal considerations of the testing program. Section 703(h), Title VII of the Civil Rights Act, which includes the Tower Amendment, states that a test will not be considered discriminatory as long as it does not by design, intent, or use discriminate on the basis of race, color, religion, gender, or national origin.

Special attention also needs to be focused on the culturally disadvantaged. For example, a test may be considered discriminatory if the members of a culturally disadvantaged group obtain significantly lower test results than their counterparts, provided both groups are equally successful on the job.

Biodata tests are being used to eliminate the adverse impact that standardized tests sometimes have on certain cultural groups. Questions asked on biodata tests are related to the examinee's academic achievement, attitudes toward work, perception of self, physical condition, and so forth. These tests generally reduce by at least 50 percent the differences in scores received by whites and minorities on traditional intelligence or aptitude tests.

The Equal Employment Opportunity Act of 1972, which is discussed later in this chapter, prohibits the use of a selection test that unfairly discriminates against any applicant.

Some organizations have routinely administered polygraph (lie detector) tests to job applicants. The passage of the Employee Polygraph Protection Act in 1988, however, severely restricts the use of the polygraph in preemployment screening. The following four standards, which must be met by the employer, have virtually eliminated the use of polygraph tests in preemployment screening except within private security firms and drug companies:

1. The employer must show that it suffered an economic loss or injury.
2. The employer must show that the employee taking the test had access to the property about which questions have arisen.
3. The employer must base the testing requirement on reasonable suspicion.
4. The employee must be notified of the details of the investigation as well as the questions he or she will be asked during the test.

Standardized paper-and-pencil honesty tests have replaced the use of the polygraph in many organizations. These tests are comprised of a number of questions related to the applicant's tolerance of others who steal, who are dishonest, and who are readily able to accept dishonesty among co-workers. In some instances, the paper-and-pencil test is accompanied by a drug test.

Types of Testing

Several types of tests are used in screening applicants. Among the more common are **performance** or **achievement tests, aptitude tests, intelligence tests,** and **personality tests.**

What do performance or achievement tests measure?

Performance or Achievement Tests. The suitability of an applicant for an office job is measured effectively by performance or achievement tests. These tests help determine how well an applicant can perform those tasks for which he or she is being considered. For example, applicants' data-entry skills can be accurately measured by giving them realistic data to enter. Applicants for clerk-typist positions might be asked to type or keyboard a series of documents as well as code and file a set of documents. For jobs that require considerable decision making, the applicants might be asked to react to several situations that require realistic decision making.

What is an aptitude test?

Aptitude Tests. An individual's potential to learn either the tasks for which he or she is being considered or the tasks he or she might be expected to perform in the future is measured by aptitude tests. Therefore, if an applicant is being considered for a position in which job holders frequently move up to a higher level position, an aptitude test may be administered.

Intelligence Tests. When mental and reasoning abilities are crucial to the success of a job holder, an intelligence test most likely will be administered to each applicant. The specialized interpretation processes these tests require have resulted in some organizations abandoning their use, especially if none of the employees is qualified to interpret the results. The use of intelligence tests has been criticized recently because such tests tend to favor applicants who have had considerable verbal and numerical experience. Therefore, applicants who have limited verbal and numerical experiences are to a certain extent discriminated against.

What do personality tests measure?

Personality Tests. Although personality tests are used less frequently in the selection process than they once were, organizations still administer these tests to individuals applying for jobs that require certain personality traits or characteristics. Some of the factors personality tests measure are interpersonal relations, motivation, ability to handle pressure, self-concept, interests, and individual needs. One of the reasons these tests are no longer used as frequently as they were in the past stems from the fact that individuals are able to determine which test responses are the most desirable. This may result in an unrealistic response that could affect test validity.

INTERVIEWING PROCESS

Considered by many to be the most crucial step as well as the most widely used tool in the hiring process, the selection interview is designed to predict an applicant's job performance based on his or her responses to a series of questions. The selection interview serves a variety of functions including the following:

What are the functions of the selection interview?

1. The interviewer can ask questions to clarify any ambiguous areas about the applicant's background.
2. The interviewer can emphasize areas of particular concern to the organization.
3. The applicant's self-expression, confidence, poise, and appearance can be readily assessed.
4. The applicant can ask additional questions about the job and the organization.
5. The applicant can emphasize certain areas about his or her background that might be helpful in making an employment decision.

Anyone who has experienced a job interview knows it can be either a frustrating or a rewarding experience. The interviewer can do much to enhance the success of the interview by doing several things. One effective way is to engage in preplanning and to become as well prepared as possible. Furthermore, at the beginning of the interview, the interviewer also needs to establish rapport with the interviewee, which can be done by doing and/or saying things that put the applicant at ease. In addition, the interviewer needs to make sure the questions he or she asks are relevant to the position of interest and that they are not prohibited by either federal or state legislation. During the closing of the interview, the applicant should be invited to ask any questions that remain unanswered. Once the interview has been completed, the interviewer should prepare written notes unless he or she does so during the interview.

Although many organizations use specialists in developing the testing aspect of the selection process, fewer organizations use individuals who are professionally trained to conduct interviews. Increasingly, organizations are beginning to discover the crucial role of the interview and are realizing the necessity for using adequately trained interviewers.

Several types of interviews are used in selecting office employees. One of the common ways to categorize interviews is by the amount of control the interviewer is able to exert during the process. In some instances, the interviewer will exert considerable control; but in other instances, the interviewer will give the applicant much leeway.

Types of Interviews

The most common types of interviews used for selecting office employees are **patterned, direct, indirect,** and **functional.**

What are the characteristics of the patterned interview?

Patterned Interview. The patterned interview generally requires the use of a form similar to the one illustrated in Figure 7–3. The form provides a list of the questions the interviewer will ask. Sufficient space is also provided on the form for the interviewer to record the interviewee's responses.

Under certain circumstances, the use of the patterned interview is especially desirable. For example, when many people are applying for the same position, the form facilitates comparing the backgrounds and/or responses of the various applicants. Furthermore, if an organization makes a practice of inviting former applicants to apply for an open position, the patterned interview form helps determine which former applicants to choose.

Perhaps the most significant advantage of using the patterned interview, provided the interviewer follows the form, is that all crucial areas are covered. The patterned interview also ensures that the interviewee will have ample opportunity to provide information about his or her background. Too often, interviewers spend excessive time discussing the organization or job, leaving too little time to get sufficient information from applicants. This practice is virtually eliminated when the patterned interview technique is used.

What are the characteristics of the direct interview?

Direct Interview. The direct interview is characterized as being conducted rather quickly because the interviewer asks only those questions directly related to the interviewee's background and his or her qualifications for a particular job. The direct interview is also characterized as being somewhat limited in the amount of information that can be collected.

The nature of the direct interview limits its use primarily to lower level office jobs or as an initial screening device. The direct interview, which is not feasible for exploring the needs, attitudes, and feelings of applicants, is most useful when a limited amount of information must be gathered rather quickly. To use this interview for any other purpose is a questionable practice.

What are the characteristics of the indirect interview?

Indirect Interview. As its name implies, the indirect interview covers a much broader range of topics than the direct interview. The indirect interview is unstructured in format, which gives the applicant considerable freedom in selecting discussion areas. Many interviewers believe the primary use of the indirect interview is to stimulate the interviewee to talk about himself or herself—to discuss needs, attitudes, and feelings.

Because of its unstructured format, the indirect interview is difficult for many interviewers to conduct. Although the interviewer is responsible for "keeping the interview on target," he or she has to be a good listener and should interrupt only when the applicant appears reluctant to provide important information or when the interviewer is asked specific questions.

Figure 7-3 Patterned interview form. Courtesy: The Dartnell Corporation, Chicago, IL.

How many times did you draw
unemployment compensation? _____ When? _____ Why? _____
Does applicant depend on self?

How many weeks have you
been unemployed in the past five years? _____ How did you spend this time? _____
Did conditions in applicant's occupation justify this time? Did applicant use time profitably?

What accidents have you
had in recent years? _____
Is applicant "accident-prone"? Any disabilities which will interfere with work?

SCHOOLING

How far did you go in school? Grade: 1 2 3 4 5 6 7 8 High School: 1 2 3 4 College: 1 2 3 4 Date of leaving school _____
Is applicant's schooling adequate for the job?

If you did not graduate from
high school or college, why not? _____
Are applicant's reasons for not finishing sound?

What special training have you taken? _____
Will this be helpful? Indication of perseverance? Industry?

Extracurricular activities. (Please omit any organizations
which reflect race, color, sex, national origin or religion.) _____
Did applicant get along well with others?

What offices did you hold in these groups? _____
Indications of leadership?

FAMILY BACKGROUND	PERSONAL SITUATION
Leisure time activities _____ Habits of industry?	When did you have last drink? _____ Sensbile?
Summer vacations _____ Did applicant keep busy?	What types of people rub you the wrong way? _____ Bias?
Group activities _____ See note after Extracurricular activities.	Ever convicted of a felony? _____
Position of leadership _____ Leader?	Charges _____ Immaturity? (This does not constitute an automatic bar to employment)

HEALTH

What serious illnesses, operations,
or accidents did you have as a child? _____
Has applicant retained any infantile personality traits due to childhood illnesses?

What illnesses, operations, or
accidents have you had in recent years? _____
Are applicant's illnesses legitimate rather than indicating a desire to "enjoy ill health"?

How much time have you lost
from work because of illness during past year? _____
Will aplicant be able to do the job?

How are your teeth? _____

Does anyone in your home suffer ill health? _____
Are spouse, children, or family relatively healthy?

Do you suffer from:
- ☐ Poor Eyesight
- ☐ Poor Hearing
- ☐ Rupture
- ☐ Rheumatism
- ☐ Asthma
- ☐ Heart Trouble
- ☐ Diabetes
- ☐ Ulcers
- ☐ Hay Fever
- ☐ Flat Feet
- ☐ Nervousness

ADDITIONAL INFORMATION: _____
_____
_____
_____
_____

Figure 7-3 (Continued)

What are the characteristics of the functional interview?

Functional Interview. The functional interview is comprised of a series of job-related questions accompanied by predetermined answers. All applicants being interviewed for a particular job respond to the same questions.

The following four types of questions are generally used in the functional interview:

1. *What-if questions.* These questions, which are generally in an oral format, involve hypothetical job-related situations. The interviewer responds to each question by stating what he or she would do with the situation or how he or she would handle the situation.

2. *Job knowledge questions.* These questions, which can be either in oral or written format, are designed to assess the interviewee's knowledge about the technical aspects of a job or the basic knowledge required to learn the job.

3. *Job sample questions.* These questions typically are performance oriented because interviewees are asked to perform a sample job task. The more closely the sample tasks match the actual job, the more effective these questions will be. In some instances, the task performance will have to be in a simulated environment.

4. *Attitude questions.* These questions are often used to assess the interviewee's willingness to do such job-related tasks as repetitive physical work, travel, work in certain environmental conditions, and so on. The content of these questions should be restricted to actual characteristics or duties of the job.

A distinct characteristic of the functional interview is the use of an interview committee. The committee is responsible for evaluating the worth of the interviewee's responses and preparing the interview questions and desired predetermined answers. The relative worth of each answer is predetermined. For example, good answers may carry a value of 5; average or marginal answers, a value of 3; and poor answers, a value of 1. The sample answers should be realistic and be based on present job requirements.

The most significant advantages of the functional interview are its reliability and accuracy in the interpretation and assessment of the interviewee's responses. It minimizes the subjectivity and inconsistency often present in other types of interviews.

What is a bona fide occupational qualification?

Regardless of the type of interview being conducted, only those questions proved to relate to a **bona fide occupational qualification (BFOQ)** can be asked. A BFOQ is a legitimate qualification—one the job holder needs to possess in order to perform the job satisfactorily. Unless the following topics have occupational relevance, questions related to them cannot be legally asked during an interview:

What types of questions cannot be legally asked during an employment interview?

1. Arrest record of the applicant.
2. Pregnancy history of the applicant.
3. Spouse, spouse's employment, or number of children the applicant has.
4. Marital status of the applicant.
5. Home ownership of the applicant.
6. Military status of the applicant.
7. Health status of the applicant.
8. Age or date of birth of the applicant.
9. Race, religion, or national origin of the applicant.

Interviewing Mistakes

Those responsible for interviewing potential employees typically conduct better interviews when they are mindful of a number of interviewing mistakes. Among these are the following:

1. Jumping to a hasty conclusion about the applicant. When an interviewer makes a hasty conclusion about an applicant, the interviewer will likely have a mind-set about the interviewee that is difficult to change. Snap impressions of individuals are often incorrect.

2. Allowing nonverbal behavior to have an undue influence. Interviewees whose nonverbal behavior is considered to be appropriate (amount of eye contact, pleasant facial expressions, head nodding, etc.) can obtain a more favorable rating than they should have. Just as important and often more so is the quality of the interviewee's verbal responses. Conversely, applicants who have less appropriate nonverbal behavior but who have excellent verbal responses are likely to be rated less favorably than they should be.

3. Possessing inadequate knowledge about the job. Interviewers should feel an obligation to their employer and the interviewees to learn as much as possible about the job for which they are conducting interviews. When an interviewer is unfamiliar with a job, attempting to select a well-qualified employee becomes more difficult.

4. Allowing negative impressions to have an undue influence. When an interviewer allows a negative impression to carry more weight in the assessment of a job applicant than a positive impression, he or she is allowing bias to enter the process. Both positive and negative impressions should be weighted equally in the overall assessment of the applicant.

5. Allowing the order of interviews to affect overall rating. Some interviewers rate less favorably than they should applicants who are interviewed immediately after an individual who interviews extremely well. Conversely, some interviewers rate more favorably than they should applicants who follow an individual who interviews very poorly. A more desirable approach is to rate each interviewee on the basis of how well he or she interviews in terms of predetermined factors rather than on how well the individual interviews in relation to others.

6. Doing too much of the talking. The interviewee should do most of the talking during an interview.

7. Not involving other employees in the interview process, especially key people with whom the new employee will work. Having several individuals participate in an interview will likely result in better coverage of relevant topics.

8. Not planning ahead of the interview the questions to be asked. Each applicant should be asked the same core of questions. Failure to prepare the list prior to the first interview will likely result in skipping some important topics.

AFFIRMATIVE ACTION PROGRAM

The process of employee selection has two crucial elements. The first is the process that enables the organization to hire the best possible individual for each opening. The second is the use of selection procedures consistent with federal or state equal employment opportunity laws.

Executive Order 11246 mandates that any organization with a federal contract exceeding $50,000 and with fifty or more employees is required to submit an affirmative action program for each of its facilities, such as a plant or field office. The plans, which must be submitted within 120 days of receiving the contract, are filed with the Office of Federal Contract Compliance Programs.

Organizations with federal contracts that range from $2,500 to $50,000 are mandated to include in their contracts an affirmative action clause, but they do not have to file a written affirmative action plan. Those with federal contracts less than $2,500 are not covered by the provisions of the Executive Order 11246.

Affirmative action programs contain several elements including utilization analysis, statistical analysis, goals, and timetables. The utilization analysis determines the number of women and minorities employed within an organization. Availability analysis, conversely, provides information about the number of women and minorities who are available to work in an organization.

To assess the adequacy of the affirmative action program, a variety of questions can be asked. Nontechnical questions dealing with employee selection include the following:

What types of nontechnical questions are to be included in written affirmative action programs?

1. Does the recruiting phase of the program attract a balance of applicants in terms of race or gender?

2. Are all jobs open to women and minorities?

3. Is a concerted effort made to place women and minorities in top-level positions?

4. Do managers and supervisors attempt to achieve a balance of applicants by race and gender? Some organizations find less effort is exerted by managers and supervisors to achieve balance than is exerted by the human resources department. In such instances, the human resources department may have to take a more active role in employee selection.

5. Does the system have the necessary machinery and procedures to effectively monitor the affirmative action program?

6. Does management regularly communicate the importance of establishing, reviewing, and updating affirmative action goals?

Other questions dealing with other personnel aspects include the following:

1. Are job standards realistic?

2. Are all employees offered the same training opportunities, or are some given greater preference?

3. Do employees receive equal pay for equal work?

4. Do all employees have an equal chance of being identified as a high-potential employee?

5. Are disciplinary policies equal for all employees, and are they uniformly administered?

6. Are personnel decisions made on the basis of factors other than age?

An important aspect of affirmative action is upward mobility. Compliance with affirmative action legislation mandates promoting to higher level positions those employees for whom the legislation exists.

Persons with major responsibilities for employee selection will find the *Uniform Guidelines on Employee Selection Procedures* useful. The *Guidelines* document, which supersedes EEOC and OFCCP Guidelines as of September 25, 1978, specifies that an employer must be able to verify the predictive

What is meant by adverse impact?

validity of its employee selection process. The *Guidelines* further require that knowledge, skills, abilities, and other worker characteristics assessed in the selection process must be necessary prerequisites for performance of critical tasks.

The *Guidelines* stipulate that an organization's selection procedures must not have an adverse impact on any protected group. If an organization's selection rate for any group protected by virtue of gender, race, or ethnic origin is less than 80 percent of the selection rate for the group with the highest selection rate, adverse impact may be present. To illustrate how the concept works, consider the following facts:

In the current year, XYZ Company hired sixty of the one hundred white applicants who applied; therefore, the white hiring rate is 60 percent.

In the current year, XYZ Company hired twenty of the forty Asian applicants who applied; therefore, the Asian hiring rate is 50 percent.

In the current year, XYZ Company hired thirty of the sixty African-American applicants who applied; therefore, the African-American hiring rate is 50 percent.

The white group had the highest hiring rate of 60 percent. If the hiring rate of the two protected groups was at least 80 percent of the white hiring rate, adverse impact is not present. The following shows the calculation of these rates:

Asian: $50/60 = 83.33$ percent (no adverse impact)

African-American: $50/60 = 83.33$ percent (no adverse impact)

Had the hiring rate for either of the two protected groups been 40 percent rather than 50 percent, adverse impact would be present because a 66.66 percent rate (40/60) would have resulted.

If adverse impact is found, the organization is compelled to determine the reasons for the impact. Among the reasons that might be investigated are the following: (1) the number of members of protected groups who apply is insufficient, (2) selection tools unfairly eliminate members of protected groups from further consideration, and (3) bias or prejudice against members of protected groups is present.

When a suit is filed against an employer for alleged discrimination, either disparate impact or disparate treatment will be the focus. Disparate impact refers to discrimination against a protected group of individuals. The 80 percent rule discussed earlier is used in determining the presence or existence of disparate impact.

How do disparate impact and disparate treatment differ from each other?

Disparate treatment, conversely, refers to discrimination against a protected individual. This type of discrimination occurs when a protected individual, although qualified, is rejected—after which the employer continues seeking applicants who have the same qualifications as the one who was rejected.

Recently, affirmative action has taken on a new dimension, resulting in its being considered more than "preferential treatment" of applicants. To a certain extent, the impetus for this appears to be a trend for the federal government to reduce the extent to which it interferes in the daily lives of Americans. Affirmative action in the broader sense means finding the most qualified employee for each given position. By increasing the diversity of its workforce, an organization is providing greater opportunities for individuals who might not otherwise get them.

FEDERAL LEGISLATION

Any individual in an organization involved with employee selection should be thoroughly aware of the federal legislation that might have an impact on the selection process. Specific legislation prohibits discrimination on the basis of age, race, national origin, and religion. Once an individual is hired, other legislation prohibits the use of an individual's gender as a salary determinant.

Civil Rights Act of 1964

Title VII of the Civil Rights Act has significant implications for the hiring process by requiring that employers or unions with twenty-five or more workers treat all persons equally, regardless of their gender, race, color, national origin, or religion. An exception to this provision allows an employer to use gender, national origin, or religion as a selection factor if justifiable as a bona fide occupational qualification. Groups protected by Title VII are women, African Americans, Native Americans, Hispanics, and Asian-Pacific Islanders. An employer who is required to abide by law must not refuse to hire an applicant or to classify applicants using gender, race, color, national origin, or religion as a basis.

Age Discrimination in Employment Act of 1967

What are the important provisions of the Age Discrimination in Employment Act of 1967?

This act, which was amended in 1978 and 1986, prohibits employers with twenty or more persons from using age to discriminate against employees and applicants who are more than forty years old. In 1986, the age cap, which had been set at 70, was lifted for most occupations. Federal employees and most private-sector employees are allowed to work beyond the age of seventy if they are able to perform their job effectively. The act forbids an employer's using a protected applicant's age as a basis for refusing to hire, for determining compensation, for discharging an employee, or for forcing retirement. Approximately one-third of the states have also passed companion legislation.

Equal Employment Opportunity Act of 1972

This act significantly amended Title VII of the Civil Rights Act of 1964. The Equal Employment Opportunity Act of 1972 has several significant implications for hiring, transferring, training, or retraining employees. This act amended the 1964 act by defining the employer as a person engaged in industry affecting interstate commerce and having fifteen or more workers. Both public and private employers are covered by the act. The Equal Employment Opportunity Commission, which is the act's regulatory agency, originally issued guidelines for the implementation of validation procedures. These guidelines are now incorporated into the *Uniform Guidelines on Employment Selection Procedures*.

Although test validation is feasible for large organizations, smaller ones have more difficulty because they have fewer employees to use in the validation process. In certain instances, when an insufficient number of employees is available, the results of validity studies conducted by other organizations, such as those cited in test manuals, may be considered acceptable if the jobs and the individuals in the two organizations are similar. This regulation has resulted in some employers abandoning the use of tests in the selection process.

Other selection devices, such as application blanks and interview sheets, that discriminate against a class of people protected by Title VII or that are discriminatory in nature are prohibited under the provisions of the Equal Employment Opportunity Act of 1972. When challenged, the employer is responsible for proving that a test or selection device is not discriminatory.

Executive Orders

What provisions of the Executive Orders affect employee selection?

Executive Order 11246 (amended by Executive Order 11375) and Revised Order No. 4 are both designed to prohibit discrimination in selecting employees. Some organizations that are excluded from abiding by the provisions of the Civil Rights Act are required to abide by the regulations of either or both of these executive orders.

Executive Order 11246 pertains to government contractors and subcontractors with a federal construction contract. The executive order forbids the following: advertising for employees by gender classifications, basing seniority lists on gender, or making personnel decisions on the basis of one's marital status. Thus, these acts require that contractors take affirmative action to ensure equal employment opportunities for all applicants. Revised Order No. 4 requires that nonconstruction organizations with fifty or more employees and federal contracts of $50,000 or larger have an affirmative action program.

Vocational Rehabilitation Act of 1973

Designed to provide equal employment opportunities for qualified people with physical and mental disabilities, the Vocational Rehabilitation Act of 1973, which was amended in 1980, has resulted in progress being made in hiring people with disabilities. Organizations with a federal contract exceeding $2,500 must include an affirmative action clause in the contract regarding the employment of persons with disabilities. This clause must state that people with disabilities will be given due consideration and will not be discriminated against either in the selection process or after they have been hired. Of more recent origin is the related ruling which suggests that the Vocational Rehabilitation Act prohibits discriminatory hiring practices against individuals with AIDS.

Vietnam Era Veterans' Readjustment Assistance Act of 1974

The Vietnam Era Veterans' Readjustment Assistance Act pertains to government contractors whose federal contracts exceed $10,000. The provisions of the act state that such employers are required to hire and promote qualified Vietnam-era veterans and veterans with disabilities. In addition, such employers are required to list vacancies with local employment services. The veterans covered by the provisions of the act are to be given referral priority.

Pregnancy Discrimination Act of 1978

As an amendment to the Civil Rights Act, employers cannot discriminate against pregnant women by firing or refusing to hire them because they are pregnant. In addition, the same benefits to which nonpregnant employees are entitled must be available to pregnant employees.

Americans with Disabilities Act of 1990

What are the implications of ADA for employee selection?

This act, which is essentially a bill of rights for individuals with physical and mental disabilities, has important implications for the selection process. Essentially, the act forbids discriminating against an individual with a disability who is otherwise qualified for the job when the employer has fifteen or more employees. The act also forbids the use of selection devices that "screen out" individuals with disabilities by virtue of their disability. Furthermore, employers are required by law to make a "reasonable accommodation" to hire and place on the job individuals who have disabilities. ADA makes illegal the refusing to hire or firing of a person because of a disability except when the impairment prevents the individual from performing the stated basic job functions.

Some employers have tried to determine a disabled person's suitability for employment by asking him or her to provide a list of the compensation claims he or she has filed over the years. Asking for such information is illegal until a conditional job offer is made—and then it is suitable only to determine whether a disabled person's prior injury/disability may prevent him or her from carrying out the stated job duties.

Civil Rights Act of 1991

With the passage and signing into law of the Civil Rights Act of 1991, employers need to exercise even more care in the hiring, promoting, and firing of employees. The act provides the right to a jury trial, in addition to punitive (the larger the number of employees in the organization, the greater the punitive damages that can be received) and expanded compensatory damages to persons who have been intentionally discriminated against. The act amends Title VII of the 1964 Civil Rights Act. For the first time, employees who are U.S. citizens and who are working abroad in a U.S. company became protected by the various provisions of the act.

A provision of the Civil Rights Act of 1991 may make it more difficult for minority applicants to prove discrimination. Section 107 of the act says that test scores cannot be modified to "alter the results of employment related tests on the basis of race, color, religion, sex, or national origin." Prior to the passage of the Civil Rights Act of 1991, some employers routinely permitted minority applicants to have lower test scores than were permitted for hiring nonminority applicants. Such adjustments are now illegal.

The need has become critical for organizations to have in place policies that identify how they will conform with various elements of this act (and other relevant acts) regarding the hiring, promoting, and firing of employees. The presence of these policies should be well publicized, and the policies should be readily available for employee use. Another important aspect of the policy is that employees who file charges, regardless of the outcome, will not be subjected to retaliatory actions in the future because they filed charges. To do so is also a violation of the act.

MAKING THE DECISION

Administrative office managers often use two approaches in deciding which applicant to extend an offer: the single-predictor approach and the multiple-predictor approach. The type and level of position being filled often determines the approach.

What determines whether a single- or multiple-predictor approach is used?

Single-Predictor Approach

When the single-predictor approach is used, one device, such as an interview or a test, will be the primary determinant in making a selection decision. To use the single-predictor approach, those responsible for hiring will want rather substantive evidence that one selection device provides results just as valid as the results provided by multiple devices. The single-predictor approach is typically restricted to use in filling positions that possess repetitive, routine tasks.

Multiple-Predictor Approach

The use of the multiple-predictor approach results in the consideration of data and information gathered from several devices (tests, interviews, background checks, references, and so on) commonly used in the selection process. Some organizations require that for an applicant to be considered as a finalist for the position, he or she must possess minimum scores on all predictors. Therefore, a score that falls below the minimum will disqualify an applicant from further consideration. The use of the minimum score technique is acceptable as long as none of its components results in adverse impact.

Other organizations using the multiple-predictor approach opt for the compensatory technique. In this situation, a good score received by the applicant on one device will compensate for a poor score on another. As a result, a greater number of applicants, including those in protected groups, will likely be able to continue longer in the selection process.

Still other organizations use a combined approach that includes a single predictor in addition to multiple predictors. To be considered for a position, an applicant must meet a minimum requirement in a single predictor (net-words-per-minute keyboarding rate, for example). Those who meet the minimum requirement in the single predictor are then further evaluated in terms of certain multiple predictors.

How does the single-predictor approach differ from the multiple-predictor approach?

In selecting an approach, the following factors should be considered:

1. Quality of the results it provides.
2. Ease with which the approach is used.
3. Degree to which the approach meets all of the requirements of federal and state legislation regarding employee selection.
4. Objectivity of the approach.
5. Degree to which the approach provides a satisfactory number of applicants from which to choose.

MONITORING SELECTION PROCESS

The employee selection process should be monitored continually. The results of the monitoring process will provide a quantity of information useful in improving the quality of the process. Two quality indicators are the following:

What is the implication of a low selection ratio?

1. **Selection ratio,** which is calculated by dividing the number of applicants by the number of individuals hired. A 3:1 or 4:1 ratio should be attained. A ratio less than 3:1 may indicate that more recruiting is needed; a ratio higher than 4:1 may indicate that initial screening is not sufficiently refined.
2. **Offer-to-hire ratio,** which is calculated by dividing the number of offers made by the number of individuals hired. The ratio should be close to 1:1. Ratios above 1:1 or 1:0 are unacceptable and may indicate that the organization either has an image problem or that the job requirements are too strenuous for employment conditions.

IMPLICATIONS FOR THE ADMINISTRATIVE OFFICE MANAGER

The responsibility of the administrative office manager for selecting office employees varies from organization to organization. In some instances, the manager will become involved at the end of the process when it is time to select the best applicant from a list of the three or four top candidates. In other instances, the manager will become involved at the beginning of the selection process.

Regardless of the step in the process at which the administrative office manager becomes involved, he or she needs to be knowledgeable about all the elements of the process. The manager also needs to be familiar with provisions of relevant federal and state legislation that will help him or her avoid actions prohibited by law.

The use of effective selection procedures is more crucial now than ever. This is true for the following fundamental reason: poor hiring decisions are costly to the organization in a variety of ways. Not only are average or below-average employees less productive over the long run, but they also may lack incentive to try to improve. Employees whose attrition rates are higher than average cause the organization to incur additional recruiting and hiring expenses. Average or below-average employees may need to be given training in certain areas, which also can be costly. Furthermore, terminating employees whose performance is substandard is becoming increasingly difficult.

One of the most effective ways for the organization to improve the overall quality of its operations is to improve the quality of its workforce. Employee selection is a good place to begin.

REVIEW QUESTIONS

1. What is the most significant disadvantage of the employee referral method of employee selection?

2. If an organization needs to hire many employees in a short time, which recruiting source is most likely to yield the greatest number of applicants?

3. In addition to assisting organizations in employee recruitment, what other types of assistance does the USES provide?

4. What are the advantages of using temporary help agencies to obtain additional employees?

5. What are the primary functions of the employee requisition blank?

6. In what ways are job descriptions and job specifications of value in the selection process?

7. What are the advantages of employee testing?

8. What impact does the Employee Polygraph Protection Act of 1989 have on employee selection?

9. In what ways do criterion validity, construct validity, content validity, and differential validity differ from one another?

10. What are the special advantages resulting from the use of patterned interviews?

11. In what ways do the Civil Rights Act of 1964, the Age Discrimination in Employment Act of 1967, the Equal Employment Opportunity Act of 1972, the Vocational Rehabilitation Act of 1973, the Vietnam Era Veterans' Readjustment Assistance Act of 1974, the Pregnancy Discrimination Act of 1978, the American with Disabilities Act of 1990, and the Civil Rights Act of 1991 impact on employee selection?

DISCUSSION QUESTIONS

1. You recently hired an employee whose performance is excellent. This individual was hired on the basis of input from three of her four previous employers. Although you requested input from each of the references listed on her application blank, you still had not heard after

several weeks from one she listed. You decided to offer her a job on the basis of the three excellent recommendations you did receive. You finally heard from the fourth company she listed. Attached to the reference sheet was a note that said the following: "We have no record that Miss Jankowski ever worked for this company." When you confronted Miss Jankowski with that revelation, she said, "Oh, I just listed that company because I didn't figure you would ever check with them. I'm sorry I was dishonest." Explain how you plan to handle this situation.

2. One of the employees you hired last year has an excellent record of performance in your company. In fact, he has received one promotion and is being recommended for his second. No other employee in your unit has been promoted as rapidly. In a casual conversation with a friend yesterday, you learned that a person with the same name as this individual was terminated from his last position because he was caught stealing company property. After he returned the stolen property, charges were dropped. You are certain this is the same individual you are so impressed with because of the unusualness of his name. At the time you hired this individual, you were under the impression he left his previous employment because he wanted to, not because he had to. Although you have no record of verifying why the individual left his previous job, you are now contemplating your next course of action. Should you talk with this individual about your recent discovery? Why?

3. One of the supervisors for whom you are responsible lists unusually heavy lifting requirements on employee requisition blanks. These requirements apparently are aimed at disqualifying women for any of the openings. How can you verify the likelihood that this supervisor is listing unusually heavy lifting requirements only to disquality female applicants? Assuming you find your discovery to be true, outline what you plan to say to the supervisor about this practice.

STUDENT PROJECTS/ACTIVITIES

1. Talk with a personnel manager to learn about the sources most commonly used when recruiting office employees in the organization in which he or she works.
2. Talk with an administrative office manager to determine what types of tests are used in screening office employees in the organization in which he or she works.
3. Going Online: Using the Internet, conduct an online search based on one of the concepts presented in this chapter or based on one of the chapter terms. Identify four or five things you learned from this material that you did not know before your search.

Minicase

The Tri-State Corporation, which is located in Cleveland, Ohio, is in the process of redesigning its applicant testing program. The company has always used tests in the selection of office employees, and the personnel manager believes the practice should be continued. You have been asked to serve on an advisory committee that is to respond to the following two questions:

1. Should different types of tests (aptitude, intelligence, and so on) be used for different levels of office employees? Why or why not?
2. What one type of test do you recommend for testing junior-level secretaries? For testing executive secretaries? Justify each recommendation.

Case

Located in Chicago, Illinois, the Zebat Corporation is the largest chain manufacturer in the state. The company manufactures a variety of chains, ranging from those used on bicycles to those used on ship anchors.

The company is known throughout the Chicago area as being one of the better companies in which to work. Because of its favorable reputation, the company has been able to use walk-ins and unsolicited applications as its only recruiting sources. The personnel manager believed until recently that walk-ins and unsolicited applications yielded results comparable to other recruiting sources. An increasing number of department heads are now complaining that they have had to hire individuals whose qualifications do not exactly match the position requirements.

1. Is the exclusive use of walk-ins and unsolicited applicants likely to be responsible for producing the situation about which the department heads complain? Explain.

2. Identify the negative aspects of using only walk-ins and unsolicited applications.

3. What other recruiting sources might the company investigate?

4. Explain how the company might assess the effectiveness of the other recruiting sources it tries.

$\mathcal{C}$hapter 8

DEVELOPING OFFICE EMPLOYEES

$\mathcal{C}$hapter $\mathcal{A}$ims

After studying this chapter, you should be able to design an effective orientation and training program for an organization, based on its needs.

$\mathcal{C}$hapter $\mathcal{O}$utline

Orientation
    Orientation Kit
Training
    Development of Training Programs
    Responsibility for Training
Principles of Learning
    Learning by Doing
    Motivation
    Knowledge of Results
    Individual Differences
Organization of Learning Experiences
    Distributed Learning
    Whole versus Part Learning
    Transfer of Learning
Training Techniques
    Information Distribution Techniques
    Simulation Techniques
    On-the-Job Techniques
Special-Purpose Training
Legal Considerations in Training
Counseling
Implications for the Administrative Office Manager

$\mathcal{C}$hapter $\mathcal{T}$erms

Active learning
Audio cassette training
Buddy system
Business games
Case method
Civil Rights Act of 1964
Closed-circuit television
College-level refresher courses
Computer-assisted instruction
Conference method
Counseling
Distance learning
Education-employer cooperative training
Employee assistance program (EAP)
Employee attitude survey
Employee development
Employee performance analysis
In-basket
Incident method
Individual differences
Information distribution techniques
Interactive video instruction
Job content analysis
Job-instruction training
Job rotation
Just-in-time training
Learning by doing
Lecture method

Motion pictures and slide presentations
On-the-job coaching
On-the-job techniques
Orientation
Orientation kits
Passive learning
Population needs analysis
Principles of learning

Programmed instruction
Role playing
Slide presentations
Simulation techniques
Training
Vestibule training
Video training
Vocational Rehabilitation Act of 1973

Employee development, which helps maximize use of human potential, is seen as a continuous process that lasts for the duration of an employee's tenure with an organization. Beginning with employee orientation, the employee development process continues with the training, counseling, appraising, and motivating of employees.

In what ways do the organization and its employees benefit from employee development?

Both the organization and its employees benefit from employee development. The organization benefits because employees are more readily able to achieve important organizational goals, such as those relating to productivity. Employees benefit because they are able to achieve their potential more quickly and easily and with less frustration, which has a positive impact on the amount of satisfaction they derive from their work.

The new technology used in the office has substantially increased the need for providing training experiences for office employees. This chapter provides a discussion of several training techniques, in addition to information about employee orientation and counseling. Motivation and performance appraisal, two other important components of employee development, are covered in subsequent chapters.

ORIENTATION

Enabling employees to adjust more readily to their new jobs and to the organization, **orientation** has a positive impact on employee productivity. As a result of the orientation process, employees are likely to make fewer costly and time-wasting mistakes. Quality orientation also enables employees to experience greater job satisfaction. Orientation is often seen as a socialization process in that it provides employees with the opportunity to become familiar with organizational values, standards, appropriate attitudes, and behaviorial patterns.

Effective orientation helps employees feel more "at home" and enhances their understanding of the nature of their job duties because it provides them with essential background information they need to perform satisfactorily. Although the content of the program will vary from organization to organization, some of the topics commonly included are the items found in the orientation checklist in Figure 8–1.

What is the "buddy" system?

One way some organizations help their new employees adjust more quickly to their job and the organization in which they work is to use a **buddy system.** Experienced employees help new employees by serving as a valuable resource. Psychologically, this system has significant advantages for new employees. Occasionally, new employees may hesitate to ask questions of their supervisors, although they are comfortable asking questions of their fellow employees. Either the new employee is referred to someone else or the experienced employee can attempt to obtain answers from another person when he or she is unable to answer the questions.

Figure 8-1 Orientation checklist.

The following are items that should be covered with each new employee within his or her first two days on the job. Generally, the supervisor or some other designated individual is responsible for covering these items. To assure complete coverage, a checkmark should be placed on the appropriate line at the time each item has been completed.

_____ 1. Welcome to the department.

_____ 2. Introduction to coworkers.

_____ 3. Tour of the department, showing location of work area, department equipment, supplies storage, lunchroom, conference room, mail, and so on.

_____ 4. Explanation of important departmental functions and the general flow of work through the department.

_____ 5. Explanation of departmental policies and procedures regarding time cards, work hours, overtime, vacation time, personal days, sick days, work breaks, lunch hour, salary review, promotions, and so on.

_____ 6. Explanation of departmental hierarchy including responsibilities of unit supervisors and department head.

_____ 7. Explanation of the employee's job title, job description and specification (provide copies of both the description and specification), job duties, accountability, and goals.

_____ 8. Explanation of how the employee should get answers to various types of questions he or she may have.

_____ 9. Explanation of how tardiness and absences are to be reported and handled.

_____ 10. Explanation of departmental and organizational policies and procedures regarding safety, health, and security matters.

_____ 11. Explanation of pay period and fringe benefits including insurance, retirement, vacation days, and holidays.

Several orientation delivery systems are used including ones that have verbal, written, and audiovisual components. Verbal orientation involves a one-on-one or a group situation. Written orientation typically involves the use of handbooks or manuals. Audiovisual presentations consist of movies or videocassette recorder tapes, slide-tape presentations, closed-circuit television, and computer-driven multimedia presentations.

To ensure the exposure of all new employees to each element of the orientation process, many organizations use a checklist to keep a record of the topics each employee has covered. The checklist is especially useful when the orientation process lasts for more than a day and when more than one person is involved with the orientation of the new employee. A representative checklist is illustrated in Figure 8–1.

Orientation Kit

What information is included in an orientation kit?

An increasing number of companies are developing **orientation kits** that supplement the employees' formal orientation experiences. Although the materials in the kit will vary, some of the commonly included items are the following:

1. Organization chart
2. Map of the premises (if the premises is large)
3. Copy of the employee handbook
4. Copy of the union contract (if the organization is unionized)
5. List of fringe benefits
6. Copy of insurance plans
7. Copy of performance appraisal form and outline of appraisal procedures
8. Copy of emergency and evacuation procedures
9. List of names and telephone numbers of key organizational employees and units

Both a human resources specialist and the new employee's supervisor will likely be included in the orientation process. The human resources specialist will often present information that all employees throughout the organization need, including such information as working hours, vacation, sick days, and so forth. The supervisor is generally responsible for orienting the new employee to his or her job and work environment.

Some organizations have found that the employee handbook distributed as part of the orientation process is interpreted by the courts as an employee contract. If the organization does not intend for the handbook to be an employee contract, a disclaimer stating such should be included in the handbook.

TRAINING

What are the advantages of using well-designed training experiences?

Training is a vital organizational function because it provides new and present employees with directed experiences that enable them to perform their job tasks more effectively. Well-designed training experiences will bring about changes in employees' attitudes, work habits, and performance levels. Among the advantages of effective training are the following: employee morale is improved, turnover is lessened, errors are reduced, employee self-confidence is increased, productivity is increased, employees adjust more readily to their jobs, and less supervision is required.

The focus of training programs has changed somewhat over the years. Previously, training was primarily concerned with the technical skills that encompass employees' jobs. Today, a certain amount of training may be of a remedial nature, and some will likely be devoted to such general topics as team building and communication skills. And depending on the situation, some training may be devoted to the effective use of technology and computer applications.

Development of Training Programs

The development of training programs consists of the following six well-defined steps.

Step 1: Determine Need for Training Program. Several factors are helpful in determining the need for a training program. The degree to which new employees are qualified for their jobs is a primary consideration. If a significant number of employees are marginally qualified, training experiences are needed. Employee attitudes about the development of a training program might also be considered. In addition, supervisory feedback is often useful when determining program need, as are the results of employee performance appraisals. Areas in which performance is generally regarded as weak or deficient are typically considered as being suitable for training.

To help determine the need for a training program, answers to the following questions will be helpful:

What should be
considered in determining
the need for a training
program?

1. What are employees not doing that they should be doing?
2. What are employees doing that they should not be doing?
3. What key expectations are the employees not achieving?
4. What are the nature of customer complaints that are employee related?
5. Are employees fully apprised about their job expectations?
6. Do employees get regular feedback regarding their expectations?
7. How far is the organization deviating from key measurable aspects of employee performance, including such aspects as error rates, manufacturing standards, employee turnover rate, operating expenses, and so forth?

Several specific types of analyses are also useful in determining the need for employee training. Included in these analyses are job content analysis, employee performance analysis, employee attitude surveys, and population needs analysis.

The **job content analysis** examines the content of present and anticipated openings. This analysis provides information about the tasks to be performed by employees, the skills employees need to perform these tasks, and the minimum acceptable employee performance standards.

For what is employee
performance analysis
used?

The **employee performance analysis** determines whether a discrepancy exists between the employees' actual performance and the minimum acceptable performance standards determined in the process of analyzing job content. This analysis is generally performed on each specific job dimension.

For what is an employee
attitude survey used?

The **employee attitude survey** is useful for determining the attitudes of employees regarding their perceived need for training. A strongly perceived need for a training program probably should be addressed. The organization's failure to address the training issue will likely result in diminished employee morale, increased turnover, and decreased productivity, all of which can result in the waste of financial resources. Although some employee attitude surveys are quite general, others solicit information about specific job dimensions.

What are the common
types of training programs
provided office
employees?

The **population needs analysis** is used to determine specific training needs of specific populations of workers. To illustrate, an organization that hires many new high school graduates may need to offer specific training experiences in areas in which this segment of its employee population is deficient. Different employee populations often have different training needs that have to be addressed.

Step 2: Define Objectives of Training Program. Before determining the nature of training experiences to provide employees, the objectives of the program have to be defined. While some training programs are designed to provide job-entry experiences, others provide retraining experiences designed to help employees improve their effectiveness.

Step 3: Determine Type of Training Program. On the basis of the perceived need for a training program and the stated objectives, determining the type of training program needed is quite simple. Following are common types of training programs provided office employees:

Why do training follow-up studies need to be conducted?

1. *Basic knowledge.* Training experiences of this type are designed to help new employees qualify for the positions for which they have been hired. In many instances, employees who are exposed to such training programs have very little, if any, knowledge about the activities that constitute their jobs. Training experiences of this nature are often seen as being remedial.

2. *Job exposure.* This type of training program is also frequently used for new employees. Individuals who are offered job exposure training programs typically have basic knowledge about their jobs but need training in certain areas. Such programs frequently involve training employees to perform certain job activities or tasks.

3. *Refresher training.* This is designed to help employees maintain a desirable level of effectiveness in performing their jobs. Changes in procedures, new technology, or in jobs make frequent refresher training desirable. In some instances, refresher training is used to upgrade employees.

Another type of training, supervisory training, is discussed in Chapter 9.

Step 4: Determine Appropriate Training Techniques. Once the need for training programs has been established and the areas suitable for training have been determined, the training techniques should be selected. Important principles of learning should be considered in selecting the appropriate training technique for the material/information being presented.

Step 5: Provide Training Experiences. After the training technique has been devised, the next step is to offer the training experiences. In some cases, these experiences might be provided by an employee of the organization. In other situations, they are provided by an outside agency through a contractual arrangement. Depending on the training techniques used, provisions may have to be made for frequent assessment of employee progress. In addition, achievement levels will have to be determined, as well as an appropriate method for measuring achievement. Without this information, the success of the training program cannot be fully realized.

Step 6: Conduct Follow-Up Studies. Upon completion of their training experiences and return to their jobs, follow-up studies of the trainees' performance should be conducted, perhaps at six-month intervals. This type of feedback is a direct indicator of the program's success. The effect of the training experience on each trainee's performance, as well as his or her attitude toward the training experience, should be assessed. Subjecting employees to training experiences that fail to meet their expectations will have a negative impact on the program's overall effectiveness.

Additional information about the following, which are indirect indicators of program success, will be helpful in assessing whether the organization's training efforts were successful:

1. Feedback from managers and staff involved with the training program.
2. Determination of how well the stated learning objectives were fulfilled.
3. Determination of the training program's impact on the measurable aspects mentioned in Step 1.
4. Calculation of the cost-benefit ratio.

Responsibility for Training

Although the human resources department in most organizations is responsible for the overall coordination of the training program, the administrative office manager or designated subordinates are often responsible for other specific aspects of training office employees. This is especially true when job exposure and refresher training experiences are provided. In many organizations, each department is responsible for its own specialized training of new employees and for training designed to upgrade employees.

PRINCIPLES OF LEARNING

Several **principles of learning** should guide the development of training programs. Program effectiveness can be maximized only when the structure of training techniques is consistent with these principles.

Learning by Doing

Why is active learning more efficient than passive learning?

Learning by doing actively involves the trainees in the learning process. In contrast to **passive learning, active learning** is a fast, efficient process for acquiring knowledge. The greater the number of senses involved in the learning process, the more active the trainee is and the better the outcome is likely to be. Trainees subjected to passive learning methods are less likely to assimilate the material being presented because they are not required to give their total attention to the situation.

Motivation

For learning to be effective, trainees must want to improve their job performance, which, in turn, will enable them to be promoted and to advance. Trainees who want to be promoted will experience greater satisfaction from their involvement in a training program than those who are involved out of fear of being dismissed because of poor job performance.

Greater satisfaction, in turn, provides greater motivation to succeed. Individuals responsible for the training experiences must provide an atmosphere that encourages trainees to want to learn and improve.

Knowledge of Results

Why do learners need knowledge of results?

Having access to learning results provides many trainees with the reinforcement they need. Many trainees find it helpful to know how closely their behavior or responses match expected behavior or responses. Knowledge of results enables trainees to continue to make correct responses or to modify incorrect responses. Correct responses should be reinforced so the trainee will continue to make them. To be most effective, feedback should be offered as soon as possible after the response has been made.

Individual Differences

Trainees vary considerably in their ability to learn as well as in their attitudes, motivation, initiative, prior knowledge, and commitment. Therefore, **individual differences** must be recognized in training endeavors. Some trainees learn more rapidly than others, some need greater amounts of practice than others, and they respond in different ways to various training techniques. Some of the training techniques discussed in a later section of this chapter provide for individual differences more effectively than others do.

ORGANIZATION OF LEARNING EXPERIENCES

Learning experiences are more effective if they build on one another and if they begin with simple experiences and proceed to the more complex ones. This is true because the trainee is able to use previous knowledge, which reinforces previous learning.

Distributed Learning

What is meant by distributed learning?

When learning is distributed, training experiences are spread over a longer period. The advantage is that most trainees learn faster and retain more than when exposed to the material over a short time. Consequently, a twenty-hour training program spread over a month tends to be more effective than the same program offered as a three-day experience.

Whole versus Part Learning

Learning in wholes versus learning in parts is a fundamental factor of concern to those who design training materials. Some job activities simply cannot be broken down into parts or components, but others readily lend themselves to the segmented approach. When feasible, learning by parts is generally more effective than learning by wholes.

Transfer of Learning. Effective learning experiences are transferable, which means that a close correlation exists between what trainees learn from their training experiences and what they actually do on their jobs. When training programs consist of experiences that have no application to or correlation with the actual jobs employees perform, transfer is limited.

TRAINING TECHNIQUES

A variety of training techniques have been developed over the years. Certain techniques are better suited for training certain individuals in certain areas than others. Included in Figure 8–2 is a list of factors that should be considered when selecting an appropriate technique for a given situation.

Figure 8–2 Factors to consider in determining an appropriate training technique

1. Nature of the tasks or jobs for which training programs are being developed.
2. Number of individuals to be trained.
3. Financial commitment the organization is willing to make for employee training.
4. Ease with which already prepared materials can be obtained.
5. Length of time needed to train individuals adequately.
6. Adequacy of the training facilities within the organization.
7. Abilities of the individuals for whom the training experiences are being developed.

Training techniques can be placed in three distinct categories: **information distribution techniques, simulation techniques,** and **on-the-job techniques.**

Information Distribution Techniques

Various information distribution techniques are used to present information, concepts, knowledge, and facts. Because these techniques do not allow for practice opportunities, they are not useful for situations where practice is required to develop and ensure mastery of the material being taught.

Lecture Method. Using one-way communication between the lecturer and audience, the **lecture method** generally consists of the lecturer's verbally presenting information to a group of trainees. Although the lecture method is effective under certain circumstances, it does not provide for individual differences because all trainees are presented the same information at the same rate. Another criticism is that trainees have little opportunity to receive feedback about their performance. Lectures provide only limited opportunity for reinforcement or practice.

The lecture method has several advantages. For example, it is one of the most economical training techniques; a large amount of information can be presented in a short time, and the trainees can be exposed to outstanding practitioners or experts.

The success of the lecture method is heavily dependent on the lecturer. In many instances, even though the material being presented is relevant and crucial for the trainees' understanding of their jobs, the material fails to have a significant impact because of the lecturer's delivery. The lecture can be made more effective by using trainee participation as well as by using visual devices during the delivery of the material.

What are the characteristics of the conference method of training?

Conference Method. Another of the information distribution training techniques, the **conference method** uses small groups headed by a conference leader. The leader's function is to provide guidance and feedback rather than instruction. Although this technique has been used more widely for training supervisors and managers, it does have a certain amount of usefulness for training office employees. The conference method is especially useful for helping office employees develop problem-solving and decision-making skills. This method can also be used to acquaint employees with new materials, to modify attitudes of employees, and to help employees overcome resistance to change.

In contrast to the rather passive nature of the trainee in the lecture method, the trainee in the conference method plays an active role because of frequent verbal interaction with other conference participants. Feedback, an important element of the conference technique, is provided by the other participants or by an individual who has been delegated that responsibility.

The conference method has been criticized because (1) it consumes a considerable amount of time before substantive results are apparent; (2) it frequently results in considerable confusion and sidetracking of the important issues unless the training sessions are highly structured; and (3) it is restricted to small groups.

Programmed Instruction. Used to train office employees in certain areas, **programmed instruction** is currently receiving a fair amount of attention. When preparing programmed instruction materials, learning objectives have to be clearly defined. After the material is divided into component parts, the instructional unit is prepared. Careful attention must be given to the ordering of the component parts; otherwise, improper sequencing is confusing to the user. Also, the information needs to be presented in small segments or units.

The instructional unit may present the material to the trainee in textbook format or in teaching machine format on a computer. After presenting small units of information, the trainee answers questions by making a response (textbook format) or by pushing a button (teaching machine format). If the trainee's response is correct, he or she is then instructed to proceed to the next unit of information. If an incorrect response is made, the trainee is given additional material on the same unit of information. Another question is subsequently presented to evaluate the trainee's mastery of the review material.

The programmed instruction training technique has three distinct advantages: The trainee obtains immediate knowledge of results, progresses through the instructional unit at an individualized pace, and takes an active role in the learning process. Among the disadvantages are high initial cost and the time consumed in developing the instructional units. Furthermore, some trainees, unless they receive adequate direction from a trainer, find pacing themselves through the material somewhat difficult.

Closed-Circuit Television. Another frequently used information distribution technique—**closed-circuit television**—enables an organization to develop its own videotapes of various procedures, processes, or methods. The trainees then view the videotapes as often as needed to master the subject matter. This technique is useful for initial learning as well as a refresher course. Videotapes custom designed for the organization enable the trainee to identify more closely with the material being presented.

Compared with lectures, closed-circuit television offers certain advantages. For example, individuals with excellent presentation skills can be used as presenters. The same may not be true of a lecturer. Furthermore, close-ups of procedures or processes can be presented on closed-circuit television, which is not always possible with the lecture method.

Motion Pictures and Slide Presentations. Although not as flexible as closed-circuit television, **motion pictures** and **slide presentations** are two other techniques used to train office employees. Closed-circuit television is more flexible because videotapes can be erased and reused, an impossibility with motion pictures and slide presentations. The use and end results of motion pictures, slide presentations, and closed-circuit television are all comparable.

Distance Learning. A new training technique, **distance learning**, involves taking the material to be taught to the trainees' work site rather than having the trainees come to the trainer's location. More often than not, distance learning will be expedited by two-way compressed video. The trainer stays at his or her work site, and the material he or she is covering is transmitted as television images through telephone lines. Being compressed, it is an economical type of training. At the receiving end, the trainees will see the trainer's motions on a television screen, but the trainer's motions will be slower than "real time," meaning they are compressed. Because it is two-way, the trainees can see the trainer when he or she is talking, and the trainer can see the trainees when they ask questions. The images can be recorded on videotape as they are being transmitted, thus enabling the tapes to be replayed at a later time.

This technique works well in a large organization with distributed employees and facilities. Rather than incurring the expense of having the individuals being trained come to the trainer's location—or vice versa—the material being taught is economically transmitted over the telephone lines.

Margin notes:

What two formats are used in presenting programmed instructional units?

What is distance learning?

College-Level Refresher Courses. Some organizations either sponsor employees or reimburse them for a percentage of the tuition cost of enrolling in **college-level refresher courses.** These courses, which cover a variety of topics, are sometimes taught at an educational institution; in other instances they are taught within the organization. An example of a commonly taught refresher course is a review class designed for individuals wishing to take a certifying examination such as the Certified Administrative Manager exam.

Simulation Techniques

Placing the trainees in an artificial representation of a real-life situation, simulation techniques require them to react as if the situation were real. Simulation training is also known as **vestibule training,** which has the following characteristics: The training usually occurs on the organization's premises away from the workstation, and it uses actual equipment and procedures.

Role Playing. When **role playing** is used as a training technique, trainees assume the roles of the individuals involved in a given situation. For example, to train employees to deal with certain human relations situations, the trainer might assume the role of an angry client and the trainee assumes the role of the employee dealing with the client. The observers who are not involved in the role-playing situation have an opportunity to evaluate the correctness or incorrectness of the role player's actions. At the conclusion of role playing, the observers and the trainer have the opportunity to discuss the trainees's handling of the situation.

How is role playing used as a training technique?

Role playing is especially useful as a training technique in areas such as human relations. Its disadvantages are as follows: It is time-consuming; only a few individuals have an active role at a given time; and because human relations situations involve so many variables, the chances are slight that the trainee will experience an identical situation on the job. The extent of the transferability of knowledge acquired through the training process to a real-life situation may become an issue.

Case Method. When the **case method** is used, trainees are given a description of certain organizational conditions involving either a hypothetical organization or the organization for which they work. The participants in the case are typically required to identify problems, to develop solutions, or to make recommendations, all of which put emphasis on the employee participation process.

The amount of information presented to the trainee varies from case to case. In some instances, the information is so brief that the trainee has to make realistic assumptions in arriving at a solution. In other instances, irrelevant information is presented in the case, which makes the trainee responsible for sorting the important from the unimportant material.

The case method is advantageous for the following reasons: The trainees who actively participate are able to obtain feedback on their suggestions and recommendations, and the technique often provides transfer from the case situation to the real-life situation. The case method has been criticized because it does not allow for the teaching of general principles, nor are the trainees generally given all the information they need for real-life problem solving.

What are the characteristics of the incident method of training?

Incident Method. Another simulation technique—the **incident method**—is closely related to the case method. In the incident method, trainees are given a few of the details about a specific situation. To obtain sufficient background information for developing a solution, trainees ask questions of the trainer. When the trainees believe they have sufficient information to make a decision, the questioning process is concluded and the trainees prepare a solution to the problem being considered. After the trainees have presented their solution, the trainer discloses any additional information the trainees failed to obtain through the questioning phase of the problem. The trainer also typically provides a solution based on all the important facts and not just those that were made accessible to the trainees.

Business Games. As a training technique, **business games** are useful for increasing trainees' understanding of the economic aspects of an industry, an organization, or a department within an organization. Games incorporate a set of rules developed from economic theory or from the financial operations of an industry or organization. These rules determine how input variables (raw materials, capital, equipment, and personnel), along with certain mediating variables (wages, finished product prices, and advertising expenditures), affect the output variables (quantity sold, amount of profit, and net worth).

Trainees have to decide what product prices to charge, how much money to allocate for advertising, what new equipment to purchase, how many additional employees to hire, and so forth. A primary advantage of business games is their realistic nature. To provide additional realism, computer usage is incorporated into many of today's business games. One of the criticisms leveled against business games is their use of "gadgetry," which tends to detract from the purpose for which the game was developed. The time-consuming nature of some games is also a disadvantage.

Games are especially well suited to help employees acquire an understanding of the various interrelations within the organization and the degree to which these interrelations affect the success of the organization's operations. Although business games are perhaps more suitable for training managers than for training office employees, the technique can be effectively modified for use in training office employees.

In-Basket. Used as a technique for training office employees, the **in-basket** is especially suited for such areas as decision making and problem solving. An in-basket contains the types of materials that would accumulate over time (perhaps two weeks) in the in-basket on one's desk. It consists of internal and external communications, customer or client complaints, reports, written records of phone messages, and other items that typically accumulate.

What are the characteristics of the in-basket method of training?

The trainee is required to do two things with each situation: determine the priority in which each situation is to be considered and devise a solution or recommendation for expediting the situation. After each trainee completes the in-basket situation, the trainer and trainees discuss various solutions and recommendations.

The in-basket technique can be made more realistic by using actual organizational situations instead of contrived ones. Although the technique does very little in teaching general principles, it is useful for developing the trainees' decision-making skills.

Computer-Assisted Instruction. Two functions—memory and storage—make it possible to store a variety of training materials in a computer. Training activities that readily lend themselves to **computer-assisted instruction** are certain kinds of drill and practice exercises, simulations, and problem solving. The same format used in programmed instruction materials is often used to present computer-assisted instructional materials.

Among the advantages of computer-assisted instruction are its low cost, simplicity, and flexibility in accommodating a wide variety of situations and trainee skill levels. Furthermore, it provides an excellent opportunity for employees to become familiar with computer usage.

Perhaps the most significant disadvantage of computer-assisted instruction is the lack of discipline among some employees to complete the instructional process.

Audio Cassette Training. As increasing numbers of **audio cassette training** systems are becoming available, audio cassette training is becoming a more prominent training technique. Cassette systems typically include one or more tapes and a textbook manual. In training systems designed to teach a computer software package, a diskette is also generally included. Cassette systems take from three to four hours to as many as forty hours to complete. Although cassette systems cover a number of topics, those involving computer operations and a variety of software packages are among the most plentiful.

Three significant advantages result from the use of audio cassette training: It accommodates trainees who learn best from an auditory approach, it is economical, and it can be used anywhere and any time trainees have access to a tape player, including in a car or plane. Two of the most significant disadvantages are that the package may include some material that may not be relevant to all trainees and the cost of developing the training package.

Video Training. Using video to train employees has become common. Included in **video training** systems are the following media: tapes, laser video disks, computer diskettes, and CD-ROMs. Generally, a trainee manual or guidebook also accompanies the medium. As a training system, the use of videos enables the trainer to see the concept being taught, learn and/or hear about the concept, and finally perform the concept.

Among the advantages of video training are its convenience, the fast learning results it provides, and its availability for future use. Cost is seen as a disadvantage of video training.

What are the advantages of interactive video instruction?

Interactive Video Instruction. Of the various employee training techniques, **interactive video instruction** is among the newest. Interactive video training generally involves the use of a computer, although the topic may not be computer related. The trainee carries on a dialogue with the computer, which he or she uses to ask himself or herself questions, to review material, and to provide responses by either touching the screen or using the keyboard. Although computer-assisted training and interactive video instruction are similar in some respects, interactive video is a more sophisticated and therefore a more costly training technique.

Among the advantages of interactive video instruction are: it results in fast learning time, and trainees are able to master more and retain more than when using some of the other training techniques. The most significant disadvantage of this training technique is the cost of equipment and materials.

On-the-Job Techniques

Training programs consisting of on-the-job techniques are popular for training office employees. On-the-job training experiences are often combined with the performance of actual job tasks. These techniques readily enable employees to transfer their training experiences to their jobs.

What are the characteristics of the education-employer cooperative training technique?

Education-Employer Cooperative Training. The **education-employer cooperative training technique** combines formal classes with on-the-job experiences. Cooperative training, which is most often found at the high school and college levels, enables trainees to be enrolled in school while being employed part time in a related job.

The students learn in their school experiences how various office tasks are performed. In their part-time jobs, they have the opportunity to put their knowledge into practice. The students receive direction from both their employers and a specially trained employee of the school, commonly known as a co-op coordinator. Because organizations frequently offer full-time jobs to the students on completion of their educational experiences, some organizations consider this training technique a valuable source of employees.

On-the-Job Coaching. When **on-the-job coaching** is used, the trainee's supervisor is the trainer. Therefore, the supervisor-subordinate relationship is also a trainer-trainee relationship. Although few would disagree with the practice of making the supervisor responsible for training subordinates in certain areas, the critics of this technique point out that being a good supervisor or manager may conflict with being a good trainer. Unless this conflict can be kept to a minimum, the individual who has dual supervisory and training responsibilities may find this technique to be somewhat disconcerting.

Figure 8–3 presents a list of suggestions designed to improve the effectiveness of employee coaching.

How is job rotation used as a training technique?

Job Rotation. Although **job rotation** is useful in training certain individuals, it is not used often as a technique for training office employees. The length of time over which the job rotation spans as well as the fairly high cost of using the technique are two disadvantages of the job rotation training technique. Trainees rotate from one area to another, giving them an opportunity to become familiar with the activities of several functional areas. The extent to which trainees perform duties in the various functional areas depends on the organization. Trainees are sometimes allowed to perform tasks in each of the areas; in other instances, they simply observe.

Job-Instruction Training (JIT). Many office jobs are comprised of tasks arranged in a logical sequence of steps. **Job-instruction training** can be quite

1. Recognize that individuals have varying needs and that they respond differently to work pressure, challenge, and change.
2. Make sure the employee is *fully* aware of his or her job responsibilities.
3. Make sure that the employee's strengths are matched with his or her job responsibilities.
4. Provide the employee with clearly defined objectives and priorities.
5. Open up communication lines with the employee by asking open-ended questions.
6. Explore with the employee what he or she and you (the supervisor) can do to make his or her job easier and more satisfying to perform.
7. Replace criticism with clarification, explanation, encouragement, suggestions, and discussions.
8. Maintain as much as possible on-the-spot accessibility.

Figure 8–3 Suggestions for improving the effectiveness of employee coaching.

useful for familiarizing employees with these tasks. This technique requires the use of specifically designed training materials, which some individuals see as a significant disadvantage. However, the fact that the materials are available, enabling the trainee to proceed at his or her learning rate, is seen as a compensating advantage.

The materials used in job-instruction training are developed around each of the sequential steps that comprise the task as well as any key points associated with each step. The following illustrates the process (Step 4) involved in changing the toner cartridge in a laser printer.

Steps	*Key Points*
4: Clean the corona wire using a small cotton swab.	The corona wire is rather fragile. Use a "soft touch" in rubbing it with the swab.

What is JIT training?

Just-in-Time Training. A new training technique, **just-in-time training (JIT),** focuses on an employee's need for immediate information related to his or her job. It is consistent with the idea that much knowledge is learned and retained when an immediate need to do so exists. It provides the employee with the opportunity to learn the application and then immediately apply it to an actual job task. The content that is covered using this process varies widely. Perhaps the most frequently used example is the built-in "help" feature in many software programs. The employee typically doesn't invoke the "help" feature of the program until he or she needs to learn immediately how to do something. Just-in-time training might not work well for certain operations where an entire process has to be stopped even for a few minutes to train one or more employees.

SPECIAL-PURPOSE TRAINING

What topics are often included in special-purpose training?

In the past, organizations were primarily concerned about training their new and present employees to perform their job tasks more effectively. The changing culture within many organizations is making desirable and in some cases mandatory training in a variety of peripheral areas including literacy training, diversity, AIDS, international business, teamwork and empowerment, customer-service attitude, and so on. A variety of training techniques, including the vast majority of those presented in the previous section, can be used to provide this special-purpose training.

Regarding literacy training, a growing number of employees are considered functionally illiterate because they are unable to read beyond the third- or fourth-grade level. Although organizations believe in becoming more socially responsible by hiring such individuals, providing literacy training is becoming more paramount. Without literacy training, many of these individuals will be locked into "dead-end" positions and therefore will not be promoted. Literacy training is a win-win situation for both the employee and the employer.

Organizations are becoming more culturally diverse. Diversity training enables individuals to become more tolerant of the views, customs, perspectives, and so on of others whose background is different. Diversity training generally results in greater assimilation of employees representing the minority cultures into the group of employees representing the majority cultures. It also enables those representative of the majority cultures to become more sensitive toward those representing the minority cultures.

An ever-increasing number of individuals infected with the AIDS virus are in the workforce, a situation that often causes anxiety among their noninfected coworkers. By helping noninfected employees become more informed about the AIDS virus, greater cooperation will likely result.

As organizations expand internationally, greater opportunities are available for employees to work abroad. Although many employees welcome the opportunity for these experiences, they will likely experience less anxiety and will be more receptive to working abroad if they have ample training. Among the topics generally covered in such experiences are aspects of the culture they will be joining, language training, business practices of the distant culture, and so on.

Teamwork and employee empowerment are two fairly new managerial concepts. However, they do not just happen because management has decided to introduce them. Training employees to be team players and to prosper in a team environment is essential. Empowerment enables employees to become more responsible for all aspects of their job. Training enables those who have not worked in such an environment previously to succeed at a higher level. Thus, they will be happier, more productive employees, resulting in greater organizational success.

As the U.S. economy continues to become more service based, an ever-increasing number of employees are dealing with customers. The highly competitive nature of many organizations suggests the need to train employees about ways to enhance customer relations. Effective customer-service training generally is very cost effective, often producing an excellent rate of return on the investment. The hallmark of many such training programs is that the "customer is always right."

LEGAL CONSIDERATIONS IN TRAINING

Several federal laws impact on organizational training programs. Denying training to individuals in protected classes—a denial that may ultimately hamper their promotion to higher level positions—is illegal. Affirmative action, which requires that all employees be given equal opportunity for advancement, also requires equality in the availability of training opportunities. The **Civil Rights Act of 1964** assures the equality of training experiences for all employees.

The **Vocational Rehabilitation Act of 1973** outlines the nature of affirmative action for individuals with disabilities. When a contract or subcontract exceeds $50,000, a detailed plan is required in which the following topics are covered: hiring, advancement, discharge, and other employment practices.

COUNSELING

What is counseling?

Another important component of the development process is employee **counseling.** In some organizations, employee counseling is carried out in a rather haphazard manner. The prevailing philosophy in some organizations is that once employees are hired, all of their needs are satisfied, they enjoy their work, and they find their jobs challenging.

Although predicting the times when employees will need conferences with their supervisors is difficult, a routine conference schedule can be developed. Supervisor-subordinate conferences may be held after employment of one month, three months, six months, and twelve months. Because of unpredictable situations, the opportunity must be made available for additional conferences when the need arises.

How can employee
conferences be made
more effective?

The effectiveness of conferences can be improved if they are conducted away from the employee's workstation, perhaps in the privacy of the supervisor's office or in a conference room. The supervisor is responsible for setting the stage for the conference, the effectiveness of which will be diminished if the employee feels uncomfortable with the situation. The supervisor must also be willing to listen to the employee and to provide suggestions and advice when sought. Both the supervisor and the employee must have respect for each other and must have an appreciation for each other's viewpoints. In addition, the supervisor must display a willingness to be helpful, a sense of fairness, and a general concern for the employee.

Many supervisors prefer to use the nondirective counseling approach, which gives subordinates the opportunity to determine the scope of the session. The supervisor listens to the subordinate but does not evaluate the substance of the subordinate's comments. A goal of the nondirective approach is to get employees to express their feelings without fear of retribution or criticism.

The subordinate's freedom of expression in the nondirective approach tends to reduce tension, anxiety, and frustration. In addition, the openness of the approach often helps the subordinates more clearly see the various dimensions of the situation.

Counseling is also an important component of **employee assistance programs** (EAPs). These are employer-provided programs in which employees needing help are provided counseling and/or treatment for such concerns as alcohol/drug abuse, gambling, healthy living, and stress. These programs are provided using several arrangements: in-house counseling or treatment, referral to specialists, and a consortium of several companies who retain the services of the specialists.

IMPLICATIONS FOR THE ADMINISTRATIVE OFFICE MANAGER

Familiarity with the various elements of employee development is becoming more important as the administrative office manager is assuming greater responsibility for certain specialized areas of the development process. Although overall responsibility in most organizations continues to be centralized within the personnel or training department, unit managers are often given responsibility for providing certain aspects of the process.

Providing quality development experiences is especially crucial to new employees. More often than not, their initial impression of the organization—which may ultimately become their prevailing impression—is affected by the quality of their early development experiences.

Managers sometimes wrongly assume that recently hired employees are adjusting well to their new situation, especially when they do not ask questions. Obviously, this assumption is incorrect because some employees are not comfortable questioning their supervisors and therefore refrain from doing so.

The philosophy that prevailed in many organizations a few years ago was that development existed only for new employees. Now, most organizations are committed to a lifelong employee development process. When managers discovered that employees' development needs increase as various situations arise—regardless of how long they have worked for the organization—the new philosophy began to prevail.

REVIEW QUESTIONS

1. What are the most common components of employee development?

2. What is typically found in an orientation kit?

3. What advantages result from employee training?

4. In what ways can the need for an employee training program be determined?

5. What types of training programs are used, and how do they differ from one another?

6. Why is knowledge of results important to trainees?

7. When determining which training techniques to use, what factors should be considered?

8. How do the lecture method and the conference method differ from one another?

9. What are the advantages of computer-assisted instruction as a training technique?

10. What are some of the topics covered in special-purpose training?

11. Why is employee counseling an important part of employee development?

DISCUSSION QUESTIONS

1. On several occasions, you, an administrative office manager, have asked your superior, a vice president, about the feasibility of installing a training program in your company. Your questions and comments have had a lukewarm response. This morning, you again asked your superior about installing a training program because you believe that a greater number of newly hired individuals are not as qualified as they were even five years ago. Although you are usually able to hire the best of the applicants for any opening, most are not totally qualified. Your superior responded to you this morning with the following comment: "We don't need a training program if we are able to hire well-qualified people. I'd rather use the money that a training program would cost to increase employees' salaries." Discuss the implications of your superior's comments.

2. The company you work for has several branch offices located throughout the country. The branch in which you work does not have a formal training program, but now some of the managers in the branch are interested in installing one. You have been designated as the individual responsible for coordinating the project. One manager suggested that you simply duplicate the training program used in another of the branches. Discuss the implications of installing a training program by duplicating the program of another branch.

3. Some discussion has occurred in your company about discontinuing the existing training program and sending employees to the local community college where they would attend classes on a tuition-reimbursement plan. Although some of the managers are in favor of the proposal, others believe that such a program would not be nearly as effective as the use of in-house training. What is your reaction to the proposal?

STUDENT PROJECTS AND ACTIVITIES

1. Talk with the personnel director of an organization about the nature of its orientation program. Who is in charge of orientation and how long does the orientation program last?

2. Talk with the director of training in an organization. How does he or she determine the nature of training needs?

3. Going Online: Using the Internet, conduct an online search based on one of the concepts presented in this chapter or based on one of the chapter terms. Identify four or five things you learned from this material that you did not know before your search.

Minicase

Office employees in the Handorf Corporation, a manufacturer of plywood and paneling products, are beginning to complain about the lack of training opportunities. They claim that on frequent occasions they have been penalized for their inability to perform certain functions, mainly because they didn't know how to perform them. They believe that if they had had the benefit of training in these areas, they would not have had the problems they are continuing to experience.

1. Besides employee opinion, what other techniques can be used to determine the need for a training program?
2. In addition to the lack of a training program, what other factors may be responsible for poor employee performance?

Case

You are a consultant with considerable expertise in the area of training programs. You just spent several days assessing the training program in Chicago-based Borowicz Corporation, a large manufacturer of equipment used in bowling alleys. After spending several days at Borowicz, you conclude that its program has several serious shortcomings.

Approximately 95 percent of the training experiences offered by Borowicz were developed primarily because of trainer interest in specific areas rather than because of trainee need. Management did not discourage this practice because of its belief that "something was better than nothing." For this reason, some training experiences have little value.

You also found out that the lecture method was widely used because of its relatively low per-trainee cost. Furthermore, you found that no employee follow-up is conducted after training because "we really don't know what to expect of employees after they have completed their training experiences."

1. What problems are found in this company with respect to its training program? Discuss the implications of each of these problems.
2. Describe in detail your recommendations for eliminating the problems that are identified.
3. What situation or situations may be responsible for the design of a training program similar to the one discussed in this case?

$\mathcal{C}$hapter 9

SUPERVISING OFFICE EMPLOYEES

$\mathcal{C}$hapter $\mathcal{A}$ims

After studying this chapter, you should be able to develop effective strategies for supervising subordinates.

$\mathcal{C}$hapter $\mathcal{O}$utline

*C*hapter *T*erms

Achievement-oriented supervision	Laissez-faire approach
Active listening	Maintenance-of-membership shop
Agency shop	Management by objectives (MBO)
Autocratic approach	Management prerogative
Behavioral theories	Mission statement
Boss-centered leadership	Outplacement services
Democratic approach	Participative management
Dues checkoff	Situational theory
Employee assistance programs	Subordinate-centered leadership
Escalator clauses	Subordinate-oriented supervision
Family Medical Leave Act (1993)	Technostress
Grievance	Union shop
Labor agreement	Vision statement

*O*ne of the common responsibilities of administrative office managers—indeed perhaps the most common one—is the supervision of subordinates. Supervision is comprised of several activities: planning, organizing, staffing, directing, and controlling. Many managers claim that their supervisory responsibilities are one of the more rewarding aspects of their job.

Supervisory effectiveness is largely influenced by the amount of leadership ability and skill the manager possesses. Some supervisory positions require greater leadership skills than others. The amount of leadership ability required of a supervisor is affected by several factors:

What factors determine the amount of leadership ability required of a supervisor?

1. Hierarchical level of the supervisor.
2. Number of individuals for whom the supervisor is responsible.
3. Nature of the work performed by the subordinates.
4. Background of the subordinates.
5. Stability of the work unit.

To appreciate fully the importance of leadership in the supervisory process, an understanding of the leadership role is needed; this is discussed in the following section.

LEADERSHIP ROLE

Leadership is one's ability to get things done through and with others. The role that leadership plays in the supervisory process can be examined by studying **behavioral theories** of leadership and the **situational theory** of leadership.

Behavioral Theories

Two behavioral theories of leadership exist: leadership styles and leadership orientation. Each theory has distinct characteristics.

Leadership Styles. Although leadership styles vary between an **autocratic approach** and a **democratic approach,** several degrees between these two approaches can also be found. Although some supervisors can be classified as being autocratic and others democratic, most use an approach that falls somewhere between the two extremes. The following illustrates the autocratic-democratic leadership continuum:

Autocratic————————————————————Democratic

What are the
characteristics of
autocratic supervisors?

Supervisors using the autocratic approach make decisions without seeking the ideas, suggestions, and recommendations of subordinates. Thus, they keep their power to themselves. Those who use this approach tend to exert extensive control over the behavior and actions of their subordinates. For example, subordinates may be disciplined before an attempt is made to determine the reasons for their misconduct. Too, autocratic supervisors rarely deviate from the norm or from the expected course of action; and they tend to be inflexible, often the cause of subordinate resentment. Over time, resentful employees may begin to restrict their productivity as a means of retaliating.

Although autocratic supervision is generally considered to be less effective than democratic supervision, its use may be appropriate when dealing with:

1. An emergency situation.
2. A situation that requires an immediate decision.
3. A new employee who is unfamiliar with the tasks he or she is expected to perform.
4. An insubordinate employee.

Democratic supervisors make extensive use of the ideas, suggestions, and recommendations of their subordinates. When the impact of a decision affects subordinates, they are likely to be invited to participate in the decision-making process even though the supervisor is the one who is ultimately responsible for the decision. This technique is officially known as **participative management.** In addition to using subordinate participation, the democratic approach is also more flexible than the autocratic approach. Those who use the democratic alternative are more likely to investigate the reasons for subordinate error or misconduct before they decide whether disciplinary action is appropriate. Too, they are likely to be more tolerant of their subordinates' mistakes than are their autocratic counterparts.

Situations for which the democratic approach is well suited include the following:

1. Sufficient time is available to permit subordinate participation.
2. Significant pending changes require considerable subordinate input.
3. Subordinates have a number of concerns they wish to express and have solved.
4. Situations or problems confronting the work group need to be resolved.

What is MBO?

The **management-by-objectives (MBO)** technique makes extensive use of democratic processes. With MBO, employees and their supervisors jointly establish objectives regarding the tasks performed by employees. At periodic intervals, the supervisors evaluate their subordinates' performance to determine progress toward goal achievement.

Situations for which the MBO technique is effective include these:

1. Work group is well educated.
2. Work group is self-motivated.
3. Work group is goal oriented.

What are the
characteristics of laissez-
faire supervisors?

A third leadership approach is the **laissez-faire approach.** Supervisors who use the laissez-faire approach generally give subordinates considerable freedom and provide very little, if any, assistance. Some supervisors who use this approach are not concerned about their subordinates. Others use it because they believe they will be more popular with their subordinates if they give them considerable freedom.

Situations for which the laissez-faire approach is well suited include these:

1. Work group is highly skilled.
2. Work group is well educated.
3. Work group is comprised of a number of temporary or leased employees.

Leadership Orientation. The leadership role can also be studied by examining the nature of the supervisor's orientation toward subordinates. Supervisors who are only concerned with the achievements of their subordinates use **achievement-oriented supervision** practices. When supervisors are greatly concerned about the welfare of their subordinates, they use **subordinate-oriented supervision.**

Achievement-oriented supervisors expect their subordinates to maintain a high output level regardless of the impact of productivity expectations on the employees. The subordinate-oriented supervisor is also concerned with output but to a lesser degree than the achievement-oriented individual. The subordinate-oriented supervisor is committed to the belief that if subordinates' needs are fulfilled, they will perform at a satisfactory level.

Situational Theory

A growing number of individuals believe the situational theory of leadership is more realistic than the behavioral theories. The situational theory is based on the belief that the amount of leadership a supervisor should exert will vary from situation to situation. Although some situations require extensive amounts of leadership, others require considerably less.

Figure 9–1 illustrates the situational theory on a continuum. As the amount of authority used by the supervisor increases, leadership becomes more boss

Margin notes:

What are the characteristics of achievement-oriented supervisors?

What is meant by the situational theory of leadership?

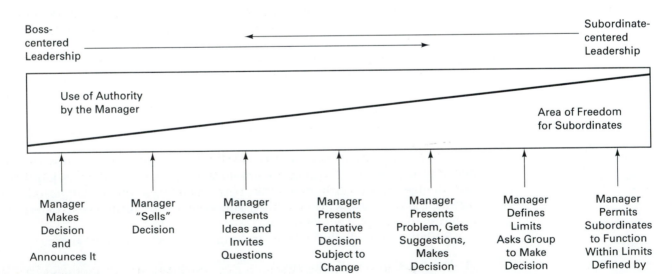

Figure 9-1 Leadership continuum. Copyright © 1958 by the President and Fellows of Harvard College. All rights reserved. Reprinted by permission of the *Harvard Business Review.* "How to Choose a Leadership Pattern," by Robert Tannenbaum and Warren H. Schmidt, March–April, 1958.

centered. Conversely, as the amount of subordinate freedom increases, leadership becomes more subordinate centered. **Boss-centered leadership** is autocratic, whereas **subordinate-centered leadership** is democratic. Any given situation will determine how much supervisory authority or subordinate freedom is appropriate.

An effective supervisor is readily able to determine how much subordinate participation is appropriate for each situation. Extensive participation is appropriate in some instances; little or no subordinate participation is appropriate in others.

FUNCTIONS OF SUPERVISION

What are the five functions of supervision?

Supervision involves five functions: planning, organizing, staffing, directing, and controlling.

 ## Planning

The amount of planning the supervisor's job involves is often directly related to the hierarchical level of his or her position. Higher level supervisors spend more time in the planning function than lower level supervisors. Furthermore, the plans developed by lower level supervisors are usually for a shorter duration than those developed by higher level supervisors. This is because the planning activities of the lower level supervisors frequently involve implementing the goals and objectives developed by higher level managers.

Supervisors are generally responsible for ensuring that their planning efforts are consistent with the organization's **mission statement** (reason for the organization's being) and **vision statement** (how the organization gets where it wants to go). In some instances, supervisors are responsible for developing both mission and vision statements for the operational areas for which they are responsible.

 ## Organizing

The organizing function involves determining which of the subordinates in the work unit are best qualified for a particular job and then assigning that job to the appropriate individuals. Consequently, organizing involves developing a staff system that facilitates the accomplishment of established plans, taking into consideration budgetary allocations for those plans. Another dimension of the organizing function is the development of an environment in which subordinates can be productive and efficient. Also, the supervisor is responsible for developing effective work processes and procedures.

What organizational principles have a role in the organizing function of supervision?

A number of the organizational principles presented in Chapter 2 are of paramount concern to the supervisor, including unity of command, span of control, chain of command, work assignment, and so on. Some of the documents the supervisor uses in the organizing function include job descriptions, job specifications, and the budget for his or her area of responsibility.

 ## Staffing

In some instances, the supervisor's staffing activities are quite extensive; in others, however, they are quite limited. Higher level supervisors frequently have considerable control over selecting new employees for their respective work units. Lower level supervisors, especially first-level supervisors, may not have as much control.

Other staffing activities of a supervisory nature involve orienting and training new employees and retraining, promoting, evaluating, and counseling all employees. Supervisors find their jobs easier when their subordinates are efficient and well trained. When they are not, supervisors will most likely have to be more concerned with the activities involved in the planning, organizing, directing, and controlling functions.

Directing

What is meant by the directing function?

Of the various responsibilities of supervisors, directing subordinates is likely the most demanding and time-consuming aspect of their jobs. Some of the activities involved in the directing function include leading, motivating, developing, and recognizing the efforts of subordinates. The directing function is concerned with the manner in which the supervisor relates to a subordinate on a person-to-person basis or to a group of subordinates on a person-to-group basis.

To maximize the directing efforts, a supervisor must not only be concerned with the goals and objectives of the organization, but also with how well the needs of each subordinate are related to the organization's goals and objectives. Although the activities in the directing function are important to lower level supervisors, they are generally not as important to higher level supervisors.

Controlling

Why is the controlling function necessary?

The controlling function involves comparing actual results with anticipated results. The activities in this function may consume a considerable portion of the supervisor's time, especially when actual results are less than what was anticipated. The supervisor is responsible for taking corrective action to remedy these situations.

Standards are used widely in the controlling process. The absence of standards against which to compare actual results diminishes the value of controlling efforts. The supervisor is also responsible for determining the validity of the standards that are used in the comparison process.

Control is generally thought to be a multifaceted process that begins with the establishment of standards (step 1). Subsequently, performance is measured (step 2) against the expectations (stated as standards), which facilitates the detection of deviations (step 3). The causes of the deviation are analyzed (step 4), and corrective action is taken (step 5).

CHARACTERISTICS OF EFFECTIVE SUPERVISORS

Over the years, several characteristics of effective supervisors have been identified. The following is a discussion of five of these characteristics: getting others to cooperate, listening to others, delegating responsibilities, understanding subordinates, and treating others fairly.

Getting Others to Cooperate

One of the most important characteristics of effective supervisors is their ability to gain the cooperation of others. Supervisors find their jobs exceedingly more difficult when their subordinates are uncooperative.

How can a supervisor gain
subordinates'
cooperation?

An effective way to gain subordinates' cooperation is to make them aware that higher level management is dependent on them for their ideas, suggestions, and productivity. In many instances, the employees who work most closely with a given work procedure are able to provide valuable contributions when changes have to be made. Management's acceptance of their ideas generally produces greater subordinate cooperation.

When employees are able to see rather quickly that their ideas are accepted and used, their cooperation is likely to increase. Accepting but not using employees' ideas may be more destructive in the long run than if their ideas and suggestions were not accepted in the first place.

Supervisors can also gain cooperation by providing as much variety as possible in the daily routine. Subordinates tend to become rather complacent and soon lose interest when their jobs lack variety.

The inability of a supervisor to justify the existence of certain policies and procedures also has a destructive impact on employee cooperation. An effective supervisor is able to answer subordinates' questions; if the answer is not known, the supervisor should make every attempt to obtain it. Much cooperation is lost by telling subordinates that something "has to be done a certain way because that is the way it has always been done." Providing subordinates with a rationale is generally much more effective.

Listening to Others

Why is listening to
subordinates important?

Another characteristic of a good supervisor is the willingness to listen to subordinates. Some supervisors have difficulty hearing out their subordinates, especially those for whom negative feelings exist. But unless subordinates are convinced their supervisors are willing to listen, the development of an effective interpersonal relationship may be difficult.

  Some supervisors are guilty of not listening to a subordinate who wishes to discuss a situation, which produces disagreement between the supervisor and the subordinate. The supervisor gives the impression that the subordinate is not in a position to question or discuss the incident, an attitude that often accompanies the autocratic approach. Another fault some supervisors have is making decisions or judgments about a situation even before the subordinate has finished talking. Such a habit reflects negatively on the supervisor because the subordinate is likely to get the impression that the supervisor has little concern for him or her or his or her ideas.

   Another undesirable listening habit of some supervisors is the injection of their comments or feelings about the situation before they are aware of all the relevant facts. The supervisor who does this is likely to "force" the subordinate to have the same beliefs as he or she does.

Listening to a subordinate is not enough. The supervisor also must pay attention to or concentrate on what the subordinate has to say. Although the supervisor may have difficulty concentrating totally on what the subordinate is saying, concentration is a crucial component of the listening process as is the emotional content of the message.

The mark of a good listener is the ability to hear what the subordinate is actually saying—and not just what the supervisor wants to hear. Supervisors who hear only what they want to hear cannot be completely objective when having to make decisions.

Active listening is generally much more effective than passive listening. Active listening requires being tuned in not only to the message being communicated but also to the feelings being communicated. It also involves responding to what the communicator is really saying, which is perhaps cloaked as a hidden message.

Delegating Responsibilities

One of the most important characteristics of good supervisors is their ability to delegate meaningful tasks to subordinates. Unless supervisors make use of delegation, they either have to do much of the work themselves or they have to depend on others to assume the responsibility for undertaking a number of their tasks. Effective delegation helps extend the supervisors' capabilities, encourages teamwork, and results in higher productivity. When delegating, the supervisor must remember the need for commensurate authority and responsibility, an important organizational principle. To make a subordinate responsible for a certain task without giving him or her the necessary authority to carry it out is counterproductive.

What guidelines enhance the effectiveness of the delegation process?

Some supervisors are hesitant to delegate, either because they do not know how to delegate effectively or because they are afraid to delegate. Supervisors are sometimes reluctant to delegate for one or more of the following reasons: (1) they believe they can perform certain tasks more effectively than those to whom they might delegate; (2) they find that it is easier to perform the tasks themselves than to teach someone else; or (3) they want the tasks done their way, which might be different from the way the subordinates might choose to do them.

The effectiveness of the delegation process can be enhanced by adhering to the following guidelines:

1. *Select the appropriate person to perform the task to be delegated.* Because all subordinates are not equally able to perform the tasks with the same level of quality, the supervisor needs to be selective in making assignments. Much of one's success in delegating can be attributed to choosing the appropriate person for each task.

2. *Select tasks that can be delegated.* A good supervisor is selective in delegating tasks. Although some tasks cannot be delegated, others should be selectively delegated. Generally, those tasks that can be delegated are routine in nature, they may involve minimal amounts of judgment, and the task steps can be easily identified. In addition to selecting the tasks to be delegated, the effective supervisor will also carefully assess the need to set any limits or restrictions on the subordinate in carrying out the delegated task.

3. *Help the person to whom tasks have been delegated.* Effective supervisors help subordinates to whom they delegate tasks. Some supervisors have the mistaken notion that if a subordinate is qualified to undertake a task, no assistance or help should be needed, which is consistent with the laissez-faire approach. Therefore, the subordinate is left alone to do the assigned tasks. Most subordinates are able to do many tasks without supervisory help, but help should be available when needed.

4. *Make sure that work assignments are fully understood.* An effective supervisor is patient with subordinates who have been delegated a task for the first time. Even though subordinates may think they fully understand their assignment, questions often arise once they begin. Once the subordinate begins the task, the supervisor may decide to stay in fairly close communication with him or her, especially when the subordinate is undertaking the task for the first time.

A supervisor who delegates tasks to subordinates is usually held responsible for task completion. Subordinates to whom tasks are assigned should have commensurate authority and responsibility to ensure task completion.

In delegating tasks to subordinates, many supervisors have difficulty accepting the fact that there is often more than one desirable or effective way to do a particular task. No matter how much a supervisor would like to have a subordinate do a task his or her way, the interpersonal relationship may be jeopardized if the supervisor requires the subordinate to follow certain procedures when others are just as effective.

Understanding Subordinates

How can supervisors develop a better understanding of their subordinates?

Because the supervisor is responsible for motivating subordinates, a thorough understanding of their needs, drives, interests, and attitudes is important. Without this background knowledge, a supervisor may have difficulty inspiring each subordinate to perform to the best of his or her ability.

 Familiarity with several aspects of each subordinate's background is desirable, including the following:

1. *Ability to think.* To understand a subordinate fully, the supervisor must be aware of the subordinate's thinking capability. The ability to sort the important from the unimportant and to organize important thoughts in a logical way is also helpful.

2. *Social traits.* For a supervisor to understand subordinates fully, an awareness of the social traits of each subordinate is needed. The supervisor needs to know which subordinates have a tendency to become aggressive, withdraw, dominate the situation, and put others at ease.

With what areas of a subordinate's background should a supervisor be familiar?

3. *Personality traits.* To have an effective working relationship with subordinates, the supervisor should have a fairly comprehensive understanding of each subordinate's personality. Without this knowledge, a supervisor has difficulty knowing how to respond to or how to supervise subordinates. An understanding of personality traits can also be used to assess the emotional needs of subordinates.

4. *Character.* Also needed is an awareness of each subordinate's character; otherwise, the supervisor can only guess at the degree to which subordinates can be trusted. Because all subordinates do not have the same amount of integrity, the supervisor may have to place greater trust in some subordinates than in others.

5. *Work habits.* Supervisors also need a knowledge of subordinates' work habits, including an awareness of who is a self-starter, who needs some direction, and who needs considerable direction. Work habits of subordinates are a significant determinant of the degree of supervision they require.

6. *Relations with others.* To understand subordinates, the supervisor must be aware of how they relate to others. This understanding is important in deciding which subordinates are able to work together on a given project, which subordinates have good public relations skills, and so forth.

Supervisors who know and understand their subordinates well can assign them tasks they are sure to enjoy. Happy, satisfied subordinates make the supervisor's job much easier. The supervisor is able to respond more effectively to the needs of subordinates when he or she is more knowledgeable about them and understands them better.

Treating Others Fairly

The last characteristic of effective supervisors to be discussed in this chapter is the fair treatment of others. The relationships between many supervisors and their subordinates have been damaged because of a lack of fairness on the part of the supervisor. A perceived lack of fairness is often as damaging to the relationship as is a real lack of fairness.

When personal feelings about subordinates sway the making of decisions, supervisors often have difficulty treating their subordinates fairly. Those individuals for whom the supervisor has strong positive feelings are likely to receive favored treatment, but those about whom the supervisor feels negatively are likely to be treated unfairly.

Effective supervisors treat all subordinates in a consistent manner in similar situations. Policies that exist for one subordinate should exist for all subordinates.

In some instances, when a subordinate is involved in a situation of a serious nature, the immediate supervisor perhaps should not be the only superior involved in deciding upon an appropriate course of action. For example, if a subordinate's conduct or actions are serious enough that dismissal is a possibility, the final decision should be made in consultation with higher level individuals. The subordinate, therefore, cannot claim that the supervisor was unfair because of prior bias or negative feelings toward him or her.

Building Teams

Why is team building important?

Research findings clearly illustrate the value of building an effective teamwork attitude among employees. Included as benefits of team building are the following: (1) employees have greater control over their jobs; (2) it encourages individual creativity and the use of creativity in solving a variety of work-related problems; and (3) it gives employees the feeling that they play a more significant role in determining what happens in the organization.

When employees work together as integral members of a team, productivity increases, quality of work improves, and employees feel they play a more significant role within the organization. The end result is a happier, more satisfied workforce. The supervisor is responsible for building a teamwork attitude, either by teaching his or her subordinates how to become better team players or by arranging for others to provide work-team indoctrination. Once a work group is committed to the work-team attitude, the orientation/instruction does not end. Rather, the orientation/instruction continues virtually for the life of the work group. At some point, instruction will change its focus from "how to" to refinement of the team-building concept.

SPECIAL SKILLS OF SUPERVISORS

What special skills should supervisors possess?

In addition to possessing the characteristics discussed in the preceding section, supervisors need conceptual, human, and technical skills, as well as skills in teaching, coaching, counseling, and communicating. These skills are often developed through supervisory training experiences made available to new supervisors or to supervisors who need or desire refresher training.

Conceptual Skills

What is the nature of the conceptual skills needed by supervisors?

The possession of conceptual skills is critical to the supervisor's success. This vital attribute enables the supervisor to perceive quickly how one phenomenon may impact on another. Specifically, conceptual skills help the supervisor determine the full impact of a change or a variety of changes. Supervisors with well-developed conceptual skills are often able to avert or eliminate situations that may later develop into problems. Possessing conceptual skills is seen by some supervisors as a "fifth" sense in dealing with organizational matters. As supervisors move higher in the organizational hierarchy, their use of and need for well-developed conceptual skills increases.

Although conceptual skills are generally learned through experiences and the educational process, some are intuitive. Skills of an intuitive nature often enable the supervisor to make the correct decision simply because it seems to be the correct decision.

Human Skills

Why must a supervisor possess effective human skills?

Also critical to the supervisor's success are skills in working effectively with others, including subordinates, peers, and superiors. Without effective human skills, the supervisor is likely to alienate others with whom he or she must work. Once the working relationship is damaged, especially in dealing with subordinates, the supervisor will likely have difficulty maximizing the cooperation of subordinates, motivating them, or maintaining their loyalty. The use of effective human skills greatly diminishes the occurrence of such problems. Effective supervisors realize the importance of building a cooperative atmosphere among the individuals and groups with which they work.

An understanding of human skills will give the supervisor greater insight into working effectively with each subordinate in each situation. Because personalities and situations vary so much, the supervisor must be able to maintain the appropriate amount of closeness or distance for each given situation. Supervisors who remain distant in every situation or who tend to have close relationships with their subordinates soon find they are considered either uncooperative or they can be taken advantage of quite easily. In either case, the subordinates will likely lose respect for their supervisors.

Human skills can be learned either through on-the-job training or through courses designed to help individuals improve their supervisory skills. Some supervisors also complete college-level courses to acquire more effective skills in working with others.

The importance of human skills to supervisory success remains rather stable at all levels of the organizational hierarchy. Therefore, supervisors at the lower levels of the hierarchy and those at the upper level have comparable needs with regard to human skills.

Technical Skills

What determines the nature of the technical skills needed by a supervisor?

The possession of technical skills is often one of the most important criteria considered in selecting an individual for his or her first supervisory position. The supervisor needs technical skills to understand certain operations or tasks. As a person moves upward in the organizational hierarchy, however, the technical skills needed diminish somewhat.

The nature of technical skills the supervisor needs is determined by his or her areas of responsibility. The ever-increasing technological nature of office functions increases the technical skills needed by office supervisors. In fact, effective supervisors thoroughly and fully understand the tasks performed by those whom they supervise. Lacking technical competence is likely to reduce the amount of influence a supervisor has over his or her subordinates. Furthermore, a lack of technical competence increases the difficulty a supervisor has in assessing subordinate performance.

Technical skills are typically acquired by means of the various training techniques discussed in Chapter 8. Some training techniques, however, are better suited for the acquisition of technical skills than others.

Teaching Skills

Supervisors responsible for teaching or training subordinates need special teaching skills. Although most supervisors could probably teach subordinates without prior training in this area, a more effective job is likely to result when supervisors have been appropriately trained.

Two important elements of teaching in which a supervisor should be skilled are demonstrating and explaining. Supervisory teaching skills are effectively learned through college and university courses and through supervisory training experiences provided by the organization.

Coaching Skills

What types of coaching skills are needed by supervisors?

The ability to coach subordinates is another of the skills needed by effective supervisors. Coaching involves a concerted effort by the supervisor to develop a subordinate. The development process is concerned with the subordinate's job and the problems related to that job. The objective of coaching is to improve job skills and to increase the subordinate's understanding of the technical aspects of the job.

A distinct difference exists between on-the-job training and coaching. On-the-job training involves teaching subordinates about the techniques of job performance, but coaching is more comprehensive. As an example, coaching might involve helping a subordinate develop managerial skills, especially if these skills are needed by an employee about to be promoted to a managerial position.

Coaching skills are effectively learned through organization-sponsored supervisory training programs.

Counseling Skills

Over the years, supervisors have counseled subordinates in a variety of areas, some of which are generally considered to fall within the domain of the supervisor-subordinate relationship. Other areas are clearly outside the scope of the relationship.

Most supervisors do not have time to provide counseling in all the areas in which their subordinates experience problems. Although the supervisor must listen to some of the subordinates' problems to maintain an effective relationship, he or she must also use good judgment in selecting the areas in which to become involved.

Increasingly, **employee assistance programs (EAPs)** are being installed in larger organizations and some smaller organizations. The rationale behind this practice is that supervisors do not have the time or the qualifications to counsel subordinates in certain areas, such as substance abuse. EAPs are discussed in detail in Chapter 16.

What is the nondirective approach to counseling?

Several counseling techniques are used, ranging from a nondirective approach in which the subordinate does most of the talking, to a technique in which the supervisor is responsible for directing the process. What is appropriate for one individual and one set of circumstances may be totally inappropriate for another individual and another set of circumstances. Regarding the supervisor's responsibility for counseling skills, he or she will know which problems to deal with and which to refer to others who are better equipped to deal with them.

Counseling skills can be learned through college and university training as well as through organization-sponsored training programs.

Communication Skills

The effectiveness of the supervisor-subordinate relationship is heavily dependent on communication. Therefore, well-developed communication skills are needed if the supervisor-subordinate relationship is to be maximized. An effective supervisor is aware of the forces that impede the communication process, namely, the following:

What forces impede the communication process?

1. *Lack of knowledge or background information.* A lack of knowledge or background information on the part of the receiver or sender will impede the communication process. Absence of knowledge often results from lack of education, intelligence, awareness about, or exposure to the topic being discussed.

2. *Inappropriate vocabulary usage.* Not everyone has the same level of vocabulary understanding. To use words that are not understood by the receiver injects a barrier into the communication process.

3. *Presence of bias or prejudice.* Showing bias or prejudice is another force that impedes the communication process. A prejudiced comment leveled against an individual impedes effective communication.

4. *Impact of filtering.* As messages pass from one individual to another, the original intent of the message may become distorted or changed in meaning. This process is called *filtering.*

Effective communication, which depends so heavily on trust, also involves the ability to show empathy and concern for others. The communication between two individuals is often hampered because either or both empathy and concern are absent.

Another way the supervisor can make the communication process more effective is to avoid developing a defensive attitude. When an open, trusting relationship between the supervisor and subordinate exists, the supervisor may at times be criticized by the subordinate. The supervisor, by becoming defensive, will create a communication barrier.

What is the direct approach in counseling?

The supervisor can further strengthen the communication process by using a direct approach when it is appropriate and an indirect approach when it is appropriate. When dealing with a sensitive situation, the supervisor may wisely use an indirect approach when communicating with a subordinate.

Courses designed to help individuals develop effective communication skills are taught at colleges and universities as well as in supervisory training programs. Because most individuals spend considerable time each day communicating, they may believe they already possess effective communication skills. Although this may be true in certain instances, many supervisors can and do profit from formal training in the communication area.

As increasing numbers of employees are working off-site (free-lance employees, telecommuting employees, and employees who work in satellite offices, primarily), maintaining effective communication with them becomes especially crucial. It is important to guard against an "out-of-sight, out-of-mind attitude" toward those employees. Although the supervisor (in some cases known as a facilitator in these situations) will likely not have as much contact with these subordinates, he or she needs to keep abreast of the projects on which they are working, offer assistance when needed, refer the employees to others in the organization who may be able to provide assistance, and so forth. Generally, employees who work off-site will feel more a part of the team if they are invited to attend department meetings.

SUPERVISORY TRAINING

Because most individuals are promoted to supervisory positions from production-oriented jobs, many can profit from supervisory training experiences. Although most have the necessary technical competence, they need to be trained in other areas. A variety of techniques, many of which are discussed in Chapter 8, are used in training supervisors.

One of the most important factors in designing training programs for supervisors is determining the areas in which they need training. Largely, these areas are determined by the nature of the organization in which supervisors are employed and the duties they are expected to perform. Because supervisors do not all need training in the same areas, some discretion should be used in selecting appropriate experiences for each individual. Topics frequently covered include the following:

What topics are frequently covered in supervisory training programs?

1. Delegating work.
2. Disciplining employees.
3. Training employees.
4. Hiring, orienting, and promoting employees.
5. Handling grievances.
6. Scheduling work.
7. Designing effective work procedures.
8. Developing effective human relations skills.
9. Developing effective communication skills.
10. Developing effective counseling skills.
11. Acquiring a working knowledge of the important aspects of relevant federal and state legislation.

Some supervisory training programs are intensive and conducted over a short time. Others are less intensive and continue for a longer time. The effectiveness of the trainer often determines the success of the training program.

SPECIAL RESPONSIBILITIES OF SUPERVISORS

Supervisors often have a number of special responsibilities that are on the periphery of the direct supervision of their subordinates. In fact, some supervisors receive more recognition for the manner with which they perform these special responsibilities than they receive for how they perform their primary supervisory responsibilities.

Career Goal Planning

Why do supervisors need to become involved in their subordinates' career goal planning activities?

Employees who perceive that they are making progress in the attainment of their career goals are often more productive and satisfied than those lacking such a perception. Effective supervisors think of themselves as having an important responsibility in helping subordinates attain their career goals. For those subordinates without clear-cut career goals, the supervisor plays a vital role in helping them in their career-planning efforts. Supervisors who are perceived by their subordinates as an impediment to the attainment of important career goals most likely will not be able to maximize the development of an effective supervisor-subordinate relationship.

For those subordinates who have clear-cut goals, the supervisor often helps them (1) assess their strengths and weaknesses, (2) develop strategic plans to attain their goals, and (3) put their plans into action. For those individuals who lack clear-cut career goals, the supervisor can often enhance the satisfaction they derive from their jobs. By helping subordinates assess their strengths and weaknesses, the supervisor is able to identify possible areas of career interest. Therefore, supervisory familiarity with the specific characteristics of various careers is helpful. Once subordinates have identified their career goal preferences, the supervisor can help them develop strategic plans and then put the plans into action.

Ethical Behavior

How is ethical behavior among employees developed?

The supervisor can make a significant impact on how ethically his or her subordinates behave. The presence of unethical behavior may also indicate the presence of illegal behavior. For example, employee theft is illegal as well as unethical. Conversely, making personal long-distance telephone calls from an office telephone—in violation of company policy—is not illegal but is unethical. Basically, ethics are rules or codes of conduct.

Some employees will engage in unethical behavior when they believe that such behavior will not be detected. Other employees will avoid unethical behavior even when the chance of having this behavior detected is minimal to nonexistent. For most employees, as the opportunity for detection of unethical behavior increases, their willingness to engage in unethical behavior decreases.

One of the most effective ways to increase ethical behavior among employees is for managers and supervisors throughout the organization to display ethical behavior themselves through their actions and words. Thus, they become important role models. A manager who tells his or her subordinates that ethical behavior is important but then engages in unethical behavior is not likely to have a significant impact on stimulating his or her subordinates to behave more ethically.

Another effective way to increase the ethical behavior of employees is to implement a code of ethics by which all employees are expected to live—regardless of job title or hierarchical level. Depending on the situation and the employees, ethical behavior might also be included as a topic in employee training programs. In some organizations, an ethics review committee is formed to determine what constitutes ethical behavior in given situations. Because the supervisor is the link between the subordinate and the next higher level in the chain of command, the supervisor is a key player in determining the extent to which employees behave in an ethical manner. Finally, rewarding ethical behavior and taking punitive action against unethical behavior is also an effective way to promote ethical behavior among employees.

Tardiness

Over time, tardiness can be quite costly to an organization. The supervisor is responsible for determining the legitimacy of tardiness-producing situations over which subordinates have no control. Examples are traffic jams, automobile malfunctions, mass transportation delays, and the like.

How should a supervisor
deal with employee
tardiness?

The supervisor can deal in a variety of ways with the actions of employees that result in their being tardy. Most supervisors believe that as the problem becomes more severe, the discipline leveled against the employee should also become more harsh. Employees may first receive an oral or written reprimand. If this does not help, the next course of action may be a pay reduction. If the problem continues, the employee may be given a week's layoff without pay. Finally, the last course of action is to discharge the employee.

Some organizations have found that the best way to eliminate tardiness is to reward employees for being punctual. The reward system may be on an individual or group basis, such as a work unit or department. Examples of rewards are time off, monetary bonus, public recognition, faster promotion, and larger salary increases.

By setting a good example, supervisors themselves can do much to help eliminate employee tardiness. Requiring an employee to be punctual when the supervisor is not punctual is difficult to justify.

The organization's cost of tardiness can be easily calculated. Assume that the employees in a given work unit were tardy 480 minutes for a month. If a standard eight-hour workday (480 minutes) exists, the equivalent of one employee's workday is lost because of tardiness during the month. If the average yearly salary of the employees in the work unit is $20,000, $83.35 (the average daily salary) is lost in a month's time because of employee tardiness ($20,000/12 = a monthly salary of $1,667 or a daily salary of $83.35).

To help control absenteeism, tardiness rates should be monitored by calculating a monthly tardiness ratio. Assuming that fifteen employees were tardy 480 minutes in a month's time, the average employee tardiness rate is 32 minutes (480/15). Tracking this figure over several months enables the supervisor to determine when tardiness is becoming a significant problem. Tardiness rates among various work units can also be compared.

Absenteeism

The employee absenteeism rate is a concern in many organizations. Absenteeism is costly not only in terms of salaries, but also in terms of lost productivity. The cost of absenteeism can reach up to $500 or more per employee per year.

In many instances, 10 to 20 percent of an organization's workforce is responsible for 75 to 80 percent of the absences. By paying particular attention to these percentages, the supervisor may be able to find more effective ways to control absenteeism.

Some absences are unavoidable, such as those caused by illness, job-related injuries, illness of a family member, and death of a family member or close friend. Although these situations create legitimate absences, some employees use them as excuses for being absent. Therefore, the supervisor must attempt to determine when an employee's stated reason for being absent is legitimate and when it is not.

A common reason for employee absenteeism is a lack of job satisfaction. Although the employee will generally offer some other reason for being absent, the real reason may be a lack of job interest. In such situations, the supervisor may take one of the following courses of action: determine ways in which the job can be made more interesting and challenging; determine whether the job requirements are considerably less than the employee is capable of performing; determine the reasons for the employee's taking the job in the first place, besides the need for money; and determine whether the working conditions are satisfactory.

How should a supervisor deal with employee absenteeism?

Supervisors can handle absenteeism in the same way that they handle tardiness. The following courses of action are frequently used in dealing with employees whose absenteeism is a problem: oral or written reprimand, pay deduction, temporary layoff, and discharge.

In many organizations, providing employees with personal days has considerably reduced absenteeism. In these organizations, employees are typically given two personal days per year. Some organizations require that the taking of personal days be approved several days in advance. Being able to plan for the employee's absence is less likely to be disruptive to the work process.

Organizations have experimented with the following ways to reward employees who have good attendance records:

What are some of the rewards used to recognize employees for good attendance?

1. Adding an extra day or two to an employee's yearly vacation time.
2. Giving an employee a monetary bonus.
3. Recognizing each employee who has a good attendance record.
4. Making available a "pool" in which an employee's chances of winning are increased each day the employee is at work.
5. Giving an employee higher salary increases and faster promotions.

How can the cost of employee absenteeism be calculated?

The cost of employee absenteeism can be calculated using the same process as that used for determining the cost of employee tardiness. Assume that a work unit is comprised of fifteen employees who have an absenteeism rate of twelve days per month. Using the same average daily salary figure of $83.35, the monthly cost to the organization is $1,000. If this average existed each month for a year's time, the cost to the organization is $12,000 ($1,000 × 12). If additional help is hired to compensate for this rate of absenteeism, an employee who earns a yearly salary of $20,000 will have to work 7.2 months ($12,000/ $1,667) to make up the work deficiency of the employees who are absent.

The monthly work unit absenteeism rate can be calculated by dividing the number of workdays employees were absent by the average number of employees in the work unit. This absenteeism average can then be compared with rates of the same work unit in other months or with the rates of other work units. Benchmark data are always useful in determining whether an absenteeism problem exists and, if so, how to deal with it.

Alcoholism and Drug Abuse

Another of the special responsibilities of many supervisors is the detection of employees who have a substance-abuse condition. In the past, many organizations discharged employees addicted to alcohol. Because of a growing awareness about alcoholism, increasing numbers of organizations have developed rather sophisticated programs designed to help their addicted employees. Most of these programs have been quite successful in helping employees once again become fully productive, wage-earning members of society. Important aspects of the organization's program are the following:

What are the important aspects of organizational alcoholism and drug-abuse programs?

1. Treatment of alcoholism as a health condition that requires medical attention.
2. Willingness to provide assistance to alcoholic employees.
3. Commitment to the employee as long as improvement is made and/or maintained.
4. Thorough communication of program elements to all employees.

Alcoholic employees cost American business and industry billions of dollars each year. Data compiled by the National Council on Alcoholism indicate that alcoholic employees are absent nearly three times more often than non-alcoholic employees. Job-related accident rates are two to four times higher for alcoholic employees. Off-the-job accident rates of alcoholic employees are four to six times higher, and accident and sickness benefits paid out are three times higher for alcoholic employees.

The National Council on Alcoholism has been helpful in getting alcoholism considered as a disease. Alcoholics are more readily accepted by society when their addiction is considered as a treatable disease instead of a personal weakness or character flaw. Being accepted by co-workers enables alcoholic employees to respond to treatment more quickly. The National Council on Alcoholism has also done an outstanding job of educating the general public about the abuses of alcoholism.

What is the nature of the supervisor's responsibilities in alcoholism programs?

Organizations that have installed programs to help alcoholics generally depend heavily on the supervisor, who is in an excellent position to detect the signs of alcoholism. Supervisors are given training to detect these signs, which include deteriorating job performance, withdrawal, increased tardiness, increased absenteeism, and so on. Because most supervisors are not in a position to help employees overcome alcoholism, the usual course of action is to refer them to the appropriate individuals, such as physicians or counselors.

The recovery rate of alcoholic employees is approximately 50 to 75 percent. With this level of success, one has difficulty trying to understand why executives in some organizations do not believe in the establishment of programs designed to help in the recovery process.

The use of drugs by employees is a fairly new problem for many organizations, which may partially explain the slowness with which organizations have developed recovery programs. On the other hand, most organizations have provided their employees with information about drug abuse. This information can be developed in-house or obtained from such agencies as the Bureau of Narcotics and Dangerous Drugs and the U.S. Public Health Service. In addition, many local police departments have narcotics divisions that make drug-abuse information readily available to organizations.

What is the nature of the supervisor's responsibilities in drug-abuse programs?

Supervisors in many organizations are responsible for detecting employees with a drug-addiction condition. The symptoms of drug abuse are typically not as noticeable as those for alcohol abuse. Some signs of drug abuse, although not foolproof, include frequent absenteeism, industrial accidents of an unexplained nature, long lunch breaks, the wearing of dark glasses to hide dilated pupils, and high pilferage rates. The supervisor must be especially careful not to accuse someone of drug addiction without the presence of substantial evidence. Supervisors who do so wrongly may be putting themselves and their employer in a precarious legal situation.

When evidence of drug addiction is found, the supervisor generally refers the individual to a professional capable of providing the needed assistance. Once the individual agrees to rehabilitation, most organizations will continue employment as long as rehabilitation progress continues.

Stress and Burnout

What is technostress?

As the personal lives of individuals become more hectic, they begin to experience increased levels of stress. More often than not, personal stress and job stress eventually become interrelated to the point that making distinctions between the two becomes difficult. Supervisory intervention may occasionally be needed. Among office employees, **technostress** (stress caused by the introduction of technology) may be more common than among their counterparts in many other areas of the organization.

Some of the more common causes of stress and burnout are having too much to do in too short a time, not having clearly defined goals, not being involved, not being challenged, and having personal problems.

The earlier the supervisor tries to help subordinates cope with stress, the less significant stress levels are likely to become. When stress becomes excessive, employees may need to seek professional assistance.

Among the ways that employees are able to cope with stress are the following:

1. Develop an appropriate attitude toward work and life in general.
2. Take an unpaid leave of absence as a means of "relaxing" and "regrouping."
3. Transfer to a less stressful position.
4. Join a therapy group.
5. Seek professional counseling.
6. Take advantage of opportunities for physical activity.
7. Take advantage of vacation time.

Burnout and stress are often related. When stress becomes excessive, employees may begin to experience burnout. Symptoms of burnout are lack of concern for the job, poor-quality work, failure to meet deadlines, frequent absenteeism and tardiness, frequent fatigue, hostile attitude, and negative feelings about work and life in general.

Sexual Harassment

What federal legislation protects against sexual harassment?

Supervisors also are responsible for avoiding the sexual harassment of their subordinates and for stressing that their subordinates avoid sexually harassing one another. Sexual harassment is most often seen in unwelcomed sexual advances, in requesting sexual favors (in exchange for a salary increase, a promotion, and so forth), and in dialogue of a sexual nature. Not only is sexual harassment illegal because it violates Title VII of the Civil Rights Act, but it also creates numerous interpersonal problems. The Civil Rights Act of 1991 allows punitive damages and emotional-distress awards for plaintiffs who win sexual-harassment lawsuits. The 1991 law also gives an individual the right to a jury trial for cases involving sexual harassment.

Supervisors are responsible for knowing what constitutes sexual harassment and for helping their subordinates become familiar with what constitutes sexual harassment. In addition to the implementation of an organizationwide policy that prohibits sexual harassment, proper education and/or training are two effective ways of dealing with the situation. Written policies regarding sexual harassment should be very clear in indicating that such behavior will not be tolerated by anyone, that harassed employees are encouraged to discuss the situation with their supervisor or some other designated employee, that the situation will be handled with confidentiality, and that harassed employees will be free from retaliation.

Several of the topics discussed in this section (especially subordinate abuse of alcohol and drugs), stress, and the residual of sexual harassment) can have a negative impact on the health and well-being of employees. In fact, some may develop health conditions that make them unable to perform their job duties. The 1993 **Family Medical Leave Act** mandates giving an employee up to twelve weeks of unpaid leave when having to deal with these conditions when the affected individual has accumulated at least 1,250 hours the previous twelve months with the same employeer.

Multicultural Issues

Organizations increasingly are becoming multicultural in terms of their workforce. As a result, supervisors—typically those who work on a daily basis with individuals of diverse cultures—are obligated to accept the diversity and to deal with it in a professional, responsible manner. Failure on the part of the supervisor to accept the diversity renders him or her less effective as a supervisor.

Some individuals of other cultures differ in fairly significant ways from the typical individual who grew up in mainstream American culture. Differences are likely to be found in various beliefs, attitudes, mores, work habits, ethics, and so forth. Not only must supervisors be tolerant of and sensitive to the differences, but also they need to work with their subordinates on accepting the differences. In some cases, getting others to accept the differences is as easy as creating greater awareness about the nature of the cultural differences. In other cases, the process is more difficult, with the supervisors having to help certain subordinates "deprogram" themselves to overcome longstanding biases, stereotyped notions, and attitudinal differences. When supervisors are able to get all their subordinates—regardless of their cultural background—to accept one another for who they are, they are dealing effectively with multicultural diversity.

How can a supervisor learn to deal with multicultural diversity?

Supervisors can learn to deal with multicultural diversity in a number of ways, including the following: attending seminars and workshops on multicultural diversity, engaging in self-study, enrolling in courses dealing with multicultural diversity, and discussing various multicultural issues with others. In most instances, supervisors take advantage of more than one of these alternatives.

DISCIPLINING EMPLOYEES

Subordinates do not always perform as expected or behave in acceptable ways; therefore, they may have to be disciplined, which is another common responsibility of the supervisor. Effectively done, disciplining a subordinate will not cause irreparable damage to the supervisor-subordinate relationship. Discipline should be seen as a teaching or enabling endeavor as well as a correcting endeavor.

The following characteristics are typical of an effective disciplinary program:

What characteristics do disciplinary processes possess?

1. It provides consistent enforcement of the organization's rules, policies, and procedures.
2. It requires that management prove guilt rather than requiring that the employee being disciplined prove innocence.
3. It provides an appeal and/or higher review process.
4. It has a specified list of penalties and/or sanctions for infractions, thus providing an element of consistency.
5. It allows the employee being disciplined to "earn" a clean record after a period of time.
6. It considers the special nuances of the situation for which an employee is being disciplined.

7. It encourages the implementation of the disciplinary process as soon as circumstances permit.

8. It matches the severity of the discipline with the severity of the situation.

9. It enables the employee to learn exactly what is required of him or her to prevent the situation from recurring.

10. The process is restricted to the problem at hand and does not involve itself with a variety of earlier problems for which disciplinary measures have or have not been taken.

11. A follow-up of the situation should be made at a specified time; and the supervisor needs to be sure he or she follows through as discussed during the interview.

Before a supervisor disciplines an employee, a thorough understanding of the situation is crucial. Discipline leveled against an employee who is unaware of the nature of the situation resulting in the need for discipline will be different from the discipline taken against an employee who is aware of the consequences of his or her actions prior to committing the offense.

An increasing number of organizations are incorporating disciplinary interviews into the employee discipline process. The use of interviews is primarily limited to the more serious situations and to recurrences of the same situation. Disciplinary interviews have the following fivefold purpose.

What are the purposes of disciplinary interviews?

1. To provide an appropriate environment in which to discuss the situation.

2. To give the supervisor and subordinate the opportunity to hear both sides of the situation.

3. To give the supervisor an opportunity to outline the nature of the disciplinary action that will be taken against the employee.

4. To provide formal, official documentation of the situation should later discharge become necessary.

5. To help teach the employee how to and why he or she should avoid repeating the situation in the future.

To help make the disciplinary interview more effective, the following suggestions are offered:

How can the disciplinary process be made more effective?

1. Prepare a written document that contains the supervisor's comments. Record the employee's comments made during the interview as well as the disciplinary action that is to be taken. Both the supervisor and employee should sign and date the document.

2. Remain unemotional and rational during the interview; don't attack or threaten the subordinate.

3. Conduct the interview in privacy so that neither party's comments can be overheard by others.

4. Discuss only the situation at hand.

5. Mention only relevant, objective facts.

6. Criticize the work, not the worker.

7. Offer growth opportunities.

8. Listen fully to the employee's side of the story.

Although disciplining subordinates involves a negative situation and is generally confrontational, the supervisor is in a position to make the best of a "bad" situation. To approach the situation with an indifferent attitude generally produces results that are less effective than they need to be.

TERMINATING EMPLOYEES

The employment of individuals is terminated for a variety of reasons, including inadequate performance, misconduct, inability to perform job duties, and job elimination. Generally, an organization will terminate an employee only after all other possible avenues have been tried. Among the alternative actions that might be tried before termination are: transferring the employee to another position, demoting the employee, making a leave of absence available to the employee, suspending the employee, retraining the employee, or giving the employee an opportunity to resign or take early retirement (if that is feasible). If the ultimate action is termination, the supervisor needs to exercise as much care—and perhaps even more care—as he or she exercises in hiring new employees.

Before a supervisor decides to recommend termination, he or she needs to understand the condition under which the employee was hired. Some employees have a written contract of employment, whereas others (namely, employees of federal, state, and local governments) are protected by civil service regulations. Still others are covered by collective bargaining agreements.

What is at-will hiring?

Another category of hiring is at-will, which means that the employee is hired to work for an indefinite length of time and that he or she has no employment rights specified in an employment contract, civil service regulations, or a collective bargaining agreement. In other words, the employee can quit at will, and the organization can terminate the employee at will. Employee handbooks, policy statements, and oral commitments at the time of hiring may constitute an implied contract. In the past, employees covered by contract, civil service regulations, or collective bargaining agreements had greater protection against termination than at-will employees. Because of significant abuse in terminating at-will employees, legislation and court decisions are now affecting this area. Extreme care has to be exercised in terminating employees who have something other than an at-will work arrangement.

Essentially, the at-will termination of employees has been replaced with just-cause termination, a process that necessitates undertaking alternative actions to avoid discharging the employee. Termination is seen as the only remaining viable alternative. The just-cause process requires upholding the following standards:

What standards must the just-cause termination process uphold?

1. The employee's termination involves a job-related or work-performance problem.
2. The employee is forewarned of the possible disciplinary consequences of his or her actions.
3. The organization's expectations and requirements of the employee are reasonable.
4. Before recommending dismissal, the supervisor makes a reasonable attempt to ascertain the extent to which the employee's performance is either satisfactory or unsatisfactory.
5. The employee is given ample opportunity to tell his or her view of the situation.
6. Any investigation that is undertaken is done so in an objective, unbiased, and fair manner.

7. The investigation provides ample evidence of wrongdoing or guilt to warrant dismissal.

8. The organization has treated similarly all other employees who are guilty of the same offense.

9. The penalty fits the offense, considering the employee's past record.

10. The penalty is carried out within a reasonable time.

If any of the standards is missing, the employee may be able to prove in a court that he or she was discharged for reasons other than just cause. When this happens, the organization may be confronted with a costly settlement.

Among the suggestions for improving the effectiveness of the termination process are the following:

What suggestions improve the effectiveness of the termination process?

1. *Use termination as the last and only remaining viable alternative.* If another alternative is available, its use should be considered.

2. *Have a written record of previous offenses, subsequent warnings, and disciplinary actions taken.* Increasingly, courts are requiring written evidence that the employee has had ample warning regarding his or her performance. The written records should also be signed by the employee as proof that he or she was made aware of the possible consequences of his or her actions. Recent court rulings also indicate the employee must be given the actual reason for termination.

3. *Follow precisely all organization-approved termination policies and procedures.* Failure to follow approved polices and procedures may result in a court's overturning the termination decision should the employee decide to file a lawsuit.

4. *Prepare a record of the termination conversation.* In some organizations, the termination conversation has to be witnessed by another employee. Even if a witness isn't required by organizational policy, having a witness present is an excellent decision. An alternative may be to have the actual termination carried out by the unit manager, with the employee's supervisor as a witness to the conversation. In other cases, the termination conversation is recorded, obviously with the employee's knowledge. Written notes of the conversation should also be prepared. Ultimately, a word-for-word transcript should be prepared from the recording.

5. *Provide new managers with information about employee termination during their orientation and training.* Ignorance about acceptable procedures for terminating employees is not a defensible excuse for making mistakes.

6. *Require that an upper-level manager or a representative of the personnel department be consulted before an employee is terminated.* An investigation of the situation may indicate that sufficient grounds for termination do not exist. Legal liability may be incurred if the termination process continues.

Because of the legalistic nature of termination and new court decisions, the organization's legal counsel should be consulted before making a termination. Most supervisors do not have time to keep abreast of recent developments in employee termination procedures.[1]

What are outplacement services?

Some organizations make **outplacement services** available to employees who are terminated. The objective of outplacement is to help individuals become reemployed as quickly and easily as possible, thus minimizing the amount of disruption in the employees' lives. Also, the more quickly a person is reemployed, the less likely he or she will continue to create a public relations problem for the organization. Consultants or consulting firms with specialization in providing outplacement are often used to provide the outplacement services.

Among some of the services provided by outplacement specialists are the following: counseling designed to help alleviate anger and frustration resulting from being terminated, coaching in how to find contacts who might be aware of suitable openings, preparing a suitable letter of application and résumé, preparing for the job interview, providing secretarial support, and advising on ways to handle salary negotiation. Because some individuals who are terminated decide to leave permanently the field in which they were working, interest assessment is another function provided by outplacement services. In some instances, arrangements for retraining may also be provided.

WORKING WITH A UNION

What are the important provisions of the labor agreement?

In addition to understanding the basic structure and functioning of unions, the administrative office manager needs to be familiar with the **labor agreement,** a document that contains the proposals accepted by both the organization's management and the union's management during the negotiation process. Although the content of labor agreements varies from situation to situation, the trend is to develop longer, more detailed agreements than in the past. The advantage of this is a decreased opportunity for misunderstandings, which likely reduces the number of grievances filed by employees against management. The labor agreement must also contain certain clauses required by the Taft-Hartley Act and the Fair Labor Standards Act.

Some of the more essential provisions of the labor agreement are discussed next.

Duration of Agreement

This section specifies the length of time the agreement is in force. Periods ranging from one to five years are common, with two- and three-year agreements being most common.

Union Security

This outlines the extent to which the union is responsible for the disciplinary control of its members. Also commonly included in this section is the identification of the type of union security found, including union shop, maintenance-of-membership shop, agency shop, and dues checkoff.

The **union shop** is the most common form of union security. This means the employee must be a member or become a member of the union within a specified time and pay dues. An individual who refuses to do so can have his or her employment terminated.

The **maintenance-of-membership shop** form of union security, which occurs only infrequently, requires that employees who voluntarily join a union must remain in good standing during the life of the agreement. Conversely, in the **agency shop** arrangement, although employees do not have to join the union, they have to pay dues because the union serves as their bargaining agent. The agency shop is often found in states with right-to-work laws that forbid mandatory union membership. **Dues checkoff** is a written agreement between the employer and the employee that allows the employer to withhold employees' union dues from their paychecks.

Management Prerogatives

What are management prerogatives?

The clause of the labor agreement that specifies the rights or prerogatives retained by management is known as the **management prerogative.** Generally, anything that is not contained in the labor agreement or restricted by law remains with the employer as a management prerogative.

Wages and Hours

Law requires that labor agreements contain a section on wages and hours. Included in this section are methods of payment, rates of pay, commissions, bonuses, and incentive pay plans. **Escalator clauses,** which provide for cost-of-living increases (commonly referred to as COLA), are also common in many labor agreements today. The Fair Labor Standards Act and the Taft-Hartley Act specify the nature of information about wages and hours that must be included in the agreement.

Promotion, Layoff, and Recall

Also commonly included in labor agreements are clauses about the promotion, layoff, and recall of members.

Discipline of Members

Situations for which employees may be disciplined, as well as the type of discipline that may be leveled for various rule infractions, are identified in labor agreements. Actions for which employees might be disciplined include intoxication, fighting, insubordination, dishonesty, and violation of company rules.

Grievances

What is a grievance?

Also outlined in most labor agreements are the procedures for filing a **grievance,** a process used when an employee charges the employer with unfair treatment. The clauses in the agreement should be carefully worded to avoid misinterpretation, which will subsequently reduce the number of grievances.

Perhaps the best way to deal with grievances is to make sure the conditions or circumstances that often give rise to the filing of grievances do not occur. However, if grievances are filed, the manner in which they are handled is likely to bear significantly on the cordiality of relations between the employer and employees. Even though the two parties carefully negotiated the agreement in good faith, grievances tend to be filed more often when employees believe they have been treated unfairly and inconsistently or when their rights as outlined in the agreement are violated. Generally, the more quickly complaints are resolved, the better.

Most well-developed labor agreements contain a section that outlines how grievances are to be handled. The procedures should be followed carefully and exactly to prevent the supervisor from becoming entangled in more problems with the union.

Strike Clauses

Some labor agreements contain clauses that prohibit striking or walking out by employees while the agreement is in force. Increasingly, unions are becoming reluctant to allow a no-strike clause to be included in a labor agreement because of the possibility of its being sued in the event of a wildcat strike.

IMPLICATIONS FOR THE ADMINISTRATIVE OFFICE MANAGER

One of the most common duties of administrative office managers is their supervisory responsibilities. The number of individuals for whom managers are responsible varies quite extensively from organization to organization.

The quality of managers' supervisory ability often affects the success of their goal-achievement efforts. Employees who respect their supervisors are generally willing to put forth more effort to achieve organizational goals than are those who have little or no respect for their supervisors.

The amount of natural supervisory talent present in administrative office managers is quite variable. While some perform excellently with little or no training, others need extensive training. In most organizations, the value put on training new supervisors is reflected in the number of supervisory training experiences that are offered.

In addition to the value of participating in a variety of training opportunities, many administrative office managers also stress the value of work experience in becoming a more effective supervisor. The more extensive their supervisory experiences, the more likely they are to develop their own personal supervisory styles.

Supervisors soon learn that the strategies they use have to be adaptable. The techniques they use in a situation one day may not be equally effective in a similar situation at another time. Much supervisory success depends on properly assessing the situation variables and then selecting the appropriate strategies for the situation.

NOTE

1. A portion of the material in the "Disciplining Employees" section and most of the material in the "Terminating Employees" section of this chapter was adapted from Zane K. Quible, *How to Select and Retain Valuable Employees* (Trevose, PA: Administrative Management Society, 1985).

REVIEW QUESTIONS

1. How do autocratic, democratic, and laissez-faire leadership styles differ from one another?

2. How do achievement-oriented supervisors and subordinate-centered supervisors differ from each other?

3. How do boss-centered leaders and subordinate-centered leaders differ from each other?

4. What is the nature of the supervisory duties in the directing function?

5. How might a supervisor gain the cooperation of subordinates?

6. How do on-the-job training and coaching differ from one another?

7. What is meant by conceptual skills, an attribute possessed by effective supervisors?

8. What kinds of topics are frequently involved in supervisory training programs?

9. What is the nature of the supervisor's responsibility for employee absenteeism and tardiness and for alcoholism and drug-abuse detection?

10. What are the differences between at-will and just-cause termination?

11. What suggestions can you offer to help a supervisor improve the effectiveness of the disciplinary process?

DISCUSSION QUESTIONS

1. Ann, an employee you supervise, has continually been among the very best subordinates with whom you have ever worked. During the last six weeks or so, you have noticed that she has become rather complacent, her work is not up to par, she is no longer outgoing, and she seems easily irritated. When you asked her one day if something was bothering her, she replied, "It's

none of your business." Because you have had such a good working relationship with Ann, you were quite surprised at her response. Although you want to help if you can, you do not want to use the same approach with her again. What different approach might you take this time?

2. Bill and Tom, two of the employees you supervise, have become close friends. You were upset this morning when Bill told you in confidence that he thinks Tom has a drinking problem. In fact, he indicated that Tom drinks a six-pack or two every evening. Although you have not noticed that Tom's work performance is affected, you would like to "nip this is the bud" before his drinking does become a problem. Outline what you plan to do with this situation.

3. Your assistant, Jim, and a secretary in your department, Mary, have been spending an increasing amount of time "in conversation" lately. They take their breaks together now—and usually without the company of others. You have become suspicious that this may be an "affair in the making," which concerns you because both are married with families. You became particularly distressed when you walked by Jim's office and saw them embracing each other. They apparently thought the door was closed, but it was open approximately one-half inch. What do you plan to do?

STUDENT PROJECTS AND ACTIVITIES

1. Discuss with an office supervisor the techniques he or she uses to get employees to cooperate with one another and with the supervisor.

2. Discuss with an office supervisor the nature of his or her experiences (other than education) that have been invaluable in acquiring the necessary skills to be an effective supervisor.

3. Going Online: Using the Internet, conduct an online search based on one of the concepts presented in this chapter or based on one of the chapter terms. Is the information you found consistent with your knowledge of that topic before your Internet search?

Minicase

Millicent Johnson is an office supervisor at the Douthit Corporation. She was appointed to this position five years ago after having worked for fifteen years in a variety of secretarial positions in the company. Unfortunately, Mrs. Johnson's supervisory performance is not as outstanding as her performance as a secretary. She is frequently rushed, often fails to meet deadlines, and seems to be overworked. Some of her subordinates volunteer to help her do certain assignments when they are available, but

she usually declines their offer because she believes she should do these tasks herself. Mrs. Johnson is a perfectionist who believes that these projects will be done correctly only if she does them herself.

1. What characteristic of good supervision is Mrs. Johnson lacking in this situation?
2. What suggestions can you provide to help her overcome this weakness?

Case

David Brock is the new administrative office manager at the Prime Insurance Company located in Philadelphia. His predecessor, Sam Worthington, was fired when he failed to comply with certain management directives. Specifically, he was asked to be stricter in supervising his subordinates so they would more fully comply with certain policies. In addition, management was greatly concerned about the con-

tinuing deterioration of the unit's productivity during Worthington's tenure and had even established certain productivity goals for his unit that were never met. Worthington's subordinates did not especially care for him as a person, but they did appreciate his letting them "do their own thing."

When Brock was interviewed for the position, he was intrigued by the challenges this situation would provide him; therefore, when a job offer was extended, he readily accepted it. Now he is beginning to have second thoughts about the wisdom of his decision.

Brock's first day on the job was a frustrating experience. He met with all of his subordinates in small groups of five or fewer employees. During these sessions, he outlined the nature of his expectations and discussed the changes he planned to implement. More than half of these small groups bluntly told him that most of the changes he planned would not work. When he questioned these groups about the reasons for their beliefs, they indicated that the employees simply would not cooperate enough to make the changes work. There is now evidence of a conspiracy to undermine Brock's authority since his first day on the job.

1. How can Brock go about eliciting subordinate cooperation in this department?

2. If he had an opportunity to relive his first day on the job, what changes might he have made in his approach?

3. Discuss ways that Brock might deal with the conspiracy against him.

$\mathcal{C}$hapter 10

MOTIVATING OFFICE EMPLOYEES

$\mathcal{C}$hapter $\mathcal{A}$ims

After studying this chapter, you should be able to design an effective employee motivation program.

$\mathcal{C}$hapter $\mathcal{O}$utline

$\mathcal{C}$hapter $\mathcal{T}$erms

*A*dministrative office managers have an important responsibility for motivating the employees for whom they are directly responsible and to facilitate the motivation of those for whom they are indirectly responsible. The motivation of employees is maximized when they are able to use their abilities and realize their potentials to the fullest extent possible. Ultimately, motivation stimulates employees to perform more effectively than they otherwise would. Generally, motivated employees perform more effectively because they want to and not necessarily because they believe they are forced to perform more effectively.

Employees who lack motivation cost organizations millions of dollars each year. They tend to be absent and tardy more frequently than their motivated counterparts. Furthermore, their turnover rates are likely to be higher, they are less productive, their work is of poorer quality, and they are less loyal to the organization. In addition, they are likely to derive less satisfaction from their jobs, and they are more difficult to supervise than their motivated counterparts.

Several basic human traits that affect motivation are discussed in this chapter, as are several popular theories of motivation. Also included is a discussion of the nature of changes in values that affect employee motivation.

BASIC HUMAN TRAITS

A number of basic human traits affect employees' job-related behavior and performance. Among these traits are ability, aptitude, perceptions, self-concept, values, interests, emotions, needs, and personality.

Ability

What is ability?

Varying considerably from person to person, employees' abilities determine how capable they are of carrying out their jobs. The amount of **ability** employees use in their jobs is affected in part by how highly motivated they are.

To help individuals fully realize their potential, the administrative office manager needs an accurate assessment or understanding of the amount of ability each subordinate has. When this information cannot be gained by any other means, one or more of several tests can be administered. A common type of test that measures an employee's ability to input data using a keyboard is to give him or her a test that involves inputting data of the same type he or she will input as part of the job. The accuracy and speed with which the data were input can be easily calculated.

Aptitude

What is aptitude?

The extent to which employees are motivated is also affected by their **aptitude,** which is a measure of their potential. Employees whose job duties are not closely matched with their aptitudes are often more difficult to motivate, which produces a situation that is detrimental to both the employees and their employer.

Perceptions

Employees bring their own views of the world to the workplace. These **perceptions,** which are influenced by the employees' personal experiences, affect their motivation.

Self-Concept

An employee's **self-concept** is basically shaped by his or her perception of self. The better one's self-concept is, the more motivated the person is likely to be.

Employees who perceive themselves to be high performers are generally willing to accept new responsibilities.

Values

Employees' **values** affect their behavior as well as their level of motivation on the job. Values are significantly influenced by the environment in which employees live and work. During the last few years, several changes have occurred in the perceived importance that employees attach to certain values. These changes are discussed in greater detail in another section of this chapter.

Interests

Individual **interests** vary significantly from person to person. Some employees lack motivation because they are not interested in their jobs. Perhaps the best way to eliminate motivation problems resulting from a lack of employee interest is to match the employee's qualifications with the requirements of his or her job. Careful screening of individuals during the hiring and promotion processes generally helps minimize the amount of mismatching.

Emotions

Employees' **emotions** or feelings affect much of what they do or say at any given moment. The way supervisors deal with employees' emotions and feelings may significantly affect their motivation level.

Needs

In what ways do employees' needs affect the motivation process?

Employees' **needs** also affect their motivation because their goals often originate from unsatisfied or unmet needs. Motivation provides employees with the "fuel" they need to attain their goals. The motivation of an employee to achieve a goal is related to (1) the importance of the goal to the individual and (2) the extent to which the need has not been met. Therefore, motivation is higher when the goal is important to the employee and when the need is largely unfilled.

Personality

Employees' basic **personality** characteristics also affect their motivation. Some of the important personality characteristics are the introverted or extroverted nature of employees, their aggressive or passive nature, whether they are tolerant or impatient, and whether they are cooperative or uncooperative.

Each of the basic human traits affects the behavior of employees as well as their level of motivation. The more familiar a supervisor is with the basic traits of each subordinate, the more effective the superior-subordinate relationship will be. Supervisors who are familiar with their subordinates' traits will also find the task of motivating them less challenging.

MOTIVATIONAL PROCESS

What impact does disequilibrium have on the motivation process?

A model of the motivational process is illustrated in Figure 10–1. The model indicates that a person's behavior is a response to **stimuli** associated with an inner state of **disequilibrium** resulting from a need, desire, or expectancy. The disequilibrium state, which is accompanied by anticipation, produces behavior or actions directed toward goal attainment. The individual anticipates that

Figure 10–1 *Motivation model.* Source: M. D. Dunnette and W. K. Kirchner, *Psychology Applied to Industry,* © 1965, p. 125. Reprinted by permission of Prentice-Hall, Inc., Englewood Cliffs, NJ.

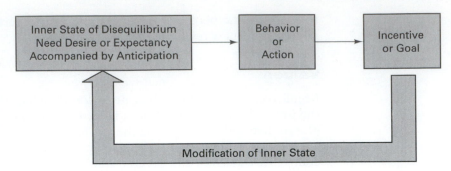

goal achievement will be a satisfying experience and that a state of **equilibrium** will be restored. Therefore, goal achievement results in the modification of the individual's inner state.

THEORIES OF MOTIVATION

Administrative office managers who understand various theories of motivation will be able to work more effectively with their subordinates than their counterparts. Most administrative office managers likely use various aspects of several of these theories in motivating their subordinates. Too, the techniques that work well in motivating one employee may not work as well in motivating another.

Hierarchy of Needs Theory

Human behavior is influenced by an individual's desire to have his or her needs fulfilled. Supervisors or managers who fail to realize this psychological fact often find their employees' behavior puzzling or bewildering. The supervisory process is more enjoyable and rewarding when supervisors clearly understand the needs of each of their subordinates.

Several schemes for classifying human needs have been developed over the years. One of the most widely used is the **hierarchy of needs theory** developed by the late A. H. Maslow.

What are the levels of needs in the hierarchy of needs theory?

Human needs, according to Maslow, exist at five basic levels. The categories are in a hierarchical order; therefore, the higher level needs are not important to the motivation process until most of the lower level needs have been satisfied. As a need becomes either mostly or totally satisfied, it no longer influences behavior, a term that Maslow called the *prepotency of the need.*

Maslow's model specifies the following categories of needs:

1. Physiological needs
2. Safety needs
3. Belonging and love needs
4. Esteem needs
5. Self-actualization needs[1]

According to Maslow, until an individual's physiological and safety needs are satisfied, his or her belonging and love needs are not important nor are esteem and self-actualization needs. The primary needs (physiological and safety) are important for survival. The secondary needs (belonging and love, esteem, and self-actualization) help individuals improve the quality of their lives.

What is involved in
physiological needs?

Physiological Needs. For humans to survive, their physiological needs must be satisfied. Included in this category are such needs as food, water, oxygen, rest, muscular activity, and freedom from extreme temperatures. Because these needs are basic or primary, higher level needs are not important until the lower level needs are mostly satisfied. For most individuals in an industrialized society, physiological needs are fairly well satisfied. Employees' salaries and wages assist them in satisfying some of these needs.

Safety Needs. After one's physiological needs are satisfied, the safety needs, which include both physical and psychological elements, become important. The safety needs of a physical nature include such items as clothing, shelter, and freedom from physical danger. Like the physiological needs, safety needs of a physical nature can be at least minimally satisfied by the salaries or wages employees receive.

What is the nature of
safety needs?

The safety needs of a psychological nature include job security and a wide variety of fringe benefits. Supplemental unemployment benefits, retirement benefits, and disability pay provide financial and emotional security, so they are classified as safety needs. The absence of these benefits may result in significant psychological insecurity.

Jobs and the environments in which they are performed satisfy the safety needs for many employees as they become quite secure in their positions. Uncertainty is created when jobs are changed or when the environment in which the jobs are performed is changed. Because many employees resist change, managers and supervisors must often help employees adjust to new situations.

Belonging and Love Needs. Once the physiological and safety needs are satisfied, belonging and love needs become important. Included in this category are the need for belonging to a group, the need for companionship, the need for love or affection, and the need for socializing.

More than ever before, employees view the environment in which they work as an important means of satisfying these needs, especially their socializing needs. When barriers within the working environment prevent the satisfaction of these needs, people tend to react by becoming frustrated.

The manager or supervisor who believes that employees must use their nonworking environments to satisfy all of their belonging needs does not fully understand the important role the working environment plays in need satisfaction. Employees want to feel they are accepted by other members of their work group and by their supervisor. An understanding of supervisor-subordinate relations as well as an understanding of group relations is helpful to supervisors concerned about the belonging needs of their subordinates.

Although money is used to purchase the things that satisfy many of the physiological and safety needs, it cannot be used to purchase the things that satisfy belonging and love needs. Although physiological and safety needs can be satisfied by physical and tangible objects, the belonging and love needs are of a more intangible nature.

Esteem Needs. Once physiological, safety, and belonging and love needs are satisfied, esteem needs become important in the motivation process. Two types of esteem needs exist: self-esteem and esteem of others. Self-esteem needs include the desire for achievement, self-respect, confidence, and mastery. The esteem of others includes such needs as recognition, attention, prestige, and status. The self-esteem needs originate within the individual, whereas esteem of others requires the recognition and attention of others.

What are esteem needs?

When individuals believe their esteem needs are being satisfied, they have a feeling of worth, importance, and confidence. When these needs are not satisfied, however, employees are likely to feel dejected, incompetent, and useless. These feelings can ultimately lead to behavior of a neurotic or hostile nature.

Some of the most long-lasting, useful techniques for motivating employees capitalize on satisfying esteem needs. For example, some employees receive the recognition they desire by being promoted to a higher level position or from having the opportunity to participate in organizational decision making.

Self-Actualization Needs. The highest level needs in the hierarchy—self-actualization needs—are the most difficult level for a majority of employees to satisfy. Before self-actualization needs become important in the motivation process, the other needs in the hierarchy must be largely satisfied. Self-actualization refers to one's desire to achieve maximum potential—or to become what one is capable of becoming.

Many different situations thwart individuals in the satisfaction of their self-actualization needs. One common situation is the job itself. Another situation is the presence of a seniority system. In such instances, employees generally have to work their way through the ranks; and until individuals with the greatest amount of seniority either resign or retire, employees with less seniority are unable to reach their aspired levels. Another situation that thwarts some individuals is their aspiration for positions requiring greater ability than they have. These employees will never be able to satisfy fully their self-actualization needs.

Some employees find that although their jobs only minimally satisfy their self-actualization needs, aspects of their personal lives enable them to fulfill some of these needs. Success in one area (personal life, for example) most likely stimulates some employees to put forth more effort in other areas (work life, as an example).

Summary. Employee motivational programs based on Maslow's hierarchy of needs are more successful than are those that fail to consider the impact of human needs on motivation. A motivated employee—one whose needs are for the most part being satisfied—is likely to be a more productive employee.

Some of the lower level needs are satisfied largely through the acquisition of money that is used to purchase such objects as food, clothing, and shelter. Therefore, most employees work to earn money for use in satisfying their lower level needs. Money, on the other hand, cannot be used to satisfy the higher level needs in the hierarchy. These needs are primarily satisfied by the individual's relationship with others and by the degree to which he or she is successful in the organization.

Although some of the basic physiological functions occur without the individual's being motivated, most conscious behavior is motivated or caused. Managers, therefore, should stimulate employees to work toward successful task completion.

Whereas lower level needs pertain to the physical body, the higher level needs are related to the mind and spirit. And lower level needs are finite for the most part while higher level needs are essentially infinite.

The primary value of Maslow's theory appears to lie in the premise that the most effective way to motivate employees is to appeal to their needs. Therefore, a supervisor who focuses on individual needs is often more successful in motivating employees to perform at desired levels than is a supervisor who ignores individual needs.

What are self-actualization needs?

What are the differences between lower and higher level needs?

Motivation-Hygiene Theory

A well-known study of employee job satisfaction, conducted by Frederick Herzberg, involved interviewing two hundred engineers and accountants in nine different companies in several different geographical locations. The outgrowth of this study is the **motivation-hygiene theory** developed by Herzberg and his associates.[2]

Interviews were conducted to determine which job aspects satisfied and which ones dissatisfied the study participants. The respondents were asked to identify those critical incidents about their work that caused them to feel exceptionally good or exceptionally bad. The researchers also probed into the reasons that caused these feelings.

With what are the job aspects that employees feel good about associated?

The research conducted by Herzberg and his colleagues found that job experiences that produced *positive attitudes* were associated with the *content* of the job. Conversely, the job experiences producing *negative attitudes* were associated with the *environment* in which the employees performed their jobs. They also found that experiences leading to *positive attitudes* were related to the *psychological needs* of employees but that experiences leading to *negative attitudes* were related to the *basic needs* of employees. Herzberg labeled those experiences leading to positive attitudes as **job satisfiers** or *motivators*. The experiences leading to negative attitudes are labeled as **job dissatisfiers** or *hygiene factors*.

Motivators. Among the factors responsible for producing positive attitudes or job satisfaction are the following:

What are Herzberg's motivators?

1. *Achievement.* Opportunity for task completion, for seeing results of effort, and for solving problems independently.
2. *Recognition.* Positive acknowledgment of task completion and individual achievement.
3. *Work itself.* Tasks that a job comprises.
4. *Responsibility.* Opportunity to be accountable and responsible for task completion and for individual performance and for being able to decide how and when tasks are to be completed.
5. *Advancement.* Advancement or promotion to higher level job or position.
6. *Growth.* Opportunity for growth and for new experiences.

Hygiene Factors. Although the motivators (satisfiers) are concerned with job content, the hygiene factors (dissatisfiers) are concerned with the environment in which the job is performed. The hygiene factors include the following:

What are Herzberg's hygiene factors?

1. *Company policy and administration.* Effectiveness of the organization and the way in which its policies are administered.
2. *Supervisors and relationships with supervisors.* Technological expertise of the supervisor as well as the fairness with which the supervisor deals with subordinates.
3. *Working conditions.* Environment of the place of work and the adequacy of equipment and supplies.
4. *Salary.* All types of compensation.[3]
5. *Interpersonal relations.* Relationship between an employee and his or her own peers.

6. *Personal life.* Impact that an individual's personal life may have on job performance and vice versa.

7. *Relationship with subordinates.* The success with which the supervisor relates to subordinates.

8. *Status.* Amount of status the job provides.

9. *Security.* Amount of security provided by the job.

An illustration of Herzberg's motivation-hygiene theory is shown in Figure 10–2.

On the basis of his research, Herzberg concluded that the absence of various job conditions is dissatisfying to employees. When present, however, these job conditions do not act as significant employee motivators (or satisfiers). Conversely, another set of job conditions, when present, produces employee satisfaction (or motivation). The absence of such conditions does not result in employee dissatisfaction, however. Thus, according to Herzberg, the various motivators (satisfiers) and hygiene factors (dissatisfiers) are not opposite ends of a continuum, but rather the factors are separate and distinct. In other words, the opposite of employee satisfaction is not employee dissatisfaction.

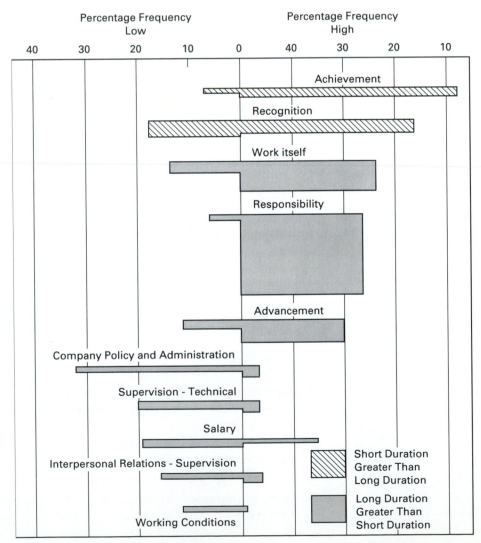

Figure 10–2
Motivation-hygiene theory.
Source: *The Motivation to Work,* by Herzberg, Mausner, & Snyderman © 1959. Reprinted by permission of John Wiley & Sons, Inc.

On what does Herzberg's theory have a major impact?

A major impact of Herzberg's theory focuses on the design of jobs. His theory supports the belief that jobs should be enriched by making work more meaningful and by providing greater opportunities for achievement, recognition, responsibility, and advancement.

Figure 10–3 presents a comparison of Maslow's hierarchy of needs model and Herzberg's motivation-hygiene model. An examination of the illustration reveals that various factors included in Maslow's hierarchy are the same factors that Herzberg has identified in his model.

Needs Theory

What are the characteristics of the needs theory?

David McClelland, who developed the **needs theory** of motivation, was more concerned with the secondary motives than with the primary motives of behavior.[4] He believed that the primary motives have a physiological base and are not acquired; therefore, a person's unconscious mind is a powerful determinant of his or her needs. The secondary motives, which are learned, have a powerful impact on one's behavior and are generally acquired from one's culture. According to McClelland, three secondary motives are of considerable importance: need for achievement, need for power, and need for affiliation.

Need for Achievement. Individuals with a high need for achievement willingly accept personal responsibility for their work and actions, and they have a strong desire for immediate feedback regarding the worth or value of their actions. Furthermore, they have a strong need to advance and to face head on those challenges that block their advancement. They also tend to be task oriented. Individuals with a high need for achievement often have difficulty

Figure 10-3 Comparison of the need-hierarchy and motivation-hygiene models. Source: Keith Davis, *Human Relations at Work*, 1972, McGraw-Hill Book Company. Reproduced by permission.

delegating authority or responsibility to others. Although these individuals thrive on challenges, they tend to set only moderate goals.

Need for Power. Individuals with a high need for power desire to control other people and have a strong influence on the behavior of others. Furthermore, they desire to be responsible for others. As a rule, individuals with a need for power seek out situations that are competitive and status oriented. Generally, they are more concerned about their self-image than about the quality of their task performance. Compared with those individuals who have a strong need for achievement, those with a strong need for power are higher risk takers.

Need for Affiliation. Individuals with a high need for affiliation tend to be socially interactive. Of great importance to them is the quality of their personal relationships, especially being liked by others. The quality of their relationships is more important than the quality of their task performance. Those with a high need for affiliation sometimes find decision making an unpleasant experience because of the priority they place on their relationships with others.

One way to maximize employee performance is to place individuals in positions that will allow them to have their needs fulfilled. To illustrate, an employee with a strong need for achievement will find greater satisfaction and consequently will likely perform better in a position that is task oriented. An employee with a strong desire for affiliation needs to be placed in a position that allows him or her to have considerable human interaction.

Various aspects of Maslow's, Herzberg's, and McClelland's theories are consistent with and support one another. For example, McClelland, Herzberg, and Maslow agree on the role that achievement plays in the motivation process. The individual need for advancement is also seen in various elements of the three theories.

Equity Theory

What are the
characteristics of the
equity theory?

According to the **equity theory,** motivation results from an individual's desire to reduce feelings of inequity that result when he or she finds (1) an imbalance in the ratio between his or her input and outcome or (2) an imbalance when comparing his or her input-outcome ratio with that of others. In either scenario, the input-outcome measure is known as a *reference ratio.* If the individual believes his or her input is greater than the outcome (represented by pay, promotion, and so on), a feeling of inequity will occur. The individual then becomes motivated to reduce input-outcome inequity. The strength of the employee's motivation is directly related to the magnitude of imbalance in his or her reference ratio.

Employees react to an imbalanced reference ratio in the following ways:

1. They alter their input level.
2. They alter their outcome expectation.
3. They change the base of their input-outcome comparison.

In summary, the two important components of the equity theory are assessment and adjustment. The employee first assesses his or her situation to determine whether or not internal balance is present. If not, then the employee seeks equilibrium by making an adjustment: He or she either increases the input level or decreases the outcome level.

Expectancy Theory

According to Victor Vroom,[5] the individual credited with developing the **expectancy theory,** the stronger the perceived relationship between effort and outcome, the higher employee motivation will be. If, for example, employees have reason to expect a good pay raise as a result of their hard work, they will be motivated to put forth the extra effort required to obtain the desired outcome.

According to the expectancy theory, employee motivation will occur when the following three conditions are present:

On what conditions is the expectancy theory based?

1. The employee believes that additional effort will be worthwhile.
2. The employee believes that higher performance will result in greater outcomes or rewards.
3. The employee places a high value on the outcomes or rewards.

Three important terms are associated with the expectancy theory:

Expectancy: This term refers to the employee's assessment that expending his or her effort will produce desired results. The greater the likelihood that expectancy occurs, the greater the amount of effort the employee will likely expend.

Valence: This term refers to how desirable the employee finds the outcome or the reward. Generally, the more desired the reward, the greater the amount of effort the employee will expend.

Instrumentality: This term refers to the desirability of a second-level outcome. Once a first-level outcome has been attained, the emergence or presence of a second-level outcome will cause the employee to continue to expend the necessary effort to achieve it. Essentially, instrumentality motivates employees to continue to push forward once a lower level goal has been accomplished.

Reinforcement Theory

Motivation is a function of the consequences of behavior, according to B. F. Skinner, who is credited with developing the **reinforcement theory.** Therefore, behavior that is reinforced tends to be repeated, whereas nonreinforced behavior tends not to be repeated.

What are the characteristics of the reinforcement theory?

A primary strategy of this theory is positive reinforcement, which is designed to increase the strength or frequency of desired behavior by positively reinforcing each occurrence of desired behavior. Reinforcement theory also uses negative reinforcement to increase the strength or frequency of desired behavior. Therefore, undesirable consequences that result from undesirable behavior tend to motivate employees to behave in a desirable manner. To illustrate, employees will improve the effectiveness of their performance to avoid being reprimanded by their supervisor.

The reinforcement theory uses two types of rewards:

Contingent reward is linked to (contingent upon) a specific incident of an employee's previous behavior. An example is rewarding an employee in some tangible way for completing a voluntary training program.

Noncontingent reward is not linked to (not contingent upon) a specific incident of an employee's behavior. An example is giving all employees (regardless of level of performance) paid holidays.

GOAL SETTING

Goals are an important component of the process of motivating employees. In fact, employees who are without goals often lack motivation; as a result, their productivity level is often substandard. Employees who have unmet goals tend to be motivated toward the fulfillment of those goals; however, the goals cease being motivational once they have been met.

Goals have several important attributes, including the following:

What are the important attributes of goals?

1. *Concreteness of goals.* A direct correlation exists between the concreteness of goals and the effort employees are willing to expend in their attainment. General goals usually have minimal impact on maximizing employee motivation. Goals that can be quantified are more powerful than those that cannot be quantified.

2. *Feedback on progress toward attainment of goals.* Employees who receive regular feedback—especially individuals who have a high need for achievement—are likely to be more highly motivated than are those who receive ineffective or minimal amounts of feedback. One of the characteristics of effective supervisors is providing subordinates with quality and timely feedback about their performance.

3. *Probability of succeeding in the attainment of goals.* The more feasible the attainment of a goal is, the more likely the employee will work toward its fulfillment. Goals with little probability of being attained result in the expenditure of little if any effort toward their attainment and may result in high levels of employee frustration. Just as overly difficult goals result in the expenditure of minimal effort, so do goals that are overly easy to attain.

4. *Participation in the setting of goals.* Employees who have an opportunity to participate in the setting of their goals are much more likely to work toward their attainment than are employees who have their goals thrust on them by their supervisor or higher level managers. Participation in goal setting increases employees' acceptance and understanding of their goals. Because employees differ from one another regarding the amount of participation in goal setting they desire, some will find this a more important attribute than others. Although employees can become largely responsible for the setting of goals, managers may sometimes need to intervene, especially when working with relatively inexperienced employees who have unrealistic expectations.

Why should employees participate in the setting of goals?

5. *Amount of dedication to the attainment of goals.* Employees who are dedicated to the attainment of goals are motivated to work harder toward their fulfillment than those who lack dedication. The amount of dedication employees have to the attainment of their goals is influenced by each of the four attributes presented previously, in addition to a host of personal characteristics. For example, an employee who plans to retire shortly is likely to be less dedicated to the attainment of a particular goal than is an employee just beginning his or her career.

ATTITUDE OF MANAGEMENT

Managerial attitude toward employees plays a significant role in employee motivation. Some managers or supervisors view employees simply as human robots whose sole function is to produce. The relationship between the supervisor and the subordinate is based primarily on units of input and output.

In most instances, the only human need that concerns these managers or supervisors is helping employees satisfy the need to be productive.

Other managers or supervisors use a paternalistic approach. These supervisors believe they know what programs, benefits, and so forth are best for their subordinates. As a result, employees have very little control over their welfare. This attitude also increases the difficulty some employees have in satisfying some of their needs.

Still other managers or supervisors use a noninvolvement approach. The belief is that managers should not be involved in helping employees satisfy their needs and that the employees themselves are responsible for the satisfaction of their higher level needs. Using this approach also prevents the full satisfaction of certain employee needs.

Managers and supervisors generally consider the humanistic approach the most appropriate. Managers and supervisors recognize that they can help employees satisfy certain needs, but other needs can only be satisfied by the employees themselves. This approach also recognizes individual differences among employees. Managers and subordinates work as a cooperative team in the satisfaction of employee needs.

CHANGING EMPLOYEE VALUES

Of all the dimensions of motivation, changes in employee values seem to be having the greatest impact on the motivational process. To illustrate, the following values were considered important by most employees as recently as the early 1970s:

What values are changing among employees?

1. Good salary.
2. High status.
3. Fast promotions.
4. Secure and stable job.
5. Strong organizational loyalty.
6. Close identification with work roles.

Employees who believed in the importance of these values were more loyal because the organizations for which they worked sponsored much of their training and skill development.

Today, organizations do not play as important a role in the training and skill development of their employees. The contemporary employee tends not to be as loyal as earlier employees because job knowledge and skills are often acquired independently of the organization.

Contemporary employees have a greater desire for:

What values do today's employees find important?

1. Having achievement recognized by the organization.
2. More leisure time.
3. Having rewards related to job performance.
4. Work that is challenging and worthwhile.
5. Participating in decisions about things that affect them.
6. Effective communication from management.
7. Job-related growth opportunities.
8. Increased job creativity.

Contemporary employees also have less concern for organizational loyalty.

When designing strategies and programs to enhance employee motivation, the administrative office manager should consider the new values that are important to the contemporary worker. What may have been motivational to employees fifteen to twenty years ago may no longer be as motivational. What is motivational to today's employees may not be motivational to employees twenty years from now.

EMPLOYEE MOTIVATION TECHNIQUES AND STRATEGIES

Several techniques and strategies are useful for motivating employees. Following is a brief description of several of these techniques or strategies. Included in Chapter 16 is a more thorough discussion of each technique or strategy. Their use can have a significant impact on increasing the productivity of office employees.

1. *Job enrichment:* Motivational strategy that enables employees to assume greater levels of responsibility for and control over their jobs while increasing their job-planning opportunities.
2. *Employee participation:* Management technique that gives employees an opportunity to participate in decisions that directly affect them.
3. *Management by objectives:* Program in which an employee and his or her supervisor jointly determine employee objectives that are to be achieved within a specified time.
4. *Flextime:* Strategy that enables employees to select the starting time of their workday.
5. *Incentives:* Motivational technique that rewards employees for increasing their productivity.
6. *Job sharing:* Management technique that allows two employees to share one position.
7. *Team building:* Strategy that stresses the need for employees to work closely together as a means of increasing their productivity.
8. *Self-managed work teams:* Management strategy in which supervisors coach subordinates and help them assume greater responsibility for their own production improvement and problem solving.

What is gain sharing?

9. *Gain sharing:* Strategy that provides employees with a monetary bonus equaling the dollar amount of cash savings that results when their productivity increases above a certain level.
10. *Telecommuting:* Strategy that enables employees to work at home or at a satellite office part or all of the time.

DOS AND DON'TS OF MOTIVATION

When creating conditions to maximize employee motivation, managers and supervisor's should remember several factors. These are presented in Figure 10–4 as dos and don'ts of motivation.

Dos	Don'ts
1. Do keep in mind the amount of ability each subordinate has.	1. Don't forget that perceptions affect subordinate motivation.
2. Do try to help subordinates achieve their maximum potential.	2. Don't forget that interests vary from subordinate to subordinate.
3. Do keep in mind the values subordinates consider to be important.	3. Don't overlook the importance of the display of subordinates' emotions and feelings.
4. Do become familiar with the needs of each subordinate.	4. Don't forget that subordinates prioritize their needs, so that higher-level needs are not important until lower-level needs have been satisfied.
5. Do remember that money can help subordinates satisfy some—but not all—of their needs.	5. Don't overlook the fact that what is motivational for one subordinate will not necessarily be motivational to others.
6. Do remember that subordinates' lower-level needs are finite for the most part but their higher-level needs are essentially infinite.	6. Don't forget that techniques for motivating subordinates that take their needs into consideration are more successful than the techniques that do not.
7. Do remember that job satisfaction originates from the content of the job but job dissatisfaction originates from the environment in which the job is performed.	7. Don't forget that subordinates' higher-level needs are largely satisfied through their interrelationships with others and by their level of success in the organization.
8. Do remember that a feeling of inequity resulting from an input-outcome imbalance may motivate some employees to engage in certain types of behavior as a means of overcoming the imbalance.	8. Don't forget that subordinates' positive attitudes about their job are associated with job content but that negative attitudes are associated with the environment in which the job is performed.
9. Do remember that the motivation of certain employees will be higher when they have reason to expect a greater reward for desired performance.	9. Don't forget that the opposite of job satisfaction is not job dissatisfaction.
10. Do remember that the work-related values employees consider to be important change from time to time.	10. Don't forget that reinforced behavior tends to be repeated while nonreinforced behavior tends not to be repeated.
11. Do know how to deal with subordinate frustration that results from lack of success in goal achievement or need satisfaction.	11. Don't forget that managers' or supervisors' attitudes toward subordinates play a significant role in employee motivation.

Figure 10–4   Dos and don'ts of motivation

HANDLING EMPLOYEE FRUSTRATION

Managers and supervisors are well aware that employees do not always succeed in achieving their goals or satisfying their needs. Some supervisors are unaware of ways to deal with the **frustration** employees experience when they are not successful in goal attainment. The greater the employees' motivation to achieve a goal or satisfy a need, the greater the level of frustration that results from their lack of success. Managers and supervisors must be concerned about employee frustration, especially when it interferes with job performance.

Frustration occurs when a barrier prevents the achievement of a goal or the satisfaction of a need. The barrier may be of either internal or external origin. Examples of internal barriers are lack of ability, aptitude, interest, or judgment. External barriers result from boring work, inadequate supervision, restrictive company policies, or poorly designed work procedures.

Manifestation of Frustration

How does frustration manifest itself?

The presence of frustration is likely to manifest itself in several types of behavior. Employees may select an alternative goal, become aggressive, experience anxiety, use a defense mechanism, or take corrective action. Managers or supervisors who understand the ways in which frustration manifests itself will be more effective in dealing with it. With proper direction from the supervisor, the employee may be motivated to follow a constructive rather than a destructive path.

Alternative Goals. When employees become frustrated because of their inability to achieve a goal, they may respond by selecting an achievable alternative goal. The motivation to achieve the new goal may be just as high as it was with the original goal, and its achievement may be just as satisfying.

Aggression. Lack of success in achieving a goal or satisfying a need results in frustration, perhaps manifesting itself in employee **aggression.** The employee may respond by verbally or physically abusing the person who is accused of preventing goal achievement or need satisfaction. Employees who respond to frustration in this way present special challenges to their manager or supervisor.

Anxiety. In some employees, frustration manifests itself in a feeling of **anxiety.** As the level of anxiety increases, so does the amount of tension experienced by the employee. In extreme cases, anxiety can cause a variety of medical problems.

Defense Mechanism. Frustration may also cause some employees to build a defense mechanism to protect their egos from psychological damage. The defense mechanism may take the form of fantasizing, rationalizing, withdrawing, or developing a negative attitude.

Corrective Action. Some employees respond to frustration by correcting the situation that produced the frustration. Employees modify or change the situations that are responsible for their lack of success. Of all the ways in which employees respond to frustration, this is generally the most mature, rational approach. Over the long run, this approach also produces positive rather than negative results.

Effective managers and supervisors are concerned about the problems that result when barriers prevent their subordinates from achieving their goals or satisfying their needs. They also need to work with subordinates who experience frustration. The supervisor's ability to help the employee sustain his or her motivation is critical when having to deal with job-related frustration.

IMPLICATIONS FOR THE ADMINISTRATIVE OFFICE MANAGER

Administrative office managers should be concerned about the level of their subordinates' motivation because motivated employees tend to be more satisfied with the jobs and with life in general, and unit goals and objectives can be more readily achieved when employees are motivated. Consequently, the level of motivation impacts not only on the organization as a whole but also on the employees themselves.

Even though the elements of motivation are basic to human life, the motivational process is complex. These elements—ability, aptitude, interests, and so on—are themselves complex, and when they interact with one another, the motivational process becomes even more complex.

The increasing managerial concern for the human element in the organization has had a positive impact on employee motivation. The human relations era that emerged several decades ago continues to provide ample proof that managers or supervisors who make subordinates responsible for self-motivation are doing an injustice to both the employer and the employees. Nowadays, managers and supervisors are more willing to assume their fair share of the responsibility for motivating subordinates.

In many instances, the strategies that are used to motivate subordinates are virtually cost free and consume little time. The failure to motivate employees is likely to create a number of serious problems for the organization, its managers, and its employees.

NOTES

1. Data are based on the Hierarchy of Needs in "A Theory of Human Motivation" in MOTIVATION AND PERSONALITY, 2nd Edition, by Abraham H. Maslow. Copyright © 1970 by Abraham H. Maslow. Reprinted by permission of Harper & Row, Publishers, Inc.

2. F. Herzberg, B. Mausner, and B. Synderman, *The Motivation to Work*, © 1959. Reprinted by permission of John Wiley and Sons, Inc.

3. New evidence indicates that salary is increasingly becoming a satisfier rather than the dissatisfier that it was a few years ago.

4. David C. McClelland, *The Achievement Motive*, Appleton-Century-Crofts, 1953. Reprinted with permission.

5. Victor Vroom, *Work and Motivation*, © 1953. Reprinted with permission of John Wiley and Sons, Inc.

REVIEW QUESTIONS

1. How do employees' needs and drives affect their motivation?

2. What impact does disequilibrium have on the motivation process?

3. What are the elements of safety needs in Maslow's theory?

4. According to Maslow, when do belonging and love needs become important to an individual?

5. What is meant by self-actualization?

6. What are the basic differences between what Herzberg identifies as job satisfiers and job dissatisfiers?

7. What is the origin of motivation in the equity theory?

8. According to the expectancy theory, what conditions must be present for motivation to occur?

9. According to the reinforcement theory, of what is motivation a consequence?

10. What are the important attributes of goals?

11. In what ways can frustration manifest itself in employees?

DISCUSSION QUESTIONS

1. In a performance appraisal interview you recently conducted with one of your subordinates, the two of you talked about motivation for a long time. You have noticed that some days her work is exceptional; on other days it is quite average. When you questioned her about her lack of consistency, she indicated that some days she is motivated and other days she is not. Do you

believe one can "turn motivation on and off" as she indicated?

2. During a recent supervisors' meeting in your company, the topic of employee motivation was discussed. Some supervisors indicated that they spend a significant amount of time trying to motivate their subordinates. Others said that motivating subordinates was not a great concern because employee motivation comes from within—and, therefore, either you are or you are not. Which group do you tend to agree with? Why?

3. In discussing your philosophy of motivation with your assistant recently, you indicated that of all the qualifications you consider in job applicants, motivation is the most important criterion. You further stated that regardless of how competent an employee is, his or her performance will be greatly diminished if he or she is not motivated. Justify why you believe that motivation is so important.

STUDENT PROJECTS AND ACTIVITIES

1. Discuss with an administrative office manager the aspects of his or her job that he or she finds most motivational. Discuss with an office employee for whom the administrative office manager is responsible the aspects of his or her job that he or she finds most motivational. Did the items they identified differ from one another?

2. Discuss with an office employee the various ways he or she handles job-related frustration.

3. Going Online: Using the Internet, conduct an online search based on one of the concepts presented in this chapter or based on one of the chapter terms. Identify four or five things you learned from the material that you did not know prior to your search.

Minicases

Many of the managers in the Babcock Corporation are concerned about the declining level of employee motivation. The absence of motivated employees is reflected in several ways including lower output, higher absenteeism, greater waste, and so forth. Some of the managers blame the company's salary administration program for these problems. Employees all receive an across-the-board increase each year. Therefore, little incentive exists for an employee to work harder than others because the additional effort will not be reflected in higher salary through a merit increase.

1. Discuss the implications of this situation on employee motivation.

2. Which theory of motivation does this situation most clearly violate?

3. What changes do you recommend be made in the salary administration program so it is consistent with the theory you identified in question 2?

Case

Emanuel Garcia is the new administrative office manager in the Gateway Corporation, a furniture manufacturer located in Albany, New York. Of the twenty-three applicants for the position, Garcia was selected primarily because of his reputation for working well with subordinates. Each of Garcia's previous employers mentioned his ability to motivate

subordinates and to get them to put forth their best efforts. Garcia's predecessor had a reputation for being quite ineffective in dealing with subordinates.

When Garcia first arrived on the job, he asked each subordinate to schedule an appointment with him so they could get to know each other better. Although the "interviews" were quite unstructured,

Garcia attempted to obtain the same information from each one. For example, he asked questions designed (1) to help him learn about the aspirations of each subordinate, (2) to find out what each subordinate liked and disliked about his or her job, and (3) to help him assess the self-concept of each subordinate.

Although some of the subordinates willingly provided answers to his questions, others were a bit more reluctant to answer, perhaps because they feared that what they said could later be held against them.

Several of the employees did mention that the company provided few opportunities for promotion and that they might have to seek employ-ment elsewhere if they expected to further their careers.

1. Do you believe Garcia overstepped his authority when he tried to extract information from each subordinate during their interviews? Explain your response.

2. What human need is being unfulfilled if employees are being denied the opportunity for promotion to higher level jobs?

3. What suggestions can you provide Garcia that will help him increase the motivation of his subordinates?

*C*hapter 11

APPRAISING PERFORMANCE OF OFFICE EMPLOYEES

*C*hapter *A*ims

After studying this chapter, you should be able to design an effective program for appraising the performance of office employees.

*C*hapter *O*utline

Uses of Performance Appraisal
Characteristics of Performance Appraisal
    Programs
Establishment of Performance Standards
Methods of Performance Appraisal
    Traditional Appraisal Methods
    New Appraisal Methods
Rating Errors
    Halo-Horns Effect
    Influence of Recent Performance
    Bias
    Central Tendency
Analysis of Appraisals
Appraisal Interviews
Employee Promotion
Implications for the Administrative Office
    Manager

*C*hapter *T*erms

360-degree feedback
Appraisal interview
Behaviorally anchored rating scales appraisal
    (BARS)
Bias
Central tendency rating error
Checklists
Computerized appraisal
Critical incidents appraisal
Employee promotion
Field staff review appraisal
Forced-choice appraisal
Graphic rating scale appraisal
Group rating appraisal
Halo-horns effect
Mixed standard scales
Narrative appraisal
Paired comparison appraisal
Peer rating appraisal
Performance standards
Results-oriented appraisal
Self-appraisal
Simple ranking appraisal

*I*nfluencing work-unit productivity directly, performance appraisal is one of the more important responsibilities of the administrative office manager. An effective appraisal system helps the organization increase its productivity and allows employees to satisfy their desire to know how well they are performing. The absence of feedback about their job performance will likely cause employees to experience frustration, anxiety, and job-related insecurity.

USES OF PERFORMANCE APPRAISAL

What are the purposes of performance appraisal?

Performance appraisal was originally designed to help identify supervisors who should be promoted and/or who should receive salary increases. Several additional uses now exist. Supervisors frequently use the appraisal process as a means of identifying their subordinates' strengths and weaknesses. Appraisal results are used when making decisions about salary increases, promotions, and employee transfers, as well as when developing strategies for increasing the employees' value to the organization.

Providing an objective basis for evaluating employees, performance appraisal helps eliminate charges of favoritism and bias. Too, the program motivates individuals to work harder as a way of obtaining higher salary increases and faster promotions.

Performance appraisal results are often used in workforce planning because appraisal data help to identify the positions that will likely become vacant as a result of employee promotion. The results of the appraisal process are also used to determine areas suitable for employee training because the appraisal data clearly identify areas in which employee performance is weak.

The performance appraisal process also helps strengthen the communication between supervisors and subordinates. By discussing the appraisal results, communication lines between the supervisor and subordinate are established. Another byproduct of the appraisal process is improved quality of supervision. Typically, supervisors who have performance appraisal responsibilities are apt to be more aware of their subordinates' strengths and weaknesses. Performance appraisal also has a positive impact on the career growth and development of employees, thus enabling them to realize their potential more quickly.

The results of performance appraisal are often used in making decisions about promoting and rewarding employees. Civil rights legislation and several court cases indicate that performance appraisal results cannot be used to discriminate unfairly against protected classes.

CHARACTERISTICS OF PERFORMANCE APPRAISAL PROGRAMS

An effective performance appraisal program possesses the following identifiable characteristics:

What characteristics should performance appraisal programs possess?

1. It must elicit a change in the behavior of employees. When they are aware of their weaknesses, employees are able to modify their behavior.

2. It must provide a basis for making compensation decisions. An effective program helps identify those employees whose contribution to the organization warrants a higher level of compensation.

3. It must provide information used as a basis for making promotion, transfer, or termination decisions. Any program that fails to provide appropriate job-change information is ineffective.

4. It must motivate employees to work harder. If the program fails to identify those employees whose contribution to the organization is considerably above average, its value is questionable.

5. It must provide feedback for use in validating various phases of the personnel program. For example, the results of the program are useful in helping determine the effectiveness of the personnel selection program.

6. It must facilitate supervisor-subordinate communication. A program's effectiveness is reduced when employees are not informed of their appraisal results.

7. It must use the appropriate evaluation base in relation to the intended use of the appraisal results. Three bases are used: (a) evaluating an employee by comparing his or her performance with the performance of others, (b) evaluating an employee by comparing his or her performance against individually determined performance objectives, and (c) evaluating an employee by comparing his or her performance against generally accepted **performance standards.**

8. The performance standards that comprise the program must be clearly stated, objective, and well understood by those doing the rating and those being rated. Performance standards that are applied differently by different appraisers and that are not well understood by those being appraised are likely to create significant problems for the organization.

ESTABLISHMENT OF PERFORMANCE STANDARDS

How are performance appraisal standards used in performance appraisal programs?

The basis against which employees are to be evaluated has to be predetermined. These evaluation standards or criteria should be made available to each individual upon employment. Otherwise, a match between an employee's actual performance and his or her expected performance may simply be a coincidence.

The use that will be made of the information gathered during the appraisal process must be considered when selecting the appraisal criteria. For example, the criteria used to determine who should be promoted are different from the criteria used to determine whether or not the employee should be discharged.

Performance standards should exist for all positions, but they are especially important in nonproduction jobs (those jobs that involve more than a quantity or quality output). In nonproduction jobs, such factors as human relations, ability to work with others, initiative, judgment, and so on are more important.

The appraisal process used to evaluate unionized employees often has a different emphasis than that used to appraise nonunionized employees. Seniority often plays an important part in determining who will be promoted in unionized organizations.

METHODS OF PERFORMANCE APPRAISAL

Some of the methods for appraising the performance of employees have been in existence for many years while others are quite new. Several methods in each of the two broad categories—traditional and new—are discussed.

Traditional Appraisal Methods

Performance traits are often the basis of the traditional appraisal methods. Unless these traits are observable, fairly standard for similar jobs within an organization, and capable of being measured objectively, the effectiveness of using a traditional rating method may be hampered. Traits measured by subjective means may create legal and morale problems for organizations.

Among the traditional appraisal methods are graphic rating scales, paired comparison appraisal, checklists, and simple ranking.

What are the characteristics of the graphic rating scale technique of performance appraisal?

Graphic Rating Scale. The **graphic rating scale,** which continues to be the most widely used performance appraisal method, requires a scale similar to the one illustrated in Figure 11–1. In completing the scale, the rater indicates the degree to which the individual being appraised possesses each specific characteristic or trait.

Three methods are commonly used to construct the evaluation section of the graphic rating scale: (1) descriptive phrases, (2) descriptive words, and (3) numerical scales.

The use of descriptive phrases provides more rating objectivity than either of the other two methods. For the trait *job knowledge,* the descriptive phrases might be "thoroughly understands the job," "more than adequately understands the job," "has sufficient knowledge of the job," and so forth. Some appraisal forms using descriptive phrases provide space for written comments about each trait.

When descriptive words are used, such as "outstanding," "excellent," "above average," "average," "below average," and "poor," raters may not be consistent with one another in their interpretation and application of these words. Consequently, what is "outstanding" to one rater may only be "above average" to another. Appraisal forms using descriptive words also frequently provide space for written comments as well as a definition of each trait, as illustrated in Figure 11–2.

Numerical scales involve a series of numbers (perhaps 1 to 6, with 1 being low and 6 being high) for appraising the performance of each individual on each trait. Assuming that all traits are weighted equally, the numerical values can be added to get a composite score for each individual. To make this method as objective as possible, the numerical values and each trait should be defined. Numerical scales can also be designed with space so the rater can provide written comments about the various traits being assessed.

The traits used in appraising employee performance must be measurable. Traits dealing with employee behavior or performance results are more measurable than are those dealing specifically with the personality of employees. Rating forms that contain irrelevant traits or that omit important traits generally result in unsatisfactory appraisal instruments.

Greater objectivity can be achieved by placing the scale values in a random order on the form. Rather than placing the highest value for each trait at the left and the lowest value at the right, the values should be reordered from one trait to the next. Therefore, the rater has to exert more care appraising employee performance, which should result in a more thorough, objective evaluation.

Also commonly included on graphic rating scales is a summary section consisting of two subsections: one for general comments about the individual being rated and the other to provide an overall rating of the individual (superior, above average, average, and so on).

Although the graphic rating scale is a fairly simple and quick appraisal method, it does possess several serious shortcomings, including the following:

What are the shortcomings of the graphic rating scale technique?

1. Unless the traits are individually weighted, each trait is considered to be of equal importance. For example, because some jobs require extensive decision making and others require very little, treating the importance of decision making equally for all jobs is not realistic.

Name _____ Social Security number _____ Present salary _____

Present position _____ Date employed _____ Date of last promotion _____

Trait				
QUALITY OF WORK Refers to neatness, accuracy, completeness of work	X Quality of work is considered above average and only rarely does any have to be redone	X Quality of work is superior and none ever has to be redone	X Quality of work is improving but is still substandard	X Much work has to be redone	X Quality of work is average and only some of it has to be redone
Comment:					
QUANTITY OF WORK Refers to volume of output	X Normally works at above average rate and wastes little time	X Works at a consistently high level with very little wasted time	X Is not able to produce at acceptable level	X Produces at an average rate but is steady and wastes little time	X Output is frequently below expected level. Wastes time
Comment:					
INITIATIVE Refers to ability to develop ideas and to ability to get things done	X Is capable of working without being told what to do	X Because of lack of initiative, always has to be told what to do	X Self starter. Never has to be told to do something	X Rarely does anything without first being told	X Develops new ways of doing things. Is resourceful
Comment:					
RELATIONS WITH OTHERS Refers to ability to get along with others	X Is respected by everyone, is helpful, and is looked upon by others as a "leader"	X Is disagreeable and does not get along well with others. Has few friends. Is a troublemaker	X Has a good attitude toward others and is liked and respected by others	X Is friendly and gets along well with others	X Is not friendly and is generally disliked by others
Comment:					
DEPENDABILITY Refers to trustworthiness and amount of supervision required	X Is always dependable, is completely trust worthy, and requires very little if any supervision	X Is not always dependable, cannot be trusted in all respects, and requires frequent supervision	X Is very trustworthy, is always dependable, and requires very little supervision	X Cannot be trusted, is not dependable, and requires constant supervision	X Can be trusted most of the time, is dependable, and requires only an average amount of supervision
Comment:					
JOB KNOWLEDGE Refers to the knowledge the individual has about the job	X Has average knowledge about job	X Knows about everything there is to know about the job	X Is very knowledgeable about the job	X Lacks job knowledge and is generally unwilling to learn	X Lacks job knowledge but is willing to learn
Comment:					

Overall rating: _____ Outstanding; _____ Above average; _____ Average; _____ Below average; _____ Poor

Summary Comments: _____

_____ _____
Today's date

Employee's signature Appraiser's signature

Figure 11-1 Graphic rating scale

Figure 11-2 Partial descriptive word appraisal form

	Outstanding	Above Average	Average	Below Average	Poor
Job knowledge Refers to the theoretical and practical knowledge as related to the present job.	X	X	X	X	X
Comments					

2. The graphic rating scale is subject to certain errors that tend to distort the rating of individuals. (These errors are discussed in the next section of this chapter.)

3. The rating scale appraises one's past performance—after it is too late to improve the quality of performance.

4. Unless the supervisor makes a special effort to help individuals overcome weaknesses identified on the graphic rating scale, some employees lack the incentive they need to improve their overall performance.

5. The graphic rating scale may contain either too many or too few traits. From six to nine traits are generally considered adequate.

A growing number of organizations are adapting their graphic rating scale to reflect the actual duties performed by employees. Thus, these scales tend to reflect closely the tasks identified on the employees' job descriptions. Rather than using a standard rating scale to appraise the performance of all employees, a different rating scale exists for various broad groups of employees or even for individual employees. Although the design of the graphic rating scale is similar throughout the organization, the actual traits listed on a given employee's rating scale reflect the most important duties that comprise his or her job. For example, an employee whose job requires considerable use of interpersonal skills will find that his or her rating scale includes this trait; however, an employee whose job requires very minimal use of interpersonal skills will likely find this trait missing from his or her rating scale.

What are the characteristics of the paired comparison appraisal technique?

Paired Comparison Appraisal. The **paired comparison appraisal** involves comparing one individual with each of the other individuals in a particular work group. Either specific traits or overall performance are considered in appraising individuals.

A chart similar to the one illustrated in Figure 11–3 is useful. The name of each individual in the work group is listed on the left side (vertically) and also in the same order across the top (horizontally). When the performance of the individual being rated is of higher quality than the individual against whom he or she is being compared, a checkmark is placed in the corresponding square. For example, according to Figure 11–3, Employee A is considered to have a higher quality of performance than Employees B, C, and D but of lesser quality than Employees E and F. Employee F has a higher performance level than Employees A, B, C, D, and E. Therefore, a checkmark is placed in the corresponding squares. The total number of checkmarks in the rows has to be determined for each individual. The greater the number of checkmarks an employee receives, the higher his or her appraisal.

Although the paired comparison appraisal method readily facilitates the comparison of individuals within a work group, it possesses some of the same shortcomings as the graphic rating scale. In addition, unless specifically identified

Figure 11-3 Rating grid

	Employee A	Employee B	Employee C	Employee D	Employee E	Employee F
Employee A	■	✓	✓	✓		
Employee B		■	✓	✓		
Employee C			■	✓		
Employee D				■		
Employee E	✓	✓	✓	✓	■	
Employee F	✓	✓	✓	✓	✓	■

Checkmark Tally: Employee A – 3
Employee B – 2
Employee C – 1
Employee D – 0
Employee E – 4
Employee F – 5

traits are used to evaluate individuals, their strengths and weaknesses are not readily apparent. This is the reason that an increasing number of organizations that use this technique are rating employees within a work group on individual traits rather than on overall performance. The number of employees who can be effectively appraised by the paired comparison method is quite small because the rating form tends to become cumbersome after more than ten to fifteen names are placed on the grid.

What are the advantages of the checklist method of performance appraisal?

Checklists. **Checklists** consist of a series of statements about various traits. The rater appraises the employee by responding to each statement. A partial checklist is illustrated in Figure 11–4.

A distinct advantage of the checklist method is that it evaluates specific items—not just broad or general traits. Although the rating errors that are characteristic of the graphic rating scale are minimized when using the checklist, both methods tend to treat the traits as being equal in weight or importance.

Simple Ranking. The **simple ranking appraisal** method ranks employees from the best to the poorest. The method is fairly simple and can be used for appraising a fairly large number of employees. To use the method, each employee's name is put on an index card, and the cards are arranged and rearranged until the proper ranking is achieved.

The advantages of this method are readily offset by its lack of specificity and usefulness to the individual being rated. Only when the rater identifies problem or weak areas for the employees do they know the reasons for a poor rating. Unless the rater uses an objective basis for appraising the individuals, bias and subjectivity may be present in the evaluation process.

Figure 11-4 Partial checklist

Trait	Yes	No
Initiative		
1. Does the individual frequently need guidance and direction from others?	___	___
2. Is the individual able to determine what course of action to follow without having to be told?	___	___
3. Is the individual a leader?	___	___
4. Is the individual a follower?	___	___
5. Does the individual accept work willingly?	___	___
Quality of Work		
1. Is the individual's work error–free most of the time?	___	___
2. Does a considerable amount of work have to be redone?	___	___
3. Is the individual's work completed on time?	___	___
4. Do the individual's work habits frequently disrupt the flow of work because of poor quality of work?	___	___

New Appraisal Methods

Although the traditional methods of performance appraisal are still frequently used in organizations, some newer methods are becoming increasingly popular. Among the newer appraisal methods are forced choice, critical incidents, peer rating, group rating, self-appraisal, narrative, field staff review, results oriented appraisals, behaviorally anchored rating scales (BARS), mixed standard scales, and computerized appraisal.

What are the characteristics of the forced-choice appraisal technique?

Forced Choice. The **forced-choice appraisal** method consists of twenty-five to forty sets of statements. From each set, the rater chooses the statement *most* descriptive and the statement *least* descriptive of the person being appraised. Figure 11–5 is an example of two sets of such statements.

Because the rater does not know which statement in each set is viewed as favorable and which is viewed as unfavorable for the individual being rated, bias and subjectivity can be almost totally eliminated. Only two statements within each set affect the person being appraised (the most and the least favorable statements), whereas the other three are treated as neutral statements. Therefore, the selection of neutral statements will not affect the individual being rated. But when the rater chooses the favorable statement, the individual's

Most	Least	
1	1	Wants to do things his or her own way.
2	2	Is valuable in a new operation.
3	3	Does not go outside area of authority.
4	4	Is viewed by peers as a leader.
5	5	Realizes capabilities of others.

Most	Least	
1	1	Needs complete information about a situation before willing to make a decision.
2	2	Would be easy to replace.
3	3	Is sensitive to needs of others.
4	4	Stands up well under pressure.
5	5	Has gone about as far as his capabilities will permit

Figure 11-5 Forced-choice statement sets

appraisal is affected positively; and when the rater chooses the unfavorable statement, the individual's appraisal is negatively affected.

The use of this appraisal method has significant advantages over the use of some of the other methods (eliminates bias and subjectivity); however, its use also has some serious limitations. The method is costly to develop and install because the statements generally have to be designed for specific job categories. The results of the appraisal are also difficult to use as a basis for employee counseling and development.

Critical Incidents. The **critical incidents appraisal** method involves formulating a list of critical job requirements for each position. To illustrate, the critical incidents for an administrative assistant might include the ability to work with others, to meet deadlines, and to perform at a quality level.

After the critical requirements have been identified, the office supervisor observes each subordinate for favorable or unfavorable displays of these requirements. The examples or incidents are immediately recorded on the appraisal form as a means of building an appraisal record for each subordinate. The favorable incidents are listed on one side, and the unfavorable incidents are listed on the other. Figure 11–6 is an example.

A distinct advantage of this method is basing the appraisal on objective facts and evidence rather than on traits that are rated subjectively. Furthermore, the rater is also required to list specific incidents in appraising subordinates. In addition, the method provides the opportunity for supervisors to discuss immediately with subordinates the favorable and unfavorable incidents.

A potential disadvantage of this method is the impression among subordinates that the supervisor keeps a "little black book" in which unfavorable incidents are recorded. This belief may create resentment among some subordinates.

Peer Rating. The **peer rating appraisal** method uses co-workers to evaluate the performance of an individual. Because peers often see a different type of behavior than what the supervisor sees, they are given an opportunity to evaluate that behavior. The technique is useful in identifying the members of a work group whose characteristics may be best suited for assuming leadership positions within an organization.

Group Rating. When the **group rating appraisal** method is used, a group of individuals who are familiar with the person being rated does the appraisal collectively rather than individually. The group generally consists of the individual's immediate supervisor, the supervisor's superior, and other persons who are familiar with the individual being appraised. The objectivity of the ap-

What are the characteristics of the critical incidents appraisal technique?

What are the characteristics of the group rating appraisal technique?

Ability to Work With Others

10/16—Mary stayed after hours to help Pat finish a project.

10/17—When several office workers were ill today, Mary helped reorganize work so deadlines could be met.

12/3—Mary asked to not be assigned to work on a particular project with Carol (for personal reasons).

Figure 11-6 Critical incidents record

praisal efforts is probably increased because more than one individual is involved in the process. This method is also effectively used in organizations in which individuals have responsibilities in two departments or work units.

Self-Appraisal. The **self-appraisal** method typically uses a rating form, such as a graphic rating scale. Both the employee being rated and the employee's supervisor complete the form. During the appraisal interview, the responses of the employee and the supervisor are compared, trait by trait. When a discrepancy occurs, an average of the two ratings is often calculated to determine the official rating.

The most distinct advantage of the self-appraisal method is the active role the employee takes in the appraisal process. Performance appraisal is for the benefit of employees; when they take an active part in the process, they are able to get a more realistic picture of their overall performance. This method also results in greater employee acceptance of the rating process.

Narrative Appraisal. Some organizations prefer to use the **narrative appraisal** method in which the supervisor prepares a written report about the employee's performance. Accompanying some narrative appraisal programs is an improvement plan that identifies how the employee will improve his or her performance in deficient areas.

The most distinct advantage of this method is that it provides detailed coverage about certain phases of the employee's job-related performance. Identified strengths and weaknesses can be covered in sufficient detail to eliminate ambiguities or incomplete information.

Making a comparison of the appraisal results of various supervisors is not possible with narrative appraisal. Because the method does not lend itself to standardization, comparing employees with one another on the basis of the written reports prepared by the raters is generally impossible. Also, the method is limited by the ability of the supervisors to prepare well-written reports.

Field Staff Review. Of the various appraisal methods discussed in this chapter, the **field staff review** method is the only one that uses an objective outside appraiser in the evaluation process. The employee being evaluated and the employee's supervisor are questioned orally by the appraiser, who is generally from the organization's human resources department. The responses of the employee and the supervisor are generally recorded on a form.

What are the steps in field staff review?

An advantage of the field staff review technique is the objective, uniform, and thorough results it provides. A potential disadvantage is the inability to perform appraisals as often as they should be provided, especially when an insufficient number of appraisers is available.

Results-Oriented Appraisal. A significant trend in performance appraisal nowadays is the use of **results-oriented appraisal.** The philosophical foundation of this appraisal method lies within the management by objectives concept, which is discussed in detail in Chapter 16. The method generally involves the following steps:

What are the steps in results-oriented appraisal?

1. Measurable performance goals are set jointly by the supervisor and the subordinate.
2. Specific courses of action are agreed on as a means of accomplishing these goals.
3. The supervisor and subordinate, at interim intervals, discuss the progress that has been made toward accomplishing these goals.

4. At the conclusion of the time period (perhaps six months to a year), the supervisor and subordinate officially evaluate the degree to which the specified goals were accomplished.

5. Goals for the next evaluation period are set.

Many organizations that have installed a results-oriented appraisal program use it in conjunction with another appraisal method, such as the graphic rating scale, to identify employee strengths and weaknesses. The performance goals are aimed at helping the employee overcome identified weaknesses.

Results-oriented appraisal can be used in organizations that do not use management by objectives. In many organizations where MBO is used, results-oriented appraisal is linked to the objectives specified by the goal-setting process of MBO. For example, if the organization has a specific goal of increasing profit, many employees in the organization are likely to have waste-reduction goals as part of their results-oriented appraisal program. Individual objectives should be developed around the following guidelines:

1. Only measurable objectives should be used. For the most part, personality traits are not suitable because they cannot be measured.

2. The number of individual objectives should be determined by the nature of the employee's performance.

3. The objectives should be achievable within a relatively short time, although they do not all have to be achieved at the same time.

4. The objectives should consist of three elements: (1) the desired results, (2) the quantity or amount of change, and (3) the time frame in which each objective is to be achieved.

Advantages of Using Results-Oriented Appraisal

What are the advantages of results-oriented appraisal?

1. The appraisal method emphasizes the future (over which the employee has some control) rather than the past (over which the employee no longer has any control).

2. The method emphasizes performance rather than personality traits.

3. The method helps identify areas suitable for training.

4. Subordinates are compared against their own progress rather than competing with their peers.

5. The method tends to strengthen superior-subordinate cooperation because the superior is in a prime position to help subordinates achieve their specified goals.

6. Employees tend to work harder when they are trying to achieve a specific goal.

7. The appraisal is tailor-made for each employee.

8. Employees are motivated to work harder for the attainment of major organizational objectives.

Disadvantages of the Results-Oriented Appraisal

1. Subordinates may set their goals too high or too low.

2. The work performed by some employees cannot be quantified or measured.

3. The use of this appraisal method may require certain managers to adjust their managerial style. In some instances, managers cannot or will not make the necessary adjustments to make the method work.

4. Some supervisors believe no need exists to counsel their subordinates because they can readily determine how well they are achieving their goals.

5. The method leads employees to work only for measurable goals and not unmeasurable goals (morale, for example).

Behaviorally Anchored Rating Scales Appraisal. The **behaviorally anchored rating scales (BARS)** technique is being used in an increasing number of organizations. This method uses a series of five to ten scales in the appraisal of employee performance. Each important job dimension has a separate scale. Among the job dimensions that might be used are the following: job knowledge, quality of work, quantity of work, initiative, dependability, and so forth. An example of one such scale is shown in Figure 11–7.

Each scale has a set of seven anchors that reflects varying degrees of job performance. The anchors are arranged in order from excellent to unacceptable. To appraise an individual's performance, the rater reads through the anchors to find the one that best reflects the quality of the individual's performance.

The BARS method produces objective and consistent results. In addition, the scales that are used for various jobs can be tailored to reflect specific job attributes. The most significant disadvantage is the amount of time consumed in developing the various scales.

Mixed Standard Scales. Similar to a number of the other performance appraisal methods discussed earlier, the **mixed standard scales** technique is also tailored to specific positions. The rating scale used in conjunction with this method contains a list of statements the rater considers in appraising the employee. The following three qualitative values are used:

+ indicates that the person being rated performs better than the performance level contained in the statement.

0 indicates that the person being rated performs exactly like the performance level contained in the statement.

− indicates that the person being rated performs worse than the performance level contained in the statement.

The individual doing the appraisal places one of the three values on the appropriate line beside each performance statement. The various performance statements, which are arranged in random order, contain positive as well as negative attributes. Once the employee has been rated, the results are analyzed to determine an overall qualitative assessment of the employee's performance. The rating scales designed for some jobs contain as many as twenty-five to thirty performance standards.

Two of the most distinctive advantages of the mixed standard scales method are that the performance statements can be tailored to specific positions and the rater only has to work with three qualitative values. Therefore, the rater does not have to decide whether the employee's performance in a certain area is *excellent* or whether it deserves a rating of a 7 or a 6. The second advantage listed earlier for the mixed standard scales method also becomes its primary disadvantage: The employee being rated is unable to determine how much better or how much worse his or her performance is than what is expected. The employee can only determine that his or her performance is better or worse than expected.

A portion of a mixed standard scale is found in Figure 11–8.

What are the characteristics of the behaviorally anchored rating scales appraisal technique?

What are the advantages of the mixed standard scales technique?

Figure 11-7 Behaviorally anchored rating scale

JOB DIMENSION: Job knowledge

☐ Excellent
Knows everything there is to know about the job; never has to be told how to do anything nor ever has to ask questions about the job.

☐ Very good
Knows almost everything there is to know about the job; knows when assistance is needed and asks for it.

☐ Good
Knows the most important elements of the job and quite a few of the less important job elements.

☐ Average
Knows some of the most important elements of the job and a few of the less important elements.

☐ Below average
Lacks knowledge about some of the most important job elements and most of the less important job elements.

☐ Very poor
Lacks knowledge about basic job elements but is willing to learn.

☐ Unacceptable
Lacks knowledge about basic job elements and is unwilling to learn.

Name_____   Supervisor_____

Department_____   Date_____

Rate each of the statements listed below, using the following values:

"+": Indicates that the person being rated performs better than the performance level contained in the statement.

"o": Indicates that the person being rated performs exactly like the performance level contained in the statement.

"−": Indicates that the person being rated performs worse than the performance level contained in the statement.

_____ 1. Always arrives at work on time.

_____ 2. Carries out work on a reasonable and timely basis.

_____ 3. Idles the time away when he or she has nothing to do.

_____ 4. Greets office callers cheerfully.

_____ 5. Has difficulty coping with job pressures.

_____ 6. Could be more meticulous in handling the details of the job.

_____ 7. Is sometimes discourteous to coworkers.

_____ 8. Returns from breaks on time.

_____ 9. Sometimes asks questions rather than trying to find answer on own.

_____ 10. Occasional carelessness sometimes results in the waste of office supplies.

_____ 11. Does not participate in "office gossip."

_____ 12. Rarely volunteers to help others.

Figure 11-8 Mixed standard scale for a secretary.

Computerized Appraisal. As with so many other operational elements of the organization, the computer is now becoming involved in the appraisal process. Among the relatively inexpensive software programs used in **computerized appraisal** are Employer Appraiser (Austin-Hayne), Performance Now (Knowledgepoint), and Review Writer (Avontos).

Appraisal software programs tend to work in the following manner: The appraiser reads through a list of rating traits. When a trait is identified as being relevant to a specific employee's job, the program will identify several subtraits that are also important. For example, the Employer Appraiser program lists "communication" as a trait, along with the following communication subtraits: written skills, verbal communication skills, listening skills, receptivity to feedback, openness, keeping others informed, and so forth. For each of the subtraits, the program provides the appraiser with a list of statements (ranging from desirable to undesirable, effective to ineffective, or good to poor aspects of the trait being rated); he or she selects the statement that most clearly reflects the employee's quality of performance regarding the subtrait. This aspect of the program resembles the behaviorally anchored rating scale process discussed earlier. The software program finishes the process by preparing a written report regarding the employee's performance. Accompanying the program is a text editor that enables the appraiser to make additions, changes, or modifications to the written report.

Some organizations also use the computer to monitor employee output that eventually becomes part of the employees' overall performance appraisal. For example, where keyboarding or data input is a critical task, the computer will keep track of the number of keystrokes an employee performs during a given period of time (perhaps hourly, daily, weekly, etc.). The more closely the employee comes to matching the performance standards expected of him or her, the more favorable the employee's productivity rating is likely to be.

RATING ERRORS

The various appraisal methods that use scoring scales (whether the scale involves descriptive phrases, words, or numerical values) are subject to human rating errors that often distort appraisal results. The rating errors usually involve judgment and occur when traits cannot be quantified or measured on an objective basis. The impact of many rating errors can be minimized with the proper training of appraisers.

Halo-Horns Effect

What is a halo-horns effect?

The **halo-horns effect** results when the rating on one trait influences the rating an employee receives on other traits. For example, if undue emphasis is placed on attitude, the halo effect occurs when those employees whose attitudes are judged to be above average are rated excessively high on all other traits. The horns effect is present when an employee whose attitude is judged to be below average is rated excessively low on other traits. The halo-horns effect can be minimized if raters consider each trait individually and do not allow the rating on one trait to influence the rating on other traits.

Influence of Recent Performance

A subordinate's recent performance is also likely to have an impact on the appraisal process. Employees whose recent performance is considerably above average (even though their earlier performance may have been below average) are likely to be rated unduly high. Likewise, employees whose performance decreases immediately before the appraisal process occurs may receive a rating that does not truly reflect the quality of their performance. The critical incidents method, which provides an ongoing appraisal of each employee, is not subject to this type of rating error.

Bias

Overcoming unconscious **bias** or prejudice is difficult for some supervisors. The appraisals of subordinates are likely to be affected by this bias, especially when their preferences are not consistent with the supervisor's preferences. Assuming that the bias is short-lived, a technique that will minimize the effect of bias involves having the supervisor appraise each subordinate two different times—perhaps two weeks apart. The results of the two appraisals are compared, and any differences are resolved.

Central Tendency

What is a central tendency error?

The **central tendency rating** error occurs when the ratings of subordinates all fall within a narrow range. Regardless of individual employee performance, all employees are rated at average or above-average levels. The presence of the central tendency rating error diminishes the usefulness of the appraisal of employee performance.

ANALYSIS OF APPRAISALS

Even though quality appraisal forms may be used in the appraisal process, the reliability and validity of the appraisal results should be determined. This analysis is especially important when the graphic rating scale and forced-choice appraisal methods are used.

How can the reliability of appraisal results be assessed?

To determine the reliability of results, employee ratings in different work units or in different jobs should be analyzed. If significant differences are found, an adjustment may be necessary. For example, some raters believe that individuals who hold more important jobs should receive a higher rating than those whose jobs they consider to be of lesser importance. Raters should always be cognizant of the fact that appraisals are concerned with how well employees perform their jobs rather than how important the jobs are within the organization.

One way to determine the validity of appraisal results is to make an analysis of the strictness or leniency with which each rater appraises his or her subordinates. Ratings made by overly strict or lenient supervisors cannot be fairly compared with supervisors whose ratings tend to fall between these two extremes. An adjustment factor may have to be used to assure the comparability of results.

Ratings can be made more reliable by determining the importance of each trait within the position. Because traits are rarely equally important, results will be more reliable if each category is assigned a specific weight in relation to its importance.

Another means of assessing the quality of the appraisal process is to follow up employees who have been promoted to high-level positions, primarily because they received high evaluations in the appraisal process. The effectiveness of the appraisal process can be verified to a certain extent if employees who received high ratings while holding one position continue to receive high ratings from another appraiser.

Using **360-degree feedback** provides some organizations with additional information about their employees, thus increasing the amount of feedback that must be analyzed. With 360-degree feedback, information about an employee's performance is solicited from virtually all others with whom the employee comes in contact during the official functions of his or her position. Insiders (supervisor, supervisor's superior, subordinates, peers) and outsiders (customers, sales representatives) are invited to complete a special rating form for this purpose. While the collected information is typically used for determining an employee's training and/or development needs, it is not used for making promotion or salary-increase decisions. These decisions, using one or more of the rating techniques discussed earlier in this chapter, are based on the information collected by the supervisor.

APPRAISAL INTERVIEWS

What is the purpose of the appraisal interview?

The success of the performance appraisal program is greatly dependent upon the appraisal form, the elimination of rating errors, and the analysis of appraisal results. The program will not be totally successful, however, unless employees are informed of the appraisal results. The **appraisal interview** is designed to inform employees of the results of their appraisal.

In many organizations, the supervisor completes the appraisal, which is then given to the supervisor's immediate supervisor for his or her approval. This practice results in several advantages: (1) if the superior does not agree with the supervisor's rating, he or she can make suggestions for modifying the rating; (2) the superior can determine areas suitable for training; and (3) the superior can become more familiar with the employees for whom he or she is responsible. After the superior approves the supervisor's rating, the evaluation form is shown to the subordinate. Following this, the supervisor and the subordinate discuss the evaluation results during the appraisal interview.

The advantages of conducting appraisal interviews are: (1) the subordinate's present performance and the areas in which improvement is desirable can be discussed; (2) the interview provides an opportunity for the supervisor and subordinate to become more familiar with one another's goals, aspirations, feelings, and attitudes; and (3) the interview tends to strengthen lines of communication between the supervisor and subordinate.

The disadvantages of the appraisal interview are: (1) supervisors who are not comfortable with the interviewing process are reluctant to conduct the interviews unless so required; (2) poorly conducted interviews are likely to cause resentment and hostility between the supervisor and subordinate; (3) some supervisors believe that conducting appraisal interviews is a low-priority responsibility; therefore, they either hurry through the interview or they fail to conduct it altogether; and (4) subordinates become defensive when criticized.

Illustrated in Figure 11–9 is a list of suggestions that will result in conducting more effective appraisal interviews.

EMPLOYEE PROMOTION

Employee promotion is viewed as a means of helping employees achieve their needs, especially the esteem and self-actualization needs identified earlier in Maslow's hierarchy of needs theory (see Chapter 10). Promotion (or advancement) was also identified as a motivator in Herzberg's motivation-hygiene theory (also see Chapter 10). Consequently, the absence of promotional possibilities is likely to result in decreased employee satisfaction.

Figure 11-9 Suggestions for improving the effectiveness of interviews

1. Start the interview by having the employee evaluate his or her performance.
2. Try to put the employee at ease immediately.
3. Emphasize strengths before discussing weaknesses.
4. Point out any strengths not identified by the employee.
5. Let the employee decide, if at all possible, how the weaknesses will be overcome.
6. Limit the areas of employee improvement to those that can be overcome within a reasonable length of time.
7. Substantiate ratings with specific examples of performance.
8. "Hear out" the individual being appraised.
9. Minimize authoritarian behavior.
10. Allow extensive two-way communication.
11. Try not to bring up topics that threaten the self-esteem of the employee.
12. Try not to cover too much material in one interview.
13. Let the employee read the written appraisal before the interview.

What is the basic difference between a major and minor promotion?

Organizations generally make two types of promotions: major and minor. A major promotion results when an employee is given a new job title, most likely in conjunction with a variety of new job responsibilities. Such a promotion results, for example, when the supervisor of records management is promoted to the position of administrative office manager. A minor promotion, conversely, results when an employee keeps his or her present job title but moves from one level to another. An example is the executive secretary, level III, who is promoted to senior executive secretary.

In organizations that have a low turnover rate, which often reduces substantially the opportunities for promotions, moving employees laterally is an option. The primary reason for using lateral moves is to motivate employees and to reduce the possibility of burnout. Perhaps an employee realizes that the opportunities for promotion in his or her present work unit are quite poor but that if he or she were to make a lateral move to another work unit, the eventual promotional opportunities are more abundant and will likely occur more rapidly.

The lateral-move technique is also frequently used in organizations that undertake a major restructuring of their work processes, resulting in a significant change in the nature of employees' jobs. When the changes are significant, some organizations terminate all their affected employees and ask them to reapply for the new positions (with a guarantee that each employee who reapplies will have a job and no one will experience a pay cut).

Decisions about employee promotion generally take into consideration both objective and subjective factors. Among the objective factors are length of time the employee has worked for the organization and has held his or her present position, nature of previous work experience, and education. Among the subjective factors are the quality of the employee's work performance, the ability of the employee to perform the next higher job, and interview ratings.

Just as hiring and performance appraisal practices must be nondiscriminatory, so must promotion practices. An organization that uses different promotion standards for different groups among its workforce is committing an illegal act. Therefore, groups of workers protected by various provisions of federal laws (Civil Rights Act, Age Discrimination Act, and so forth) must be promoted using guidelines free of bias or discrimination. The promotional standards and/or criteria that are used must be applied uniformly throughout the organization, regardless of who is being promoted. The following suggestions help assure bias-free, nondiscriminatory promotion practices:

What suggestions help assure a bias-free nondiscriminatory promotion practice?

1. Allow employees to bid on job openings communicated to all employees throughout the organization.

2. Base the written performance appraisal on written job-related performance standards with which the employee is familiar.

3. Discuss the written performance appraisal with the employee, at which time he or she is asked to sign the appraisal. (This document is likely to be a critical one should an employee either file a discrimination charge against the supervisor and/or organization or sue the organization because of its promotional practices.)

4. Track the promotions of employees categorized as members of a protected group as identified in the federal and state legislation.

5. Have supervisors keep a log of subordinates' work performance—both desirable and undesirable—and attendance and tardiness.

Although the employee expects the organization to use fair, uniform, and consistent promotion procedures, he or she also has a number of responsibilities. Among these are an understanding of the lines or channels of promotion, expectations of his or her present position, duties and responsibilities comprising the next higher position, and qualifications needed by employees in the next higher position.

Increasingly, organizations are maintaining computerized data banks that contain information useful in making promotion decisions. These banks, which are used as an internal recruiting source, are accessed to determine which of the present employees possess the qualifications needed for the vacant position. From the list of qualified employees, those who are considered as deserving of a promotion are then further assessed to determine their suitability for the vacant position.

IMPLICATIONS FOR THE ADMINISTRATIVE OFFICE MANAGER

Performance appraisal is one of the most useful tools available to administrative office managers who wish to improve the operating efficiency of their units. Employees who overcome the weaknesses identified by the appraisal process are often able to perform at higher levels than previously.

Well-designed performance appraisal programs are psychologically worthwhile to employees. The absence of job-performance feedback denies employees the opportunity to satisfy the need of knowing how well they are performing.

Administrative office managers are vitally involved in designing many organizational performance appraisal programs. For example, they commonly serve on advisory committees that provide input into program development. The background, training, and performance appraisal experiences of these individuals provide them with the necessary qualifications for making a significant contribution to this area.

At the unit level, managers must be especially careful to avoid using subjective appraisal practices. Regardless of how well designed an organization's program is, much of its success will be destroyed by managers who are not objective in their appraisal efforts. Imagined subjectivity is often as damaging to the appraisal process as actual subjectivity.

REVIEW QUESTIONS

1. What are the various uses of the performance appraisal?

2. What are the characteristics of effective performance appraisal programs?

3. What suggestions can you offer that will be useful in designing an objective graphic rating scale?

4. What are the advantages and disadvantages of the paired comparison, checklists, and simple ranking methods of performance appraisal?

5. Why are employees opposed to the critical incidents method of performance appraisal?

6. What is the unique characteristic of the field staff review appraisal technique?

7. What guidelines should be followed when establishing the goals for the results-oriented appraisal method?

8. What kinds of rating errors are likely to occur when appraising employees' performance? Give examples of each type of error.

9. How can reliability and validity of an appraisal rating form be determined?

10. What suggestions can you provide for improving the effectiveness of performance appraisal interviews?

11. What is the basic difference between a major and a minor promotion?

DISCUSSION QUESTIONS

1. You are the administrative office manager in your company. You believe in giving your subordinates a pat on the back when they do well. During a recent performance appraisal interview, one of your subordinates was quite surprised to receive an average rating. He indicated that you frequently told him he was doing well, yet his official appraisal indicated average performance. Outline your response to him. How do you justify the discrepancy?

2. You have been at odds with one of your subordinates for several months. Although this individual does good work, you consider him to be a troublemaker. You have tried to keep your dislike for him from affecting your appraisal of his performance. During the appraisal interview you just completed, however, he said, "Just because you don't like me, you don't have to take it out on my appraisal. I don't think my performance has deteriorated as much as your appraisal of me indicates it has. I am going to discuss this with Ms. Snodgrass (your superior)." If this employee takes the matter up with Ms. Snodgrass, how are you going to defend your appraisal?

3. You are a supervisor of ten employees in the office services department. Performance appraisal is a task you do not enjoy because you dislike giving anyone a poor rating even if it is deserved. One of your former employees was transferred six months ago to another department. This individual essentially did the same job as she did in your department. The employee's new supervisor called you this morning to question why the employee had received above-average ratings from you when she performs considerably below average in her new job. Although you would like to rationalize the reason for her performance, you know that the problem likely stems from your practice of appraising employees' performance higher than it should be. You have decided that, in the future, you will have to give more accurate ratings. How are you going to justify lower ratings to employees in the future when their performance is just as effective (or more so) than it was in the past?

STUDENT PROJECTS AND ACTIVITIES

1. Obtain employee appraisal forms from two different organizations. What are the similarities in the content found on the two forms? The differences?

2. Talk with an administrative office manager to learn how he or she diminishes the impact of rating errors when appraising employee performance.

3. Going Online: Using the Internet, conduct an online search based on one of the concepts presented in this chapter or based on one of the chapter terms. Identify four or five things you learned from the material that you did not know prior to your online search.

Minicase

The Rudman Corporation manufactures a variety of lawn-care tools and equipment. Several years ago, many of the management functions were decentralized, which gave unit managers almost total autonomy in managing their units. The new president has decided that because the organization is growing rapidly, certain management functions should be centralized. He hopes that will provide better, more effective coordination of the various functions. One of the first functions to be central-ized is employee performance appraisal. At last count, twelve different appraisal techniques were being used in the various units.

1. Comment on the desirability or undesirability of the decentralized appraisal process currently being used in Rudman Corporation.
2. What advantages result from a centralized appraisal process?

Case

During the last year, the First American Bank in Tulsa, Oklahoma, has had a 20 percent increase in its workforce. If the volume of business increases as much this year as last, the bank projects its workforce will have to increase an additional thirty to thirty-five individuals this year. Although most of the new people who have been hired are office employees, a few have been hired at the management level. The same ratio between management and office employees is expected to be needed among new employees this year as in recent years.

The rapidly increasing number of employees is "straining" several of the bank's management functions including its performance appraisal program.

At the present time, a graphic scale is used to appraise employee performance. The form was originally developed for an insurance company nearly fifteen years ago and has not been changed during the fourteen years the bank has used it.

The executive vice president has asked you, the administrative office manager, to provide her with information about the results-oriented performance appraisal approach.

1. How might the First American Bank sell its employees on the use of the results-oriented approach after the graphic rating scale approach has been used for so long?
2. What suggestions can you offer to help assure the success of the results-oriented appraisal approach, assuming it is the one that is selected?
3. Most likely, supervisors will need some specialized training in specific elements of the results-oriented program. Identify and discuss some of these elements.

*C*hapter 12

ANALYZING JOBS OF OFFICE EMPLOYEES

*C*hapter *A*ims

After reading this chapter, you should be able to design an effective program for analyzing the jobs of office employees.

*C*hapter *O*utline

The Nature of Job Analysis
Uses of Job Analysis
Job Analysis Program
    Questionnaire Method
    Interview Method
    Observation Method
    Combination of Methods
Describing the Job
    Job Description
    Job Specification
    Uses of Job Descriptions and Job
        Specifications
Implications for the Administrative Office
    Manager

*C*hapter *T*erms

Critical incidents technique
Interview method
Job analysis
Job description
Job information worksheet
Job specification
Observation method
Questionnaire method
Time and motion study
U.S. Employment Service

*I*n some organizations, managers and supervisors are becomimg less familiar with the various duties performed by their subordinates. When this happens, job analysis becomes more important. One of the reasons managers and supervisors are not as familiar with various aspects of their subordinates' jobs is that they most likely have not actually held all the positions for which they have managerial or supervisory responsibility. In addition to providing input useful in job structuring, analysis also results in better control and coordination of employee output.

THE NATURE OF JOB ANALYSIS

How do job descriptions and job specifications differ from each another?

Job analysis is the formal process of collecting information about the components of a job. The information collected through job analysis is used to prepare job descriptions and job specifications. A **job description** is the written document that outlines the duties and responsibilities of a job. A **job specification,** conversely, refers to the document that outlines the personal qualifications an employee must possess to perform the duties and responsibilities of a particular job. The description pertains to the job, but the specification pertains to the job holder.

USES OF JOB ANALYSIS

What are the uses of job analysis?

Job analysis has several uses as an important administrative management function. The information collected in job analysis is ultimately used in recruiting, selecting, and placing employees in positions that match their qualifications. In addition, job analysis is used to help determine qualifications of employees; and it facilitates employee performance appraisal because job analysis data are useful in determining realistic performance standards. Job analysis also plays an important role in employee promotion and transfer. Furthermore, job analysis is used to identify areas in which new or existing employees may need training.

Job analysis is also used to standardize the same job performed by several employees. Control over employee production is improved because standardization increases the efficiency with which employee output is measured. As a result, employees have greater assurance their work load is consistent with normal expectations. Because it improves the quality and quantity of job-related information shared with employees, job analysis also provides an important human relations function. Finally, by providing data about the relative difficulty of the various job tasks, job analysis is used in the development of equitable salary scales.

Although the job analysis process may identify inefficient use of time and motion in office procedures, it should not be confused with a time and motion study. By providing data relating to specific jobs, a **time and motion study** is primarily an industrial engineering function. Job analysis, conversely, is an administrative management function. The basic purpose of a time and motion study is to identify waste and inefficiency, whereas the basic purpose of job analysis is to identify job duties and responsibilities. Jobs that contain wasteful motions and that are inefficient should be subjected to time and motion study before they are analyzed. Otherwise, the analyzed results will be based on nonproductive functions, making the analysis process invalid.

JOB ANALYSIS PROGRAM

What must be considered before beginning a job analysis program?

An effective job analysis program requires important preparatory work, including a clear identification of program objectives, purposes, and procedures to be followed in collecting data. Before starting the analysis procedures, the following four items must be considered: (1) the jobs that will be included in the analysis, (2) the order in which the jobs will be analyzed, (3) the nature of the information to be collected, and (4) the method to be used in collecting the information. To minimize their resistance to the program, detailed information about the objectives, purposes, and benefits of the program must be communicated to employees.

The cooperation and support of employees will be obtained more quickly when they are made aware of the following benefits of job analysis:

1. It provides an objective basis for determining the importance of each job, determining the rate of pay for each job, and appraising the performance of each employee.
2. It enables each employee to better understand job duties and responsibilities that his or her position comprises.
3. It facilitates making more equitable employee work load assignments.
4. It assists employees in areas where self-improvement is appropriate.
5. It aids supervising employees because each job is clearly defined.

Successful job analysis programs are comprised of a number of well-designed steps, including the following:

What are the steps involved in job analysis programs?

1. Determining the use or uses that will be made of the collected information. Because some of the methods used to collect information are better suited for certain types of information than are the other methods, being familiar with the uses of collected information is critical.
2. Becoming familiar with available background information. Among the types of background information with which the analyst needs familiarity are the organization chart, existing job descriptions, and systems and/or process charts that show how various job tasks are interrelated and intertwined.
3. Determining which jobs are to be analyzed. When only a portion of an organization's positions are to be analyzed, a systematic means should be used to determine which jobs to analyze. Generally, all the positions in a given work unit or department are analyzed at the same time.
4. Collecting the data. Before the data are actually collected, those who will be collecting the data as well as those from whom the data are collected should be familiarized with the process.
5. Verifying the accuracy of the collected data. Two employees who have identical or near identical jobs will sometimes provide contradictory data about their positions. The data collected through job analysis and subsequently used to prepare job descriptions and job specifications need to be as accurate as circumstances will allow.
6. Developing the preliminary job descriptions and job specifications. After they have been developed, they should be examined by both the supervisors and the employees who are familiar with positions to which they pertain.
7. Finalizing the job descriptions and job specifications. Once finalized, the documents should be shared with the employees as well as job applicants to whom they pertain.

A significant determinant of the success of the job analysis program is the reliability of the collected information. Three methods are frequently used to collect information: **questionnaire, interview,** and **observation.** In some instances, a combination of two or more methods may be appropriate.

Questionnaire Method

Employees who are most familiar with the job being analyzed generally complete the data-gathering questionnaire, which typically consists of a series of questions, often in short-answer format. The success of this method depends on the employee's ability to make a correct interpretation of the questionnaire items and to provide accurate and easy-to-classify answers.

Questionnaires used to collect information from employees are typically designed by the administrative office manager, by the organization's job analyst, or by a consultant. Regardless of who prepares the questionnaire, its design will have a significant impact on the success of the program.

The design of the questionnaire is determined by the number of employees who are expected to complete it. In organizations with a small workforce, a simplified questionnaire that includes the following items may be sufficient.

How are job analysis questionnaires designed/developed?

- Title of job
- Description of job
- Tasks performed daily, weekly, monthly, quarterly, and annually
- Special requirements (skills, experience, knowledge) for the job
- Special work performance for the job

A questionnaire with more detail may be needed when the number of employees expected to complete it increases. An example of such a questionnaire is illustrated in Figure 12–1.

The analysis of some jobs is facilitated by studying the special methods, forms, and reports used by the employees, especially when the items are used extensively in a particular job. Failure to analyze these items adequately may result in the preparation of unrealistic job descriptions and specifications. If special methods, forms, and reports are crucial components of an employee's job, the questionnaire should be designed to make note of these during the data-collection process.

A successful job analysis program requires the gathering of accurate and complete information. Situations to guard against are omission of important facts, inclusion of inaccurate information, or statements that misrepresent the importance of certain job attributes. Questionnaire design may play an important role in assuring complete and accurate information.

For what situations is the questionnaire method used?

Situations for which the questionnaire method is especially appropriate are the following:

1. When the job being analyzed can be described quite easily.
2. When the job being analyzed consists mostly of physical activities rather than human relations or personality factors. (Employees often have difficulty assessing the importance of job-related human relations or personality factors.)
3. When a considerable number of jobs are to be analyzed.
4. When the questionnaire can be precisely and clearly worded.
5. When job information has to be obtained quickly.

Figure 12-1 Job analy-
                 sis questionnaire

Your Name _____   Supervisor's Name _____

Title of Job _____   Today's Date _____

Level of Job _____   D.O.T. Number _____
                                             (To be filled in by analyst)
Department _____

A. *Description of Duties:* Please describe the duties and responsibilities of your job as you understand the situation. In your description, please be as specific as you can in telling what your job consists of, the importance of each duty and responsibilty, and the frequency with which each is performed. The following suggestions may facilitate your response:

1. Divide your job into specific duties and steps.

2. In describing each step, indicate from whom the work is obtained, explain the nature of the operation, indicate to whom the finished work is given, and indicate the frequency of the operation.

   (If the space provided below is not sufficient, please continue on the reverse side of this page.)

B. *Educational Requirements:* Please place a check mark (✓) beside the amount of education required for the job you hold.

No education requirement _____   College degree _____

High school diploma _____   Years of college work required _____

Some college work _____   Other _____ (Please specify)

C. *Skills Required:* Please indicate the nature of any skill requirements for the job you hold, including the level of skills required.

     Nature of skills   *Level required*
_____
_____
_____

D. *Experience Requirements:* Please indicate the nature of any job experience requirements for the job you hold, including the number of years required.

     Nature of experience   *Years of required experience*
_____
_____
_____

E. *Job Knowledge Requirements:* Please indicate the nature of any job knowledge (specific or general) for the job you hold, including the appropriate sources for obtaining the required knowledge.

     Job knowledge requirements   *Source of gaining knowledge*
_____
_____
_____

F. *Equipment/Tools Used:* Please list the equipment and tools used in the discharge of your job, including the frequency of usage and the amount of skill required in using the equipment and tools.

   Equipment/Tools   *Frequency of use*   *Skills required*
_____

An alternative to developing a questionnaire for use in job analysis is the use of a standardized questionnaire. Among the more common standardized job analysis questionnaires are the Position Analysis Questionnaire (PAQ), the Task Abilities Scale, and the Management Position Description Questionnaire. The instruments used in each of these techniques are research based, and their use helps increase the reliability and validity of the survey results.

Figure 12-1
(*Continued*)

G. *Materials and Forms Used:* Please list the materials and forms used in the discharge of your job, including the frequency of use.

Materials and forms used	Frequency of use

H. *Source of Supervision:* Please identify, by title only, the individual(s) responsible for supervising your work, including the degree to which you are supervised.

Supervisor's title	Degree of supervision

I. *Contact with Others:* Please indicate with whom (outside your own department) you come in contact, the nature or purpose of the contact, and the medium through which the contact is made (phone, person, etc.). Include only company employees.

Contact with	Nature of contact	Medium of contact

J. *Working Conditions:* Please indicate to what extent your work is performed in undesirable or hazardous conditions. Consider such items as noise, temperature, air, lighting.

K. *Physical Requirements:* Please indicate the nature of any physical requirements for the job you hold.

L. *Responsibility Requirements:* Please indicate the nature of any responsbility you have for exercise of judgments, direction of others, and public relations.

M. *Physical Effort Requirements:* Please place a check mark (✓) in the appropriate columns.

	Very Frequently	Frequently	Sometimes	Seldom	Never
Walking					
Sitting					
Lifting					
Reaching					
Stooping					
Standing					
Other_____					
Other_____					

N. *Other Considerations:*
1. How long does it take to become familiar with this job?
2. What is the next job in the promotion channel?
3. What is the present salary for this job? (Give range)
4. Please provide any other information you care to that would assist in analyzing this job.

What are the characteristics of the Position Analysis Questionnaire?

The PAQ contains 194 elements in six major areas: information input, mental processes, work output, relationship with other persons, job context, and other job characteristics. Employees respond to each of the 194 elements using a scale with six choices: *Does not apply, nominal/very infrequent, occasional, moderate, considerable,* and *very substantial.* The PAQ helps identify the behaviors involved in the performance of job tasks, duties, and responsibilities. Because the PAQ is completed by a trained analyst, greater uniformity in how employees respond to various questions can be attained.

The questionnaire method facilitates the rapid collection of a large amount of information. Some organizations, however, supplement the questionnaire method with a combination of interviews and observations to assure the collection of accurate information.

A potential disadvantage of the questionnaire method is the construction of an instrument that is too complex, confusing, or long to be effective. These conditions may result in the collection of inaccurate information. Another disadvantage is the tendency for some employees to overestimate or underestimate the importance of the jobs they perform. Finally, the information gathered on the questionnaire has to be collated and synthesized, which tends to be a time-consuming process.

Interview Method

The interview method involves questioning employees about their job duties and responsibilities. Three types of interviews exist: they can be conducted one on one with individual employees; they can be conducted with a group of employees who perform the same job; or they can be conducted with one or more individuals who supervise the employee whose job is being analyzed. Interviews are typically conducted at either the employee's workstation or at a site selected by the interviewer. Those conducted at the workstation enable the interviewer to observe the job during the interview process, which, in effect, combines the interview and observation methods of gathering job information.

In the same way that a printed questionnaire facilitates the questionnaire method, a **job information worksheet** facilitates the interview method. The items included on the job information worksheet are similar to those included on the questionnaire. Accuracy and completeness of information can be increased by reading employees' responses back to them. Some organizations also have supervisors confirm the accuracy of the information provided by their subordinates.

The interview method of gathering job information is appropriate in the following situations:

For what situations is the interview method suited?

1. When the number of employees whose jobs are to be analyzed is quite small.
2. When the job being analyzed is quite complicated. (This method enables the interviewer to ask questions of the employees until he or she sufficiently understands the job duties and responsibilities.)
3. When the interviewer's data-collection efforts are enhanced by observing the employee at work while talking with him or her about job tasks.
4. When the job being analyzed is largely comprised of human relations and personality factors.

The primary advantage of using the interview method is the interviewer's ability to collect all the desired facts about a particular job. The occurrence of incomplete or omitted information, which is sometimes found in the questionnaire method, is rare when using the interview method.

A disadvantage of the interview method is the time-consuming task of talking with each employee. The data-collection process is likely to be much slower than when using the questionnaire method. Furthermore, unless rapport is readily established between the interviewer and the employee, the completeness and accuracy of the employee's responses may be affected.

Observation Method

A third method of gathering job information involves observing the employee at work. Observations can take place either at the employee's workstation or at the various locations where the employee works. The analyst records the observations on a job observation sheet, which includes many of the same items found on a job questionnaire or the job information worksheet.

The observation method is appropriately used in the following instances:

For what situations is the observation method used?

1. When the nature of the job prohibits the employee's absence from his or her workstation.
2. When, because of the complexity of the job, the analyst has difficulty analyzing the job on the basis of the information gathered through a questionnaire or interview.
3. When the number of jobs to be analyzed is small.

The primary advantage of the observation method is the accuracy of the information gathered by the analyst. In addition, the analyst is able to observe the employee for the needed length of time without interrupting the work flow.

A disadvantage of this method results from the time-consuming process of gathering information. Another possible disadvantage is the uncomfortable feeling some employees experience while being observed. Furthermore, some employees change their work patterns when they know they are being observed, which has the potential for distorting the results.

Combination of Methods

To obtain information about a particular job, two or more of the previously described methods can be combined. Using a combination of methods usually assures accurate and complete input because of the ease with which information collected by one method can be verified by the second method. Therefore, details omitted while using one method will usually be obtained through the use of a second method. Having available more accurate, complete information may offset the disadvantages of using a more time-consuming, costly process.

What are the characteristics of the critical incidents technique?

An adaptation of the combination method is the **critical incidents technique,** which involves obtaining records of behavior (incidents) that led to either effective or ineffective job performance. These incidents are collected in a variety of ways including the use of questionnaires and interviews from both supervisors and employees. After the incidents are available, they are then grouped and placed into several categories. The list of critical incidents identifies the behaviors that employees in various positions need for successful job performance.

DESCRIBING THE JOB

One of the important outcomes of the job analysis program is the identification of duties and responsibilities comprising a particular job. When employees' duties are not formally determined or are not put into writing, management has less control over employee performance. In some cases, an employee might perform only those duties he or she is willing to perform. Formal, written job descriptions help ensure that employees are performing their assigned duties. Descriptions also prevent job holders from gradually changing the nature of the job. Furthermore, descriptions help prevent misunderstandings between employees and their supervisors about specific job duties. The job needs to be described as it presently exists and not as the preparer of the description wishes it to be.

Job descriptions and specifications can be combined into one document, or they may be maintained as two separate documents. Presenting them separately is advantageous when the information in the description and specification is used for different purposes, as is commonly the case.

Job Description

The use of clear, concise statements is crucial in preparing job descriptions. The following are offered as suggestions for writing effective job descriptions:

How can a job description be made more effective?

1. A simple, direct sentence structure should be used.
2. A functional verb in the present tense should be used to begin each sentence. Examples of such verbs are *plans, prepares, originates,* and so forth.
3. Conciseness can be achieved by eliminating all unnecessary words and phrases.
4. The description should focus on the skills involved in performing the job as well as on the tools and equipment that are used.
5. Job titles that appear in the description should be printed in all capital letters.
6. The content in the description should accurately reflect the nature of job duties.
7. The job description should be as thorough as possible.

Job titles in job descriptions should compare closely with the listings in the *Dictionary of Occupational Titles (D.O.T.),* a document prepared by the **U.S. Employment Service** in the U.S. Department of Labor. The latest edition of the *D.O.T.,* which was published in 1991, contains data on approximately twenty thousand jobs. Also now available is a Windows version of the *D.O.T.* that facilitates a computerized search and retrieval of information.

The *D.O.T.* descriptions help standardize organizational job titles and descriptions, which is useful in reporting a variety of statistical information. In selecting the *D.O.T.* number to place on the job description, the number in the *D.O.T.* description that most closely matches the organization's description is used.

Figure 12–2 illustrates the *D.O.T.* job description for a clerical position.

Although job descriptions are not presented in a standard format, they typically consist of the following sections:

What sections are typically found in job descriptions?

1. *Job identification.* This section includes the title of the job, the level of the job, the department in which the job is found, the comparable *D.O.T.* number, and the date on which the job description was approved and adopted.
2. *Summary of job.* This section is a brief summary of the job. Sufficient information should be included in the summary so one can clearly differentiate between the job being described and other similar jobs.
3. *Duties of job.* This section clearly describes the primary duties and responsibilities of the job, as well as their frequency of occurrence. To prevent ambiguities and possible misunderstanding, uncommon duties and responsibilities should be explained in sufficient detail and with sufficient justification. Although the following items may be included in other sections of the job description, they may also be included as part of this sec-

Figure 12-2 D.O.T. job description. *Dictionary of Occupational Titles.*

203.362-022 WORD PROCESSING-MACHINE OPERATOR (clerical) word processor.

Operates word processing equipment to record, edit, store, and revise correspondence, reports, statistical tables, forms, and other materials, utilizing clerical skills and knowledge of word processing functions. Reads instructions to determine procedures to be followed regarding material to be prepared or revised and required format for finished copy. Depresses keys on word processing equipment to adjust controls for spacing, margins, and tabulation, and places tape cassette, diskette, or other magnetic recording medium in holder. Keyboards (types) original material into machine memory, typing from printed copy, machine dictation, or related sources. Reads proof copy of material entered into machine memory, and depresses keys to correct typographical errors, print out final copy, and record material onto magnetic medium. Locates medium in file when revisions are required, places medium in holder and presses keys to insert (type), delete, correct, reposition, or reformat designated material. May operate equipment that extends word processing capabilities, such as cathode ray tube (CRT) displays, single or multiple printers, or optical character recognition (OCR). Important variations are kinds (trade names) of word processing equipment operated. May operate electronic typewriters with limited editing capabilities. GOE 07.06. 02 PD S 08 09 10 12 13 15 M1 L3 SVP 4 SOC 4624

tion: (a) identification of the tools and equipment, forms, and materials used in carrying out the job; (b) title of the individual responsible for supervising the job holder and the degree of supervision received; and (c) relationship of the work flow, transfer, and promotion characteristics between the job being described and other similar jobs.

A description is illustrated in Figure 12–3.

Job Specification

Like the material in the job description, the content of the job specification is not presented in a standard format. The writing guidelines given for presenting job descriptions are also appropriate for presenting job specifications.

What sections are typically found in job specifications?

Job specifications typically consist of some or all of the following parts:

1. *Job identification.* This section includes the title of the job, the level of the job, the point value of the job (if appropriate), the department in which the job is found, the comparable *D.O.T.* number, and the date on which the job specification was approved and adopted. In addition, a column may be provided on the right side of the specification for the purpose of recording the number of points assigned each factor during the job evaluation process.

2. *Experience requirements.* This section is used to specify the minimum experience requirements. In addition to specifying the nature of the requirements, the statement should include the required number of years of experience.

Figure 12-3 Job description

Title of Job _____ Secretary _____	D.O.T. Number _____ 201.368 _____
Level of Job _____ Level III _____	Date Approved _____ 11/30/XX _____
Department _____ Office Services _____	

SUMMARY OF JOB: The individual holding this job performs secretarial duties for the manager of the department. Since the job involves relieving the manager of some of his or her administrative duties, a considerable amount of the work is administrative in nature. The individual also supervises other office employees.

DUTIES OF JOB:

Most Frequent Duties: (Comprising at least 70 percent of work day)

1. Taking dictation and transcribing materials
2. Keeping manager's appointments calendar
3. Supervising other office employees
4. Working with office budget
5. Answering correspondence
6. Protecting confidentiality of materials
7. Acting as RECEPTIONIST for manager's callers
8. Answering telephone
9. Preparing weekly salary data
10. Allocating work among others

Least Frequent Duties: (Comprising not more than 30 percent of work day)

1. Filing documents and materials
2. Preparing reports
3. Designing interoffice forms
4. Evaluating subordinates
5. Duplicating materials
6. Maintaining petty cash

TOOLS AND EQUIPMENT USED:

Typewriter, computer, calculator, copy machine, dictation equipment

FORMS AND REPORTS USED ON JOB:

Departmental budget, payroll forms, personnel evaluation forms, petty cash disbursements, and other office reports as called for

SUPERVISED BY: DEPARTMENT MANAGER

RELATION TO OTHER JOBS:

This position is related to all other secretarial and clerical jobs in the department, since the individual is responsible for assigning work to other employees.

Since this position is the highest secretarial position in the department, promotion possibilities include a secretarial position in the central offices or as an ADMINISTRATIVE ASSISTANT.

3. *Educational requirements.* Identified in this section are the minimum educational requirements for the job holder. Any required courses or technical training should also be listed.

4. *Human relations requirements.* This section specifies human relations and personality factors required of the job holder. Although the nature of these factors is difficult to assess, many times they are critically important in the performance of a particular job. Typically included are personality traits, initiative, ambition, resourcefulness, and cooperation.

5. *Job knowledge requirements.* This section identifies any job knowledge requirements not covered in the experience and educational sections. Typically included are such items as tools, equipment, and materials.

6. *Responsibility requirements.* This section provides a description of the areas of responsibility for the job being described. The extent of the responsibility should also be included in the description. Possible areas of responsibility are safety, equipment and materials, other employees, work of others, quality of work, and cost reduction.

7. *Skill requirements.* Provided in this section is a list of the skills required to perform the job. If different skill levels exist, the level of skill required should also be identified. Examples of skill levels are variable typing or keyboarding rates and machine operation rates.

8. *Physical effort requirements.* This section of the job specification describes the nature of the physical effort requirements including such factors as walking, sitting, lifting, reaching, stooping, and standing. The specification should stipulate the amount of physical effort required and the amount of time consumed by each type of physical effort.

9. *Environmental conditions.* Described in this section are the conditions and surroundings under which the job is performed. Factors to be included are lighting, air, temperature, and noise levels.

A representative job specification is illustrated in Figure 12–4.

Only justifiable personal requirements should be included in a job specification. Sometimes specifications are prepared that include more strenuous

---

Title of Job	Secretary	D.O.T. Number	201.368
Level of Job	Level III	Date Approved	11/30/XX
Department	Office Services	Point Value	270

RATING
Points

EXPERIENCE REQUIREMENTS: A minimum of 3 years' previous experience is required.

40

EDUCATIONAL REQUIREMENTS: A high school diploma is required and some college work is desirable.

30

HUMAN RELATIONS REQUIREMENTS: Ability to get along well with people, to meet people, to be creative, and to cope with stress stiuations.

40

JOB KNOWLEDGE REQUIREMENTS: Ability to perform bookkeeping functions and to use calculating equipment, in addition to regular secretarial requirements.

50

RESPONSIBILITY REQUIREMENTS: Responsibility for assuring the quality of work of others, as well as being responsible for assuring the maintenance of equipment.

50

SKILL REQUIREMENTS: Ability to type 60 words a minute and ability to take shorthand at 100 words a minute.

50

PHYSICAL REQUIREMENTS: Must be able to sit for long periods of time.

10

Figure 12-4 Job specification

requirements than may be necessary. Trying to justify a keyboarding rate of 70 words a minute is difficult when a 50 words-per-minute rate is adequate for the demands of the job.

State and federal laws prevent the use of age, sex, race, religion, and color as a basis for identifying job requirements. Job specifications should be reviewed periodically to determine whether any requirements are discriminatory or ambiguous.

With the enactment of the Americans with Disabilities Act, employees are required to have requisite skills, background, and experience to perform the essential functions of the job. The ADA states that the employer must make "reasonable accommodation" so that a disabled person can perform these job functions unless doing so will result in an "undue hardship." Although the ADA does not require that employees have job descriptions and job specifications, their presence is often helpful should any legal questions arise.

Uses of Job Descriptions and Job Specifications

What uses are made of job descriptions and job specifications?

The value of job descriptions and specifications is determined by how they are used. Both documents should be readily available to job holders and their supervisors.

Appropriate Uses of Job Descriptions

1. To inform the job holder about the duties and responsibilities of his or her job.
2. To assist the job holder in improving his or her job performance.
3. To assist the job holder in preparing for promotion or transfer.
4. To facilitate orientation and training of new employees.
5. To assist in the arbitration of employee grievances.

Appropriate Uses of Job Specifications

1. To facilitate recruitment and selection of employees, especially in screening job applicants.
2. To facilitate the job evaluation process.

IMPLICATIONS FOR THE ADMINISTRATIVE OFFICE MANAGER

The administrative office manager has important responsibilities in job analysis activities. In many organizations, the administrative office manager serves as a key member of the job analysis advisory committee. In addition, managers are often responsible for communicating information to their subordinates about key aspects of job analysis activities including benefits, uses, and so forth. The manager is also responsible for motivating his or her subordinates to provide accurate responses in job information collection efforts.

The absence of job analysis information can be a serious impediment to the effective management of organizational functions and to employee supervision. For example, when job information is unavailable, managers cannot be sure that positions are properly designed or that employees have equitable work loads. Nor can they be sure that employees' salaries are properly related to the importance of job duties.

The absence of job analysis information unnecessarily compounds the employee selection process. Job descriptions and job specifications that are prepared on the basis of job analysis information are integral components of the employee selection process. The absence of job descriptions also compounds the difficulty of employee supervision because neither the supervisor nor the employee can be certain of the official duties that a job comprises. Lack of certainty about appropriate job duties often creates disagreements, which may impede the development of effective supervisor-subordinate relations.

REVIEW QUESTIONS

1. How do job analysis, job descriptions, and job specifications differ from one another?

2. Are time and motion studies related to one another? Explain.

3. Identify the benefits of job analysis.

4. To what situations is the questionnaire method of job analysis especially suited?

5. To what situations is the interview method of job analysis especially suited?

6. To what situations is the observation method of job analysis especially suited?

7. What suggestions can you offer for writing effective job descriptions?

8. In what ways are job descriptions and job specifications used?

DISCUSSION QUESTIONS

1. You were recently talking with a friend who works in another company. During the conversation, you indicated that you were heading the company's job analysis committee, which is currently getting ready to undertake a thorough job analysis. When you indicated that you needed to collect this information because all job specifications and descriptions were being reviewed, he indicated that in his company descriptions and specifications are revised by several managers when they feel changes need to be made. He further indicated that no input from job analysis is used in revising job descriptions and specifications. Discuss the implications of the way in which job descriptions and specifications are revised in the company in which your friend works.

2. You are a member of a committee charged with revising the job descriptions and job specifications in the company in which you work. In revising the lowest level clerk-typist position, one committee member insisted that the minimum education requirements for this position should be a two-year associate of arts degree. When you questioned him about his position (you believe that a high school degree is all that is needed for this position), he indicated that it was time to upgrade office positions—and the way to do that was by increasing minimum education requirements. Discuss the wisdom of upgrading an office position by means of increasing the educational qualification of the job holders.

3. You are the new administrative office manager in a small company. In looking at the current job descriptions and specifications, you noticed that they do not seem to be especially accurate or reasonable. When you asked your assistant about the descriptions and specifications, she indicated that your predecessor, working alone, revised them several months before he retired. When you asked why they were revised by a committee of one, she indicated that your predecessor wanted to be able to structure the positions as he wanted and, therefore, no input from others was desired. She further indicated that your predecessor was rather opinionated about various points, including how various office personnel should perform their jobs. Discuss the implications of the manner in which the descriptions and specifications were prepared.

STUDENT PROJECTS AND ACTIVITIES

1. Obtain a job analysis questionnaire used in analyzing the jobs of office employees. How does its content compare with the content of the job analysis questionnaire found in this chapter?

2. Obtain the job descriptions for two comparable jobs. What are the similarities in the identified tasks? The differences?

3. Going Online: Using the Internet, conduct an online search based on one of the concepts presented in this chapter or based on one of the chapter terms. Identify four or five things you learned from the material that you did not know before your search.

Minicase

The Drieden Corporation, a manufacturer of fine china, is about to undertake an extensive analysis of its jobs. The individual in charge of job analysis knows that many things can either "make or break" the program. In the interest of conducting a successful program, you have been asked to provide a list of suggestions that will be useful in helping assure the success of the job analysis program.

1. What suggestions do you plan to put on your list?

2. Of the suggestions you listed in Minicase Question 1, identify three suggestions that you believe are the most important and explain why you believe they are a top priority.

Case

A few years ago, Dartmouth Industries, a toy manufacturer in Buffalo, New York, undertook a thorough analysis of its jobs. For a variety of reasons, this endeavor was generally regarded as having created several problems, some of which continue to prevail. A large share of the problems that resulted can be attributed to the human resources manager who was in charge of the job analysis efforts.

The human resources manager, according to many sources, was using job analysis to "get even" with the employees because of their entering into collective bargaining. The sources believed that because the human resources manager was indeed the one who "lost" on collective bargaining, he would "win" on job analysis.

Even though this manager continues to work for Dartmouth, some of the negative sentiment to-

ward job analysis has subsided. Obviously, no one wants the same mistake to be repeated during the pending job analysis efforts.

1. What suggestions can you make to help assure the pending job analysis efforts will not have the image problems found in the earlier efforts?

2. What might have been done during the earlier efforts to help eliminate the creation of image problems associated with undertaking a job analysis program?

3. Why would it be almost impossible for the human resources manager to use job analysis to get even with employees?

Chapter 13

EVALUATING JOBS OF OFFICE EMPLOYEES

Chapter Aims

After studying this chapter, you should be able to design an effective program for evaluating the jobs of office employees.

Chapter Outline

Job Evaluation Methods
    Ranking
    Job Grading
    Factor Comparison
    Point Evaluation
Adopting a Job Evaluation Method
Job Evaluation Committee
Implications for the Administrative Office
    Manager

Chapter Terms

Compensable factors
Factor comparison
Job classification
Job evaluation
Job grading
Key jobs
Monetary comparison scale
Nonkey jobs
Nonquantitative method
Point evaluation
Quantitative method
Ranking
Standard job description

Job evaluation is used by organizations to provide information about the relative worth of jobs, which, in turn, helps determine the monetary worth of the jobs. The process of evaluating jobs uses the information collected through job analysis, the topic of Chapter 12.

What are the benefits of a formally established job evaluation progam?

A formal job evaluation program is beneficial for several reasons. Job evaluation provides an objective determination of the value of each job. Determining job worth by any other means may produce subjective results. In addition, employees are more likely to accept the relative values of their positions when job worth is determined by job evaluation. Too, it gives employees a greater appreciation for and understanding of the relationship between the demands of their jobs and their compensation. Another benefit is that it helps reduce the number of employee complaints about wage inequities. Job evaluation is also used in identifying lines of authority and patterns of advancement within an organization. Finally, it can be used to identify areas appropriate for new employee orientation and training as well as to facilitate employee transfer.

JOB EVALUATION METHODS

How do the nonquantitative and quantitative job evaluation methods differ from one another?

Two types of job evaluation methods are used: nonquantitative and quantitative. A **nonquantitative method** of job evaluation involves evaluating a job as a whole job rather than evaluating it on the basis of its parts. When job parts or job factors provide the evaluation basis, however, a **quantitative method** is being used. The two most popular nonquantitative methods of job evaluation are ranking and job grading. Of the quantitative methods, factor comparison and point evaluation are the most popular.

Compensable factors are used in the evaluation process. These are the factors that jobs share in common with one another and that provide the evaluation basis. Examples of compensable factors are working conditions, physical effort, skill requirements, decision-making requirements, and so forth. The nonquantitative methods typically use job difficulty as their one compensable factor. The quantitative methods use a variety of compensable factors, including those listed earlier.

Ranking

What are the characteristics of the ranking method?

Of the various job evaluation methods, the simplest and oldest method is the **ranking** or order-of-merit system. The job description and specification for each job (see Chapter 12) are used in the evaluation process. After the relative importance of all the jobs being evaluated is determined, each job is assigned to a specific job level. The individual or the committee doing the evaluating is responsible for determining the number of job levels.

Three steps constitute the ranking method: (1) determine the number of different levels to be used in the job evaluation process; (2) by means of a ranking device, rank the various jobs from the most important to the least important; and (3) assign each job to one of the predetermined job levels.

Figure 13–1 illustrates two aspects of the ranking method of job evaluation: (1) the rank of each job, from the least important to the most important, and (2) the level to which each job is assigned. After the jobs are ranked, the next step involves determining the range of pay for each of the job levels. For an organization to remain competitive, it has to provide salaries comparable to those paid by other organizations in the community. Methods of gathering information about salary rates in other organizations in the community are covered in Chapter 14.

Figure 13-1 Ranking
method of job evaluation

Job title	Job level
Messenger	1
Mail Clerk	2
Requisitions Clerk	2
File Clerk	3
Data Entry Operator I	3
Micrographics Clerk	4
Data Entry Operator II	5
Correspondence Secretary I	5
Administrative Secretary I	6
Correspondence Secretary II	6
Administrative Secretary II	7
Correspondence Secretary III	7
Computer Programmer	7
Administrative Secretary III	8
Executive Secretary	8
Administrative Assistant	9
Systems Analyst	9

Figure 13–2 illustrates the range of pay for each job level included in Figure 13–1. For example, job level 6, which includes the administrative secretary I and the correspondence secretary II positions, was found to have an average monthly salary of $2,600 in other organizations in the community. In the organization for which this salary scale was prepared, job level 6 has a monthly salary range of $2,400 to $2,950, with $2,625 per month as the midpoint salary. Creating a salary range for each job enables an organization to compensate employees on the basis of their quality of performance and longevity with the organization.

The ranking of jobs is frequently done by means of index cards. The title of each job is placed on a separate card, and the cards are then arranged and rearranged until they are sorted in the order of job importance.

The ranking method is frequently limited to situations in which a minimum number of jobs is to be evaluated. The method becomes too cumbersome when more than twenty-five to thirty jobs are being considered. Because the ranking method is a fairly quick and inexpensive evaluation method, it is also appropriately used when time and financial cost are important considerations.

The use of the ranking method has several advantages: it is readily understood by employees, it is a fairly quick and simple method to use, and it is fairly inexpensive to install.

Job Level	Average Salary Paid for Job Level in other organizations	Salary Range		
		Minimum	Midpoint	Maximum
1	$1,500	$1,300	$1,525	$1,750
2	1,700	1,500	1,725	1,950
3	1,900	1,700	1,925	2,150
4	2,100	1,900	2,125	2,350
5	2,300	2,100	2,325	2,650
6	2,600	2,400	2,625	2,950
7	2,900	2,700	2,925	3,350
8	3,300	3,000	3,325	3,750
9	3,700	3,300	3,725	4,150

Figure 13-2 Salary
ranges

What are the
disadvantages of the
ranking method?

The use of the ranking method also has several disadvantages. It does not provide a highly refined index of job worth because comparisons are made on the basis of the job as a whole job and not on the basis of its parts or factors. The importance of the job may be influenced by the job holder. In addition, job ranking may be influenced by the going wage and salary rates rather than by actual importance.

Job Grading

The **job grading** method (also known as **job classification**) is another of the nonquantitative methods of job evaluation. The job grading method is used in the federal civil service system.

What are the
characteristics of the job
grading method?

The grading method involves evaluating jobs on the basis of a number of predetermined classes or grades. Several factors affect the number of classes or grades used including the nature of job duties, responsibilities, skills, and knowledges. Once the predetermined classes have been set, standard job descriptions are prepared. More objectivity can be achieved if an organization compares its **standard job descriptions** with those of similar organizations.

What is a standard job
description?

The competitive salary ranges are developed in much the same way as the ranges are developed for the ranking method. Each job is then compared with the standard job description to determine the level of best fit.

Generally, different standard job descriptions have to be developed for each of the family groups found in an organization. These groups typically include clerical, stenographic, sales, accounting, and data processing categories.

Figure 13–3 illustrates a standard job description for clerical positions.

To summarize, the job grading method is comprised of the following four steps:

1. The predetermined classes of jobs are designated.
2. A standard job description is prepared for each of the predetermined classes.
3. The jobs are placed into the various predetermined classes.
4. Each job is compared with the various levels outlined on the standard job description to determine the level into which the job should be placed.

Figure 13–4 illustrates the job grading method of evaluating clerical, stenographic, and data processing jobs. For example, the lowest level clerical job is assigned level 1, while the lowest level stenographic and data processing positions are assigned to levels 3 and 2, respectively. The highest ranked data processing position (systems analyst) is considered more important than the highest ranked clerical and stenographic positions. The file clerk position, for example, is most comparable with level 3 on the standard job description. For this reason, the file clerk has been graded as level 3.

When is the job grading
method typically used?

The job grading method is appropriately used in the following three situations: (1) when the organization has too many jobs for the ranking method to be used effectively; (2) when the organization consists of several different family groupings of jobs (clerical, stenographic, data processing, accounting, for example); and (3) when time and cost are of some consideration.

The job grading method is rather inexpensive to use. It is an easy method to explain to employees, and employees tend to accept the evaluation results quite readily.

A disadvantage of the job grading method results when overlap occurs between two of the levels in the standard job descriptions. The whole job is evaluated without regard for the proportionate importance of specific job parts

Figure 13-3 Standard job description

Level 1

Job duties include mail sorting, simple typing, some filing. There is almost no responsibility for decision making and use of judgment. The job requires no special equipment or special skills or knowledges.

Level 2

Job duties include working with records (other than indexing or coding) and typing. There is very little responsibility for decision making and use of judgment. No specialized equipment is used, nor are any special skills or knowledge required.

Level 3

Job duties include indexing and coding records and filing records, as well as typing. There is some responsibility for decision making and judgment, some specialized equipment is used, and a knowledge of indexing and coding rules is required.

Level 4

Job duties include typing, machine calculations, filing. There is an average amount of responsibility for decision making and use of judgment. This level requires the use of various calculating machines.

Level 5

Job duties include complex typing, machine calculations, and filing. There is an above-average responsibility for decision making and use of judgment. A knowledge of calculating machines is required.

Level 6

Job duties include typing and transcription. There is a considerable amount of responsibility for decision making and use of judgment. This level also requires the use of dictation-transcription equipment, and special skills and knowledge required include ability to operate word processing equipment and ability to proofread and use punctuation and grammar properly.

Level 7

Job duties include typing and complex transcription. There is extensive responsibility for decision making and use of judgment. The use of dictation-transcription equipment is required as is the ability to proofread and to use punctuation and grammar properly.

Figure 13-4 Job grading method of job evaluation

Level	Clerical	Stenographic	Data processing
1	Mail Clerk		
2	Requisitions Clerk		Data Entry Operator I
3	File Clerk	Secretary I	
4	Clerk Typist I		Data Entry Operator II
5	Clerk Typist II	Secretary II	
6	Word Processing Typist I		
7	Word Processing Typist II	Executive Secretary	Computer Programmer
8			
9		Admin. Assistant	Computer Technician
10			
11			Systems Analyst

or factors. Also, the importance of a particular job may be somewhat biased by current rates of pay or by certain job holders. Another disadvantage seen by some organizations is the need to prepare the standard job descriptions that facilitate the process.

Factor Comparison

What factors are typically included in the factor comparison method of job evaluation?

As a quantitative method of job evaluation, **factor comparison** determines the relative worth of jobs on the basis of their parts (compensable factors) rather than on the basis of whole jobs. Although the factors vary from organization to organization, the most frequently used compensable factors are:

1. Skill requirements
2. Mental requirements
3. Physical requirements
4. Responsibility requirements
5. Environmental requirements

The factor comparison method consists of six well-defined steps:

What steps constitute the factor comparison method of job evaluation?

Step 1. **Key jobs** are identified.
Step 2. Key jobs are ranked compensable factor by compensable factor.
Step 3. Salary is apportioned among each compensable factor, and key jobs are ranked accordingly.
Step 4. The factor ranking of each job is compared with its monetary ranking.
For what is a monetary comparison scale used?
Step 5. A **monetary comparison scale** is developed.
Step 6. **Nonkey jobs** are evaluated using the monetary comparison scale as a basis.

Step 1. For this step, fifteen to twenty key jobs are usually considered a sufficient number. The key jobs should be somewhat standard (comparable to similar jobs with the same title within other organizations), they should vary in difficulty and importance, and salary rates for the key jobs should be internally and externally consistent.

Step 2. This step consists of ranking the key jobs, factor by factor, using job importance as a basis for the ranking. The ranking technique discussed previously is also suitable for ranking jobs when using this method. To ensure greater consistency of results among raters when a committee is responsible for the ranking process, common definitions should be developed for each of the factors. For example, the common definition of skill might be as follows: a technical proficiency (usually physical or manual) developed either through education or actual experience or by a combination of both. The factor ranking (FR) of jobs can be facilitated by preparing a chart similar to that in Figure 13–5. (For expediency, fewer than the normal number of jobs will be used to illustrate this method.)

Illustrated in Figure 13–5 is the factor ranking of each of the five key jobs. For example, although the skill requirements for the executive secretary are the most extensive, they are the least extensive for the messenger.

Figure 13-5 Factor ranking of key jobs

	Factor ranking				
	Skill	Mental	Physical	Responsibility	Environment
Executive Secretary	1	1	4	1	4
File Clerk	4	4	2	3	3
Data Entry Operator	3	3	3	4	1
Messenger	5	5	1	5	2
Secretary I	2	2	5	2	5

How are differences in the factor rankings and monetary rankings of key jobs resolved?

Step 3. This step consists of apportioning the monetary worth of the key jobs among each of the factors. The importance of each factor to each key job is the basis of the apportionment. The job evaluation committee determines the relative importance of each job factor, and the more important job factors will receive a greater proportion of the total salary. For example, Figure 13–6 indicates that skill is the most important factor in the executive secretary position because it receives a greater proportion of the total salary. As illustrated, the executive secretary position pays an average monthly salary of $3,115. Of the total monthly salary, $735 is paid for skill requirements, $625 for mental requirements, $565 for physical requirements, $655 for responsibility requirements, and $535 for environmental conditions.

Following the apportionment of the total monthly salary among each of the factors, they are then ranked according to their salary components. These results are illustrated in Figure 13–6 under the monetary ranking (MR) columns. As an example, the executive secretary position with a $735 allocation for skill ranks first among the key jobs, whereas the messenger with a $515 allocation ranks last.

Step 4. This step involves comparing the factor ranking and monetary ranking of key jobs. A chart similar to the one illustrated in Figure 13–7 facilitates the comparison. The figures in the factor ranking column come from Figure 13–5; the figures in the monetary ranking column come from Figure 13–6.

When a disagreement exists between the factor rankings and the monetary rankings, adjustments are made to bring the rankings into agreement with each other. The job evaluation committee must decide whether to adjust the factor ranking or to change the salary apportionment, an action that will affect the monetary ranking. In Figure 13–7, the rankings for mental requirements of the file clerk and the data entry operator illustrate a situation in which the rankings did not agree during the preliminary evaluation procedures. The numbers in parentheses represent the new rankings. For example, the original factor

	Average Monthly Salary	Skill		Mental		Physical		Responsi- bility		Environ- mental	
		Prop.	MR	Prop.	MR	Prop.	MR	Prop.	MR	Prop.	MR
Executive Secretary	$3,115	$735	1	$625	1	$565	4	$655	1	$535	4
File Clerk	$2,885	$565	4	$555	3	$595	2	$585	3	$585	3
Data Entry Operator	$2,935	$615	3	$545	4	$585	3	$575	4	$615	1
Messenger	$2,795	$515	5	$525	5	$615	1	$535	5	$605	2
Secretary I	$2,995	$715	2	$585	2	$555	5	$615	2	$525	5

Figure 13-6 Proportion and monetary rank of each factor

Figure 13-7 Comparison of factor ranking and monetary ranking of key jobs

	Skill		Mental		Physical		Responsibility		Environment	
	FR	MR	FR	MR	FR	MR	FR	MR	FR	MR
Exec. Secretary	1	1	1	1	4	4	1	1	4	4
File Clerk	4	4	(3)4	3	2	2	3	3	3	3
Data Entry Operator	3	3	(4)3	4	3	3	4	4	1	1
Messenger	5	5	5	5	1	1	5	5	2	2
Secretary I	2	2	2	2	5	5	2	2	5	5

ranking for mental requirements for the file clerk was 4, and the data entry operator was ranked as 3. To bring the rankings into agreement, the factor rankings of the two positions were reevaluated, and the numbers in the parentheses represent the final rankings.

Step 5. The fifth step in the factor comparison method is the development of a monetary comparison scale similar to the one shown in Figure 13–8. This scale facilitates determining the worth of each nonkey job. The monetary worth

Salary	Skill	Mental	Physical	Responsibility	Environmental
$825					
815					
805					
795					
785					
775					
765					
755					
745					
735	Exec. Sec.				
725					
715	Sec. I				
705					
695					
685					
675					
665					
655				Exec. Sec.	
645					
635					
625		Exec. Sec.			
615	Dt. Ent. Op.		Messenger	Sec. I	Dt. Ent. Op.
605					Messenger
595			File Clerk		
585		Sec. I	Dt. Ent. Op.	File Clerk	File Clerk
575				Dt. Ent. Op.	
565	File Clerk		Exec. Sec.		
555		File Clerk	Sec. I		
545		Dt. Ent. Op.			
535				Messenger	Exec. Sec.
525		Messenger			Sec. I
515	Messenger				
505					
495					

Figure 13-8 Monetary comparison scale

of each of the five factors constituting each key job is then placed on the scale. This information is obtained from the proportion column in Figure 13–6.

Step 6. The final step consists of evaluating each of the nonkey jobs, using the monetary comparison scale as a reference point. The position of each key job on the monetary comparison scale serves as a guide for evaluating the nonkey jobs. As each nonkey job is evaluated, factor by factor, the monetary value of each factor is entered on the scale. Evaluation is facilitated by examining the relationship between the job being evaluated and the jobs already entered on the scale. The monetary worth of each nonkey job is determined by totaling the monetary values assigned to each factor.

The factor comparison method of job evaluation is primarily used when job factors vary too much to use one of the whole-job evaluation methods. It is appropriately used in organizations with a large variety of jobs to be evaluated.

Advantages of the Factor Comparison Method

What are the advantages of the factor comparison method?

1. It provides more accurate results than either the ranking or job grading methods of job evaluation because it compares compensable factors against compensable factors.
2. Because different evaluative factors may be selected, factor comparison can be designed to meet the specific needs of the organization.
3. The actual worth of each compensable factor is easily determined.
4. The evaluation of nonkey jobs is simplified greatly by using a device such as the monetary comparison scale.

Disadvantages of the Factor Comparison Method

1. Periodic adjustment of salary rates may result in the development of inequities in the organization's salary structure.
2. Inequities in salary rates of key jobs will affect the evaluated worth of nonkey jobs.
3. An incorrect interpretation of the importance of any one of the factors can cause a serious error in the evaluated worth of a job.
4. Because of the complicated nature of the method, explaining the system to employees is sometimes difficult; and employees sometimes have difficulty understanding the system.

Point Evaluation

What are the characteristics of the point evaluation method of job evaluation?

The most commonly used evaluation technique is the **point evaluation** method in which jobs are evaluated on the basis of such compensable factors as job skills, effort, responsibilities, and working conditions. The factors are divided into degrees, and each degree is assigned a specific number of points.

Figure 13–9, as an example, illustrates (1) the four typical compensable factors, (2) the subfactors that constitute each of the compensable factors, (3) the degrees for each of the subfactors, and (4) the number of points allocated to each of the degrees. The percentages found beside each of the four primary job compensable factors indicate the importance of each factor to the whole job.

A reasonable amount of judgment must be exercised in selecting *compensable* factors and subfactors used in point evaluation. In large, complex organizations, several plans may have to be developed, because what is appropriate for evaluating office jobs, for example, is not appropriate for evaluating factory

Figure 13-9 Allocation of points for job factors

Factors	First degree	Second degree	Third degree	Fourth degree	Fifth degree
Skill (30%)					
1. Education	10	20	30	40	50
2. Experience	10	20	30	40	50
3. Job knowledge	15	30	45	60	75
4. Manual dexterity	5	10	15	20	25
Effort (25%)					
5. Physical	10	20	30	40	50
6. Mental	10	20	30	40	50
7. Visual	5	10	15	20	25
Responsibility (30%)					
8. Equipment/tools	8	16	24	32	40
9. Materials/products	10	20	30	40	50
10. Work of others	5	10	15	20	25
Job conditions (15%)					
11. Surroundings	10	20	30	40	50
12. Hazards	5	10	15	20	25
13. Safety of others	5	10	15	20	25

jobs. The compensable factors and subfactors that are chosen must be appropriate for the needs of the organization as well as representative of the jobs. Generally, eight to sixteen subfactors are sufficient for this method.

What information is found in the point manual?

Point Manual. The point evaluation method requires the preparation of a manual that describes each of the degrees into which the subfactors have been divided. The manual also lists the number of points allocated to each of the degrees.

Care should be taken to select only subfactors pertinent to the jobs being evaluated. Likewise, care should be taken to eliminate subfactors that tend to overlap with others, that cannot be clearly defined, or that tend to evaluate personal rather than compensable factors.

When selecting the appropriate number of degrees, two conditions should be considered: the relative importance assigned to each subfactor and the ease with which individual degrees can be defined. Although Figure 13–9 shows five degrees for each subfactor, in some instances, subfactors are divided into as few as three degrees or as many as eight degrees.

What methods are used to assign points to the degrees in the point evaluation method?

Two methods are generally used to assign the number of points to each degree: (1) the straight arithmetic method by which the points increase by a constant amount (for example, 10, 20, 30, 40 or 8, 16, 24); and (2) the geometric progression method by which the points increase by a constant percentage (such as 3, 6, 12, 24). Figure 13–10 illustrates a partial point manual with descriptions for office jobs.

A variety of trade associations, management consulting firms, and companies have developed point manuals. Among the more widely used manuals are those prepared by the National Metal Trades Association and the National Electrical Manufacturers Association. When one of the prepared manuals is adopted, care must be taken to ensure that it meets the specific needs of the organization in which it is being used.

Evaluating the Jobs. The last step involves evaluating each job. The job specification is compared subfactor by subfactor with the degree or level descriptions in the point manual. When the appropriate degree is determined, the

Figure 13-10 Point manual (office jobs)

EDUCATION: This subfactor is concerned with the nature of the educational experience of the employee. High school equivalency certificates will be accepted in lieu of a high school diploma. As far as college work is concerned, community college and business and/or technical school attendance is accepted. Work taken in adult education programs does not count as college-level work.

Degree	Points	Description
1st	10	Less than high school diploma
2nd	20	High school diploma but no college work
3rd	30	High school diploma and not more than 2 years (60 semester hours) of college work.
4th	40	High school diploma, at least 2 years (60 semester hours) of college work, but no college degree
5th	50	College graduate

EXPERIENCE: This subfactor is concerned with the amount of time that it takes an employee to obtain and develop skills necessary to perform a particular job. It is assumed that the individual already possesses the required job knowledge before starting the time element involved in the experience factor. Any previously obtained experience, either inside or outside the organization, is recognized.

Degree	Points	Description
1st	10	Up to and including three months' experience
2nd	20	Over three months' but less than one year of experience
3rd	30	Over one year but less than two years' experience
4th	40	Over two years' but less than four years' experience
5th	50	Over four years of experience

PHYSICAL: This subfactor is concerned with the amount of physical effort expended in carrying out the duties of the job. In determining the appropriate level to which a particular job is to be assigned, "normal" efficiency in carrying out the duties should be used as a guideline.

Degree	Points	Description
1st	10	This level involves a balance of physical effort: sitting, standing, or walking. Included in this level are those office jobs with a normal amount of physical effort.
2nd	20	This level involves expending a considerable amount of physical effort through the job holder's moving around a considerable amount.
3rd	30	This level involves expending physical effort through one continuous activity, such as sitting, typing, machine operation, etc. Some lifting may be involved; the job holder typically works for a long period in one position.
4th	40	This level involves a considerable amount of walking or standing, especially for long periods
5th	50	This level involves continuous standing in one place or a considerable amount of walking or lifting for long periods.

actual job factor is then assigned the corresponding number of points. Each point value is also entered on the job specification. After each compensable factor has been evaluated, the relative worth of the job is determined by adding the total number of points assigned to the various factors. The total point value for each job is subsequently converted into salary rates, as illustrated in Figure 13–11.

Figure 13–11 Salary
range: point evaluation

Total Points	Midpoint	Minimum	Maximum
0–300	$2,100	$2,000	$2,200
301–320	$2,150	$2,040	$2,260
321–340	$2,200	$2,080	$2,320
341–360	$2,240	$2,120	$2,360
361–380	$2,270	$2,140	$2,400
381–400	$2,320	$2,170	$2,470
401–420	$2,400	$2,240	$2,560

What steps constitute the point method of job evaluation?

To recap, the point method of job evaluation involves five steps. First, the factors and their relative worth are determined. Second, the factors are then divided into subfactors. Third, the point manual is developed, specifying the number of points assigned to each degree for the various subfactors. Fourth, the job specification of each job is compared subfactor by subfactor with the degree descriptions in the point manual as a means of determining the appropriate number of points to assign each subfactor. Finally, the points assigned to each subfactor are added to determine the worth of the job. The higher the number of points a job receives, the greater is its importance.

The point evaluation method is appropriately used in organizations that have a considerable number of diversified jobs. When intraorganizational problems require the use of a sophisticated job evaluation method, this one is appropriate.

Advantages of Using the Point Evaluation Method

What are the advantages of the point evaluation method?

1. Of all the methods, it is the most difficult to manipulate; and only minimal opportunity exists for pressure to be exerted on the individual or committee doing the evaluating.

2. The method has a high degree of objectivity and consistency of results.

3. Salary increases can be given that do not affect the evaluated jobs because the point values of the jobs stay the same until the components of the job are changed.

4. Because of the flexibility in selecting subfactors, degrees, and points, developing a system tailor-made for the organization is possible.

Disadvantages of Using the Point Evaluation Method

What are the disadvantages of the point evaluation method?

1. Developing a point manual can be a difficult, time-consuming task.

2. Hiring specially trained personnel to install the system may be necessary.

3. Selecting and writing definitions of degrees is not an easy task.

4. Allocating points among each of the subfactors may be somewhat arbitrary.

ADOPTING A JOB EVALUATION METHOD

A variety of organizations have developed job evaluation programs that others can adopt. However, adopting a program without first making certain it meets the organization's needs is not recommended. A program that is successful in one organization may be unsuccessful in another unless certain modifications are made. The following should be closely examined when modifying an existing program:

1. The nature—specific and general—of the jobs in the organization.
2. The duties and responsibilities that constitute the jobs in the organization.
3. The procedures used to determine salary rates.
4. The philosophy of the organization's management regarding the job evaluation program.

JOB EVALUATION COMMITTEE

The nature of job evaluation makes desirable the use of a committee that is typically responsible for designing the program and revising it when the need arises. The use of a committee adds credibility to the program because of the common perception that programs developed by a committee have a broader support base than those developed by only a few individuals. The committee is also generally responsible for monitoring the program to ensure compliance with various operating policies.

When evaluating job worth, many organizations prefer that committee members work independently of one another. The results of their evaluation efforts are then reviewed collectively by the various committee members before developing the final results. Although each committee member has considerable input, committee decisions override individual decisions.

What are the advantages of using job evaluation committees?

The advantages of using a committee are that (1) the results of the program tend to be more objective, (2) the employees are more likely to accept a program developed by broad-based representation, and (3) the results tend to be more accurate.

IMPLICATIONS FOR THE ADMINISTRATIVE OFFICE MANAGER

The administrative office manager often has important job evaluation responsibilities, which include serving on the organization's advisory committee and the job evaluation committee. The advisory committee is ongoing and is generally headed by the individual who has overall responsibility for job evaluation efforts, most likely someone in the human resources department. The job evaluation committee, conversely, is not ongoing but rather functions periodically for the purpose of engaging in job evaluation efforts.

Administrative office managers can eliminate some undesirable situations by assuring comparability of the relative value and the monetary value of the jobs for which they have responsibility. When discrepancies between these two values exist, employees' morale may shrink; they may begin to restrict their output; and turnover, absenteeism, and tardiness levels tend to be higher.

Administrative office managers are well qualified to take an active role in organizational job evaluation activities. Their background and training provide them with the knowledge they need to accept important responsibilities and to assume crucial leadership roles in this area.

REVIEW QUESTIONS

1. Identify the benefits provided by a job evaluation program.

2. Explain why the job ranking method is considered a nonquantitative method, whereas the factor comparison method is considered quantitative.

3. Compare and contrast the job evaluation techniques discussed in this chapter in terms of the following:

   a. Number of jobs for which each method is suitable.

   b. Any special apparatus required by each method.

   c. Special characteristics of each method.

   d. Validity of results of each method.

   e. Special conditions for which the use of each method is appropriate.

4. Why is the use of a committee advantageous in undertaking a job evaluation project?

DISCUSSION QUESTIONS

1. You, the administrative office manager in the company in which you work, currently serve on its job evaluation committee. Among the jobs being evaluated are several in the accounting department including three levels of accounting clerk positions. At a recent committee meeting, the manager of the accounting department indicated that he would like to see these positions downgraded. When asked why, he reminded the committee members that the five accounting clerks recently challenged him on a new departmental policy he implemented last year. He also indicated that he needs to show them who is boss. Discuss the use of job evaluation to retaliate against disgruntled subordinates.

2. Several years ago, the company in which you work used factor comparison to evaluate the worth of its jobs. The complexity of the process created a great deal of confusion among employees. After a time, most just accepted the results. The problem arose because the salaries of the key jobs were not competitive with those of other similar companies in the community. The company has had several good financial years, which has enabled it to make significant gains in the competitiveness of its salary program. Last year, the company suffered a significant downturn in its profitability, which resulted in minimal salary increases. A number of the employees are again blaming their "salary woes" on the factor comparison job evaluation technique that was used several years ago. What is your reaction to the employees' attitudes toward factor comparison?

3. The rumor is running rampant throughout the company in which you work that the office employees in the president's and vice presidents' offices are paid more than employees in identical jobs in other offices of the company. Several individuals believe that the "higher level executives will always take care of their own." You, the administrative office manager, know that this is not true because the company has an effective job evaluation program and that the salaries paid to individuals in every office position do conform with the salary ranges established by job evaluation. What might explain the fact that certain individuals in certain jobs in these offices get paid more than their counterparts in other offices?

STUDENT PROJECTS AND ACTIVITIES

1. Discuss with an office employee how he or she perceives the value of job evaluation.

2. Discuss with an administrative office manager how he or she perceives the value of job evaluation.

3. Going Online: Using the Internet, conduct an online search based on one of the concepts presented in this chapter or based on one of the chapter terms. Identify four or five things you learned from the material that you did not know prior to your online search.

Minicase

Several supervisors in Jaminez Import Company, which is located in San Diego, believe that an evaluation of all office jobs should be undertaken. These supervisors also know that management will likely not approve their request unless factual evidence is available to support their belief that a job evaluation project is necessary.

1. Identify several signals that these supervisors might use as evidence that the evaluation of office jobs is necessary.
2. What factors should these supervisors weigh in determining which job evaluation method to use in the event that their request is approved?

Case

The Briarwood Dairy Company, which is located in Milwaukee, Wisconsin, is one of the largest dairy processors in the Midwest. Approximately ten years ago, the company undertook a thorough job evaluation project. Employer-employee relations before the job evaluation were not especially cordial, and the relations have been less cordial since. In fact, on several occasions, the employees have been on the verge of unionizing. In many instances, management has "backed off," which undoubtedly diminished temporarily the amount of employee interest in unionizing.

It now appears that a thorough job evaluation again needs to be undertaken. Management knows that if it does not proceed with caution, the employees most likely will unionize.

1. What suggestions can you provide that will be helpful to management in undertaking a job evaluation project that these employees will accept?
2. What should management do to get the employees to accept the job evaluation results once they are implemented?
3. Once the results have been implemented, in which ways can management evaluate their effectiveness?

Chapter 14

ADMINISTERING SALARIES OF OFFICE EMPLOYEES

Chapter Aims

After studying this chapter, you should be able to design an effective program to administer the salaries of office employees.

Chapter Outline

Salary Administration Program
    Goals of Salary Administration Program
    Policies and Procedures of Salary Administration Program
    Responsibility for Salary Administration Program
Determining Salary Structure
    Factors Affecting Salary Structure
    Developing Wage Curve
Incentive Pay
    Types of Incentive Pay Plans
Performance-based Pay
Legally Required Benefits
    Social Security
    Workers' Compensation
    Unemployment Compensation
    Disability Insurance
Fringe Benefits
    Paid Holidays
    Paid Vacations
    Sick Leave
    Paid Personal Days
    Educational Assistance
    Life Insurance Programs
    Health Care Insurance
    Disability Insurance

Health Maintenance Organizations
Preferred Provider Organizations
Medical and Fitness Facilities
Maternity Leave
Employee Assistance Programs
Pension Plans
Profit Sharing
Child Care Services
Car Pools
Cafeteria Services
Company Discounts
Wellness Programs
Eldercare
Reimbursement Account Programs
Time-off Bank
Federal Legislation
    Fair Labor Standards Act
    Equal Pay Act
    Walsh-Healey Act
    Davis-Bacon Act
    Pregnancy Discrimination Act
    Pension Reform Act
    Age Discrimination in Employment Act
    Economic Recovery Tax Act
    Deficit Reduction Act

Consolidated Omnibus Budget Reconciliation
  Act
Family and Medical Leave Act of 1993

Implications for the Administrative Office
  Manager

$\mathcal{C}$hapter $\mathcal{T}$erms

401(k) Plan
Ability to pay
Age Discrimination in Employment Act
Collective bargaining
Consolidated Omnibus Budget Reconciliation Act
Cost-of-living index
Davis-Bacon Act
Deficit Reduction Act
Defined-benefit Pension Plan
Defined-contribution Pension Plan
Economic Recovery Tax Act
Equal Pay Act
Fair Labor Standards Act
Family and Medical Leave Act of 1993
Fringe benefits
Gain sharing

Going rates
Individual incentive
Key contributor program
Legislation
Merit pay
Pension Reform Act
Piecework plan
Preferred provider organizations
Pregnancy Discrimination Act
Relative worth of the job
Reimbursement account programs
Salary scattergram
Time-off bank
Walsh-Healey Act
Wellness programs

$\mathcal{I}$n many organizations, employee compensation consumes as much as 80 percent of their operating budgets. The need to effectively manage the salary administration program is obvious as is the need to provide employees with salaries sufficiently high to maintain an effective working relationship.

An organization's job evaluation program is the source of input for developing an effective salary program. Once the relative worth of jobs has been determined, a salary administration program helps ensure that employees receive equitable compensation. Inequities are likely to result when salary decisions are made by a process other than a formal salary administration program.

Equitable, fair compensation is important to employees for the following reasons.

Why is equitable, fair compensation important to employees?

1. It is a basic determinant of their worth to the organization.
2. It provides a measure of status and recognition.
3. It directly affects their standard of living.
4. It is a reward for the time and effort they contribute to the organization.

Employees who believe the relationship between the compensation they receive and the services they provide the organization is out of balance will likely react in one or more of the following ways: their productivity will decrease, their morale will deteriorate, and their turnover rates will increase.

SALARY ADMINISTRATION PROGRAM

An equitable salary has a positive impact on employees' output and morale. The salary administration program, which is responsible for determining equitable compensation, is also helpful in recruiting, selecting, and retaining capable employees. As the quality of employees improves, so does the organization's ability to produce higher quality goods or services at lower prices.

Goals of Salary Administration Program

Efficient, effective salary administration programs operate within the framework of several well-defined goals, namely the following:

What are the common goals of salary administration programs?

1. *To provide a systematic determination of equitable compensation for employees.* Effective programs provide a sound foundation for determining equitable employee compensation. Such programs also help reduce the number of salary-related grievances filed by employees.

2. *To help the organization conform with existing legislation pertaining to employee compensation.* Legislation affecting employee compensation is frequently enacted, and existing legislation is periodically amended. Fewer violations of this legislation will occur when the director of the salary administration program is responsible for ensuring program compliance.

3. *To help the organization control its salary costs.* A well-designed salary administration program benefits the organization by helping it control its salary costs. The program helps provide balance between the worth of each job and the salary paid for that job. Therefore, salary programs help organizations more readily operate within their salary budgets.

4. *To help reduce employee turnover.* When an organization's salary structure is neither internally equitable nor externally competitive, employee turnover tends to increase significantly. A salary administration program helps minimize problems of this nature.

5. *To motivate employees to perform at an optimum level.* Providing employees with various financial or nonfinancial incentives motivates them to become more efficient and productive. The guidelines, procedures, and policies used to reward deserving employees are important components of the salary administration program.

6. *To promote good employer-employee relations.* When employer-employee relations are cordial and pleasant, employees tend to be more cooperative and supportive. Management-union disagreements often originate in the organization's compensation process. A sound salary administration program minimizes disagreements; however, when they arise, an effective program helps resolve problems quickly without having to resort to arbitration. Effective programs also ensure that employees receive a fair day's salary for a fair day's work.

Policies and Procedures of Salary Administration Program

Decision making in well-designed salary administration programs is guided by policies and procedures that help assure consistency and fairness. The policies also provide management with the necessary authority to achieve desired goals and objectives.

Many organizations adopt a salary structure that uses a range for each job grade or level. To ensure the equal, fair treatment of all employees, policies and procedures must be developed to help determine where a newly hired employee or a recently promoted employee should be placed within the salary range. Policies outlining the advancement of employees from one salary range to another should also be available.

Other policies and procedures should exist that specify the organization's plans for periodic review of its salary structure and its various job classifications. A policy is also needed that identifies the appropriate steps to be used when filing a compensation-related grievance.

What is the result of an absence of clearly defined policies and procedures to guide the salary administration program?

The absence of clearly defined policies and procedures may result in the use of factors other than individual performance as a basis for making merit increases. The policies and procedures by which these decisions are made must be thoroughly communicated to employees.

The policies and procedures regarding salary increases also need to be clearly defined. Salary increases usually consist of either (1) a flat increase of a certain number of cents per hour or (2) a percentage-of-salary increase.

The use of the flat rate enables employees with lower salaries to get a larger percentage increase than employees with higher salaries. In time, unless adjustments are made, the salary differential between the lower and higher paid employees will diminish, resulting in salary compression or even inversion. Some claim that when the salary differentials diminish significantly, employees will no longer have as much incentive to prepare themselves for the higher paying jobs or for those jobs that typically require higher skill levels. This situation may eventually result in a scarcity of skilled employees.

Fringe benefits, another function of the salary administration program, must also be guided by well-defined policies and procedures. For example, in some organizations, paid holidays are considered a fringe benefit. When an employee is absent from work the day before or after the paid holiday, policies should specify the conditions under which the employee will or will not be paid for the day of absence.

Policies regulating shift or overtime pay should also be developed. Federal legislation specifies minimum rates for overtime pay, but some organizations pay more than the minimum rate in certain situations. If, for example, an organization has a salary differential for day and night shifts, regulating policies should be clearly defined.

In unionized companies, in what documents are fringe benefits typically discussed?

In a unionized organization, many of the policies regulating various phases of employee compensation are written into the union-management contract. Fewer misinterpretations will result when these policies are clearly and specifically worded.

Also needed are policies that guide the incentive pay programs or performance-based programs. Many organizations, for example, provide employees with a variety of bonuses. To determine the actual amount of the bonus payment, a formula based either on a percentage of total profit or a percentage of total profit in excess of a specified amount is commonly used.

Responsibility for Salary Administration Program

Salary administration programs that operate with centralized control are administered uniformly. The hierarchical placement, duties, and responsibilities of the director of the salary administration program are largely determined by three factors: the size of the organization, the nature of goods or services produced by the organization, and the types of jobs for which the director is responsible.

Even though responsibility for the salary administration program in many organizations rests with the personnel department, the administrative office manager is often extensively involved. The manager frequently serves on the advisory committee that assists the director of the salary administration program. The members of advisory committees often have a broad understanding of the technical aspects of certain jobs and are therefore able to supply the salary administration program director with information regarding important job requirements and compensation rates.

In small organizations, the human resources manager frequently has over-all responsibility for the salary administration program, in addition to other personnel-related functions. In larger organizations, the salary administration program is headed by a full-time director. In some organizations, the director of the salary administration program reports to the personnel director, while in others, the human resources manager and the director of the salary administration program are co-equals.

DETERMINING SALARY STRUCTURE

Determining an appropriate salary structure, which is a fairly complex process, begins with an examination of the various factors that impact on the salary program.

Factors Affecting Salary Structure

What factors affect the salary structure?

The following provides a discussion of the significant factors affecting the salary structure that must be considered. Included in the discussion are such factors as the relative worth of the job, going rates, cost-of-living index, legislation, collective bargaining, organization's ability to pay, and level of productivity.

Relative Worth of Job. Employees rightfully expect their salaries be properly related to the demands of their jobs and to the salaries paid to employees performing other jobs in the organization. If not, salary inequities are likely to occur, a situation that most likely will impact negatively on employee attitudes. The **relative worth of the job** is determined by means of job evaluation procedures, which were discussed in Chapter 13.

Going Rates. When **going rates** are used to determine the salary structure, employees consider themselves to be treated more fairly, and they accept the results more readily. Occasionally, the going rates for comparable jobs can be obtained from prepared salary surveys. The unavailability of these surveys may mean that the organization will have to conduct its own salary survey.

The following discussion provides important information about several prepared salary surveys.

Edward N. Hay and Associates compiles *Compensation Comparisons—Industrial and Financial Management*, an annual update of salary trends for exempt executive, management, and technical employees. The information for the survey is gathered from a comprehensive sample of national and international firms. Differences between exempt and nonexempt positions are discussed in the "Federal Legislation" section of this chapter. Persons in these positions are "exempt" from receiving extra compensation for overtime work.

What is an exempt employee?

The Administrative Management Society Foundation annually updates its *Directory of Office Salaries*, which includes twenty commonly found office and data processing positions. The survey includes weekly salary data for the twenty jobs in the largest cities in the country, in addition to including regional average salaries and nationwide averages for each of these positions.

In 1973, the Administrative Management Society conducted its first annual management survey, the *AMS Guide to Management Compensation*. This survey, which is now conducted by the Administrative Management Society Foundation, provides salary data on twenty key exempt middle-management positions as well as information on fringe benefits, length of workweek, paid vacations, holidays, and pension plans.

Numerous local chambers of commerce and trade associations compile salary data for jobs found in their localities. Using the results of these surveys, when they are available, will save many organizations considerable time, effort, and money.

The absence of published salary data may result in an organization's having to conduct its own survey. Without this vital salary information, the organization has no way of knowing whether its salaries are competitive with those of other organizations in the community.

When designing a salary survey, the following guidelines will be helpful:

What guidelines are helpful in designing a salary survey?

1. If only a portion of the total number of organizations in a community is to be surveyed, special provision must be made to assure the random selection of those that are to be included.

2. The number of organizations to be surveyed must be large enough to be representative of the lot from which the sample is drawn.

3. For best results, the organizations to be surveyed should be of the same classification and approximate size as the organization conducting the survey. For example, banks should survey other banks, manufacturing organizations should survey other manufacturing organizations, and so forth.

4. The questionnaire must be designed to gather the desired information. Frequently included in salary surveys are the following:

What information is typically collected in a salary administration questionnaire?

   a. Number of employees in the firm.

   b. Number of employees in each job category on which the salary data are based.

   c. Salary range for each job category.

   d. Number of hours per week for each job included in the survey.

   e. The pay policy for employees who work on holidays.

   f. The type and monetary worth of supplemental pay (includes bonuses, profit sharing, stock options, and pension plans).

   g. The holidays for which employees receive pay.

   h. The organization's policy regarding vacations with pay, sick leave, insurance, salary increases, overtime, incentive pay, and shift differential pay.

5. To provide some assurance that jobs are comparable, the relevant job descriptions should be obtained from the organizations being surveyed. Even though jobs in several organizations have comparable titles, they may differ significantly in terms of duties and responsibilities.

After collecting the relevant job information, a median or average salary for each job can be computed. The organization is then able to decide how competitive its salary structure is in comparison with the salary structures of other organizations.

Cost-of-Living Index. During inflationary times, the **cost-of-living index,** which is calculated by the federal government, is frequently used by an organization in developing its salary structures. The use of the cost-of-living index as a salary determinant results in a periodic upward adjustment of salaries, which enables employees to maintain their purchasing power. Therefore, employees' salaries increase by the same amount as the cost-of-living index.

In unionized organizations, the salary structure may be mathematically tied to the cost-of-living index by an escalator clause written into the union-management contract. For example, some contracts stipulate that when the cost-of-living index increases by a certain percentage, employees' salaries will automatically increase by a specified amount. Although the cost-of-living index is popularly used as a salary determinant during inflationary times, it is generally not popular with unions during times of economic stability.

Legislation. Another determinant of the organization's salary structure is the compensation-related **legislation** enacted at both national and state levels. Provisions of this legislation affect minimum salary rates, overtime pay, child labor, fringe benefits, and so on.

What legislation impacts on salary administration programs?

Some of the more significant legislation—including the Fair Labor Standards Act, the Equal Pay Act, the Walsh-Healey Act, the Davis-Bacon Act, and the Pension Reform Act—are discussed in the "Federal Legislation" section of this chapter.

Collective Bargaining. When the employees of an organization belong to a union, their salaries are determined by a **collective bargaining** process. Although going rates, cost-of-living increases, and job worth most likely will be considered in the bargaining process, the salary rates agreed on will reflect the degree of "give and take" between the two parties. Organizations with unionized employees frequently set salary trends that nonunionized organizations follow as a means of maintaining a competitive salary structure.

Organization's Ability to Pay. Also affecting the organization's salary structure is its **ability to pay** salaries and wages. Generally, this ability is affected by such factors as competition and the overall profitability of the industry. The more keen an organization's competition is, the less able it is to pay top salaries and wages. Likewise, as the industry with which the organization is associated experiences declining profits, the ability to pay top salaries and wages becomes more prohibitive.

Level of Productivity. An organization's level of productivity affects the amount of money available to pay employees. As an organization's productivity increases, so does the amount of money potentially available for increasing wages and salaries. Directly linking the amount of salary increase to productivity improvement often motivates employees to improve their performance. Salary increases paralleling comparable increases in productivity will not increase an organization's labor costs. When salaries increase faster than productivity increases, however, the organization's labor costs will consume a larger percentage of the total operating budget.

What impact does productivity have on salary administration?

Developing a Wage Curve

After the relative worth of each job has been determined by one of the job evaluation methods discussed in Chapter 13, the monetary worth of the job can be determined. For example, when the job ranking method of job evaluation is used, the relative importance of each job influences the predetermined level into which each job is placed. By using the procedures presented in this chapter, the monetary worth for each of the levels is determined. The job grading method uses the same basic procedures to determine the monetary worth of jobs.

When the factor comparison method is used, the monetary worth of each key job is first determined. This information provides a basis for determining the monetary worth of the nonkey jobs. When the point evaluation method is used, the point value of each job determines its monetary worth. Because point evaluation is the most frequently used method of job evaluation, it will be used to illustrate the salary determination process.

Salary Scattergram. Determining the monetary worth of each job begins with preparing the **salary scattergram,** such as the one illustrated in Figure 14–1. The scattergram shows the relationship between the relative worth and the monetary worth of each job. The horizontal axis of the scattergram identifies the points value or relative worth of the jobs, but the vertical axis identifies the monetary worth.

What is the function of a salary scattergram?

The relative worth (point value) and monetary worth (salary) of each job are plotted on the scattergram. For example, if a two-hundred-point job pays a salary of $2,400, a dot is placed on the scattergram at the intersection of these two values. After all the jobs are plotted, a correlation line is drawn on the scattergram where an approximately equal number of dots appear above and below the line. The scattergram clearly identifies the relationship between the relative importance of various jobs and their monetary worth.

The external competitiveness of an organization's salary structure is assessed by comparing its correlation line with the correlation line of a composite of several other organizations in the same community. If the organization's salary structure is lower than the composite line, the organization will need to make adjustments in its salary program if it is to remain competitive. Such an adjustment is illustrated in Figure 14–2.

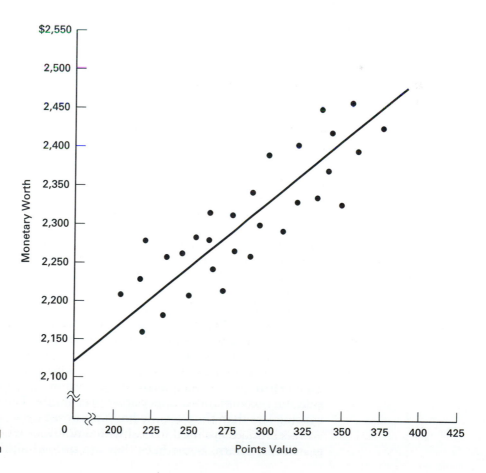

Figure 14–1
Scattergram

Figure 14-2 Salary comparison and adjustment

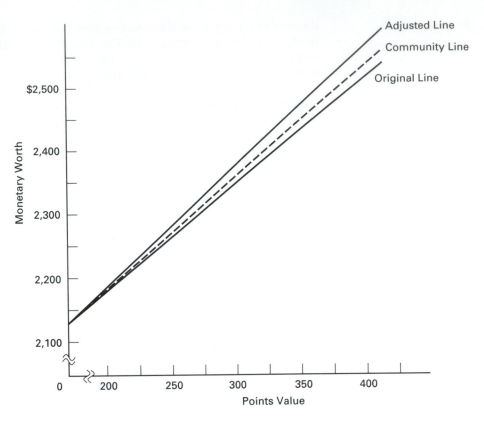

Establishing Salary Range. Once the correlation line has been officially established, the next step involves setting the upper and lower limits of the salary range for each pay grade. This is easily done by placing a line a fixed percentage amount (10 percent, for example) above the correlation line and another line the same percentage amount below the correlation line.

How is the salary range established?

Figure 14–3 illustrates the upper and lower limits of each pay grade, using a salary range of 10 percent on either side of the midpoint (correlation) line. At the lowest and highest ends of the midpoint line, base points 10 percent above and 10 percent below are placed on the chart. The upper and lower limits of the salary range can then easily be determined by connecting the two base points above and the two below the midpoint line. For each points category, rectangular-shaped boxes that intersect the upper and lower limit lines are then drawn on the figure. Once this is done, the rectangular-shaped boxes readily identify the upper and lower limits of each salary range.

Why are overlapping rates used?

Most salary structures are designed with overlapping rates for adjoining job categories. This concept is illustrated in Figure 14–3. The jobs in the 300- to 320-point category receive a salary of $2,125 to $2,280. The salary range for the adjoining category (321 to 340 points) is $2,170 to $2,235. These two ranges overlap by $50. The use of salary structures with overlapping rates enables employees with considerable experience to be paid an amount equal to or higher than a relatively inexperienced employee in the next higher category.

When an organization undertakes a thorough job evaluation and adjusts its salary structure, the suggested compensation for some employees may fall outside the recommended upper and lower limits. The salaries of the employees earning less than the suggested minimum are generally adjusted upward. Several techniques are used to deal with employees who earn more than the suggested maximum. Sometimes they are trained and promoted to higher level

Figure 14-3 Salary ranges

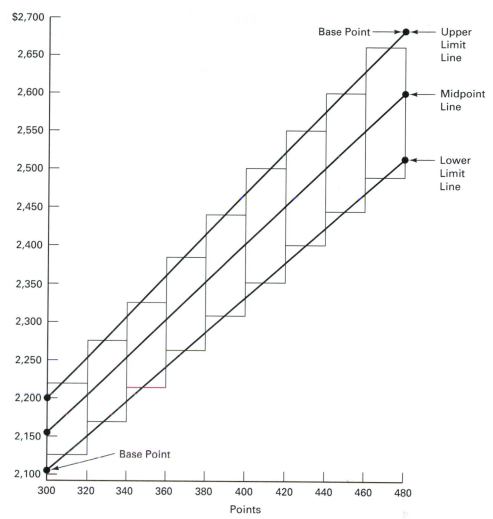

jobs more commensurate with their present salaries. In other instances, the employees are promoted as quickly as circumstances allow, which will help achieve parity between their job responsibilities and salaries. Some organizations will award smaller and/or less frequent salary increases to these employees until their salaries fall into the recommended range for their job responsibilities.

Planning for Salary Increases. Procedures for increasing employees' salaries have to be built into the organization's salary administration program. Salary progression enables employees to move upward within their range and facilitates increasing their salaries when they are promoted from one job level to another. Keeping employees informed about procedures for increasing their salaries is essential.

How are employees' salaries typically increased?

Employees' salaries are usually increased in three ways: at specific time intervals, by merit, or by a combination of specific time intervals and merit. The use of time intervals enables employees whose performance is satisfactory to receive automatic salary increases at regular intervals, most likely once or twice a year.

The merit method, which ties the quality of an employees' performance to the amount of his or her increase, is also used frequently to increase employees' salaries. Thus, employees whose work is distinctly superior receive a larger salary increase than those employees whose work is considered above average.

The use of the combination method results in the increase of salaries at specific time intervals until employees reach the midpoint or average salary for their respective salary ranges. For an employee to reach the upper limit of the range, his or her performance must be outstanding. Therefore, salary increases are automatic from the lower limit to the midpoint of the range, but merit increases are necessary for an employee to receive the salary at the top of the range.

A growing number of organizations that use the combination approach increase the salaries of all employees a fixed percentage—4 percent, for example—and the remainder of their salary increase is comprised of **merit pay.** Employees tend to be more highly motivated to improve their performance when their merit pay is directly related to job performance. One way to link job performance and merit pay is to give those employees whose performance is outstanding an 8 percent merit increase added to their fixed-amount increase; those whose performance is rated above average, a 6 percent merit increase; and so forth. Employees whose job performance is rated average or below generally are not eligible for merit increases.

INCENTIVE PAY

An increasing number of organizations are presently installing employee incentive pay plans that take into consideration the employees' performance in relation to work standards established through work measurement procedures. Properly designed incentive pay programs benefit both the organization and its employees. The organization's productivity is increased, which improves its profitability; and the employees are able to increase their compensation.

The following characteristics are typical of effective incentive pay plans:

What are the characteristics of typical effective incentive pay plans?

1. Employees are convinced that a direct correlation exists between their level of performance and the amount of incentive pay they receive.
2. Employees are aware of the precise level at which they must perform to be eligible to receive incentive pay.
3. Management thoroughly communicates its expectations to employees.
4. Incentive pay is given only to those employees who increase their effectiveness.
5. Employees are fully convinced that they will benefit substantially as a result of improved performance.

When incentive pay plans are put in place, quality and quantity of output improve, costs decrease, and employee morale improves.

Types of Incentive Pay Plans

Two broad types of incentive pay plans are found: individual and group. Individual plans are more common than group plans.

Individual Incentive Plans. A common type of individual plan is the **individual incentive** that involves measuring each employee's output; individual rewards are based on that output. Although individual incentive plans are not as readily available to office workers as they are to workers in other types of industry (textile, steel, and clothing, for example), an increasing number of organizations are installing incentive plans for their office employees.

How do partial plans differ from whole plans?

Some individual incentive pay plans are partial plans, whereas others are whole plans. The determining factor is how much of the employee's total compensation is based on his or her output. With partial plans, a portion of the amount of an employee's paycheck is based on his or her output that exceeds the minimum threshold amount. With whole plans, the entire paycheck is based on the amount of the employee's output. A common type of whole plan is a piecework plan.

The **piecework plan,** a type of individual incentive, was common during the early decades of the last century and is regaining its popularity in some industries. The piecework plan pays employees a standard rate for each unit of output. Some piecework plans use a differential system that enables higher producing employees to receive a higher rate than the lower producing employees.

How are compensation rates determined in incentive plans?

Two types of rate determination are used in individual incentive plans: (1) units of production and (2) time required to complete a unit. The units of production rate is commonly used for office employees, especially for those whose jobs primarily involve data entry (either numerical or alphabetical). The computer system they use automatically counts their keystrokes, which serve as the basis of their incentive pay.

Incentive plans based on the amount of time required to complete a unit are typically used for longer cycle jobs with mental or creative task components. Some of the more successful individual incentive plans reward employees by paying one amount for a given level of production and an increased amount after the individual's output exceeds that level. For example, employees whose output exceeds the minimum level might be paid an additional 25 cents for every two hundred keystrokes up to ten thousand keystrokes, but 27 cents for every two hundred keystrokes above ten thousand.

Among the advantages of piecework plans are these: Calculating output is simple, employees readily understand them, and they can provide a powerful incentive to employees for improving their performance. Piecework plans also have disadvantages: Their use is restricted to manual work that is performed continuously without variation, they cause employees to be more concerned about output and less concerned about quality, and when employees' jobs change, the entire piecework plan may have to be reworked.

Group Incentive Plans. The growing interdependence of employees' jobs makes group incentive plans more desirable than individual incentive plans in some organizations. These plans are often based either on the amount of profit earned by the organization or on the amount of cost reduction it realizes.

Group incentive plans based on the profit earned by the organization tend to motivate employees to increase their productivity, either by increasing their output or by decreasing their inefficiency. A percentage of the increased profit is returned to deserving employees as a reward for helping their employer increase its profitability.

In what ways can participants of group incentive plans be rewarded?

Employees participating in a group incentive plan can be rewarded in several different ways. One common way is to set standards for members of the group; when the standard is met, employees are paid on the basis of the pay received by the highest producing employee, the lowest producing employee, or the average output rate for the group. Another way is to set a composite standard for the group; when the group meets its production standard, all employees receive the same monetary reward.

Another type of group incentive pay plan is based on cost reduction. The members of a work unit whose output costs are less than the threshold amount are rewarded financially. Although most of the amount saved is divided among the employees, most employers retain a portion of the savings to help pay for other programs that ultimately benefit the employees.

PERFORMANCE-BASED PAY

How do performance-based pay plans differ from incentive pay plans?

A basic difference between the incentive plans discussed earlier and performance-based pay plans is that the latter tend to place greater emphasis on key employees than do the incentive plans. Another distinction is that the performance-based plans reward total performance rather than just one component of an employee's job, such as output. Some performance-based plans are better suited for rewarding employees who have a management status than are the typical incentive plans.

One type of performance-based pay plan is the **key contributor program.** This program is designed to retain key employees, often those with management status, whose special skills and contributions to the organization have a significant impact on its overall performance. Among the types of rewards made to the key contributors are a hiring bonus, cash benefits, stock option plan, and increased salary, perhaps as high as 140 to 160 percent of the normal salary. Although a sizable portion of the organization's employees might be rewarded under an incentive pay plan, only a handful are likely to benefit from the key contributor plan.

What is gain sharing?

Gain sharing, another of the performance-based plans, is a goal-based, organizationwide plan that involves employees extensively in the plan's operation. The plan is generally based on employee-generated costs in relation to company sales. Whenever the employee-generated costs are less than the threshold amount, the difference is divided among the employees. Results are reported frequently—perhaps weekly—with rewards distributed monthly.

Organizations that use gain sharing can adopt one of three different standardized plans—Scanlon, Rucker, or Improshare—or they can develop their own. Regardless of which alternative is used, those responsible for designing and/or installing the program need to be familiar with the concept before they begin.

With gain sharing, production-oriented employees know that if they increase the efficiency of their output and sales-oriented employees know that if they increase sales volume, then they all will be able to share the "gain." Although an incentive plan sometimes entices employees to increase the quantity of their output without regard to its quality, performance-based plans focus on the quality of output. If production increases at the expense of quality, sales will decrease, thus reducing the amount of "gain" to be shared among the employees.

LEGALLY REQUIRED BENEFITS

What benefits are legally required?

Employers are required by federal and state law to provide certain benefits for their employees. Among these benefits are Social Security, workers' compensation, and unemployment compensation. In addition, several states have enacted a mandatory disability insurance program.

Social Security

Officially known as the Old-Age, Survivors, Disability, and Health Insurance program, the Social Security program taxes most employers and employees.

The Federal Insurance Contributions Act, which initiated the Social Security program, has been amended to include Medicare, a health insurance program for the elderly and disabled.

Qualifying recipients of Social Security receive their payments monthly. Now that the program is tied to the cost-of-living index, recipients' payments increase as living costs increase. The tax levied on employers and employees also increases periodically.

Workers' Compensation

The workers' compensation program is designed to protect employees and their dependents against losses resulting from job-related injury or death. Early in the development of this concept, workers' compensation was levied only against employers. Now, however, in an increasing number of states, the program is supported by both the employer and employee.

Unemployment Compensation

Another of the legally required programs is unemployment compensation. This program provides a stipend for unemployed persons. In some states, employers make the full contribution, whereas in other states, both employers and employees contribute to the program.

Disability Insurance

An increasing number of states require participation in the disability insurance program. The cost of this program is generally borne by both the employer and employee. The program provides payments to employees who become disabled as a result of a job-related injury.

FRINGE BENEFITS

What percentage of payroll do fringe benefits typically consume?

Fringe benefits are supplemental compensation in excess of the direct compensation employees receive for performing a specific job. The amount of fringe benefits paid employees has increased rather dramatically over the years. According to the *Employee Benefits* survey conducted regularly by the U.S. Chamber of Commerce, the average amount paid by all organizations (manufacturing and nonmanufacturing) for fringe benefits is around 40 percent of the total payroll. Consequently, for an employee making $60,000 per year, the organization will spend another $24,000 on his or her fringe benefits.

The availability of fringe benefits has a positive impact on employees' morale and loyalty to the organization. Employees are more satisfied with their jobs, and their productivity often increases as a result of receiving fringe benefits. Furthermore, benefits provide an element of job security. To help sustain employees' positive feelings about fringe benefits, an increasing number of organizations are providing frequent and detailed information about the benefits they provide their employees.

A growing number of organizations give employees an opportunity to select the ones that best meet their needs from available benefits. This cafeteria approach, as it is called, gives each employee a lump sum of money, and he or she selects the benefits that will best meet individual needs. With the increased number of families in which both husband and wife work, this approach is highly desirable. Rather than having duplicate fringe benefits, such as medical insurance coverage, the husband and wife can each decide which benefits to receive from each employer.

Some of the most frequently found fringe benefits provided employees are discussed in the paragraphs that follow.

Paid Holidays

Organizations commonly pay employees for national holidays that fall on working days. For example, many employees are compensated for New Year's Day, Memorial Day, Independence Day, Labor Day, Thanksgiving, and Christmas. In many organizations, employees are paid for Fridays when holidays fall on Saturday and for Mondays when holidays fall on Sunday. Some organizations also pay employees for the following holidays: President's Day, Martin Luther King Jr.'s Birthday, and Veteran's Day. In addition, some organizations observe special state holidays.

Paid Vacations

Many organizations also pay their employees while they are on vacation. In most instances, the length of the paid vacation is determined by the employee's longevity with the organization. Exempt employees frequently receive longer paid vacations than nonexempt employees because exempt employees are not eligible to receive overtime pay. Some organizations also give employees a paid vacation day on their birthdays.

Sick Leave

What trend is emerging with unused sick leave?

Another fringe benefit frequently provided employees is sick leave. Most organizations provide a specified number of days of sick leave per year. In some organizations, employees are permitted to accumulate sick days from one year to the next. In other instances, employees can extend their paid vacations by adding their unused days to their vacation time. In still other instances, when employees retire, they are paid for unused sick days accumulated over the years. A trend is emerging that rewards (generally financially) employees for not using their sick days. For example, some organizations buy back from each employee each year the sick days he or she did not use. However, this practice may cause some employees to come to work when they are quite sick. Unless closely controlled, some employees have the tendency to abuse sick-leave benefits.

Paid Personal Days

An increasing number of organizations are giving employees a certain number of paid personal days that can be used as they wish. Employees given paid personal days are less apt to use sick days for reasons other than illness. When an employee has no more personal days, his or her wages are likely to be reduced for absences that exceed the maximum allowed.

Educational Assistance

What is the nature of the educational assistance fringe benefit?

Many organizations pay a portion or all of the tuition costs incurred by employees who attend school part time. Of these, most also help pay for the cost of books and supplies. Some stipulations that are frequently part of the employer-employee educational assistance agreement are (1) the course must be directly related to the employee's job or to a higher level job for which the employee is trying to qualify; (2) the employee must successfully complete the course; (3) the course must be taken at an institution approved by the organization; and (4) the employee, after completing the course, must continue working for the organization for a specified length of time, perhaps a year or two.

Life Insurance Programs

Another common benefit employees receive is life insurance paid either partially or wholly by the employer. In many instances, the amount of life insurance provided each employee is related to his or her salary (perhaps equal to two years' salary). Some plans permit employees to purchase additional insurance (above the maximum provided by the employer) at their own cost. In addition to death benefits, many life insurance programs also provide dismemberment or accidental death benefits.

Health Care Insurance

Group medical, surgical, dental, prescription drug, and vision benefits are also paid either partially or wholly by many employers. Although some provide coverage for all the members of an employee's immediate family, others provide dependent coverage for a nominal cost. Accidental death and dismemberment benefits may also be provided employees as part of their medical insurance coverage. Too, an increasing number of organizations are making major medical insurance available to their employees. Major medical coverage is used when the limits of health insurance coverage have been reached.

Disability Insurance

Disability insurance is also provided by some organizations. This coverage provides payments to employees who become disabled by a job-related accident or by a sickness that prevents their continuing to work. Its primary aim is to provide income protection or compensation for loss of salary when employees are unable to work because of illness or an accident.

Health Maintenance Organizations

What is the function of a health maintenance organization?

As an alternative to group health care insurance benefits, an increasing number of employees have an opportunity to enroll in health maintenance organization (HMO) plans. HMOs, which stress preventive medicine, provide free office calls for their subscribers. Hospital coverage is also provide by the HMO. Those who opt to use the services of the HMO are no longer under the care of their private health care professionals. HMOs generally receive a preset annual fee for each enrolled employee. The HMO keeps the fee regardless of how little of it might be used. The charges incurred by employees who use HMO services at a higher than average rate are partially offset by the unused charges accumulated from employees whose medical expenses are lower than average.

Preferred Provider Organizations

Commonly known as PPOs, **preferred provider organizations** contract with employers, insurance companies, or third-party payers, to provide reduced-fee medical services. Unlike HMOs, PPOs allow individuals to select their healthcare providers from among those participating in the plan. Individuals working with participating providers will receive health care at a lesser cost than they will working with nonparticipating providers. Contrasted with HMOs, individuals with PPOs have a much wider choice of health-care providers from which to choose.

Medical and Fitness Facilities

A growing number of organizations are providing medical and fitness facilities. A portion of the cost of each of these facilities may have to be borne by the users. Some medical facilities provide only first aid, but others provide a sick-room service. In some organizations, the medical facility is operated by nurses; in others, it is operated by a full medical staff.

The fitness facility provides employees an opportunity to participate in fitness programs and health-related seminars. In other instances, the organization may pay for a portion of the cost incurred when employees participate in off-premise fitness programs. This benefit is receiving an increasing amount of attention because organizations have discovered that healthy, fit employees are able to attain higher productivity, they are absent less often, and their long-term medical costs are lower than their counterparts. As a result, any investment in such programs is usually offset by employees' increased productivity.

Maternity Leave

Many organizations provide their employees with maternity leave, even though they do not come under the provisions of the Family and Medical Leave Act of 1993. In some cases, the leave can be paid up to the limits of the employee's accumulated sick leave or vacation leave. An increasing number of organizations also are providing paternity leave for their male employees, who may also be able to use their sick leave or vacation days to receive a paid leave. Some firms also provide their employees with leave for use when adopting a child. A growing number of organizations are reimbursing their employees for a portion or all of the cost incurred in child adoption.

Under the provisions of the **Family and Medical Leave Act of 1993,** which affects all U.S. businesses with fifty or more employees, employers have to provide their employees—both males and females—with twelve weeks of unpaid leave per year in certain situations. Among the situations are the following: having a child; adopting a child; assuming responsibility for a foster child; caring for an ill child, spouse, or parent; or the employee's having a serious illness. Furthermore, the employee is guaranteed that he or she will be able to return to an equivalent job upon returning to work.

Employee Assistance Programs

What is the function of employee assistance programs?

Many organizations of sufficient size to have full-time attorneys and accountants permit their employees to use their services on a limited basis. For personal situations of a complicated nature, employees will most likely be referred to professionals outside the organization.

Included as part of some employee assistance programs is a counseling and referral service. These programs are commonly used by employees who have an addiction (alcohol, drugs, gambling, and so forth) and by those with emotional problems.

Pension Plans

Another common fringe benefit provided employees is a pension plan. A number of important aspects involving pension plans are governed by regulations in the Pension Reform Act, which is discussed in greater detail later in this chapter.

How do defined-benefit and deferred-contribution plans differ?

One type of pension plan is the **defined-benefit plan,** which uses a formula to calculate the amount of retirement a person will receive. Thus, the employee is able to predict his or her eventual retirement benefits. A **defined-contribution plan,** on the other hand, identifies how much the employer will contribute toward the employee's pension plan. It does not provide a formula that enables the employee to calculate the amount of his or her retirement.

Another type of pension plan is the **401(k) plan** that allows employees to put a portion of their compensation into a company profit-sharing or stock bonus plan. Because the amount that an employee contributes to his or her 401(k) plan is based on pretax dollars, the employee is able to reduce his or her federal and perhaps state tax liability.

Profit Sharing

An increasing number of organizations are installing profit-sharing plans that enable employees to share a specified amount of yearly profits. A portion of the increased profits is usually retained by the organization for use in supporting various operations. In some instances, employees receive a cash payment; in others, they receive stock in the organization. The latter is known as an *employee stock option plan.* Employees who receive stock typically make a greater commitment to the organization's success because doing so makes their stock more valuable.

Child Care Services

To accommodate working mothers, many organizations provide child care centers for the children of their employees. Certain restrictions—for example, age and health status of the child—are frequently imposed by the organization.

Car Pools

A growing number of organizations are making employees' participation in car pools increasingly attractive. Some organizations provide choice parking places to employees who belong to car pools, whereas others provide free parking for those who participate in a pool. Still other organizations use van pooling, which involves giving employees a ride to and from work in an organization-owned vehicle.

Cafeteria Services

Eating facilities are provided by organizations, primarily for the convenience of their employees. In some instances, these cafeterias operate on a break-even basis, resulting in reduced meal costs for employees. From the cafeterias in some organizations, employees are able to obtain take-out food for their evening meal.

Company Discounts

As a benefit for their employees, some organizations make their products or services available at reduced costs. The discount may range anywhere from 10 percent to being able to purchase the product or service at cost.

Wellness Programs

Why are wellness programs receiving considerable attention?

Either as a stand-alone program or as a supplement to their fitness facilities, **wellness programs** are being installed in an increasing number of organizations. These programs are geared toward the employee's maintaining a total health program. In some of these programs, routine physicals are an important component, as is dietary and health maintenance counseling.

Wellness programs that work provide a desirable return on their investment in terms of reduced health insurance claims. Increasingly, organizations find it much more desirable to provide financial resources through a wellness program that helps employees maintain a healthy lifestyle than it is to pay the insurance claims (and have the related expense incurred by absent employees) when they do not maintain a healthy lifestyle. Employees who smoke and those whose weight is not within a normal range incur significantly more insurance claims than do those who do not smoke and those whose weight is within a normal range.

In some organizations, the eradication of smoking is an important aspect of wellness programs. Accordingly, an increasing number of organizations (1) permit smoking only in designated areas or (2) ban smoking on organization premises. Some organizations are also paying bonuses to employees who quit smoking, but others are paying for the employees to attend seminars aimed at helping attendees quit smoking.

Eldercare

An increasing number of organizations are becoming cognizant of the rapidly growing number of elderly in the United States, many of whom are dependent on their offspring for varying amounts of their care. To accommodate as much as possible those employees with dependent elderly parents, some organizations implement flextime programs that enable employees to delay the starting time of their work day. Thus, an employee is able to provide whatever parental needs may be necessary before going to work. Other organizations allow employees to establish a flexible spending account (a provision of the Deficit Reduction Act discussed in the "Federal Legislation" section of this chapter) in which a given percentage of pretax dollars can be deducted from their paychecks to provide care for either dependent children or dependent elderly parents.

Reimbursement Account Programs

What are reimbursement accounts?

An ever-increasing number of organizations are installing **reimbursement account programs** that are financially advantageous to both the employees and the employer. Employees have deducted a predetermined amount from each paycheck. Because the amount deducted is not considered as taxable income, employees' tax obligation is reduced. For example, for every $1,000 an employee at the 28 percent income tax bracket puts into a reimbursement account, his or her tax obligation is reduced $280. In addition, the employee and the employer both save on Social Security taxes.

When the employee has either a medical expense not covered by his or her insurance coverage or a dependent-care expense, the reimbursement account is used to reimburse the employee for the amount of these expenses. Reimbursement can be obtained for deductibles, co-pay, and such noninsured expenses as dental care, eye care, or prescription drugs.

Time-Off Bank

One of the newest fringe benefits made available to employees is the **time-off bank.** Rather than giving employees a specified number of vacation days, they are given hours in their time-off bank that they can use for vacation, personal time, illness, or additional holiday time. In most cases, the hours in the time-off bank are a composite of vacation days, personal days, and paid sick-leave days. The number of hours an employee is eligible to have put in his or her time-off bank is often determined by the hierarchical level of the job and the employee's longevity with the organization.

In most organizations, employees are permitted to spend their accrued time in hours, days, or even weeks if their time accrual is sufficient. Generally, employees are also able to move all or a portion of their unspent hours forward into the next year. Some organizations also pay employees for their unspent hours at the end of each year, upon their retirement, or when they terminate their employment.

FEDERAL LEGISLATION

The provisions of federal legislation are also important considerations in developing a salary administration program. Among the more important acts are the Fair Labor Standards Act and its amended act, the Equal Pay Act; the Walsh-Healey Act; the Davis-Bacon Act; the Pregnancy Discrimination Act; and the Pension Reform Act. The important provisions of these acts that impact on the salary administration program are discussed in this section.

Fair Labor Standards Act

How does the Fair Labor Standards Act impact salary administration?

According to the **Fair Labor Standards Act,** employees who are covered by the act must be paid at least the legal minimum wage. The act also contains specific provisions for overtime pay, equal pay for equal work, and minimum ages of children who can be hired.

The act as originally passed by Congress applied only to companies involved with interstate commerce. With a number of amendments passed over the years, the act now encompasses almost all firms in the United States.

An important provision of the act is its distinction between exempt and nonexempt employees. A common misconception is that all salaried employees are exempt from minimum wages and overtime pay, while nonexempt employees (employees paid by the hour) are covered by the minimum wages and overtime pay provisions of the act. The act identifies four exempt job categories: executive, administrative, outside sales, and professional. In these categories, other criteria—which vary among the categories—must be present to make an employee fully exempt. For example, in the executive category, the additional criteria that need to be present to classify an employee as exempt are the following: have management responsibilities, supervise employees, have authority to hire and fire or to make recommendations to hire and fire, devote certain percentage of work time to managerial duties, and receive a minimum weekly salary. Even though an employee may be salaried, to be exempt his or her job must also possess these additional criteria.

Another important provision of the act involves compensating employees who work more than 40 hours in a given week. The act requires that employees who are paid for their overtime hours be paid at a rate of 1.5 times their regular salary. Employees who receive time off for working overtime must receive 1.5 hours off for every hour worked over 40 hours per week.

Equal Pay Act

What is the important
provision of the Equal
Pay Act?

The **Equal Pay Act** of 1963, which amended the Fair Labor Standards Act (FLA), applies to the same employers as the FLA. Under the provisions of the Equal Pay Act, an employer cannot have unequal pay policies or fringe benefits for men and women who perform equal jobs that require equal skill, effort, and responsibility and that are performed under similar working conditions. The Equal Pay Act also makes it illegal for an employer to reduce the salary rates of employees of one gender as a means of eliminating salary differentials.

Walsh-Healey Act

The **Walsh-Healey Act** covers employees working on government contracts that use materials and equipment in excess of $10,000. The act also stipulates that employees must receive at least the minimum wage, that they must receive overtime pay, and that child labor must not be used.

Davis-Bacon Act

The **Davis-Bacon Act,** passed in 1931, is also known as the Prevailing Wage Law. The act sets minimum wages for persons employed by contractors working for the federal government on projects worth more than $2,000. The minimum wage rate is established at the prevailing level of pay for other similar jobs in the area.

Pregnancy Discrimination Act

Passed in 1978, the **Pregnancy Discrimination Act** forbids employers from mandating that pregnant employees take a maternity leave at a prescribed time during their pregnancy, regardless of their ability to carry out their job duties. The act also gives employees the right to return to their jobs after giving birth, and their retirement benefits and seniority must remain intact.

Pension Reform Act

How does the Pension
Reform Act impact salary
administration?

The **Pension Reform Act,** officially known as the Employee Retirement Income Security Act of 1974, has a significant impact on organizations' pension plans. The act does not require an organization to have a pension plan; however, if it does, the plan must meet the requirements outlined in the act. Organizations that offer a pension plan are required to meet a minimum funding standard, which means they must contribute at least a minimum amount to a qualified defined benefit or money purchase pension or to an annuity plan.

An organization can have an exempt, fully insured plan if certain requirements are met during the plan year. One such requirement is that the plan be funded exclusively with individual insurance or annuity contracts. Another requirement is that the contracts must provide for the payment of level annual (or more frequent) premiums from the time an employee becomes a participant in the plan until the employee reaches retirement age or ceases participation in the plan.

If the organization's plan is subject to the provisions of the act, all employees who have reached the age of twenty-five and who have worked for the organization for one year (one thousand hours in industries of an intermittent or seasonal employment nature) are covered.

The following outlines some of the more important provisions of the act. Pension plans must be vested, which means that employees are entitled to the amount they contribute to their pension plans, in addition to a share of their employer's contribution, under one of the following options: (1) fully vested after ten years of continuous service; (2) partially vested after a time (for example, after five years of service, 25 percent vested); after ten years, 50 percent vested; and after fifteen years, 100 percent vested; (3) vesting under the "forty-five rule," which means that after five years of service, the employee is entitled to 50 percent vesting when the sum of the employee's age and years of service exceeds forty-five, with added vesting for additional years of service until the employee is entitled to 100 percent vesting. (For example, an employee who has ten years of service and whose age and service equal or exceed fifty-five is entitled to 100 percent vesting.)

In most cases, employees who are hired after a mandatory retirement age are also covered by the act. Employees who change jobs can take their vested benefits with them. If the new employer approves, the vested benefits can be transferred to the new employer's retirement program, although such transfers are limited to once every three years. The annual benefit payable to any employee covered by the act may not be greater than the lesser of $75,000 or 100 percent of the employee's average compensation for the three consecutive calendar years in which the employee received his or her highest salary.

The benefits of the plan must be communicated to the employees in a summary plan description that contains the following:

What information about benefits must be communicated to employees in a summary plan description?

1. The name of the plan; the common name of the plan; the employer and address; the type of plan; how the plan is administered; the administrator's name and address; the date of the plan's fiscal year; the employer identification number; the name and address of the person responsible for the legal services of the organization; and the names, titles, and addresses of the plan's trustees.

2. Requirements for participation and the benefits; description of joint and survivor benefits; service requirements for accruing full benefits; how benefits are prorated for less than a year's service; and who pays for the plan.

3. Identity of any organization that maintains the plan's funds or provides benefits; the manner in which claims are to be filed; the procedure to follow when a claim is denied; and whether or not the plan is insured under the Pension Benefit Guaranty Corporation.

Age Discrimination in Employment Act

According to the provisions of the 1986 amendments to the **Age Discrimination in Employment Act,** neither male nor female employees who work for a private business with at least twenty employees can be forced to retire. An exception is top-level executives who can be retired at seventy years of age.

Economic Recovery Tax Act

Passed in 1981, the **Economic Recovery Tax Act** allows employees, depending on their yearly income and filing status, to contribute up to $2,000, tax deductible, to an employer-sponsored pension, profit-sharing, or savings account or to an individual retirement account (IRA). Beginning in 1998, employees can contribute up to $2,000 per year in a nondeductible account, known as a Roth IRA, that grows tax free.

Deficit Reduction Act

The **Deficit Reduction Act** that was passed in 1984 taxes some benefits, especially flexible spending plans. In return for reduced pay, however, one type of flexible spending plan gives employees the choice between several nontaxable benefits.

Consolidated Omnibus Budget Reconciliation Act

An important provision of the **Consolidated Omnibus Budget Reconciliation Act** passed in 1985 gives terminated or laid-off employees the right to maintain health insurance by paying their own premiums for up to eighteen months. Coverage is extended to employees with reduced work hours, a situation that might otherwise make them ineligible for coverage.

Family and Medical Leave Act of 1993

What does the Family and Medical Leave Act of 1993 provide employees?

The Family and Medical Leave Act of 1993, which covers employers with fifty or more employees, is primarily used by employees to take an unpaid leave upon the birth of a child, when they adopt a child, or when they have an ill child, spouse, or parent who needs their assistance. It guarantees employees twelve weeks of unpaid leave during a year's time; employees must have worked for their current employer a minimum of twelve months and have worked a minimum of 1,250 hours during the year before the leave begins. In some instances, an employer can require that an employee use any available paid leave as part of the twelve-week leave if any is available.

IMPLICATIONS FOR THE ADMINISTRATIVE OFFICE MANAGER

The degree to which employees are satisfied with their salaries often affects the interest they take in their jobs. Dissatisfaction can result in increased turnover, higher levels of absenteeism and tardiness, and reduced productivity. Unfortunately, when problems do arise in the salary administration program, rebuilding employee confidence can take a long time.

The administrative office manager in many organizations, especially in larger ones, plays an important advisory role in the salary administration program. In some of these organizations, the administrative office manager also has certain functional responsibilities for the program, which may include conducting salary surveys and helping determine new salary schedules.

In some organizations, the administrative office manager determines the amount of merit increase for each employee for whom he or she has either direct or indirect responsibility. In other instances, the manager determines the amount of merit increase for those subordinates for whom direct responsibility exists and merely approves the merit increase for those employees for whom he or she is indirectly responsible. The amount of increase for these employees is determined by their immediate supervisor.

REVIEW QUESTIONS

1. What is the nature of the relationship between job evaluation and salary administration?

2. How does a salary administration program help employees perform at an optimum level?

3. What types of policies should be developed to improve the efficiency of the operation of the salary administration program?

4. In a large organization, who is generally responsible for salary administration? In a small organization?

5. Which of the prepared salary surveys are suitable for determining going rates for the following:

   a. Office or clerical employees?

   b. Middle management?

   c. Exempt employees?

   d. Data processing employees?

6. How can the salary range for specific jobs be determined?

7. How can an organization be sure that its salaries are competitive with salaries paid by other organizations in the community?

8. What characteristics are typically found in effective incentive pay plans?

9. Why do organizations make fringe benefits available to employees?

10. Which provisions of the Fair Labor Standards Act have special significance for salary administration?

11. What workers are covered by the Walsh-Healey Act? By the Pension Reform Act?

DISCUSSION QUESTIONS

1. Several of the employees in the company in which you work have been with the company for many years. These employees also perform considerably above average. Because they are at the top of their salary ranges, their yearly salary increases are limited to the amount of increase in the upper limit for their ranges. Their superiors are upset about this because they believe these employees should receive a merit increase. Several have suggested that these employees "simply be taken off the salary scale so they can receive decent salary increases." Discuss the implications of this suggestion.

2. One of your subordinates just left your office after complaining to you that his salary is lower than another recently hired employee who has the same job title as his. The employee who is dissatisfied indicated that he felt his salary should be higher because he has been with the company for four years. How can you justify the situation of an employee with four years of experience who receives a lower salary than a new employee who has the same job title?

3. The company in which you work uses its ability to pay as the only criterion in determining how much money will be made available for its yearly salary program. Over the long run, what are the implications of "ability to pay" as the only criterion that is considered?

STUDENT PROJECTS AND ACTIVITIES

1. Obtain from two organizations in your community (perhaps a large organization and a small organization) a list of the fringe benefits they provide their employees. What are the similarities in the benefits that are provided?

2. Discuss with an administrative office manager the nature of the incentive pay program offered the employees in the organization in which he or she works.

3. Going Online: Using the Internet, conduct an online search based on one of the concepts presented in this chapter or based on one of the chapter terms. Identify four or five things you learned from this material that you did not know before your online search.

Minicase

The Shane Corporation, which is located in Curtis, Nebraska, is the largest employer in the community. At the present time, more than 300 individuals are employed by the corporation. Increasingly, the employees are filing grievances related to their dissatisfaction with the salary program. Most employees believe their salaries are not properly related to job requirements and that job importance and job pay are not consistent. The organization knows that part of the problem lies with the evaluated worth of the jobs. The fact that the salaries are not competitive within the community also has an adverse effect. Because no printed salary information exists for the community in which the Shane Corporation is located, a salary survey will have to be conducted.

1. What steps will be involved in conducting the salary survey?
2. What suggestions can you provide to help ensure the success of the survey?

Case

The salary administration program at Mandez Bakery, Inc., was formally established about ten years ago. You were recently appointed to a committee responsible for determining a new salary structure. The project has progressed to the point that the salaries for comparable jobs in the community have been determined. Figure 14–4 is the salary scattergram depicting the relationship between the salaries and evaluated worth for each job in the Mandez Corporation. Figure 14–5 depicts the correlation line for comparable jobs in the community. The company strives to pay salaries above the community average, which are depicted by the line in Figure 14–5.

1. Determine what you believe would be an appropriate correlation line (midpoint) for salaries in the Mandez Corporation.
2. On the basis of the new midpoint line, prepare a salary range at 10 percent above and below the midpoint. Prepare a salary range chart to depict this information.

Figure 14-4 Relationship between salaries and evaluated worth for each job in Mandez Bakery

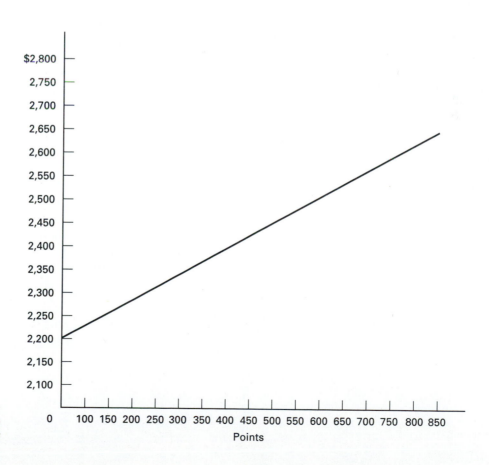

Figure 14-5 Correlation line for comparable jobs in community

$\mathcal{C}$hapter 15

MEASURING OUTPUT OF OFFICE EMPLOYEES

$\mathcal{C}$hapter $\mathcal{A}$ims

After studying this chapter, you should be able to design an effective strategy for measuring the output of office employees.

$\mathcal{C}$hapter $\mathcal{O}$utline

Nature of Work Measurement
    Objectives of Work Measurement
    Advantages
    Characteristics of Measurable Office Activities
Work Measurement Program
Work Measurement Techniques
    Production Records
    Work Sampling
    Time Study
    Micromotion Study
    Predetermined Standard Time Data
Performance Leveling
Work Standards
    Advantages of Work Standards
    Types of Standards
Implications for the Administrative Office
    Manager

$\mathcal{C}$hapter $\mathcal{T}$erms

Continuous timing
Descriptive standards
Lapsed timing
Microchrometer
Micromotion study
Performance leveling
Predetermined standard time data
Production records
Quality standards
Quantity standards
Random observations
Stopwatch study
Time log
Time study
Time study sheet
Work measurement
Work sampling
Work standards

Work measurement is used to help determine what constitutes a fair day's work from both the employer's and the employee's standpoint. Employers need evidence that employees are producing at an acceptable level, and employees need assurance that they are being compensated equitably in relation to their output.

The information collected through the work measurement process is used in setting work standards, which specify expected quantities of output within a given amount of time. Such information enables an organization to compare actual productivity of its employees with expected productivity.

Several methods are used for measuring work. Some office activities are measured by counting the number of units employees produce. Others require more sophisticated measures, such as those presented in this chapter.

What is the function of work standards?

NATURE OF WORK MEASUREMENT

Because an increasing number of administrative office managers are becoming more concerned about work efficiency and productivity, the measurement of office activities is receiving greater attention than in the past. Greater control over office operations can be exercised when work standards are used for comparing actual results with anticipated results. Although standards can be developed to measure the effectiveness of most office activities, developing standards for nonmeasurable activities is not possible.

Objectives of Work Measurement

By determining a reasonable level of productivity, work measurement is especially useful in assessing how well an employee's actual output compares with expected output. Work standards are used to express expected output or production levels.

What are the objectives of work measurement?

Another use of work measurement is to aid the planning and scheduling of work. By using work standards, the administrative office manager is able to determine a realistic amount of time for task or job completion. The standards can also be used to determine the number of employees who will be needed to complete a project within the allotted time. Work measurement provides the basis for determining whether additional employees are needed for the timely completion of a project.

Another objective of work measurement is to help determine the efficiency of work methods and processes. The task of determining whether the employee is overproducing or underproducing is made easy by comparing an employee's output level with generally accepted standards. If employees consistently produce less than expected, an attempt should be made to determine the reasons for the low production levels. If the reason can be attributed to employee inefficiency, the need for an employee training program might be investigated.

Additionally, work measurement helps determine the cost of office operations. Unit cost is calculated by dividing total cost by the number of units produced. Unit output costs are used in two ways: to facilitate the comparison of an organization's performance data with comparable data of other organizations and to aid the budget-preparation process. The amount that should be budgeted for each activity or work process is easily estimated by projecting the total units of output that will be produced during the budget period and then multiplying this projection by the unit output cost.

Finally, work measurement helps determine equitable employee workloads. By using standards to determine load, greater equity in assigning work can be ensured. Equally important is a greater employee understanding of expected performance, which has a positive impact on morale.

Advantages

What are the advantages of work measurement?

A work measurement program results in several significant advantages. Greater control over work processes and methods is possible. Work measurement helps determine the appropriateness of the number of employees assigned to a work unit as well as the efficiency with which individuals produce. Greater efficiency in planning work is possible, and backlogs can be avoided by using the results of work measurement in scheduling work. Finally, the results of work measurement can be used to help simplify work processes.

Characteristics of Measurable Office Activities

What are the characteristics of measurable office activities?

The measurement of office activities requires tasks that can be isolated and counted. Thus, the tasks that comprise specific office jobs must be identifiable. To ensure accurate results, office tasks must be fairly consistent from one measurement to another because fluctuations can readily destroy the reliability of measurement results. Office tasks should also be of sufficient quantity to justify the cost of measurement. The measurement of low-volume office tasks that are expensive to measure typically is not justified.

Activities that require considerable amounts of judgment and decision making are typically unmeasurable. Because the time consumed in performing these tasks varies so widely, measurement results may not be sufficiently reliable to develop accurate standards. Although office tasks involving considerable creativity are difficult to measure, methods have been devised for use in developing standards for such nonroutine creative jobs as drafting and editing.

WORK MEASUREMENT PROGRAM

The installation of a work measurement program involves considerable planning and a thorough investigation of various alternatives. The number of options available enables organizations to develop programs tailored to their specific needs.

Selling a work measurement program to employees and gaining their support are critical to the program's success. Without employee acceptance, program success will be diminished, sometimes quite significantly.

What techniques are available for selling employees on the value of a work measurement program?

Several techniques are successfully used in selling work measurement programs. Employees desire information about the nature of job-related changes they may have to make. Employees also desire to learn whether the work measurement results will be used by the organization in assessing the need to retain or eliminate their positions. Assuring employees that the results of work measurement will not cause anyone to be terminated is often critical to employee acceptance of the program. Attrition can often be used to make any needed staffing adjustments.

Among the other techniques used to gain employee support are group meetings in which the participants discuss the merits of a work measurement program, case studies about other organizations that have successful work measurement programs, and detailed information about the installation of the work measurement program. Once the decision has been made to install the program, employees should receive from a top-level executive a memo or letter in which information about the program is clearly outlined.

The following is a step-by-step plan for installing a work measurement program:

What steps are involved in installing a work measurement program?

1. *Make preliminary plans.* The objectives of the program should be outlined, the work measurement techniques should be selected, and the timetable for installing the program should be determined. If consultants are needed to help install the program, contracting for such services should be considered at this point.

2. *Hire employees.* The duties and responsibilities of the individuals who are responsible for the program should be determined before their selection.

3. *Gain acceptance of and support for the program.* The individuals involved with the installation and operation of the program should be used extensively in gaining acceptance of and support for the program.

4. *Collect important data.* If the selected work measurement technique requires gathering data from various work units, the individuals responsible for data collection should be familiarized with the mechanics of the technique.

5. *Analyze collected data and develop standards.* Once the necessary data have been collected, they should be analyzed, and standards should be developed accordingly. If the work measurement program uses predetermined standards purchased from an outside source, the appropriate standards for the various office activities should be developed during this step.

6. *Train supervisors and managers.* Each supervisor and manager in the organization who is directly or indirectly responsible for an employee whose job is affected by work measurement should receive training on the use of work measurement and the implementation of standards.

7. *Instruct employees.* Once supervisors have received training in the implementation and use of standards, they should inform their subordinates of expected levels of production.

8. *Follow up.* Successful work measurement programs are evaluated periodically, with the follow-up occurring more frequently during the early stages of the program. Management needs to know how actual results compare with expected results. When actual results do not compare favorably, the reasons for the discrepancy should be determined, and the program should be modified accordingly.

WORK MEASUREMENT TECHNIQUES

Several work measurement techniques are used to develop work standards. When selecting an appropriate technique to use, the following criteria should be considered:

What criteria should be considered in selecting an appropriate work measurement program?

1. The intended use of the standards.
2. The degree of accuracy required of the standards.
3. The cost the organization is willing to incur in developing the standards.
4. The nature of the work for which standards are desired.
5. The degree to which individuals responsible for the program understand the elements of work measurement and work standards.

Among the work measurement techniques available are production records, work sampling, time study, micromotion study, and predetermined standard time data.

Production Records

As a work measurement technique, the use of **production records** is rather simple and quick. It uses employee production records to determine the amount of time needed to complete a particular job.

Figure 15–1 illustrates a **time log** that is helpful when using the production records technique. The log enables each employee to keep a record of the work he or she produces and the amount of time taken to produce the work. Each task the employee performs is entered in coded form on the time log (column 1). The number of units produced (column 2) and the amount of time taken to produce the units (column 3) are also entered on the time log. The time increments are usually expressed in units of five or ten minutes.

Each employee should keep a time log for as long as needed to smooth out or balance any unusual fluctuations. In most instances, a period of two weeks is considered a minimum amount of time for recording data.

On accumulating the production records of all the employees, a calculation is made of the total units they produce and the total amount of time taken to produce the units. By dividing the total units produced by the total time taken to produce the units, a unit output standard can be determined. In some instances, the standard will be adjusted either upward or downward as a means of pacing an employee's performance against the average standard. This is done

What is the function of a time log?

What is the minimum time to maintain a time log?

Activity 1	Units Produced 2	Time 3
D	1	8:00
		8:10
A	15	8:20
		8:30
		8:40
C	2	8:50
		9:00
D	1	9:10
F	15	9:20
		9:30
		9:40
		9:50
		10:00
		10:10
		⋮
		12:00

Figure 15–1 Time log

by a leveling process discussed in detail in the "Performance Leveling" section of this chapter.

When the various tasks in a work process change or when the conditions under which work is performed change, the standards most likely will have to be adjusted. This is the reason for routinely investigating the validity of the standards determined by this technique.

Sometimes, department production records kept over a period of time are also used to determine work standards. For example, the log regularly maintained in most word processing centers might be sufficient to set work standards. These logs are frequently used to keep track of the time taken to transcribe the contents of a magnetic dictation belt or tape. By approximating the number of words on a belt or tape and by knowing how much time the transcription process takes, a words-per-minute typing standard can be developed. Allowances have to be made, however, for variations in the speed of dictation, the complexity of the material, and so forth. The greater the number of uncontrolled variables, the less accurate this technique is likely to be.

Among the advantages of the production records technique are the following: It is simple, easily understood, and inexpensive to use. Therefore, it is the only financially feasible technique for many organizations. In addition, standards can be quickly developed and implemented without the need for specially trained individuals.

A disadvantage of using the production records technique is the possibility that it may contribute to setting inaccurate standards when employees fail to maintain accurate time logs. Also, the standards developed by this technique are readily affected by changes in work processes. Therefore, employees may have to keep time logs quite regularly for use as input in adjusting standards. Furthermore, because it determines "what is" rather than "what should be," adjustments may have to be made.

What are the advantages of the production records technique?

Work Sampling

What are the characteristics of the work sampling technique?

Using a statistical base, the **work sampling** technique requires **random observations** to determine the amount of time consumed by each element of an office procedure. The statistical element of work sampling is based on the following law of probability: If a procedure is observed randomly a sufficient number of times, the results will be as reliable as when the procedure is observed continuously over a period of time. An important aspect of the work sampling technique is the accurate identification of the type of activity being performed by an employee at the time of each random observation.

Observations are considered random if the employee or employees being observed are randomly chosen and if the time of the observations is randomly determined. These random observations are used to determine what percentage of the total process each activity or task consumes.

The filing of insurance applications is used to illustrate the work sampling method. The filing process involves five distinct activities. A total of one hundred random observations was determined to be a sufficient quantity. Random observations are made to determine the percentage of the process that each activity consumes. Figure 15–2 illustrates this relationship. For example, of the one hundred random observations, activity A was observed twenty times; activity B, ten times; activity C, forty times; and so forth. The total filing process consumed 500 minutes. Therefore, if activity A constitutes 20 percent of the total process in terms of the number of observations, activity A should also constitute 20 percent or 100 minutes of the total time consumed by the filing process. (This is determined by multiplying 500 minutes by .20.)

A Activity	B Observations	C Percent	D Time (min)	E Units Produced	F Standard (D ÷ E)
A	20	20	100	250	.4
B	10	10	50	100	.5
C	40	40	200	200	1.0
D	20	20	100	50	2.0
E	10	10	50	125	.4
Totals	100	100	500	725	

Figure 15-2 Illustration of work sampling method

Records also have to be examined to determine the number of units produced during each activity. This is illustrated in column E of Figure 15–2. During the 500 minutes consumed by the filing process, 250 units were produced during activity A, 100 units during activity B, and so forth. To determine the standard for activity A, the amount of time (100 minutes) is divided by the number of units produced (250). Therefore, a standard of .4 is derived for activity A. Consequently, one unit is produced during each .4 of a minute or every 24 seconds.

The random selection of the employees and the times they are to be observed can be greatly expedited by using a table of random numbers. These tables and directions for their use can be found in statistics books.

Determining Sample Size. The appropriate sample size is critical to the success of the work sampling technique. The appropriate number depends on the following: (1) the portion of time the smallest activity consumes in the total work process, (2) the degree of tolerance required, and (3) the reliability of results required.

What factors are considered in determining appropriate sample size?

The smaller the portion of time consumed by the smallest activity in the total work process, the greater is the need for a larger sample. This is because a sufficient number of observations needs to be made to ensure the reliability of results; an insufficient number of observations will likely result in insufficient reliability. Generally, the activity that is selected should consume a minimum of 5 percent of the total time. Any activity consuming less than 5 percent is sometimes eliminated from consideration.

Referring to the degree of accuracy required, tolerance is another of the critical elements to be considered when determining appropriate sample size. As the need for a higher tolerance increases, so does the number of observations that have to be made. Conversely, a lower tolerance results in the need for a smaller number of observations.

The degree of reliability required also affects the number of observations that need to be made. Situations that require greater reliability will require a larger number of observations.

The following illustrates the impact of variances among three factors that need to be considered in determining the appropriate sample size. If the smallest activity in the work process consumes 25 percent of the total process and if 90 percent accuracy and 80 percent reliability of results are required, 510 observations will be needed. On the other hand, if the smallest activity consumes 5 percent of the total process and if 95 percent accuracy and 80 percent reliability are desired, 12,840 observations will be needed. These numbers are obtainable from appropriate tables in statistics books.

What are the advantages of the work sampling technique?

Advantages and Disadvantages of Work Sampling. The advantages of the work sampling technique are as follows:

1. The results are highly accurate, provided that random observations are made.
2. The technique does not require the services of a highly trained analyst.
3. The technique is fairly reasonable in terms of its installation cost.
4. The results can be gathered rather quickly.
5. Work sampling is well suited for long-cycle work processes.

Among the disadvantages of the work sampling technique are the following:

1. Some employees have a tendency to perform differently if or when they know they are being observed. If unusual performance occurs frequently, the results of work measurement could be affected significantly.
2. Procedures consisting of numerous minute activities are not suitable for work sampling.
3. To set standards, production records have to be used to determine units of output. Such output records are not always readily accessible.
4. The use of work sampling is sufficiently complex that a trained analyst is needed.
5. Various elements of the process are somewhat difficult for employees to understand. As a result, employees may not fully support the program.

Time Study

Also known as **stopwatch study** or stopwatch time study, **time study** uses a stopwatch in the data-gathering process. To improve the effectiveness of this technique, all wasted motions should be eliminated before the work process is analyzed. Standards based on inefficient work processes are of little value because they simply perpetuate the inefficiency.

The time study technique involves the following three steps:

What steps are involved in the time study technique?

1. Break the job down into its basic elements.
2. Record on a **time study sheet** the amount of time consumed by each element of the work process. This step is repeated for several cycles of the work process.
3. Determine the appropriate standards on the basis of the time consumed by each element of the work process.

Figure 15–3, which outlines the process for calculating payroll, illustrates a time study sheet used in conjunction with the time study technique. The time study sheet is completed by entering into the appropriate columns the amount of time consumed by each of the elements of the work process. Five cycles of the process were timed, according to the information on Figure 15–3. In an actual situation, more than five cycles may be needed.

What is the difference between continuous timing and lapsed timing?

The time study technique uses two timing techniques: **continuous timing** of the entire process or **lapsed timing** for each element of the entire process. When the continuous technique is used, the analyst simply records the stopwatch reading at the conclusion of each element of the process in the "R" (reading) column of cycle 1. For example, in cycle 1, the first element was completed when the stopwatch showed 15 seconds; the second element, 37 seconds; the third element, 92 seconds; and the fourth, 110 seconds. The amount of time consumed by each element is then entered in the "T" (time) column. The first

| Work Process Calculating Payroll | | | | | | | | | | | | | | | | | Analyst's Name: L. Davis | |
| Date: September 3, 20 xx | | | | | | | | | | | | | | | | | Worker's Name: Sandy Evans | |

Elements	Cycle																Standard	Notes
	1		2		3		4		5		6		7		8			
	T	R	T	R	T	R	T	R	T	R	T	R	T	R	T	R		
Determine Total Hours Worked	15	00 15	16	126	15	234	14	342	15	451							15	
Multiply Hours Worked by Base Rate of Pay to Arrive at Gross Pay	22	37	21	147	21	255	22	364	26*	457*							22	*Put wrong value in machine – had to start over (lost 4 seconds)
Calculate Deductions	55	92	53	200	55	310	54	418	54	511							54	
Subtract Deductions to Get Net Pay	18	110	19	219	18	328	18	436	18	529							18	

Figure 15-3 Time study sheet

element consumes 15 seconds; the second, 22 seconds (37 minus 15); and so forth. The timing of the work process is repeated a sufficient number of cycles to compensate for erratic performance.

The use of the lapsed time technique requires that the analyst reset the stopwatch to "0" at the completion of each element of the process. These figures are immediately recorded in the "T" column. Unlike the continuous method, no subtraction is required when the lapsed time technique is used.

The validity of standards is directly affected by the performance of the employees whose output is being timed. In some organizations, the employees who are most respected by their coworkers are the ones timed because of the assumption that the standards will have greater credibility among all employees. If the employees who are timed are also the most skilled workers, the standards most likely will have to be leveled to accommodate the less skilled employees. The leveling process is discussed in the "Performance Leveling" section of this chapter.

Another important characteristic to consider when selecting employees to participate in the timing process is the consistency with which they perform their jobs. An erratic performance is likely to have a negative impact on the reliability of the standards. If the procedure being measured lacks efficiency, the inefficiency should be eliminated before subjecting the procedure to time study. Otherwise, the time study data will not be accurate.

What advantages result from the use of time study?

Time study has the following advantages: (1) it results in the development of accurate standards; (2) it produces more accurate results when measuring work processes comprised of minute elements than either the production records technique or the work sampling technique; and (3) it results in the development of standards that can be readily used for assessing the performance of employees.

Among the disadvantages of time study are the following: (1) The measurement process often requires the use of a trained analyst, which adds to the cost of the work measurement program; (2) office employees tend to have a negative reaction to standards determined by the stopwatch technique; and (3) the technique is not useful for measuring time-consuming elements of a work process.

Micromotion Study

Of the various work measurement techniques, **micromotion study** is the only one that uses a visual recording (either a motion picture or a videotape) of the work process being analyzed. This technique is especially appropriate for work processes that involve both people and machines. An analysis of the visual recording reveals inefficiency in task performance as well as task elements that need to be simplified.

When the primary purpose of micromotion study is to provide data for setting standards, the visual recording is analyzed to determine the amount of time consumed by each element of the work process. Time calculation is carried out in two ways:

1. Multiplying the number of frames on which an element appears by the speed of the film as it advances through the camera provides the amount of time each element consumes. This result becomes the standard for the element. To illustrate, if two thousand frames advance through the camera per minute and if a particular element of the process appears on two hundred frames, the standard would be one-tenth of a minute (six seconds).

2. Using a stopwatch, measure the amount of time consumed by each element of the work process.

What is a microchrometer?

A **microchrometer** may be needed when the elements of the work process are minute. The microchrometer, which is a special timing device attached to the camera, enables the unit of time to be photographed on each frame of the motion picture. The standard for each element is determined by subtracting from the time that appears on the first frame of a particular element the time that appears on the last frame of the element.

The tendency for micromotion to be an expensive work measurement technique often restricts its use to high-volume, costly work processes. Many believe its use cannot be justified except for processes that possess the volume and cost characteristics mentioned earlier.

The advantages of micromotion study are as follows: (1) it is extremely accurate; (2) it is well suited for analyzing the most minute elements of a work process; and (3) it can also be used to simplify work processes because wasted motions appear on the recording.

The micromotion study technique also possesses several disadvantages: (1) it is more costly than some of the other work measurement techniques; (2) its use is limited to high-volume, costly work processes; and (3) it requires the services of a trained analyst. These disadvantages preclude some organizations from selecting micromotion study as a work measurement technique.

Predetermined Standard Time Data

From where are predetermined standard time data obtained?

The **predetermined standard time data** technique is the only one discussed in this chapter that typically uses data obtained from external sources. Predetermined standard time data are generally purchased from management consulting firms or from work measurement associations. The purchased data are used as a base for setting the organization's work standards. In rare instances, an organization may develop its own predetermined standard time data, a process that requires the use of individuals who have extensive training in work measurement.

The predetermined standard time data technique is based on the following premise: When motions are performed under identical conditions, the time values of the motions will be constant from one situation to another. Therefore, an organization can use predetermined standard time data to set standards for basic motions, provided the motions are performed under the same conditions as when the predetermined standard times were set.

When using predetermined standard time data, the analyst uses the following steps:

What steps constitute the predetermined standard time data technique?

1. The work process is broken down into its most minute elements.
2. Each element is analyzed in terms of the motion involved.
3. To determine the appropriate standard, each motion of the work process is compared with the purchased predetermined standard time data. This step is repeated for each element. Figure 15–4 illustrates one of the tables found in one system.
4. The standard for the entire process is found by adding the standard times for each of the motions.

Internally and externally developed predetermined standard time data are generally developed by either stopwatch time studies or by micromotion study. The use of either of these techniques generally provides accurate data.

Several predetermined standard time data systems are available. Included are such systems as Motion-Time Analysis, Methods Time Measurement (MTM), Basic Motion Time Study, Universal Maintenance Standards, and Master Clerical Data (MCD). Although the same basic principles were originally used in developing each of the systems, certain elements of the various systems differ significantly.

The data illustrated in Figure 15–4 represent one of the thirteen tables found in the MTM system. The time measurement unit (TMU) used in MTM is one hundred-thousandth of an hour. Because the time units are so minute, MTM is not well suited for many common office work processes. For example, grasping and putting a sheet of paper into working position can involve three or four different MTM motions.

Master Clerical Data, which is an adaptation of MTM, classifies clerical work into thirteen distinct elemental categories. The data in the categories are used to provide input for determining standard times for various elements of clerical work processes. Figure 15–5 illustrates the standards for a portion of the MCD system.

The use of predetermined standard time data results in several advantages. The technique results in accurate standards. Once the predetermined data are available, additional work measurement analyses do not have to be completed when a work process is changed or when a new work process is developed, even though new standards have to be calculated. Because of the specificity with which the standards are developed, employees accept the results more readily than when some of the other less sophisticated techniques are used. Finally, the application of the technique is fairly rapid.

Several disadvantages also exist. The technique is costly because of the necessity of using highly trained analysts and expensive predetermined standard time data. Certain office operations, primarily those of long cycle, are not adaptable to the predetermined standard time data technique. Also, when predetermined standard time data are developed internally, the technique is time consuming and is likely to be a costly process.

Figure 15-4 Pre-determined standard time data. Copyrighted by the MTM Association for Standards and Research. No reprint permission without written consent of the MTM Association, 16-01 Broadway, Fair Lawn, NJ 07410.

TABLE II - MOVE - M

Distance Moved Inches	Time TMU				Wt. Allowance			CASE AND DESCRIPTION
	A	B	C	Hand In Monitor B	Wt. (lb.) Up to	Dynamic Factor	Static Con-stant TMU	
3/4 or less	2.0	2.0	2.0	1.7				
1	2.5	2.9	3.4	2.3	2.5	1.00	0	A Move object to other hand or against stop.
2	3.6	4.6	5.2	2.9				
3	4.9	5.7	6.7	3.6	7.5	1.06	2.2	
4	6.1	6.9	8.0	4.3				
5	7.3	8.0	9.2	5.0	12.5	1.11	3.9	
6	8.1	8.9	10.3	5.7				
7	8.9	9.7	11.1	6.5	17.5	1.17	5.6	B Move object to approximate or indefinite location.
8	9.7	10.6	11.8	7.2				
9	10.5	11.5	12.7	7.9	22.5	1.22	7.4	
10	11.3	12.2	13.5	8.6				
12	12.9	13.4	15.2	10.0	27.5	1.28	9.1	
14	14.4	14.6	16.9	11.4				
16	16.0	15.8	18.7	12.8	32.5	1.33	10.8	
18	17.6	17.0	20.4	14.2				
20	19.2	18.2	22.1	15.6	37.5	1.39	12.5	
22	20.8	19.4	23.8	17.0				
24	22.4	20.6	25.5	18.4	42.5	1.44	14.3	C Move object to exact location.
26	24.0	21.8	27.3	19.8				
28	25.5	23.1	29.0	21.2	47.5	1.50	16.0	
30	27.1	24.3	30.7	22.7				
Additonal	0.8	0.6	0.85		TMU per inch over 30 inches			

PERFORMANCE LEVELING

Why is performance leveling sometimes necessary?

Designed to determine what constitutes a fair day's work, the results of work measurement are of concern to both the employer and the employee. To accomplish this purpose, standards may have to be adjusted by using a process known as **performance leveling**. Adjusting standards will help ensure that they are reasonable.

Because most work measurement techniques gather data on continuously performed work processes, the techniques may not take into consideration the individual differences between employees, the effect of fatigue on employees, interruptions, coffee breaks, rest periods, and so forth. To make standards as reasonable as possible, they may have to be leveled to compensate for these conditions.

Full attainment of standards is desirable, although rarely can that goal be achieved even under the best of conditions. When standards are set too high for all employees to reach, including the most productive employees, the results of the work measurement program will likely be negligible. This situation makes performance leveling desirable.

The use of trained analysts for performance leveling is advantageous. The knowledge and experience of these individuals adds considerably to the accuracy of the leveling process. If trained analysts are not available (for example, when the production records technique is used), the individuals in charge of the work measurement program may have to adjust the standards several times until they are appropriate for the circumstances.

TYPICAL MCD–MOD–I ELEMENTS

A	ARRANGE PAPERS		
COLLATE			
TWO SHEETS		ACT	42
ADD'L. SHEETS		ACA	27
SORT			
GROUPS		ASG	47
PIGEONHOLES		ASP	69
ALPHABETICALLY			
0 THRU 19		ASA01	72
20 THRU 29		ASA02	79
OVER 30		ASA03	85

G	GET AND ASIDE		
GET ONLY			
BATCH OF PAPERS (Loose)		GGB	31
JUMBLED OBJECT		GGJ	27
MEDIUM OBJECT		GGM	18
SHEET OF PAPER		GGS	21
ASIDE ONLY			
TO FIXTURE		GAF	23
TO OTHER HAND		GAH	20
TO PILE		GAP	32
TO TABLE		GAT	15
COMBINED GET & ASIDE			
BATCH TO FIXTURE		GBF	54
BATCH TO PILE		GBP	63
BATCH TO TABLE		GBT	46
JUMBLED TO FIXTURE		GJF	50
JUMBLED TO OTHER HAND		GJH	47
JUMBLED TO TABLE		GJT	42
MEDIUM TO FIXTURE		GMF	41
MEDIUM TO OTHER HAND		GMH	38
MEDIUM TO TABLE		GMT	33
SHEET TO FIXTURE		GSF	44
SHEET TO OTHER HAND		GSH	41
SHEET TO PILE		GSP	53
SHEET TO TABLE		GST	36

B	BODY ELEMENTS		
ARISE and SIT		BAS	208
SEATED TURN		BST	122
BEND and ARISE		BBA	61
WALK PER STEP		BWS	17

M	MAILING		
FOLD			
INSERT			
NO-SEAL			
REGULAR ENVELOPE	MFIN01	195
MANILA ENVELOPE	MFIN02	240
STRINGED ENVELOPE	MFIN03	226
SEAL			
REGULAR ENVELOPE	MFIS01	275
MANILA ENVELOPE	MFIS02	340
IDENTIFY			
LABEL/STICKER			
DRY	MIL01	49
WET	MIL02	85
STAMP			
NORMAL PER TIME	MIS01	13
SELF-INKING	MIS02	56
DATE SET	MIS03	49
OPEN			
SEALED			
FOLDED			
REGULAR ENVELOPE	MOSF01	192
MANILA ENVELOPE	MOSF02	199
UNFOLDED			
REGULAR ENVELOPE	MOSU01	132
MANILA ENVELOPE	MOSU02	169
UNSEALED			
FOLDED			
REGULAR ENVELOPE	MOUF01	101
MANILA ENVELOPE	MOUF02	110
STRINGED ENVELOPE	MOUF03	148
UNFOLDED			
REGULAR ENVELOPE	MOUU01	41
MANILA ENVELOPE	MOUU02	80
STRINGED ENVELOPE	MOUU03	118
UNFOLDED			
INSERT			
SEAL			
REGULAR ENVELOPE	MUIS01	130
MANILA ENVELOPE	MUIS02	258
NO-SEAL			
REGULAR ENVELOPE	MUIN01	50
MANILA ENVELOPE	MUIN02	158
STRINGED ENVELOPE	MUIN03	145

F	FASTEN/UNFASTEN		
BINDER			
DUO-TANG			
FASTEN		FBDF	125
UNFASTEN		FBDU	77
THREE RING			
OPEN		FBTO	31
CLOSE		FBTC	31
CLIP			
PAPER			
PLACE		FCPP	75
REMOVE		FCPR	43
RUBBER BAND			
PLACE		FRP	129
REMOVE		FRR	16
STAPLE			
HAND			
FIRST		FSHF	77
ADDITIONAL		FSHA	35
TABLE			
FIRST		FSTF	37
ADDITIONAL		FSTA	20
REMOVE			
FIRST		FSRF	84
ADDITIONAL		FSRA	52

H	HANDLE PAPER		
JOG			
CARDS			
UP TO 1" THICK		HJC01	5
OVER 1" THICK		HJC02	9
SHEETS			
UP TO 1" THICK		HJS01	8
OVER 1" THICK		HJS02	12
PUNCH			
THREE HOLE		HPT	30
SHIFT			
FLIP OR TURN		HSF	23
GENERAL		HSG	27
TEAR			
CARE		HTC	32
NO-CARE		HTN	23

O	OPEN AND CLOSE		
BINDER			
COVER			
8 1/2 X 11		OBC01	48
DRAWERS and DOORS			
DESK DRAWER		ODD	62
FILE DRAWER		ODF	78
TOPS			
FLAPS		OTF	95
HINGED LID		OTH	35
LOOSE LID		OTL	71

Figure 15–5   Master clerical data. Courtesy: Serge A Birn Company.

The following illustrates how the leveling process is used. Assume that a standard for filing documents was set at forty per hour. This standard was set using predetermined standards. Because none of the presently employed file clerks is able to attain that standard, the rate was leveled to thirty-five units per hour. Now, 80 percent of the file clerks regularly attain that rate. Obviously, attainable standards are less damaging to employee morale.

WORK STANDARDS

What should be remembered in setting work standards?

A primary objective of work measurement is to collect data for use in setting standards for office work. Unless care is exercised in performing work measurement activities, the reliability of the resulting standards is likely to be affected. The use of input in some form other than that derived from accurate work measurement is not recommended.

Work standards should not be set at a level that only the most efficient, productive employee can attain. Nor should they be set at such a low level that each employee is capable of effortlessly attaining the standards. Rather, they should be set at a level that provides a sufficient incentive for the employee to perform well but also at a level where the average employee can be reasonably successful. If the standards are to be used effectively, they must be acceptable to the employees. In many instances, the most difficult and time-consuming task in developing standards involves gaining employee acceptance.

Advantages of Work Standards

The use of work standards provides several important benefits.

What advantages result from the use of work standards?

1. They help increase the efficiency with which employees perform their jobs.
2. They help inform employees of their expected production levels.
3. They assist managers in making personnel decisions, because the employees who are performing beyond expected levels of production can be readily identified.
4. Because employees are aware of the procedures for performing their jobs, less supervision is needed and greater control over the work process is possible.
5. They provide the basis for incentive wage systems.
6. They help improve employee morale by making employees aware of what is expected of them.

Types of Standards

Among the types of standards used in offices are quantity, quality, and descriptive standards. Although work measurement is used only to develop quantity standards, the others are important for various kinds of office work or functions.

Quantity Standards. **Quantity standards** are expressed as units of output per unit of time. For longer work cycles, the unit of time is usually expressed in hours. For shorter work cycles, the unit of time may be expressed in minutes or even seconds.

Two types of quantity standards exist: subjective and engineered. Subjective standards are based on an educated guess or supposition. Therefore, no scientific or research processes are used in their calculation, which sometimes causes their accuracy to be challenged. Engineered standards, conversely, are much more precise because they are based on the results of work measurement. Although subjective standards are more arbitrary, engineered standards are more accurate, reliable, and acceptable.

Quality Standards. Although not determined by work measurement, **quality standards** are crucial in an office. They are used to measure the accuracy and acceptability of work. For example, quality standards are helpful in determining the suitability of typewritten or keyboarded work and the accuracy of filing, arithmetical calculations, and data entry. Although adherence to strict quality standards will result in the redoing of some work, the enforcement of the standards will likely be cost-effective in the long run.

What are descriptive standards?

Descriptive Standards. Like quality standards, **descriptive standards** are not determined by work measurement. These standards are used to identify acceptable descriptive characteristics of areas or objects within an office. For example, descriptive standards are used to determine the appropriate amount of office space for the different categories of employees. To illustrate, a vice president is entitled to more square feet of floor space than a clerk-typist.

Some organizations also use descriptive standards to identify the size and type of working areas or desks to which the various categories of employees are entitled. They are also used in purchasing office supplies, equipment, and items that may have an effect on the working environment—for example, the lighting in the office.

IMPLICATIONS FOR THE ADMINISTRATIVE OFFICE MANAGER

The availability of a work measurement program and realistic work standards helps administrative office managers supervise their subordinates. When standards are available, concern for what constitutes a fair day's work can be greatly diminished.

Employees have assurance that their expected production rates do not exceed their level of responsibility and compensation rates. The employer has assurance that it is getting its "money's worth" from the employees. In essence, work measurement and standards remove much uncertainty in the organization's production processes.

For the administrative office manager, getting employees to accept the work measurement program and standards is generally the most significant problem. Employee acceptance is fundamental to program success. Much of the time and effort the administrative office manager devotes to the program, especially in the preliminary development stages, is concerned with obtaining employee acceptance. If employees are made aware of the program benefits and are convinced that they will be treated more fairly, many of their concerns can be eliminated.

REVIEW QUESTIONS

1. How can work measurement be used to determine the efficiency of work methods and procedures?

2. How can work measurement be used to provide a greater amount of control over work processes and methods?

3. How is work measurement useful in determining equitable workloads?

4. How do the production records technique and the work sampling technique of work measurement differ from one another?

5. What is the difference between the continuous and lapsed-time methods of timing work for the time study method of work measurement?

6. Because predetermined standard time data frequently use data purchased from an outside source, how can one justify their use in other organizations?

7. Why is performance leveling necessary?

8. Discuss the various uses of work standards.

9. What are descriptive standards?

DISCUSSION QUESTIONS

1. You, the administrative office manager of the company in which you work, were recently appointed by your superior to head a task force designed to investigate the feasibility of installing a work standards program. Top management has become increasingly concerned about the deteriorating productivity of its employees. In your first task force meeting, several members indicated that before a work standards program is installed, something needs to be done about the quality of employees who are being hired. These individuals indicated that work standards will have no impact on individuals whose job skills are so weak that they will never be able to achieve the work standards. What is your reaction to this type of situation?

2. Assume that you concur with the task force members in Discussion Question 1 who claim that the more immediate problem facing your company is, in fact, poor quality employees—and not a lack of work standards. As the administrative office manager, outline how you plan to solve the dilemma. The plan you develop will be presented to top management for its approval and subsequent implementation.

3. Assume that top management approved the plan for improving the quality of the employees in the company discussed in Discussion Question 2. Quantitative data show that the company's productivity has increased during the year that your plan has been in place. Top management is again talking about the need for the installation of a work standards program. Employees' resistance to such a program is rapidly increasing because they believe they are now working as efficiently and as productively as they can. Therefore, they believe the use of work standards would become punitive. You have been given the responsibility of developing a strategy for use in overcoming employee resistance. What elements are going to be included in your "strategy"?

STUDENT PROJECTS AND ACTIVITIES

1. Discuss with an administrative office manager the process used in setting work standards in the organization in which he or she works.

2. Discuss with an office employee who has participated in work measurement processes the value he or she perceives for work measurement.

3. Going Online: Using the Internet, conduct an online search based on one of the concepts presented in this chapter or based on one of the chapter terms. Identify four or five things you learned from the material that you did not know prior to your online search.

Minicase

The Blevins Bakery Company, which is located in Deerfield, Illinois, has grown quite rapidly in the last few years. Several management practices and programs found in most firms of a comparable size are not found in Blevins. Perhaps the fact that most of management's effort has been devoted to expansion rather than operations' improvement explains why a work measurement program has never been implemented.

1. What advantages will result in the implementation of a work measurement program?

2. What are the components of such a program?

Case

The Taylor Rubber Corporation, a manufacturer of vehicle tires, belts, and hoses, is located in Cleveland, Ohio. Except for the performance of four of its administrative units, management is quite satisfied with the organization's overall accomplishments. The performance of the office employees in these four units contrasts sharply with that in the other units. The employees in these four units are not as productive as their counterparts in the other units. They work at a slower pace, their work contains errors, and some of their work has to be redone.

Several of the managers believe that the installation of a work standards program in these four units would be beneficial. These same managers acknowledge that installing work standards in only these four units may cause these employees to be-lieve that they are being "picked on." These managers also acknowledge that if the standards were installed throughout the organization, the employees in the other units may become resentful, which would adversely affect their performance.

1. Should the standards program be implemented in only the four units or throughout all units within the organization? Justify your response.

2. If the decision is made to install standards throughout the organization, how can you justify this action to those employees whose performance is adequate?

3. If the decision is made to install standards in only the four units, how can you justify this action without alienating the employees?

Chapter 16

IMPROVING PRODUCTIVITY OF OFFICE EMPLOYEES

Chapter Aims

After studying this chapter, you should be able to design an effective program that enables employees to improve their productivity.

Chapter Outline

The Productivity Dilemma
The Productivity Improvement Program
    Characteristics of Successful Programs
    Steps in Developing a Productivity Improvement Program
    Measuring Office Productivity
Productivity Improvement Techniques
    Job Design
    Flextime
    Job Sharing
    Management by Objectives (MBO)
    Job Security
    Employee Participation
    Quality Circles
    Quality of Work Life (QWL)
    Employee Assistance Programs
    Communication
    Burnout Reduction
    Incentives
    Mental and Emotional Stress Reduction
    Team Building
    Problem Solving
    Time Management
    Alternative Workweek
    Total Quality Management (TQM)
Implications for the Administrative Office Manager

Chapter Terms

Alternative workweek
Burnout
Communication
Cost-benefit ratio
Employee assistance programs (EAP)
Employee empowerment
Employee participation
Flextime
Horizontal loading
Incentives
Job design
Job enrichment
Job rotation
Job security
Job sharing
Job simplification
Management by Objectives (MBO)
Measurement data
Mental and emotional stress
Per unit cost
Problem solving
Productivity improvement program
Productivity manager
Quality circles
Quality of work life (QWL)
Team building

Time management
Total Quality Management (TQM)
Vertical loading

*A*dministrative office managers are typically responsible for helping office employees maximize their productivity. To do this, a well-designed, structured program is needed. A formal approach to productivity improvement generally ensures a favorable return on the organization's financial investment in the program.

The familiarity of administrative office managers with the new technology that helps increase employee output enables them to play a vital role in the development of productivity improvement programs. They are also familiar with the various management practices that have a favorable impact on employee productivity. In some organizations, the administrative office manager coordinates the productivity improvement program. In other organizations, the administrative office manager serves on the productivity task force that is likely coordinated by the **productivity manager.**

What is productivity?

By definition, *productivity* is the result obtained from dividing output by input. Consequently, the more output an organization obtains from constant levels of input, the better its productivity.

Included in this chapter is a discussion of several topics, including various elements of productivity improvement programs. The chapters in the next section contain information about the technology that has a positive impact on office productivity.

THE PRODUCTIVITY DILEMMA

Awareness about the United States' productivity dilemma increased significantly during the mid- and late-1970s and early-1980s when its productivity began to stagnate. The productivity dilemma in this country received even more attention when most industrialized countries continued to increase their productivity during the years that U.S. productivity declined. An overall deterioration in productivity levels is particularly troublesome because of its negative impact on the country's economic vitality. Although productivity in the United States is improving, some of the Asian countries are currently fairing better.

The following situations are responsible for the productivity dilemma in the United States:

What conditions are responsible for the stagnation of productivity in the United States?

1. Constraining nature of government regulations, actions, and policies.
2. Declining work ethic.
3. Declining research and development expenditures.
4. Declining capital investment.
5. Increasing number of service workers.
6. Changing characteristics of workforce.
7. Constraining practices, policies, and attitudes of management.

An administrative office manager interested in improving office productivity will find that reducing the constraining practices, policies, and attitudes of management is the one area among those listed above about which he or she can do something.

THE PRODUCTIVITY IMPROVEMENT PROGRAM

Establishment of a formal **productivity improvement program** is an effective way for an organization to increase its productivity. The use of an informal approach will likely result in fewer desirable outcomes.

Included in this section is a discussion of the following program elements: characteristics of successful programs, steps in developing programs, and measuring office productivity.

What are the characteristics of successful productivity improvement programs?

Characteristics of Successful Programs

Successful productivity improvement programs possess several common characteristics, including:

1. *Top-management support.* Without the endorsement and support of top management, any effort expended in improving productivity will likely result in less than maximum results. Top-management support is a most crucial program characteristic. In addition to endorsing the changes that must be made to improve productivity, top management must also be willing to allocate the necessary financial resources to the program.

2. *Employee commitment.* Employees who are committed to improving their productivity are an important ingredient of successful productivity improvement programs. Once the program begins functioning, employees have a large impact on its success or failure. The greater the level of employee commitment at the beginning, the better the chances for program success. Effort must also be devoted to maintaining that support once the program begins functioning.

3. *Top-priority status.* Another hallmark of effective productivity improvement programs is their top-priority status. These programs generally attain faster, more significant results than programs carrying lesser status.

4. *Productivity goals.* Successful productivity improvement programs possess measurable productivity goals that are reasonable and attainable. While the organization has broad goals, employee goals must also be formulated. Employees who are aware of their expected performance are generally found to be more highly motivated to achieve predetermined goals.

5. *Employee participation.* One of the most effective ways to increase employees' desire to improve their productivity is to involve them in the process of program design. Participation generally increases program success. In addition, employees are often able to contribute excellent ideas about ways they can increase their productivity. Once the program is functional, employees should be continually encouraged to contribute their ideas for increasing their productivity.

What impact do employee rewards have on productivity improvement programs?

6. *Employee rewards.* Productivity improvement programs that reward employees for increasing their productivity are more successful than those that provide no rewards. Faster promotions, incentive pay, profit sharing, and recognition are among the types of rewards successfully used. The fact that rewards are available may be perceived by employees to be just as important as the type of rewards they receive.

7. *Program leadership.* Overall authority and responsibility for the coordination of a productivity improvement program are generally assigned to one individual. Many organizations also use a task force that serves in an advisory capacity to the individual who has overall responsibility for the program.

8. *Program communication.* In successful productivity improvement programs, there is extensive communication between management and employees. Lack of information often produces employee anxiety about the need for establishing a program. Communication will help diminish the concern of employees that they are being manipulated by management. In addition, communication between employees and management is useful when modifying the program. Employees should be given ample feedback about all program accomplishments, including those that fall short of expectations.

9. *Measurement techniques/devices.* Another characteristic of successful productivity improvement techniques is the use of appropriate measurement techniques/devices. While some of the work performed in offices is easily measured or counted, other activities (such as creative effort) are difficult to measure. Determining the success of productivity improvement efforts is more difficult when activities cannot be accurately measured.

Steps in Developing a Productivity Improvement Program

The development of a formal productivity improvement program should proceed through several logical, well-defined steps:

What steps are involved in developing a productivity program?

Step 1. Carry Out Preliminary Planning. Careful planning during this first step will help ensure successful results once the program becomes operational. In fact, unless a solid foundation is laid at this stage of program development, designing a quality program is difficult, if not impossible. Once top management approves the development of a program and appoints the productivity manager, various activities within this step can be undertaken.

An important activity is the identification of the program's objectives. Although top management may provide some broad objectives, additional specific objectives should be formulated by the task force. The nature of the general and specific objectives will be affected by the amount of financial resources management commits to the program. The specific objectives should be expressed in quantitative, measurable terms, which will facilitate the eventual assessment of program accomplishments.

Also important in preliminary planning is determining the program's scope, which will identify the departments or units that are to be included in the improvement efforts. The scope will be affected by the availability of financial resources and need. To determine which units will benefit most from productivity improvement, surveys, observations, and work analyses are often used.

The individuals who will be involved extensively in the productivity improvement program should also be identified at an early stage in the developmental process. Besides the administrative office manager, others who can make significant contributions to the task force are individuals with expertise in data processing, systems design, and human resources utilization.

Providing input and direction into the development and operation of the program are two responsibilities of the task force. It may also be responsible for developing or carrying out certain tasks. Common responsibilities of the task force are formulating specific program objectives and productivity goals, monitoring program results, approving productivity improvement suggestions initiated at lower organizational levels, and developing control procedures that help ensure the success of the program.

In some organizations, input is obtained from committees within those departments or work units extensively involved in productivity improvement efforts. Common responsibilities of these groups include providing pertinent data and information to the task force, identifying areas/activities in need of improved productivity, developing productivity improvement initiatives, and communicating with all unit employees about productivity improvement efforts.

Keeping employees abreast of developments will increase their acceptance of the program. Managerial communication should begin during this stage and continue throughout the duration of the program.

Why does the current situation have to be assessed?

Step 2. Assess the Current Situation. Before an organization can make any changes to improve its productivity, the current situation has to be assessed. This process involves measuring the present productivity performance of department functions and employee activities. In addition to helping reveal areas/activities in need of change, preliminary **measurement data** can also be used as a benchmark to evaluate program results after the changes have been implemented. The pre- and post-comparison of data will help determine whether efforts to improve productivity are successful.

Why do the interrelationships between employees, equipment and machines, and work processes need to be analyzed?

Assessing the current situation involves identifying and analyzing the nature of the various departmental work processes and procedures. Also important is the analysis of the efficiency of the interrelationships between employees, equipment and machines, and work processes. Examining the nature of these interrelationships helps identify which elements may be responsible for restricting productivity. Those areas or activities creating problems should be included in the productivity improvement program.

The department or unit manager is often responsible for coordinating the assessment of the activities under his or her control. Before undertaking the assessment, though, the program's staff should thoroughly orient the manager about proper procedures to be followed. Having the manager rather than the productivity unit staff conduct the assessment is recommended because the manager is more likely to understand the internal functions of his or her department than is an outsider. Involving department employees as much as possible in the assessment process is also helpful.

In addition to assessing department functions, evaluating the way in which employees perform their assigned duties is important. Special attention will be focused on those activities that impede employee productivity. In some instances, employees simply lack the motivation to increase their productivity; in other instances, various elements of their work processes impede their output. Effort should be made to eliminate the negative effect of either of these two situations on employee productivity.

The next major section provides more detailed information about the process of measuring office productivity.

At the conclusion of this step, a fairly comprehensive list of areas and activities potentially targeted for inclusion in the productivity improvement program will have been formulated.

What factors can be used to prioritize the areas and activities being considered for productivity improvement efforts?

Step 3. Select Areas/Activities. From the comprehensive list of areas/activities identified in step 2, those in greatest need of improvement are selected. The amount of financial resources allocated to the productivity improvement program may also have to be considered in determining the feasibility of including various areas/activities. Conceivably, the cost of improving the productivity of certain areas or activities may exceed the availability of financial resources.

When the inclusion of all the areas on the comprehensive list is not possible, objective criteria should be used to prioritize those being considered. The criteria that are used in the prioritizing process include (1) the extent to which the area/activity encompasses the entire organization, (2) the projected amount of improvement that is possible, (3) the cost-benefit ratio of each improved area/activity, and (4) the quantity of work in the area that is being considered for change or the frequency with which various activities occur.

At the conclusion of this step, a new list is compiled of the areas/activities to be included in the productivity improvement program.

Step 4. Develop Alternative Solutions. Generally, several alternatives will be available to help increase the productivity of the various areas/activities that were selected in the previous step. As the number of alternatives identified increases, so does the amount of planning flexibility that is available.

The task force and the various internal unit committees play a key role in identifying the alternative solutions. The more expertise the group members have in both the technological and human resource areas, the more useful their input will be.

An assessment should be made of the potential impact of each of the alternative solutions on related areas/activities. Those alternatives with a potentially negative impact should be eliminated from consideration. The calculation of a **cost-benefit ratio** for each of the alternatives will be useful in weighing their relative advantages and disadvantages.

What is the function of the cost-benefit ratio?

After each alternative is carefully assessed and evaluated, the one identified as having the greatest potential for productivity improvement is chosen. The task force plays a key role in identifying the best alternative for improving the productivity of the various areas/activities.

Step 5. Design the Solution. Once the alternative solution is selected, the next step involves designing the solution. In some instances, the design process is fairly simple and takes little time and effort. In other instances, the design process is rather complex and time consuming.

When the chosen solution requires new equipment and/or extensive changes in work procedures, the design process will be more complex. Involving equipment vendors and systems specialists in the design process may be worthwhile. In some instances, involving individuals who have expertise in areas other than those affected is also useful.

Top management's approval of certain solutions is required before the design process gets underway, especially when solutions require significant amounts of new equipment or extensive changes in existing procedures. For less involved solutions, middle management approval may be sufficient.

Step 6. Develop an Implementation Plan and Implement the Solution. Occasionally, the development of a plan for implementing a solution will consume nearly as much time and effort and will be nearly as involved as the design process. The more thought and planning that go into the development of the implementation plan, the more easily the solution can be implemented. The complexity of the implementation plan corresponds to the complexity of the situation.

The success of a new solution is often affected by the level of commitment unit managers and employees have for its succeeding. Therefore, they are often involved in the development of the implementation schedule. Their input may make a significant difference in determining whether or not the solution is successful.

Other important aspects of this step involve installing the new equipment, training or retraining of employees, "debugging" the new system, obtaining software, and so forth. Also important is determining the dates by which various activities should be completed and identifying the individual(s) responsible for carrying them out.

The last part of this step is the implementation of the solution, a process made easier when the previous steps are carried out as suggested and in an organized manner.

Step 7. Conduct a Follow-Up of the Solution. Once the solution has been in operation for a few months, it should be evaluated to determine how well its actual performance compares with expected performance. Pre- and post-measurements can be compared to determine whether objectives are being attained. When actual results are less than what was expected, the reasons for the discrepancy should be determined before any modifications are made.

Measuring Office Productivity

Several techniques are available for use in measuring the tasks performed by office employees. While several techniques have existed for a number of years, others are fairly new. A number of measurement techniques were discussed in detail in Chapter 15.

Measuring the productivity of various office activities is a crucial element of step 2 (assess current situation) when designing a productivity improvement program. The productivity status of an area or activity has to be assessed before any recommendations for improvement can be made. Making changes on the basis of a perceived need rather than a carefully measured need is not recommended because doing so is generally counterproductive.

Several characteristics of specific office tasks determine the ease with which they are measured. An easily measured task possesses the following characteristics: it can be isolated, which helps determine the point at which it begins and ends; the amount of effort involved in performing the task and the amount of time consumed in completing it are fairly uniform from one undertaking to another; and the task is easily countable.

The two types of office tasks that are not as readily measured as tasks with a manual or physical nature are those that involve a fair amount of creativity and those that use considerable amounts of judgment. The tasks that require greater levels of creativity and judgment are those for which some of the newer measurement techniques have been developed.

Several types of data can be obtained through the measurement process. One type of data is quantitative in nature, which is calculated by dividing the amount of time consumed in producing the units by the total units of output produced. When both a quantity and quality measure of office productivity are desired, the productivity rate will have to be adjusted to reflect the amount of poor-quality work that has to be redone.

In some instances, the availability of cost data is helpful. This is calculated by using the **per unit cost** of materials and pro-rating the cost of labor, equipment, and overhead. Computing the per unit cost is necessary when calculating cost-benefit ratios of either existing procedures or various alternative procedures being considered.

Following are suggestions for increasing the effectiveness of productivity measurement:

1. Determine the measurement objective (quantity, quantity and quality, or cost) before selecting the measurement technique.
2. Consider the characteristics of the area/activity being measured and select the simplest, easiest-to-use technique that circumstances will allow.

What types of office activities can be easily measured?

How can the effectiveness of productivity measurement be determined?

3. Train those who are responsible for measurement to use the various techniques properly.

4. Use a sufficiently long measurement period to compensate for any abnormal fluctuations in the workload.

Data gathered during the measurement process are used in several ways. One important use is to help identify those areas/activities in need of improved productivity. The data are also used to provide a benchmark to make comparisons of office productivity before and after the various solutions have been implemented. Furthermore, the data are used to help identify viable solutions for increasing productivity.

When the measured results indicate a need to improve the productivity of an area/activity, the following four broad options are available:

Office technology: The productivity of office employees can often be increased when they use the new equipment that enables them to perform their tasks faster and with less effort.

Work processes and procedures: Office employees can improve their productivity by using efficient work processes and procedures. Several of the chapters in this text contain sections concerned with improving the efficiency of various work processes and procedures.

Working environment: The environment in which employees work can be designed to stimulate their desire to become more productive. Information about designing an effective working environment is also covered in several chapters in this text.

Personnel: Employees who have positive attitudes about their jobs and the organizations for which they work tend to be more productive than those with negative attitudes. The following section provides a discussion of several techniques that help improve employee attitudes about their jobs and their employers.

PRODUCTIVITY IMPROVEMENT TECHNIQUES

Office productivity can be enhanced by increasing the output of office employees. Frequently, the performance of employees either impedes or enhances the productivity of the office function, regardless of the effectiveness of the automated technology they use, the efficiency of the work processes that comprise their jobs, or the environment in which they work.

Included in this section is a discussion of the following productivity improvement techniques: job design, flextime, job sharing, Management by Objectives (MBO), job security, employee participation, quality circles, quality of work life, employee assistance programs, communication, burnout reduction, incentives, mental and emotional stress reduction, team building, problem solving, time management, and alternative workweek.

Job Design

Job design clearly affects the amount of satisfaction employees derive from their work and the level of productivity they attain in performing their job functions. Employees generally want their jobs to possess several characteristics, including task variety, importance, and autonomy. Furthermore, they want to be able to identify with their job as well as to receive feedback regarding their job performance. Designing jobs with these characteristics will have a positive impact on employee productivity.

Several job-related approaches are successfully used to help employees improve their productivity. The following are included among these approaches.

Job Rotation. The use of **job rotation** as a technique for improving productivity enables employees periodically to exchange their work assignments with others. This technique enables the organization to maximize the opportunities for employee growth and development. Not only does the job satisfaction of employees improve, but also their productivity increases. Furthermore, employees benefit from the additional training they are likely to receive. Another advantage is a reduction in the monotony employees experience with their jobs when they perform the same tasks for an extended time.

Psychologically, job rotation has a positive impact on the productivity improvement efforts of many employees who use it as a way of temporarily exploring other jobs. Those who enjoy the jobs they rotate into frequently apply for those positions when they become open because they are more fully aware of their strengths and weaknesses for a particular position. The employer also benefits from having employees who are cross-trained, and a higher level of interdepartmental cooperation may result because of the rotational experiences of employees. Finally, it also helps the work units within the organizations that use it avoid stagnation because "new" employees tend to bring with them new or different points of view.

Job Simplification. Another aspect of job design that has a positive impact on productivity improvement efforts is **job simplification.** This technique involves removing repetitive, dull tasks from jobs as well as removing such impediments as awkward work flow and communication barriers. Much of the new office technology is capable of handling the repetitive, mundane tasks employees used to perform manually.

Job Enrichment. Of the various job-design approaches useful for improving productivity, **job enrichment** may provide the best long-term results. Enrichment enables employees to assume greater levels of responsibility for and control over their jobs while increasing their job planning opportunities. Essentially, job enrichment humanizes employees' jobs by giving them greater opportunities to experience achievement, recognition, and job growth. The end result of enrichment is that it gives employees more challenging work. Enrichment is related to **employee empowerment,** which fully authorizes and "enables" employees to do their jobs. Therefore, empowerment gives employees the authority, skills, and decision-making responsibilities to carry out their jobs.

Job enrichment and job enlargement should not be confused with each other. Whereas job enlargement provides employees with a broader range of job duties without corresponding increases in responsibility and control, job enrichment provides a broader range of duties with corresponding increases in responsibility and control. Job enlargement has little impact on improving employee productivity. In fact, it may have the opposite effect because employees tend to become more bored with the job tasks.

Horizontal loading, similar to job enlargement, gives the employee more duties with identical or similar types of task characteristics. **Vertical loading,** on the other hand, which is similar to job enrichment, provides the employee with a job comprised of duties having varied characteristics. From a psychological standpoint, vertical loading has a more beneficial impact on employee productivity than horizontal loading.

In what way can job rotation be used to improve employee productivity?

What is job enrichment?

The enrichment of jobs is successful for several fundamental reasons. Employees become motivated because of increased opportunities for achievement, responsibility, recognition, and so forth. Furthermore, jobs that are enriched have greater variety, which has a positive impact on the employees' job satisfaction. When jobs are enriched, their intrinsic rewards increase. Overall job enrichment results in higher productivity, lower error rates, greater job satisfaction, and improved worker-management cooperation.

Job enrichment is most successful when jobs consist of natural units of work; the employee can be given control over his or her job tasks; the employee can be rewarded for assuming increased responsibility; the employee is not satisfied with his or her present job; jobs consist of fragmented tasks that can be combined; and the employee believes his or her job makes a meaningful contribution to society.

The process of enriching jobs consists of three steps. The first step is to identify the natural units of work. If employees' jobs enable them to complete these natural units, they will most likely have a feeling of greater control and responsibility for task completion than when they perform several but not all of the tasks that comprise their positions.

The second step in the enrichment process involves training employees to complete the natural units of their work. In some instances, employees can be trained to assume the entire work process immediately. In other instances, employees will assume the new work process gradually. The supervisor generally determines the pace with which employees are able to assume responsibility and control for their enriched jobs.

The third step is to gather feedback about the success of the job enrichment efforts once the employees begin performing their newly designed positions. This feedback is useful when changes have to be made.

Flextime

What are the characteristics of flextime?

Also having a positive impact on employee productivity is a technique known as **flextime.** This concept enables employees to select their starting times, usually within a two- to three-hour period. Consequently, employees are able to begin working as early as 6 A.M. or as late as 9 or 10 A.M. Even though the employees' starting times are flexible, most programs require employees to work a span of hours per day, perhaps from 11 A.M. to 2 P.M. These are known as core hours, and all employees are expected to be at work unless they have a prearranged excused absence. A few programs allow employees to accumulate excess hours that can be used later when they need to be absent from work. All guidelines regarding the program need to be clearly and thoroughly communicated to employees.

Scheduling is simplified when employees are required to report to work at the same time each day for a week's duration. Some organizations also have policies prohibiting participation of employees whose output provides input for other employees. This policy is especially prevalent in situations in which productivity of the work unit might be hampered because of the variability of employee starting times, and an insufficient number of employees are available to work.

Advantages of Flextime

What are the advantages of flextime?

1. It significantly decreases the rate of absenteeism and almost totally eliminates tardiness.
2. Production increases because employees are responsible for a full working day regardless of when they arrive on the job.

3. Employees experience greater job satisfaction because flextime helps them fulfill some of their human needs.

4. Employees experience less frustration in going to and from work because public transportation facilities and highways may be less congested during their travel time.

5. Employees whose leisure activities require several hours of daylight are able to plan their work schedules around their leisure-time schedules.

6. Employees can use their own time for scheduling appointments with doctors, dentists, lawyers, accountants, and so forth.

7. Flextime reduces employee tension levels caused by the pressure of meeting strict work schedules.

Disadvantages of Flextime

1. An employee whose output becomes another employee's input may not be permitted to participate in the flextime program. In some instances, larger inventories of processed work are maintained so productivity is not hampered when employees take advantage of variable starting hours. As a work-scheduling concept, flextime tends to work better for some types of positions than others.

2. Planning employees' work schedules may become cumbersome, especially in organizations that use multiple shifts.

Job Sharing

What are the characteristics of job sharing?

Increasing numbers of organizations are using **job sharing** to help employees increase their productivity. Job sharing is a technique in which two people share what was originally a full-time job. Individual salaries and fringe benefits are pro-rated according to the amount of each employee's work contribution. Job sharing is especially attractive to those individuals who want to or have to work but who also have such significant family responsibilities as caring for children or elderly relatives. Increasingly, older employees who want to continue to work but not on a full-time basis find the job-sharing technique attractive.

Job sharing results in several advantages. It reduces absenteeism and tardiness because employees can often work around those situations that keep them from going to work or prevent their arriving on time when they have a full-time position. If a job characteristically has certain times when the presence of both part-time employees would be advantageous, such arrangements can often be made. In addition, one employee may be able to work a full day to accommodate the work partner's personal schedule.

Many organizations have found that the combined output of two individuals sharing one job exceeds the output level expected of one full-time employee. When working a portion of a day, employees may be able to sustain higher productivity levels because they are not likely to experience the same level of fatigue experienced by those who work a full day.

Job sharing also has some disadvantages. The amount of employer paper work increases, as does the number of records that must be maintained. Perhaps the most significant problem is the splitting of fringe benefits. By dividing some benefits between two employees, such as insurance, for example, the amount of coverage may not be sufficient. To obtain adequate coverage, the employees may have to pay for a portion of the cost of the fringe benefit, whereas full-time employees are likely to have the full cost of their coverage paid for by the employer. The division of benefits is to a certain extent simplified in organizations that use the cafeteria approach to fringe benefits. Coordinating the tasks performed by each employee may also create some difficulties.

Management by Objectives (MBO)

What are the characteristics of Management by Objectives?

Another successful technique that helps employees improve their productivity is **Management by Objectives (MBO).** The supervisor and employee jointly determine the objectives the employee is to achieve within a specified time period. The supervisor and employee also determine the strategies for achieving the objectives and the criteria that will be used to measure the employee's achievements.

Generally, the objective-setting process should be a joint effort between the employee and the supervisor. Although the supervisor may not always participate in the objective-setting process, he or she must review and approve subordinates' objectives.

On a regular basis, perhaps every three to six months, the employee and the supervisor will discuss the employee's success in attaining the previously defined objectives. The time between the review sessions should be long enough that the employee can see progress but sufficiently short that he or she does not lose sight of the objectives. If the employee has been successful, a new objective may be defined. Objectives that are not attained by a specified date are either continued during the next evaluation period or modified after considering the employee's current performance.

Employees find MBO desirable because it gives them the chance to become involved in the decision-making process. Having an opportunity to participate motivates employees to exert greater effort toward the attainment of their objectives.

Advantages of MBO

What are the advantages of Management by Objectives?

1. It satisfies human needs, thus providing employees with the necessary motivation to achieve their objectives.
2. It helps employees become more involved within the organization because they believe their jobs take on added importance.
3. It provides employees with definite objectives toward which they should work, thus eliminating ambiguous work assignments.
4. It helps employees take considerably greater interest in performing their jobs because they have an opportunity to participate in defining their objectives, they are given the latitude to achieve their objectives, and they know their performance will be assessed in relation to how successful they are in achieving their objectives.

Disadvantages of MBO

1. The objective-setting process is time consuming. Some supervisors resent the amount of time an effective MBO program takes.
2. The desired results are sometimes not reached because of lack of supervisory involvement in working with employees.
3. The absence of a definite reward system prevents some employees from making a positive response to the technique.

Job Security

Some individuals are reluctant to increase their productivity because they fear fewer employees will be needed as a consequence. Although many of these employees readily admit that they could be more productive, the absence of **job security** often keeps them from increasing their output. Productivity improvement efforts most likely will not be successful when employees have to be continually concerned about the impact of their increased output on the stability of their employment.

Within a typical organization, the office function is one in which employees can be reasonably assured that their employment will not be terminated if they increase their output. The large number of office employees throughout the organization and their characteristically high attrition rates facilitate making staffing adjustments when the need arises.

Employees will more likely accept a variety of other changes designed to improve organizational productivity if they do not have to be concerned about the effect of these changes on their employment status. Not only does job security stimulate greater employee productivity, but also it improves employee morale and attitudes.

Employee Participation

Another effective way to help employees improve their productivity is to involve them in decision-making processes, a technique officially known as **employee participation.** Nowadays, employees want to be involved in decisions that directly affect them. In many instances, they can make a significant contribution because they are more knowledgeable and much better informed about certain job aspects than their supervisors.

Furthermore, when employees' input is sought, they are less likely to resist pending changes and more likely to cooperate. Participation also gives employees greater control over their jobs and enables them to express themselves more creatively.

What prerequisites must be present for successful employee participation?

For employee participation to be successful, two prerequisites must be present. First, management, although not bound by employees' suggestions, must consider their input in making decisions. Second, employees must be convinced that management wants the benefit of their input in the decision-making process.

Generally, employees tend to accomplish what they want to accomplish. Employee participation often gives employees the motivation to accomplish more than they might otherwise want to accomplish. Furthermore, the ideas, suggestions, and recommendations generated by the employees who will be affected by the input often stand a better chance of being implemented than those imposed by management.

Quality Circles

Of the various techniques used successfully to improve employee productivity, **quality circles** are one of the newest. A circle is a voluntary group of eight to twelve employees who perform similar or related work. The members of the circle meet on a regular basis to identify, analyze, and develop solutions to a variety of their work-related problems. The meetings, which are generally held on company time, are often scheduled weekly for approximately an hour. The success of quality circles is affected in part by the manner in which these meetings are organized and operated. Before employees become involved with a circle, they should thoroughly understand the purpose, composition, and benefits of the concept.

The quality circle leader, who is responsible for conducting the weekly circle meetings, is typically the supervisor of a work unit. By having a good grasp of the nature of the problems brought before the group, the leader will help the members define, analyze, and solve work-related problems. During the meetings, the leader should disassociate himself or herself as a work unit supervisor, which enables him or her to function as a group member rather than as a manager or supervisor.

Most organizations that use quality circles appoint a facilitator who is responsible for working with circles and for coordinating the activities involved in using the technique. The facilitator is also responsible for providing training experiences for circle leaders as well as for preparing a variety of written materials for use in improving the effectiveness of the technique.

Advantages of Quality Circles

What are the advantages of quality circles?

1. They help employees become more productive.
2. They increase the opportunities for employees to grow and develop.
3. They are economical to use.
4. They help increase employee job satisfaction.
5. They improve the communication between management and employees.

Disadvantages of Quality Circles

1. Some circles try to deal with problems outside the members' areas of expertise, thus reflecting poorly on the concept.
2. Some circles lack top management support, although they have the support of lower level management, which likely will result in their being less successful than they should or could be.
3. Some supervisors whose subordinates participate in quality circles believe their authority is usurped by the process.

Quality of Work Life

What is meant by quality of work life?

As a management process, the **quality of work life (QWL)** concept impacts on the following elements of an employee's position: working conditions, economic rewards and benefits, interpersonal relations, and a variety of organizational contributions. The outcome of the QWL technique is the improvement of employees' attitudes and morale, which will impact positively on their productivity. When their quality of work life is improved, employees have more positive feelings toward their jobs and the organization for which they work; as a result, they are generally more willing to be more productive.

By using the QWL technique, an organization is able to improve its operating effectiveness in many ways, including reducing production costs; improving employee productivity; reducing absenteeism, tardiness, and turnover; and improving quality of work.

Organizations that use the QWL technique often appoint a joint management-labor committee responsible for providing important program direction. The committee may also be responsible for identifying areas that need improvement, for identifying strategies that will help improve the quality of work life for employees, and for providing periodic evaluations of the technique.

Some of the strategies used to improve the quality of employee work life are flextime, MBO, job enrichment, job security, job rotation, Total Quality Management (TQM), and employee participation.

Employee Assistance Programs

One of the values of **employee assistance programs (EAPs)** is their impact on employee productivity. These programs provide counseling to employees whose personal problems have a negative impact on their job performance. The counseling is provided by individuals with the necessary specialized training.

Among the types of situations for which employees receive assistance are substance abuse (alcohol and drugs), nervous disorders, gambling addiction, emotional problems, mental health problems, family relations problems, marital problems, physical health conditions, care for children and aging dependents, and legal concerns. Nearly any type of personal problem that prevents employees from performing at their maximum can be included in the program. In some cases, primary problems (marital problems, for example) give rise to secondary problems (substance abuse, for example).

While employee assistance programs require a specially trained staff, most organizations find that the savings resulting from increased productivity more than offset staffing costs. A favorable cost-benefit ratio helps justify the implementation of an EAP.

A number of alternatives are available for providing employee assistance programs. In some organizations, all EAP services are provided by an internal staff. In other organizations, some of the services are provided in house and others are provided out of house. A less-common arrangement is the consortium plan that provides a collaborative plan sponsored by the participating organizations.

What alternatives are available for offering EAPs to employees?

Communication

Another effective technique for improving employee productivity is increasing the quantity and quality of **communication** between management and employees. Feedback is an important part of the communication process.

Employee productivity is often impeded because management fails to communicate its expectations to employees. In most cases, management doesn't purposely withhold information from employees. Rather, management either takes for granted that employees are aware of its productivity expectations or it miscalculates the amount of information employees desire.

Feedback provides a vital function in productivity improvement efforts. It helps reinforce the productive behavior of employees, and it is useful in correcting undesirable behavior that hampers employee productivity.

E-mail, which has become so commonly used throughout many organizations, is often the communication tool of choice for supervisors and/or managers to communicate regularly with their subordinates. In many cases, e-mail messages are more likely to be read than are general memoranda distributed on a wide basis.

Burnout Reduction

Employees experiencing **burnout** are generally unable to perform at their maximum capacity. Burnout, which results from stress-related physical and mental fatigue, can be experienced by any employee at any stage of his or her career. However, certain personality types—specifically those with high energy levels and strong self-actualization needs—tend to be more susceptible.

Some of the causes of burnout result in its perpetuation. For example, stress and anxiety, two common causes, tend to fuel burnout. A reduction of stress and anxiety often helps an employee eliminate his or her burnout condition. Symptoms of burnout include fatigue, forgetfulness, physical problems (headaches, stomach problems, and backaches), job boredom, and poor attitude.

Several cures are available for burnout, stress, and anxiety, including professional counseling, a leave of absence, rotation or promotion into another position in the organization, and reduction in the number of assigned job duties.

How can burnout be reduced?

Incentives

The more employees are rewarded for increasing their productivity, the more likely they will try to improve their performance. Several types of **incentives** have been developed to reward employees for increasing their productivity. While some plans are based on group performance, others are based on individual performance (see Chapter 14). In plans based on group performance, all members of the group share the rewards for increasing the group's productivity. An individual-based plan rewards the individuals who increase their productivity.

Following are several guidelines that will be helpful when implementing an incentive pay plan:

1. The reward system must be easily understood.
2. The rewards should be distributed quickly after predetermined levels of employee productivity have been attained.
3. The rewards should increase in proportion to increases in productivity.
4. The rewards should be sufficiently large to motivate improved performance.
5. The rewards should be distributed fairly often.

To help keep employees continually aware of the benefits of improving their productivity, they should receive frequent communication about the incentive pay program. The absence of such communication may diminish employee interest in the program.

Mental and Emotional Stress Reduction

What factors cause mental and emotional stress among employees?

Employees with unusual levels of **mental and emotional stress** typically are unable to maximize their productivity. Mental and emotional stress may be caused by unsatisfactory interpersonal relations, low self-esteem, tension, stress, worry, job boredom, job isolation, job insecurity, and unpleasant work conditions. One of the most effective ways to reduce mental and emotional stress is to eliminate the source or cause of the problem. Stress also leads to burnout conditions.

When employees experience severe levels of mental and emotional stress, they may need professional help, such as that made available by counselors in employee assistance programs, by psychologists and psychiatrists in the community, and by self-help groups. Another technique for reducing stress is the use of accurate job descriptions so employees are fully aware of the duties and responsibilities of their job before they accept it. Another technique is to ensure the adequacy of the physical environment, including lighting, seating, and noise control.

Flexible work schedules and rotation of work assignments are also successfully used by some organizations to reduce employee stress. Providing employees with the opportunity to attend stress-reduction programs, seminars, and meetings is another useful technique.

Supervisors play a key role in identifying subordinates who are experiencing mental and emotional stress. Among the symptoms are reduced job performance, increased absenteeism, moodiness, and inability to concentrate. Before referring the subordinate to specialists who can provide professional help, the supervisor should have ample evidence that the stress condition actually exists.

Team Building

When the members of a work group wish to become more productive, the team-building technique is effective. **Team building** enables a work group to identify, diagnose, and solve its own problems. In other words, the team members are empowered to assume greater responsibility for their jobs.

Team building helps a work group increase its productivity in one or more of the following ways: by improving the performance of individual members of the work group, by improving the interpersonal relations among the members of the work group, and by improving the effectiveness of work procedures as a means of attaining group goals.

Crucial to the success of the team-building technique is a consultant, most likely an outsider but sometimes an internal resource person. The consultant plays several important roles: facilitator, change agent, resource person, trainer, and analyst. The consultant should avoid prescribing solutions because this denies the members a valuable opportunity to grow and develop. Rather, the consultant should identify several alternative solutions and then let the group select the one it believes is best for the circumstances.

Also crucial to the success of the team-building technique are (1) a team leader who is committed to the team-building concept, (2) the support of top management, (3) the involvement of each team member, (4) a feeling of personal security of each team member, and (4) allowing adequate time for the process to work.

Advantages of Team Building

What are the advantages of team building?

1. It eliminates situations that impede employee productivity.
2. It sensitizes team members to the impact of their behavior on the performance of the group.
3. It develops a team spirit that motivates members to perform as effectively as possible so the group can achieve its goals.

The most significant disadvantages result from the time-consuming nature of the process and the expense of bringing in an outside consultant.

The self-managed work-team concept is an adaptation of the team-building technique. These teams, which are given a high degree of autonomy, are often able to set their own production goals (which are based on centralized volume goals), set their own work hours, choose the members of their teams, initiate transfers and discharges, and so forth. The self-managed team concept produces among employees the belief that they own their jobs, which results in their wanting to perform as productively as possible.

The use of self-managed work teams has lessened the need for authoritarian control when dealing with subordinates. This approach gives the supervisor an opportunity to focus on productivity improvement and problem solving rather than on punitive or disciplinary actions.

Problem Solving

Another technique employees find helpful for improving their productivity is effective **problem solving.** The use of such an approach is especially important when dealing with complex situations.

What steps are involved in problem solving?

An effective problem-solving approach begins with identifying the problem. Those involved with the situation must be able to differentiate between the problem and its symptoms, as the two are often confused. While solving the problem will usually eliminate the symptoms, treating the symptoms rather than solving the problem may be counterproductive over the long run. Once the problem is identified, it can be defined, which involves identifying the main issues involved in the situation.

After problem identification and definition, the next step involves collecting information about the problem. The more complete this information is, the more effectively the problem is likely to be solved. Information is collected by several means: examining records, interviewing others, and observing others. Before undertaking a subsequent step in the problem-solving process, every effort needs to be made to ensure that this step is complete.

After the information has been collected, the next step involves analyzing the information. This is often the most time-consuming step in the process. An attempt is made to determine how each bit of information affects the problem, that is, how the parts affect the whole. Maintaining a sense of objectivity during this phase will enable those involved with the situation to maximize their efforts. Analysis involves looking at relationships and interrelationships, comparisons and contrasts, and similarities and differences.

Before the information is analyzed, the criteria that will be used to evaluate the effectiveness of the various solutions need to be identified. The absence of these criteria will make it difficult—perhaps impossible—to compare one solution with another.

After completing the analysis of information and the identification of the criteria steps, those involved with the problem are able to begin identifying solutions to the problem. Depending on the situation, this step may be carried out by several individuals. The various solutions to the problem might be identified by means of the brainstorming technique. After the various alternatives have been identified, the next step involves selecting the best alternative for solving the problem. The criteria that were identified earlier are used in selecting the best solution.

Once the best solution has been identified, it is implemented. After a period of time has passed, an evaluation is made of the effectiveness of the solution. The results of the "solved" problem are compared against the criteria that were identified earlier. This will help determine the effectiveness of the solution. This step may also identify the need for fine tuning or making some minor adjustments in the solution.

Time Management

The extent to which an individual is an effective manager of time is a significant determinant of his or her productivity level. One key to effective **time management** is being able to estimate accurately how long the completion of various tasks will take. For routine tasks, this is easily done by keeping track of the amount of time a specific task takes to complete. By timing task completion several times and calculating an average of the results, a realistic assessment can be made.

How can an individual become a better manager of his or her time?

What is the key to effective time management?

Another key to effective time management is proper daily planning. A daily task list should be prepared, either at the end of the previous day or at the first undertaking of the current day. The task list identifies which tasks the individual needs to complete during the day. Also included on the list is the priority for getting each task completed that day. An "A-B-C" priority scheme is often used. A task assigned an "A" priority must be completed that day, while a "C" task carries the least critical priority. The unfinished tasks on the current day's task list are placed on the next day's list, along with the current priority or a new priority.

By being aware of how much time a particular task takes to complete, the individual is able to use his or her task list to schedule the timely completion of the task. This helps the individual more effectively meet deadlines and due dates, which will have a positive impact on how well he or she manages time.

The individual will also experience less job-related stress if he or she is aware of the amount of time typically taken to complete a task.

Following are some specific suggestions for the effective management of time:

1. Complete the most difficult tasks first.
2. Develop a daily routine during which time similar tasks are completed, such as making phone calls or answering correspondence.
3. Delegate work to others when and where appropriate.
4. Maintain a project calendar that identifies deadlines/due dates for major projects or tasks.
5. Simplify work flow.
6. Use "waiting" or idle time effectively.

Alternative Workweek

Some organizations are instituting workweeks other than the traditional eight-hour, five-day workweek. Most common is the four-day, thirty-six- or forty-hour workweek. An **alternative workweek** of thirty-six hours results in a nine-hour day, while a workweek of forty hours results in a ten-hour day. For those employees who value a three-day weekend, the alternative workweek is desirable. Increased employee productivity results from the decreased absenteeism or tardiness of employees who have to use part of their normal workday for taking care of their personal matters.

From a management perspective, an alternative workweek may increase problems associated with work scheduling and employee supervision. To deal with this situation, some organizations are open only four days a week, which helps reduce overhead costs. Perhaps only a skeleton workforce is present on the day that the organization's offices are closed.

Total Quality Management (TQM)

What are the two critical ingredients of TQM?

Although the primary outcome of **Total Quality Management (TQM)** is not necessarily to help employees become more productive, several of its ingredients have the residual outcome of productivity enhancement. Overall, TQM is designed to help an organization improve the quality of its products and/or services as well as everything the organization does to get its products and/or services into the hands of its customers. Thus, TQM is an organizationwide program.

Two critical ingredients of TQM, teamwork and empowerment, have a positive impact on employee productivity. Employee empowerment gives the employees the right to recommend changes that will have a positive impact on their output. Once management accepts the recommended changes, employees are then given the responsibility to determine how they should be implemented. Over the long run, employees are responsible for determining the success of the recommended changes and finetuning them to ensure their success. By empowering employees in this manner, which does not result in managerial abdication, they are more extensively committed to ensuring the success of the recommendations they implement. Because management does not have to be as greatly concerned about day-to-day operations (this is now an enhanced responsibility of the employees), it can spend more time focusing on planning for the future.

TQM, as a concept, stresses continual improvement rather than simply meeting objectives or maintaining the status quo. For that reason, it is considered a continuous, ongoing program that is appealing to many employees.

IMPLICATIONS FOR THE ADMINISTRATIVE OFFICE MANAGER

The amount of responsibility administrative office managers have for productivity improvement varies from organization to organization. Some are responsible only for coordinating the productivity improvement efforts within their own units. Others have organizationwide responsibility through their involvement as a member of the task force that advises the productivity manager. And some administrative office managers serve as the coordinator of the productivity improvement programs within their organizations.

The contributions of administrative office managers to the improvement of organizational productivity are unmistakable. Their familiarity with the new technology that impacts significantly on productivity improvement and their awareness of the variety of strategies used in managing employees enable them to perform a vital function.

A number of alternatives are available for increasing organizational productivity, especially in the process of managing employees. The majority of the managerial techniques that facilitate increasing employee productivity are quite economical because they don't require large cash outlays. The primary cost is in the expenditure of time and effort.

Organizations generally find that when a high priority is placed on productivity improvement, attained results are well worthwhile. In fact, most organizations can no longer afford to ignore their productivity performance, because over the long run, the impact of productivity on profitability can be substantial.

REVIEW QUESTIONS

1. What is productivity?
2. What is responsible for the stagnation of productivity in the United States?
3. What are the characteristics of effective productivity improvement programs?
4. Why is the use of employee participation desirable in the development of a productivity improvement program?
5. What important activities comprise the preliminary planning phase of a productivity improvement program?
6. What broad options are available for improving the productivity of an area or activity?
7. What are the advantages and disadvantages of the flextime concept?
8. In what way can job security have a positive impact on productivity improvement?
9. How do quality circles function?
10. What is the purpose of employee assistance programs (EAPs)?
11. Why does team building work as a technique for improving employee productivity?
12. What two ingredients of TQM have a positive impact on employee productivity?

DISCUSSION QUESTIONS

1. Why do the "constraining practices, policies, and attitudes of management" have a negative impact on productivity in the United States?
2. The company in which you work is presently installing a productivity improvement program. Many of the employees believe that management's desire to install the program stems from the notion that regardless of how productive employees are, room for improvement always exists. The employees believe that they are considerably above average in their productivity. Therefore, management must have some ulterior motive for installing the program—such as increasing its profitability—at the expense of the employees. What can be done to help mobilize the employees behind

the implementation of a productivity improvement program?

3. You work in a company that implemented a successful productivity improvement program several years ago. At the time the program was installed, management did not make any promises about sharing the increased productivity with the employees. Management's response was, "Let's wait and see." For the last three years, the firm has been more productive than ever before. Increasingly, the employees are asking for a share of the increased profit resulting from increased productivity, and management keeps putting the employees off. Analyze this situation from an employee's viewpoint and management's viewpoint and discuss how you think the issue should be resolved.

STUDENT PROJECTS AND ACTIVITIES

1. Assemble a list of five of the techniques designed to improve employee productivity. Show the list to an office employee and ask him or her to rate these techniques in terms of how effective each is in enticing the employee to increase his or her productivity.

2. Talk with an employee in an organization that uses the flextime concept. What does the employee like best about the concept? Like least?

3. Going Online: Using the Internet, conduct an online search based on one of the concepts presented in this chapter or based on one of the chapter terms. Identify four or five things you learned from the material that you did not know prior to your online search.

Minicase

Donald O'Mallary, one of five vice presidents in the Swift Telephone Company, is responsible for appointing employees to serve on the company's productivity task force. He is well aware of the significant contribution this task force can make in assuring the success of the company's productivity improvement program.

1. What qualifications should be possessed by the individuals O'Mallary appoints to the task force?

2. When he invites these individuals to serve on the task force, what should he tell them about the importance of the productivity improvement program that will help convince them to accept this invitation?

Case

Mary Lemincz was recently appointed coordinator of the productivity improvement program in the Bonnick Corporation, which is located in Dallas. Bonnick is one of the largest U.S. manufacturers of oil-drilling equipment.

Lemincz enthusiastically accepted the appointment as productivity coordinator. She has had tremendous support from many employees thus far. In fact, because of this support and the extra effort these employees have put into the development of the program, the project is actually ahead of schedule.

At its last meeting, Lemincz mentioned that the task force will soon begin thinking about developing productivity measurement techniques. She acknowledged to the members of the task force that this will not be easy because of the nature of the measurement process.

1. What suggestions can you offer Lemincz that will be helpful to her in developing the measurement process of the productivity improvement program?

2. Why is productivity measurement crucial during the program development phase and also once the program is operable?

3. What uses are made of the measurement data?

*C*hapter 17

SYSTEMS ANALYSIS

*C*hapter *A*ims

After studying this chapter, you should be able to evaluate the effectiveness of an office system.

*C*hapter *O*utline

The Systems and Procedures Concept
    Definitions
    Objectives
    Advantages and Disadvantages
    Characteristics of Systems
    Elements of Systems
New Developments in Systems and Procedures
    Design
The Systems and Procedures Staff
Designing or Modifying Systems
Systems and Procedures Tools
    Workload Chart
    Flow Process Chart
    Office Layout Chart
    Right- and Left-Hand Chart
    Operator-Machine Process Chart
    Horizontal Flow Process Chart
    EDP Block Diagram
Implications for the Administrative Office Manager

*C*hapter *T*erms

EDP block diagram
Flow process chart
Horizontal flow process chart
Integrated systems
Knowledge management
Methods
Office layout chart
Operator-machine process chart
Procedures
Right- and left-hand chart
Subsystem
System
Workload chart

*U*sing **integrated systems** has enabled many organizations to control increasing office costs and improve their operating efficiency. Among the functional or operational areas typically incorporated into the integrated system are sales, production, marketing, purchasing, and finance. With their inclusion in an integrated system, these areas become interrelated, which generally results in the improvement of the organization's operating efficiency.

Integrated systems are often comprised of several subsystems, which commonly encompass the organization's functional areas. In a manufacturing-oriented organization, these subsystems often include sales, marketing, and purchasing. When the operating functions are not interrelated but are maintained as separate entities, each function operates as a system rather than as a subsystem. As a rule, the more interrelated the organization's systems are, the more efficient they are. Most systems—whether integrated or not—make extensive use of computer technology.

THE SYSTEMS AND PROCEDURES CONCEPT

What components are incorporated into functional systems?

Several components—including employees, equipment, and forms or materials—are incorporated into functional systems and subsystems. Through systems analysis, the interrelationships of the components are studied in an attempt to simplify work processes and to provide a solid foundation for managerial decision making.

In many organizations, the systems concept encompasses a broad range of activities. For example, in large organizations, it is common to find the following activities either directly or indirectly related to the systems function:

> Administrative auditing
>
> Budgeting
>
> Forms management
>
> Job standards
>
> Manpower planning
>
> Office layout and design
>
> Operations research
>
> Procedures analysis
>
> Promotion and training
>
> Quality control
>
> Records management
>
> Standardization of operating processes
>
> Systems design
>
> Telecommunications
>
> Time and motion study
>
> Work measurement
>
> Work sampling
>
> Work simplification

Definitions

What is a method?

A **system** is a series of **subsystems** comprised of interrelated **procedures** that help achieve a well-defined goal. While procedures consist of related **methods** necessary to complete various work processes, methods consist of specific clerical or mechanical operations or activities. Figure 17–1 graphically illustrates the relationships between a system and its subsystems, procedures, and methods.

Objectives

The objectives for developing and using systems vary from organization to organization. The following, however, identify the major objectives of using the systems concept:

1. To maximize the efficient use of the organizational resources.
2. To control operating costs.
3. To improve operating efficiency.
4. To help achieve the objectives of the organization.
5. To help carry out the various functions of the organization.

Advantages and Disadvantages

What advantages result from systems utilization?

Several advantages result from using the systems concept: (1) various functions of the organization are better coordinated; (2) wasteful, unproductive, and uneconomical activities are eliminated; (3) the operating efficiency of the organization is improved; and (4) more effective control can be exerted over various activities and functions.

The following are among the potential disadvantages of systems usage: (1) a certain amount of operating flexibility may be destroyed; (2) any inefficiency that is built into the system likely will disproportionately increase as

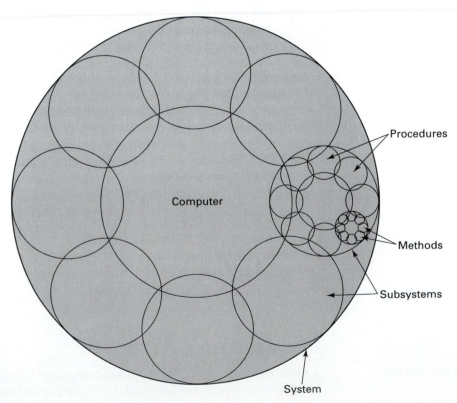

Figure 17-1 Design of a system

work flows through the system; (3) and a totally integrated system may be affected somewhat when changes are made in one of its subsystems.

Characteristics of Systems

Well-designed systems are:

What characteristics do well-designed systems possess?

1. *Flexible.* Although an effective system is structured, it should be sufficiently flexible to accommodate special or unusual circumstances.
2. *Adaptable.* If a system is well designed, changes in the system can be made without destroying or hindering its functioning.
3. *Systematic.* An effective system is systematic and logical.
4. *Functional.* For a system to be effective, it must serve the purpose for which it was intended.
5. *Simple.* A system should be as simple as circumstances will allow.
6. *Resourceful.* A well-designed system makes appropriate use of organizational resources.

Elements of Systems

What are the five elements of systems?

Systems are comprised of several elements: input, processing, and output, as well as two related elements—feedback and controlling. Each element plays an integral role in moving work through the system.

Input. The flow of work through a system begins with the input of some type of resource. In the office area, common types of input are data, information, and materials. Included as part of input are the requisite employee skills and knowledge as well as the equipment employees need to carry out the various methods and procedures comprising the system. In many instances, the output of one system becomes the input for another system.

Processing. The transformation of the input into desired output takes place during the processing element, which involves the methods and procedures that comprise the system. Common processing activities involve counting, computing, sorting, classifying, and retrieving data/information.

Output. Interaction between the input and processing elements produces output, commonly in the form of either paper or an electronically stored document. Output is often the data/information that employees use in carrying out their job responsibilities. The quality of the output is likely to have a significant impact on the overall efficiency and profitability of the organization. This output is often the input of another system.

Feedback. During the time that data and/or information are being processed through the system, feedback enables the system to determine whether results are meeting expectations. For example, if unit costs exceed the acceptable standards, additional controls may have to be invoked, which is another element of the process. Feedback enables the system to evaluate the effectiveness with which input is being processed prior to preparing the output. The amount of needed feedback varies from system to system. The more crucial the system is to organizational survival, the more critical feedback becomes.

Figure 17-2 Purchasing subsystem

Procedure 1:	Requisition supplies
Methods:	A. Fill out purchase requisition
	B. Obtain necessary authorization
Procedure 2:	Obtain quotations from possible vendors
Methods:	A. Fill out quotation forms
	B. Send forms to prospective vendors
	C. Catalog respective bid quotations on receipt
Procedure 3:	Order supplies
Methods:	A. Fill out purchase order
	B. Send purchase order to vendor
Procedure 4:	Receive order
Methods:	A. Check order to verify quantities and acceptability
	B. Deliver supplies to appropriate department
	C. Notify accounts payable of receipt of order
Procedure 5:	Pay vendor
Methods:	A. Prepare payment voucher
	B. Prepare check
	C. Send check to vendor

What comprise the external dimensions of control?

Controlling. Another of the vital elements of some systems, controlling has both internal and external dimensions. The internal dimensions are the organizational policies and procedures to which the system must adhere. The external dimensions, on the other hand, involve local, state, and federal rules and regulations that impact on the system as well as ethical and moral considerations. As a rule, the more effort that goes into systems design, the less important feedback and controlling elements are because they have been planned for during the development of the system.

A Purchasing Subsystem: An Illustration. A system designed for purchasing office supplies is presented to illustrate the systems concept. The various procedures and methods that constitute a purchasing system are shown in Figure 17–2. Each of the system's components—employees, forms, equipment— is found in this system.

NEW DEVELOPMENTS IN SYSTEMS AND PROCEDURES DESIGN

What is knowledge management?

The increasing amount of technological integration used in designing operating systems and procedures is responsible for the evolution of what is known today as **knowledge management.** As an evolving concept, knowledge management is emerging from what used to be commonly known as document management, and it involves capturing and communicating information to those who seek it or who need it. Basically, knowledge management involves providing information to the right persons at the right time.

Increasingly, knowledge management will use a Web-based workflow. In fact, the vast majority of an organization's procedures that involve the processing of documents will become Web based. Incorporating "push-technology," certain information will be made available or delivered to users without their soliciting it. When and where needed, the procedures will accommodate technology-based collaboration, using e-mail, scheduling, and collaborative software.

The software used to facilitate the technologically integrated procedures must possess a number of characteristics:

1. *Work-assignment delivery:* The system must facilitate fairly robust messaging capability, allowing the delivery of work tasks from one person to another throughout the organization.

2. *Interconnectivity of departments and/or work units:* The system must not only allow but also facilitate the transmittal of significant quantities of messages per hour, both vertically and horizontally.

3. *Accommodation of existing data:* The system must accommodate and facilitate the incorporation of existing data because insufficient organizational resources or time are available to adapt the existing data.

4. *Cost effective:* The system must be cost effective, perhaps resulting in a cost of less than $100 per employee whose job functions are incorporated into the system.

The following example illustrates how this concept functions: Assume that sales representatives in an insurance company complete insurance applications at their local sites, using either a desktop or laptop computer. Suppose that either the wrong type of information was entered at a certain location within the application or that a certain piece of information is missing, but the sales representative didn't realize it before electronically transmitting the application to the underwriting department. Without human intervention, the electronic system will send the sales representative an e-mail message requesting either the correct or the missing information, along with a screen image of the original application. (Older systems typically required that an employee in underwriting either prepare a written message to be sent to the sales representative or call the sales representative with his or her request to obtain correct or missing information.) Using the same screen of information the sales representative completed earlier, the incorrect or missing information can be added, at which time the application will be resubmitted electronically to the underwriting department. If all needed information is now available, the application will be "pushed" to an underwriter who will evaluate it and subsequently approve or disapprove the application or recommend modification. The underwriter's decision can be electronically transmitted to the sales representative who can then inform his or her client that the application was approved, disapproved, or needs to be modified.

THE SYSTEMS AND PROCEDURES STAFF

Several alternatives are available for staffing the systems and procedures function within an organization. To a large extent, the most appropriate staffing alternative is governed by:

What factors govern the selection of the most appropriate staffing alternative for systems analysis and design?

1. The size of the organization.
2. The type (manufacturing, service, etc.) of the organization.
3. The organization's commitment to the total or integrated systems approach.
4. The philosophy of top management toward the systems and procedures function.
5. The type and extent of technology incorporated into the system or systems.

Alternatives for staffing the systems and procedures function include (1) use of outside consultants (includes individuals employed in firms specializing in the design of systems as well as consultants employed as service representatives by office equipment or supplies vendors; (2) use of a full-time systems staff; or (3) use of a part-time systems staff.

Outside consultants are frequently hired on a retainer basis in much the same way that the organization's lawyer might be retained. Consultants generally provide recommendations but leave final decisions about the configuration of the systems to management.

Use of outside consultants results in several advantages. Most significant is the expertise consultants are able to provide. Because consultants are outsiders, they can be objective in making recommendations. And when retained over a period of years, outside consultants are able to keep their clients' systems up to date. The most significant disadvantage of using outside consultants is the high cost of their services. Another disadvantage may result from their unavailability at needed times.

What advantages result from employing a full-time systems staff?

Use of a full-time staff enables the organization to develop and improve on a continual basis all of its systems and work processes—not just the most important ones. A full-time staff is also advantageous when problems arise and immediate assistance is needed. But for some organizations, the cost of employing a full-time staff is not economically feasible. The conflict that may arise between line managers and the systems staff is another potentially significant disadvantage.

Individuals who belong to a full-time staff are known as *systems analysts.* They must have some of the following qualifications: understanding of data/ information processing and work flow; familiarity with analysis, design, and installation of systems; knowledge of departmental functions and operating processes; and ability to conduct research.

When an organization is too small to warrant the use of outside consultants or a full-time staff, the systems function is often assigned to an individual who functions in some other capacity. Most likely this individual is the administrative office manager. The primary advantage of this alternative—its economy—is sometimes overshadowed by the individual's inability to carry out the assignment effectively because of insufficient time or expertise.

DESIGNING OR MODIFYING SYSTEMS

The development of a new system or the modification of an existing system is enhanced by following a series of well-designed, sequential steps. While the development of new systems uses only steps 1, 4, and 5, steps 1 through 5 are appropriate for the modification of an existing system.

What steps are involved in systems design?

1. *Define clearly the process to be studied.* A clear definition and delineation of the process results in an analysis suitable for the situation being studied. Studies are often conducted because of one or more of the following problem situations: bottlenecks in work flow, criss-crossing or backtracking work flow, inefficient work flow, inefficient use of organizational resources (both human and nonhuman), and duplication of effort. In some cases, the study of work processes has to be restricted to repetitive, high-volume tasks.

2. *Outline the details of the present process.* Before the system can be modified, the present process has to be clearly outlined. The process can be outlined in narrative form or by using one of the charts described in the next section of this chapter. Outlining the present process on the appropriate form requires that each step be identified and broken down into its minute parts. Completeness of the step can be ensured when the following questions are answerable: who, what, when, where, why, and how.

3. *Analyze the present process.* The next step involves analyzing the process. Questioning the necessity of each step helps identify those that can be simplified, eliminated, or combined with others. When work processes consist of complex steps, simplification becomes a primary focus. And sometimes when one step can be eliminated, subsequent steps can also sometimes be eliminated.

4. *Outline the improved process.* Once the present process has been thoroughly analyzed, then the improved process is clearly outlined, generally on the same type of form or chart used for the original outline. As much as possible, care should be taken to simplify the design of the improved process. In many cases, the improvement can be tried during a "trial run" before it is officially adopted. Modifications can be made, and determining the degree to which the proposed process is an improvement over the present process is possible.

5. *Install the new process.* After a decision has been made to implement the new process, it is ready for installation. Some employees may need to be convinced that the new process is actually an improvement over the old, which is typically the responsibility of the supervisor. The new process should be subjected to periodic follow-up and review. Doing so will facilitate making any needed modifications in the various elements of the process.

In some instances, problem solving is used to design or modify systems. The problem-solving steps outlined in Chapter 16 are appropriate for use.

SYSTEMS AND PROCEDURES TOOLS

A number of tools are available for use in modifying existing systems or for developing new systems. When selecting a tool for either purpose, care should be taken to ensure its appropriate use.

Workload Chart

What information do workload charts provide?

Also referred to as a *work distribution chart*, the **workload chart** is a useful tool for developing efficient systems and for simplifying work processes. A workload chart will identify the following:

1. The major activities performed by a given work unit.
2. The amount of time the work unit as a whole spends on each activity.
3. The activities performed by each employee and the amount of time he or she spends performing the activities.

Answers to the following questions should be sought when analyzing the information provided by the workload chart:

1. Is the work unit performing the work it is intended to perform?
2. Are employees performing too many duplicate operations?
3. Are the tasks that each employee performs of a related nature?
4. Are the special skills and talents of the employees being used to the fullest extent?
5. Are the major functions of the work unit actually consuming the greatest amount of work time and effort?

Figure 17-3 Daily log

Employee's Name	Esther Jones	Department	Purchasing
Employee's Title	Clerk – Typist	Today's Date	9/23/xx

Clock Time	Time Consumed	Activities
8:00 – 8:30	30 minutes	Type report
8:30 – 8:45	15 minutes	Type quotations
8:45 – 9:15	30 minutes	Type Purchase orders
9:15 –10:15	60 minutes	Type letters (follow-up)
10:15–10:30	–	Take break
10:30–12:00	90 minutes	Compile data for report

6. Are the employees' workloads evenly distributed?

7. Are the employees productive?

8. Is the flow of work efficient?

The workload chart helps identify areas of inefficiency that should be corrected prior to developing a system. A basic purpose for using the systems concept is violated if inefficient procedures or methods are allowed to be built into the new system.

What is the relationship among the workload chart, a summary log, and an activity list?

Information needed to complete the workload chart should be collected over a typical work period, perhaps one to two weeks. Each employee records on a daily log sheet, such as the one illustrated in Figure 17-3, the activities he or she performs. At the end of the information-collecting period, a summary log, such as the one illustrated in Figure 17-4, is prepared.

Following each employee's completion of the summary log, an activity list is compiled. The purpose of the activity list is to identify the activities performed by the entire work unit. A partial activity list is illustrated in Figure 17-5.

Employee's Name	Esther Jones	Department	Purchasing
Employee's Title	Clerk – Typist	For Period Ended	9/27/xx

Activities	Hours	Minutes
Type quotations	5	
Type Purchase orders	21	30
Type letters (follow-up)	6	15
Compile data	1	30
Receive callers	2	
Type reports	3	
Keep vendor interview appointments	1	30
Answer phone	1	30

Figure 17-4
Summary log

Figure 17-5
Activity list

Department	Purchasing	For period ended	9/27/XX

Number of employees _____ 5 _____

Activities performed	Activity code
File	A,B,C,D,E,F
Type follow-up letters	D
Review receipt of orders	C
Answer telephone	F
Compile data	F
Prepare payroll	F
Type reports	F
Type purchase orders	B
Type quotations	E
Duplicate materials	F
Review purchase requisitions	B
Approve purchase requisitions	B
Handle personnel matters	F

Illustrated in Figure 17–6 is a workload chart prepared from the information presented in the summary log and the activity list. Each activity is assigned a code, and the activities are then entered in coded form in the "activity number code column" at the far left of the chart. The activity column provides a brief description of the activity, and the "hours column" lists the total amount of time consumed by the various activities. Each employee in the work unit is provided a separate column that lists the activities he or she performs and the amount of time each activity consumes.

Examining the activity column in Figure 17–6 reveals that activities are listed in descending order of time consumption. In the employees' section of the chart, the individuals with the highest level of job importance are listed at the left, and those with the least amount of importance are listed at the right.

Flow Process Chart

What information do flow process charts provide?

Also frequently used to analyze and simplify work is the **flow process chart,** a tool especially helpful for identifying each step in a specific work process. The various steps in the process are categorized and identified by one of the following symbols:

Operation: Changing the physical or chemical characteristics of an object. Examples of operations are erasing, stapling pages together, keyboading, underlining, and circling words.

Transportation: The movement of an object from one location to another. An example of transportation is giving the word originator a letter to be signed.

Inspection: Verifying data or checking an object. A common example is proofreading.

Delay: A situation that causes the next step in the process to be delayed. A letter awaiting signature is an example.

Storage: Storing and/or protecting an object. Filing is a typical example of storage.

Each of the operation steps in a particular work process can also be classified as a *get ready, do,* or *put away* step. Special attention should be focused on

Activity Code	Activity	Hours	Susan Brown Purchasing Agent	Hours	Jack Adams Buyer	Hours	Ralph Anders Audit Clerk	Hours	Esther Jones Clerk-Typist	Hours	Mary Green File Clerk	Hours
A	Interview vendors	49	Interview vendors	12	Interview vendors	25			Receive vendors Keep interview appointment sheets	2 1	File literature	9
B	Review requisitions Approve requisition Prepare purchase orders	44	Review requisitions and proposals Approve requisitions Dictate memos explaining disapproval	7 2 5	Approve purchase orders	1			Type purchase orders	21	File approved requisitions File purchase orders	4 4
C	Verify receipt of orders, audit invoices, approve invoices	42			Review receipt of orders	1	Compare invoice with receipt of order forms and note discrepancies Audit invoices Approve invoices for payment	15 15 3			File receipt of order forms File invoices	4 4
D	Follow-up	12	Review major discrepancies	1	Dictate follow-up letters and review of discrepancies	3			Type follow-up letters	6	File follow-up letters	2
E	Obtain quotations	11			Request quotations	1	Maintain quotation forms	3	Type quotations	5	File quotations	2
F	Miscellaneous	42	Appointments Reading brochures Preparing reports Personnel matters Preparing payroll	2 3 5 2 1	Reading brochures Compiling data	8 1	Compiling data	4	Compiling data Typing reports Answering phone	1 3 1	Miscellaneous filing Duplication material	2 9
TOTALS		200		40		40		40		40		40

Figure 17-6 Workload chart

Why should special
attention be focused on
"do" steps?

the *do* steps: By eliminating these, the *get ready* and *put away* steps are also eliminated. The justification for a step can be determined by assessing it in terms of who, why, where, how, and when. Steps that cannot be substantially justified should either be eliminated or combined with other steps.

The flow process chart briefly describes the nature of each step in the process, identifies the distance that objects are transported, and provides the amount of time consumed by each delay step. To facilitate the analysis, the symbols representing each step are connected with a line, and those symbols depicting *do* operations are darkened. After the work process is outlined on the chart, the process is analyzed to determine where simplification may be appropriate. Each step should be subjected to several questions: Is the step necessary? If so, why? Can the step be eliminated, simplified, or combined with another step? Is each step properly sequenced within the total process?

After the process has been analyzed, the right-hand part of the flow process chart is prepared to outline the proposed work process. The present and proposed processes are then summarized in the upper-left corner, as Figure 17–7 illustrates.

Office Layout Chart

Frequently used in conjunction with the flow process chart, the **office layout chart** is well suited for visualizing work flow. The layout chart clearly identifies backtracking, criss-crossing, and inefficient work flow patterns.

The layout chart is actually a scale drawing of the present office layout, and the flow of work is depicted by using lines to connect the various workstations. When the layout and the flow process charts are used in conjunction with one another, layout charts should also be prepared for the proposed work flow.

Figure 17–8 illustrates layout charts for the present and proposed work flow that were outlined in Figure 17–7.

Right- and Left-Hand Chart

What information do right-
and left-hand charts
provide?

The **right- and left-hand chart** is used to identify hand movements in a particular work process. Similar to the flow process chart, hand movements are classified into various categories:

Operation: The movement of the hand at one location, such as grasping an object, stapling, writing, keyboarding, or using a calculator.

Transportation: The movement of the hand when transporting an object from one location to another. Examples include inserting a document to be faxed into the fax machine's hopper and placing an object in an out-basket.

Hold: Holding an object while the other hand is used to do something to the object. An example is holding several sheets of paper with one hand while using the other hand to operate a stapler.

Delay: The situation of an idle hand while the other hand is in motion. An example would be a motionless hand while the other hand holds a letter being proofread.

What are the distinct
sections of a right- and
left-hand chart?

The right- and left-hand chart consists of four distinct sections. The upper-left corner is the layout section, which is used to illustrate the arrangement of materials involved in the work process. For example, in Figure 17–9, which illustrates the manual collation of five sheets of paper, the five sheets are identified as 1, 2, 3, 4, and 5.

	Present	Proposed	Difference
○ No. of Operations	8	7	1
⇨ No. of Transportations	4	2	2
□ No. of Inspections	3	1	2
◻ No. of Delays	1	1	–
▽ No. of Storages	1	1	–
Distance Traveled	149	117	32

Job __Processing Credit Applications__

Forms Used __–__

Charted by __L. Davis__

Department __Office Services__

Date __11/30/xx__

Present Method	Operation Transportation Inspection Delay Storage	Distance in Feet	Time in Minutes	Present Method	Operation Transportation Inspection Delay Storage	Distance in Feet	Time in Minutes
Credit applications opened by mail clerk	● ⇨ □ ◻ ▽			Credit applications opened by mail clerk	● ⇨ □ ◻ ▽		
Credit applications alphabetized	● ⇨ □ ◻ ▽			Mail clerk scans applications for completeness	○ ⇨ ⊠ ◻ ▽		
Credit applications transported to credit clerk	○ ⊠ □ ◻ ▽	17ft.		Credit applications alphabetized by mail clerk	● ⇨ □ ◻ ▽		
Credit clerk scans applications for completeness	○ ⇨ ⊠ ◻ ▽			Credit applications transported to credit clerk	○ ⊠ □ ◻ ▽	17ft.	
Credit clerk contacts references	● ⇨ □ ◻ ▽			Credit clerk contacts references	● ⇨ □ ◻ ▽		
Credit clerk waits for references	○ ⇨ □ ⊠ ▽		1 week average	Credit clerk waits for references	○ ⇨ □ ⊠ ▽		1 week
Information provided by reference entered on application	● ⇨ □ ◻ ▽			Information provided by reference entered on application	● ⇨ □ ◻ ▽		
Applications transported to supervisor	○ ⊠ □ ◻ ▽	15ft.		On routine applications, credit clerk decides on desirability and limit	● ⇨ □ ◻ ▽		
Supervisor inspects applications	○ ⇨ ⊠ ◻ ▽			Application sent to data processing	○ ⊠ □ ◻ ▽	100 ft.	
Supervisor decides on desirability of applicant	● ⇨ □ ◻ ▽			Information keypunched on card	● ⇨ □ ◻ ▽		
Supervisor assigns credit limit	● ⇨ □ ◻ ▽			Application stored	○ ⇨ □ ◻ ▼		
Applications transported back to credit clerk	○ ⊠ □ ◻ ▽	17ft.		Credit card prepared	● ⇨ □ ◻ ▽		
Credit clerk inspects application	○ ⇨ ⊠ ◻ ▽				○ ⇨ □ ◻ ▽		
Application transported to data processing	○ ⊠ □ ◻ ▽	100 ft.			○ ⇨ □ ◻ ▽		
Information keypunched on card	● ⇨ □ ◻ ▽				○ ⇨ □ ◻ ▽		
Application stored	○ ⇨ □ ◻ ▼				○ ⇨ □ ◻ ▽		
Credit card prepared	● ⇨ □ ◻ ▽				○ ⇨ □ ◻ ▽		

Figure 17-7 Flow process chart

Figure 17-8 Office layout chart

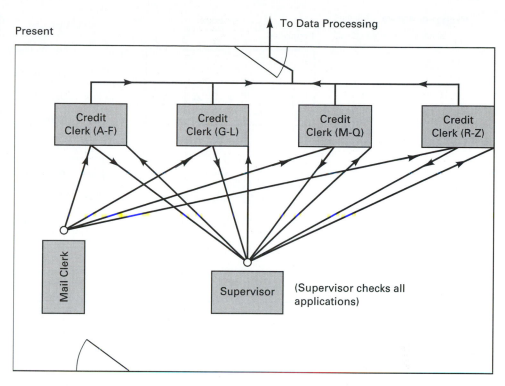

Present

To Data Processing

Credit Clerk (A-F)   Credit Clerk (G-L)   Credit Clerk (M-Q)   Credit Clerk (R-Z)

Mail Clerk

Supervisor   (Supervisor checks all applications)

Proposed

To Data Processing

Credit Clerk (A-F)   Credit Clerk (G-L)   Credit Clerk (M-Q)   Credit Clerk (R-Z)

Mail Clerk

Supervisor   (Supervisor checks only nonroutine applications)

Scale: 1" = 5'

Figure 17-9 Right-
and left-hand chart

Proposed

1	2	3	4	5

Job _Collating 5 pages_

Forms Used _Sheets of paper_

Charted by _D. Evans_

Department _Office Services_

Date _11/30/xx_

	Present		Proposed		Difference	
	LH	RH	LH	RH	LH	RH
◯ No. of Operations	6	6	4	4	−2	−2
⇨ No. of Transportations	3	2	3	2	0	0
☐ No. of Inspections	−	−	−	−	−	−
◗ No. of Delays	−	−	−	−	−	−

LEFT HAND	Operation / Transportation / Inspection / Delay		Operation / Transportation / Inspection / Delay	RIGHT HAND
Grasp page 1	⊗ ⇨ ☐ ◗	1	◯ ⇨ ☐ ◗	
Transport to page 2	◯ ⊗ ☐ ◗	2	◯ ⇨ ☐ ◗	
Place page 1 on top of 2	⊗ ⇨ ☐ ◗	3	◯ ⇨ ☐ ◗	
Grasp page 1 and 2	⊗ ⇨ ☐ ◗	4	◯ ⇨ ☐ ◗	
Transport pages 1 and 2 to 3	◯ ⊗ ☐ ◗	5	◯ ⇨ ☐ ◗	
Place pages 1 and 2 on top of 3	⊗ ⇨ ☐ ◗	6	◯ ⇨ ☐ ◗	
	◯ ⇨ ☐ ◗	7	⊗ ⇨ ☐ ◗	Grasp pages 1,2 and 3
	◯ ⇨ ☐ ◗	8	◯ ⊗ ☐ ◗	Transport pages 1,2 and 3 to 4
	◯ ⇨ ☐ ◗	9	⊗ ⇨ ☐ ◗	Place pages 1,2 and 3 on 4
	◯ ⇨ ☐ ◗	10	⊗ ⇨ ☐ ◗	Grasp page 1,2,3 and 4
	◯ ⇨ ☐ ◗	11	◯ ⊗ ☐ ◗	Transport pages 1,2,3,4 to 5
	◯ ⇨ ☐ ◗	12	⊗ ⇨ ☐ ◗	Place pages 1,2,3,4 on 5
	◯ ⇨ ☐ ◗	13	⊗ ⇨ ☐ ◗	Grasp page 1,2,3,4 and 5
Joggle pages 1, 2, 3, 4 and 5	⊗ ⇨ ☐ ◗	14	⊗ ⇨ ☐ ◗	Joggle page 1,2,3,4 and 5
Transport pages 1 – 5 to pile	◯ ⊗ ☐ ◗	15	◯ ⇨ ☐ ◗	
Place pages 1 – 5 on pile	⊗ ⇨ ☐ ◗	16	◯ ⇨ ☐ ◗	

The upper-right corner of the chart provides space for identifying the nature of the job being analyzed. The summary section appears below the layout and identification sections. Space is provided for summarizing the present process, the proposed process, and the differences between the two processes.

The lower two-thirds of the form is used to summarize the movement of the right and left hands in relation to one another. Space is provided for a brief description of each motion, and the symbols representing the various motions are connected with lines.

Following the careful outlining of the present work process, the necessity and efficiency of each step in the process is considered. After the process has been analyzed and the various motions have been appropriately eliminated, combined, or simplified, the proposed process is outlined on a second right- and left-hand chart. The various motions are then summarized in the proposed area of the summary section. The differences between the present and proposed methods are also noted in the summary section.

Operator-Machine Process Chart

What information do operator-machine process charts provide?

The **operator-machine process chart** is used to study the relationship between an operator and the machine he or she uses. Its use is primarily limited to analyzing high-volume, repetitive work processes.

As is true with the other process charts discussed in this chapter, the primary reason for using this chart is to analyze a work process, focusing on opportunities to eliminate, simplify, or combine as many steps as possible. By reducing idle time, higher levels of productivity can be realized.

Illustrated in Figure 17–10 is the operator-machine process chart, which consists of a summary section, an identification section, a layout section, a parts section, and a section used to illustrate the various steps in the work process. The left-hand activity column is used for operator activities; the right-hand activity column is used for machine activities.

In the middle of the chart is the time column used to depict the amount of time each activity consumes. The lines in the time column represent a standard unit of time, perhaps one to six seconds. The columns on either side of the time column are darkened to identify inactivity either on the part of the operator or the machine.

Horizontal Flow Process Chart

What information do horizontal-flow process charts provide?

The **horizontal flow process chart** is useful for illustrating work processes that involve multicopy forms (such as purchase orders, invoices, and credit applications). These charts follow the movement of each copy of the form, starting with the point of origin, moving through the various steps in the flow of work, and ending with the disposition of each copy of the form. The symbols used in the horizontal flow process chart are similar to those illustrated in Figure 17–11.

Figure 17–12 is a horizontal flow process chart that illustrates a purchasing subsystem, including the preparation of the purchase requisition and the purchase order, sending the purchase order to the vendor, and transmitting copies of the purchase order to the receiving and accounting departments. These two departments will also prepare horizontal flow process charts to illustrate the flow of work through them.

When designing new systems, the horizontal flow process chart is useful for outlining the various procedures in each subsystem. It is also useful when modifying an existing system.

Figure 17–10
Operator-machine
process chart

OPERATOR-MACHINE PROCESS CHART

Job _Opening letters by machine_

Machine Used _Letter opener_

Forms Used _____

Charted by _D. Evans_

Department _Mail room_

Date _11/30/xx_

	Operator		Machine	
	Time	%	Time	%
Work	42	58	30	42
Idle	30	42	42	58

Layout	Parts

LETTER BIN   LETTER OPENER   TABLE

Operator	Time*	Machine
Operator joggles handful of letters and inserts in opener		IDLE
IDLE		Opener opens 100 letters in 30 seconds
Puts opened letters on table		IDLE

*Each Line Represents 6 Seconds

Clerical Operation. A manual offline operation not requiring mechanical aid.

Magnetic Tape. Used when I/O is magnetic tape.

Document. Paper documents and reports of all varieties.

Display. Information displayed by plotters or video devices.

Transmittal Tape. A proof or adding machine tape or similar batch-control information.

Auxiliary Operation. A machine operation supplementing the main processing function.

Communication Link. The automatic transmission of information from one location to another via communication lines.

Processing. A group of program instructions which performs a processing function of the program.

Input/Output. Any function of an input/output device making information available for processing, recording processing information, tape positioning etc.

Decision. The decision function used to document points in the program where a branch to alternate paths is possible based upon variable conditions.

Punched Card. An I/O function, representing all kinds of punched cards.

Program Modification. An instruction or group of instructions which changes the program.

Processing. A major processing function.

Perforated Tape. Paper or plastic tape, chad or chadless.

Online Keyboard. Information supplied to or by a computer utilizing an online device.

Sorting, Collating. An operation on sorting or collating equipment.

Input/Output. Any type of medium or data.

Offline Storage. Offline storage of either paper, cards, magnetic, or perforated tape.

Flow Direction. The direction of processing or data flow.

Predefined Process. A group of operations not detailed in the particular set of flow charts.

Terminal. The beginning, end, or a point of interruption in a program.

Connector. An entry from, or an exit to, another part of the program flow chart.

Offpage Connector. A connector used instead of the connector symbol to designate entry to or exit from a page.

Flow Direction. The direction of processing or data flow.

Figure 17-11   Flow charting symbols

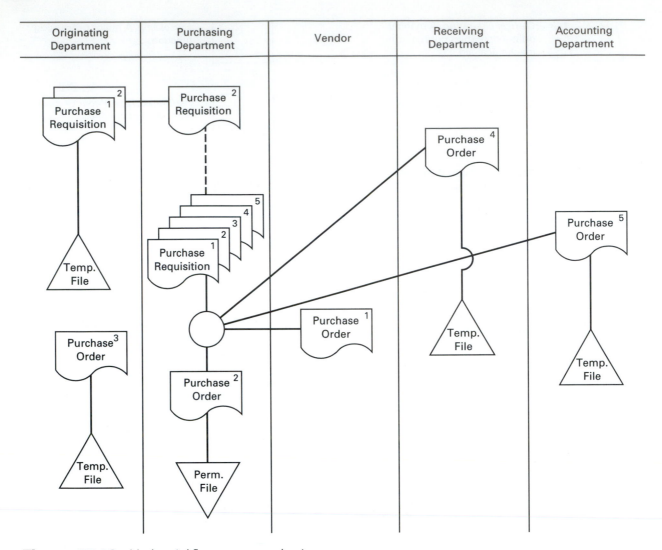

Figure 17-12   Horizontal flow process chart

EDP Block Diagram

Because many systems are computer based, a variety of programs must be prepared to facilitate the orderly processing of data and information.

For what are EDP block diagrams used?

Before preparing a computer program, an **EDP block diagram** is frequently prepared to assist the programmer in organizing ideas about solving business problems in an efficient, sequenced manner. The diagrams are also useful when a program malfunctions or has to be modified. EDP block diagrams use standardized symbols, such as those illustrated in Figure 17–12.

Although the EDP block diagram illustrated in Figure 17–13 is not readily transferable into a computer program, the basic fundamentals of the diagram are illustrated. The processes that a student may go through in getting ready to go to class, in getting ready for the class to start, and in getting ready to leave the class are illustrated in the diagram.

Depicted by diamond-shaped symbols, the decision steps of the diagram involve either a *yes* or *no* decision. In the case of a *yes* decision, the process then proceeds to the next step in the vertical sequence of the diagram. In the case of a no decision, an alternative step (called *branching*) is used until the appropriate situation occurs that allows the process to continue sequencing through the

Figure 17-13 EDP block diagram

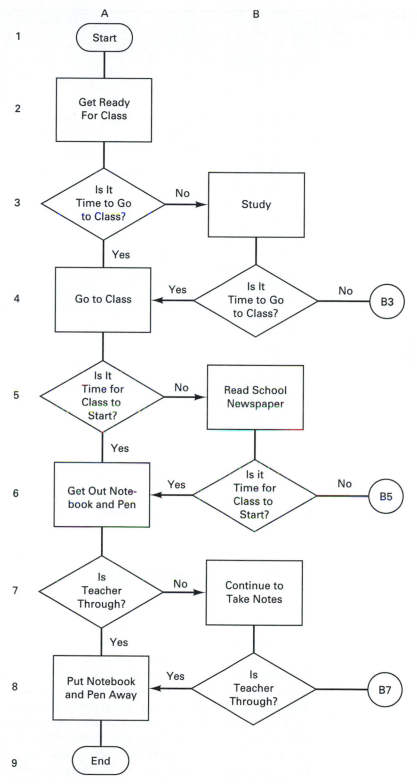

Figure 17-14 Uses of systems analysis tools

	Work Load Chart	Flow Process Chart	Right- and Left-Hand Chart	Operator-Machine Chart	Horizontal Flow Process Chart	EDP Block Diagram
Analysis of employee or departmental activities	x					
Useful for nonintricate work processes	x	x				
Identification and analysis of steps in specific work processes		x	x	x	x	x
Identify nature of each step in work process		x	x	x	x	x
Identify distance that objects or employees move		x				
Identify amount of time of each step	x			x		
Identify ways to eliminate, combine, simplify steps	x	x	x	x	x	x
Identify hand movement in work process		x	x	x		
Identify relationship between operator and machine				x		
Identify activity of each copy of a multicopy form					x	
Identify steps of a computer program						x

vertical listing of steps. For example, in Figure 17–13, the student will continue to study until the time arrives to leave for class.

Figure 17–14 summarizes some of the characteristics of each of the systems analysis tools.

IMPLICATIONS FOR THE ADMINISTRATIVE OFFICE MANAGER

The level of responsibility that administrative office managers have for systems analysis varies from organization to organization. Generally, the alternative used by the organization for staffing its systems analysis function determines the administrative office manager's level of responsibility for this area. The greatest amount of involvement tends to be in organizations that use a part-time staff headed by the administrative office manager.

Familiarity with the organization's operating units is crucial for those involved with systems analysis and design. This is especially true nowadays because of the trend toward developing and implementing integrated systems. Those who are involved in systems development also should be familiar with work flow, data processing, and fundamentals of analysis and design.

Systems analysis provides an opportunity to specialize for those who wish to do so, as do several of the other areas for which administrative office managers are responsible. Some prefer the more specialized nature of systems analysis and design over the more general nature of administrative office management.

REVIEW QUESTIONS

1. What is meant by the integrated systems concept?

2. What are the objectives of the systems concept?

3. What are the characteristics of a well-designed system?

4. What advantages result from using outside consultants for designing a system?

5. Explain the use of the daily log sheet.

6. In a flow process chart, why is the elimination of the do steps in a work process advantageous?

7. What special situations are identified by office layout charts?

8. For what type of systems analysis is the horizontal flow process chart especially suited?

DISCUSSION QUESTIONS

1. When a group of employees in your unit recently heard that the company in which you work was going to implement several systems designed to reduce operating costs, they became quite concerned. Their basic complaint was that systems tend to standardize or make uniform operating procedures—and how could several people who perform the same tasks be expected to perform those tasks in the same manner? They also indicated that they each have their special "shortcuts" for performing these tasks and that, as individuals, their own procedures are the most efficient for each of them. What is your reaction to the thinking of these employees?

2. The organization in which you work is presently undertaking a systems analysis project that will culminate in the design and implementation of one or more systems. The group that you supervise was selected to participate in the data-collection process, using a daily log to collect the data. When you attempted to collect the log from one of your subordinates, she said, "I am not going to complete that stupid thing. As long as I do my work well—and you keep telling me that I do—how I spend my day is no one's business. Besides, I know management is doing this just to try to prove that the company is not getting its money's worth from the employees." Discuss how you plan to deal with this situation.

3. You are a senior systems analyst-designer in a consulting firm that has clients all over the country. The president of a company you worked with two years ago just called you to say that the system you installed in his company is producing less-than-desirable results. Instead of helping the company reduce its operating costs, the system seems to be having the opposite effect. This puzzles you very much as you collected more information than you usually do before you design and implement systems. You noticed during your data-collection efforts that many of the employees seemed to be skeptical of management's intentions, which prompted you to collect more information than you otherwise would have. Although discrepancies existed in some of the data you collected, you resolved the differences with managers and supervisors before you began designing the system. Identify some of the possible reasons the system is not producing the results you expected.

STUDENT PROJECTS AND ACTIVITIES

1. Talk with a systems analyst who has been intricately involved in the development of a system used in an organization. Have this individual discuss with you the development of the system—from the beginning to the end.

2. Compare the purchasing subsystem presented earlier in this chapter with that of an existing organization. What are the similarities and differences between the two?

3. Going Online: Using the Internet, conduct an online search based on one of the concepts presented in this chapter or based on one of the chapter terms. Identify four or five things you learned from the material that you did not know prior to your online search.

Minicases

For several months now, the new manager of the credit application unit of Johnson Manufacturing Company has been aware that several of the unit's work procedures are inefficient. The first procedure to be assessed is the credit approval process. At the present time, five different individuals are involved in the credit approval process. Before credit is approved or denied, two of the five individuals work with each form at two different times.

1. What analysis tool(s) would be useful in analyzing the present process?

2. Identify the characteristics of each tool that you identify in Question 1.

Case

Recently, the Merrimac Insurance Company, which is located in Hartford, Connecticut, completed several cost analysis studies and found an alarming increase in the cost of processing insurance claims. Merrimac's rates are about 15 percent higher than the national average.

A recent study completed by several systems analysis experts indicated that much of the cost can be attributed to inefficient work flow. Part-time employees are frequently hired to help process the backlog.

The following outlines the steps involved in processing the claims:

1. The claim is received in the mailroom.
2. The claim is transported to the claims department, a distance of 401 feet.
3. The claim is opened and then assigned to a claims clerk according to an alphabetical sequence.
4. The claim is transported to a claims clerk, a distance of fifteen feet.
5. The claims clerk briefly scans the claim.
6. The customer's file is retrieved from the file area, a distance of fifty feet.
7. After checking the customer's folder for coverage, premium status, and history of claims, the claims clerk approves the claim and makes a notation on the folder.
8. The claim is transported for final authorization to the supervisor, a distance of twenty feet. (Because of the backlog, this regularly results in a two-day delay before the supervisor gives final approval.)
9. The authorized claim is transported to data processing, a distance of 160 feet.
10. The customer's folder is refiled.

You have been assigned the responsibility of charting the process as it presently exists.

1. What analysis tools would be appropriate for charting the process?
2. Using an appropriate tool, chart the process and make recommendations for simplifying it.
3. Chart the proposed process using an appropriate tool.

$\mathcal{C}$hapter 18

COMPUTER TECHNOLOGY

$\mathcal{C}$hapter $\mathcal{A}$ims

After studying this chapter, you should be able to design an effective computer system for an organization.

$\mathcal{C}$hapter $\mathcal{O}$utline

Computer Generations
Classifications of Computers
    Classification by Category
    Classification by Size
Components of Computer Systems
    Input
    Storage
    Arithmetic/Logic Unit
    Control Unit
    Output
Computer Instructions
Distributed Data Processing
Managing Computer Problems
    Computer Power Problems
    Computer Viruses
Implications for the Administrative Office
   Manager

$\mathcal{C}$hapter $\mathcal{T}$erms

Analog computers
Arithmetic/logic unit (ALU)
Assembler
Artificial intelligence
Audio communication
Audio response
Bar code input
Binary code
Byte
Cathode ray tubes (CRT)
Central processing unit (CPU)
Computer output laser disk (C.O.L.D.)
Computer output microfilm (COM)
Compiler
Computer viruses
Control unit
Digital computers
Distributed data processing
Expert systems
Floppy disks
Fourth-generation languages
Handwriting pads
Hardware
Impact printer
Input
Integrated circuits
Light pen
Magnetic hard disks

Magnetic ink character recognition (MICR)
Magnetic strips
Magnetic tape
Mainframe computers
Mark-sense forms
Midsized computers
Monitors
Mouse
Nonimpact printers
Object program
Optical cards
Optical character recognition (OCR)
Optical laser disks
Output
Personal computers
Point-of-sale (POS) terminals
Printer-plotters

Problem-oriented language
Procedure-oriented languages
Random-access memory (RAM)
Scanner
Server
Software
Source program
Symbolic languages
Storage
Supercomputers
Terminals
Touchscreen
Touch-tone phone
Turnkey systems
Video capture card
Voice annotation
Voice input

*E*ither directly or indirectly, computers have a significant impact on virtually every aspect of our working and personal lives. They make our jobs easier to perform and increase the satisfaction we derive from many aspects of our personal lives. The widespread use of the computer-driven Internet for both work and pleasure assures our lives will continue to be affected significantly by computer technology. The odds are quite good that our future will be affected just as much by computer technology as our past has been.

No invention during this century has had a more revolutionary impact on many of the work processes and procedures used in the business world than has the computer. By installing their own data processing system or by using the services of a computer service bureau, even today's smallest organizations have access to data processing capabilities.

Where was the first computer developed?

Development of the first electronic computer, the ENIAC (Electronic Numerical Integrator and Computer), was begun at the University of Pennsylvania in 1943 and completed in 1946. This device was developed to solve complex ballistic firing problems of guided missiles and artillery shells. The first commercial electronic computer, the Remington Rand Univac I, was dedicated on June 14, 1951, at the U.S. Bureau of Census and was assigned the task of completing the 1950 census. The first business enterprise to install and use computer applications on a daily basis was the General Electric Company at Appliance Park, Kentucky, which installed a Remington Rand Univac computer in 1954. Since that time, literally hundreds of thousands of computer applications have been developed for use in hundreds of thousands of organizations.

COMPUTER GENERATIONS

Computer technology, which has progressed through three recognizable phases, is presently in a fourth generation or phase. Distinct characteristics of each can be identified.

The first generation of computers, which spanned the years 1952 to 1958, used vacuum tubes that consumed large amounts of electricity and generated considerable heat. Data input was generally restricted to punched cards, and internally stored programs were limited to magnetic cores or rotating drums.

The first-generation computers were used primarily by organizations for the mechanical processing of various clerical and accounting procedures. The cost of executing 1 million instructions on first-generation equipment was approximately $4.50, and the typical maximum capacity of internal memory was a mere 4,000 characters.

How do the characteristics of the second generation of computers differ from the first generation of computers?

The second generation of computers, which were marketed from 1958 through 1963, used solid state transistor cards rather than the vacuum tubes of the first generation. Transistor usage greatly reduced the physical size of computer equipment. Magnetic tape drives were developed during the second generation, and the magnetic core memory devices became much more functional. In addition, the second generation saw the development and use of symbolic computer languages as well as the use of such random access storage devices as magnetic cards and disk files. The second generation of computers enabled many organizations to develop a systems approach for the processing of data. Processing speeds reached 30,000 instructions per second, the cost of executing 1 million instructions was reduced to 30 cents, and the maximum capacity of internal memory increased to 30,000 characters.

How do the characteristics of the third generation of computers differ from the fourth generation of computers?

The third-generation era lasted from 1964 to 1969. During this time, miniature circuitry chips were used in the construction of electronic computers. Other developments of the third generation are (1) unlimited random access storage capability, such as disks, and (2) the availability of many prewritten computer programs. The introduction of minicomputers was one of the major developments of this generation. The impact of the third-generation computer on business applications was most significant in the development and refinement of the total systems approach for the processing of data. The number of instructions that could be executed per second increased nearly seven times (200,000) while the cost of executing 1 million instructions decreased to 5 cents. Maximum capacity of internal memory increased to 512,000 characters.

The current generation of computers, which appeared in 1970, has resulted in the further simplification and refinement of the systems approach. In addition, fourth-generation computers make greater use of microprogramming, which involves the rapid assembly and use of complex control and processing operations. Fourth-generation computers also use microscopic integrated circuits, which increase equipment operating speeds. Large-scale integration (LSI) and very-large-scale integration (VLSI) allow an ever-increasing number of circuits to be placed on a chip, which significantly reduces equipment manufacturing costs. Today's supercomputers are capable of executing three trillion instructions per second at less than 1 cent per million of instructions. These computers have an internal memory capacity of 2.5 terabytes (1 terabyte is the rough equivalent of one thousand gigabytes).

What is a terabyte?

Another characteristic of fourth-generation computers is the associative memory capability, which means that storage locations are identified by their content or subject matter rather than by their position. With the earlier computers, storage locations were identified by their positions.

Data processing equipment has gone from computational speeds of seconds, to milliseconds (one-thousandth of a second), to microseconds (one-millionth of a second), to nanoseconds (one-billionth of a second), to picoseconds (one-trillionth of a second). Many computer systems now routinely process data in picoseconds.

What are the characteristics of the fifth generation of computers?

Work on fifth-generation equipment is currently underway. Among the characteristics being speculated for this equipment are the following: widespread use of **artificial intelligence,** megachips, and advanced parallel processing capability. Artificial intelligence will allow computers to learn from their mistakes. The megachips likely to be found in fifth-generation equipment will have over 1 million storage locations. The parallel processing capability will allow several computers to process numerous instructions simultaneously, unlike today's equipment that is capable of processing only one instruction at a time.

Artificial intelligence allows computers to mimic human behavior, including such behavior patterns as the ability to reason, learn, self-improve, and simulate sensory and mechanical capabilities. The artificial intelligence found in today's fourth-generation systems is quite elementary when compared with the sophistication of the artificial intelligence expected to be found in the fifth-generation systems. Artificial intelligence will give computers the ability to reason, accumulate knowledge, and simulate human sensory capabilities.

Among the categories of artificial intelligence are the following:

1. Expert system (enables the computer to help with problem solving).

2. Natural languages (allow the user, using a natural human voice, to communicate with a computer).

3. Human sensory simulation (allows a computer to help perform basic human sensory functions, such as speaking, seeing, and hearing).

4. Robotics (uses a computer to operate devices).

Of these various categories, expert systems are seen as having the greatest application for usage in the business world.

What are expert systems?

Expert systems will be commonly found in the fifth-generation era. These are programs that capture the experiences, decision processes, and thought processes of experts in specific areas, ranging from automobile maintenance, to space planning, to computer systems design, to surgery.

Expert systems are created by a process that involves interviewing experts in a specific field. The experts' knowledge is translated into a series of rules and strategies. Because most expert systems will involve artificial intelligence, the system's knowledge base continually grows because it learns from user feedback. In this sense, the system continues to learn through learning. This technology allows managers and expert systems to become partners in problem solving. The end result is that as knowledge is accumulated by the system, fewer bad decisions will be made. Expert systems work with knowledge rather than information.

To illustrate how an expert system works, consider the use of such a system in office space planning. The program might first ask the user to enter several "parameters," such as the number of square feet in a given work area, number of employees to be located in the area, hierarchical level of the various employees, and the typical amount of furniture/equipment each employee has. After this information has been input into the system, the user might be asked to respond to several questions about the following topics: type of lighting system, location of electrical outlets, nature of employee interaction, amount of contact with outsiders, and so forth. Given the needed information, the system will be able to recommend the optimum type of layout structure (open, traditional, etc.) and even the amount of square feet and ideal location for each employee.

CLASSIFICATIONS OF COMPUTERS

The electronic computer is the backbone of data processing systems. To understand the electronic data processing concept, an understanding of electronic computers is essential, including their classifications. Computers can be classified by category and by size.

Classification by Category

The categorical classification of computers includes digital computers and analog computers. Each has distinct characteristics and uses. Increasingly, computer usage involves digital rather than analog equipment.

Digital computers are used primarily to count numbers. Data are represented by strings of numbers, which, in turn, are expressed by electrical impulses. Therefore, the digital computer is most often used for processing business data. The digital computer is capable of calculating and manipulating discrete variables.

Digital computers get their name from the fact that the basic unit of storage is the binary digit or bit. Binary digits have only two settings, usually represented by a "0" or a "1." The use of binary code is explained later in the "Storage" section of this chapter.

While digital computers are used to count numbers, **analog computers** are used as measuring devices. The analog computer, which is most appropriate for use in scientific research, operates on continuous values, such as voltages, temperatures, and speeds. While the digital computer is capable of calculating answers with 100 percent accuracy, the analog computer is not as precise. The accuracy of the analog computer is limited by the precision with which the continually variable physical quantities can be controlled.

How do the characteristics of analog computers differ from those of digital computers?

Classifications by Size

Computers can also be classified according to their size. Common sizes are personal computers, of which several types exist, midsized computers, mainframe computers, and supercomputers. The basic differences among the computers in each of the categories are in the computer power each category is able to generate, equipment costs, expansion capabilities, processing speeds, and types of input, output, and storage capacity.

Personal Computers. Several types of **personal computers** are found today: desktop computers, network computers, notebook and laptop computers, pocket computers (also known as a palmtop PC), and personal digital assistants (PDAs).

Desktop units are equipped with a central processing unit (CPU), a monitor, a keyboard, and a mouse. The CPU is stored in either a vertical case, known as a *tower*, or a horizontal case. Additional functionality can be readily obtained, such as a network card or modem, speakers, internal tape drives, and so on.

What is a server?

A specialized type of desktop unit is the **server,** which basically functions as a host computer in a computer network and provides programs and data in response to requests it receives. For example, rather than putting word processing capability on each desktop computer, the program is installed on a server, which provides the user with the same capability it would have if it were installed on his or her desktop unit. Servers tend to have fast operating speeds as well as large hard-disk drive capacity.

Network computers are relatively inexpensive because they are not equipped with disk drives; and they have smaller processors and less internal memory than other types of computers. The software individuals use on these computers is stored on a server at a remote site and is available through a computer network.

Notebook units are quite small, generally fitting into a briefcase and perhaps weighing less than three pounds. Laptop computers, on the other hand, are larger; and they weigh considerably more, perhaps as much as eight pounds. Some individuals use laptops as their primary computer; generally, notebook computers are too small to function well as a primary computer for individuals who use them frequently or extensively. Notebook units may be equipped with a port replicator, and laptop units may be equipped with a docking station that contains a conventional-sized keyboard, monitor, and mouse. The notebook's and laptop's central processing unit becomes the CPU for the port replicator or the docking station.

For what is a docking station used?

Also known as pocket PCs, palmtop computers can literally fit into a pocket or purse. They function primarily to maintain one's appointment book, schedule, and e-mail. Input is generally character-by-character using a stylus.

Personal digital assistant computers (PDAs) are generally more functional than palmtop computers. Some are equipped with a built-in cellular phone that facilitates sending faxes, making an Internet connection, and sending e-mail. Input of information is generally done by a stylus, touching the keys on the on-screen keyboard, or by using a reduced-feature keyboard. PDAs generally support appointment scheduling, personal phonebook, to-do list, diaries, spreadsheets, and so forth. Cabling facilitates connecting the PDA to another computer for data transfer or to a printer to prepare hard copy.

Today, the minimum memory of personal computers is 128KB (kilobyte). Just a few years ago, the minimum memory was 4KB. A **byte** usually stores one alphabetic character or two numeric characters. A fully functioning personal computer can be purchased today for as little as $400. Except for the desktop and network computers, the other types of personal computers are portable, which means they can be made operational by use of a battery, although most computers that operate on battery can also be operated using an electrical connection.

Personal computers generally have a limited number of input and output devices. Included are a keyboard used for the inputting of data into the device, a mouse, a disk drive for data storage, and a monitor used for soft-copy output. A common peripheral device attached to computers is a printer used to prepare hard-copy output. Increasingly, personal computers are being equipped with hard disks capable of storing up to as much as 22GB (gigabytes) of data.

Personal computers are used in offices in two basic ways: as a stand-alone device for the processing of data/information or as an intelligent terminal attached to the organization's computer network. An increasing number of personal computers are used as dedicated computers in organizations. This means their use has a specific dedicated function, such as monitoring the organization's environmental control system, controlling the organization's telephone system, and so forth.

An illustration of a personal computer is presented in Figure 18–1.

Figure 18-1 Personal computer. Photo Courtesy Gateway, Inc. © 1999.

Midsized Computers.

Midsized computers, which until recently were generally referred to as minicomputers, are typically free standing in design. Basically, they are mainframe computers in miniature form. These devices are often equipped with a printer, in addition to the keyboard, a monitor, and a disk drive. Primary data storage consists of a hard-disk drive. Prices range from $10,000 to $250,000. Midsized computers are generally multiuser systems that can support as many as 500 on-line terminals. Compared with personal computers, midsized computers have considerably higher processing speeds.

What is the price range of midsized computers?

Like their personal computer cousins, midsized computers are typically **turnkey systems.** This simply means that all components of the system are bundled, and the user simply has to unpackage the equipment, plug it in, turn it on, and load it with the desired programs. The operation of midsized computer systems is easily learned.

Midsized computers are often used to process business transactions, such as accounts payable and receivable, payroll, inventory control, purchasing, and sales, as well as to perform complex design (computer-aided design or CAD) functions. Also, they can be interfaced with more powerful equipment or operate independently of any other equipment.

A midsized computer is illustrated in Figure 18–2.

Mainframe Computers.

In the early 1960s, many organizations began installing **mainframe computer** systems capable of amassing enormous amounts of computing power. These systems use a wide array of input and output devices as well as several types of internal and external memory/storage devices. In comparison to the other sizes of computers, mainframe computers process data at much faster rates. Mainframe computers typically have a primary storage capacity of millions of bytes. Their cost ranges from $200,000 to several million dollars. The smallest of the mainframe computers are sometimes called *small business computers.*

What is the price range of mainframe computers?

Mainframe computers are often used as host computers, which means they serve as a centralized switching device and, using a network system, operate enterprisewide. An example of an enterprisewide system is the organization's human resources system. Mainframe computers are also capable of simultaneously supporting thousands of online terminals.

Figure 18–3 illustrates a mainframe installation.

Supercomputers.

The largest of the mainframe computers are referred to as **supercomputers.** Their price ranges from $1 million to nearly $100 million, and they have extremely large primary memories, some as large as hundreds

Figure 18–2 Midsized computer. Courtesy: International Business Machines Corporation.

Figure 18-3 Mainframe computer. Courtesy: International Business Machines Corporation.

of millions of bytes. Capable of processing hundreds of millions of instructions per second, most organizations are unable to justify the use of such powerful equipment. Some supercomputers now have processing speeds and computing capacities ten times greater than large mainframes. Only a handful of companies manufacture supercomputers, which are used to process scientific data more often than business data.

What are the characteristics of super computers?

COMPONENTS OF COMPUTER SYSTEMS

What are the components of the central processing unit?

Computer systems consist of the following components: input unit, storage unit, central processing unit (CPU) comprised of the arithmetic/logic unit (ALU) and the control unit, and output unit. These components are known as the computer hardware. The computer software, which is discussed in the "Computer Instructions" section of this chapter, consists of computer programs and instructions. The relationships between each of the hardware components are illustrated in Figure 18–4.

Figure 18–4 depicts the flow of information and/or electric pulses between the various components. The **central processing unit (CPU)** houses three of the five hardware components: control, storage, and arithmetic-logic. Input and output are not part of the CPU of the computer. Each of the five compo-

Figure 18-4 Components of electronic computers

nents is discussed in detail in the following sections. Some of the input media and devices are also used for data storage and as output media or devices. The multifunctional media and devices are discussed in detail in the "Input" section of this chapter.

The central processing unit is able to process data much more rapidly than the computer is capable of reading the data from most of the input media or devices. The CPU is also able to process data much more rapidly than the data appear in output form. Buffering the data compensates for the difference between input and processing rates and between processing and output rates. This means that data are temporarily put into storage to compensate for the differences in the operating speeds of the equipment.

Input

What characteristics of input media exist?

The computer functions by converting letters, numbers, and symbols that humans are capable of reading into data the computer is capable of reading and processing. Paper media, magnetic media, and electronic devices are used to **input** data into computers. The following list identifies the types of media and devices that comprise each of the three main categories of data input:

Paper

Magnetic ink character recognition
Optical character recognition
Mark-sense forms

Magnetic

Magnetic tapes
Magnetic strips
Magnetic hard disks
Floppy disks
Magnetic drums

Electronic

Keyboard terminals
Monitors
Point-of-sale terminals
Touch-tone phone
Audio communication
Optical laser disks
Computer mouse
Light pen
Touchscreens
Voice input
Handwriting input
Bar code input
Scanners
Optical cards

Magnetic Ink Character Recognition (MICR). Also classified as a paper input medium, **MICR** uses magnetically charged numbers imprinted on paper. MICR is used by banks and other financial institutions as a primary means of processing the millions of checks that are written each day. The numbers on the bottom of checks contain iron oxide magnetizable particles. Blank checks are imprinted with the routing symbol, the transit number, the individual's account number, and the check number.

On what types of documents is the MICR process used?

The first bank to receive a check after it has been written imprints the check's amount in MICR numbers at the bottom of the check. The check is now ready for processing through regular banking channels. The bank that receives the check may transfer it to a Federal Reserve Bank, which then transfers it to the bank on which it was written. Figure 18–5 illustrates the meaning of MICR numbers.

Magnetic ink character recognition reader-sorter units read the imprinted numbers and sort checks by bank number and by account number. Sorting rates range from approximately 180 to 2,000 documents per minute. Before the numbers are read into the reader-sorter, the checks pass through a strong magnetic field, causing the iron oxide to become magnetized. The read heads sense the characters, after which the characters are read into the CPU of the computer or transferred to another input medium for later processing.

What are the advantages of MICR?

One advantage of MICR is the high degree of accuracy with which documents are read. Even though they are often folded, contain staple holes, and are covered with a variety of stampings, they are read with a high degree of accuracy. Another advantage of MICR is the ability of humans to read the characters, which is not possible with some of the other types of input media.

The MICR system also has some disadvantages. Because MICR was developed primarily for the banking industry and because it uses only fourteen characters needed by the banking industry, the system is not useful for other

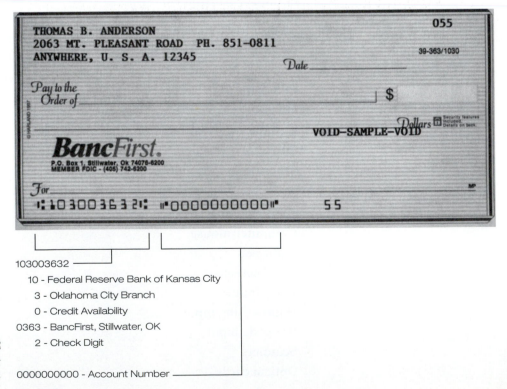

Figure 18-5 MICR numbers. Courtesy: Banc-First, Stillwater, OK.

103003632

10 - Federal Reserve Bank of Kansas City

3 - Oklahoma City Branch

0 - Credit Availability

0363 - BancFirst, Stillwater, OK

2 - Check Digit

0000000000 - Account Number

purposes. Alphabetic characters are not available in the MICR system. Second, clerical involvement is sometimes needed when the preprinted numbers are not sufficiently magnetized with iron oxide particles. Therefore, the check has to be reprocessed. In addition, the magnetized numbers on checks are sometimes printed in the wrong location, which requires their reprinting before the check can be processed through the reader.

Optical Character Recognition (OCR). Another input medium that uses paper is **OCR.** Whereas MICR consists of only fourteen numbers and symbols, all printed characters can be used in OCR systems. In addition, OCR does not require the use of the special magnetized print. OCR equipment can read data appearing in three formats on source documents: typed, printed, and handwritten. Figure 18–6 illustrates OCR letters, numbers, and symbols.

Increasingly, OCR is being used to input data/information into organizational databases, especially externally originated data/information. The content of reports and other business documents can be scanned by OCR readers as long as they are printed or typed in an OCR-compatible print/type style. Once the data/information are stored in the database, they can be used in several different ways. For example, suppose some statistical data stored in the database are appropriate for inclusion in a report being prepared by a manager. Depending on the type of word processing system on which the report is being prepared, the manager may be able to use the word processing software to access the desired data. After the data have been accessed, they can be easily inserted at the desired location in the report. Thus, the manager will not have to keyboard the desired data.

Like the other types of input media and devices, certain advantages result from using OCR. First, the original source document can be used for input into the computer without first having to transfer the information onto some other input medium or device. Second, it reduces the amount of human effort involved in the electronic processing of data. Third, OCR data are easily read by humans. And, finally, the equipment needed to imprint OCR characters on documents is inexpensive.

To a certain extent, OCR is limited because of the rather strict type fonts and character sizes that must be used, although newer equipment is more flexible. If an incorrect type font is used or if the characters are larger or smaller than those the reader is capable of reading, the system may not work. In addition, when OCR characters are imprinted on paper with a typewriter equipped with a special font, extreme care must be exercised when correcting errors. Another limitation is the high cost of heavy-duty OCR readers. Light-duty readers that require manual movement of the read head can be purchased for as little as $100.

Common types of OCR scanners are (1) those that scan labels, such as price tags; (2) page scanners that scan material on a typewritten or printed page; and (3) document scanners that scan different sizes of documents, such as billing invoices.

What are the characteristics of optical character recognition?

ABCDEFGHIJKLMNOPQRSTOVWXYZ
abcdefghijklmnopqrstuvwxyz

Figure 18-6 OCR-compatible characters. Courtesy: International Business Machines Corporation.

чⵏ⌐≄%|⅋∗{}——=+■/?❜❞;:.¬
1234567890

What are the
characteristics of mark
sense?

Mark-Sense Forms. When using **mark-sense forms,** preprinted shapes (such as squares, rectangles, or circles) are darkened with a writing instrument, most commonly a No. 2 lead pencil. These forms are then run through optical equipment. As the equipment "senses" the darkened areas, the system keeps a tally of the number of each area it reads. The end result is the preparation of a report that identifies the number of times each darkened area appears on a mark-sense form. The use of mark-sense forms in test taking is also common. In this situation, a report detailing the number of incorrect responses subtracted from the correct responses will be prepared for each mark-sense form run through the scanning device. An example of a mark-sense form is shown in Chapter 22.

Magnetic Tape. In high-speed, large-volume computer applications, **magnetic tape** is the most widely used type of input. Magnetic tape, which is also the most common external data storage medium, is used as an output medium as well. The iron oxide coating on one side of the magnetic tape receives the electromagnetic pulses, which enables data, appearing as binary digits, to be recorded on the tape. Because the pulses can be erased and new pulses stored on magnetic tape, this input medium is reusable.

How are data entered
onto magnetic tape?

Data are entered on magnetic tapes either directly or indirectly. For example, data that are transferred by a converter from mark-sense forms to magnetic tape are transferred indirectly, while key-to-tape units, which use a keyboard, are direct. The information contained on the source document is keyed into the unit, and as each key is depressed, two things occur simultaneously: (1) the electromagnetic pulse is recorded as a binary digit in one of the tracks or channels on the tape; and (2) the letter, number, or symbol appears on a screenlike display unit that facilitates verifying its accuracy.

In some instances, instead of keying data directly onto the magnetic tape, data are keyed first onto either a hard-disk drive or floppy disks. Before the data are fed into the CPU, they are transferred onto magnetic tape.

Key-to-tape units prepare either standard-size magnetic tape or smaller-sized magnetic tape found in special cartridges or cassettes. Before the data on the smaller size tape can be fed into the CPU, it may be necessary to use a converter to transfer the data to a standard-sized magnetic tape.

Magnetic tape units are used for data input (reading) and for output (recording or writing). Such units, which are referred to as *tape drives,* must contain as many read-write heads as there are tracks on the magnetic tape being used. If the magnetic tape contains nine tracks, which is a common size, the tape drive must also contain nine read-write heads. As the electromagnets pass over the binary digits stored as pulses on the tape, the data are fed into the CPU. A tape drive is illustrated in Figure 18–7.

What are the advantages
and disadvantages of
magnetic tape?

Among the advantages of using magnetic tape are the following: Data can be stored much more compactly on a tape than on cards or floppy disks (to illustrate, a standard reel of magnetic tape has the same storage capacity as five hundred single-sided, double-density floppy disks); magnetic tape is relatively inexpensive to purchase; magnetic tape is one of the fastest input media; and the likelihood of misplacing a magnetic tape is small in comparison to the likelihood of misplacing floppy disks.

Use of magnetic tape results in certain disadvantages, one of which is the inability of people to read the data recorded on the tape. In addition, the environmental conditions for using magnetic tape are more strict than those required for using MICR forms. For example, minute specks of dust can cause the data on the tape to be misread, and tapes can be mistakenly erased.

Figure 18-7 Magnetic tape drive. Courtesy: Hewlett Packard Company.

Furthermore, it may be necessary to control humidity levels in a computer room where magnetic tape is used. When the data needed for a certain processing operation are at the end of the tape, all the data on the tape must first pass through the tape reader. Therefore, because of its sequential nature, information recorded on magnetic tape cannot be accessed randomly. Before self-locking tape systems were invented, tapes were sometimes stretched, crinkled, or contaminated by computer operators. The magnetic nature of the tape means that data can be erased or distorted with a magnet.

Magnetic Strips. Found on the back of credit cards and some ID badges, **magnetic strips** provide a fast, accurate method of data input. The data stored on the strip allow the user to communicate with the computer. In some instances, the data contained on the strip provide an element of security, which prevents the fraudulent use of the card or badge.

Magnetic Hard Disks. Similar to several of the other input media already discussed, **magnetic hard disks** are used during input, storage, and output. The disk is used to store the computer's operating system, its application software, and data.

Unlike magnetic tape, which requires sequential accessing, magnetic hard disks permit random accessing of data. Therefore, data can be accessed from a disk without all of the disk contents having to be read up to the location where the desired data are stored. Random accessing of data on a disk is much faster than the sequential-accessing nature of magnetic tape.

How does random accessing differ from sequential accessing?

Magnetic disks, the diameters of which range in size from five to thirty-six inches, are made of thin metal plates covered on both sides with a magnetic recording material. A disk pack contains several of these disks, typically ten to twenty. Data are accessed from the disk pack by arms that, upon command from the computer, move to the location of the data. The read-write heads located on the arms then read and transfer to the computer the electromagnetic pulses contained in the tracks on the disk. During the read-write process, heads do not come into contact with the disk. If they do, a head crash occurs, which may destroy the readability of the entire disk pack.

While some disk drives contain only permanent access arms with multiple read-write heads for each disk contained in the disk pack, others contain an access arm with an attached read-write head for each disk surface. The arms in a multiple-access unit move simultaneously. Consequently, if the computer directs an access arm to the seventh track on the fourth disk, all the arms move to the seventh track of their respective disks. The read-write heads on the No. 4 access arm will then read and transfer the desired data to the computer. A disk drive is illustrated in Figure 18–8.

Several advantages result from the use of magnetic hard disks. One of the most significant is their random-accessing capability, which shortens data retrieval time. Another advantage is that disks in several disk packs can receive data from one input operation, which simultaneously updates the data stored on several disks. In addition, related data stored on several disk packs can be accessed as the data are required for a processing operation.

The most significant disadvantage of magnetic hard disks is their cost. When compared with the same amount of data storage space on magnetic tapes, disks are considerably more expensive. However, the cost of storing data on disk packs has decreased from one generation of equipment to the next.

Figure 18–8 Disk drive. Courtesy: Burroughs Corporation.

Two main types of hard disk drives are found on personal computers: external and internal. Although the internal drives are most common, a new variation is the removable hard drive that is internal, yet it uses a removable disk cartridge, making that part of it external.

Floppy Disks. **Floppy disks,** which are made of a flexible plastic material, vary in size, although 3.5 inches is most common. They are permanently encased in a plastic container. A keyboard, such as a terminal keyboard, a personal computer keyboard, or a keyboard attached to a dedicated word processor, is used to input information on a floppy. To correct an error, one simply "backspaces" over the error as it appears on the screen and then depresses the correct keys on the keyboard. After the information is keyboarded, it is "read" from memory onto the disk. This process facilitates permanent disk storage of the keyboarded material.

Perhaps the most significant advantage of floppy disks is the ease with which they are handled. They are easily placed in and removed from the disk drive, they are easily mailed, they permit the easy correction of errors, they can be reused, and they are easily maintained. Another significant advantage is their low cost.

When compared with magnetic disks, the amount of storage capacity on floppy disks may be a potential disadvantage. Although floppy disks can store data in either single or double density (high density) and on one or two sides, they do not store nearly as much information as a magnetic hard disk. Floppy disks commonly store up to 1.44MB of data. Another disadvantage is their tendency to be somewhat vulnerable to fingerprints, spilled liquids, smoke, close contact with a magnet, dirt, and dust. However, with adequate protection, these concerns are minimal

What is a super drive?

A new type of floppy disk drive, referred to as a super drive, is now available. It accommodates very high-density floppy disks capable of storing 120MB of data on a 3.5-inch floppy disk. Also available are ZIP drives, both internal and external, that store up to 250MB of data on a ZIP disk.

Keyboard Terminals. **Terminals,** which are connected on-line to the computer, are capable of transforming the letters, numbers, and symbols humans are capable of reading into codes the computer is capable of reading. This type of terminal may not be suitable for the mass input of data because they are entered only as rapidly as the operator is able to keyboard.

Some keyboards, such as console terminals, are attached on-line to a computer in the same room while others are attached off-line (by means of telephone equipment) to computers hundreds of miles away. To illustrate the use of these terminals, consider the process of making hotel and motel reservations. To determine whether or not a room is available, the operator uses the terminal to enter the data into the computer. The appropriate data are retrieved from the computer's storage facility and are then transmitted by the terminal to the operator. If a room is available and if reservations are then desired, the operator uses the terminal to transmit the appropriate data to the computer.

What are the advantages and disadvantages of keyboard terminals as an input medium?

The use of keyboard devices for on-line data input has several distinct advantages. As input devices, they are rather inexpensive. In addition, these terminals can be used to communicate with a computer over a distance of many miles. Another advantage is the ability to obtain hard copies of data input and output. On the other hand, using keyboard devices to communicate with the computer is extremely slow, directly correlated with the user's keyboarding speed. Therefore, they may not be well suited for inputting massive amounts of data, which presents another disadvantage.

Monitors. As an input/output (I/O) device, **monitors,** which use **cathode ray tubes (CRTs),** are attached to virtually every desktop personal computer. Too, monitors with larger display areas have become much less costly.

Monitors, like keyboard terminals, can be located a distance from the computer facility. Some of these terminals may be used as input devices (for on-line update) or as inquiry-response devices (that is, the data are displayed only for inquiry purposes).

In some instances, an input tablet, which consists of a grid comprised of hundreds of copper wires, is attached to a monitor. The grid is covered with a glass or plastic shield, and the paper on which the illustration appears is placed on the shield. Using a special pen to trace over the lines on the paper, the copper wires enable the unit to transmit electrical impulses to the computer's storage unit. To change a line on the electronically stored illustration, the special pen is used to erase the original line prior to moving the new line to the desired location.

An electronic light pen may also be used to transmit illustrations to a computer. This pen, which contains a photocell, is used to trace the illustration directly onto the monitor screen. Electronic responses between the terminal screen and the photocell in the light pen are transmitted to the computer. The light pen can also be used to add, delete, or modify lines on illustrations or in tabular information.

The use of monitors results in several distinct advantages. Monitors provide a noiseless system, and output is displayed rapidly on the screen. In addition, they are the only input device suitable for the input of line drawings. Another advantage is the ease with which illustrations can be modified. Disadvantages of monitors used as an input device are their inability to operate when the CPU is inoperable, their inability to make backup copies of data that may be lost during the inputting process (which means that such data will have to be rekeyed), and the growing concern of the unhealthy nature of long-term CRT usage. In addition, as input devices, monitors are not suitable for on-line inputting of large volumes of data into the computer.

Figure 18–9 shows a flat-screen monitor.

Figure 18-9 Monitor.
Courtesy: LG Electronics
USA.

When purchasing monitors, several of their attributes need to be considered, including the following:

What attributes should be
considered in selecting
computer monitors?

Interlaced vs. noninterlaced: Noninterlaced monitors result in less flickering.

Refresh rate: The higher the refresh rate (70 Hz or higher is recommended), the less flickering will be noticed.

Dot pitch: Refers to how far apart individual dots of the same color are on the screen. A smaller dot pitch will produce a sharper, clearer image.

Resolution: Refers to the amount of information available on a screen. SVGA (800×600 resolution) has become the standard.

Flat vs. conventional screens: Flat screens produce less glare and less distortion, which may be important when using CAD/CAM applications.

Safety standards: The Swedish rating of MPR-II is becoming standard, meaning that the monitor emits radiation in the extra low frequency or very low frequency range.

Point-of-Sale Terminals. An increasing number of stores and businesses are using **point-of-sale (POS) terminals** rather than cash registers. In some stores, as much as 70 to 80 percent of the required operating data can be captured at the point of sale. These devices are attached on-line to a computer and most likely are also used to facilitate the authorization to accept a check or credit card. As the required data for the sale are captured, they are stored in the system for later use in preparing summary reports. In some companies, the captured data originating from the sales are used to facilitate automatic reordering when a sufficient number of specific items have been sold.

In addition to performing the same functions as cash registers, POS terminals have the following capabilities: They provide computerized inventory control; provide credit information about a charge customer; print credit card charge slips; and, by means of a sensing wand, read and transmit to the computer the price found on the magnetized price tags that are attached to merchandise. The most common type of tag, such as those found on items in food markets, uses the universal product code (UPC). From an efficiency standpoint, the most significant advantage of POS terminals is their elimination of the need to depend on a mechanical means to input data into the computer. Thus, a time-consuming, labor-intensive step is eliminated. Calculations are performed by the computer, and the terminal prints the results automatically on a sales receipt. The most significant disadvantage of POS terminals is their inoperability when the system's computer is down.

Figure 18–10 illustrates a point-of-sale terminal.

Touch-Tone Phone. The use of a **touch-tone phone** as a data input system is likely to increase. When the various keys on the phone are depressed, the tones can be used to activate devices that input data into a computer. This system will undoubtedly be used extensively to facilitate banking transactions, to check account balances, to pay bills, to place orders, and to do accounting arithmetic.

Two significant advantages result from using this type of data input device. One is the convenience of the device, and the other is its low cost. Perhaps the most significant disadvantage is that errors can be easily made, especially if people are not totally familiar with the uses of the system.

Audio Communication. As an input medium, **audio communication** facilitates the transformation of standard telephones into data terminals. Portable audio terminals onto which telephone handsets are placed communicate with

Figure 18-10 Point-of-sale terminal. Courtesy: International Business Machines Corporation.

computers. These terminals are usually battery operated, and they transmit data through a telephone communication medium (copper lines, fiber optics, and microwaves, for example) to receiving units that ultimately feed data into computers.

Data are input into the system by means of the terminal keyboard. Output is in the form of prerecorded voice responses transmitted through telephone lines to a speaker in the portable terminal.

This terminal device is especially useful for traveling salespeople, who, for example, might need to communicate with the home office about the availability of certain products that a customer wishes to order. The portable terminal is also used to place the order.

Audio communication that uses portable audio terminals is advantageous for several reasons. Electronic equipment can be used to communicate information that individuals previously have had to communicate. It is a convenient system to use because any telephone can be transformed into a terminal. In addition, data can be kept up to date, and they are readily obtainable. However, the portable audio terminal is not designed for mass input of data, which, to a certain extent, limits its use.

Optical Laser Disks. Another of the electronic media used to input data into a computer are **optical laser disks.** Using a keyboarding device, data are entered and stored as binary digits on the disk. While some binary digits create pits in the disk surface, others do not. During the process of inputting data into the computer, a laser beam is used to read the configuration of the pit.

Optical laser disks have become more useful with the availability of technology that enables their contents to be erased. Typically, a laser beam is used to erase data that have been magnetically recorded on the disk.

The most significant advantage of optical laser disk technology is the potential storage capacity. A double-sided optical laser disk is capable of storing four billion bytes. To store the equivalent amount of information on double-sided floppy disks requires more than 15,000 floppies.

A common application of optical laser disk technology is CD-ROM, the acronym for compact disk–read-only memory. Because of the read-only-memory feature, data on the disk can only be read; they cannot be manipulated or changed. A single CD-ROM has a storage capacity of 680MB. Compared with other technologies, CD-ROM enjoys a significantly more dense storage capacity. Technology is now available that facilitates the recording of CD-ROMs at the user site.

Computer Mouse. An increasingly common type of data/information input into a computer involves the use of a **mouse,** a small plastic box hard-wired to a computer. On the bottom of the box is a ball that rolls as the box is moved. Moving the box moves an arrow or pointer on the screen. Thus, if the user moves the mouse to the left, the arrow moves to the left on the screen. The use of a mouse enables the operator to place the arrow "on top" of his or her desired processing command. Then the operator depresses the "enter" key on the mouse, and the command is read into the computer. The alternative is to enter the same command using a keyboard, which may be more time consuming. In some applications, the mouse can be used to draw lines or objects on the screen. Some computers, especially notebook and laptop computers, use either a track ball or a touch pad as an alternative to a mouse.

What is a light pen?

Light Pen. The **light pen** has a very useful function in some applications, such as working with engineering or architectural drawings. The pen is used in conjunction with the CRT monitor. When the pen is placed close to the screen, the cursor locks onto the position of the pen. To modify a drawing, the user simply moves the light pen to the desired location, which takes the line on the screen with it, thus adjusting its location.

Touchscreens. To use a **touchscreen,** another input device, the various alternatives available to the user appear on the screen. The alternatives are often shown as icons on a menu. The user simply touches the desired alternative shown on the screen. The heat-sensitive nature of the screen causes the area being touched to close an electronic circuit, which facilitates the reading of the information in that circuit into the computer.

What is voice input?

Voice Input. Projected by some to become the most common future input system, **voice input** is currently receiving a fair amount of attention, especially with the bundling of a voice-response component with the word processing program of a widely used office suite software program. When using voice input, an individual speaks into a microphone attached to a device that transforms each word into a digitized format. The digitized codes representing each word can then be stored in computer memory.

Voice input equipment is currently available that can accommodate a 30,000-word vocabulary. The equipment interactively learns the vocabulary and speaking style used by an employee. With the required pause between each word, the equipment is capable of creating text at an approximate rate of 140 words per minute.

Closely related is equipment that enables drivers with cellular telephones to operate their phones with voice-response commands rather than push-button commands. Thus, users can access their voice messaging system while driving a car, without having to take their eyes off the road. The system can also be used to make calls or to have the system call them back if they have voice messages waiting but don't want to receive them at that time.

An adaptation of voice input is called **voice annotation,** which allows a user to record a voice message at specific locations in a written document being displayed on a computer monitor. Suppose, for example, as a supervisor, you are on-screen editing a subordinate's report. Rather than handwriting a comment about a change you recommend, you can insert a voice comment at that location. Then, when the subordinate continues revising the document, he or she hears the comment instead of reading it.

Handwriting Input. Available now are **handwriting pads** that recognize handwritten characters when interfaced with a personal computer. About the size of clipboards, although thicker and heavier, these writing pads can be carried around by the user. Data are entered on the pad by a writing instrument that resembles a pen. As the data are entered, they appear on the computer screen and are saved to storage with the "save" command.

Figure 18–11 illustrates a handwriting pad.

What are handwriting pads?

Bar Code Input. An increasing number of applications found in many organizations accommodate **bar code input** of data into the computer. Various units of data/information can be contained in bar code format, which is subsequently entered into the computer by means of a scanning device, such as a light pen or a bar code reader.

In organizations that have bar code technology, a common application might be departmental checkout of supplies. Each item in supply has a bar code identification. The checkout operation involves scanning the department's bar code identification and each item being checked out. Bar code input greatly simplifies the process of charging each department for the supplies it uses. Too, bar codes are used as an integral component of document management systems that are discussed in Chapter 21.

Scanners. For data/information not originally stored in an organization's computer system, the use of a **scanner** eliminates the need to input the material using a manual procedure such as keyboarding. For example, if a report is received from someone outside the organization but the information found in the report will be useful to employees, a scanner is used to digitize the report's content, which is then stored in the system. At that point, the text data can be manipulated by means of a text editor, and numerical data can be placed in spreadsheet form. Scanners also digitize line drawings, photographs, and other graphics, which facilitates their electronic storage.

What is the purpose of a scanner?

Figure 18-11 Handwriting pad. Courtesy: GRiD Systems Corp.

Optical Cards. Used as a storage device as well as an input device, **optical cards,** which are about the size of a credit card, hold 100MB of data, which is roughly equivalent to 40,000 pages. Special readers are used to input the data from the card into the computer system. A less-sophisticated version of the optical card is found on the magnetic strip on the backside of charge cards. The strip includes information such as the cardholder's name and account number. To input the information into the system, the user simply moves the card through a special card reader.

Video Capture Card. One of the newest input (and output) technologies is the **video capture card** to which a Web-based camera can be attached. This technology facilitates low-resolution videoconferencing through the Internet. Video capture cards also facilitate the input of "data" from TV broadcasts, taped video played on a VCR, and live video from camcorders.

Summary. While some of the input media and devices discussed in this section are used only for data input purposes, others are used also for output purposes, while still others are used for input, storage, and output. Several other multipurpose media and devices are identified in the sections that follow.

Storage

What is RAM?

There are two types of computer **storage** components: primary and secondary.

RAM (random-access memory) is a temporary type of primary storage that the computer uses as it performs specific functions. Once the computer no longer needs the information temporarily stored in RAM (both data and computer instructions), that information "evaporates" to make room for subsequently needed information. During a processing operation, and depending on the capacity of the computer's RAM, the information may move in and out of RAM several times. Because RAM is volatile, its contents disappear when the computer loses power. The majority of personal computers sold today have a minimum of 128MB of RAM.

In personal computers, internal storage is facilitated by means of solid-state **integrated circuits,** also known as *chips*. As many as 7.5 million transistors are etched into one silicon chip, which is approximately one-half of an inch in size. These chips are mounted on the computer's mother board, which contains a number of chips designed to perform specific functions.

The following terms are associated with the internal memory of personal computers:

RAM (random-access memory): Refers to memory used to store data or instructions. The user can alter the data or instructions held in RAM.

ROM (read-only memory): Refers to memory in which permanently encoded data or instructions are stored. The user cannot alter the contents of ROM.

Certain types of hybrid, erasable ROM are now available:

EROM (erasable read-only memory): Can be erased using ultraviolet light.

PROM (programmable read-only memory): Can be programmed with a special device commonly called a ROM programmer.

EPROM (erasable, programmable read-only memory): Can be erased and programmed with special devices.

Cache memory, also found in personal computers, is used to increase the movement of work through the computer. It serves as a high-speed holding area for the program instructions and the data that are being processed. When compared with RAM, cache memory is considerably more expensive.

Secondary storage is permanent storage. A number of secondary storage devices are used, including a number of those also used for input processes that were discussed in the previous section. Among the most common of these secondary storage devices are the hard disk drive (internal), floppy disk (external), and CD-ROM/DVD (external).

How is binary code used?

Before data that humans are capable of reading can be processed by the computer, they have to be converted into an appropriate coded format. Thus, once these data (either primary or secondary) are stored in the computer, they appear as **binary code,** which uses 0s and 1s to represent each letter, number, and symbol. To illustrate, the number 9 is converted to a combination of 0 and 1 codes, as are the letter *C* and the comma symbol.

Binary counting occurs in a right-to-left direction, starting with a 1, and each position to the left of 1 doubles in value. In a right-to-left direction, the following represents binary counting:

128, 64, 32, 16, 8, 4, 2, 1

Computer components operate with their electric switches continually closing (0) and opening (1). Electric pulses are either absent (0) or present (1). Microcircuits are either not conducting (0) or conducting (1). The code of 1 is used to represent a *yes* or *on* position, while a 0 is used to represent a *no* or *off* position. The number 13 is represented by a binary code of 001101; 15, by 001111; 19, by 010011; and so on. Figure 18–12 illustrates the binary codes for numbers 1 through 10 and letters *A* through *Z*.

Arithmetic/Logic Unit

What is the function of the arithmetic-logic unit?

The **arithmetic/logic unit,** another of the components of the CPU, is capable of performing addition, subtraction, multiplication, and division operations. The ALU is also capable of comparing the size of data. During processing operations, data are transferred upon command from storage to the ALU where they are manipulated and returned to storage. During one processing operation, data may be transferred back and forth several times between the ALU and storage.

Data that are transferred from storage to the ALU are held during manipulation in either accumulator or storage registers. For example, if the computer is being used to calculate payroll, the number of hours worked is transferred to a register known as the *accumulator*. The hourly rate of pay is also transferred to a storage register. At this point, the amount in the accumulator (hours worked) and the amount in the storage register (hourly wage) are transferred to the adder, which multiplies the hours by the wage rate to determine the amount of gross wages. This figure is then transferred back to the accumulator, where it is held until needed again. Eventually, this figure will have to be transferred back to the adder, where the amount of deductions is subtracted from gross wages. The amount of net wages is stored until the output operation is performed. The adder is capable of performing all four arithmetic operations.

Control Unit

What is the function of the control unit?

The **control** unit, which is another of the components of the CPU, performs three main functions: selection, interpretation, and execution of the program instructions. Specifically, the control unit:

Figure 18-12 Binary codes for numerical and alphabetical characters

Decimal	Binary					
	32	16	8	4	2	1
1	0	0	0	0	0	1
2	0	0	0	0	1	0
3 (2 + 1)	0	0	0	0	1	1
4	0	0	0	1	0	0
5 (4 + 1)	0	0	0	1	0	1
6 (4 + 2)	0	0	0	1	1	0
7 (4 + 2 + 1)	0	0	0	1	1	1
8	0	0	1	0	0	0
9 (8 + 1)	0	0	1	0	0	1
0 (8 + 2)	0	0	1	0	1	0

A	11 0001
B	11 0010
C	11 0011
D	11 0100
E	11 0101
F	11 0110
G	11 0111
H	11 1000
I	11 1001
J	10 0001
K	10 0010
L	10 0011
M	10 0100
N	10 0101
O	10 0110
P	10 0111
Q	10 1000
R	10 1001
S	01 0010
T	01 0011
U	01 0100
V	01 0101
W	01 0110
X	01 0111
Y	01 1000
Z	01 1001

1. Instructs input devices to read data into storage.
2. Locates data held in storage and transfers them to memory.
3. Instructs the arithmetic/logic unit to perform certain operations on the data.
4. Informs the arithmetic/logic unit of the location of data stored in memory.
5. Informs the output devices which information is to be printed or transferred to some other medium where it will be stored.

Output

Many of the input media and devices are also used for **output.** Those media and devices with dual input and output functions that were discussed in the "Input" section of this chapter are not discussed again in this section. Rather, they are simply listed, and the discussion in this section is limited to those devices that perform only output functions.

Following are the media and devices capable of performing both input and output functions:

Media

Magnetic tape

Magnetic hard disks

Floppy disks

Optical laser disks

Optical cards

Computer output laser disks (C.O.L.D.)

Devices

Keyboard terminals

Monitors

Point-of-sale terminals

Audio communication devices

The discussion of output devices in this section includes impact printers, nonimpact printers, printer-plotters, computer output microfilm (COM), computer output laser disk (C.O.L.D.), and audio response output.

Impact Printers. The **impact printer** is a commonly used output device. After the data have been processed in the CPU, an impact printer is used to prepare a hard (paper) copy of the results. In comparison to some of the other types of output devices, the impact printer is relatively slow, although some of the newer printers are now capable of printing up to 3,000 lines of 132 characters per minute. The impact printer functions by pressing a typebar against a ribbon that comes in contact with paper. The impact printing process, although much faster, is similar to the typewriting process. Dot matrix printers are among the most common type of impact printing device used today.

Nonimpact Printers. **Nonimpact printers,** which function without typebars, are much faster than impact printers. The faster nonimpact printers are capable of printing at rates in excess of 60 pages per minute, and mainframe page printers are capable of printing approximately 500 pages per minute. Among the common types of nonimpact printers are ink-jet printers and laser printers.

Two types of ink-jet printers are found: those using squirts of ink and those using wax that changes from a solid state to a liquid state and back to a solid state on the paper during the printing process. Printers that use liquid ink in the printing process come equipped with small jets through which squirts of ink are forced.

Another type of nonimpact printer—the laser printer—uses a dry toner in the printing process. Of the two, laser printers are now used more often in businesses than ink-jet printers. In the home office market, however, ink-jet printers are more common than laser printers. Figure 18–13 illustrates a laser printer.

Color printing is now available with both laser and ink-jet printers. Color ink-jet printers are much more economical to purchase than color laser printers. The primary advantage of using color in the printing process is the impact it creates on the reader.

A disadvantage of using nonimpact printing devices is their inability to make multiple copies of the same page, which is possible with dot-matrix print-

What is a potential disadvantage of nonimpact printers?

Figure 18–13 Laser
printer. Courtesy: Hewlett-
Packard Company.
Reprinted with permission.

ers. And the shape of characters formed on ink-jet printers occasionally lack
uniformity, although the quality of work produced by ink-jet printers has improved dramatically over the years.

Printer-Plotters. Used primarily to prepare graphic illustrations, such as
scientific and engineering drawings, **printer-plotters** are also capable of printing characters. This type of equipment, which is quite expensive, is valuable to
a growing segment of the data processing market.

Computer Output Microfilm. When **computer output microfilm (COM)**
is used, output is in the form of microfilm rather than paper. Two methods of
preparing COM are available. One method uses a magnetic medium, such as
magnetic tape, on which output data are recorded. The magnetic medium is
processed through equipment that decodes the data and prepares the COM. The
other method uses a microfilm recorder that contains a cathode ray tube similar
to the screen found on monitors. As data are processed through the CPU, the
characters are displayed on the CRT and are subsequently photographed by a microfilm camera. Comparatively, COM prepares output much faster than printers.

What is COM?

Audio Response. Used as a type of computer output, **audio response** involves translating computer output into spoken language. Among the common
applications are equipment maintenance or diagnostic instructions or directives, telephone number changes, pay telephone charges, time and temperature
readings, proofreading of numbers in spreadsheets, and so forth.

In some audio-response systems, all possible messages are prerecorded,
and the computer selects the one that is appropriate for the given situation. In
other instances, such as when reporting telephone number changes, the computer assembles each message as the need arises.

Computer Output Laser Disk. To overcome some of the storage constraints of computer output microfim (COM), organizations are using **computer
output laser disk (C.O.L.D.)** as a storage medium. While a significant amount
of information can be stored on the laser disk, perhaps the most significant advantage is that the disk can be put onto a server, making its contents available to
anyone who can access the server. Compared with COM, which can be accessed
by only one person at any given time, C.O.L.D. is much more versatile.

What is C.O.L.D.?

COMPUTER INSTRUCTIONS

Up to this point, the content discussed in this chapter has pertained to **hardware**—the physical devices, machines, and equipment found in computer installations. **Software,** which is needed to operate the hardware, refers to the application programs and the systems programs.

The first step in developing a computer program is to define the problem. To do this, the alternatives for preparing a solution to the problem have to be determined. Identifying the input data needed to solve the problem as well as determining the appropriate ways for processing data are both considered in preparing the solution.

The second step in developing a computer program involves preparing a flowchart, such as the one illustrated in Figure 18–14. Flowcharts, which are also known as *decision tables,* are used to outline what has to be done with the data to obtain the desired output. The information on the flowchart is then usually converted into instructions the computer is capable of understanding.

Although many programs use words that have meaning to people, these programs have to be translated into instructions the computer is capable of understanding. This is accomplished through a translation process.

Five different types of programming languages have been developed: symbolic languages, procedure-oriented languages, problem-solving languages, fourth-generation languages, and visual languages. Each type has played an important role in electronic data processing.

When a **symbolic language** is used, the translation of the **source program** into an **object program** is performed by a third program known as an **assembler.** When either a **procedure-oriented language** or a **problem-oriented language** is used, a **compiler** translates the source program into an object program.

The following outlines the steps involved in reading a program into the computer and the subsequent processing of the data:

What steps are involved in developing computer programs?

1. The compiler program is read into the CPU. The compiler, which may be recorded on such a medium as the computer's hard disk drive, is usually supplied by the computer manufacturer.

2. The source program, which is recorded on an input medium, is read into the CPU.

3. The compiler program translates the source program into an object program, which is subsequently recorded on an output medium or device (tapes and disks, for example).

4. The object program is read into the CPU.

5. Using one of the input media, the data to be processed are read into the CPU.

6. The data are processed according to the object program's instructions and are stored until the control unit directs an output device to record the processed data.

What are examples of symbolic languages?

Symbolic languages, which resemble machine instructions, use mnemonic codes to identify various operations. Examples of symbolic languages are AUTOCODER and SPS (Symbolic Programming System).

Procedure-oriented languages involve descriptions of a set of procedures to be used in solving the problem. Some examples are BASIC (Beginner's All-purpose Symbolic Instruction Code); COBOL (Common Business-Oriented Language); FORTRAN (Formula Translation); and PL/1 (Programming Language 1).

Problem-oriented languages, on the other hand, describe the nature of the problem. The language used in the program is similar to the language of the

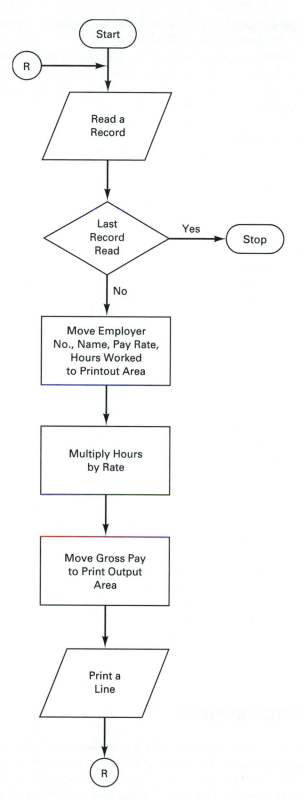

Figure 18–14 Flow process chart. Courtesy: Methods Research Corp., Ocean Township, NJ 07712.

Start

Read a Record

Last Record Read — Yes → Stop

No

Move Employer No., Name, Pay Rate, Hours Worked to Printout Area

Multiply Hours by Rate

Move Gross Pay to Print Output Area

Print a Line

R

problem that is to be solved. An example of a problem-oriented language is RPG (Report Program Generator).

What are the characteristics of fourth-generation languages?

Developed in the late 1970s and early 1980s, **fourth-generation languages** were developed to overcome some of the problems inherent in the procedure-oriented languages. A prime characteristic of fourth-generation languages is that they allow the user to focus on what is to be accomplished rather than on how it is to be accomplished, which is a trait of the earlier programming languages. Another characteristic of fourth-generation languages is their design for specific applications, such as spreadsheets, graphic presentations, and financial modeling. Some examples of fourth-generation languages are Focus, Ramis II, Microsoft Chart, Encore, and System W.

Visual languages are another type of programming language. These languages use visual programming, which replaces text-based instructions with symbolic icons that represent common programming functions. Visual Basic is a popular visual programming language.

Although a detailed discussion of programming languages is beyond the scope of this book, a short discussion of COBOL is presented to aid the reader's understanding of computer processes.

COBOL was designed primarily for the processing of business data and is now a widely used programming language. Rather than using codes or symbols to represent processing functions, COBOL uses English words. Thus, a source program written in COBOL will contain such words as ADD, SUBTRACT, CALL, and FILE. A compiler is then used to translate the source program into the object program, enabling the computer to understand the instructions contained in the program.

A COBOL program contains four divisions: identification, environment, data, and procedure. The identification section of a program written in COBOL typically includes the following types of information: the name of the program, the author of the program, the date on which the program was written, and the date on which the program was compiled.

The environmental division is used to identify for the compiler the types of equipment available for compiling the source program and for processing the object program. The computer doing the translating may or may not be the same one used to run the object program. The environment division also describes the input/output devices that are to be used in the processing of data.

The data division describes the files from which the program is to retrieve the data that are to be processed. This division also identifies the characteristics and format of the data to be processed.

The procedure division is the location of the actual programming of the problem. This is the part of the program that appears in the flowchart prepared earlier.

DISTRIBUTED DATA PROCESSING

What is distributed data processing?

An increasing number of organizations are using **distributed data processing,** a concept that began evolving in the early to mid-1970s. Distributed data processing is a network comprised of several to thousands of personal computers. Each personal computer has the ability to process data independently at the user site as well as the ability to communicate with the other computers. The concept enables computer power to be placed where it is most often needed—at the user site.

Distributed data processing is actually a third-generation data processing system (not to be confused with equipment generations). The first generation involved a totally decentralized data processing system, often using now-obsolete accounting machines. New computer equipment developments provided the impetus for the second generation, which generally involved large centralized computer systems. The third generation, which has become very popular, got its impetus from the development of the personal computer. Fourth-generation data processing systems will make extensive use of expert systems.

Essentially, the design of data processing systems has now gone full circle, starting with decentralization and returning to decentralization. Although both the first- and third-generation systems are decentralized, many differences between the two systems exist, especially in terms of equipment, operations, applications, functions, and characteristics.

The equipment used in the second-generation systems—powerful, fast, expensive, and often massive—necessitated centralized operations. In many organizations, the structure of the centralized operations makes the development of management information systems (MISs) a logical process. A MIS is advantageous from the standpoint of providing an enormous database that managers throughout the organization find useful in their decision-making efforts.

How do third-generation systems differ from second-generation systems?

The equipment found in third-generation systems better meets the needs of some organizations than second-generation systems. Second-generation systems are often unable to meet organizations' needs because (1) the system reaches an ultimate size beyond which it cannot be further expanded, (2) all system users must conform to the parameters of the system, (3) they are more costly than third-generation systems, and (4) they may not be able to provide managers with the timely information they need to facilitate their decision making.

What reasons exist for implementing distributed data processing?

Four strong cases for implementing distributed data processing are: (1) processing control is returned to the user; (2) in contrast to a large centralized computer facility, the use of personal computers is more economical; (3) the user department can design processing operations that meet its specific needs; and (4) by installing processing equipment at the user site, data do not first have to be transmitted to another location.

Organizations that use distributed data processing will not necessarily have only personal computers. In fact, most distributed data processing systems also use mainframe equipment. The four types of distributed data processing systems are: (1) personal computers that communicate with mainframe equipment; (2) personal computers that communicate with other personal computers; (3) personal computers that function in an audit-entry capacity; and (4) personal computers that function in a stand-alone capacity.

When personal computers are used to communicate with a mainframe centralized computer, they more often than not function as satellites added to the central system. Perhaps the central system has expanded to the point where adding more equipment to the mainframe is impractical. The personal computers process data at the user site as well as interact with the central computer system. In many cases, after personal computers process the data at the user site, they input summary data into the central system.

Systems in which personal computers communicate with other personal computers are generally comprised of only personal computers. Because a mainframe does not exist in most cases, one of the personal computers functions as the network controller. The organization's database may be maintained in three ways: by one personal computer, by each personal computer having its own database, or by each personal computer controlling a part of the database, with all personal computers having access to it.

Typically, when personal computers function in an audit-entry capacity, they are used to enter data into the organization's data system. They are also often used to verify the data in an off-line manner. Used in this way, personal computers provide economical processing of data as well as a fast and efficient means of data entry.

Personal computers that are used in a stand-alone capacity process data independently of all other computer equipment. They are not able to communicate with other devices, nor are they used to input data into a centralized database as they are sometimes used in other types of distributed data processing systems.

The use of distributed data processing results in several distinct advantages:

What are the advantages of distributed data processing?

1. Distributed data processing gives the user department control over the processing of data. Processing data at the point where the results are used is logical. Also, when user departments are made responsible for data processing, more attention is likely to be given operating efficiency and cost-benefit ratios.

2. Distributed data processing is likely to result in reduced data processing costs. Over the long run, the unit cost per computation is likely to be less than comparable costs incurred when using large centralized facilities. In addition, communication costs involved in computer operations are lower because data will be processed "on site" rather than being transmitted to a centralized facility for processing.

3. Distributed data processing systems can be easily expanded or contracted to meet changing user needs. Whereas large-scale centralized operations are not easily modified to accommodate changing user needs, a distinct advantage of personal computer systems is the ease with which they are modified. The modular nature of personal computers is a characteristic generally not found in a large-scale system.

4. User departments are not at the "mercy" of a centralized computer facility. In centralized operations, jobs tend to be processed on a priority basis. When user departments have access to their own personal computers, data can often be processed more quickly.

5. Decentralized data processing systems are less vulnerable. In contrast to centralized systems that affect the entire organization when they are inoperable, a malfunctioning personal computer will not have a serious impact on the organization's ability to process data.

The use of distributed data processing in organizations that have a centralized computer facility transfers a considerable amount of responsibility to the user, including data entry, input/output control, and processing, maintenance, and programming. Centralized operations retain technical support and control over hardware, software, databases, and communications. The most successful distributed data processing systems consist of both centralized and decentralized responsibility.

MANAGING COMPUTER PROBLEMS

A number of problems affect the operation of computers. The impact of these problems can be minimized by using appropriate management. Among the most bothersome problems are electrical power problems and computer viruses.

Computer Power Problems

Electrical power problems can have a devastating effect on computers, especially if the power problems cause a total computer crash, resulting in the loss of a significant amount of data/information. Computer equipment requires power that fits rather rigid specifications. When the power fails to conform with these specifications, equipment, software, and data/information can experience varying degrees of damage.

Among the types of power problems are the following:

What types of power problems plague computers?

1. *Sags:* A short-term significant decrease in voltage, which results in loss of data/information, creates software glitches, and causes keyboard lockup.
2. *Brownouts:* A longer term significant decrease in voltage, which will generally result in total computer failure.
3. *Oscillations:* The superimposing of high-frequency noise on the electrical waveform, which results in equipment damage, loss of data/information, and glitches in the software.
4. *Surges:* A short-term increase in voltage, exceeding the maximum specification, which causes overheating of equipment, sometimes resulting in equipment failure.
5. *Spikes:* A short-time significant increase in voltage, which can cause massive damage to the equipment.

To avoid the excessive voltage problems, protection devices are useful. These devices simply prevent excessive voltage from reaching the equipment.

Power failure is avoided by installing standby power units, which generate power to replace what is lost or reduced. Most of these units contain battery backup that protects the system until the generator is activated.

When installing a system designed to prevent computer power problems, working with an electrical consultant is recommended. The specialization these individuals have enables the organization to install a system tailored to its specific needs.

The use of mirroring software enables an organization to restore the data on a hard drive should the drive crash because of power failure or mechanical failure. This software provides real-time data replication on another server so that when a crash occurs, the other server takes over as though nothing had happened. Mirroring software has enabled many organizations to continue to function with virtually no computer downtime when a drive crashes.

Computer Viruses

Perhaps more annoying to computer users than power problems—especially to personal computer users—are **computer viruses.** These viruses can destroy massive amounts of data/information in a desktop unit or disrupt an entire network operation.

Three broad categories of viruses exist: file infectors, boot sector viruses, and multipartite viruses. File infectors attach to or replace executable programs. Programs become infected when they are executed with a virus that is residing in the computer's memory or when the programs are opened. Boot sector viruses, on the other hand, are restricted to magnetic media, such as floppy disks and hard drives. When an infected boot sector program is read on the floppy disk or on the hard drive, the virus enters the computer's memory and subsequently infects sectors other than the boot sector of the hard drive. Multipartite viruses infect both boot sectors and files on floppy disks or on a hard drive.

Following what suggestions helps one avoid problems with computer viruses?

Suggestions for dealing with viruses include the following:

1. Avoid using software from unreliable sources.
2. Avoid exchanging floppy disks between computers.
3. Avoid letting others use your computer, especially if they want to use their own software.
4. Back up the data frequently.
5. Back up new software immediately—and then use only the back up copy.
6. Stop using the computer immediately if abnormal operations begin to occur.
7. Use a virus detection/eradication software package.
8. Be especially careful of software downloaded from the Internet.
9. Be alert to the fact that computer viruses are often transmitted by e-mail messages.

Once viruses become present in a computer system, they can multiply rapidly, sometimes affecting the entire system. In dealing with computer viruses, a proactive posture is much preferred to a reactive one.

IMPLICATIONS FOR THE ADMINISTRATIVE OFFICE MANAGER

Increasingly, administrative office management functions are becoming computer oriented. Miniaturized computer chips, which are found in much of the new equipment, expand the computer's capability and increases its power. And most of the new functional operating systems for which the administrative office manager is responsible are now computer driven.

A basic understanding of computer technology is crucial for administrative office managers. They also need a basic understanding of the role of electronic data processing in the various systems that impact on the office function. Administrative office managers need this background so they can make intelligent decisions about various aspects of the areas for which they are responsible.

Although the basic electronic data processing concept remains relatively unchanged since its origination, important changes have taken place in equipment capability, power, and cost and in the nature of the systems that use electronic data processing. As automated office systems mature, even more changes will take place in the way electronic data processing is used in the office function.

REVIEW QUESTIONS

1. What are the differences between artificial intelligence and expert systems?
2. What are the characteristics of the current generation of electronic computers?
3. How do digital computers differ from analog computers?
4. What are the various size classifications of computers?
5. How do OCR and MICR differ as input media?
6. What is a point-of-sale terminal?
7. What functions does the arithmetic/logic unit perform?
8. How do source programs and object programs differ?
9. What are the four main divisions of a COBOL program, and what is contained in each?

10. Why is distributed data processing desirable?

11. How can the impact of computer viruses be minimized?

DISCUSSION QUESTIONS

1. You work in a small office that presently uses no computer equipment. A number of your job tasks (typing correspondence, keeping financial records, and so forth) could be performed more efficiently, however, using a personal computer instead of the manual processes you presently use. When you recently talked with the owner of the company about the purchase of a personal computer, he said, "Convince me you need one, and I will think about it." Outline the sales pitch you plan to use in persuading the manager to purchase a personal computer.

2. You are a sales representative in a large company that manufactures industrial carpeting. To place orders you receive from the customers in your territory, you simply call your company's toll-free number. Thus, you can tell the purchaser immediately the in-stock status of the carpeting being ordered as well as anticipated delivery dates. Sometimes you are on hold for several minutes until the order dispatcher is available to talk to you. In other cases, you have to dial the toll-free number several times before you can "get through." You proposed to management that each sales representative be given a laptop computer capable of communicating directly with the company's computer. Thus, when an order is placed, the sales representative would use the laptop computer to obtain the necessary information as well as use the computer to place the order. You believe this would save considerable time. What advantages and disadvantages are likely to result if the decision is made to switch from the old procedure to the proposed procedure?

3. The company in which you work has a rather antiquated computer system. Data input is done with punched cards. The current president is rather traditional and believes that equipment should not be replaced until it wears out—regardless of how inefficient it may be. He finally agreed to consider updating the computer system's data input, storage, and output system to magnetic tape. What advantages will the magnetic tape result in when compared with the punched cards? What disadvantages will the magnetic tape have when compared with a magnetic hard disk system?

STUDENT PROJECTS AND ACTIVITIES

1. Talk with the director or manager of a large-scale computer operation. What are this individual's common job responsibilities?

2. Obtain the promotional brochures for two competing personal computers. In what ways are the two devices similar to one another? Different from one another?

3. Going Online: Using the Internet, conduct an online search based on one of the concepts presented in this chapter or based on one of the chapter terms. Identify four or five things you learned from the material that you did not know prior to your online search.

Minicase

The Durham Company is a large supplier of automobile parts. When the traveling sales representatives receive an order from a customer, they telephone it to the appropriate regional warehouse. Frequently, items in the warehouse have an out-of-stock status. A minimum of two days passes before the sales representative learns that an item is temporarily out of stock. By that time, several other customers may have ordered the same out-of-stock items. Because the company is greatly concerned about its customer relations, several managers believe that if the customers were to know the availability status of a given item immediately, the negative impact would be less than when the customer finds out two days later that the item is not available. Therefore, the company desires to provide its representatives with a device that will enable them to communicate directly with the company's computer when placing orders and when determining inventory levels.

1. What input device do you recommend?
2. How is the device used?

Case

Jack Hemingway, president of Hemingway Company, recently appointed a group of employees to serve on a computer systems study committee. The company, which manufactures electrical components for automobiles, is interested in upgrading its present computer facilities because they are no longer adequate. The system has been expanded to capacity, primarily because of the organization's recent rapid growth and because of its desire to make greater use of operating systems.

You, the administrative office manager, have been appointed to serve on the computer systems study committee. Your specific responsibilities involve investigating the various types of input media that are presently available for input and storage of data.

1. What types of magnetic media might be appropriate?
2. What are the advantages and disadvantages of the media that might be appropriately used?
3. Of the media that are appropriate, which is your preference? Why?

$\mathscr{C}$hapter 19

TELECOMMUNICATIONS TECHNOLOGY

$\mathscr{C}$hapter $\mathscr{A}$ims

After studying this chapter, you should be able to design an effective telecommunications system for an organization.

$\mathscr{C}$hapter $\mathscr{O}$utline

The Nature of Telecommunications
    Communication Channels
    Transmission Modes
    Networks
    Transmission Speeds
    Duplexing
    Modems
Telephone Systems
    Types of Telephone Systems
    Alternative Telephone Services
    Grade of Service
    Telephone Features and Options
    Other Devices Using Telephone Lines
Call Processing
    Telephone Interconnect Equipment and Services
Intraorganizational Communication Devices
    Telewriter
    Intrafax
    Closed-circuit Television
    Paging Systems
Management of Telecommunication Services
Controlling Telecommunications Costs
Telecommuting and Telecommunications
The Internet
    History of the Internet
    Internet Characteristics
    Internet Services
Implications for the Administrative Office Manager

$\mathscr{C}$hapter $\mathscr{T}$erms

800 service
Analog mode
Asymmetric Digital Subscriber Line (ADSL)
Bandwidth
Baud
Broadband channels
Bus network
Call processing
Cellular phone technology
Centrex
Closed-circuit television
Coaxial cable
Communication channels
Communication networks
Dial-up access
Digital mode
Duplexing
Electronic mail
Facsimile (fax) devices
Fax broadcast
Fax on demand
Fiber optics
FTP (file transfer protocol)
Grade of service
HTML (hypertext markup language)
Hyperlinks
Hypertext
Interconnect

Interconnectivity
Internet
Internet fax
Internet Relay Chat (IRC)
Internet Service Provider (ISP)
Internet telephone
Intrafax
Integrated Services Digital Network (ISDN)
Key system telephones
Listserv
Local area networks (LAN)
Metropolitan area networks (MAN)
Microwaves
Modem
PABX
Paging systems
PBX
PC conferencing
Picturephone

Ring network
Satellites
Star network
Telecommunications
Telecommuting
Teleconferencing
Telnet
Telewriter
Twisted-pair wiring
URL (uniform resource locator)
Usenet
Videoconferencing
Voice messaging
Whiteboard
Wide area networks (WAN)
Wideband Data Service
Wireless radio frequencies
World Wide Web

*M*any of the new developments affecting administrative office management are possible because of the **interconnectivity** of equipment used by employees in performing their job functions and responsibilities. This interconnectivity makes it possible for employees to complete many of their job tasks just as easily and effectively when they are a thousand miles from their office as when they are on the premises. The convergence of computing and telecommunications technology is rapidly expanding the capabilities of both computers and telephones. The Telecommunications Act of 1996 is playing an important role in the emerging telecommunications technology, resulting in the availability of more technology with increased accessibility and at a lower cost.

Telecommunications—the transmission of information using telephone technology—is largely responsible for making equipment interconnectivity possible. In many organizations, especially smaller ones, the administrative office manager is often responsible for determining the need for and function of telecommunications equipment and services. In larger organizations, this function may be performed by the manager of telecommunications services. Of the various areas comprising the administrative office management field, telecommunications is now one of the most technical.

THE NATURE OF TELECOMMUNICATIONS

Telecommunications involves the transmission of voice, data, and images from one location to another. Before computers were readily available, telecommunications primarily involved voice communication over telephone lines. However, during the last several years, telecommunications has expanded to include additional channels and formats, truly making it a multimedia system. This section provides a discussion of several topics related to telecommunications, including communication channels, transmission modes, networking, transmission speeds, duplexing, and modems.

Communication Channels

For what are communication channels used?

The primary function of **communication channels** is to facilitate the transmission of voice, data, or images to computers or other remotely located peripheral equipment. Among the communication channels are twisted-pair wire, coaxial cable, microwaves, satellites, fiber optics, and wireless radio frequencies. If the telecommunications potential is to be maximized, special consideration has to be given to selecting an appropriate channel for specific situations. The various channels are not all equally suited for all situations.

Twisted-Pair Wire. The oldest of the communication channels is **twisted-pair wiring.** It uses two insulated copper wires twisted around one another, primarily to prevent noise interference from electrical circuits. Twisted-pair wiring is used for voice and data communication over standard-grade telephone lines.

Static on standard-grade lines is sometimes excessive, which may result in the transmission of data errors. When this occurs, a special conditioned line may need to be leased to reduce transmission errors and increase data transmission rates. Today, many organizations lease dedicated lines, which provide them with exclusive, full-time use of these lines.

The use of twisted-pair wire requires a physical connection between the sender and receiver. Compared with microwave, satellite channels, and wireless radio frequencies that do not require a physical connection, this requirement is seen by some as a disadvantage.

Coaxial Cable. Composed of either copper or aluminum wires, **coaxial cable** is another of the communication channels. The outer surface of coaxial cable is typically a metallic sheathing covered with a plastic coating that protects the data-transmission wires from electrical interference. A coaxial cable measuring three inches in diameter may contain as many as one hundred different wires. Large-diameter coaxial cable is used for underwater intercontinental communication systems.

Small-diameter coaxial cable is often used in local area networks, which are discussed in the "Transmission Modes" section of this chapter. The small-sized cable is also used widely in cable television systems.

Microwaves. While twisted-pair wiring and coaxial cable require a physical connection, microwave technology does not. Transmitted as high-frequency radio waves, **microwaves** travel from the sending location to the receiving location using a series of antennas located not more than 30 miles from one another. Microwave technology is used extensively in sections of the country where the antennas, which are on tall towers, have been installed.

Because microwaves travel in a straight-line path, the sending and receiving antennas have to be located in a precise line of sight. Even a small variance can cause an interruption of service or interference.

Satellites. Located approximately 22,300 miles above the earth's surface are a number of earth-orbiting **satellites** used to transmit voice, data, and image signals. These satellites are geosynchronous, meaning that they travel at the same orbital speed as the earth. Therefore, they are always positioned above the same earth location. Satellite technology is similar to microwave technology in that it is also a line-of-sight medium. Satellite transmission is much faster and less expensive than twisted-pair wire and coaxial cable technologies.

Satellites that support organizational telecommunications efforts are all privately owned by such carrier companies as AT&T, COMSAT, RCA, and Western Union. Users of the satellite pay a fee. In the future, an increasing number of businesses will have their own satellites. Some organizations are likely to enter into a cooperative arrangement with a handful of other businesses in the joint ownership of a satellite.

For what type of communication process is twisted-pair wiring typically used?

What are the characteristics of microwave technology?

What are the characteristics of satellite technology?

With satellite technology, a signal is transmitted from an earth station to the satellite, from which the signal is transmitted back to another earth station. The signal may return directly to the recipient's location, or it may have to travel through another channel (such as microwave) before it reaches the recipient's location.

Fiber Optics. One of the newest of the communication channels is **fiber optics,** a technology that uses hair-sized glass fibers to transmit high-frequency laser (light) pulses. Although the signal is transmitted as a beam of light, the nature of fiber optics allows the beam to round corners. Repeaters are used to strengthen signals transmitted over distances of more than fifty miles.

When compared with other communication technologies, fiber optics enjoys the following advantages: (1) it is safer to use in some installations because it involves the transmission of light rather than electrical current; (2) it is not subject to electromagnetic or radio frequency interference; (3) it provides greater security for the transmission of data because fiber optics cannot be "bugged"; and (4) the fiber optics cable is lightweight and compact. A cable comprised of approximately 150 fibers—measuring an inch in diameter and weighing less than six ounces per foot—can carry nearly 100,000 simultaneous two-way phone conversations. Fiber optics cables carry ten times as many signals as a three-inch coaxial cable and a thousand times as many signals as a microwave system.

What are the characteristics of fiber optics technology?

Wireless Radio Frequencies. Technology using **wireless radio frequencies** transmits data and/or telephone signals through the air. An antenna attached to the device (whether it be a telephone, a local area network, or a pen-based handwriting recognition device) enables it to send and receive signals.

Employees who are typically away from their desks during the workday find a cellular phone that uses radio frequencies to be a very convenient device. These calls are assessed at the usual cellular call charge. However, once the employee enters the building, the convertible phone automatically transforms into a wireless PBX-system-based device that enables any caller to get in phone contact with the employee any time the employee has the phone in his or her possession. Calls made/received on the phone within the premises are not subject to the cellular call charge because the phone is simply functioning as a cordless telephone.

Two primary advantages result from the use of wireless radio frequency devices: (1) the ease with which contact between two individuals can be maintained and (2) not having to install wires, cables, or fibers to facilitate telecommunications. Disadvantages are that transmission is (1) not secure, meaning that it can be intercepted by others; and (2) subject to static and other types of interference.

What advantages result from the use of wireless radio frequency devices?

Transmission Modes

Data are technologically communicated in either digital or analog modes. The differences between the two are explained and illustrated here.

Digital. Because most business computers are digital in nature, they transmit data as digital signals. Data are transmitted as discrete pulses of electrical current (approximately five volts) through a communication medium. However, before data can be transmitted, they have to be converted into binary code. This means that each alphabetic character, number, and symbol is converted to a series of 1s or 0s capable of being understood by the computer. A more detailed discussion of binary code is found in Chapter 18. A binary code of 1 is transmitted as an electrical pulse, while a binary code of 0 is transmitted as the absence of a pulse.

How do digital and analog modes differ from one another?

Over longer distances, the use of the **digital mode** for transmission of data has the following disadvantages: (1) the strength of the signals tends to weaken as they are transmitted over distance; (2) the presence of static or noise on the line can affect the accuracy of the data that are transmitted; and (3) the longer the distance that data are transmitted, the greater the power required. These disadvantages are overcome somewhat by using an analog mode, which is the common mode used in telephone systems.

Analog. While the digital mode transmits data as electrical pulses, the **analog mode** transmits data as low- and high-pitched sounds. The binary code of 1 is transmitted as a low-pitched sound, while the 0 is transmitted as a high-pitched sound. This is the means by which the disadvantages of the digital mode are eliminated.

Most significant among the disadvantages of the analog mode is its inability to accept digital signals. This problem is remedied by using a modem at the sending location that converts digital signals into analog signals and reconverts the analog signals into digital signals at the receiving location.

Figure 19–1 illustrates the difference between the digital and analog modes.

Networks

The availability of **communication networks** has accelerated the development of new ways of completing a variety of office tasks. The ability to transmit data and information between two sites provides almost endless opportunities for employees to carry out their job tasks more efficiently and easily than ever before.

What are the three types of networks?

Three types of networks are found: local area networks (commonly called (LANs), metropolitan area networks (MANs), and wide area networks (WANs; also called long-haul networks). While LANs are used to interconnect computers and peripheral equipment located up to a few hundred feet from one another, metropolitan area networks are used to interconnect devices within a restricted geographical area (such as within a large metropolitan area). Wide area networks, on the other hand, are used to interconnect computers and peripheral devices located thousands of miles from one another. Each computer connected to a network must contain a network interface card (NIC) or an adapter card, which facilitates the sending and receiving of data from another computer.

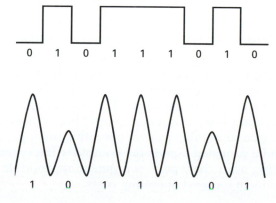

Figure 19-1 Transmission modes

Local Area Networks. The discussion of **local area networks** includes the functions for which LANs are used and the types of LANs that are found. Among the uses of LAN are to

What are the common functions for which local area networks are used?

1. *Expedite communication.* Increasingly, employees in an organization are able to communicate with one another using their personal computer terminals. This communication mode is used as an alternative to face-to-face conversations or telephone calls, both of which create communication difficulties when the receiver is not readily available. The use of a personal computer to communicate with another individual is possible through using electronic mail or electronic messaging, for example. The LAN is used to interconnect the computer devices, thus facilitating their ability to communicate.

2. *Share computer and peripheral devices.* The cost of today's equipment makes desirable the sharing of as many computer and peripheral devices as possible. Not only is shared equipment likely to be used more efficiently, but also it is likely to have more extensive use. Rather than attaching a printer to each personal computer, a LAN can produce the same level of functionalism by connecting a number of personal computers to one printer.

3. *Share computer files.* Increasingly, organizations are storing their data and information electronically. Through the LAN, these stored computer files are available to all authorized users. Electronic filing is discussed more fully in Chapter 21.

4. *Reduce software costs.* The vast majority of software programs are available today for use on file servers (computers with fairly extensive hard disk drive capacity). A LAN makes the connection between the file server and the user, which allows him or her to use the software program. Rather than having to purchase a separate software program for each personal computer, which will be considerably more expensive, a site license can be obtained to "serve" the software to desktop computers, using the LAN.

The three common types of local area networks are star networks, ring networks, and bus networks. The differences between each are considerable. Figure 19–2 illustrates each type of network.

Using coaxial cable to interconnect computer terminals and other peripheral devices with the host computer, the **star network** acts as a switcher for the various functions that are performed. Data files and software are stored in the host computer. The LAN facilitates accessing both stored data/information and software.

What are the characteristics of the star network?

Advantages of the Star Network

1. Data/information as well as software and certain hardware devices are centralized. User sharing of hardware and software is cost effective.

2. Users can be given the type of terminal that best meets their needs. Those whose job responsibilities can be performed on a terminal that does not need to possess its own operating intelligence can generally use what is known as a *dumb terminal*. The operating intelligence of these terminals originates from a host computer. Those whose job responsibilities require a device containing its own operating intelligence (called a *smart terminal*) can be provided a personal computer interconnected to a host computer. Giving users the type of equipment appropriate for the tasks they perform results in reduced operating costs.

Figure 19–2 Types of local area networks

Star

Ring

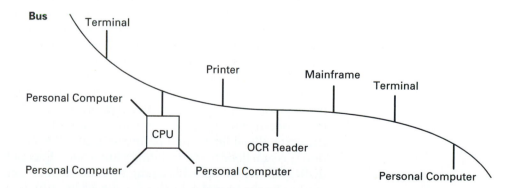

Bus

Disadvantages of the Star Network

1. The devices are generally interconnected by coaxial cable, which means that significant amounts of cabling must be installed in floors, walls, and ceilings. Installing coaxial cable after a building has been constructed is typically quite expensive.

2. If the host computer fails, the devices that depend on the host for their operating intelligence will be inoperable. The devices that possess their own operating intelligence may continue to be operable, although not for tasks that require software or data/information stored in the host computer or on a file server.

What are the characteristics of the ring network?

A **ring network** interconnects a number of devices to a continuous network cable. The various devices attached to the ring are all of equal importance; therefore, the ring network differs significantly from the star network, which uses a host computer. Certain devices in the ring may also have an exclusive interconnection (called a *mesh network*) with one another.

The most significant advantage of the ring network is its reliability. Because this network does not require a host computer, individual computer workstations will continue to be operable even if a problem occurs in the network. The most significant disadvantage of the ring network is the special care that needs to be exercised in coordinating communication so messages do not become garbled because of signal intermixing during their transmission. Communication controllers are used to prevent the garbling.

What are the characteristics of the bus network?

In a **bus network,** computers and peripheral devices are connected to a network cable. The cable is not continuous as it is with the ring network, nor does the bus network depend on a host computer, as the star network does. For these reasons, some consider the bus network to be the most ideal of the three types of networks.

Two advantages of the bus network are: (1) the reduced amount of network cable that is required, especially when compared with the ring network, and (2) its ability to function without a host computer. Both result in cost reductions.

The most significant disadvantage of the bus network results from timing or scheduling the transmittal of data/information through the channel. Mistiming can result in data collision. This problem is eliminated by using a device that assures the availability of a channel before beginning the transmission of data.

Wireless LAN technology is now available. Personal computers can send data to peripheral equipment, such as printers, as far away as 150 feet. Using radio signals that can be transmitted through walls, the connected devices are not limited to a line-of-sight arrangement. One reason to consider the use of a wireless LAN is to overcome the inconvenience of installing cable in locations that lack accessibility. Another advantage of using a wireless LAN is the ease with which peripheral devices can be moved to a new location within the premises. However, wireless systems generally have higher up-front costs and slower operating performance than their wired counterparts.

Critical to the success of a LAN is its current functionality as well as its ability to grow, keeping in mind the ever-present need to be cost effective. Increasingly, organizations that occupy large buildings are using fiber-optic cabling in the vertical and horizontal pathways that connect the data communication station on each floor to the building's hub room. Except for the personal computers dedicated to high-speed imaging or data transmision, Category 5 cable, considered to be the "standard cable," is generally sufficient to connect most personal computers to the fiber-optic cable. Category 5 cable is a cost-effective alternative to the more expensive alternative of connecting with fiber-optics cabling.

Metropolitan Area Networks. Using high-speed fiber-optic lines, **metropolitan area networks** serve a larger geographical area than a LAN but a smaller area than a WAN. Although they are not as common as LANs or WANs, MANs are generally found only in larger metropolitan areas, as the name implies. The entities attached to a MAN generally share some common feature, such as being a government unit, for example. Perhaps all the city, county, and state entities located in a given metropolitan are interconnected by a MAN. Other entities that may be interconnected with MANs are educational facilities (public and private; elementary, secondary, and college) and medical facilities (hospitals, medical centers, doctors' offices, and health-related organizations).

MANs are installed primarily to facilitate the sharing of information among the interconnected entities. Rather than having to request the information on hard copy, the requesting party, with the proper authorization, is able to retrieve a screen image of the desired information from which a paper copy can be prepared if needed.

Wide Area Networks. Organizations typically use a **wide area network** to interconnect computer equipment and peripheral devices at their headquarters with the equipment at remotely located branches. The interconnection facilitates communication between employees and equipment at the two locations. Contrasted with LANs and MANs, WANs typically have more users, and they are more multifunctional because more extensive resources are generally interconnected.

WANs are used for

What are the common functions for which wide area networks are used?

For what are WANs used?

1. *Centralized electronic filing.* Data/information generated at the remote sites that might be of value to individuals at other sites are often transmitted to the headquarters where they are stored in the organization's database. With proper authorization, users at other sites are then able to access and use this information.

2. *Remote data entry.* The use of a WAN allows data to be entered at a remote site but transmitted to a centralized location where they are processed. For example, point-of-sale terminals are often interconnected to a WAN that transmits data to a centralized computer where processing and storage take place. Using this type of system may be considerably less expensive than purchasing a computer for this purpose at each remote site.

3. *Centralized software storage.* Some organizations install the software at the centralized location from which it is transmitted through the WAN each time it is needed at a remote site. This is an alternative to installing an individual copy of the program on one or more computers at each remote site.

4. *Electronic communication.* The WAN is used for electronic communication in much the same way as the LAN. For example, the WAN facilitates computer conferencing (a conference between two individuals in which their computers are used for sending and receiving their "conversation"), electronic mail, electronic messaging, and data/information exchange.

Among the types of communication channels typically used in WANs are conditioned telephone lines, fiber optics, microwaves, and satellites. A common type of WAN is the hierarchical network in which local personal computers and terminals are interconnected with regional midsized computers or a mainframe computer. The regional computers are interconnected with a national mainframe.

Transmission Speeds

An important determinant of how well computer applications function is the speed with which data are transmitted from one location to another. The transmission speed is especially significant when an application has many users, such as in an airline reservation system or with automatic teller machines. As the number of users increases, so must the data transmission speed. Otherwise, the users will have to wait for their response, which diminishes the cost effectiveness and efficiency of the system.

The two important determinants of data transmission speed are baud and bandwidth.

Baud. By definition, **baud** refers to the number of signal changes per second that a communication channel will allow. Common baud rates are now 28,800, 33,600, and 56,000 bits per second. A baud of 33,600, for example, means that 33,600 signal changes occur each second.

What is bandwidth?

Bandwidth. Bandwidth refers to the data transmission capacity of the channel. Generally, the wider the band, the more data it can carry during a specific unit of time.

Generally using coaxial cable, microwaves, satellites, and fiber optics, **broadband channels** are capable of transmitting millions of characters per second. To accomplish these speeds, digital data may have to be converted to and transmitted as analog signals. However, with the installation of digital cable in a growing number of communities (most likely at least initially to support cable television), the data will not have to be converted, which means data are communicated at much faster rates than has been possible in the past. For example, when high-definition television becomes readily available, programming will be received through digital cables that will also provide a fast digital telephone connection simply by providing data dial-tone capability. With dial-tone capability, digital cable becomes available for voice and data transmission. On-demand television programming will also be provided through video dial-tone capability on the digital cable. While coaxial cable that supports cable television is a one-way transmission medium (inbound), digital cable will become a two-way medium (both inbound and outbound).

Competition between cable television providers and telephone companies to serve and to hold on to their customer base has resulted in the phone companies making available new technologies to counter the large bandwidth of digital cable. Increasingly, **Integrated Services Digital Network (ISDN)** and **Asymmetric Digital Subscriber Line (ADSL)** capability are becoming available; both support data and voice transmission at much faster rates than has been possible using traditional telecommunications technology. Both technologies permit simultaneous data and voice transmission on the same line, the equivalent of having two phone lines.

Three types of ISDN services are or will be available:

What three types of ISDN services are or will be available?

1. *Basic rate ISDN*, which is designed primarily for those (homes and small offices) not needing an especially high-speed transmitting or receiving capability. With this level of service, one or two 64Kbps (kilobytes per second) channels are available, in addition to a 16Kbps signaling channel. With two-channel service, data are communicated at 128Kbps until the service also needs to accommodate a voice call. At that time, one channel is used for transmitting/receiving data; the other channel supports voice transmission.

2. *Primary rate ISDN*, found mainly in organizations, requires a T1 line, which operates at a rate of 1.544Mbps. It provides up to twenty-four 64Kbps channels.

3. *Broadband ISDN*, which requires the use of fiber optics, provides a maximum transmission rate of 622Mbps. Its use will primarily be in large organizations that need a high-level transmitting and receiving capability.

ADSL, which, like IDSN, also uses existing copper telephone lines, is capable of transmitting 8Mbps contrasted with the 10Mbps capability of digital cable. However, when contrasted with the current technology available to many users, which transmits at 33Kbps transmission speeds, the ability to transmit at rates of 8Mbps is a huge increase.

While technology is currently available to provide huge broadband capability, its usage is dependent upon the provider's making the necessary installation to support the new technology. Therefore, the organization's ability to access the technology is directly controlled by the providers.

Duplexing

In telecommunications, **duplexing** determines how messages are sent—on a discrete basis or on a simultaneous basis. In a half-duplexing arrangement, data are sent and received between two locations on a discrete basis. Therefore, while the equipment at one location "sends," equipment at the other location "receives." In a full-duplexing arrangement, data can be both sent and received simultaneously. Therefore, "sending" and "receiving" can occur at the same time.

Modems

What is the function of a modem?

Because most business computers are digital and most telephone systems continue to be analog, a **modem** (acronym for modulator-demodulator) is needed. The modem converts digital signals into an analog format so they can be transmitted over phone lines, microwaves, satellites, and so on. At the receiving location, a modem reconfigures the analog signals into a digital format so they can be accepted by a digital computer.

Modem protocols are controlled by the International Telecommunications Union, which has set the most recent modulation protocol (V.90) to communicate at a maximum rate of 56Kbps. An earlier protocol (V.34) allowed a communication rate of 28.8Kpbs. When two modems with unlike modulation protocols are being used, transmission takes place at the rate of the slower modem.

TELEPHONE SYSTEMS

Included in this section is a discussion of the various types of telephone systems as well as alternate telephone services, grades of service, telephone features and options, other related telephonic devices, interconnect, and telegraphy.

Types of Telephone Systems

Each of the types of telephone systems used in organizations—key system, PBX, PABX, and Centrex, has its own special characteristics and uses.

Key System. **Key system telephones,** an inexpensive alternative to PBX, PABX, and Centrex systems, use handsets that are equipped with buttons or keys. The user, therefore, is able to perform a number of functions rather than depending on a receptionist or operator to perform these functions. Key system telephones are becoming much more sophisticated, often possessing a number of the features found in other more expensive systems.

PBX. In a **PBX** (private branch exchange) system, all incoming and outgoing calls go through the switchboard. However, a PBX system does not require the use of an operator for making interoffice calls.

PABX. The **PABX** system, or private automatic branch exchange, also uses a switchboard or console. The operator receives incoming calls and connects the caller with the recipient. With a PABX system, employees dial their own outgoing and interoffice calls. PABX systems are more widely used than either PBX or Centrex systems.

Centrex. The **Centrex** (central exchange) system requires neither a switchboard nor a console for the completion of calls. All employees have their own telephone number. Employees also make their own interoffice calls, typically by dialing the last four or five digits of the telephone number of the individual or department they wish to contact.

What are the characteristics of Centrex telephone systems?

Of the three systems, Centrex is the most private because employees do not share telephone lines with others. It is also possible to obtain an itemized list of call charges for each telephone in the organization. Thus, fewer long-distance nonbusiness telephone calls are likely to be made. In Centrex systems, operators are generally used to provide number information service.

Several types of Centrex equipment are available. With Centrex I equipment, operators are needed to transfer calls. Centrex II does not require an operator to transfer calls, and it enables the user to make three-party calls and place a caller on hold while consulting another person.

Centrex tends to be the most expensive telephone system discussed in this chapter. Some organizations, as a cost-cutting measure, have replaced their Centrex system with a PABX system.

Alternative Telephone Services

Over the years, several alternative telephone services have been developed, including Wideband Data Service and cellular phone systems.

Wideband Data Service. **Wideband Data Service** selects the appropriate band for the type of data or image being transmitted. For example, the slower that words or data are being transmitted through the lines, the narrower the band can be; however, faster transmission rates require wider bands. Rather than leasing a band sufficiently wide to handle the transmission of all types of data, a Wideband Data Service provides several band widths. Thus, the user has access to the appropriate band for a specific type of data. For example, computers that are communicating with one another at rates of 200,000 words per minute need a wider band than equipment transmitting at 100 words per minute. The wider the band, the more costly it is to use. Image transmission typically requires a wider band than data or voice transmission.

What is Wideband Data Service?

Cellular Phone Systems. The advent of **cellular phone technology** makes it possible to use phones from almost any location. As the technology continues to develop, equipment is becoming smaller in size and lighter in weight. The vast majority of cellular phones being sold today use digital rather than analog technology, which improves transmission quality as well as increases the number of services that are available (caller ID, messaging, voice mail, and so forth).

Cellular phone systems use radio transmitters. In the more populated areas of the country, radio transmitters are located in designated service areas (cells) that have a radius of eight to ten miles. At the center of each service area is a transmitter.

When a call is placed on a cellular phone, the signal "informs" the transmitter in the service area that a phone channel is needed. Once the connection is made with the phone channel, the signals are transmitted using conventional telephone lines, microwave technology, and so forth.

When a call is placed from a mobile phone to another mobile phone in the same service area, the transmitter serves as both the transmitter and receiver. If the call is made from a conventional phone to a mobile phone in a distant service area, conventional technology is used between the sending location and the transmitter in the area serving the location of the mobile phone. Once the signals reach the service area, the radio transmitter makes the "connection" between the transmitter and the mobile telephone.

The critical component of cellular phone systems is the radio transmitter. If a transmitter is within eight to ten miles of a call's origin, a cellular phone can be used to make local, long-distance, and even international phone calls.

Cellular technology is developing rapidly to accommodate traveling employees and/or telecommuters. Now available are cellular devices that allow the user to plug a modem, laptop computer, or facsimile (fax) device into a cellular phone. Some providers of cellular service now offer an encryption feature that provides a totally private voice and data transmission. The lack of a secure transmission channel destroys the confidentiality of a phone conversation.

800 Service. Increasingly, organizations are using both inward and outward 800 lines. To the inbound caller, using an 800 line is a toll-free call. The rate paid by the organization for 800 service is based on a variety of factors, each of which needs to be assessed in determining the appropriate configuration for cost-effective 800 service. As the number of 800 service phone numbers reached the maximum number possible, two new companion prefix numbers have been placed into service: 877 and 888.

Grade of Service

What is meant by grade of service?

The number of telephone circuits available is known as **grade of service.** An insufficient grade of service means that the organization does not have an adequate number of trunk lines on its PBX and PABX system to handle the volume of calls it receives. Grade of service is not a concern with Centrex systems. Three or fewer busy signals per one hundred call attempts provide a sufficient grade of service.

Grade of service not only applies to incoming calls, but also to outgoing and interoffice calls. For example, if busy signals are heard often when the outgoing call access (usually 9) is dialed, more outgoing trunk lines may have to be installed. On telephone systems other than Centrex, an insufficient number of links will produce a busy signal when attempting to make interoffice calls.

By attaching to telephone lines special meters that record the number of times busy signals occur during a given period, an organization can assess the adequacy of its grade of service. The ratio of busy signals to completed calls can be calculated to determine grade-of-service adequacy.

Telephone Features and Options

A variety of telephone features and options are now available.

1. *Automatic route selection.* The system automatically selects the best, most economical route for long-distance phone calls.
2. *Automatic station restriction.* The system prohibits making long-distance calls from certain phones.

3. *Automatic identification of outward dialing.* The system identifies the phone extension that was used to make long-distance phone calls.

4. *Call blocking.* This feature makes it possible to "block" incoming calls. The call recipient isn't aware that the call was placed because his or her phone doesn't ring when calls are made from the "blocked" numbers.

5. *Call forwarding.* The system automatically routes external incoming calls and internal calls to other designated on-premises or off-premises phones.

What is call pickup?

6. *Call pickup.* The system permits an individual to receive an incoming call on any phone. The call recipient, after being paged over the PA system, uses any convenient phone to dial the appropriate code, thus being able to access the call.

7. *Call return.* This feature enables the system to redial the last number that called the employee.

8. *Call tracing.* This feature enables the local phone company to determine the phone number from which an unidentified caller placed a call.

9. *Call waiting.* The system sounds a tone or lights up a lamp to indicate that another call is awaiting the individual whose phone is currently in use. In the more sophisticated systems, call waiting maintains a running log of the number of waiting calls a person has. When necessary, the employee, with the push of a button, can obtain supervisory assistance to help reduce the backlog.

10. *Caller ID.* This feature identifies on an LED screen (either built into the telephone or in an attached device) the phone number from which an incoming call originated.

11. *Distinctive ringing.* The system uses a distinctive ringing to signal the user of the special status of certain calls (such as return calls).

12. *Direct inward dialing.* The system automatically completes incoming calls without the assistance of an operator.

13. *Direct outward dialing.* The system automatically transfers outgoing calls without the assistance of the operator.

14. *In-conference transfers.* The system automatically transfers an individual's calls to another person when the former is in conference or does not wish to be interrupted.

15. *Repeat dialing.* This feature allows the system to keep dialing a busy phone number at predetermined intervals (perhaps every minute).

16. *Speed dialing.* The system allows users to make frequently called local or long-distance calls by dialing a prescribed two- or three-digit number.

17. *Station billing system.* The system provides a printout of the phone numbers called by each user, the date of each call, and the duration of each call.

What is station hunting?

18. *Station hunting.* The system automatically transfers calls to another person when the phone is not answered within a specified number of rings.

19. *User code.* The system matches the services an employee is entitled to use with the service he or she is attempting to use. Unless the required code is provided and the service is within the employee's authorized service limits, the call cannot be completed.

Other Devices Using Telephone Lines

In addition to telephones, several other communication devices found in offices also require the use of telephone lines. While some of these devices use "voice-grade" lines, others require the use of heavier duty lines capable of transmitting high-speed data communication. The following devices also use telephone lines: teleconference and videoconference devices, PC conferencing, Picturephone, fax devices, e-mail, and voice messaging.

Teleconference and Videoconference Devices. As an alternative to holding face-to-face conferences among an organization's executives, a growing number of firms use **teleconferencing** and **videoconferencing,** especially organizations that have executives in several locations throughout the United States.

How do teleconferencing and videoconferencing differ from each other?

Teleconferencing uses telephones to connect any number of remotely located individuals, which enables them to communicate by voice only. Videoconferencing transmits images of these individuals as well as their voice communication.

High-quality videoconferencing technology continues to be an expensive investment. The most costly equipment component of a videoconferencing system is the coder-decoder used to translate video images from an analog mode into a digital mode. After translation, the digital computerized signals are transmitted over either high-speed digital lines or satellites. Two types of coder-decoder equipment are used: full motion and limited motion. Full-motion transmission provides a real-time image, just as it appears to the camera, on the television screen. Limited-motion transmission is much slower, with fast or sudden movement (including rapid lip movement) either appearing as a blur or not appearing at the receiving location.

Low-quality videoconferencing is now possible between two personal computers to which Web cameras are attached. Although the screen image is small and the transmission speed is slow, resulting in the blurring of motion images, this technology has some utility in certain office procedures.

A videoconference is shown in Figure 19–3.

PC Conferencing. Using at least two personal computers, **PC conferencing** facilitates simultaneous transmission of video, data, and voice. Because of telecommunications interconnectivity, the two personal computers involved in the conferencing can be thousands of miles from each other. An adaptation of PC conferencing involves the **whiteboard,** which is a shared, on-screen workspace used by participants to discuss a drawing, photograph, or handwritten material.

Figure 19–3 Video-conference. Courtesy: American Telephone and Telegraph.

Another adaptation enables two or more individuals to share an application so they can work on the same material (text and/or graphics) simultaneously.

Picturephones. Another of the devices that uses telephone lines is the **Picturephone.** This device, which incorporates a televisionlike screen and a telephone, enables the sender and receiver of a call to see each another as they talk.

Facsimile (fax) Devices. Telephone lines are also used to interconnect **facsimile (fax) devices.** Generally, organizations are using dedicated fax lines to which their fax devices are attached. Doing so eliminates having to call the recipient to tell him or her to activate the fax device so the material can be transmitted. If a dedicated line is not used, a fax/tel switch will be useful. This switch can determine whether the incoming call is a fax or a telephone call. If it is a fax, the switch activates the fax device to receive the document. If it is a voice call, the telephone rings in the normal manner.

What is a dedicated fax line?

Some of the more sophisticated fax devices can operate unattended. Such devices are capable of automatically dialing up to fifty phone numbers stored in memory. An advantage of such units is their operability at night when long-distance toll charges tend to be the least expensive.

Fax devices in use today use three types of print technology: thermal-transfer (some use plain paper while others use special paper), ink-jet, and laser and light-emitting-diode (LED) machines. Costwise, the thermal devices are the least expensive, while the laser and LED devices are the most expensive.

A fax device is pictured in Figure 19–4.

Among the more recent developments in fax technology are the following: fax on demand, Internet fax, and fax broadcast. These developments add to the functionality of using fax as an important communications tool.

What is fax on demand?

Fax on demand enables an outside party to call an organization that has the capability of transmitting information "on demand." Once connected to the fax-on-demand equipment, the outside party uses the keys on his or her phone to transmit the numeric code of the desired document. Almost instantly, the organization's fax transmits the requested information to the outside party. Except for the effort expended by the outside party in making the original call, the entire process is automated. An increasing number of organizations are installing fax on demand as a customer support service for providing instructions, manual supplements, technical assistance, and so forth.

Internet fax uses the Internet to fax material from one location to another. Bypassing the normal fax-transmission process that uses telephone lines for

Figure 19–4
Facsimile. Courtesy:
Pitney Bowes.

which long-distance tolls are charged, Internet fax diverts the transmission process to the Internet, resulting in "free" faxing (free after paying the monthly Internet Service Provider's access charge). The fax is ultimately received as an attachment to an e-mail message. The receiver can view the material on a personal computer's monitor or print it.

Fax broadcast enables a sender to transmit the same message to a number of different recipients. Its use is appropriate when immediacy and message importance are a concern. Although the same message can be sent by e-mail, sending it by fax assures more timely receipt as well as its being viewed as a more important document than if it were sent as an e-mail message.

Fax broadcast service companies are now being founded throughout the country. Rather than transmitting in-house the same message to a number of recipients, the message along with the fax numbers of the recipients are transmitted to a service company. The high-speed capability of the service company's equipment assures the message will likely be transmitted more quickly and efficiently than if it were transmitted in-house. Fax broadcast service companies are often a cost-effective alternative to the organization's having to install equipment that will effectively handle large message loads.

E-Mail. The use of **electronic mail** is an efficient way to distribute information between the sender and one or more recipients. With an Internet connection and an e-mail address, electronic messages can be sent between individuals regardless of their location throughout the world.

Organizations that have e-mail capability tend to use one of the following three alternatives: a proprietary e-mail software program, e-mail capability provided by an Internet Service Provider (ISP), or a free e-mail account. Four common proprietary programs are Lotus Notes, Microsoft Mail, Microsoft Exchange, and Eudora. Subscribers to America Online, an ISP, are provided e-mail capability. Free accounts are available from Hotmail, Excite, and Yahoo!.

Keyboarding the message is as easy as keyboarding material using word processing software. Electronic mail software programs function by enabling the sender to keyboard the message after entering the recipient's name and the message subject. Depending on the system traffic and the physical distance between the sender and the receiver, the receiver may receive the message in a matter of seconds or in several hours. The message is "stored" in the system until accessed by the reader.

What are some of the common features found in e-mail programs?

E-mail software programs are rapidly becoming more versatile. Some of the features commonly found are spell checking, message forwarding, message archiving, e-mail directory, attaching other files to the e-mail message, notifying the recipient of awaiting messages, and notifying the sender that his or her message has reached the receiving location. Another desirable feature is the ability to reply to the original sender without having to re-enter his or her e-mail address or subject. Each subsequent reply to the original message simply "builds" on the original message.

Employees at a remote location who have access to a computer with a modem and the necessary e-mail companion software are able to access e-mail sent to the office. This feature is especially desirable for employees who travel extensively, work at home, and telecommute. A new alternative access system allows a person to access his or her e-mail messages by phone, as the text in e-mail messages is converted to voice. The user replies to the e-mail message using a voice rather than a text message.

A number of issues relating to e-mail have arisen over the last several years. Increasingly, these issues are being addressed in many organizations as relevant policies are being implemented. Among the issues are use of the organization's e-mail system for personal use, privacy of e-mail, and limits on amount of material that can be archived. These issues are often covered in the form of policy and are outlined in the employee manual.

What are the nature of some of the policies being implemented by organizations regarding e-mail usage?

Increasingly, organizations are implementing policies that prohibit employees from using their e-mail system to send personal messages. The reason for this is that when e-mail is used for personal messages, the organization's resources are diverted from their primary purpose (that of carrying out official organizational tasks). Employees who use their working time to send and receive personal e-mail messages, depending on the extent to which this is done, can cost their employer a considerable sum of money over a year's time. In addition to the cost of diverted employee time is the cost associated with transmittal and storage of the messages.

In most organizations, e-mail messages are not private and can be accessed and read by any employee in the organization who has administrator rights to the e-mail system. E-mail privacy does not exist because increasingly organizations are implementing policies which state that all e-mail messages are considered as business messages. However, most organizations enter e-mail message depositories only when they have a compelling reason to do so. If message confidentiality is a concern or could become a concern, the originator should perhaps consider using another communication medium to transmit the message. An employee needs to remember that the content of e-mail messages can be used "against" him or her in a variety of ways, including in a court of law. A good rule of thumb regarding the use of e-mail as a communications tool is that people should avoid using it to send a message unless they are comfortable sending the same message on a postcard.

The volume of e-mail messages transmitted daily throughout large organizations requires extensive storage capacity, especially when long messages are sent to hundreds of individuals. Employees should refrain from sending messages to multiple readers unless the content is important and appropriate for these individuals. To help combat the capacity problem, messages should be kept short, perhaps limited to one screen of content. Employees are encouraged to archive important messages as soon as possible after their receipt and to delete the unimportant ones. E-mail system maintenance is becoming a more important task for all who use it, just as the filing of paper documents has been for decades.

What are the characteristics of voice messaging systems?

Voice Messaging. One of the more widely used telecommunications services is **voice messaging,** which allows individuals to send and receive phone messages when they are not in their office or when they are in their office but don't want to be disturbed.

Voice messaging systems convert spoken words into digitally encoded information recorded on a magnetic medium. The computer technology that drives the system allows the messages to be transmitted according to the sender's instructions or holds the messages in memory until they are accessed by the recipient. The telephone keypad is used to control basic operational functions, such as recording, playing back, forwarding, saving, and deleting messages.

Two types of voice messaging systems are found: One type uses an add-in board in personal computers while the other uses equipment, added to the telephone system, that is dedicated to voice messaging. The add-in board type is less expensive but is also less versatile than the dedicated system.

Voice messaging can be used in a number of ways. As the sophistication of the system increases, so does the number of ways in which the system can be used. One use of the system is broadcasting, which transmits the same message to as many as 250 individuals. The individuals to receive the message are identified by an identification code, and each person whose code is entered into the system automatically receives the message. Another use is to transmit a message at a predetermined time, which is automatically done by the system.

Messages can also be automatically redirected to other individuals simply by entering the appropriate directions (most likely pressing 0, 1, 2, or 3 on the keypad) into the system. Depending on the system, an individual may have the ability to use a touch-tone phone to access his or her messages twenty-four hours a day. This is done simply by dialing the appropriate telephone number and using the keypad to enter a confidential identification number. In some instances, the system periodically calls the user, notifying him or her of waiting messages. In accessing the voice messaging system, a user has the option of listening to a stored message at that time, having a message permanently stored on a magnetic medium, delaying the playback of any stored message, or erasing the message from the system.

The newest development in voice messaging is a system that integrates voice messaging and fax with electronic mail. Thus, users are able to share text, image, and voice data/information, with all messages being delivered into one's e-mail inbox.

Voice messaging virtually eliminates the "telephone tag" problem that plagues many individuals in many offices. It also accommodates individuals who need to communicate with other individuals in other time zones, and it may reduce the number of secretarial support staff needed through a reduction in the number of handwritten messages that have to be prepared regarding incoming phone calls.

Call Processing

What is meant by call processing?

Designed to improve the manner in which in-coming calls are expedited in an organization, **call processing** is becoming a vital function. Call processing is typically comprised of several integrated components, including an automated attendant, automated call distribution or queuing, and voice messaging. The caller uses the keypad on his or her phone to activate these components, which use interactive voice response technology.

When answering an organization's phone, the automated attendant tells the caller to depress a specified key on the keypad to route the call to the desired individual/department. Should the caller need to talk to a human attendant, the appropriate key is mentioned during the recorded message. Some systems have an audio directory that enables the caller to obtain the recipient's extension simply by entering the first two letters of his or her last name.

Customers/clients are becoming increasing frustrated by their inability to talk with an employee when the automated system does not provide them with their desired option. In designing these automated attendant systems, all possible combinations of situations should be carefully planned so callers are made to feel they are not in an endless queue. Regardless of how many options are available, one option that needs to be provided is that of talking with a human.

What is the automated attendant feature?

The automated call distribution feature is activated when all of the organization's employees in a given unit are busy (customer service representatives, for example). This feature locks calls into the queue in the order in which they are received, thus assuring the caller that he or she will be connected with an employee when one becomes available. Music is generally heard by those waiting in queue.

Voice messaging, discussed in detail earlier in this chapter, is another component of an increasing number of call processing systems.

To help the organization better manage its telephone service, some call processing systems also provide weekly management reports that identify the times when the system was its busiest, the average length of calls (in minutes and seconds), and the number of calls received. For systems that use a human rather than an automated attendant, other data often available include the number of calls that were abandoned when the caller hung up, the amount of time callers were placed on hold, and the busy rate.

Telephone Interconnect Equipment and Services

What is telephone interconnect?

In 1968, a court decision gave individuals the right to obtain telephone equipment and long-distance calling services from sources other than the Bell System. Obtaining such equipment or service in this manner is known as **interconnect.** Organizations, as a result, may either lease or purchase telephone equipment from an independent equipment supplier or obtain long-distance calling services from an independent carrier. Some of the long-distance interconnect carriers are MCI, Sprint, and Allnet.

Among the important considerations when selecting interconnect equipment or services are the reliability of the supplier and the quality of equipment and/or service the supplier is able to provide. The system can be no better than the equipment and/or service provided by the supplier.

Advantages of Telephone Interconnect

1. Over time, the organization may be able to reduce costs significantly by using interconnect equipment and/or long-distance calling services.
2. Interconnect devices are often more flexible than the equipment leased from a telephone company, which helps the organization maximize the efficiency of its operations.

Disadvantages of Interconnect

1. When purchasing interconnect equipment, the service provided by some suppliers tends to decrease, which may result in a less-than-optimum situation.
2. Equipment that is owned may be difficult to dispose of once it becomes obsolete.
3. The service provided by some interconnect equipment suppliers and/or long-distance calling services compares poorly with the quality of service generally provided by AT&T or a Bell subsidiary.

INTRAORGANIZATIONAL COMMUNICATION DEVICES

Several devices are used to transmit data and information within an organization. Included are such devices as telewriter, intrafax, closed-circuit television, and paging systems.

Telewriter

As an internal device, the **telewriter** is used to transmit handwritten messages between two sites fairly close to each another. This device is especially useful

Figure 19–5
Telewriter. Courtesy:
Teleautograph.

for transmitting messages between an organization's office and warehouse or plant. As the words are written on paper attached to the writing table of the device, they are converted to electrical impulses. At the receiving location, these impulses activate the unit to prepare a duplicate paper copy of the message.

Figure 19–5 illustrates the telewriter device.

Intrafax

What is intrafax?

Another fax device is **intrafax,** which is used internally within an organization. It can be used to transmit duplicate copies of all types of forms, letters, drawings, and other kinds of documents between various offices in an organization.

Closed-Circuit Television. The use of **closed-circuit television** is increasing in organizations. Closed-circuit television is used to transmit information as well as to provide security for the premises. To transmit information between two locations in the organization, information is placed in front of the closed-circuit camera. The image is transmitted instantly to the television monitor at the receiving location. Depending on the equipment being used, the material being transmitted can be saved on a computer-readable magnetic medium.

Paging Systems

A number of **paging systems** are used extensively in organizations. One type uses the organization's public address system. The employee's name or identification code is broadcast through the public address system, along with the message. Another system uses portable pocket-sized paging devices. While some of these devices only beep, others permit either one- or two-way audio communication. Some can be used to page a person several miles from the base unit.

MANAGEMENT OF TELECOMMUNICATIONS SERVICES

The growing complexity of telecommunications services within many organizations necessitates their proper management. Therefore, an increasing number of organizations are formally managing their telecommunications systems, generally resulting in a significant reduction of their telecommunication costs.

Among the outcomes of the installation of a telecommunications management system are the following:

What is likely to be the result of proper management of telecommunications services?

1. An understanding of how the various elements of the telecommunications system fit together, resulting in the most efficient system possible.
2. A consolidation of various technical aspects of the system, resulting in greater efficiency.
3. The use of a system that enables managers to have the needed information readily available at the time it is needed.
4. The use of a system that is as technologically advanced as the various system components will allow and that will enhance the organization's telecommunications system in the future, not impede it.
5. Coordinated development of the entire system rather than a fragmented approach that affects parts of the system.

Among the benefits of telecommunications services management are the positive impact it has on telecommunications costs and the ongoing development of a system that grows with the organization as the technology becomes available. Manager of telecommunication services is a high-level position that provides another career opportunity for the administrative office manager.

CONTROLLING TELECOMMUNICATIONS COSTS

Because telecommunications within an organization is so pervasive and because it is technologically oriented, some effort needs to be expended in controlling telecommunications costs. A number of suggestions can be offered to help control telecommunications costs, including the following:

How can telecommunications costs be controlled?

1. Coordinate all aspects of the telecommunications system, thereby ensuring the compatibility of existing components and the expandability of the system when the need arises.
2. Investigate alternative long-distance carriers to determine which one can best meet the organization's needs in the most cost-effective manner. When evaluating long-distance carriers, the following are factors that need to be evaluated:
   a. Billing in six-second increments rather than rounded-up, full-minute increments.
   b. Billing plans for day/night/weekend calls.
   c. Billing plans for intrastate/interstate/international calls.
   d. Nature of ancilliary services (calling cards, prepaid debit cards, Internet access) provided.
   e. Length of time company has been in business.
   f. Number of states in which the carrier is licensed to provide service.
3. Consider the use of reconditioned equipment when new equipment is needed.
4. Determine whether equipment purchasing or leasing is most cost effective.
5. Install a long-distance call monitoring system.
6. Install only the phone features that can be justified from a cost-effective standpoint.
7. When remodeling or building a new facility, design the telecommunications system to accommodate future expansion.

TELECOMMUTING AND TELECOMMUNICATIONS

What is telecommuting?

Over the years, a number of developments in telecommunications have been responsible for the increasing popularity and growth of **telecommuting,** which enables employees to work at a remote site (typically in their home, in a satellite office, or on the road). Among the two most important developments making telecommuting possible are the ability to interconnect a personal computer (or a laptop or notebook) to a telephone line that enables the communication process.

Adding to the attractiveness of telecommuting is the positive impact it has on meeting the requirement of the 1970 Clean Air Act, amended in 1990, that stipulates any organization with 100 or more employees in one location must reduce its employees' commute time by 25 percent when the organization is located in areas with severe ozone levels. By allowing some employees to telecommute part or all of the time, organizations are more readily able to meet this requirement of the amended Clean Air Act.

Among the types of employees who are often given the opportunity to telecommute are the following:

1. Individuals involved with sales and/or marketing.
2. Individuals who are primarily responsible for data entry.
3. Individuals who interact over the telephone with customers/clients or potential customers/clients.
4. Some physically challenged individuals who find that working at home better accommodates their challenges.
5. Individuals with small children.
6. Individuals who do not have high levels of interaction with other employees in performing their job responsibilities.

Some organizations find that as many as 50 percent of their employees have jobs that could lend themselves well to telecommuting. In some instances, telecommuting enables organizations with space problems to avoid having to obtain more office work areas for their employees. Investing in the equipment and technology to facilitate telecommuting is less expensive than obtaining more work space. This is how some organizations save two dollars for every dollar they invest in equipment and technology for telecommuters.

Although the technology made available to each telecommuting employee should be determined by his or her specific job responsibilities, the following are among the devices/services that might be provided: personal computer (or laptop for employees whose job responsibilities involve considerable traveling), a cell phone (primarily for those whose job involves considerable traveling), fax capability, a scanner, a copier, a dedicated phone line (ISDN line when data transmission is extensive), e-mail capability, and Internet access.

The use of telecommuting is not without its issues. Among some of the issues are these:

What are some of the issues that arise with telecommuting?

1. Does the organization provide its employees with ergonomically designed furniture so that the telecommuters cannot hold the employer liable for health-related problems that may arise?
2. Does the telecommuting arrangement violate any local zoning ordinances, union regulations, OSHA requirements, or insurance stipulations?
3. Does the telecommuting arrangement have any tax implications for employees who use their home office to carry out their work responsibilities?

4. Are the telecommuters aware of work expectations, policies, and so forth?

5. How often should the program be assessed to assure it is providing the organization with a good return on its investment?

Although the telecommuting arrangement is advantageous for a number of reasons, most of which have been implied or stated in the previous paragraphs, it does have some disadvantages, including the following:

1. Some employees telecommute simply to avoid on-premise supervision, which may become problematic.

2. Some employees believe telecommuting alienates them from their co-workers.

3. Some employees miss the human interaction available when they work on the premises.

4. Some employees believe telecommuting adds to their home stress level.

5. Some employees believe it has a detrimental impact on their promotability.

THE INTERNET

What is the Internet?

The **Internet** has become a pervasive force in today's world. As a global network of connected computers, the Internet is made functional through interconnecting LANs worldwide. Using a personal computer, anyone with Internet access can exchange information with another individual in any part of the world who also has a personal computer and Internet access. During the last few years, the Internet has transformed many of the things (both job and non-job-related) people do on a daily basis and will likely do so even more extensively in the future.

The LANs that comprise the Internet are maintained by corporations, universities, Internet Service Providers, government agencies, and so forth. Information in a LAN that an organization wishes to protect from outsider access is maintained behind a firewall, which is a software program that restricts who is able to access the information through the Internet. While properly designed firewalls provide high levels of security, they might not provide absolute security of information accessible through a LAN.

History of the Internet

Although the Internet has existed conceptually since the early 1960s, only in the mid-1990s did it become a popular and powerful communications tool. Until 1995, the Internet backbone was financially supported by the National Science Foundation, which prohibited any commercial traffic on it. University personnel were the main early users of the Internet, primarily for communication and information exchange. In 1995, with the lifting of the commercial ban, the Internet has developed rapidly, providing its users with a wide array of information and services. Accessing information on the Internet became much easier with the advent of Web graphical browsers, the first of which appeared in 1994. Internet2, a high-speed optic network, became functional in early 1999. With the increased development of new technology, it will eventually operate at 9.6GB per second.

Internet Characteristics

One of the marvels of the Internet is its ability to operate seamlessly and blindly with regard to the type of computer platforms being used. Common computer platforms used today are PC, Macintosh, Linux, and Unix. Internet technology removes the incompatability of these systems so that information created by a Macintosh is as functional using a PC system as it is using a Macintosh. Without this feature, information created on a Macintosh, for example, would only be accessible using a Macintosh, a feature that would severely limit the usefulness of the Internet.

The Internet uses a set of standards, formally known as *protocols*, that make the sending and receiving of information possible. Using client and server programs, information is sent and received. The client program, such as a Web browser, is stored on the user's personal computer. The server program is located on another computer (server) at another site. When the client program requests specific information stored on the other computer, the server program functions by "serving" it, using telecommunications techology in the process. Different Internet services use different client programs. For example, the client used to access information using a Web browser is different from the client used to send and receive e-mail messages.

What are protocols?

The same protocol that organizations use to access the Internet is being used to develop what is known as *intranets*. These internal networks are based on the same protocol as the Internet and facilitate communication, collaboration, and the management of the organization's information resources. Thus, they are increasingly viewed as being the organization's "backbone." The advantage is that employees have internal access to the same familiar services as they have on the Internet, but the intranet is not accessible from outside the organization. For example, information that is to be available to all employees can be developed as a Web-based document and viewed on a Web browser. Because of the ease with which hypertext documents are created, Web-based documents can be created for use by just a few employees or for the entire organization, but their work is not viewable by outsiders.

Individuals access the Internet in a variety of ways, all of which involve the use of telecommunications. The Internet is commonly accessed in the following ways:

1. *LAN access:* Employees in organizations that have a LAN are able to access the Internet through the LAN, assuming the organization provides Internet access as a feature of the LAN. Accessing the Internet through a LAN is fast.

2. *Cable access:* With the rapid deployment of digital cable for cable TV subscribers, the ability to access the Internet through the same cable is possible. This means of access provides one of the fastest processes for downloading information from the Internet.

What is dial-up access?

3. *Dial-up access:* Most home users of the Internet currently connect to it using **dial-up access.** Using an ISDN line provides faster Internet access than an analog phone line. Some small organizations also use the dial-up process when leasing dedicated lines from an **Internet Service Provider (ISP),** which provides them with a continuous, direct Internet connection.

4. *Shell access:* As the least expensive means of gaining Internet access, the shell alternative requires a phone line and a modem. The shell facilitates the connection with a Unix computer platform, enabling the user's computer to operate as a terminal. The user may subsequently be able to access a computer that is connected to the Internet, thus giving him or her Internet access.

Internet Services

A variety of Internet services currently exist, and others likely will be introduced in the future. The two most commonly used services are e-mail and the World Wide Web (WWW).

E-Mail. E-mail has become a standard communicating tool in many organizations, and its use will likely continue at an even faster pace into the foreseeable future. Approximately half of the U.S. population currently uses e-mail, which is the fastest growing Internet service in terms of users.

World Wide Web. Although the **World Wide Web** is used by individuals to carry out their official job functions, it is also widely used as a non-job-related resource. The amount of material accessible on the Web is increasing at a rapid rate. One reason is that virtually anyone can "publish" material on the Web simply by uploading it to a Web server.

Much of the material accessible on the Web is in **hypertext** format and uses **hyperlinks,** which are underlined or highlighted words or phrases that when accessed display the information comprising the link. Thus, rather than being organized in a linear manner (a characteristic of print media), hypertext with hyperlinks uses a branching approach. The hypertext document is created using **HTML (hypertext markup language)** code. By inserting the appropriate code at the appropriate location in the document, the page will appear as the developer wished. New code features are being introduced fairly regularly. Simple code is easy to learn. However, to incorporate more advanced features in a Web page requires fairly extensive knowledge of such scripting languages as JavaScript.

Web-based material is accessed by means of a Web client, also known as a Web browser. If the user knows the address of the material, called a **URL (uniform resource locator),** he or she can readily access it. Telecommunications technology is used to transmit the request to the server where the information is stored; it is also used to retrieve and transmit the desired information to a computer at the user's location.

Increasingly, individuals are using the Web as an information resource. Thus, they use it in much the same way that library patrons use a card catalog (traditional or electronic) to locate desired information. To locate the desired information, they use the search feature of a Web directory (such as Yahoo! or Netscape), or they use a search engine (such as Northern Lights or Snap). These services tend to work on the basis of keywords or key terms. For those documents in which the desired word or term appears, the user will receive a listing on his or her screen that provides some information about the resource, along with a hyperlink (URL). To access a resource, the user simply "clicks" on the link; in a manner of seconds, the material will appear on his or her computer screen.

While people use the Web in a wide variety of ways and for a variety of reasons, an increasing number of individuals are using it for access to a variety of free Web-based applications. The entity providing the free applications generates revenue from the advertisements it has placed on the Web site. For example, some individuals use a Web-based e-mail service, such as Netscape's WebMail or Microsoft's HotMail. Some individuals also use a Web-based calendar/scheduling function. Instead of storing their appointments on a paper-based calendar or on an electronic calendar at their site, they use a Web-based calendar, such as When or calendar.Yahoo. Individuals also use Web-based keyboard chatting and Web-based telephoning, both of which are free.

The odds are quite good that in the future, Web-based word processing programs, spreadsheet programs, and database programs will also be available as applications. Rather than having to store the appropriate software on their personal computer's hard drive, people will use the Internet to access the application that performs the desired functions. The main advantage of using Web-based applications (such as e-mail, calendaring, and so forth) is that they

What is HTML?

are available any time and anywhere as long as an Internet connection is accessible. Thus, a user may not need a full-fledged personal computer with software. A terminal that provides Internet access may be sufficient for him or her to perform the desired tasks.

Figure 19–6 illustrates a Web site as viewed on a browser.

FTP (File Transfer Protocol). Using an **FTP (file transfer protocol)** client, such as WS-FTP, one can transfer files to the Internet. The process of transferring files to a server is called *uploading;* the process of transferring files from a server is called *downloading.* A variety of different types of files can be transferred using FTP, such as ASCII files, program files, graphics files, and files saved in various proprietary formats. Material displayed in hypertext format is actually an ASCII file. Large files are often stored on the server in a compressed format so they consume much less storage space. Once downloaded, they will need to be "unzipped" unless this takes place automatically during the downloading process.

The popular Web browsers facilitate the downloading of anonymous FTP files stored on a server. They are considered anonymous because their use is unrestricted. Care should be exercised in downloading files from the Internet because a computer virus may be present in the downloaded material. Immediately upon downloading, the material should be scanned for the presence of a computer virus.

Usenet. Comprised of thousands of newsgroups pertaining to thousands of different topics, the **Usenet** is basically an Internet (offline) discussion forum. Individuals who have a question or who wish to provide input about a certain topic post the question or information to the relevant newsgroup. Readers of the newsgroup who have information to share about the question or who wish to reply to the original comment will post a response to which others may in turn respond. The replies to the original message are known as *threads.* Although some

What is FTP?

What is the Usenet?

Figure 19–6 Web site

newsgroups are relevant to job-related concerns/issues employees have, many are unrelated. Therefore, most people probably use newsgroups more often for non-job-related purposes than for job-related purposes.

Newsgroups require their readers/users to subscribe to them. Once subscribed, using a Usenet client (perhaps a Web browser), one can access all the posted messages, including the original and response messages. Messages posted most recently are usually displayed first. Once a message has been accessed, its identifier changes color so the reader/user can easily determine whether or not that material has been read.

Listserv. Considered as an Internet mailing list, subscribing to a list brings all posted messages directly to each subscriber's desktop. The original and reply messages are received as e-mail. With Usenet, the subscriber has to "go after" the messages; but with **listserv,** the messages come to the subscriber, which many individuals find more convenient. However, depending on the lists to which a person subscribes, his or her mailbox may become cluttered quite quickly with these messages, especially when the current topic(s) generate considerable discussion.

Internet Relay Chat (IRC). As an Internet service, **IRC** enables individuals to "join" an in-progress chat group or to start a new chat group. It provides online (real-time), text-based communication capability. Employees who are located throughout the country but who wish to confer with one another about a certain topic can do so by using IRC. To join, they will need to know the chat group's name (also called the *channel*) and where they can locate it. A number of Internet Service Providers make IRC available to their subscribers. All individuals accessing a certain chat group will need to be subscribers to the same ISP.

Internet Telephone. To bypass a long-distance telephone carrier, some people use the **Internet telephone** process to make long-distance calls. However, the limitations of the system do not make it a viable alternative as an organization's long-distance phone service provider. Both parties involved in the call need to be "signed on" their computer at the same time. They communicate with each other using a microphone and the computer's speakers.

Voice clarity is sometimes affected, and echoes, delayed transmission, or word clipping sometimes occurs. Attaching a Web camera to the personal computer allows low-grade videoconferencing, a feature used extensively by some employees in some organizations.

What is telnet?

Telnet. Telnet is another service accessible using the Internet that enables employees to log into a remote computer. As a terminal emulation protocol, **telnet** enables one to work from a personal computer as though it were a terminal linked directly to the host computer, which makes it an interactive session. Telnet may be used to search databases, execute commands, run programs, and so forth.

IMPLICATIONS FOR THE ADMINISTRATIVE OFFICE MANAGER

Telecommunications is becoming more important in the modern office as organizations develop and install sophisticated office systems. Telecommunications, through interconnectivity, enables the various devices used within these systems to communicate with one another.

Organizations that are preparing to instill a sophisticated office system should plan carefully. To maximize efficiency, an organization should carefully assess its needs and then select telecommunications devices, services, and functions that best satisfy these needs.

The technical expertise of the administrative office manager is helpful in designing efficient telecommunications systems. In most instances, the efficiency of the system will be affected by the accuracy with which telecommunications needs are assessed. The administrative office manager plays a key role in assessing these needs; and once they have been determined, equipment manufacturing representatives, phone company personnel, and consultants are helpful in determining how these needs can be best fulfilled. The administrative office manager often serves as the liaison between the organization and outside experts.

REVIEW QUESTIONS

1. What types of communication channels are used in telecommunications?

2. How do digital and analog signals differ from one another?

3. For what functions are LANs, MANs, and WANs used?

4. How do half and full duplexing differ from each another?

5. For what are modems used?

6. In what ways do key system, PBX, PABX, and Centrex telephone systems differ from one another?

7. What type of technology do cellular phones use?

8. Explain how teleconferencing and videoconferencing differ from one another.

9. What components comprise a computer phone system?

10. Explain how a fax device is used to transmit documents.

11. What are some of the features commonly found on e-mail systems?

12. What are the advantages of telecommuting?

13. What Internet services are currently available?

DISCUSSION QUESTIONS

1. The company in which you work has grown rapidly during the past few years. This has necessitated hiring additional employees—and installing additional telephones. Rather than installing additional lines, several employees share the same extension. This means some of the telephone lines are in almost constant use. As a result, outsiders frequently get a busy signal when calling the company. What technological concept is less than adequate for your company? What suggestions do you have for assessing the adequacy (or lack thereof) of the company's telephone system?

2. Several years ago, the company in which you work installed a PBX telephone system. At that time, the decision was made to continue the use of PBX because the company already had a switchboard operator "on board." This operator is now about to retire. The company will soon have to install another telephone system because the present system cannot be further expanded. The company will soon have to decide whether to purchase another PBX system or switch to a PABX system. How might the company be able to justify the cost of a PABX system, assuming that the initial financial outlay will be greater than the outlay for a PBX system?

3. In the company in which you work, you are considered the individual most knowledgeable about communication networks. The executive vice president recently asked you to prepare a report on LANs. He will use this information in deciding whether or not to investigate the feasibility of installing a LAN. Technologically, the installation of a LAN will be possible as provisions were made for one during the construction of the building, which is now three years old. The company also purchases only one brand of office and computer equipment, which means that incompatibility of equipment will not be a concern. On what basis are you going to justify the installation of a LAN? (You have been in favor of such an installation for two years.)

STUDENT PROJECTS AND ACTIVITIES

1. Talk with a vendor of telephone equipment and systems to determine what new technology is being used in the company's products.
2. Interview a manager of telecommunications, primarily to learn about the nature of his or her job duties.
3. Going Online: Using the Internet, conduct an online search based on one of the concepts presented in this chapter or based on one of the chapter terms. Identify four or five things you learned from the material that you did not know prior to your online search.

Minicases

The Davidson Corporation, which is located in Las Vegas, Nevada, is in the process of studying its present PBX telephone system. The communication demands of the organization are not adequately met by the present telephone system. Undoubtedly, when a new system is installed, either a PABX system or a Centrex system will be selected.

1. What are the characteristics of PABX and Centrex systems?
2. What factors should be considered to help determine which system to choose?

Case

The Boeckeler Corporation, a distributor of hospital and surgical supplies, is located in New Britain, Connecticut. It is the largest distributor of its kind in the Northeast.

The new president of the corporation, who has been on the job for eighteen months, has asked each unit in the organization to investigate ways of containing its recurring costs. He specifically asked various unit managers to investigate the feasibility of purchasing its present equipment rather than leasing it. Two years ago, the company leased 40 percent of its office equipment. The reason for leasing so much equipment was to make capital available for expansion of its warehouse.

The organization's purchase of the equipment now appears feasible. This includes the purchase of the telephone equipment presently leased by the company.

1. In what ways might the purchase of the telephone equipment be advantageous for the company?
2. In what ways might the purchase of the telephone equipment be disadvantageous for the company?
3. Assume the company decides to purchase the telephone equipment. What suggestions can you provide that will help ensure the company's satisfaction with the system it purchases?

$\mathcal{C}$hapter 20

APPLICATIONS SOFTWARE

$\mathcal{C}$hapter $\mathcal{A}$ims

After studying this chapter, you should be familiar with the various types of applications software used in the office.

$\mathcal{C}$hapter $\mathcal{O}$utline

A Historical Perspective
Types of Applications Software
Sources of Applications Software
Use of Integrated Applications Software Programs
Common Applications Software Used in the Office
Word Processing Software Programs
    The Beginning of a Revolution
    Steps in the Word Processing Cycle
Spreadsheet Software Programs
    Functions of Spreadsheets
    Features of Spreadsheet Software Programs
Database Software Programs
    Database Software Program Characteristics
    Features of Database Software Programs
Presentation Software Programs
    Output Options
    Creating Output Using Presentation Software
Desktop Publishing Software Programs
    Preparing Camera-Ready Copy
    Features of Desktop Publishing Software
Scheduling Software Programs
Implications for the Administrative Office
    Manager

$\mathcal{C}$hapter $\mathcal{T}$erms

Applications software
Automatic hyphenation
Automatic word correction
Automatic word wrap
Beta version software
Blank slide
Browse view
Camera-ready copy
Cell
Cell address
Clip-art library
Commercial software programs
Database software
Date fields
Desktop computers
Desktop publishing software (DTP)
Dictation
Disposition
Fields
Formula bar
Formula replication
Grammar and style checker
Graphics creation
Horizontal applications software
Hypertext markup language (HTML)
Integrated software
Justification
LCD projector

List view
Logical fields
Macros
Merge
Numeric fields
Object linking and embedding (OLE)
Office suite software
Origination/formatting
Portable document format (PDF)
Presentation software
Public domain software
Query by example (QBE)
Query function
Revision
Scheduling software
Shareware programs
Site license
Slides
Software license

Software piracy
Spell checking
Spreadsheets
Stand-alone software
Structured Query Language (SQL)
Systems software
Templates
Text fields
To-do list
Transparencies
Type/font library
Vertical applications software
Voice response
What-if function
Word processing
Word originators
Word processing specialists
WYSIWYG

*T*he emergence of personal computers and the development of telecommunications technology that facilitates equipment interconnectivity are changing the way many office tasks are performed. These changes, which are found within all levels of the organizational hierarchy, are likely to continue at a rapid pace into the foreseeable future. In fact, more changes have occurred in this area within the last fifteen years than occurred in the previous one hundred years.

Many of the changes found in the way office tasks are performed result from the ability to capture and store data, beginning with their initial keyboarding or system input using voice response. Once the data are captured and stored, they can be used subsequently in many different ways, in many different configurations, and by many different employees who have proper authorization to access the data. Subsequent use of the data often requires minimal human effort in creating a new document, which means that fewer support personnel may be needed in the future.

The affordability of personal computers and the ease with which they perform a wide variety of office tasks are largely responsible for growing numbers of employees doing an increasing amount of their own office production work, such as keyboarding their own letters, entering data into a spreadsheet, creating graphics for a presentation, and so forth. This, in turn, has changed the role and function of many administrative assistants. No longer do these assistants spend a significant amount of time transcribing dictation or keyboarding handwritten material originated by those for whom they work. Rather, they have taken on new responsibilities, such as conducting research, compiling research data, writing reports, editing others' work, and so forth.

What primarily has been responsible for the change in the way many office tasks are performed?

A HISTORICAL PERSPECTIVE

With IBM's development in the early 1960s of an electronic device called the MTST (Magnetic Tape Selectric Typewriter), the ability to capture and store keyboarded material became possible. Although this early technology was obviously primitive when compared with today's technology, it essentially began a revolution. The work performed on this early equipment was done by employees who were specially trained to use it. And its cost and lack of versatility made it impractical to put one of these devices on each employee's desktop.

Shortly after the introduction of the MTST came the development of the **word processing** concept. As originally developed, *word processing* was defined as the mix of people, equipment, and procedures to transform thoughts and ideas into printed copy. Today, the meaning of *word processing* has evolved into a different context where basically it refers to a software program used on a personal computer. In many organizations, word processing centers were installed; employees who originated material (preferably using dictation) had this material keyboarded by a specialist in the word processing center. Because the initial keyboarding of the document resulted in the capture and storage of the material, word originators found the process of editing their documents much easier. Because the document was stored, only the changes had to be keyboarded, which resulted in considerable saving of employees' time and better quality written work.

The ability to capture and store keyboarded material that revolutionized the text processing function, along with the miniaturizing of computer technology (primarily transistors and chips) led to the next significant change in the way office tasks were performed. With the introduction of the personal computer in the late 1970s and 1980s, a variety of office tasks could now be performed at employees' desks. Just as word processing resulted in the ability to capture and store text, new applications resulted in the ability to capture, store, and subsequently perform arithmetic functions on much of the numerical data with which employees worked.

In today's offices, the marriage of computer and telecommunications technology, coupled with a wide variety of applications software, allows employees to perform much of their work wherever they are regardless of the time of day (or night). Each new version of the applications software seems to make it more functional, easier to use, and in many cases more highly integrated with other applications software. Today, a vast amount of software is readily available, with more being introduced regularly, to support a large number of the tasks employees perform in their daily routines.

What is the definition of the original concept of word processing?

TYPES OF APPLICATIONS SOFTWARE

Employees use **applications software** to perform a wide range of their tasks. It differs from the **systems software** used to make the personal computer operational. Examples of systems software used on PC-compatible computers are Microsoft Windows and Linux; on Macintosh computers, it is called Mac OS. Examples of applications software include WordPerfect, PowerPoint, and Lotus Notes.

Two basic types of applications software exist: horizontal and vertical. Of the two types, **horizontal applications software** is more commonly used in a wide variety of organizations. **Vertical applications software,** on the other hand, is designed for a specific type of business or a specific function within a broad range of organizations. Examples of horizontal applications software are word processing and spreadsheet programs. Examples of vertical applications software are the patient scheduling, billing, and insurance claims processing software used by medical and dental offices. Another example is the software used for payroll processing.

What two types of applications software exist?

In selecting applications software of either the horizontal or vertical type, a number of factors need to be considered:

1. Is the program appropriate for its intended use?
2. Is the program bundled with a number of additional features that will not be used, making it cost ineffective?
3. Is the program vendor reputable and likely to stay in business for the foreseeable future?
4. Is the program accompanied by a quality user manual?
5. Is the program supported by technical assistance?
6. Is the program's cost appropriate for the amount of use the program will have?
7. Is the program compatible with the capacity of the equipment on which it will be installed?

SOURCES OF APPLICATIONS SOFTWARE

Although the vast majority of programs employees use to perform their job functions are commercial, a wide variety of shareware and freeware programs are also available. As a rule, software available from each of the three sources is copyrighted, which means that the purchaser cannot make copies for other users without violating the copyright accompanying the software. Doing so results in **software piracy,** which is a federal offense in the United States.

What is software piracy?

Commercial software programs are available for purchase from retail establishments, directly from the developer, by downloading from the Internet, and bundled with new equipment. In each of these alternatives, the software has to be paid for before it is available for use. Once the program is installed on a personal computer, the user is asked to register it with the developer, a feature that may be required to receive technical support.

What is shareware?

Shareware programs, contrary to what some individuals believe, are also copyrighted, but the user is generally able to try a shareware program before having to purchase it. After a free trial period, the user either has to remove the program from his or her personal computer and perhaps return the software or pay a nominal fee for its use. The registration fee may provide the user with limited technical support as well as announcements about program updates. The vast majority of shareware programs are downloaded from the Internet. As a rule, shareware programs do not have as many "bells and whistles" as commercial software programs do.

Freeware programs, which are also generally copyrighted, are given away. The copyright feature prohibits someone from selling the program for a profit. Generally, freeware has fewer "bells and whistles" than shareware.

Another type of program, **public domain software,** is not copyrighted and can be sold or modified without the developer's permission. In some instances, before a software program is finalized and made available for purchase, the developer offers a preliminary or beta version of the software to interested parties. **Beta version software** is typically in its final stages of testing. It generally still has some computer bugs in it, and users are asked to notify the developer of these bugs. As a rule, beta software expires on a given date or after the passage of a certain amount of time.

What is beta version software?

With the ever-increasing use of telecommunications technology, some software will likely be "served" from a commercial server. Rather than using a networked version of the software installed on an organization's computer or on the hard drive of a personal computer, the applications software is "served" through the Internet to its user. In some cases, software is free to users because ads on the server are used to support software maintenance. When having to pay for the use of this software, two different plans exist for charging the user: charging a predetermined amount each time the user accesses the software or charging him or her based on the length of time it is used. One of the advantages of using software in this manner is its availability for use whenever and wherever an individual can access the Internet, a feature that well accommodates the traveling employee.

Organizations typically install the software they purchase on a network server or on the hard drive of personal computers. When installed on a network server, all individuals who are authorized to access the server will likely be able to use the software. But when the software is stored on the hard drive of an employee's personal computer, it will be accessible only to the individual using that computer at any given time. With the appropriate software, equipment, and telecommunications service, the individual may be able to access server-based software from a remote location such as from his or her home or from a motel room when traveling. Being able to access and use server-based software, either on or off the premises, requires the proper functioning of the server and the network. When either the server or the network is not functioning properly, employees are not able to access or use the software.

How is a software license used?

Software generally is accompanied by a **software license,** which provides the right to install and use the program on only one computer. When a **site license** is purchased, the organization is able to install and use the program on the specified number of computers, although the program will likely be installed on one server and then accessed through a network.

USE OF INTEGRATED APPLICATIONS SOFTWARE PROGRAMS

What is integrated software?

During the last few years, the trend has been for software developers to integrate two or more software programs into a package or a suite. Until that time, individual programs were generally developed as **stand-alone programs.** On the other hand, **integrated software** is one program capable of performing several functions. An example of an integrated program is word processing software that contains graphics and communications capability. An example of **office suite software** is a bundled package that contains word processing, shreadsheet, database, presentations, and scheduling components.

Most software suites, including Corel Office, Lotus SmartSuite, and Microsoft Office also contain one or more integrated programs. Developers are currently making these programs available as suites (bundled with different combinations of programs) or as stand-alone programs. Therefore, if a user knows that he or she will use only two of the components as individual programs (word processing and spreadsheet, for example), purchasing only these two components will likely be less expensive than purchasing the entire suite.

When evaluating various office software suites for possible purchase, the ease with which functions performed in one program can be "brought" into another program should be assessed. For example, suppose an employee is preparing a report, using word processing software to capture and store the report's text. Also suppose the report includes a number of tables containing data stored in a spreadsheet. The suite should quickly and easily facilitate the importing of the spreadsheet data into the text of the report at whatever location the employee wishes. Also suppose the employee decides to include some

What function does OLE
provide?

graphics in the written report. The suite should enable the employee to create
the graphics using the graphics function of either the word processing program
or the spreadsheet program and then importing the illustrations into the written report. The ability of the office suite software to perform as just described
is made possible by **object linking and embedding (OLE),** which is accomplished by the automatic window display of the menus and toolbars that are
relevant to the type of data with which the employee is currently working.
When dealing with text, the software displays menus and toolbars related to
text processing. But when the employee switches to the graphics function of
the word processing software, the menus and toolbars change to reflect the
graphics function.

The growing presence of the World Wide Web in our lives, both work and
personal, means that more of the material employees create will likely be uploaded to the Web as a means of sharing it with other users as nonpaper-based
documents. Because people use different computer platforms (Windows, Macintosh, Linux, and Unix, primarily) to access this material, it has to be put into
a file format that provides a readable display using a Web browser regardless
of the equipment on which the material was created and the server that "serves"
the material. This is accomplished by storing Web-based material in ASCII
(American Standard Code for Information Interchange) format, which allows
individuals accessing the material using a computer with Windows to view it
just as easily as people accessing it using a Macintosh computer.

**What is the primary use of
HTML?**

Hypertext markup language (HTML) is used to facilitate the creation of
Web-based documents. It contains a number of codes that cause the material to
appear and to function in a prescribed manner. For example, surrounding text
with the following code will cause it to appear in a bold format: <b>text</b>.
Therefore, the word *text* will appear on the screen in a bold format. The software
programs that came bundled in the earlier office software suites contained a
utility that converted the material into HTML format, automatically inserting
the appropriate code at the appropriate location. Therefore, if in a document the
word *text* appeared in bold, the conversion automatically inserted <b> before
and</b> after the word *text*. Although these programs did not work perfectly,
they did a fairly effective job of inserting the desired code in most of the locations throughout the document. Generally, someone familiar with HTML code
had to edit the entire document, fixing the code where it was not functioning
properly or inserting the appropriate code where it was missing. Increasingly,
the suite developers are changing the file formats used in their programs so they
are HTML compatible without having to undergo the file conversion process.
When this feature works perfectly, no "clean-up" work will be necessary.

COMMON APPLICATIONS SOFTWARE USED IN
THE OFFICE

**What typically determines
which applications soft-
ware programs an
employee has available
on his or her computer?**

Employees use a number of different applications software programs in various functional areas of today's organizations. The programs they actually use
or perhaps have access to may be determined by their job functions and responsibilities. If they have access to office suite software, which an increasing
number of employees do, all components of the suite will be available. Depending on the licensing agreement with the developer, the software will either
be installed on the hard drives of their personal computers or "served" to them
through a network, with the software installed on the network server.

Following is a list of the applications software programs commonly used
in an office environment:

- Word processing
- Spreadsheets
- Databases
- Presentations
- Desktop Publishing
- Scheduling

WORD PROCESSING SOFTWARE PROGRAMS

With the availability of word processing equipment, a revolution began in the way many office tasks were carried out or performed. The equipment has changed forever many office tasks that had remained unchanged for decades.

The Beginning of a Revolution

What was the primary function of word processing specialists?

Because of the expense of the early word processing equipment, these devices tended to be centrally located; and they were operated by employees, known as **word processing specialists,** who had specialized training to use them. The majority of the documents created by employees were no longer keyboarded by secretaries or clerk-typists physically located near the **word originators.** Employees within all levels of the organization were encouraged to make extensive use of the word processing facilities. Because standard office typewriters that had been the sole production tool up until that time were no longer used as extensively as in the past, they began to disappear quite rapidly. A few standard office typewriters are found in many of today's offices, and they have two primary functions: to fill in paper-based forms and to prepare gummed mailing labels.

With the widespread use of word processing, employees, who were known as word originators, were encouraged to use **dictation** in the origination process. In many organizations, dictation equipment was accessible twenty-four hours a day. In these systems, the telephone was the dictation input device, and the keys on the keypad were used to operate such equipment functions as *record, review,* and *erase.* The dictation was stored on large-capacity recording devices in the word processing center; the word processing specialists spent a significant portion of their work day either keyboarding the dictation or making revisions in the documents they had already keyboarded. Word originators were discouraged from submitting handwritten material to be keyboarded for two reasons: the difficulty word processing specialists experienced in reading originators' handwriting and their ability to transcribe dictated material faster than they were able to keyboard handwriting.

What is the primary reason many organizations dismantled their word processing centers years ago?

In time, the large centralized word processing facility found in many organizations began to be replaced by several smaller centers located throughout the premises. This was done primarily because many of the word processing specialists felt isolated, and the equipment became increasingly affordable. In fact, in this model, the word originators and the word processing specialists likely knew one another; but in the earlier model, word originators and word processing specialists most likely never met one another.

The introduction of the Apple II desktop computer in the late 1970s provided the impetus for yet another revolution. Affordable **desktop computers** could now be placed on employees' desks. Therefore, an ever-increasing number of employees began to have access to desktop computers, either Apple- or IBM-brand equipment. Although the equipment was used only for a few functions, primarily because of a lack of software, employees soon discovered that the availability of word processing software enabled them to compose their own documents using their computer keyboards.

The technology had now developed to the point where errors were corrected and/or changes in wording were made simply by backspacing over the error or deleting the unwanted material. Once the error disappeared on the screen, it also disappeared from the document. Employees soon found they could "compose effectively at the keyboard" or at least as effectively as when they used dictation to originate a new document. And with a little practice, they could certainly compose at the keyboard faster than they could handwrite the same material. As this model for expediting office work increased in popularity, the use of word processing centers with the specialized word processing equipment began to disappear. Today, equipment dedicated to performing only the word processing function is virtually nonexistent.

What is the primary use of voice response in word processing?

It is too early to determine whether the **voice response** capability bundled with some of the popular word processing software (or that can be used in conjunction with word processing software) will begin another revolution, that of using dictation rather than the computer's keyboard to originate documents. Compared with the early versions of the voice response software, today's version is quite sophisticated, allowing dictation at rates approaching 160 words per minute and with a fairly accurate response record.

Word processing is one of the most widely used—if not the most widely used—functions for which personal computers are used. And of the various components of office software suites, word processing continues as the most commonly used component.

Steps in the Word Processing Cycle

Word processing is comprised of three fairly distinct steps: **origination/ formatting, revision,** and **disposition.** In preparing a document, once the originating/formatting is done, the originator may do on-screen editing and then print the document to ready it for disposition. However, most word originators prefer to edit and revise a portion of their work (especially longer and more complex documents) using a printed copy. Therefore, once the desired changes are marked on the paper copy, they are keyboarded prior to the final disposition/printing and delivery of the document.

Origination/Formatting. Although many originators do most of the document formatting during the originating step, some prefer to do most of it as a separate step after the first draft of the document is prepared. The ease with which documents can be reformatted enables the originator to make changes at any stage of the document-creation process.

What is WYSIWYG?

Today's word processing software has "what-you-see-is-what-you-get" (**WYSIWYG**) capability, which is a fairly recent addition. Therefore, when the originator decides to put text in bold format, it shows on the screen in bold. Changes in font type and size are reflected on the screen as well, so the printed copy of the document will appear just as it does on the screen.

How does automatic word correction work?

Another desirable feature of today's programs is **automatic word-wrap.** When a line is filled with text, the software automatically carries text to the next line without the operator's having to insert what is known as a hard return at the end of the line. In addition, other desirable features used during the originating process are **spell checking** and **automatic word correction.** Misspelled words are highlighted on the screen, which gives the originator an opportunity to correct the error before continuing. The automatic word correction feature identifies the error and corrects the word automatically. An example is the keyboarding of *hte* for *the*. When automatic word correction is enabled, the software automatically makes the correction for the originator.

As material is keyboarded, it is held in the computer's RAM (random access memory) until permanently saved to another medium. Error correction is fast and easy, often done by simply backspacing over the error to erase it and then keyboarding the correct text. Word processing software can be scheduled to save a temporary file of the material as often as the originator wishes—perhaps as often as every minute. This is a desirable feature that prevents the loss of keyboarded material should a power failure occur. Subsequent editing of saved (stored) material requires "reading" the document back into the computer's memory to facilitate making changes.

Revision. A number of helpful software features also facilitate the editing/revising of keyboarded material. One frequently used feature allows the originator to block text (also known as *highlighting*) to do the following: delete, copy, or move that text; change its font or size; change its font characteristics (bold, italics, or underlined format); change the vertical or horizontal spacing of the text; place the text in a box or in columns, and so forth.

During revising/editing, some originators also make use of another common software feature, the **grammar and style checker.** The software is capable of finding fairly simple grammar errors as well as such writing style errors as keyboarding the same word two times in succession and using the same word too many times in a short paragraph. Although these two features are helpful, they have limitations for which careful proofreading and an adequate knowledge of grammar/punctuation usage are the only acceptable alternatives.

A number of other helpful features are commonly found on the word processing programs found in today's office software suites:

1. **Automatic hyphenation:** This feature can be enabled so the program inserts hyphens and automatically divides words when they do not fit in their entirety at the end of a line.

2. *Footnotes:* This feature automatically inserts footnotes at the bottom of the page on which the superscript reference appears.

3. *Tables:* This feature facilitates the creation of columns in tables, aligning the numbers in the columns on the decimal or on the number's right side when all numbers are whole.

4. *Table of contents:* By marking text, usually headings and subheadings, with the appropriate code, the program automatically creates a table of contents.

5. *Index:* By marking text with the appropriate code, the program creates an index with the terms in alphabetical order.

6. *Web format conversion:* Once a document has been originated and saved, it can be converted to HTML format to facilitate its uploading to the World Wide Web.

7. **Graphics creation:** The program accommodates the insertion of graphics into a document as well as prepares certain types of graphics aids (bar charts, for example) that can be easily inserted into a document.

8. **Justification:** The program adjusts each line to fill the horizontal space allocated to the line; therefore, the lines on the right-hand side of the page end evenly, except for a partial line at the end of a paragraph. Material can also be justified vertically so the same amount of blank space appears at the top and bottom of each page.

What is the primary function of a grammar and style checker?

What function is performed by the table of contents feature of word processing software programs?

9. **Merge:** This feature permits the automatic merging of information found in two separate files. An example is the merging of the names and addresses of the recipients of a letter with the body of the letter.

10. **Macros:** A useful feature of word processing programs is the ability to use either built-in or user-defined macros, which are basically subprograms within the main program. An example is the date macro, which, when invoked (perhaps by depressing the control key and another key), enables the user to depress the *D* key, and the macro automatically inserts the current date at that location.

What is the primary function of templates?

11. **Templates:** This feature provides the originator with a predesigned format for a number of different types of documents, including résumés, interoffice memoranda, agendas, calendars, and so forth.

Disposition. As the final step in the word processing cycle, disposition is quite variable. It generally involves saving/storing the file on a magnetic medium as well as distributing the content of the file, using a variety of processes. In the early days of word processing, distribution generally involved using a printer to prepare a hard copy of the document and then transmitting the document through the U.S. Postal Service or through internal mail within the organization.

With the increasing availability of fax equipment, transmission by fax has become popular. More recently, with the increased use of e-mail technology, documents prepared using a word processing program are often sent as attachments to e-mail messages. Some individuals are predicting that Web-based distribution may become the most common means of document distribution for a growing number of employees. Rather than sending a hard copy of the documents they prepare using a word processing program or faxing the documents to the recipient or sending them as attachments to e-mail messages, the documents are converted to HTML format and subsequently uploaded to a Web server. Anyone who has access to the Internet and a Web browser and who knows the URL of the documents and is authorized to access them is able to read their contents.

Certainly, word processing has made the task of writing/composing easier for many people. And because of the ease with which material can be revised before it is considered in "final" form, word processing enables word origina-

How has the use of word processing improved the quality of written work found in many organizations?

tors to prepare higher quality work. Before the availability of word processing, making significant changes in a typed document generally resulted in retyping either a portion or all of it. For that reason, some originators were reluctant to make extensive revisions in their work, often resulting in work of lesser quality.

Shown in Figure 20–1 is a copy of the screen image of the paragraph shown above, in manuscript form, as it was created using the WordPerfect software program. The entire manuscript for this text was saved as files on floppy disks, which were used to create each page of this textbook. The material saved on the floppy disks was imported into a desktop publishing software program, which eliminated the necessity of typesetting the text, a process that was commonly found as recently as ten to twelve years ago in the publishing industry. Desktop publishing software is covered in a later section of this chapter.

SPREADSHEET SOFTWARE PROGRAMS

What are the three capabilities of spreadsheet software programs?

Many employees use **spreadsheets** to increase their productivity. Spreadsheets are created using a software program designed to process or manipulate information found within tables comprised of columns (vertical) and rows (horizontal). The program is capable of (1) presenting the data (alphabetic and nu-

Figure 20-1 Screen image of a document created using word processing

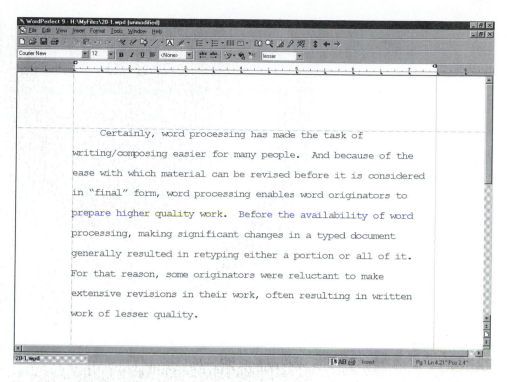

meric) as they were entered; (2) presenting the results produced by manipulating the information, such as calculating the average of a column of numbers; and (3) presenting the data in a rearranged order.

Many employees use the **"what-if" function** that spreadsheet programs offer. This function works in the following manner: Suppose an administrative office manager wanted to determine what effect placing several small desktop copiers throughout the organization might have on overall copying expenses. Currently, employees do all of their copying on two larger copiers in an inconvenient location for many of them. They waste time walking to and from these copiers and waiting in line to use them.

By determining the amount of time it takes to make one copy under the present process versus the predicted time the process would take if several copiers were installed will enable the administrative office manager to make a number of desired calculations. In fact, he or she can make calculations based on "what if" three desktop copiers were strategically placed? Four desktop copiers? Five desktop copiers? etc. Because the spreadsheet program facilitates recalculation of rows and columns in complex tables, once the administrative office manager has the program properly designed to perform these calculations, with a minimum of keystrokes, the outcome of the various alternatives (three, four, or five copiers) can be readily calculated. At some point, the installation of an additional desktop copier (perhaps the fifth or sixth one) will be found not to be cost effective in terms of its rental or purchase cost, because the per-unit cost of a copy begins to increase.

Functions of Spreadsheets

Most employees use spreadsheet programs to do more than simply display entered data. Other functions for which spreadsheet programs are used include performing arithmetic functions on either columns or rows of data, performing a variety of statistical calculations on the data, and preparing a variety of graphic aids, such as pie and bar charts. Another useful tool that spreadsheet programs offer is the sorting of the content of columns. Text data can be alphabetized; numerical data can be sorted in an ascending or descending order.

Features of Spreadsheet Software Programs

As shown in the screen image in Figure 20–2, the spreadsheet working window is designed as follows: The vertical columns are identified with alphabetic letters: Column A, B, C . . . AA, AB . . . DD, DE, and so forth. The horizontal rows are identified with numbers: 1, 2, 3, 4, 5, and so forth. The intersection of the row and column provides a rectangular-shaped area, known as a **cell;** each cell has a specific address: A1, A2, A3, B1, B2, B3, and so forth. The **cell address** of the highlighted cell in Figure 20–2 is *B11*. Data (alphabetic or numeric) are entered into a cell by placing the cursor in the cell and keyboarding the desired information. The keyboard arrows are used to move either to the left or right, up or down. However, before data can be entered into a specific cell or before the content of a cell can be altered, the cursor has to be located within the cell.

A variety of different cell formats are available, which, when invoked, put the cell contents automatically into the desired format. To illustrate, entering 1234.56 will appear in the cell as $1,234.56 if the currency and comma separator formats have been chosen for that cell. This feature reduces the number of data-entry keystrokes that must be performed.

All arithmetic functions (addition, subtraction, multiplication, and division), as well as a variety of statistical applications, can be performed on numerical data. Some functions, such as the addition of a column of numbers or row of numbers, are performed simply by highlighting the numbers in the column or row to be added and then clicking on the summation key in the toolbar. Other arithmetic and statistical functions are performed by entering the appropriate formula in the formula bar. For example, a formula can be entered in the **formula bar** that calculates the average of the nine numbers in

How are columns and rows identified in spreadsheet software programs?

What is the formula bar found in spreadsheet software programs?

Figure 20–2 Screen image of a spreadsheet worksheet

Column B of Figure 20–2. An example of such a formula, which is shown in the formula bar, is: =SUM(B2:B10)/9. This formula tells the program to add the nine numbers in Column B and then divide that sum by 9 to calculate the average. Once the formula has been created and used, changing a cell's contents will automatically adjust the answer derived by the formula. The formula automatically inserts the new calculation in the appropriate cell.

Formula replication is another useful feature of spreadsheet programs. When the same formula needs to be entered into a number of cells, the replication feature, using the copy and paste function of the program, places the same formula in each cell, making the necessary adjustment in the cell addresses. Thus, the user doesn't have to key the same formula a number of times. For example, if the formula =SUM(B1:F1) were copied and pasted into row 2 of a spreadsheet, the replication feature would automatically adjust the formula to be =SUM(B2:F2); row 3, =SUM(B3:F3), and so on. When using replication, if one of the elements of the formula needs to remain a constant (known as an *absolute value*), that can be easily accomplished by placing the $ symbol before each element of the constant; for example: D4. Formulas that contain an absolute value are not adjusted during replication.

A highly desirable feature of the latest versions of the common spreadsheet programs is their ability to present worksheets in HTML format without having to use a conversion utility. Thus, a file can be saved by the normal process, and then the file can be uploaded to a Web server, making it viewable using a Web browser. The spreadsheet data appear the same whether they are viewed with a Web browser or in the spreadsheet program.

In a formula in a spreadsheet software program, how is a constant value identified?

DATABASE SOFTWARE PROGRAMS

What is a database?

A database is a collection of information (both alphabetic and numeric) stored in an organized manner. A **database software** program facilitates data entry, storage, maintenance, retrieval, and so forth.

A database can be likened to an index that appears at the back of a textbook. Each entry in the index is considered a record that contains two units of information: one field contains the descriptor; the other field contains the page number or numbers on which the descriptor is found. Another example is an employee file maintained as a database by an organization. The record is the composite of information stored about the employee, and each piece of stored information is considered as a field. One field, therefore, likely contains the employee's name; another field contains his or her Social Security number, another field contains his or her department, another contains his or her office phone number, and the last field might contain his or her e-mail address. Because one of the advantages of using databases is their ability to provide instant record retrieval, being able to retrieve an employee's e-mail address (query function) simply by keying that employee's last name and perhaps a few letters of the first name should be possible.

Database Software Program Characteristics

A well-designed database possesses a number of identifiable characteristics:

1. It facilitates retrieval of the desired information instantly and in the desired format.

2. It permits the storage of data in a secure manner so records are inaccessible to unauthorized users.

3. It allows the easy maintenance of data stored in the database, including adding records, updating records, and deleting records.

4. It eliminates redundant information so that the information can be used in a variety of ways.

5. It provides a data-validation feature during data entry so that the incorrect type of information is not entered into a field; therefore, the entering of alphabetic data in a field designed for numeric data is not possible.

What is a basic determinant of the usefulness of a database?

To a certain extent, the usefulness of a database is determined by its basic design. Considerable thought needs to be devoted to the contents its users will find helpful once the database becomes a reality. In some instances, the database designer may have to "live in the future" to determine what records will be needed at some point, although they are not currently needed. In such situations, these records should perhaps be entered at the time the database is created rather than added later, which would likely be a more time-consuming process.

Features of Database Software Programs

The validation process used in data entry often helps eliminate the possibility of entering the incorrect type of data. When the various **fields** are created, the type of information that will be entered within them is defined. Among the types of fields are **text fields** (which can contain both alphabetic and numeric data), **numeric fields** (into which only numeric data can be entered), **date fields** (into which only a date can be entered), and **logical fields** (into which only a "yes" or a "no" can be entered). Therefore, if someone tries to enter numerical data in a logical field, the validation process will prevent that from occurring.

Shown in Figure 20–3 is the screen image of a table created using a database software program. Had the person creating the table erroneously tried to insert alphabetic information in the *Work Phone* column, the program would

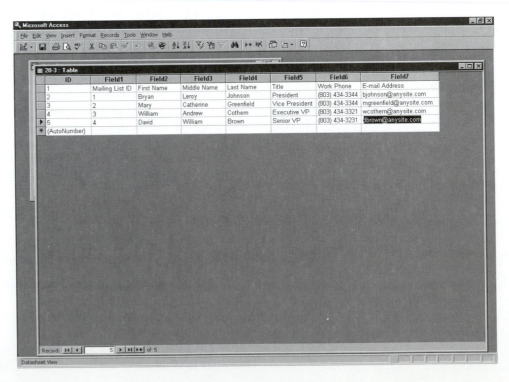

Figure 20–3 Screen image of a database table

not have allowed it because this field was preset to accept only numeric information. Once the information found in this table is stored in the database, it can be used in a variety of ways, including the preparation of the report shown in the screen image in Figure 20–4. Note that the report lists the employees' last name first but that the table listed their first name first. Also note that the report includes only the information requested by the user and that it is presented in alphabetic order, not in the mailing list ID order that was used in the table in Figure 20–3.

Once a database is loaded with data, it becomes a useful source of information, assuming, of course, that users can easily and quickly retrieve it. Three retrieval options are available: the database user can scan its contents, using the **"browse" view;** the user can generate lists, using the **"list" view;** or the user can obtain the desired information with the **"query" function.**

The "browse" process is simply that; the user examines the data contained in the various records, such as a screen image similar to the one shown in Figure 20–3, one field or record at a time. The larger the database, the less practical this option is.

The "list" process enables the user to "construct" a table in which the fields are column heads, and records are listed line by line. In some searches, the list process is quite useful because once the data are in a table format, they can be sorted in a variety of ways. For example, if the data in a certain column are alphabetic in nature they can be sorted in alphabetical order. If the data are numerical, they can be sorted in numerical order. Assume, for example, the user decided to sort the data in a table on the basis of the date that each of the company's 300 employees began working. By sorting the data in this table on the basis of the starting date column and having the sort function arrange the data in ascending order, the user can quickly determine which employees have worked for the company the longest. The screen image shown in Figure 20–4 is a report prepared using the list view, with the data put in alphabetic order, beginning with the employees' last name.

For what is the "browse" view function used in a database software program?

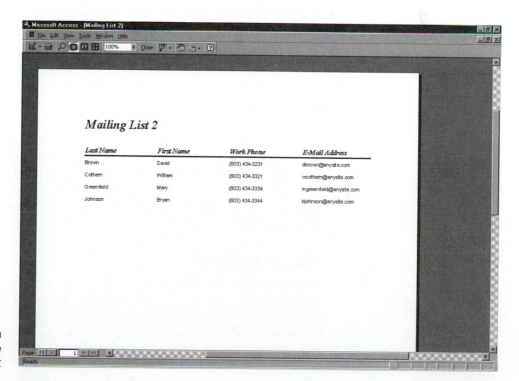

Figure 20–4 Screen image of a database report

How is the query by
example used?

The "query" process is the most complex of the three options for searching a database, but it is often the most productive process when undertaking complex searches. A common query process is known as **query by example (QBE).** To search for information, the user keys into a blank query form the information he or she wishes to match. Once this has been done and the query is submitted, in a matter of seconds the results are displayed on the screen.

Another query technique is the **Structured Query Language (SQL),** which enables the user to search for a specific record or for a group of records that possess the stated search criteria. As an example, when searching a database for a specific record that contains an employee's e-mail address, keying in the employee's name will retrieve his or her record, which contains the e-mail address. A more complex search would be undertaken when the user wishes to obtain a list of employees in a managerial or administrative position who have completed a master's degree. Using the appropriate search process, a list of these employees will be readily provided.

Once the desired information has been retrieved from a database, it can be viewed on the screen; it can also be printed as a report. Database software programs provide a number of formatting options for a printed report. Probably the most common format is to print the data in columns with the column heads corresponding to the field names. The integrated nature of office software suites facilitates merging the names and addresses in a database into a form letter prepared using word processing. Other records from the database can also be merged into the letter. For example, suppose a bank that provides its customers with a credit card wishes to send a personalized letter to each card holder. Such database records as name and address of each card holder as well as the card holder's account number are merged into the form letter.

Some organizations allow outsiders (such as customers) to access online certain records within their databases. For example, an increasing number of vendors provide their customers with the ability to do online tracking of the status of their order. Therefore, the customer can determine when the vendor received the order, when the order was filled, and when the order was shipped. At that point, the customer may be able to track the movement of the order from the vendor's location to the final destination if the order is shipped by a company that provides online tracking. UPS and FedEx are examples of companies that provide online tracking.

PRESENTATION SOFTWARE PROGRAMS

Employees who make presentations, even short ones, have discovered the value of supplementing their spoken words with visual aids. **Presentation software** programs facilitate the preparation of these visual aids. Because the software program facilitates preparing "soft" copies of the visual aids (in addition to hard copies—handouts, for example—if and when needed), changes in the aids can be made almost up to the minute the presentation begins.

Output Options

What are the output
options available on
presentations software
programs?

A number of options are available with regard to the types of output that presentation software is capable of creating. It can create a paper copy of each visual aid, which is generally used as a master to prepare **transparencies** displayed by an overhead projector. (As an alternative, one can print directly on a special type of transparency, thus bypassing the intermediate step of first preparing a paper copy.) The software can provide the presenter with three to six smaller images of the **slides** comprising the presentation. These slides are printed on a page that he or she uses during the presentation. These same pages can also be used as the master for preparing paper handouts for those attending the presentation. Too, the software can be used to prepare slides displayed using an **LCD projector** attached to a computer. The slides displayed using an LCD projector can be truly multimedia in nature by incorporating sound, motion, and so on. Finally, output can also be in the form of 35mm slides.

Creating Output Using Presentation Software

The process of creating output, called *slides,* is greatly simplified by the presentation software program. The user has a number of options in preparing the slides; these options should be considered carefully when determining basic slide design.

The first option is to determine whether to use a template, which is a ready-made format that comes with the software. With a template, the user simply keys the information to be displayed on each slide. Information can be text, numerical, or a graphic aid, such as a pie or bar chart. The basic design (shape of objects, color combinations used, and so forth) of the template cannot be changed, however. Although the template designs are visually attractive, they sometimes create difficulties in viewing slide content during the presentation. This is especially true in rooms that don't have the most desirable viewing environment because the projector screen area of the room cannot be darkened sufficiently to enhance the display. Too, some rooms have to be darkened so much that participants are bothered. The user has control over size of font used, text color, and font style. The larger the room in which the presentation is being made, the less likely it is that a template will be used because of potential viewing difficulties.

Another option is the "**blank**" **slide** alternative. Although this option provides no built-in design features, it can be used to prepare some very attractive slides for use in presentations using LCD projection equipment. When beginning with a blank slide rather than a template, a number of options are available, such as using a slide that automatically inserts bullets at the beginning of each new item, a slide that does not insert bullets, or a slide that produces a graphic aid, such as a bar or pie chart. In many presentations, several of the slide options are likely to be used. Once a slide has been created, a number of other features can be added to it, including these:

What are some of the features that can be added to slides once they are created?

1. The background color that will be displayed as well as the size, type, color, and characteristics of the text.

2. The manner in which the information on the slide appears on the screen during the presentation. All of the information can be made to appear at once, or it can be made to appear when desired, which is known as the *build feature.* To activate the build feature, a slide format incorporating bulleted lists must be used, which allows this animation effect.

3. The manner in which each item on the slide appears on the screen, which is known as the *transition effect.* The items can appear letter by letter, known as the *typewriter effect,* or as a camera shutter, with the information in the middle of the slide appearing first, moving outward, and so forth.

4. The inclusion of motion on a slide, which may make its use more effective. This is accomplished by incorporating a video clip onto the slide, which is somewhat more complex that simply putting text on it.

Shown in Figure 20–5 is a screen image of a slide that was created using Microsoft's PowerPoint presentation software program. A blank slide was used that provided space for the slide's heading (Agenda) as well as automatically

Figure 20-5 Screen image of a presentation slide

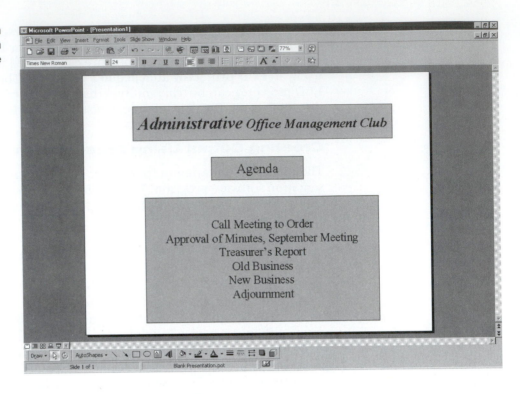

inserted a bullet at the beginning of each new line. If the animation feature is activated during the presentation, the various bulleted items on each slide will appear one by one as the presenter depresses the *page down* key on the keyboard or clicks the mouse button.

For what is the automatic display feature used?

Depending on the nature of the presentation, the use of the automatic display feature may be desirable. Invoking this feature allows the presentation to run by itself without the need for human intervention. Its use is desirable for display booths at conventions, for example. Because presentations can run by themselves, employees are available to answer questions, to hand out materials, and so forth. The amount of time each slide is to appear on the screen is predetermined and set, thus assuring that viewers have ample time to read the material on each slide. Today's version of the software programs also permit adding sound (voice, music, and so forth) to each slide as it is displayed.

As has been the case with several of the other components of office suite software, files created using presentation software can be uploaded to a Web server without requiring conversion to another format. In fact, with Internet access and a Web browser, the slides created for a presentation can be "served" through the Internet and displayed on a Web browser interconnected to an LCD projector. The alternative to this is to store the file on either a floppy disk or the hard drive of a computer. Because the slides comprising the presentation are displayed by the presentation software program, one can do anything with the slides, (print, save the file to a disk for later reading, etc.) that can be done with them when they are viewed offline using the presentation software.

DESKTOP PUBLISHING SOFTWARE PROGRAMS

Although the popular word processing software programs have incorporated desktop publishing capability, dedicated **desktop publishing software (DTP)** is the program of choice in preparing an increasing number of documents in

What is the primary function of desk-top publishing software?

many organizations. This is because word processing software is somewhat limited when compared with the capability of desktop publishing software. When preparing brochures, pamphlets, ad pieces, manuals, and so forth, desktop publishing software is much more versatile. It eliminates the earlier, tedious, often cumbersome process of typesetting material and then manually pasting up each page.

Preparing Camera-Ready Copy

Most printing processes require the preparation of what is known as **camera-ready copy,** which is used to prepare the plates that enable the document to be printed professionally, perhaps using the offset printing process. Using desktop publishing software, which is dedicated to the process of producing camera-ready copy, will likely result in the creation of a higher quality document from a production standpoint than is possible with word processing. The fact that word processing is primarily concerned with text while desktop publishing is more concerned with total document composition is a major reason why the latter is generally preferred.

Most individuals who use desktop publishing software find it desirable to prepare the text with a word processing program and to make revisions in the text. Once that is done, the material is copied and pasted into the document being created with the DTP program.

For what is word processing commonly used in conjunction with DTP?

Desktop publishing software facilitates the process of creating the basic design and layout of each page of the document, whether it has one page or a thousand pages. When a number of pages have the same basic layout, the design can be easily replicated on each of these pages. In preparing the layout of each page of the document, separate frames are created for text, pictures, art, rules/dividers, and so forth. After the frames have been put in place at their desired location, they are filled with the desired content, whether it is a picture, art, text, or a divider. At this point, the page is considered to be "pasted up." When photographs are placed into documents created with desktop publishing software, they are generally scanned to create a digital file of the image. The image is then imported into the frame where it will appear in the document.

Features of Desktop Publishing Software

A number of desirable features are available on desktop publishing software, including these:

1. Design templates, which enable the user to construct pages without having to create their basic design.
2. **Clip art library,** which consists of hundreds or perhaps thousands of ready-to-use images. In most cases, the clip art can be sized to fit the frame (space) in which it will be placed.
3. **Type/font library,** which provides the user with perhaps hundreds of different typefaces in different sizes and with different characteristics, such as bold, italics, and so on.

Figure 20–6 is a screen image of a page layout created with desktop publishing software to prepare camera-ready copy for a brochure announcing a conference program. When the master is prepared, the text represented symbolically on the screen image will print as the actual text.

The output of a document created using desktop publishing software can be in the form of hard copy or soft (electronic) copy. When hard copy is

Figure 20-6 Screen
image of the layout of
a brochure created
using DTP

Heading

Lorem ipsum dolor sit amet, consectetuer adipiscing elit, sed diam nonummy nibh euismod tincidunt ut laoreet dolore magna aliquam erat volutpat. Duis autem vel eum iriure dolor in hendrerit in vulputate velit esse molestie consequat, vel illum dolore eu feugiat nulla facilisis at vero eros et accumsan et iusto odio dignissim qui blandit praesent luptatum zzril delenit augue duis dolore te feugait nulla facilisi.

Lorem ipsum,

Dolor sit amet
Consectetuer adipiscing

Subhead

Lorem ipsum dolor sit amet, consectetuer adipiscing elit,
sed diam nonummy nibh euismod tincidunt ut laoreet

dolore magna aliquam erat volutpat. Duis autem vel eum iriure
dolor in hendrerit in vulputate velit esse molestie
consequat, vel illum dolore eu feugiat nulla facilisis at vero

eros et accumsan et iusto odio dignissim qui blandit praesent
luptatum zzril delenit augue duis dolore te feugait nulla facilisi.
Lorem ipsum dolor sit amet, consectetuer adipiscing elit,
sed diam nonummy nibh euismod tincidunt ut laoreet
dolore magna aliquam erat volutpat. Duis autem vel eum
iriure dolor in hendrerit in vulputate velit esse

molestie consequat, vel illum dolore eu feugiat nulla
facilisis at vero eros et accumsan et iusto odio

Subhead 2

luptatum zzril delenit augue duis dolore te feugait nulla
facilisi.Lorem ipsum dolor sit amet, consectetuer
adipiscing elit, sed diam nonummy nibh euismod
tincidunt ut laoreet dolore magna aliquam erat volutpat.
Duis autem vel eum iriure dolor in hendrerit in vulputate
velit esse molestie consequat, vel illum dolore eu

feugiat nulla facilisis at vero eros et accumsan et iusto
odio dignissim qui blandit praesent luptatum zzril delenit
augue duis dolore te feugait nulla facilisi.
Lorem ipsum dolor sit amet, consectetuer adipiscing
elit, sed diam nonummy nibh euismod tincidunt ut
laoreet dolore magna aliquam erat volutpat. Duis autem

Subhead 2

vel eum iriure dolor in hendrerit in vulputate velit esse molestie consequat, vel illum dolore eu feugiat nulla facilisis
at vero eros et accumsan et iusto odio dignissim

Subhead 2

qui blandit praesent luptatum zzril delenit
augue duis dolore te feugait nulla facilisi.
Lorem ipsum dolor sit amet, consectetuer
adipiscing elit, sed diam nonummy
nibh euismod tincidunt ut laoreet dolore

magna aliquam erat volutpat. Duis autem vel eum iriure dolor in

hendrerit in vulputate velit esse molestie consequat,
vel illum dolore eu feugiat nulla facilisis at vero eros

et accumsan et iusto odio dignissim qui blandit praesent
luptatum zzril delenit augue duis dolore te feugait nulla facilisi.

prepared, it will likely be made on a printer, such as a laser or ink-jet printer (either black and white or color), using a high dots-per-inch resolution. When an electronic copy is prepared, it appears in HTML format so the material can be uploaded to the World Wide Web and then viewed using a Web browser. As an alternative to the HTML format, the document can be saved in the **portable document format (PDF),** a proprietary format of Adobe Corporation, and then uploaded to the World Wide Web where it can be accessed on a Web

What is PDF?

browser. When viewing the document, the reader will need to use Acrobat Reader, which can be downloaded for free from Adobe.

SCHEDULING SOFTWARE PROGRAMS

Employees use **scheduling software** programs instead of paper-based calendars to keep an electronic record of their appointments. One of the significant advantages of using the software programs is that when a team or a committee leader is attempting to set up a meeting, the electronic calendars of those who are expected to attend can be accessed automatically by the software program to determine the times each is available. Once that information is known, the leader can use the software program to enter the important data about the meeting (day, time, duration) into each member's electronic calendar. Software programs are also available that notify each of these individuals about the meeting by e-mail. These programs also enable their users to maintain a daily **to-do list.**

Critical to the success of using the scheduling software is the need for employees to keep their schedules updated. When some employees make appointments or schedule events that they do not enter into their electronic calendar, the system will indicate they are available for an upcoming meeting or event when that may not be the case. This often results in the "double booking" of employees' time, generally resulting in unnecessary frustration to those who are inconvenienced.

A widely used feature of the scheduling software is the preparation of a variety of paper-based output, including a daily calendar, showing the times of each appointment scheduled for that day; a weekly calendar; and perhaps a monthly calendar. This facilitates scheduling events during times that employees are unable to access their electronic calendars. However, for the system to function properly, they need to remember to enter their new appointments into the system just as soon as they can.

Several widely used software programs dedicated to maintaining a schedule are available, including OnTime. An example of a program that combines e-mail and the scheduling components is Lotus Notes. An increasing number of individuals are using Web-based scheduling, which enables them to access their schedule, regardless of their actual location, simply by accessing the World Web Web. An example of Web-based scheduling is Yahoo's calendar, an example of which is shown in the screen image in Figure 20–7. Web-based calendars are free to their users; they derive their financial support from the online advertising that accompanies them. Increasingly, these programs also enable their users to maintain a to-do list as well as *notify* to add an appointment to the schedule by e-mail.

Regardless of the system used—Web based or system based—it needs to be user friendly. It also needs to facilitate updating, editing, and deleting items, as well as the ability to obtain paper output. Another useful feature is the ability to include recurring events in the schedule but having to key them only once, letting the system automatically schedule these events. For example, suppose a team leader has asked that members of her group be available to meet every Wednesday morning from 9–10 from January 15 through May 20. The recurring-event feature of the scheduler puts this event on each person's schedule for the duration of this time period, although the crucial information was entered into the system only once.

What often determines whether or not electronic scheduling functions effectively?

Figure 20-7 Screen image of web-based scheduling. Reproduced with permission of Yahoo! Inc. © 1999 by Yahoo! Inc. YAHOO! and the YAHOO! Logo are trademarks of YAHOO, Inc.

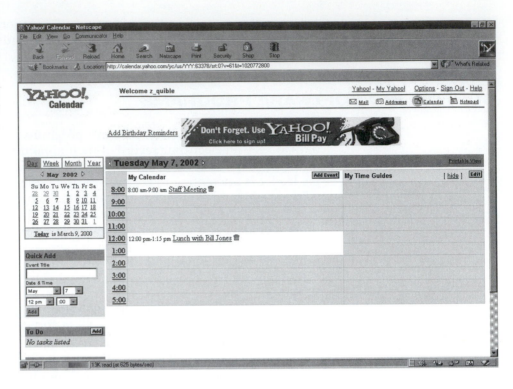

IMPLICATIONS FOR THE ADMINISTRATIVE OFFICE MANAGER

The applications software programs discussed in this chapter are designed to help their users, including the administrative office manager, to become more productive in carrying out their job responsibilities. The extent to which the programs are used to their fullest capability will likely determine whether employees succeed in that regard. As the programs become more full featured, an increasing number of individuals seem to be using the "just-in-time-training" technique to master all the features they need. Employees become readily proficient using the programs' features they commonly use, and the just-in-time technique is available for those features they use infrequently and that they may not always remember how to perform. Among the sources for this type of training are the Help feature built into the software programs, a user's manual that accompanies the program, and a variety of "how-to" books readily available for purchase. In addition, large organizations that have a Help Desk facility can also provide their employees with needed assistance.

REVIEW QUESTIONS

1. Why are an increasing number of employees in many organizations doing more of their own office production work?

2. How does the original concept of word processing differ from today's concept of word processing?

3. Explain how applications software differs from systems software.

4. What factors need to be considered in selecting applications software?

5. How do stand-alone software, integrated software, and office suite software differ from one another?

6. What are the three common steps involved in the word processing cycle?

7. Prepare a list of some of the common features of word processing software, and explain their function.

8. What is the value of the "what-if" feature found in spreadsheet software programs?

9. On spreadsheet software, how is the address of a cell determined?

10. What characteristics should a well-designed database possess?

11. Through what three methods are data in a database retrieved?

12. How do the templates found in presentation software differ from the blank slide option?

13. For what is desktop publishing software typically used?

14. What are the two common sources for maintaining an electronic schedule?

DISCUSSION QUESTIONS

1. You and another employee of the company in which you work were recently discussing the use of word processing software. You indicated that you felt you were fairly proficient using the features you commonly use but that you were not especially proficient with infrequently used features. The other employee indicated that she tries to be as proficient as she can with all features regardless of how frequently or infrequently she uses them. Discuss why the other employee's approach actually may be counterproductive and what suitable alternative could be considered.

2. You are one of the officers of a student organization on your campus. Over the years, your financial records have been maintained manually, primarily using bookkeeping ledger paper. Given the accessibility of computers and software, you now believe the financial records should be computerized. Discuss what software program will be most helpful to maintain the organization's financial records as well as various uses the organization might make of the software in terms of the management of the organization's operations.

3. In the administrative office management course you are currently taking, you are expected to make a seven- to ten-minute presentation about a topic related to this area. In discussing this assignment with another student in the class, he indicated that he had decided to use transparencies and the overhead projector. You indicated you plan to create slides using a presentation software program and then display them during the actual presentation using a computer and LCD projector. Discuss why you believe your approach will result in a more effective presentation than the one made by the other student.

STUDENT PROJECTS AND ACTIVITIES

1. Obtain brochures or sales literature outlining the functional specifications and capabilities of two competing applications software programs discussed in this chapter. Compare their similarities and differences.

2. Interview an individual whose job function requires the use of desktop publishing software. Discuss how he or she determines with any given job whether to use the desktop publishing feature of a word processing program or a stand-alone DTP program.

3. Going Online: Using the Internet, conduct an online search based on one of the concepts presented in this chapter or based on one of the chapter terms. Identify four or five things you learned from the material that you did not know prior to your online search.

Minicase

You were recently discussing the word processing concept with a friend. You indicated that during the time you've used word processing software, you've developed fairly good skills for composing documents at the keyboard. Your friend, on the other hand, indicated that she still finds preparing a handwritten copy of the document prior to keyboarding is easier for her. Although most individuals who use word processing software develop fairly proficient composing-at-the-keyboard skills, some do not; apparently your friend is one of those individuals.

1. Compared with the document-creation process used by your friend, what are the advantages of your document-creation method?

2. What alternative input method can you recommend to your friend that might make her task of creating documents easier?

Case

Delvin Company, a paint manufacturer located in Old Lyme, Connecticut, has not provided many of its employees with access to desktop computers. Input for document creation is either dictated or handwritten; office personnel, using desktop computers and word processing software, are responsible for transcribing the dictation or keyboarding the handwritten material. Financial and production data are entered into the system using terminals attached to the company's mainframe computer. Employees generally have found this process satisfactory because they didn't know how to use nor did they want to learn how to use desktop computers. Although as these employees retired and were replaced with younger employees comfortable and familiar with using computers, the company has continued to use its existing procedures.

As the newly hired administrative office manager for the company, you believe a number of processes have to change. One immediate change is to provide employees with a desktop computer if their job functions can be performed more efficiently using the equipment. Management has tentatively agreed with your recommendation to make desktop computers readily available. However, management also has two main concerns: (1) With an increasing number of employees doing more of their own office production work, what should it do with the potential surplus of office employees who have been doing this work in the past and who may not be needed with the implementation of your recommendation? (2) Should the applications software that employees use to carry out their job functions be installed on their desktop computers, or should the company install a network and load the software onto a server, making it available in this manner?

1. What suggestions can you provide that will help deal with a potential employee surplus should that occur when employees are given desktop computers?

2. What are the pros and cons of installing the applications software employees will use on a server connected to the network?

3. What are the pros and cons of installing the applications software on employees' desktop computers?

4. What suggestions can you offer that will help provide a smoother transition from the current process to the new process, assuming it is implemented?

*C*hapter 21

RECORDS MANAGEMENT AND MICROGRAPHICS

*C*hapter *A*ims

After studying this chapter, you should be able to design an effective records management program for an organization.

*C*hapter *O*utline

The Records Cycle
Organizing a Records Management Program
    Objectives of the Records Management
        Program
    Policies of the Records Management Program
    Organization of the Program
    Filing Systems
    Personnel
    Records Retention
    Storage and Retrieval of Records
    Records Retrieval
    Disposition of Records
    Evaluating the Records Management Program
The Records Management Manual
Document Management
Imaging Systems
    Scanned Images
    Micrographics
    Electronic Images
Implications for the Administrative Office
    Manager

*C*hapter *T*erms

Aperture cards
Centralized control
Charge-out system
Compound documents
Computer-assisted retrieval (CAR)
Computerized records retrieval
Computer output microfilm (COM)
Computer output to laser disk (C.O.L.D.)
Decentralized control
Filing
Film strips
Finding ratio
Front-projection readers
Image processors
Imaging systems
Jacketed film
Lateral equipment
Microfiche
Micrographics
Microimage format
Mobile filing equipment
Open-shelf file
Performance standards
Planetary camera
Power filing equipment
Processor camera
Rear-projection readers
Record processor

Records
Records inventory
Records management
Records management manual
Records retention
Roll film
Rotary camera

Rotary power files
Structural power files
Transfer
Use ratio
Vertical equipment
Vertical rotary files

*T*he ever-increasing volume of an organization's records and information that must be maintained requires an effective program. A well-designed, efficient records management program can significantly reduce an organization's operating costs. Furthermore, an efficient records management program helps ensure the proper care of an organization's records. Finally, an effective records management program enables the organization to control its records before the records begin to control the organization.

Improperly maintained records in hard-copy form are more likely to be misplaced or destroyed by mistake or have their confidentiality breached. Improperly maintained records stored electronically may become inaccessible and also have their confidentiality breached. The quantity of records stored electronically in many organizations is increasing rapidly. One reason for this is the number of e-mail messages that are sent daily, many of which are stored at least for a short time. Too, many e-mail messages contain attached files. An effective program provides the protection of an organization's records accumulation.

What is a record?

Records refer to informational documents in both paper and electronic formats that are used to carry out various functions. Records include forms, letters, e-mail messages, memoranda, reports, and manuals. **Records management** refers to the activities involved in controlling the life cycle of a record, beginning with its creation and ending with its ultimate disposition. **Filing** refers to the activities involved in rough sorting of paper-based documents, locating the proper folder for the document, and placing the document in the folder.

An effective records management program results in several significant advantages for the organization:

1. It better serves its clients or customers.
2. It increases employee productivity.
3. It accomplishes its work load with fewer employees.
4. It centralizes its records and information, thus making them readily available to all employees who need them.
5. It eliminates duplicate records and information.
6. It reduces its records storage space.
7. It complies with reporting regulations at the federal, state, and local levels.
8. It keeps better track of and control over its records and information.
9. It avoids costly litigation and liability issues.

The emergence of data processing has resulted in new applications used to store and retrieve information. Before organizations used data processing, storage and retrieval of information involved paper-based documents. Increasingly, information is now being stored electronically on a magnetic medium or optical disks, using a process known as **image processing.**

What is micrographics?

Records management also encompasses **micrographics,** the process of making miniature film images of paper documents. The film on which the microimage appears is available in several different formats. A process known as **computer-assisted retrieval (CAR)** is often used to retrieve microrecords. Micrographics is discussed in detail in a later section of this chapter.

The loss of an organization's records often results in its demise. Situations that can make the records management program particularly vulnerable are its failure to

1. Provide data backup.
2. Store backup copies of vital records off site.
3. Maintain information security or system access.
4. Maintain physical security where needed.
5. Provide adequate fire detection and suppression systems.
6. Provide adequate managerial control over the program.

THE RECORDS CYCLE

What stages comprise the records cycle?

Informational documents, including records, typically proceed through the life cycle illustrated in Figure 21–1. One of the most important functions of the *creation stage* involves controlling the development and adoption of new forms. New forms and records should be approved for use only when they can be substantially justified. The creation stage is also concerned with developing efficient methods of entering data on documents, a task of critical importance. Another important function of the creation stage involves determining the length of time records should be stored before they are destroyed.

The *utilization stage* of the records cycle is concerned with developing efficient procedures for use in retrieving and delivering desired records to their desired location at the desired time. Consideration is also given to developing efficient procedures for the movement of documents through their respective work flows. The effectiveness with which a document is used in this stage is greatly affected by the quality of the information it contains. For information stored electronically, utilization involves making accessible to the user the

Figure 21-1 Records cycle

records he or she is authorized to use and making inaccessible those he or she is not authorized to use.

The *storage stage* involves developing efficient procedures for using filing equipment and the space occupied by the equipment. To maximize efficiency and convenience, records should be stored in a location readily accessible to users. Storage is also concerned with protecting records against disaster or unauthorized use.

The *retrieval stage* is concerned with locating requested records. In addition to "signing out" documents removed from the files, retrieval involves tracking down documents not returned to the files within a reasonable time. For records stored electronically, retrieval involves using appropriate keyboard commands to access the desired information.

The *disposition stage* involves preserving valuable documents, especially those vital to the smooth operation of the organization. Disposition also involves transferring records from a high-cost storage area to a low-cost storage area as well as properly destroying records no longer having any value to the organization. Microrecording documents is also an important function of this stage. Records that are stored electronically can be permanently archived or purged when they have fulfilled their useful life. In most organizations, less than 5 percent of their records need to be permanently stored.

ORGANIZING A RECORDS MANAGEMENT PROGRAM

In addition to becoming increasingly aware of the rapidly growing number of records created and the costs incurred, managers are also becoming more aware of the benefits of implementing an efficient records management program. The following sections provide information about various program components of managing records stored in a nonelectronic format.

Objectives of the Records Management Program

What are the objectives of records management programs?

One of the first priorities in developing a records management program is to clearly identify a set of program objectives, such as the following:

1. To provide control over the records cycle, that is, the creation, utilization, storage, retrieval, and disposition of records.
2. To develop efficient procedures for each stage of the cycle.
3. To eliminate needless storage of duplicate records.
4. To reduce costs in each stage of the records cycle.
5. To develop realistic standards for employee performance and program evaluation.
6. To develop employee appreciation for the value of a records management program.
7. To standardize procedures and equipment used in the records management program.

Policies of the Records Management Program

After the objectives of the records management program have been developed, general operating policies should be adopted. Policies are used to guide decision making about various aspects of the program. Because vague or ambigu-

Why are policies needed that are designed to guide the records management program?

ous policies often result in ineffective or improper actions, policies should be clearly worded. The following are examples of the kinds of policies frequently included in records management programs:

1. The records management program, which has management's support, is considered to be an integral organizational function.
2. Each record created in the organization comes under the jurisdiction of the records management program and, therefore, is subject to centralized control.
3. The records management program shall operate under the procedures outlined in the records management manual.
4. Records must receive adequate protection at all times.
5. The administrative office manager has primary responsibility for the records management program, but ultimate responsibility lies with the appropriate functional vice president.
6. Efficiency will have precedence over cost when making decisions about work flow.

Organization of the Program

The type of control and the location of records storage determine the organization of the records management program. Some programs operate under **centralized control** while others operate under **decentralized control.** Records can be stored in a records depository (centralized) in the organization or within the various work units (decentralized).

How does centralized control differ from decentralized control?

Centralized Control. When a records management program uses centralized control, the overall authority and responsibility for the program is vested in one individual. Centralized control usually increases the formality of the program. In a centrally controlled program, records can be stored either centrally or decentrally.

Centralized storage, which means that records are stored in a central location within the organization, is advantageous for the following reasons:

What are the advantages and disadvantages of centralized storage?

1. The number of duplicate records that are stored is reduced considerably. Ideally, no duplicates are stored.
2. The equipment is more efficiently used, resulting in the need for fewer file storage units.
3. The organization can take advantage of the cost savings that accrue from the use of standardized equipment and procedures.
4. The program uses trained employees who file documents accurately.
5. The retrieval, retention, and transfer of records is better controlled.
6. The records pertaining to a particular subject are stored in one place.
7. The program operates continuously and is not hampered by employee absence.
8. Obscure records are obtained more quickly because their whereabouts are known.

The following are disadvantages of centralized storage:

1. The records may be more vulnerable because they are stored in one central location.
2. The time spent in transporting frequently used records to and from the central storage area may delay their immediate use.

3. If records cannot be immediately obtained, those who need them may be inconvenienced.

4. The confidentiality of records may be more difficult to maintain. More organizations are storing confidential records decentrally.

Decentralized storage means that records are kept within the various work units until the time has arrived for their destruction or transfer to low-cost storage areas. The following are advantages of decentralized storage:

What are the advantages and disadvantages of decentralized storage?

1. Confidential records are stored in work units throughout the organization and, therefore, are less vulnerable.

2. Because the records are stored on site, valuable time is not consumed in transporting records.

3. Because each work unit is primarily responsible for the storage of its own records, flexible procedures can be developed.

The following outlines the disadvantages of decentralized storage:

1. Some work units are likely to develop their own procedures rather than using those of the system, which may produce operating inefficiencies.

2. Duplicate filing equipment may be required.

3. Filing equipment may not be efficiently used.

Several factors should be considered when deciding whether to store records centrally or decentrally. Among the more important ones are attitude of top management toward the storage of records, competence of personnel, size and type of the organization, philosophy of the organization with regard to centralization and decentralization, and the number and kinds of records stored.

Decentralized Control. With decentralized control, each work unit assumes responsibility for the management of its own records. Decentralized control results in duplication of equipment, records, and personnel effort, as well as results in a lack of consistency in methods and procedures. In most cases, when control is decentralized, so is the storage of records.

Filing Systems

Another critical component of the records management program is the filing system or systems that are used. The filing system involves systematically classifying, coding, arranging, and placing records in storage and facilitating their quick and easy retrieval when requested by a user. Most organizations use standardized filing rules approved by the American Records Management Association. Cross-referencing of materials is also frequently involved in the filing process.

What types of indexing systems are used in records management programs?

Two general filing methods exist—alphabetic and nonalphabetic. The alphabetic method consists of three specialized indexing systems—filing by *name, subject,* or *geographic area;* the nonalphabetic method is comprised of *numerical* and *chronological* indexing systems. Figure 21–2 illustrates the various systems.

Most organizations use one of the alphabetic indexing systems. Each of these three systems uses alphabetic sections (A, B, C, D, etc.). Filing rules are used to determine the appropriate alphabetic section under which each record will be filed. Each system also uses two types of folders—individual and miscel-

Figure 21-2 Alphabetical and nonalphabetical indexing systems

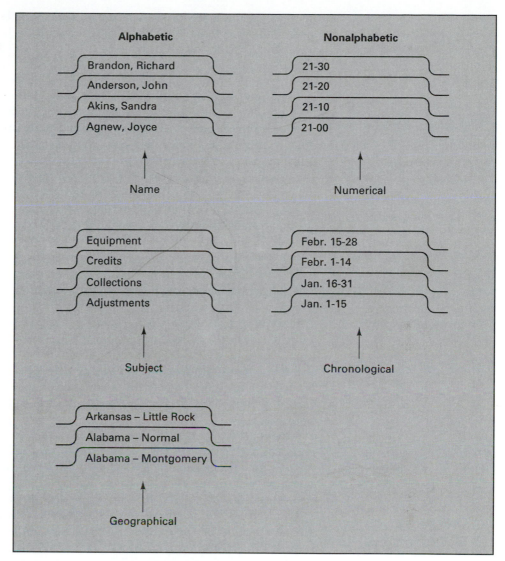

laneous—for each alphabetic section. When a specified number of records (usually five) is filed under a particular category, a separate individual folder is then prepared. For example, when the specified number of records pertaining to "Adjustments" has accumulated, a file folder labeled "Adjustments" is prepared.

Using the foregoing example, until the specified number of records pertaining to "Adjustments" is filed, records pertaining to this subject are filed in the "A" miscellaneous folder, along with other records of insufficient quantity to warrant the use of an individual folder. Records within each miscellaneous folder are filed alphabetically, with the most recent record filed as the first record in each category.

Both numeric systems use a numbering system. Numeric systems are used extensively for filing records that are numbered serially and for records on which the date is an important information item. Examples of records filed by numerical systems are purchase orders, sales slips, and invoices.

When the numerical indexing system is used, each category is assigned an individual number. To illustrate, a separate category is provided for each salesperson in an organization. The records pertaining to the salespersons are filed by their individual numbers. Cross-referencing is crucial in the numerical system. In the example just used, the name of each salesperson and his or her number are recorded on 3- by 5-inch index cards. Because the cards are filed alphabetically, the cross-reference index is used to determine the categorical number under which a particular individual's records are filed. Although time is consumed when having to use the cross-reference index, the system is useful when the secrecy and confidentiality of records must be maintained.

With the chronological indexing system, records are filed by a significant date. In some cases, this indexing system is used to follow up situations that require attention by a specific date. In other cases, the system is used for filing such records as daily reports and sales summaries. When the chronological indexing system is used, the record being filed is placed in front of all others in the file folder; thus, the file is arranged with the most recent record on top of the accumulation and the least recent record on the bottom.

Personnel

What types of positions are found in records management programs?

The personnel needs of the records management program are greatly influenced by two factors: the type of program structure used and the size of the organization. Centralized storage uses personnel who work with records on a full-time basis; in decentralized storage, personnel may work with records on a part-time basis. When converting from decentralized storage to centralized storage, some organizations find that more personnel are needed to staff the records management program. Over the long run, the expertise and specialization provided by full-time personnel will most likely offset the increased labor costs.

In small organizations that use centralized control and storage, overall responsibility for the records management program frequently rests with the administrative office manager. All day-to-day operations are likely performed by one employee, usually a file clerk. As organizations increase in size, greater specialization takes place. Responsibility for the program still rests with the administrative office manager, with a file supervisor likely managing the day-to-day operations of the center. The support staff is comprised of file clerks, requisition clerks, and messengers.

The file clerks are responsible for filing and retrieving records. The requisition clerks approve requests after determining whether the requests are valid and whether the individuals making the request have proper authorization to view the record. The requisition clerks are also responsible for the follow-up of materials not returned by the due date. Messengers deliver requested records and return records to be refiled.

In large organizations, a records manager—rather than the administrative office manager—assumes responsibility for the management of records. The mechanical aspects of the program are carried out by the support staff.

A growing number of individuals who work with records management are earning the designation of a Certified Records Manager (CRM), a program sponsored by the Institute of Certified Records Managers. Certification requires the passage of a five-part test covering (1) records management principles and program organization; (2) records generation and control; (3) active records retrieval, systems, and equipment; (4) records disposition/protection; and (5) technology of records management. In addition, the candidate must have a minimum of three years' full-time or equivalent professional experience in records management; a baccalaureate degree (or an equivalent substitution); and a recommendation from a Certified Records Manager.

Records Retention

What does records
retention specify?

Records retention, another important component of the records management program, uses retention schedules to specify the length of time that records and documents must be retained by an organization.

Benefits. A systematic records retention program is beneficial in several ways:

1. Considerable cost and space savings result from transferring inactive records to low-cost storage areas and from ultimately destroying records no longer useful to the organization.

2. Retrieval of records is simplified because fewer active-status records are stored.

3. Systematic destruction of records prevents their being destroyed prematurely.

4. Equipment for storing records—both active status and inactive status—is more efficiently used.

Conducting the Records Inventory. Prior to developing a records retention schedule, an important task involves determining the nature and volume of all records created. This is the major reason for conducting the **records inventory.** To conduct the inventory by sorting through files, record by record, would result in considerable time consumption and effort. An overall view of what has been created and filed is usually sufficient. To facilitate the process, a records inventory form similar to the one illustrated in Figure 21–3 is useful.

Why is a records inventory
conducted?

If the records are stored decentrally, cooperation of each department head is essential; otherwise, the inventory is likely to be somewhat inaccurate. Often a liaison is appointed within each department to assist the personnel conducting the inventory.

Classifying the Records. Upon completing the records inventory, the next step in the development of a comprehensive records management

Name or Title of Record	Form Identification No. (if Used)	Type of Copy (Original, Carbon Copy, etc.)	Location	Number of Location of Carbon Copies (if in Existence)	Indexing Method	Volume (in Linear Feet)	Inclusive Dates of Records	Frequency of Use and by Whom

Figure 21–3 Records inventory form

program involves classifying records according to their value or worth to the organization. A widely used classification scheme, which was developed by the National Fire Protection Association,[1] uses the following two categories to classify records: vital and important.

Vital records are considered to be irreplaceable. A reproduction of vital records does not have the same value as their originals. Vital records are needed for the continued existence of the organization.

How do vital records differ from important records?

Important records are those for which a reproduction is obtainable, often with considerable expense and labor or delay.

Scheduling Retention Periods. The records retention schedule, which is frequently used in a records management program, specifies the length of time each record is to be kept prior to its destruction. It does not designate when records should be transferred from active status to inactive status. Therefore, if the retention schedule indicates that a certain record has a life of three years, the record will be eligible for destruction after that length of time has passed.

The development of the records retention schedule involves several well-defined steps:

What steps are involved in developing a records retention schedule?

1. Getting authorization to develop the schedule.
2. Conducting a records inventory to determine the kinds, volume, and location of records.
3. Developing a records classification scheme to determine the value of each kind of record.
4. Developing a tentative retention schedule.
5. Securing top management's approval of the schedule.
6. Distributing the approved schedule to appropriate individuals.

Generally, a committee is appointed to develop the schedule. In smaller organizations, a representative from each work unit might be appointed to serve on the committee. In larger organizations in which the appointment of a representative from each work unit would be too cumbersome, an individual may represent several work units.

In addition to relying on the judgment of the committee members to develop the records retention schedule, several other factors should be considered. Because some records have a legal life of a specified length, the statute of limitations should be considered. Statutes, which vary from state to state, specify the legal life of certain records. *The Guide to Records Retention Requirements*, published annually by the U.S. Government Printing Office, lists retention periods required by departments of the federal government. The legal life of other records is specified by federal legislative acts—the Walsh-Healey and Fair Labor Standards Acts, for example.

After the tentative records retention schedule has been developed but before it receives final approval, the organization's tax specialist, attorney, and chief financial officer should closely scrutinize the schedule. The insight of these individuals is helpful. In some instances, one or more of these specialists is appointed to serve on the committee that develops the records retention schedule.

As with all programs and policies, the records retention schedule should be reviewed periodically to determine whether revision is necessary. As additional legislation is passed and as the use and quantity of records change, the schedule may need to be updated.

An example of a records retention schedule is presented in Figure 21–4.

Figure 21-4 Records retention schedule. Courtesy: Electric Wastebasket Corporation, New York, NY 10036.

Record Retention Timetable

LEGEND FOR AUTHORITY TO DISPOSE

AD – Administrative Decision

ASPR – Armed Services Procurement Regulation

CFR – Code of Federal Regulations

FLSA – Fair Labor Standards Act

ICC – Interstate Commerce Commission

INS – Insurance Company Regulation

ISM – Industrial Security Manual, Attachment to DD Form 441

LEGEND FOR RETENTION PERIOD

AC – Dispose After Completion of Job or Contract

AE – Dispose After Expiration

AF – After End of Fiscal Year

AM – After Moving

AS – After Settlement

AT – Dispose After Termination

ATR – After Trip

OBS – Dispose When Obsolete

P – Permanent

SUP – Dispose When Superseded

*After Disposed   ** Normally   † Govt R&D Contracts

TYPE OF RECORD	RETENTION PERIOD (YEARS)	AUTHORITY
ACCOUNTING & FISCAL		
Accounts Payable Invoices	3	ASPR-STATE, FLSA
Accounts Payable Ledger	P	AD
Accounts Receivable Invoices & Ledgers	5	AD
Authorizations for Accounting	SUP	AD
Balance Sheets	P	AD
Bank Deposits	3	AD
Bank Statements	3	AD
Bonds	P	AD
Budgets	3	AD
Capital Asset Record	3*	AD
Cash Receipt Records	7	AD
Check Register	P	AD
Checks, Dividend	6	
Checks, Payroll	2	FLSA,STATE
Checks, Voucher	3	FLSA,STATE
Cost Accounting Records	5	AD
Earnings Register	3	FLSA,STATE
Entertainment Gifts & Gratuities	3	AD
Estimates, Projections	7	AD
Expense Reports	3	AD
Financial Statements, Certified	P	AD
Financial Statements, Periodic	2	AD
General Ledger Records	P	CFR
Labor Cost Records	3	ASPR, CFR
Magnetic Tape and Tab Cards	1**	
Note Register	P	AD
Payroll Registers	3	FLSA,STATE
Petty Cash Records	3	AD
P & L Statements	P	AD
Salesman Commission Reports	3	AD
Travel Expense Reports	3	AD
Work Papers, Rough	2	AD
ADMINISTRATIVE RECORDS		
Audit Reports	10	AD
Audit Work Papers	3	AD
Classified Documents: Inventories, Reports, Receipts	10	AD
Correspondence, Executive	P	AD
Correspondence, General	5	AD
Directives from Officers	P	AD
Forms Used, File Copies	P	AD
Systems and Procedures Records	P	AD
Work Papers, Management Projects	P	AD

Revised and printed by Electric Wastebasket Corp. © 1983

Figure 21-4
(*continued*)

TYPE OF RECORD	RETENTION PERIOD (YEARS)	AUTHORITY
COMMUNICATIONS		
Bulletins Explaining Communications	P	AD
Messenger Records	1	AD
Phone Directories	SUP	AD
Phone Installation Records	1	AD
Postage Reports, Stamp Requisitions	1AF	AD
Postal Records, Registered Mail & Insured Mail Logs & Meter Records	1AF	AD, CFR
Telecommunications Copies	1	AD
CONTRACT ADMINISTRATION		
Contracts, Negotiated Bailments, Changes, Specifications, Procedures, Correspondence	P	CFR
Customer Reports	P	AD
Materials Relating to Distribution Revisions, Forms, and Format of Reports	P	AD
Work Papers	OBS	AD
CORPORATE		
Annual Reports	P	AD
Authority to Issue Securities	P	AD
Bonds, Surety	3AE	AD
Capital Stock Ledger	P	AD
Charters, Constitutions, Bylaws	P	AD
Contracts	20AT	AD
Corporate Election Records	P	AD
Incorporation Records	P	AD
Licenses - Federal, State, Local	AT	AD
Stock Transfer & Stockholder	P	AD
LEGAL		
Claims and Litigation Concerning Torts and Breach of Contracts	P	AD
Law Records - Federal, State, Local	SUP	AD
Patents and Related Material	P	AD
Trademark & Copyrights	P	AD
LIBRARY, COMPANY		
Accession Lists	P	AD
Copies of Requests for Materials	6 mos.	AD
Meeting Calendars	P	AD
Research Papers, Abstracts, Bibliographies	SUP, 6 mos. AC	AD
MANUFACTURING		
Bills of Material	2	AD, ASPR
Drafting Records	P	AD [†]
Drawings	2	AD, ASPR
Inspection Records	2	AD
Lab Test Reports	P	AD
Memos, Production	AC	AD
Product, Tooling, Design, Enginnering Research, Experiment & Specs Records	20	STATUE LIMITATIONS
Production Reports	3	AD
Quality Reports	1AC	AD
Reliability Reports	P	AD
Stock Issuing Records	3AT	AD, ASPR
Tool Control	3AT	AD, ASPR
Work Orders	3	AD
Work Status Reports	AC	AD

Figure 21-4
(*continued*)

TYPE OF RECORD	RETENTION PERIOD (YEARS)	AUTHORITY
OFFICE SUPPLIES & SERVICES		
Inventories	1AF	AD
Office Equipment Records	6AF	AD
Requests for : Services	1AF	AD
Requisitions for Supplies	1AF	AD
PERSONNEL		
Accident Reports, Injury Claims, Settlements	30AS	CFR, INS, STATE
Applications, Changes & Terminations	5	AD, ASPR, CFR
Attendance Records	7	AD
Employee Activity Files	2 or SUP	AD
Employee Contracts	6AT	AD
Fidelity Bonds	3AT	AD
Garnishments	5	AD
Health & Safety Bulletins	P	CFR
Injury Frequency Charts	P	AD
Insurance Records, Employees	11AT	INS
Job Descriptions	2 or SUP	CFR
Rating Cards	2 or SUP	CFR
Time Cards	3	AD
Training Manuals	P	AD
Union Agreements	3	WALSH-HEALEY ACT
PLANT & PROPERTY RECORDS		
Depreciation Schedules	P	AD
Inventory Records	P	AD
Maintenance & Repair, Building	10	AD
Maintenance & Repair, Machinery	5	CFR, AD
Plant Account Cards, Equipment	P	AD
Property Deeds	P	AD
Purchase or Lease Records of		AD
Plant Facility	P	
Space Allocation Records	1AT	AD
PRINTING & DUPLICATING		
Copies Produced, Tech. Pubs., Charts	1 or OBS	AD
Film Reports	5	AD
Negatives	5	AD
Photographs	1	AD
Production Records	1AC	AD
PROCUREMENT, PURCHASING		
Acknowledgments	AC	AD
Bids, Awards	3AT	CFR
Contracts	3AT	AD
Exception Notices (GAD)	6	AD
Price Lists	OBS	AD
Purchase Orders, Requisitions	3AT	CFR
Quotations	1	AD
PRODUCTS, SERVICES, MARKETING		
Correspondence	3	AD
Credit Ratings & Classifications	7	AD
Development Studies	P	AD
Presentations & Proposals	P	AD
Price Lists, Catalogs	OBS	AD
Prospect Lines	OBS	AD
Register of Sales Order	NO VALUE	AD
Surveys	P	AD
Work Papers, Pertaining to Projects	NO VALUE	AD

Figure 21-4
(*continued*)

TYPE OF RECORD	RETENTION PERIOD (YEARS)	AUTHORITY
PUBLIC RELATIONS & ADVERTISING		
Advertising Activity Reports	5	AD
Community Affairs Records	P	AD
Contracts for Advertising	3AT	AD
Employee Activities & Presentations	P	AD
Exhibits, Releases, Handouts	2 - 4	AD
Internal Publications	P (1 copy)	AD
Layouts	1	AD
Manuscripts	1	AD
Photos	1	AD
Public Information Activity	7	AD
Research Presentations	P	AD
Tear-Sheets	2	AD
SECURITY		
Classified Material Violations	P	AD
Courier Authorizations	1 mo. ATR	AD
Employee Clearance Lists	SUP	ISM
Employee Case Files	5	ISM
Fire Prevention Program	P	AD
Protection - Guards, Badge Lists, Protective Devices	5	AD
Subcontractor Clearances	2AT	AD
Visitor Clearance	2	ISM
TAXATION		
Annuity or Deferred Payment Plan	P	CFR
Depreciation Schedules	P	CFR
Dividend Register	P	CFR
Employee Withholding	4	CFR
Excise Exemption Certificates	4	CFR
Excise Reports (Manufacturing)	4	CFR
Excise Reports (Retail)	4	CFR
Inventory Reports	P	CFR
Tax Bills and Statements	P	AD
Tax Returns	P	AD
TRAFFIC & TRANSPORTATION		
Aircraft Operating & Maintenance	P	CFR
Bills of Lading, Waybills	2	ICC, FLSA
Employee Travel	1AF	AD
Freight Bills	3	ICC
Freight Claims	2	ICC
Household Moves	3AM	AD
Motor Operating & Maintenance	2	AD
Rates and Tariffs	SUP	AD
Receiving Documents	2 - 10	AD, CFR
Shipping & Related Documents	2 - 10	AD, CFR

Storage and Retrieval of Records

What factors should be considered in deciding what type of storage equipment to use?

Another factor that affects the success of the records management program is the equipment used for storing records. When acquiring storage equipment, every attempt should be made to secure equipment that will be satisfactory for its intended use.

Standardization of storage equipment, a characteristic of centrally controlled programs, helps ensure similarity of equipment size, durability, capacity, and design features. Of particular significance for storing vital and important records is the maximum temperature the equipment is able to withstand.

Various criteria should be considered before deciding upon a particular kind of storage equipment, including the following:

What categories of storage equipment are used in records management programs?

1. The nature of the records being stored, including size, quantity, weight, physical composition, and value.
2. The frequency with which records are retrieved.
3. The length of time that records are stored in both active and inactive status.
4. The location of storage facilities (centralized and decentralized).
5. The amount of space allocated for storage and the possibilities for expansion.
6. The type and location of storage facilities for inactive records.
7. The layout of the organization.
8. The degree to which stored records should be protected.

Types of Storage Equipment. Equipment designed for mass storage of records is categorized as vertical, lateral, and power. Each category consists of a variety of different types of equipment.

Vertical equipment is the type most commonly used in records management programs. Of the various types of vertical equipment, standard four-, five-, and six-drawer file cabinets continue to be the most widely used. These cabinets use approximately 2.5 square feet of floor space, and a like amount of additional space must be allowed for opening drawers. A distinct advantage of the standard file cabinet is the ease with which it may be moved with its contents intact. However, in time, the space-wasting feature of the drawered cabinets will likely make them obsolete for storage of large accumulations of records.

Another type of vertical equipment often used in records management programs is the **open-shelf file.** Although it maximizes the use of space (the files frequently extend from floor to ceiling) and improves storage efficiency, this equipment is recommended only for records that are filed and removed with the folders intact. This type of equipment is not well suited for situations where individual documents are frequently removed from folders. Open-shelf filing is illustrated in Figure 21–5.

Figure 21–5 Open shelf filing. Courtesy: Aurora Steel Products, Inc.

For what is vertical
equipment often used?

How does lateral
equipment differ from
vertical equipment?

Several types of **vertical rotary files** have also been developed. In a comparable amount of floor space, this type of equipment holds considerably more records than the standard file. Because of the rotary feature, retrieval is fast and convenient. Figure 21–6 illustrates vertical rotary filing.

Vertical equipment is most often used for storing inactive records in low-cost storage areas. Records are frequently stored in cardboard containers on steel shelves that extend from floor to ceiling. The containers are often the same ones used to transfer records from high-cost storage areas to low-cost storage areas.

Although vertical in structure, **lateral equipment** uses lateral pull-out drawers that require considerably less space than standard file cabinets. Storing records in drawers rather than on open shelves may expedite retrieval. Because lateral equipment can be insulated and equipped with doors that lock, some consider lateral equipment to have distinct advantages over open-shelf files. Figure 21–7 illustrates lateral filing equipment.

Power filing equipment, although not necessarily new, is now being used with greater frequency. Comparatively, the initial investment is considerably higher with power filing equipment than with other types of storage equipment. Some types of power equipment reduce the number of personnel needed in the records management function, and the resulting savings from labor costs can be used to offset the cost of the equipment.

The following questions should be assessed when evaluating the suitability of power equipment:

1. Structurally, will the floor withstand the weight of the equipment?
2. Because the installation of this type of equipment is permanent, have future storage space needs received adequate attention?
3. What effect will power outages have on the system; for example, can the system be operated manually, although perhaps not conveniently?
4. Do the equipment and physical environment provide adequate protection and security for the stored records?
5. In the event of equipment malfunction, are service representatives located nearby?

Figure 21-6 Rotary filing equipment. Courtesy: Acme Visible Records Inc., Crozet, VA.

Figure 21-7 Lateral filing equipment. Courtesy: TAB Products Co.

Three types of power equipment are available: (1) rotary power files designed to accommodate a particular size of card or form; (2) structural files designed to accommodate all kinds of forms and records; and (3) mobile files.

Organizations frequently use **rotary power files** for storing information about customers or clients and patient records in hospitals or doctors' offices, for example. Power is used to rotate the mechanism until the desired file bin is accessible; the file clerk then retrieves the requested record. Figure 21–8 illustrates a rotary power file.

Structural power files are typically used to store all types of records—not just one type as is characteristic of rotary power files. Some of the newer heavy-duty files are equipped with an electronic eye. At the push of a button, the transport mechanism scans and locates the desired storage container. A retrieval mechanism then moves the storage container to the console operator, who removes the requested record. Structural power files are often custom designed to meet the special needs of a particular records management program. A structural power file is illustrated in Figure 21–9.

Mobile filing equipment is classified as a power unit, even though some units are operated manually. Because mobile files eliminate the need for aisle space, they are especially useful where storage space is limited. Shelves are stored back to back against one another. A rail system facilitates the forward or backward movement of shelf units, which creates aisle space between two units. Aisle space has to be created between the shelf on which the desired record is stored and the adjacent shelf. Only one aisle can exist within the unit at any time, which makes the remainder of the shelves in the unit inaccessible. When using mobile filing equipment, especially power equipment, care should

How does one retrieve a document from a mobile file?

Figure 21-8 Rotary power files and computer interface. Courtesy: White Office Systems.

Figure 21-9 Structural
power file. Courtesy:
Supreme Equipment and
Systems Corporation.

also be exercised to assure that its safety devices always operate satisfactorily. Unless they are operating as they should, a person may become trapped in the aisle between two shelves as they are being closed. Figure 21–10 illustrates a mobile filing system.

Records Retrieval

Records retrieval, which refers to the activities involved in locating and removing tangible records from the files, involves the following steps: (1) the individual who desires a record fills out a request slip, which is transported to the central storage facility (as organizations install e-mail systems, the request more than likely will be sent as an e-mail message); (2) the requisition clerk approves the request and asks the file clerk to retrieve the record; (3) the record is transported either by messenger or by a mechanical device to the individual making the request; and (4) the record is returned to the central storage area when no longer needed. The procedures for manual retrieval are similar for both power and nonpower equipment.

Many organizations are now using a **computerized records retrieval** and **charge-out system.** The computerized system, which is often powered by a

What is the primary
function of charge-out
systems?

Figure 21-10 Mobile
filing system. Courtesy:
TAB Products Co.

desktop computer, is used to keep an inventory of all checked-out records. The inventory lists the name of the person who checked out the record, the date the record was checked out, the due date, and the names of others who have asked to check out the record upon its return. Before the requisition clerk submits the request to the file clerk, the computer is used to determine the availability of the record.

These computerized systems can also be used to perform other tasks such as maintaining the records retention schedule, maintaining the transfer schedule, and providing use-analysis statistics.

Disposition of Records

Disposition refers to the ultimate fate of records. For example, some records are permanently stored. Some are transferred to low-cost storage areas where they may be permanently stored or eventually destroyed. And some are micro-recorded while others are immediately destroyed. The four major methods of records disposition are protection, **transfer,** microrecording, and destruction.

What types of records disposition exist?

Protection

The value attached to vital records is a basic factor in determining the type of protection these records receive. Most vital records are protected by storing them in fire-resistant safes and vaults. If this protection is inadequate or un-available, vital records can be duplicated and the copies stored in secure off-site locations.

When evaluating an off-site storage location, a number of factors should be considered, including the following:

1. Safety and security measures provided by the facility, including fire, water, and burglar systems.
2. Environmental conditions, including lighting, temperature, and humidity control systems.
3. Protection provided against paper-eating rodents and insects.
4. Measures provided for dealing with emergency situations, such as power failures, severe weather conditions, and so forth.
5. Ability to provide around-the-clock input and removal of records.

In some instances, these off-site storage facilities also offer certified destruction of obsolete records as well as document scanning and conversion services.

Transfer. Transfer refers to changing the status of records from active to in-active. In many instances, as soon as the status of records has changed, they are transferred from high-cost to low-cost storage areas.

A basic factor used to determine when records should be transferred is their frequency of use. For example, records that are used at least three times a month should be considered active. If a record is referred to two or fewer times a month, it is still considered active but should probably be stored in the less accessible areas of the storage center (for example, in the lower drawers of file cabinets). Records that are referred to not more than once a month are often considered inactive and are, therefore, transferred to low-cost storage areas. In all probability, most of the records found in active status will not be more than two years old.

How do perpetual and periodic transfer differ from one another?

The two most common methods of records transfer are *perpetual* and *periodic*. When the perpetual method is used, records are continuously transferred to low-cost storage areas. The records are constantly examined; and when their age or frequency of use renders them inactive, they are transferred.

When periodic transfer is used, the files are examined at frequent intervals (perhaps every four months); and the inactive materials are transferred. An adaptation of the periodic transfer method is the *duplicate equipment technique* that requires a double set of files and equipment. The current year's records are stored in one set of file cabinets. The previous year's records are filed in the other set of cabinets, which are located beside the current year's files. After a year has passed, transfer takes place. The current year's records (now a year old) become the previous year's records. The previous year's records (now two years old) are transferred to low-cost storage or destroyed, and the now-empty cabinets are used for the filing of the current year's records.

Microrecording. Microrecording, a means of records disposition, is used primarily for two reasons: (1) it can significantly reduce the amount of space needed to store records, and (2) it is a means of making duplicate copies of those records sufficiently important to justify keeping duplicate copies.

Destruction. When records have been maintained for the length of time stipulated by the records retention schedule, their suitability for destruction should be evaluated. Several destruction methods are available. In warmer climates, the heating requirements of some buildings can be partially or wholly provided by incinerating records. Other organizations shred records and sell the paper for packing and other industrial purposes.

In what ways are records destroyed?

For ecological reasons, many organizations use paper recycling to dispose of records. The U.S. paper industry hopes to recover and reuse more than 50 percent of the nation's waste paper. This goal responds to an Environmental Protection Agency guideline which states that printing and writing grades of paper must contain at least 50 percent recycled waste paper. Technology is now available that enables recycled paper to be of sufficient quality that it can be used for good-quality letterhead paper.

When records are destroyed, a certificate of destruction is usually prepared that identifies the date on which the document was destroyed. Special procedures may have to be used when destroying confidential materials.

Evaluating the Records Management Program

Records management programs—especially those that have been implemented recently—should be periodically evaluated. The longer a program exists, the less frequently it may need to be evaluated. A new program is typically evaluated six or nine months after implementation.

What information do finding and use ratios provide?

The **finding** and **use ratios** are frequently used to evaluate the condition of the files in which records are stored. The finding ratio is used to determine how many requested records are actually found and is calculated with the following formula:

$$\text{Finding ratio} = 100 - \frac{\text{Number of records not found}}{\text{Number of records found}}$$

s MANAGEMENT AND MICROGRAPHICS**463**

Thus, if two hundred requested records were found and two were not, a finding ratio of 99 percent would result. The suitable range for a finding ratio is 97 percent or higher. Ratios less than 97 percent indicate that one or more of the following conditions may exist: (1) records are misfiled, (2) records are not properly indexed or coded, (3) records are not promptly returned for refiling, and (4) the whereabouts of records are not known because of improper charge-out procedures.

The use ratio is helpful in assessing the frequency of record use as well as determining whether too many unused records are filed. It is calculated by using the following formula:

$$\text{Use ratio} = \frac{\text{Number of records used}}{\text{Number of records not used}}$$

A ratio of 20 percent or higher is generally considered satisfactory. The following situations may be responsible for a low use ratio: (1) too many records are being maintained in active status when they should be transferred to inactive status, and (2) individuals are using duplicate records rather than requesting records from the central storage area.

Using **performance standards** is another means of evaluating the effectiveness of the records management program. Comparing employees' performance against reliable standards provides information about the efficiency of employees in carrying out various mechanical aspects of the program. Comparison reveals whether or not the employees are performing at an acceptable or an above-average rate. Training in appropriate areas may be desirable for those whose performance is unacceptable.

Figure 21–11 illustrates performance standards for filing and other related activities. These standards were developed under certain conditions; and unless the organization is able to duplicate these conditions, adjustments may need to be made.

Comparing the operating costs of the records management program with standard operating costs is another way to evaluate its effectiveness. Acceptable costs vary among organizations and between geographical areas, but the following guidelines are typical:

Salaries: 75–80 percent

Equipment and supplies: 15–20 percent

Space: 5–10 percent

Tasks	Units per Hour
Type 3 × 5 inch cards, labels, or tags	100
Code one-page letters	200
Sort 3 × 5 inch cards	300
Sort indexed or coded correspondence	250
File 3 × 5 inch cards	180
File correspondence	250
File vouchers numerically	700
Retrieve 3 × 5 inch cards	180
Retrieve correspondence and prepare charge-out forms	70

Figure 21–11 Filing standards.

Source: Wilmer O. Maedke, Mary F. Robek, and Gerald F. Brown, *Information and Records Management*, 2nd ed. (Encino, CA: Glencoe Publishing Co., 1981), p. 165. Reprinted with permission.

THE RECORDS MANAGEMENT MANUAL

What content sections are often found in records management manuals?

The **records management manual** is a vital document in the records management program. After the manual has been prepared, it should be approved and then updated periodically as program changes are made. The manual should also be available to each employee who works with records.

The following are appropriate content sections of the manual:

1. Objectives of the records management program.
2. Statement of policy of the program.
3. Organizational structure of the program.
4. Filing systems used in the program and the types of records filed under each system.
5. Personnel structure of the program.
6. Records retention schedule.
7. Procedures for retrieving records and information.
8. Disposition of records, including protection, transfer, microrecording, and destruction.
9. Procedures for evaluating the program.
10. Document management systems (if used).
11. Image systems (if used).

DOCUMENT MANAGEMENT SYSTEMS

What is a common component of document management systems?

Because of the ever-increasing number of records stored in organizations, the need exists to develop efficient ways to manage those documents. As a result, document management software was developed to aid the process of properly managing an organization's record accumulation. A common component of these management systems is the bar-code labeling of the documents stored within the system, even if the document is stored as a microrecord or as a digital image. As paper records are created and moved into storage, a bar-code label is placed on each record or on the file folder label.

Once the records are bar-coded, tracing their movement in and out of the document depository involves scanning the label and keying in either the destination or the recipient's code. If the document or folder is passed from its original recipient to another person before it is returned to the records depository, placing scanners in offices is useful for tracking the movement of the document or folder should follow-up become necessary.

An integral part of document management is the indexing of documents and/or key words within the documents. When employees might find certain documents helpful and if the documents are digitized and stored electronically, a key word search can be undertaken that identifies all the documents within the organization that contain the key word(s). At that time, each of the documents stored in hard-copy format can be retrieved and checked out by scanning the bar-code labels attached to the documents or file folders. Paper documents that have been digitized (by scanning) can be retrieved and displayed on the monitor of a desktop computer. Documents/records created on a microcomputer (word processing, spreadsheets, databases, e-mail messages, and so forth) can bypass the scanning process if they are archived on a magnetic medium or optical disk.

The goal in document management systems is to make them "seamless," regardless of the various types of media used for document storage. Therefore, the procedures would be identical when retrieving records stored in paper form, as a microimage, or on a magnetic or optical medium.

Because new developments in document management systems are occurring at a rapid pace, a careful study of their capabilities and the organization's needs is critical before a purchasing decision is made. Failure to study the situation carefully and thoroughly will likely result in the purchase of a system that provides less than optimum results.

IMAGING SYSTEMS

To what does imaging system refer?

As used in the management of an organization's records accumulation, **imaging systems** refer to scanned images, micrographics, and electronic images. Generally, the original paper-based document is not considered an "image"and, therefore, is not a component of an imaging system. Records comprising the imaging system are nonpaper, although they may have originally been paper based and can be easily reconstituted as a paper-based document simply by printing the image. Included in this section is a discussion of scanned images, micrographics, and electronic images.

The cost of document/image storage varies considerably with the medium on which the record is stored. Some storage systems use CD-ROMs as the storage medium. A 600MB CD-ROM can store approximately 250,000 pages of text while the DVD (Digital Versatile Disk) can store more than a million pages of text on a 5 1/4-inch platter. Cost savings result from the density with which these technologies store images. Storing records in electronic format costs a penny to $1 per megabyte, while storing records as microimages costs $1 to $3 per megabyte. Storing documents in their paper format costs $10 to $20 per megabyte.

Images stored electronically, are becoming increasingly accessible through the Internet or an intranet for those who are authorized to access them. Accessing images in this manner increases dramatically the efficiency of an organization's image retrieval system, especially when the organization has a number of remote locations separated by thousands of miles.

Document/image creation increasingly will contain hypertext links, making it possible to configure a particular document for its primary users. Thus, documents created in this manner possess added value for their users because they can be tailored to individual user needs. These kinds of documents are known as **compound documents.**

What is a compound document?

Scanned Images

Today's optical scanning equipment is used to scan paper documents, which produces a digital image. Once a document is captured as a digital image, its electronic storage is a simple process. Critical to the success of scanned documents is the ability to locate readily the scanned images. This is accomplished by an indexing process.

Systems are now available (they include both the hardware and software) that facilitate the document scanning process. These systems scan the document, allow the naming of each document using a variety of descriptors, store the image electronically, index the information, and provide various levels of image security. Retrieval of the document is done by keying into a computer the document information, and the system lists all documents filed under that descriptor. Once the document is displayed using the appropriate display equipment, it can be read, printed, e-mailed, or faxed.

Micrographics

Micrographics, another component of imaging systems, is used to increase the efficiency of a records management program. Among the most desirable aspects of using micrographics is the significant amount of space saved when storing documents in microimage format. The contents of 100 standard file drawers can be reduced to two drawers when storing contents in microimage format, which results in a 98 percent reduction in the amount of document storage space.

Today, in many organizations, as some records are microrecorded, they are simultaneously scanned using a high-speed image input device. This process digitizes their contents for storage on a magnetic medium or on an optical disk. Once the document has been digitized, it can be used as any other stored information is used. Under these circumstances, the digitized copy of the document likely is the one employees use, while the microrecord is used as a backup and for permanent storage. Once a digitized record is no longer considered to be active or has reached an age when it should be purged from electronic storage, the microrecord provides permanent storage.

Determining the Feasibility of a Micrographics System. Before an organization makes a decision about installing a micrographics system, its feasibility has to be determined by assessing technical, financial, and efficiency factors.

Technically, microrecording certain documents may not be feasible because of limitations imposed by such factors as document size, physical condition, or readability. Although microrecording certain documents may be feasible in other respects, the inability to overcome certain technical constraints may prohibit their being microrecorded.

How is the feasibility of micrographics usage determined?

To assess the financial feasibility of micrographics, the cost of storing records in hard-copy format and/or electronic format can be compared with the cost of preparing and storing microimages. Included are equipment costs, materials costs, and labor costs. The financial feasibility of micrographics will also be affected by the break-even point. The point at which greater economy can be achieved by storing a document in microimage format rather than hard-copy or electronic format will need to be determined. If the break-even point arrives after a document is eligible for destruction, then converting the document to microimage format is generally not financially feasible.

To assess the efficiency of a micrographics system, the convenience of using micrographics is assessed. Of special concern are the ease and speed with which desired microimages are retrieved and the convenience of magnifying the images, thus making them readable. Some types of equipment streamline the retrieval process, which reduces the amount of manual retrieval effort.

What types of microimage formats are available?

Microimage Formats. Another important decision that will have to be made when installing a micrographics program is which **microimage format** to use. Figure 21–12 illustrates the major types of microimages used today: roll film, aperture cards, jacketed film, microfiche, and film strips.

Of the various types of microimage formats, **roll film** continues to be the most widely used as well as the most economical. The film can be stored on a reel or in a cassette, cartridge, or magazine.

Figure 21-12 Types of microimages. Courtesy: Infosystems Magazine, Hitchcock Publishing Company.

16mm Roll Film   35mm Roll Film   Aperture Cards

Jacketed Film   Microfiche   Film Strips

Crucial to the success of a roll-film system is the indexing procedure used in retrieving the desired image. One of the more sophisticated systems is Miracode, developed by Eastman Kodak Company. A binary code index notation is made adjacent to each frame on the filmstrip. To find a specific frame, the film is inserted into a reader, and a keyboard is used to enter the binary code index of the desired frame into the machine. In a matter of seconds, the desired frame is mechanically retrieved and displayed on the screen.

Another means of indexing microimages involves the use of flash targets, which are suitable for use on reel or cartridge microfilm. The film is divided into segments of twenty feet, and each twenty-foot length is numbered consecutively, beginning with number 1. When retrieving a microimage, the segment number is used to find the general location of the microimage, and manual screening is used to find the specific image. The Miracode system locates an image faster than the flash target system.

Although **aperture cards** are generally used to store one image, several images can be affixed on a card. The image is mounted in the hole on the card, and identifying data can be keypunched into the card. The keypunched holes are "read" by the card sorter, thus facilitating the mechanical retrieval of the desired card.

A jacket consists of two thin pieces of clear plastic into which strips of microfilm can be inserted. The jacket, which typically has four channels, holds the strips in place. **Jacketed film** is especially useful for the temporary storage of microimages. Strips can be easily removed from the jacket, which makes it reusable. If a permanent, tamperproof image is desired, a microfiche copy of the jacket can be prepared. Jackets are not suitable for mechanical retrieval.

As many as several hundred images can be stored on a **microfiche,** which is a piece of film commonly measuring 4 inches by 6 inches. If a reduction ratio of 24 to 1 is used, ninety-eight images of hard copy, each measuring 8 1/2 by 11 inches, can be recorded on one microfiche. But if a reduction ratio of 42 to 1 is being used, 325 pages of material can be recorded on one microfiche of the same size.

What are the characteristics of aperture cards?

Typically, microfiche are indexed by displaying the contents of the fiche in one of the frames, most likely the one in the lower right corner. While letters of the alphabet are used to identify rows, numbers are used to identify columns. To display the contents in frame B-10, the grid coordinate mechanism on the reader is set at B-10.

Film strips are short pieces of microfilm on which microimages are stored. They are generally prepared as roll film and then cut into short sections that contain a specified number of images.

Other Features of Micrographics Systems.

Micrographics systems may use several other features, including computer-assisted retrieval (CAR) and computer output microfilm (COM).

The efficiency of a micrographics system is greatly affected by its retrieval process. Generally, organizations that have an extensive micrographics system use CAR. A computerized index of each document stored in microimage format is maintained.

For what is CAR used?

To retrieve the microrecord, the title of the desired image is entered by terminal keyboard into the computer system. The computerized index is scanned to locate the reel number (or microfiche number) of the desired document, and this number is displayed on the terminal screen. The micrographics clerk then retrieves the appropriate reel (or microfiche) from the storage rack. The reel (or fiche) is inserted into the reader, and the appropriate frame is then located either manually or automatically by a system, such as the Miracode system.

An illustration of a CAR system is shown in Figure 21–13.

A computer output microfilm (COM) system bypasses the paper printout process found in most computer systems. As the data are processed by the computer, the output results are displayed on an internal cathode ray tube. A special camera that produces either microfilm or microfiche is used to photograph each screen display of data/information. The **computer output microfilm (COM)** process prepares output twenty to twenty-five times faster than paper output is prepared on impact or laser printers.

For what is COM used?

The primary advantages of using COM are its origination and retrieval speed; the increased data availability because microimages are easily and inexpensively created; the decreased cost of data distribution; the reduction of storage space; and the environmental consideration of not having to dispose of large amounts of paper.

Figure 21–13
Computer-assisted retrieval. Courtesy: Canon, U.S.A., Inc.

As an alternative to COM, **computer output to laser disk (C.O.L.D.)** is becoming an increasingly popular storage medium. Rather than outputting to a microrecord, output is to a laser disk, which stores up to 200,000 pages on a disk. When compared with COM, three significant advantages result: density of storage, document viewing can take place simultaneously at many different locations, and records can be indexed, which facilitates the searching and accessing process.

Equipment Used in Micrographics Systems.   The equipment used in micrographics is the most costly aspect of installing these systems. Needed equipment includes cameras, image processors, and readers (reader-printers).

Two basic types of cameras are used in the microrecording process: rotary and planetary. A **rotary camera** automatically feeds documents through the machine. The camera operator places the document on the feed tray, and the document is microrecorded as it moves through the machine. Most rotary cameras have a 12-inch document width restriction.

A **planetary camera** is useful for microrecording large documents, such as engineering drawings and blueprints. The most significant difference between the planetary camera and the rotary camera is in document feeding. While documents are not automatically fed through the planetary camera, they are through the rotary camera. The operator places the document to be microrecorded on the camera's overhead flatbed, makes the exposure, and then removes the document. A document being microrecorded on a rotary camera continually moves through the camera; but on a planetary camera, the document is stationary during the microrecording process.

The **processor camera,** which is a variation of the planetary camera, is useful for microrecording large documents. The unique feature of this camera is its capability of automatically mounting an image in an aperture card. The entire process takes about 40 seconds, which makes this camera especially attractive when an immediate image is required.

New camera technology makes possible the updating of microfiche as well as the ability to obtain an instant image. The camera that possesses these two capabilities is known as a **record processor.** By means of an electrostatic image-fusing system, outdated images can be overprinted with such words as PAID or VOID. At any time, new images can be added to unused frames on the fiche. Two categories of records appear to be well suited for updating: certain personnel records and insurance records.

Figure 21–14 illustrates a micrographics camera.

Most of the new image processors move the film through the following steps: developing, washing, fixing, washing, and drying. Perhaps the biggest difference between the various processors on the market today is the way in which the film is moved through the equipment. Some processors move the film through in a straight-line path while other processors move the film through in a serpentine path.

The ultimate usability and acceptability of a micrographics system is often influenced by the image reader. Unless the users of the reader are easily and quickly able to obtain good quality displays of the image, they most likely will not be satisfied with the system.

The two broad categories of readers are **front-projection readers** and **rear-projection readers.** Within each category, a variety of readers are available to accommodate the various types of microimage formats.

Some readers are equipped with a printing device that enables the user to obtain a hard copy of an image. The user simply pushes the "print" button

How do rotary and planetary cameras differ from each another?

What is the function of an image processor?

Figure 21–14 Micrographics camera. Courtesy: Eastman Kodak Company.

on the reader; and in a matter of seconds, a hard copy can be obtained. Figure 21–15 illustrates such a reader/printer.

What factors need to be considered to determine which documents to microrecord?

Factors to Consider in Determining Which Documents to Microrecord. After installing the micrographics system, decisions will have to be made about which documents to microrecord. Answering the following questions will be useful in making these decisions:

1. *How long is the record to be kept?* Generally, records must be kept for at least four years before microrecording is financially feasible. For each year longer than four years that records are retained, microrecording becomes increasingly desirable.
2. *Will the physical characteristics of certain records prevent their being microrecorded?* The quality of the microimage will be no better than the quality of the original. Dark colors sometimes do not photograph well when black-and-white film is used.
3. *Will the microimage be admissible as evidence in legal courts?* Increasingly, microimages are becoming admissible as court evidence; but before original copies are destroyed, appropriate state and federal laws should be checked.
4. *Does a sufficient volume of certain records exist to warrant their being microrecorded?* Generally, the greater the number of records, the more advantageous microrecording is apt to be.
5. *Considering the frequency of use, would the original record be more convenient to use than a microimage?* If efficient procedures are used, the original record and the microimage should be about equally convenient.

Figure 21-15 Micrographic reader-printer. Courtesy: Canon U.S.A., Inc.

Electronic Images

Storing documents electronically eliminates much of the paper that held information in the past. Although paper continues to be the most common medium for storing information in the majority of organizations, its use in the distant future will likely decrease at a rate comparable to the increase in the use of imaging.

Imaging systems involve the capture, storage, and retrieval of information in two different formats: electronically as digitized documents or as micrographic images. The emergence of new technology is stimulating interest in and growth of this critical area of records management. The new technology permits the simultaneous scanning and microrecording of images, thus making them available in the two formats (microimage and digitized as electronic). Other technology permits the digitizing of records previously stored as microimages. Once a record is digitized, it can be manipulated in the same way that any other computer-stored information can be manipulated. Furthermore, stored images subsequently can be moved through other electronic peripherals, such as fax devices and laser printers.

Depending on the way the digitized records are indexed, a key word search can be conducted that identifies all records in the database that contain the key word. Thus, if the user wishes to retrieve all electronic images involving "ABC Company," the company's name is entered into the system as a key word. Other documents can also be retrieved by their specific file name (letter to John Brown on December 12, 2000, for example). In this case, the following file name might be entered into the system: Brown, John/letter/12–12–00. The system will then retrieve the letter and display it on the user's desktop computer monitor.

What are the benefits of imaging systems?

Imaging systems offer a number of benefits, including the following: the dependablity of microimaging, the sophistication of optical-disk technology, the significant reduction in storage space required, and the less opportunity for misplacement or loss of documents. Another advantage results from increased employee efficiency because fewer hours are required to maintain the stored information, and employees with access rights enjoy almost instantaneous retrieval of the desired information.

IMPLICATIONS FOR THE ADMINISTRATIVE OFFICE MANAGER

The nature of the administrative office manager's responsibility for records management varies from organization to organization. While some managers have day-to-day responsibilities, others have overall responsibility. In the latter situation, the records manager usually has responsibility for the daily activities of the program.

A basic understanding of records management is needed by managers and especially by those who have functional responsibility for the area. No longer can managers hold on to the mistaken notion that records management is solely a clerical task. Like so many other managerial responsibilities, the effectiveness of the records management program is directly related to the amount of attention it receives.

The most significant challenge facing those who are responsible for records management is the concept of imaging systems. Technology is developing at a fast rate; administrative office managers with extensive records management responsibilities need to keep abreast of these developments.

The information created and stored within an organization is often considered to be its lifeline. If that information is not effectively managed, organizational success can be hampered.

NOTE

1. Reprinted with permission from NFPA 232-1980, Standard for the Protection of Records, Copyright © 1980, National Fire Protection Association, Quincy, Massachusetts 02269. This reprinted material is not the complete and official position of the NFPA on the referenced subject, which is represented only by the standard in its entirety.

REVIEW QUESTIONS

1. Review the differences between records management and filing.

2. What is meant by records disposition?

3. In deciding whether the storage of records should be centralized or decentralized, what factors should be considered?

4. What kinds of filing systems are available for use in a records management program?

5. What kind of employees are likely to be used in a centralized storage facility?

6. Explain the perpetual, periodic, and duplicate equipment methods of records transfer.

7. How can the effectiveness of a records management program be evaluated?

8. What kinds of microimage formats are now available, and what are the characteristics of each?

9. What is CAR?

10. What is COM?

11. What is image processing?

DISCUSSION QUESTIONS

1. You are the supervisor of records management in the company in which you work. Occasionally, one of the file clerks you supervise is careless when filing, which results in the misfiling of records. Although you believe that this person is a good worker, is fun to be around, and is eager to learn, you wish she would be more careful in filing. Discuss how you plan to handle this situation.

2. As the supervisor of records management in the company in which you work, you are hearing an increasing number of complaints about the inefficiency of the records management program. The complaints you are hearing are unfounded, as you have statistical data to prove that they are not legitimate. You believe the problem stems from the fact that two years ago when the company installed a centralized storage area, several unit managers were upset, and the present complaints are a backlash of that decision. The two more frequently heard complaints are that never-used records are being stored and that some records cannot be found—or at least not found as quickly as those making the requests would like. Discuss how you plan to respond to these erroneous charges.

3. The company in which you are a manager uses decentralized storage and control of its records. When you were out of the office for three days last week, the new office supervisor took it upon herself to clean out the files as a means of keeping busy. She indicated that files containing materials at least three years old were removed and put into temporary storage boxes until the contents can be destroyed. She did not want any materials destroyed until you returned. Discuss the implications of her actions.

STUDENT PROJECTS AND ACTIVITIES

1. Tour the records storage area of a large organization. What types of filing equipment were used? Does the equipment maximize the efficiency with which records are stored?

2. Tour the records storage area of a small organization. What types of filing equipment were used? Does the equipment maximize the efficiency with which records are stored?

3. Going Online: Using the Internet, conduct an online search based on one of the concepts presented in this chapter or based on one of the chapter terms. Identify four or five things you learned from the material that you did not know prior to your online search.

Minicase

The Mundorf Corporation used a decentralized records management program until approximately eighteen months ago. The records manager who was responsible for installing the new centralized program left the company a year after it was installed. At the time she left, the program was functioning well. She left before she had the opportunity to evaluate the program formally, however. You have been asked by the executive vice president, who is responsible for the records management program, to suggest techniques to evaluate the effectiveness of the program.

1. Provide a detailed discussion of each technique.

Case

About five years ago, the Beyer Corporation, which is located in Omaha, Nebraska, designed and implemented a decentralized records management program. Except for confidential records, all documents are stored centrally. The program was designed and implemented by Alan Cole, who left

Beyer about two years ago when he accepted a position as vice president for corporate relations in a milling company located in a neighboring state.

Over the past several months, Brock Johnson, Cole's successor, has been hearing a growing number of complaints about the centralized system. The following complaints are heard most frequently:

1. Records cannot be retrieved rapidly enough.

2. Some records that have been requisitioned have not been found.

3. Determining the whereabouts of records that have been checked out from the central storage area is not always possible.

4. Some employees keep duplicate copies of records in their offices so they don't have to wait for records requisitioned from central storage.

5. Discrepancies exist in the subject categories into which records should be filed.

6. Employees who work in centralized storage find the work boring and monotonous.

The company is now thinking about returning to a decentralized storage system whereby records would be stored in various departments.

1. On the basis of the information presented, do you believe the company should retain centralized storage or return to a decentralized storage system? Why?

2. If the company decides to keep the centralized storage system, what courses of action would you recommend to alleviate the problems that have been cited?

3. What factors should be considered in deciding whether to keep the centralized system or to install a decentralized system?

*C*hapter 22

FORMS DESIGN AND CONTROL

*C*hapter *A*ims

After studying this chapter, you should be able to develop effective forms for use in an organization.

*C*hapter *O*utline

Forms Control Program
  Step 1: Cataloging Forms
  Step 2: Classifying Forms
  Step 3: Analyzing Forms
  Step 4: Eliminating Forms
  Step 5: Consolidating Forms
  Step 6: Developing Design Guidelines
  Step 7: Developing Forms
  Step 8: Printing Forms
  Step 9: Maintaining Perpetual Supply
    Inventory
Types of Office Forms
  Continuous Forms
  Unit-set Forms
  Carbonless Forms
  MICR Forms (magnetic ink character
    recognition)
  OCR Forms (optical character recognition)
  Mark-sense Forms
  Electronic Forms
Forms Design
  Design Elements
  Forms Design Software
  Forms Design Illustrated
Professional Forms Services
Implications for the Administrative Office
  Manager

*C*hapter *T*erms

Analysis
Ballot-box design
Bar code
Box design
Carbonless forms
Cataloging
Classification
Continuous forms
Data-entry method
Electronic forms
Fan-fold forms
Forms control program
Grade of paper
Grain of paper
Mark-sense forms
MICR
OCR
One-time carbon
Prenumbering
Professional forms services
Removable side strip forms
Roll forms
Software-based forms
Statute of limitations
Unit-set forms
Web-based forms

*T*he efficiency of transactions that involve the use of forms is often affected by the forms' quality, including their design. In many instances, the best way to improve transaction efficiency is to improve the quality of the forms. Today, increasing numbers of organizations are replacing their paper forms with electronic forms, a trend that will become much more common in the future. Electronic forms are discussed in detail in a subsequent section of this chapter.

Most of the forms used in an organization perform a vital function. Those without a vital function typically are poorly designed, or they have minimal value; their discontinuation should be considered.

Forms are a vital component of the integrated systems discussed in Chapter 17. The design of forms used in integrated systems is especially crucial because of the need for forms to be compatible with the equipment and software used in the system and with other related forms.

FORMS CONTROL PROGRAM

What are the common objectives of forms control programs?

Because administrative office managers are frequently involved with forms design, their involvement with **forms control programs** seems logical. Forms control programs that have the benefit of advisory committees are being used with greater frequency. An essential prerequisite of these programs is top-management support.

The following objectives are typical of forms control programs:

1. To guard against the development of unneeded forms.
2. To eliminate unneeded existing forms.
3. To assist in the development and design of efficient forms.
4. To consolidate and simplify existing forms when appropriate.
5. To provide a continuous review of existing forms.
6. To facilitate the development of efficient work procedures that involve the use of forms.

The implementation of operating systems in an organization generally requires the standardization of organizational forms. Consequently, the systems staff and individuals involved with forms design and control should work together. Otherwise, the effectiveness of the system will be diminished.

Several distinct steps are involved in the design of an efficient forms control program. These steps are presented in chronological order.

Step 1: Cataloging Forms

The **cataloging** of forms enables those individuals responsible for the forms control program to determine the nature, type, and purpose of the forms used throughout the organization. The individuals responsible for forms control collect from each department or work unit several copies of each of its forms. The cataloging procedure will reveal the following:

What information is provided by forms cataloging?

1. The primary purpose of each form.
2. The forms used by each department or work unit.
3. The frequency of use of each form.
4. The number of copies of a multiple-copy form set.
5. The routing of each copy of a multiple-copy form set.

6. The final disposition of each copy of a multiple-copy form set.
7. The primary method of entering data on each of the forms.
8. The relationship among various forms.

Each form is assigned an identification number during Step 1. Generally found in the lower left corner, the number usually appears in a coded format. Typically, each department within an organization is assigned a numerical code. Each form within a given department is then assigned a specific identification number. To illustrate, the following number is coded as follows:

23-010

(The number "23" refers to the marketing department; "010" refers to the tenth form developed in the marketing department.)

Some organizations also include in the identification number the month and year that the form was last revised as well as the number of forms printed the last time the supply was replenished. This appears as follows:

23-010 Rev. 1/00 4M

"Rev. 1/00" means the form was revised in January 2000, and "4M" means that 4,000 copies of the form were last printed.

Step 2: Classifying Forms

What is the purpose of forms classification?

The use of a forms **classification** scheme facilitates the analysis of the forms assembled during the cataloging process. Forms are typically classified by function and by number.

Classifying forms by function means they are organized according to their specific purpose. For example, all forms pertaining to sales are grouped together, all forms pertaining to accounts receivable are grouped together, and so forth. When completed, the functional classification enables those responsible for forms design and control to analyze the similarities and differences among the various forms.

Classifying forms by number involves assembling the various forms according to the identification number assigned to each form in Step 1. Although using a number classification scheme generally is not helpful when comparing the similarities and differences between forms, it facilitates building a master file useful for cross-referencing purposes as well as for assigning the identification number to new forms.

Step 3: Analyzing Forms

Forms **analysis,** which often results in reducing the cost of creating and processing a form, is an integral aspect of a forms control program. The analysis process involves studying each form in terms of its function.

Forms analysis provides answers to the following questions:

What information is provided by forms analysis?

1. What is the primary purpose of the form?
2. Does the form contain the necessary information to fulfill its purpose?
3. Do the design specifications on the form accommodate its data entry, transmittal, filing, and retrieval requirements?
4. Does the form contain any extraneous information?

Forms analysis should take place before a new or revised form is officially approved or before an existing form is restocked. Ideally, each form is subjected to an analysis every two or three years.

Step 4: Eliminating Forms

If the forms analysis reveals that certain forms either are no longer used or need to be used, their elimination should be considered. In some instances, certain forms may not be needed because the purpose for which they were designed is now being served by another form. Or perhaps a form is no longer used because it is not compatible with the organization's systems and procedures.

Step 5: Consolidating Forms

Forms analysis may reveal a similarity of some items on certain forms. In some instances, the development of one new form that consolidates two or more currently existing forms may be possible. The consolidating process is facilitated by the use of a grid similar to the one illustrated in Figure 22–1, which identifies the various items found on several forms.

An examination of the grid reveals several items are found in common on the various forms being analyzed. The greater the number of common items, the more easily forms can be consolidated.

Step 6: Developing Design Guidelines

What design guidelines should be remembered?

Before new forms are designed or existing forms are revised, design guidelines should be developed. These guidelines will be helpful in designing forms compatible with one another. The following identifies several design guidelines:

1. When the same information appears on several forms, it should appear in the same location on each form (for example, the name and address of the organization).

	FIRM NAME AND ADDRESS	SHIP TO	SEND TO	QUANTITY	DESCRIPTION	CATALOG NUMBER	PRICE	TOTAL PRICE	SUGGESTED VENDOR	TERMS	SUB TOTAL	TAX
PURCHASE REQUISITION				X	X	X			X			
PURCHASE ORDER	X	X	X	X	X	X	X	X		X	X	X
RECEIPT OF GOODS				X	X	X	X	X		X	X	X

Figure 22–1 Data comparison grid

2. Information that is to be transferred from one form to another should appear in the same sequence on both forms. (For example, the columns common to both a purchase requisition and a purchase order should appear in the same order on both forms.)

3. When control of forms is important, the forms should be numbered sequentially. (For example, numbering checks helps guard against their misuse.)

4. The design of the form should be guided by such characteristics as simplicity, practicality, and ease of use.

Step 7: Developing Forms

When new forms are being developed, their need has to be justified. In addition, their design should be consistent with the guidelines covered in this chapter.

Step 8: Printing Forms

In the past, many organizations had their forms duplicated by printing companies. Because increasing numbers of organizations are installing extensive reprographics units with the specialized equipment needed to print forms, this step is more likely to be done in-house. An exception may be the use of electronic forms when hard copies of forms may not be needed.

Step 9: Maintaining Perpetual Supply Inventory

What is the primary reason that a perpetual supply inventory is maintained?

The last step in the forms control program is the development of procedures for use in maintaining a perpetual supply inventory. This helps keep a sufficient supply of forms on hand. When the supply reaches the minimum level, it is replenished. Effective inventory procedures also prevent a surplus of forms.

TYPES OF OFFICE FORMS

Several types of office forms exist. Those presented in this chapter include continuous, unit-set, carbonless, MICR, OCR, mark-sense, and electronic.

Continuous Forms

Many of the forms used in offices today are classified as **continuous forms.** Although these forms are attached to one another, the perforations separating each form facilitate their detachment from one another. Three types of continuous forms are available: **fan-fold, roll,** and **removable side strip.**

Figure 22–2 illustrates each of these three types.

The fan-fold type is a multicopy set, the roll type is a single-copy form, and the removable side-strip form may be either a single or multiple copy.

What are the characteristics of fan-fold forms?

Fan-fold forms are distinctive because the copies are made by bellow folding a single sheet of paper several times. Carbon paper is interleaved between the various copies. The forms are generally perforated on the sides, the top, and the bottom, which facilitates separation of the various copies from one another.

The multiple-copy removable side strip form has a separate sheet of paper for each copy. The side strip serves two purposes: The holes in the strip are used to feed the forms through the printing device, and they hold the original and

Figure 22-2 Types of continuous forms

Fan-fold   Roll

the multiple copies of the forms together until the various copies are separated from one another.

The roll type is restricted to single-copy forms because of the tendency for multiple-copy forms to become misaligned when rolled. Continuous letterheads, a type of roll form, can be used on high-speed impact printers. The perforations facilitate the separation of one letterhead from another.

Continuous forms are especially suited for automated printing equipment, such as computer printers and automatic typewriters. A considerable amount of time is saved because continuous forms are automatically fed through the equipment, eliminating the need to insert each form in the equipment.

Cards in a continuous format that can be processed by computer equipment are also now available. These cards, which are commonly used for customer billing, are printed on heavy paper stock. The removable side strips on both sides facilitate automatic feeding through the printing device. After data entry, the cards are separated from one another. The portion of the card that is generally returned with the customer's payment can then again be processed by card-reading equipment.

Unit-Set Forms

What are the characteristics of unit-set forms?

Unit-set forms are maintained as separate forms and may be either single or multiple copy. The multiple-copy variety frequently uses a one-step carbon removal technique in which all carbons are removed at one time. At the top of each form set is a perforated strip to which the various sheets of carbon are attached. The carbons are shorter than the copies of the form. Carbon is removed by grasping the perforated strip with one hand and the bottom of the copies with the other. During removal, the carbons remain attached to the perforated strip.

A unit set form is illustrated in Figure 22–3.

Unit-set forms are versatile. Certain portions of the carbon copies can be deleted in either of two ways: (1) by not carbonizing these portions of the carbon copy or (2) by omitting the section on each copy that is to be deleted. The latter process is easily accomplished by eliminating the paper where the deleted portions would have appeared had paper been there. This is done by using sheets of different sizes to construct the unit-set form.

Carbonless Forms

Carbonless forms use a process in which the back side of one copy and the face side of the next copy have special coatings. When pressure is applied to the form, the chemical coatings interact, which causes an image of the information written on the original copy to appear on the carbon copy. Until recently, the images on carbonless copies appeared in blue, a color that does not always photocopy well. New chemicals are available that produce black images, thus facilitating the photocopying of these forms.

Although the cost of making copies by this method is approximately 15 percent higher than with other methods, the carbonless process results in significant advantages. For example, portions of copies can be easily deleted by not applying the coatings to these areas. Because carbon paper does not have to be inserted between the various copies of the form, the form set is thinner. Not only can more copies be made, but the sets also consume less storage space. Furthermore, because carbon paper is not used, the process is cleaner and is less likely to result in smudged copies. The carbonless form also enables one to detect erasures, which decreases the likelihood of unauthorized changes being made on the forms. Furthermore, because no carbon is used, maintaining confidentiality is not the concern that it is with carboned forms.

What advantages result from the use of carbonless forms?

MICR (Magnetic Ink Character Recognition) Forms

MICR forms are used primarily by banks and other types of lending institutions to expedite the storing and processing of numerical data found on banking documents. Numbers are imprinted on the documents with a magnetic ink. Special equipment reads these numbers and then transmits the data to the computer or to other processing equipment.

OCR (Optical Character Recognition) Forms

Whereas the MICR forms are used only for numerical data, **OCR** forms use both alphabetic and numerical data. As the data are read on the OCR form, they are transmitted to the computer where processing takes place. Although machines are generally used to enter data on the OCR forms, handwriting, to a

Figure 22–3 Unit-set form

limited extent, can be used. Considerable precision must be used in the development of forms using the OCR concept. Improper alignment can cause the equipment to misread the data.

A related type of form has a **bar code** imprinted on it. A scanner is used to read the bar code, which inputs the scanned information into the organization's information system. A variety of information is included in bar codes. A common one is the form's number.

Mark-Sense Forms

How are mark-sense
forms processed?

A **mark-sense form,** such as the one illustrated in Figure 22–4, is useful for certain applications. Special scanning equipment reads pencil marks on the form. These forms are especially advantageous for information comprised mostly of numerical characters. The data-entering process becomes quite cumbersome when a considerable amount of alphabetic information has to be entered.

Electronic Forms

Of the various types of forms used widely in organizations, the newest and fastest-growing type are **electronic forms.** Two types of electronic forms are used: **software-based forms** and **Web-based forms.**

Two main options are available for creating software-based forms. One option is to scan (using an OCR scanner) an existing paper-based form, which prepares a form template in electronic format. During data entry, an actual image of the form appears on the employee's computer screen. Data entry into the various form fields can be accomplished using either specialized data entry software programs or a word processing software program. When needed, the information found in various fields of the form can be captured and automatically stored in a database, which makes the information available for subsequent use. Printed copies of the completed form can be prepared using either laser or dot-matrix printers. The printed copies can be prepared using either blank paper or preprinted blank forms. Once the form is scanned and stored, the template is available to any employee who needs to access it.

Another software-based option simply provides for the employee on his or her computer screen the fields on a given form for which data need to be entered. In the option discussed in the last paragraph, the employee sees an actual screen image of the form. In this option, the employee sees only the fields for which data need to be supplied. When printing a form, the software merges the data and the form by overlaying the data into the appropriate sections of the form. Where needed, the entered data can be captured and transmitted to a database.

Why is the use of Web-
based forms increasing?

The use of Web-based forms is increasing rapidly because of Internet technology. Web-based forms are used both internally and externally in many organizations. The forms are created using HTML coding, which basically provides an "electronic document." CGI-script is commonly used in the transmission of the data to a Web server. Increasingly, Java script is also used in creating and processing Web-based forms. Some or all of the data entered onto the form can be captured and stored in the organization's database, making it available for subsequent use. Web-based forms generally do not have the same format appearance that non-Web-based forms do.

Among the advantages of using electronic forms are the following:

What are the advantages
of using electronic forms?

1. Filling in the variable information on an electronic form is quicker than handwriting or using a typewriter to fill in a paper form.

2. The need to keep an inventory of paper forms is greatly diminished because fewer paper copies of forms will likely be prepared.

REGISTRATION SECTION REQUEST FORM ■ MICHIGAN STATE UNIVERSITY ■

OFFICE OF THE REGISTRAR

NAME _____

LAST   FIRST   MIDDLE

STUDENT NUMBER

INSTRUCTIONS
1. Using a #2 pencil, *write* and *mark* student number in box at right.
2. Write and mark in the boxes below the sequence number for each lecture, laboratory or recitation (disregard the hyphen printed in the sequence number).
3. Write and mark the number of credits (CR column) for each lecture, laboratory or recitation. For a Variable credit course (VA) write and mark the exact number of credits you are carrying in that course.
4. If you are visiting or repeating a course, mark the visitor or repeat circle.
5. If you are taking a course for Credit-No Credit, use the box designated as such in the lower right corner.
6. See example ar right for proper marking. Be certain to fill in each circle completely.
7. Complete this form by marking the boxes on the far right for the total number of sequence boxes used and the inital of your last name.

EXAMPLE 0 3 0 4 1 2 SEQUENCE NUMBER

MAKE HEAVY BLACK MARKS
THAT FILL CIRCLE COMPLETELY

FOR ACCURACY IN YOUR
SCHEDULE, AVOID STRAY MAKRS

ERASE COMPLETELY
ANY ENTRY CHANGED

Lectures, Labs and Recitations all carry the same credit on this form
(not for fee assessment, but for the purpose of early enrollment)

SEQUENCE NUMBER | CR | VISITOR | REPEAT

MARK TOTAL NUMBER OF SEQUENCE BOXES USED

MARK FIRST INITIAL OF YOUR LAST NAME

USE ONLY FOR CREDIT-NO CREDIT OPTION ➤

MSU is an Affirmative Action/Equal Opportunity Institution

Michigan State University Prining
O 13938

Figure 22-4 Mark-sense form. Courtesy: Michigan State University.

3. The need to enter redundant information on several different forms is greatly reduced. Once the information has been captured and stored in the organization's database, the information can be automatically pulled into other forms as the need arises.

4. The need to file paper copies is greatly reduced, thus decreasing filing time and storage space.

5. Information stored on electronic forms can be retrieved more readily than that stored on paper copies.

6. The template of an electronic form can be easily and quickly revised as the need arises.

FORMS DESIGN

The efficiency with which information is entered on a form depends on its design. Poorly designed forms are difficult to complete, especially for individuals who are unfamiliar with the use to be made of specific forms. Poorly designed forms increase the likelihood that errors will be made.

Extreme care must be exercised when designing forms that are part of an organization's operating system. Forms that are not compatible with the system or with other related forms destroy the efficiency of various work processes. For this reason, many organizations often use the services of professional forms designers when new forms are needed. These designers help ensure the compatibility of the forms with the organization's operating system.

Depending on the qualifications of the organization's internal staff, the services of outside forms designers may not be needed. And because of the limited function of some forms or their infrequent use, trying to justify the cost of hiring professional designers may not be possible.

Before actual work begins on designing the form, the following information is needed:

1. *The purpose of the form.* The purpose of the form must be defined before the following can be determined: the type of information to be included on the form, the number of copies that will be needed, the routing of each copy, and the nature of completion directions or instructions that are needed. In addition, the form's purpose will determine the necessity for using certain control procedures, such as prenumbering or authorization signatures.

Why does the nature of the equipment that will be used in processing a form need to be determined before the form is designed?

2. *The nature of the equipment on which the form will be processed.* The equipment on which the form will be processed may restrict its size. The type of equipment will also determine whether or not automatic feeding of the form is possible. In addition, the nature of the equipment will determine whether the paper on which the form is printed has to possess certain characteristics and the amount of space needed for inserting the information on the form.

3. *The relationship between the form being studied and any other previously developed forms.* If the form being developed is related in any way to other forms, care must be taken to ensure their compatibility. The sequencing of items should be identical, especially if the information from one form has to be later transferred to another form.

What impact do statutes of limitation have on forms design?

4. *The length of time that various copies must be legally retained.* If the **statute of limitations** requires that a certain form be kept for a long time, the paper on which it is printed must be sufficiently durable to withstand the time element. This will directly influence the quality of paper on which the form is printed.

Figure 22–5 Item
alignment

Incorrect	*Correct*
Name:	Name:
Address:	Address:
City:	City:
State:	State:

Design Elements

After the four background characteristics have been considered, the design process may begin. Among the factors to be considered are those discussed in the paragraphs that follow.

Adequate Identification. The name of the form should be clearly displayed on the form. In addition, if the form is an external one, the organization's name, address, and telephone number should also appear on each copy. Other than printing the organization's logo or trademark on the form, the use of symbols or pictures should be kept to a minimum.

Alignment of Items. The items on a form should be aligned so that only a minimum number of tab settings have to be made, especially on forms for which a typewriter is commonly used for data entry. Ideal alignment enables one tab set to be used several times. Figure 22–5 illustrates the incorrect and correct way of aligning items on a form.

In the incorrect illustration in Figure 22–5, a single tab set will not accommodate each item. By aligning the items as shown in the correct illustration, one tab set will accommodate all the items. Over time, properly aligned items will conserve considerable physical effort.

Preprinting. As much information as possible should be preprinted on forms. Doing so simplifies the task of entering information and enhances the completion of the form. When information can be preprinted, the individuals who complete the form simply check the desired items. This is illustrated in Figure 22–6. The use of **ballot-box design** in the correct illustration is a useful time-saving technique.

Why are some forms prenumbered?

Prenumbering. For several reasons, the **prenumbering** of forms is advantageous because employee time and effort are conserved; greater control can be exercised over the use of the form; and if necessary, the processed forms can be easily rearranged in numerical order. Forms are typically prenumbered in the upper right corner.

Figure 22–6 Ballot-box design

Incorrect	*Correct*
Please state which shipping method you prefer_____	☐ Parcel post ☐ Land freight ☐ Air freight ☐ Other_____

Types of forms frequently prenumbered are purchase orders, checks, payment vouchers, invoices, and so forth.

Instructions. Because of the complexity of some forms or because the individual using a certain form may not be familiar with its completion procedures, the inclusion of instructions on the form is helpful. Generally, external forms are the only ones on which instructions are needed. Employees, either through training or use, are familiar with internal forms, thus eliminating the need for instructions.

When needed, instructions should be placed as close as possible to the items to which they pertain. If this is not possible because of insufficient space, the instructions may be placed on the back side of the form or on a separate sheet. If instructions cannot be placed near the information to which they pertain, their location should be noted so they can be readily found.

Identification Number. All forms should have an identification number, which is often located in the lower left corner. The number might consist of a department number, the number of the form within the department, the adoption or last revision date, and the quantity of forms printed during the last printing. The following, which contains the four elements just mentioned, illustrates an identification number:

212:017 Rev. 9/00 4M

Type of Carbon. When selecting the appropriate type of carbon for making copies of a form, the following factors should be considered:

What factors need to be considered in determining the appropriate carboning method?

1. The frequency of use of the form.
2. The number of copies of the form that must be made.
3. The confidentiality of the form.
4. The opportunity for tampering with the data on the form (erasing and retyping, for example).
5. The method for entering data on the form.
6. The nature of the equipment through which the form has to be processed during completion.

Several methods exist for making carbon copies: carbonless, one-time carbon, carbon roll fastened to the equipment, and single-sheet carbon. When justified, using the carbonless system to make copies results in several advantages that were outlined in the "Types of Office Forms" section.

One-time carbon is the type used in continuous or unit-set forms. In terms of quality, one-time carbon is a low-grade type and is used only once. Because the carbon is inserted between the various sheets of the form during its manufacturing process, considerable employee time is saved.

Although carbon rolls are not used frequently, some machines are equipped with a carbon roll device. The carbon feeds through the equipment independently of the movement of forms through the machine. Therefore, employees do not have to insert carbon paper between each copy of each form.

Because some forms are not used frequently enough to justify one of the carbonizing methods listed earlier, the single-sheet carbon method is used. High-grade carbon can be reused a number of times. A carbon sheet has to be

Figure 22–7 Box design

Last Name	First Name	Middle Initial
House Number	Street	
City	State	ZIP Code

inserted manually between each copy of the form, which can make this method quite time consuming.

Data-Entry Method. The **data-entry method** on a form has a significant impact on the spacing between the items and the design of the form.

Why does the primary method of data entry need to be considered in forms design?

1. *Spacing.* The primary method for entering data should be considered when determining the amount of vertical and horizontal space to provide between items. If a typewriter is the primary data-entry method, the vertical spacing between items should be consistent with regular typewriter spacing. Otherwise, employee time and effort are wasted when having to align the typewriter's printing device with each line of the form. Double spacing (three lines to an inch) is the recommended vertical spacing when using the typewriter as the primary data-entry method.

   Sufficient horizontal space must also be provided when the typewriter is used as the primary data-entry method. Ample space should be provided to accommodate the longest alphabetic or numerical item to be typed in each section of the form.

   When handwriting is used as the primary data-entry method, more horizontal space must be provided on the form than is needed when a typewriter is used. Three lines to an inch is the recommended vertical spacing.

2. *Design format.* The primary data-entry method must also be considered in designing the format of the form. For example, if the primary data-entry method is a typewriter or some other mechanical printing device, a **box design** is preferred. This design, which is shown in Figure 22–7, simplifies aligning the form when it is placed in the typewriter. By placing the identifying tabs in the upper left corner rather than below each box, the typist does not have to space down to read what is to be typed and then space back up to type the desired information.

   Line design, which is illustrated in Figure 22–8, is the preferred design format when handwriting is used as the primary data-entry method. In line design, the identifying tabs may appear below the lines.

Paper. For several reasons, the paper on which forms are printed must be considered. The type of paper has a significant impact on the ability of forms to withstand the passage of time and ease with which forms can be handled.

Last Name	First Name	Middle Initial
House Number	Street	
City	State	ZIP Code

Figure 22–8 Line design

Paper possesses three basic qualities: weight, grade, and grain. The effect that each of these qualities has on forms design is as follows:

1. *Weight.* The weight of paper on which forms are printed determines their durability. Weight is determined by how much 500 sheets (a ream) of paper stock measuring 17 by 22 inches weigh. If the ream weighs twenty pounds, the paper is referred to as twenty-pound paper. If it weighs sixteen pounds, it is sixteen-pound paper. The ream is then cut into different sizes, depending upon the desired size of the form. A ream of twenty-pound standard-sized letterhead paper (8 1/2 by 11 inches) weighs five pounds. The lightest weight paper suitable for the circumstances should be used.

   Because many forms have multiple copies, paper weight is especially important because it will determine the number of copies that can be made. The weight of paper may also have an impact on postal costs.

2. *Grade.* The **grade of paper** on which forms are printed determines their durability and how well they will withstand the passage of time. Paper grade is determined by the type of materials—cloth and/or sulphite—used in manufacturing. As the cloth content increases and the sulphite content decreases, the paper's grade improves. Paper consisting of 100 percent sulphite lasts up to fifteen years; 25 percent cloth, fifteen to twenty-five years; 50 percent cloth, twenty-six to fifty years; and 100 percent cloth, fifty years or longer.

   The grade of paper on which forms are to be printed should be determined by (1) the number of years the organization is legally required to keep a particular form; (2) the frequency of use of the form (greater cloth content makes the paper less brittle); and (3) the primary data-entry method.

   In addition to the physical content of paper, its finish may also be an important consideration. The finish is apt to determine the ease with which erasures can be made, how rapidly ink will soak into the paper, and the overall appearance of the paper. Although several types of finish are available, a bond finish is one of the most commonly used. Bond paper has greater internal strength than nonbond paper and is relatively easy to erase because of its fairly smooth finish.

3. *Grain.* The **grain of paper** refers to the fibers contained in the paper. Fibers run through paper in either a vertical or horizontal direction, depending on how the paper is cut. When equipment is used for data entry, special consideration should be given to the direction of the fibers in the form. The grain of paper should be vertical in forms that are fed automatically through the equipment. Therefore, the grain of paper should run the same direction that the paper is fed through the equipment. The paper is more likely to misfeed when the grain is in the opposite direction that it feeds through the equipment.

Color. Colored paper and ink in printing forms should be kept to a minimum and used only when justifiable. Colored paper is often used in multiple-copy form sets, especially when different copies of the form are to be routed to different places. By printing each copy of the form set on paper of a different color, the sorting process is greatly simplified. Light-colored stock should be used because it provides a better contrast with the ink.

The use of several colors of ink is generally not recommended. Not only does the cost of printing increase, but also the different colors are apt to distract from the form's purpose. Generally, black is the most desirable color of ink, although limited use of other ink colors can be justified when certain sections of a form need to be emphasized.

How is the weight of paper determined?

What impact does the grade of paper on which forms are printed have on forms design?

Why does the grain of paper have to be considered in forms design?

What should be remembered about the use of color in forms?

Size. The size of the form is determined largely by the amount of data that will be entered on it. When a typewriter is used for data entry, forms can generally be smaller than when the primary data-entry method is handwriting. Another factor to consider is the size of the type used on the form. The size of the paper stock from which the forms are cut may also be of some importance. To keep trim waste to a minimum, the size of the paper stock should be considered in determining the size of the forms. Possible restrictions placed on form size by the equipment that will be used in processing the forms should also be considered.

Print Type Size. While many printing type styles are available, the number of different styles used on a form should be kept to a minimum. When several type styles are used, items of equal significance should be printed with the same type size and style. Items needing emphasis can be printed in a bold or italics type style, which will make them more distinctive.

Some states have passed legislation setting minimum type sizes for certain portions or areas of forms. The type size restrictions generally pertain to items having a financial or legal significance, such as portions of conditional sales contracts.

For what is shading used in forms design?

Shading. To emphasize certain portions of forms, areas are sometimes shaded. The more distinctive areas draw the user's attention to the emphasized material.

Adequate Margin Size. The method of data entry should be considered in determining adequate margin size. This is especially true when the typewriter is the primary data-entry method. A sufficient bottom margin should be provided to prevent slippage of the form in the typewriter when entering material at the bottom of the form.

Forms Design Software

Increasingly, designers are using forms design software to prepare nonelectronic forms. These are the traditional forms that use paper, unlike the electronic forms discussed earlier that may or may not appear on paper.

What factors need to be considered in selecting a forms design software program?

In selecting a forms design software program, the following factors must be considered:

1. The hardware on which the software will be used, including its memory capabilities.
2. The ability of the software program to accept scanned information.
3. The format features provided by the software program, including the following:
   a. Ability to accommodate variations in vertical and horizontal spacing.
   b. Availability of a variety of font types and sizes.
   c. Ability to make "combs" (putting vertical lines on a horizontal rule to serve as dividers for individual letters or numbers).
   d. Presence of a zoom feature.
   e. Ability to accept logos (needs a graphic import capability).
   f. Ability to provide a template into which information is keyed, after which a paper copy of the form is prepared on a laser printer.
   g. Ability to imprint bar-codes on forms.

In some instances, forms design software provides a template for use in creating electronic forms. In other cases, it is used only to prepare the master needed for the quantity printing of forms on which information is generally either handwritten or typewritten.

Forms Design Illustrated

Figure 22–9 is presented to illustrate several of the forms design factors covered in the preceding discussion. The encircled numbers on the form correspond

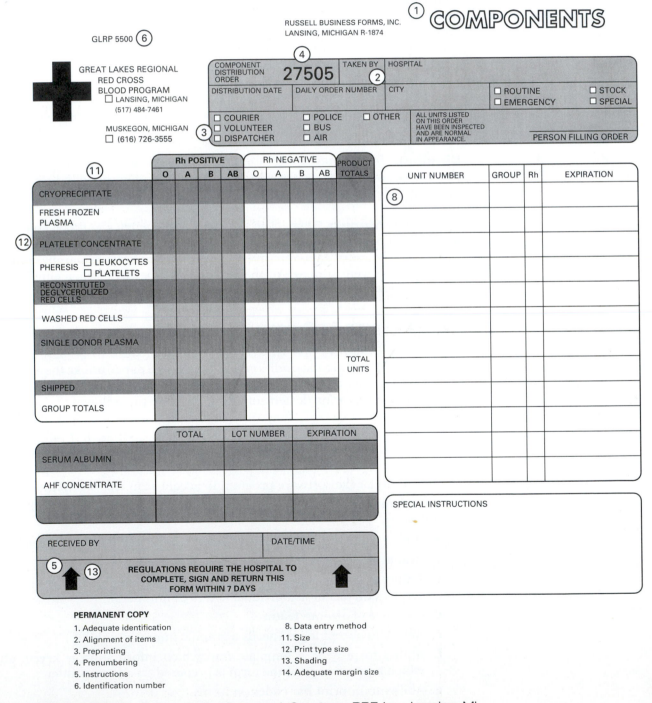

Figure 22-9 Forms design illustrated. Courtesy: RBF, Inc., Lansing, MI.

with the numbers of the various factors covered in the preceding discussion. The form in Figure 22–9 is a three-part unit-set form. One-time carbon is used for making carbon copies.

1. *Adequate information.* The name of the form (Components) is clearly presented on the perforated strip at the top of the form. The name of the organization and its phone number appear in the upper left corner, along with its logo.
2. *Alignment of items.* The form illustrates the alignment of items (hospital and city), which reduces the number of tabs that must be set on the equipment.
3. *Preprinting.* A considerable amount of preprinting (method of transporting, components, and use of components) is shown on the form. The form also makes use of ballot-box design for these items.
4. *Prenumbering.* The sequential number of the form (01255) appears on the form.
5. **and 13.** *Instructions and shading.* Instructions appear in the lower left corner near the items to which they pertain. The instructions are highlighted by shading and arrows.
6. *Identification number.* The identification number of the form (GLRP 5500) appears on the perforated strip in the upper left corner.
8. *Data-entry method.* Because the data-entry method is primarily by typewriter, this fact was considered in the design process. The form accommodates the typical vertical spacing found on typewriters. The form also illustrates the design format recommended when typewriters are used for data entry.
11. *Size.* The size of the form accommodates the various types of equipment that will be used for processing and storing it.
12. *Printing type styles.* Items of equal emphasis on the form are presented in equal type sizes.
14. *Adequate margin sizes.* To prevent slippage, an adequate bottom margin appears on the form.

PROFESSIONAL FORMS SERVICES

The use of **professional forms services** should not be overlooked, especially when the organization has several sophisticated systems. Using professional forms services becomes perhaps even more crucial for designing forms that are an integral part of these systems.

What services do professional forms services provide?

Forms services provide a variety of functions for their clients. The two most common ones are forms design and production. After the purpose of a form and its function within an operating system are identified, the specialist designs the form. Following the design and approval of the form, the service makes arrangements for producing the form. The forms specialist can also offer many suggestions for forms revision, which enables the organization to use forms compatible with one another as well as with its operating systems.

Some professional forms services also provide a variety of other functions. They may provide warehouse facilities for storing their clients' forms supply. They also keep their clients supplied with a sufficient quantity of forms. When the supply of forms stored in the warehouse reaches a certain level, the forms service automatically reorders a new supply. The forms service thus assumes responsibility for the storage and perpetual supply inventory of clients' forms.

IMPLICATIONS FOR THE ADMINISTRATIVE OFFICE MANAGER

The widespread installation of integrated systems is responsible for the design and control of forms becoming a more important administrative office management responsibility. Forms are an integral component of these systems, and every effort should be made to ensure that they enhance rather than destroy the operating efficiency of the systems in which they are used.

The involvement of the administrative office manager in forms design and control can vary from total responsibility to no responsibility. Those who are involved may be responsible for directing the forms control program as well as for designing the forms. Both these responsibilities require a thorough understanding of the elements of forms design and control.

In some instances, professional forms designers are used in the design process. The individuals who serve as the liaison between the organization and the professional designer—whether it is the administrative office manager or some other employee—must have a basic understanding of the forms design process. Those who are not familiar with this process may find their liaison role to be a challenging experience.

For those managers who are knowledgeable about the design process, forms simplification, consolidation, and elimination may be a more challenging task than forms design. This task is simplified somewhat when each manager in the organization becomes concerned about the efficiency of the forms for which he or she is responsible.

REVIEW QUESTIONS

1. What are the objectives of a forms control program?

2. What is involved in the cataloging of forms?

3. Why is the prenumbering of forms useful?

4. What device commonly is used in entering data into electronic forms?

5. When instructions are included on forms, where should they be placed?

6. What techniques exist for making carbon copies of forms?

7. Why should the data-entry method be considered when designing forms?

8. How is the weight of paper determined?

9. How do the grade and grain of paper differ?

10. What factors need to be considered in selecting a forms design software program?

DISCUSSION QUESTIONS

1. As the manager of the forms control program in the organization in which you work, you are responsible for selecting seven individuals to serve on the program's advisory committee. What background characteristics should these individuals possess in order to make the maximum contribution to the committee?

2. You and another employee in the organization in which you work were discussing integrated systems. The individual with whom you were talking said that he was under the impression that a system is designed around the forms that are used in an organization—and not the forms around the system. Discuss the implications of the other employee's ideas about the relationship between systems and forms design.

3. You are working on a special project for your employer. One of your responsibilities is to make a collection of all the forms that are used in the organization and prepare a forms classification. When you explained the nature of this project to one of the department heads, he said, "You've got to be kidding! Someone is allowing you to waste your time doing this?" Defend the importance of your project.

STUDENT PROJECTS AND ACTIVITIES

1. Arrange to have an individual responsible for forms design demonstrate the design process, from beginning to end.

2. Obtain a comparable form (such as a purchase order or an invoice) from two different organizations. In what ways are the forms similar? Different?

3. Going Online: Using the Internet, conduct an online search based on one of the concepts presented in this chapter or based on one of the chapter terms. Identify four or five things you learned from the material that you did not know prior to your online search.

Minicase

Jamison Importers is a fairly small wholesaler of items sold in gift stores located throughout the nation. The firm is in the process of developing a new invoice that will be processed on its new computer. The organization is hoping to design an invoice that also incorporates a shipping label. The president of the company has asked you, the office supervisor, for a written report in which you are to:

1. Identify the type of form you recommend, along with a rationale for your decision.

2. Identify the kind of carbonizing process you recommend and your reasons for choosing that process.

Case

The Borowitcz Manufacturing Company, which is located in Memphis, Tennessee, has hired you, a consultant, to help design efficient office procedures. When you were contacted a few weeks ago about this project, you were told that the office function "has several areas of operating inefficiency."

After you spent several hours analyzing various aspects of the organization's operations, you have concluded that a forms control program is badly needed. Forms are continually being developed that seem to lack full justification. Many of the forms are also poorly designed.

In talking with several managers in Borowitcz, you have gotten the impression that they will not be in favor of implementing another regulatory program unless its need can be totally justified. Consequently, you know that if you are to be successful in getting your suggestion approved, you will have to build a strong case for the development of a forms control program. In the report you are to prepare for Borowitcz, you decide to:

1. Discuss the benefits of a forms control program as a means of trying to convince management of the need for such a program.

2. Discuss the strategies that can be used to help increase employee acceptance of the program once it is implemented.

Chapter 23

OFFICE REPROGRAPHICS AND MAIL SERVICES

Chapter Aims

After studying this chapter, you should be able to design an effective reprographics service and a mail service for an organization.

Chapter Outline

*C*hapter *T*erms

Addresser-printers
Conveyor system
Courier services
Desktop publishing
Diazo copying
Diffusion transfer copying
Electric mail carts
Fiber optics copying
Gelatin transfer copying
Information Based Indicia Program (IBIP)
Offset process duplication

Online mailing service
Pneumatic tube system
Production standards
Reprographics centers
Satellite centers
Spirit process duplication
Stabilization copying
Stamping-sealing equipment
Stencil process duplication
Thermography copying
Xerographic process copying

*T*he equipment used in **reprographics centers** is undergoing fairly significant change, primarily because of technological advances. New technology enables the equipment to produce higher quality work at a faster rate and at a lower per unit cost. The technology also makes the equipment easier to use, and the documents produced using the new technology often have a more appealing visual appearance than the early technology was able to provide.

What is the primary function of reprographics centers?

Reprographics centers are designed to provide copying and duplication services. Day-to-day management responsibility is generally assigned to the center supervisor, while the administrative office manager typically has overall managerial responsibility for the center.

In addition to covering the topic of reprographics, this chapter discusses several mechanical devices used to transmit internal correspondence and provides information about the mailroom. While the mailroom supervisor is typically responsible for the day-to-day operations of the mailroom, another of the administrative office manager's overall responsibilities is its effective management.

ORGANIZATION OF THE REPROGRAPHICS CENTER

The efficiency of the reprographics center, similarly to most other administrative office management functions, is likely to be determined in part by its organizational structure. Operating efficiency can come closer to its maximum potential when the center is properly organized and managed. The appropriate organization for a reprographics center is determined in part by the various needs it fulfills.

Determining Needs

The administrative office manager and/or the supervisor responsible for the present reprographics unit are generally responsible for determining the center's needs. To a large extent, the needs are affected by the organization's copying and duplicating requirements. In most cases, these requirements are assessed by analyzing the nature and quantity of copied and duplicated materials.

What factors are considered in determining the needs of the reprographics center?

To determine needs, the following factors should be considered:

1. The number of copies needed of various documents prepared in the organization.

2. Special production requirements of the copying or duplicating process (such as color requirements, reducing or enlarging requirements, and types of paper on which the copies are to be made).

3. The overall quality of the original document (such as typewritten or prepared on a computer printer, line drawings, and photographs).

4. The desired quality of the copying or duplicating processes.

5. The turnaround time needed for obtaining copies.

6. The nature of specialized production jobs.

Unless this phase is carefully considered, a newly installed center most likely will not be efficiently organized nor will the equipment in the center be optimally appropriate for various production jobs.

Centralized Control

A common characteristic of most reprographics centers is the centralized control of the unit. Typically, the administrative office manager has overall responsibility for and control over the operation of the center. The day-to-day operation of the center, however, is frequently the responsibility of a supervisor.

Primarily to facilitate user accessibility, reprographics centers generally are centrally located in the organization. Because most of the departments are likely to use reprographics services, location is of primary importance. In organizations that occupy several floors of a building, locating several **satellite centers** throughout the premises may be desirable. These centers most likely contain only a portion of the equipment found in the main center. Smaller production jobs are performed in the satellite centers while major jobs are most likely performed in the main center. In some cases, departments that make extensive use of copiers may find it essential to install their own desktop-sized copiers.

When compared with decentralized control, centralized control of the center offers the following advantages:

What are satellite centers?

What advantages result from centralized control?

1. Greater control over the reprographics function is possible.

2. The center is likely to operate with greater efficiency.

3. The selection and utilization of the equipment is likely to be more efficient.

4. The process of purchasing and replenishing supplies is likely to be performed more efficiently.

Personnel

The quality of the services produced in the reprographics center is directly related to the care with which personnel produce the work. Because many of the processes are quite specialized, the employment of individuals who are skilled in and knowledgeable about reprographics is critical. Otherwise, maximum use of the equipment and implementation of effective work procedures may not be possible.

A number of techniques are used to teach personnel how to operate the equipment found in the reprographics center. For the less sophisticated devices, manufacturers generally provide short, comprehensive training sessions. For more sophisticated equipment, the personnel may need to complete a formal education program provided by a variety of schools, including high schools, technical schools, community colleges, and four-year colleges and universities. Participants in these educational programs frequently enroll in a printing or graphics program.

Operators of heavy printing equipment commonly work for several years as a printer's apprentice. Heavy equipment is more likely to be used in firms that specialize in printing.

Layout

What type of work flow is recommended for a reprographics center?

The layout of the reprographics center also needs to be considered. Because a considerable amount of work produced in the center involves several steps, the flow of work through the center must be planned. The most efficient pattern is to have a straight-line work flow that eliminates backtracking and criss-crossing of jobs in progress.

The specialized nature of the equipment found in reprographics centers makes desirable the use of the various services provided by equipment manufacturers. Representatives of these manufacturers are not only able to provide excellent suggestions for the layout of a reprographics center, but also they are able to help an organization develop efficient operating procedures.

Planning the layout of the center involves (1) determining the placement of the equipment in the center, (2) providing washroom and darkroom facilities, if needed, and (3) providing adequate storage space for the enormous amount of supplies that are typically needed in printing and duplicating operations. In addition, certain environmental conditions are also important in the center, including adequate ventilation to assure air quality control and acoustical control.

Policies and Procedures

The policies and procedures used in operating the center are mainly concerned with the delivery of user services.

Those who use the services of the reprographics center are generally required to complete a requisition form. The form is a work order that includes the following items: the number or name of the document being reproduced; the desired reproduction method, the number of pages in the master copy, the number of copies needed, special directions (such as color of paper, ink, reduction, collating, and stapling), the name of the department to be charged, the name of the individual making the request, and authorization.

Another important procedure involves the handling of confidential materials. To maintain the integrity of this material, some centers assign the processing of confidential work to certain individuals who can be trusted and who are held responsible for maintaining its confidentiality. Any breach in confidentiality can then be easily traced to the guilty party.

What types of policies should be established for the reprographics center?

The reprographics center must also establish a policy governing the processing of high-priority items. This policy is needed because some employees believe that each item they send to the reprographics center has a high priority, requiring immediate attention. Most centers operate on a first-in, first-out basis, except for legitimate high-priority or rush jobs. For a job to be classified as high priority, some centers require that the job be certified as such by several individuals. This procedure eliminates the likelihood that some employees will abuse the privilege of rush production.

Designing the process for determining the appropriate copying or duplicating method for each job is another procedure that needs to be developed. The basis for determining the appropriate method is influenced by the number of copies that are to be made, the intended use of the copies, and the turnaround time needed.

Maintenance of Equipment

The specialized nature of the equipment found in reprographics centers requires quality maintenance that extends its life and improves the quality with which work is produced. Improper maintenance is often responsible for increasing the center's operating costs and producing poor-quality work.

Equipment operators are able to provide a wide variety of routine equipment maintenance, which helps keep the equipment clean and properly adjusted. More complex maintenance is provided by specially trained individuals. In some cases, these individuals are employed by the organization; but in most cases, they work for equipment vendors and provide the maintenance service on a request basis.

Standards

For the reprographics center to be financially feasible, its efficiency is paramount. One way to judge the center's efficiency is to determine how well **production standards** are attained. These standards, which can be obtained from many of the manufacturers of the equipment found in the center, identify the per-hour number of copies that various devices are reasonably capable of producing. Without the use of standards, the organization has no way of knowing whether the reprographics center is operating efficiently. If the actual results are considerably less than the expected level, the administrative office manager and/or the reprographics center supervisor must determine the reasons for the difference. Where needed, appropriate action must be subsequently taken.

In some instances, the reprographics center supervisor will determine the standards rather than using those available from the various equipment manufacturers. To do this, the center's output has to be recorded over a period of time. These records can then be used to determine either hourly or daily output rates for each employee in the center and the need for additional employees. Each time the volume of work increases to the point that one more employee is needed, the reprographics center supervisor can use these data to justify hiring additional help.

In addition to production standards, the reprographics center must also be concerned with cost standards. Factors that must be considered in developing these standards include cost of operating equipment (lease or depreciation), cost of supplies, operator costs, and the cost of the space occupied by the center. When the per-unit costs exceed normal costs, the administrative office manager or the reprographics center supervisor should determine the reasons for the excessive costs.

Cost Control

The nature of the reprographics center makes cost control not only desirable but also crucial. The existence of many potential areas of costly waste in the center requires giving continual attention to cost-control measures. The following suggestions are useful for controlling costs:

1. Use the most economical duplicating and copying processes the jobs will allow.
2. Request or produce only as many copies as are needed.
3. Keep the equipment in proper adjustment so that very few, if any, pages are ruined in the duplicating or copying processes.
4. Print on both sides of the paper when possible.
5. Use the services of the reprographics center for a particular project unless some outside organization is able to provide more economical service.
6. Take advantage of quantity purchasing of supplies.

What use is made of production standards in a reprographics center?

How can costs be controlled in the reprographics center?

Equipment

The equipment that is used also has a significant bearing on the efficiency of the reprographics center. The center's equipment also determines to a great extent the types of services the center is able to provide. A wide variety of equipment is presently on the market, much of which varies considerably in terms of the operational processes.

Subsequent sections in this chapter provide a detailed discussion of the copying process, duplicating process, and imprinting process. Also included is a discussion about some of the auxiliary equipment found in reprographics centers.

THE COPYING PROCESS

The presence of efficient copying equipment has undoubtedly been greatly responsible for the paperwork explosion occurring in organizations. For the most part, the equipment has resulted in significant advantages, although certain disadvantages also result. Perhaps the two most significant disadvantages are the ease with which unneeded extra copies of documents are made and the use of the organization's equipment to make copies for personal use. Preparing extra copies and personal-use copies adds to operating costs and costs for storing and/or disposing of the extra copies.

A common means of categorizing copying equipment is by the type of paper it uses. While some copying equipment requires special sensitized paper, other copying equipment uses plain paper.

Copying Equipment Requiring Sensitized Paper

What types of copying processes use sensitized paper?

Several copying processes require the use of sensitized paper. Among these processes are diffusion transfer, gelatin transfer, stabilization, diazo, and thermography.

Diffusion Transfer. Also called a wet-copy process, **diffusion transfer** requires the use of two chemically coated sheets of paper for each copy that is made. One of the sheets is a negative coated with a silver halide gelatin, making the sheet sensitive to light. The other sheet is the positive. The face of the document being copied is placed against the gelatin side of the negative sheet. These two sheets are then exposed to an intense light. The image areas of the original absorb light rays while the nonimage areas of the original document reflect light back to the negative, thus forming an image on the negative.

After the negative has been exposed, it is placed face-to-face against the positive sheet, and the two sheets are then passed through a developing solution. A reaction of this solution with the image on the negative sheet causes the image to transfer by diffusion to the positive sheet. The two sheets are then passed through rollers to remove excess developer. The negative is discarded; and after the positive sheet has been allowed to dry for a few minutes, the copy is ready for use.

Compared with some of the other copying processes, this method results in several disadvantages: a developing solution is needed, copies have to dry before they are usable, and the process is quite slow.

Gelatin Transfer. Sometimes known as dye transfer, **gelatin transfer** also requires the use of special paper and developing chemicals. The face of the

What are the
characteristics of the
gelatin transfer process?

original document is placed against the surface of the negative sheet, which is coated with a gelatin substance. The original and the negative are exposed to light, allowing the nonimage areas of the original to reflect to the negative. The exposed negative is then passed through a chemical solution that causes gelatin in the exposed areas to harden. The unexposed areas of the negative remain soft, and as the negative is passed through the chemical solution, these areas become a dye. As the dye areas of the negative come into contact with the copying paper, the dye transfers to the paper, which creates a likeness of the original on the paper. Up to ten copies of the original can be made before the dye either dries or is spent.

This process has the same disadvantages as the diffusion transfer process.

Stabilization. Whereas the diffusion and the gelatin transfer processes require both negative and positive sheets, the **stabilization** process does not. This process involves the reflection of light from the original document onto sensitized paper. The copy paper is first passed through a developing chemical and then through a stabilization chemical, which permanently affixes the image on the copy paper.

Stabilization is especially suited for copying photographs. Like the other processes already discussed, disadvantages of this process include: required use of chemicals, copies have to be dry before they are usable, and the process is slow.

Diazo. Especially well suited for making copies of architectural and engineering drawings, **diazo** requires the use of an original document in a translucent state. Therefore, it can only be used to copy those documents that have printing on one side of the page. The original document is placed against a copy sheet coated with a diazonium compound. The two sheets are then exposed to light. The nonimage areas allow the light rays to pass through to the coated copy paper, which activates the decomposition of the diazonium compound. The copy paper is then exposed to a chemical; and while the decomposed areas remain neutral, the active areas (image areas on the original) react and cause an image to appear on the copy sheet.

Although it is one of the least expensive copying processes, diazo is marked by several disadvantages, including the use of ammonia fumes in the development process and the slowness with which the process works.

What are the
characteristics of the
thermography process?

Thermography. Another of the copying processes requiring the use of sensitized paper is **thermography.** This process works on the principle that dark areas or substances absorb heat, whereas light areas or substances do not. This process is also known as the *infrared* or the *heat-transfer process*. When thermography is used, the original document is placed beneath the copy paper. As the original and the copy paper are exposed to infrared rays, the image or printed areas of the original hold heat, causing the copy paper to darken in these areas. The original images are produced on the copy paper. Because this process requires the use of writing and printing substances that hold heat long enough to transfer the image to the copy paper, some types of ink and colors cannot be used.

Among the more serious disadvantages of this process are the restriction of its use to heat-sensitive substances and the tendency of thermography copy papers to darken and become brittle with age.

Copying Equipment Using Plain Paper

What copying processes
use plain paper?

Two copying process presently available use plain paper: the **xerographic process** and **fiber optics.** For routine types of office copying, these processes are generally considered as being superior to the other processes that require sensitized copy paper or liquid chemicals.

Xerographic Process. The basis of the xerographic process is the physics principle of unlike electrical charges being attracted to each other and like charges being repelled from each other. The process, by means of a camera, transmits the image of the original document to a selenium-coated drum that is positively charged. The nonimage areas of the original document allow light to strike the drum, which causes the positive charge in those areas to dissipate. The image areas of the drum, on the other hand, hold their positive charge. A negatively charged black powder is then spread over the drum; and because unlike electrical charges attract each other, the powder adheres to the image areas. A plain sheet of paper with a positive charge is then passed over the drum, which transfers the images to the paper and creates a likeness of the original document. The black powder is permanently affixed to the paper by means of a heat transfer process.

Some of the newer, more advanced copiers replace the traditional light source with a laser or CRT light source. A toner is used to produce the image that appears on the drum, and the image is transferred to paper. The toner is affixed to the paper by means of a heat transfer process.

Among the features commonly found on today's plain-paper copiers are image reduction, image enlargement, automatic document feed, duplexing (facilitates copying on both sides of a sheet of paper during one pass through the copier), collating, and stapling.

Other new, less common features found on copiers include automatic paper folding; adhesive binding; automatic hole punching; facsimile; built-in image editing (allows certain areas of the document to be copied and other areas to be deleted; spot color (allows the addition of one color to a portion of a black-and-white copy); digital editing (the copy scans the image to convert it to digital signals, which makes possible the subsequent alteration of the image); and remote monitoring and diagnostics (an internal modem permits the copier to send usage data from a branch office to a home office or, when the copier is malfunctioning, send diagnostic data from the installation site to a service center).

Many new plain-paper copiers use microprocessors to perform a variety of functions. Among these are diagnostic capabilities, density control, and user prompts. For example, the prompt may give the user the following verbal instruction: "Please load with more paper." When the paper supply has been replenished, the microprocessor-controlled prompt will say, "Thank you."

Full-color copier technology is currently developing at a fast rate. This technology, which permits the interfacing of full-color copiers with microcomputers and facsimile machines, is resulting in the continual decrease in the per-page cost of full-color copying. Like black-and-white copying, full-color copying also uses xerographic technology. Other technologies used are electrophotographic (image is produced by using chemicals on photographic paper) and thermal transfer (uses heat and pressure to fuse onto the surface of paper the colors that are found on a coated ribbon). The xerographic and electrophotographic technologies produce better quality copies than does the thermal transfer process.

What features does digital copying provide?

The digital copying process provides a number of useful features unavailable on analog equipment, including stretching, shrinking, or slanting text material; enlarging (up to 200 percent) and reducing material (down to 50 percent); overlaying one image on another; mirror imaging; color converting; reverse imaging; and deleting of material while copying other material from the same image.

With digital equipment, the image being copied is "scanned" once, with the subsequent printing of the desired number of copies. Thus, each copy is considered as a first-generation copy. Analog equipment copies the document repeatedly, with each copy being a second-generation copy. Of the two types of equipment, digital equipment generally provides better quality work.

The following categories of plain-paper copiers are available: low volume, medium volume, and high volume.

What categories of plain-paper copiers are available?

Low-volume copiers are designed to produce 1,000 to 20,000 copies per month at rates of 10 to 30 copies per minute. The copiers, which are small enough to fit on a desk top, are found distributed throughout the premises. Some of the low-volume copiers use microprocessor controls.

The medium-volume copiers are used to produce 20,000 to 50,000 copies per month. They operate at a faster rate (30 to 60 copies per minute) than the low-volume copiers, and generally they are centrally located. Medium-volume copiers are likely to possess more functions than their low-volume counterparts.

The high-volume copiers are used to produce 50,000 to 100,000 copies per month and operate at rates exceeding 60 copies per minute. They are always used in a central location. Of the three categories, high-volume copiers perform the greatest number of functions.

The newest generation of plain-paper copiers are the electronic or intelligent printers/copiers, which actually are nonimpact printers and copiers integrated into one device. This equipment may receive digital input from a word processor, computer, or CRT unit, from which it prepares a hard copy. In some cases, the printing will take place immediately. In other instances, the information will be stored in the system's memory, which is capable of holding up to 1,000 pages. Printing will be completed later. Another feature of the printer/copier is its ability to store a variety of graphics and forms for later use. Color printer/copier devices are also now available that permit printing in color from a computer as well as color copying. Although this equipment is more expensive than equipment that does not permit computer interfacing, where justifiable, it is well worth the extra cost.

A new copier device is available that combines the following functions: copying, scanning, facsimile, computing, and printing. Eventually, this device will be able to massage, change, and redistribute all of the information received—including paper documents, images, graphics, computer data/information, and mail—in an organization.

Following are the more common features found on today's copier equipment (even some of the low-volume copiers):

What are some of the common features found on today's copying equipment?

Automatic document feed

Enlargement or reduction of document size

User access codes

Dual-page copying (primarily for copying book pages)

Duplexing

Interrupt memory

Job memory

Automatic paper-size sensor

Multiple paper drawers

Production run counts

Sheet bypass

When selecting equipment, these features should be considered if their use can be justified. Features that cannot be justified or that would be used rarely should probably not be considered as they will increase equipment and maintenance costs. As an alternative, some organizations will obtain one or two devices with some or all of these features; their other devices provide fewer of these features.

Some organizations that cannot justify obtaining high-volume specialized copier equipment that possesses the features just identified use outsourcing for some of their copying. In determining which jobs to outsource and which to do internally, the following factors should be considered: needed turn-around time, needed number of copies, nature of the work, and confidentiality of the work.

Figure 23–1 illustrates a plain-paper copier using the xerographic process.

When selecting or comparing copiers, the following factors should be kept in mind:

What factors should be considered when selecting copiers?

Copier applications

Equipment reliability

Equipment cost

Image quality

Copier volume

Vendor reputation

Vender service response time

Fiber Optics. The newest development in copying processes is the use of fiber optics. The process functions in the following way: the conventional mirror lens assembly on a plain-paper copier is replaced with a fiber optics mechanism. The optic tubes transmit light from the original document to a drum. Each fiber carries a minute portion of the document image. The toner, which produces the image, is fused to the paper as the document is prepared.

Figure 23-1 Plain-paper copier. Courtesy: Xerox Corporation.

Monitoring Copier Usage

The accessibility of copiers is directly related to their use for personal copying. Among the suggestions for reducing copier misuse are:

1. Set the per-page cost of personal copies as low as possible, assuming that if the cost is sufficiently low, employees will be more inclined to pay for personal copying.
2. Restrict copier usage to certain individuals who will do all copying for the organization.
3. Use copiers that require the user to enter a PIN (personal identification numbers) into the control panel before the equipment becomes operational. As an alternative, magnetic debit cards that can be recharged can be used to make the equipment operational.
4. Remove convenience copiers and install satellite copy centers, with use being restricted to individuals who work in the centers.

THE DUPLICATION PROCESS

At one time, the difference between copying and duplicating was fairly clear-cut. The major distinction was in the number of copies the equipment was used to make. To illustrate, a copying process was typically advantageous for making fewer than thirty copies of an original, while duplicating processes were used for larger quantity jobs. But because of new copying technology, an increasing number of organizations are now using copiers for all but their largest production jobs.

What types of duplication processes exist?

The three major types of duplicating processes found today are the spirit process, the stencil process, and the offset process. As time passes, the spirit and stencil processes will be used less commonly in offices.

Spirit Process

What is used in making copies with the spirit process?

This process is suitable for making fewer than 300 copies from one master. Of the three duplicating processes, the **spirit process** is the least expensive. It requires the use of a spirit master, which consists of two sheets: the carbon backing sheet and the face of the master. As the master face is written on, drawn on, or typed on, the carbon adheres to its backside (in reverse image). When ready for use, the master is placed carbon side up on the duplicator drum. The master is moistened with a special alcohol solvent, which causes a small portion of the carbon to transfer to each sheet of copy paper upon its passage through the duplicator. The master can be used to print copies until all of the carbon is depleted.

Spirit masters can also be prepared by a thermal process. The original document and a thermal master are fed through a device that causes the image areas of the document to hold heat. The build-up of heat then causes the carbon on the thermal master to adhere to the face of the master. Typically, fewer copies can be made from thermal masters than from the spirit masters prepared in the conventional manner.

The spirit process is quite flexible. Several colors of carbon can be placed on one spirit master, which provides multicolor printing in one pass through the machine. The masters also can be stored and reused. In addition, portions of the master can be removed after some of the printing has been done. This facilitates use of the same master for two different production jobs that have identical information. To eliminate a section, the portions can either be cut out of the master or covered with tape, or the carbon in those areas can be scraped from the master. The colors produced by the spirit process are not as vivid as those produced by stencil duplication.

Stencil Duplication

Like the spirit process, **stencil duplication** is also rather inexpensive. Stencil duplication is suitable for making up to 2,500 copies from one master. The stencil consists of a fiber substance coated with wax. When the stencil is typed, written on, or drawn on, the wax is pushed aside, which enables ink to pass through the exposed areas. The stencil is attached to a drum covered with an ink-soaked pad. The ink, which passes through the exposed areas of the stencil, is transferred to the copy paper as the paper and stencil come into contact with one another. If properly cared for, the stencil can be stored and reused.

How is color printed using stencil duplication?

When color duplicating is desired, a separate stencil may have to be made for each needed color. For example, a stencil may have to be prepared to transfer the red areas to the paper, another for the blue areas, and so forth. Therefore, if a duplicating job involves four different stencils, the paper has to pass through the duplicator four times.

In some instances, producing multicolor documents may be possible simply by applying the various colors of ink to the appropriate areas of one ink pad. This eliminates having to make separate stencils for each color because all colors will be printed in one pass through the machine. This technique is not suitable when the various ink colors are near one another on the ink pad as the inks have a tendency to blend with one another.

Stencils can be prepared on an electronic stencil-making device. The same images that are found on the original document are burned into the stencil. Electronic stencil-making devices are also capable of making halftone illustrations.

More copies can be made from a stencil master than can be made from a spirit master. In comparison to the spirit process, the stencil duplication process is less convenient for multicolor duplication.

The advent of digital duplicators has given the stencil-duplication process a renewed life in an increasing number of organizations. These duplicators use a digital scanning process to prepare the required stencil. Once the stencil is prepared, the device automatically mounts it and then unmounts it when the desired number of copies have been printed. As a result, it is cleaner to use than the old stencil duplicators. Compared with copier technology, digital duplicators have the following advantages: They produce no ozone or radiation, and they use water-based ink (unlike their predecessors that used a petroleum-based ink). The quality of work produced by digital duplicators makes them suitable for company newsletters, manuals, reports, and so forth.

Offset Process

Although more costly and more intricate than either the spirit process or stencil duplication, the **offset process** is more extensively used than either of the other two duplication processes. Depending on the conditions, several thousand copies can be made from one master.

What are the characteristics of the offset process?

The offset process is based on the chemical principle that water and grease do not mix. The image areas on the printing master hold the greasy printing ink, while the nonimage areas hold water, which repels the ink. The inked images are transferred or offset to a rubber blanket or roller. As the duplicating paper comes into contact with the roller, the image is transferred to the paper.

Offset masters, which are prepared in a variety of ways, are either paper or metal. Some of the paper masters are direct image and can be drawn on, typed on, or written on. Paper masters can also be prepared photographically by a master maker while the metal plates can only be prepared photographically by a plate maker. A much larger number of copies can be produced from a metal plate than from a paper master.

Many offset duplicators are highly automated. Some of the features found on these duplicators are the ability to cut sheets of paper from a paper roll; perforating, slitting, and collating attachments; a counter that stops the duplicator when the desired number of copies have been prepared; automatic insertion and ejection of paper masters; and automated machine cleanup.

Of the three primary duplication processes, offset offers the best quality of work. In most cases, the quality of offset duplication is nearly as high as the quality of the original. Because offset equipment is more specialized, operators need to be well trained. In relation to the spirit and stencil processes, the per-unit cost of offset duplication is somewhat higher.

Copy Printer

What are the characteristics of a copy printer?

Copy-printer equipment, which incorporates the offset printing process, is a new development in reprographics equipment. This device is especially well suited for high-volume, short-run, repetitive jobs. It is designed for situations in which five to a thousand copies are needed and is well suited for organizations printing from 150,000 to 500,000 copies per month.

Copy-printer equipment has an extensive number of automated features. The operator simply places the original in the machine and inputs the number of copies to be made. The machine automatically completes the job. The machine, therefore, is capable of electrostatic master making, master feeding, and offset duplicating, all without operator assistance. In addition, most copy printers are also capable of reducing the original to a smaller sized copy as well as sorting the copies into sets.

THE IMPRINTING PROCESS

The imprinting process is used to add information to an already existing document. Several imprinting processes are available, including those discussed in the following paragraphs.

Signature Machines

Two types of signature machines are presently available. One machine uses a ribbon to imprint a signature on a document. This is the type of machine frequently used to affix signatures to checks. Another type uses a template of the individual's signature. As the stylus follows the signature contained in the template, a mechanical pen produces the signature on the document. This device is especially useful for placing original signatures on important mass mailings, for example.

Although not a machine, a third means of affixing a signature to a document is to digitize the individual's signature and store it as a file on a magnetic medium, such as the hard drive of a desktop computer. When needed, the file is accessed; and the signature is inserted at the appropriate location in the document. This process can be used to imprint the signature of the originator to a letter, for example, as the document is being printed.

Impression Stamps

For what are impression stamps used?

These stamps are used when a small amount of repetitive data needs to be recorded on documents. Examples are date stamps, signature stamps, name and address stamps, and authorization stamps. For small jobs, an impression stamp is generally more convenient than other printing processes.

Numbering Devices

Numbering a series of documents sequentially is often desirable. The use of a mechanical numbering device is much quicker and neater than numbering by hand.

AUXILIARY EQUIPMENT

During the last few years, a considerable amount of auxiliary equipment has been developed for use in reprographics centers. While some of this equipment mechanizes the duplicating process to a greater extent than ever before, other equipment expands the process so a greater variety of jobs can be performed. The following provides a discussion of some of the more significant developments.

Automatic Collators

These devices have considerably reduced the amount of manual effort expended in many offices. Automatic collators, which can be attached to offset duplicators, copiers, and intelligent copiers/printers, mechanically collate pages as they leave the device. Each page is transported to the appropriate bin in the collator. At the end of the production cycle, the bins will contain one copy of each page that has been duplicated/copied. As the collated sets are removed from the collator, they can be stapled, thus completing the job. However, if most copying jobs involve multiple pages that need to be collated and stapled, consideration should perhaps be given to purchasing copying equipment that has a built-in collating feature.

Binders

What is meant by perfect binding?

Instead of binding documents with staples or spirally binding documents, a recent development is the adhesive binding of documents. This process, which is also known as *perfect binding,* involves putting a thin layer of adhesive along one edge of the document to be bound. The adhesive holds the pages together.

Desktop Publishing

The newest development in the photocomposition process is known as **desktop publishing.** Primarily used for internal and lower volume external documents, desktop publishing creates documents with a professional appearance. A microcomputer and desktop publishing software program are used to input material into the system. The document, the output of which is typically prepared on a laser printer capable of producing high-quality work, has the appearance of a typeset document. When multiple copies are needed, an original of the document is often used as a master. The process facilitates the inclusion of graphics, photographs, and various sizes and styles of type.

Folding Equipment

Rather economically priced equipment is now available that folds documents. While some equipment folds only one sheet at a time, other equipment folds multiple sheets. Several different folding arrangements may be possible, although folding pages in halves or thirds is most common.

MECHANICAL DEVICES FOR TRANSPORTING INTERNAL CORRESPONDENCE

While some of the internally created documents stay within the departments in which they are generated, others must be transported to other departments. In addition to a messenger service, a variety of mechanical devices are used. The more common types of mechanical devices are pneumatic tubes, conveyor systems, and electric mail carts.

Pneumatic Tubes

What mechanical devices are used for the internal transmission of documents?

The use of a **pneumatic tube system** requires a network of tubes located throughout the premises. To install a tube system after a building has been completed adds greatly to the cost of the system.

　　Documents to be transported from one department to another are placed in special carriers that travel through the network of tubes. Less sophisticated tube systems generally have a central receiving-distributing point that interconnects the tube network throughout the departments in the organization. More sophisticated pneumatic systems incorporate an automatic dialing tube unit. The user dials the destination point and inserts the carrier into the tube. Once it begins traveling, the carrier is automatically switched from one tube to another until it reaches its destination. The more sophisticated systems eliminate the central receiving-distributing point required in the less sophisticated systems.

Conveyor Systems

The **conveyor system** is an effective mechanical device for transporting documents from one location to another on the same floor. This device consists of a continuous conveyor belt on which several multilength channels are placed. Each workstation has its own channel. After the document is placed in the appropriate channel, the belt moves it to the desired station where it falls into a receiving tray. The number of workstations that can receive documents is limited to the number of upright channels that are contained in the system.

Electric Mail Carts

What is used to guide electric mail carts through the premises?

Some organizations use **electric mail carts** rather than employees to distribute incoming mail or to collect outgoing mail from the various departments. The carts, which follow either copper wires imbedded in the floor or fluorescent paint on the floor surface (including carpet), can be programmed to stop at various locations, perhaps for a period of twenty seconds. If additional time is needed, an employee can push a "stop" button. Pushing the "start" button enables the cart to continue its route. These devices automatically stop when an object gets in their way.

　　Some electric mail carts are equipped with a recorder unit that can be used to broadcast any kind of prerecorded information. The more sophisticated carts are also capable of riding unassisted on elevators. Figure 23–2 illustrates an electric mail cart.

THE MAILROOM

Considerable diversity exists among mailrooms found throughout organizations. In fact, of all the areas of administrative office management, the greatest diversity most likely will be found among organizations' mailrooms.

To a large extent, the structure of the mailroom is determined by the size and needs of the organization. Smaller organizations are generally able to function with one individual who has responsibilities other than processing incoming and outgoing mail and delivering internal correspondence. In larger organizations, one or more employees have a full-time responsibility for mail services. The personnel, layout, and equipment requirements of the mailroom are determined by several factors:

What factors determine the personnel, layout, and equipment requirements of the mailroom?

1. The number of employees in the organization.
2. The correspondence volume of the organization. The volume is affected by the type of organization.
3. The speed with which the mail must be handled. Organizations that receive large sums of money through the mail each day may require faster mail-handling procedures than others.
4. The nature of the outgoing mail that is processed in the mailroom. Correspondence mailed in standard-sized envelopes that does not need to be weighed requires less processing time than materials that must be weighed or that require special handling because of the mailing container.

Typical functions of mailrooms are the processing of incoming and outgoing mail, internal pickup and delivery of mail, distribution of internal correspondence, and receipt and shipment of parcels. The extent to which each of

Figure 23-2 Electric mail cart. Courtesy: Bell & Howell, Inc. Automated Systems, Division, Zeeland, MI.

these functions is performed in the mailroom has a significant impact on a number of its features.

Adding to the smooth functioning of an organization's mailroom is the preparation and use of a mail services manual, which is distributed throughout the organization. As with any operating manual the organization develops, the content should be thorough and clearly understandable so mailroom personnel do not have to spend time engaging in further elaboration or clarification about its content. Among the topics typically included are mailroom operations, mailroom policies and procedures, services provided, outgoing mail preparation, specific directions for various types of mailings, mail classifications, and mail-delivery options.

Mailroom Personnel

What determines the personnel mix found in mailrooms?

The type and number of personnel required in the mailroom are determined by the size of the organization and the variety of functions performed by the mailroom. When one or more full-time employees are needed, a supervisor is typically responsible for day-to-day operations, while the administrative office manager is more likely to have ultimate responsibility for its operation. Other types of employees found in mailrooms are senior mail clerk, mail clerk, delivery clerk, and messenger.

The senior mail clerk may be responsible for opening and routing to the appropriate recipients mail that is addressed either to the organization or to a position/title (such as manager of human resources) rather than to a named individual. This person needs to have a thorough understanding of the organization's various operational functions as well as have a familiarity with the individuals who work in each of the functional areas. In addition, the senior mail clerk may be responsible for other routine duties commonly performed in the mailroom.

A primary responsibility of the mail clerk is to rough sort incoming mail into predetermined categories, such as by floor or by department. The mail clerk is also frequently responsible for operating the various mailing machines, in addition to performing other routine duties.

The delivery clerk is generally responsible for the mail for a specific area or group of departments in the organization. This employee may also be responsible for pickup and delivery of internal correspondence as well as for sorting outgoing mail.

The messenger is typically responsible for special-request delivery of materials and mail. In some instances, the messenger may be responsible for transporting the rough-sorted mail from the mailroom to the appropriate delivery clerks. In addition, the messenger may, upon request, be responsible for running errands inside or outside the organization.

What is an "outsourced" mailroom function?

As an alternative to employing their own mailroom staff, some organizations are using outsourcing, which involves having an outside organization perform some or all mailroom functions. Some organizations have all mailroom functions performed by outsourcing. Other organizations have only a few functions performed by outsourcing, such as presorting or preparing mass mailings. When an outsourcing service is used, it can be housed on or off the organization's premises.

Mailroom Layout

Because of the amount of physical activity involved in the mailroom, layout can have a direct bearing on its efficiency. For this reason, special consideration needs to be given to mailroom layout.

The functions performed by the mailroom determine the areas that should be considered in planning its layout. For example, space should be provided for removing mail from mail sacks. To accommodate those who wish to work in a standing position, the dumping table typically has raised sides and may be higher than a normal table. After the mail is dumped, the next process may be to align the various envelopes so they can be run through the mail opener. Mail that is marked "personal" or "confidential" has to be removed before the mail is mechanically opened. In some organizations, the envelopes are opened by the individuals to whom they are addressed.

The sorting area also needs to be considered in designing the layout of the mailroom. If the mailroom is responsible for the rough sorting of incoming mail but not for the final sorting, less space is needed than when the mailroom is responsible for both sortings. Pigeonhole racks speed up the sorting process. Additional space is also needed for packing and wrapping parcels, in addition to stamping, sealing, and sorting outgoing mail.

When designing the layout of the mailroom, special consideration should be given to its work flow. The processing of mail should move from one point to the next with a minimum amount of physical effort and distance. The efficiency of the design of the mailroom—typically, a U-shaped arrangement is recommended—greatly determines the speed and accuracy with which the mail is processed. Figure 23–3 illustrates the layout of a well-designed mailroom.

Mailroom Equipment

Much of the new equipment being manufactured for processing incoming and outgoing mail greatly reduces the amount of physical effort involved in mail

Figure 23–3 Mailroom layout. Courtesy: Pitney Bowes.

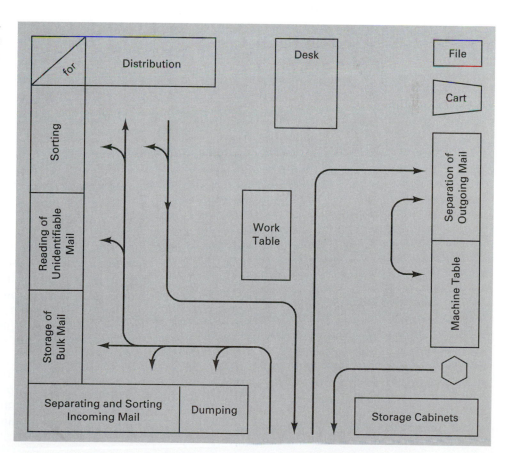

What types of equipment are found in the modern mailroom?

processing. Some of these new developments combine several functions into one piece of equipment. For example, equipment is available that performs all of the following functions: stamping, postmarking, sealing, counting, and stacking.

Several categories of equipment are found in the modern mailroom, some of which are discussed next.

Addresser-Printer Equipment. This type of equipment is used to print mailing addresses on envelopes and other types of mailing containers. **Addresser-printers** vary considerably in terms of their mechanical operation. Some are manually operated, but most are electrically powered. All addresser-printers require the use of data plates, which are about the size of a plastic credit card. These plates, which are made of metal, plastic, or foil, are capable of holding at least 320 characters. To imprint names and addresses on mailing containers, a tray containing the data plates is inserted into the addresser-printer. As the plate comes in contact with the mailing container, an impression is made on the envelope when the ribbon inserted between the raised characters on the data plate is pressed against the envelope.

Increasingly, addresser-printer equipment uses a dot-matrix printing device or an ink-jet printer interfaced with a computer, rather than the address plates common among earlier equipment. This equipment facilitates the easy maintenance of an up-to-date mailing list.

Opening Equipment. A considerable amount of employee time can be saved by using automatic opening equipment. The opener trims off a small part of the envelope. Care has to be taken to make sure that the opener does not also cut the contents of the envelopes.

What function does stamping-sealing equipment provide?

Stamping-Sealing Equipment. A wide variety of **stamping-sealing equipment** is now available. While some of the equipment only stamps and seals envelopes, other more sophisticated equipment performs the following additional functions: postmarking envelopes, stacking envelopes, recording the amount of postage used, and counting the number of envelopes processed. In addition, some postage meters are equipped with attachments for signing and backstamping.

Historically, stamping-sealing equipment has consisted of mechanical components, in addition to the detachable postage meter. To purchase postage using this system, the meter is taken to a U.S. Post Office where it is reset and resealed. The capacity of some postage meters is as high as $9,999.99. Each time an envelope is processed through the meter, the amount of postage affixed to the envelope is subtracted from the meter.

A new development in the stamping process allows an organization to purchase electronic postage, officially known as the **Information Based Indicia Program (IBIP),** through the Internet. The digital stamp is affixed to the envelope using a software program, a desktop computer, and a printer. Three areas of information are imprinted on the envelop as it is prepared: the recipient's name and address, the bar code that represents the ZIP code or ZIP code + 4, and the digital stamp.

An account is established for each desktop computer in the organization for which the use of electronic postage is authorized. The Internet is used to charge the account; and each time a digital stamp is affixed to an envelope or mailer, the amount of the stamp is deducted from the account that is maintained on the desktop computer. The account can be recharged twenty-four hours a day, seven days a week.

In addition to reducing the amount of physical effort involved in preparing outgoing mail, the use of stamping-sealing equipment is advantageous for another reason. When this equipment is used, envelopes that require more than the minimum amount of postage are generally weighed, thus assuring the accuracy of the amount of postage affixed to the envelope.

Automatic Envelope Emptiers. Equipment is also available that automatically removes the contents of envelopes. In addition to removing envelope contents, the devices are also capable of automatically disposing of empty envelopes. These devices are adjustable so that envelopes of different sizes can be processed.

Label Preparation Equipment. Another type of equipment often found in the mailroom prepares labels. The printing mechanism of the label preparation equipment is typically activated by a magnetic medium, such as that used by data processing equipment. Names and addresses are contained on the medium; and as it is read by the equipment, names and addresses are printed on labels. Pressure-sensitive labels are commonly used, and equipment can be obtained that mechanically affixes the labels to the mailing container.

The most recent technology used in designing label-preparation equipment incorporates ink-jet printing. The printer is attached to a computer, and the outgoing pieces to be addressed are loaded in the printer's hopper. These printers are designed to handle all sizes and thicknesses of mail. In addition to entering the address on each piece, the printer also adds the appropriate bar code for each ZIP code. Compared with using pressure-sensitive labels, ink-jet address printers are faster and more economical.

Inserting Equipment. This type of equipment is used to stuff inserts into envelopes. Some of the equipment being manufactured is also capable of folding up to six sheets of paper before inserting the material into an envelope.

Electronic Scale. Many organizations have found the use of electronic scales for weighing mail to be an effective cost-saving device. These scales display the actual amount of postage needed on the item being weighed. Electronic scales do not require as much subjective judgment as earlier scales.

Bundling Equipment. The purpose of this equipment is to tie and bundle packages. Because this equipment is capable of performing at a much faster rate than humans, it can save an organization a considerable amount of time in preparing outgoing mail.

Figure 23–4 illustrates mailroom equipment.

Conserving Mailing Costs

Organizations are using a number of techniques to conserve their mailing costs. The majority of these techniques use new mailing technology. Among the techniques are the following:

1. Imprinting of POSTNET bar codes on the envelope. The use of ZIP + 4 (the original five-digit ZIP-code number and the newer four-digit number) on a specified quantity of first-class envelopes entitles the organization to a discount. The bar code must be capable of being read by the U.S. Postal Service's scanning equipment, which means that it needs to be placed in a specified area. Additional discounts are available to users who, in addition

What technology is used in printing labels?

How can mailing costs be conserved?

Figure 23-4 Mail-room device. Courtesy: Ascom Hasler Mailing Systems®, Inc.

to using ZIP + 4, presort their first-class mail before delivering it to their local post office. When designing a ZIP + 4 system, U.S. Postal Service employees should be consulted about the latest regulations governing the ZIP + 4 program. If a large volume of the four-digit routing numbers have to be added to an organization's mailing database, the most economical process is to invest in a national ZIP + 4 directory on a CD-ROM. With the appropriate software, the system will automatically add the four-digit numbers to the already stored five-digit ZIP code.

2. Affixing the proper amount of postage to each piece of mail. The use of new electronic scales helps assure that each mailed item receives the proper amount of postage. This suggestion is especially appropriate when mailing parcels and first-class items weighing more than one ounce.

3. Keeping mailing lists up to date. Out-of-date mailing lists are costly, especially when the items cannot be forwarded. Normal forwarding time is one year.

4. Using light-weight mailers. A number of new light-weight mailers are now available, especially those that accommodate unfolded 8 1/2-by-11-inch sheets of paper.

5. Using fax delivery, when possible, rather than an overnight delivery service.

6. Investigating the use of alternative delivery services for parcels.

Courier Services

For what are courier services used?

As an alternative to the traditional delivery method by the U.S. Postal Service, **courier services** are used extensively by some companies. Among these are delivery by Federal Express, Burlington, Purcolator, United Parcel Service, and Greyhound. The advantage of using these services is the speed with which mail and packages can be delivered.

Online Mailing Service

An **online mailing service** enables an organization to prepare documents on the premises but then transmit them electronically via the Internet to an online mailing service that will print, fold, insert, and address the mail. The organization is charged a per-unit fee for each processed item that includes the postage. In deciding whether to use an online mailing service, the organization will likely undertake a financial analysis designed to determine whether this work can be processed more economically on or off the premises.

IMPLICATIONS FOR THE ADMINISTRATIVE OFFICE MANAGER

Two areas for which the administrative office manager is commonly responsible are reprographics and mail services. In large organizations, each area is likely to have a full-time supervisor, with the administrative office manager maintaining overall responsibility.

The more extensively these areas are designed around organizational needs, the more efficient they will be. And operational efficiency is directly related to cost efficiency. Among the factors affecting operational efficiency are equipment, procedures, personnel, and layout.

When contrasted with the equipment found a few years ago in these two areas, today's equipment is much easier to operate. In fact, many of the judgmental decisions that the operator had to make using yesterday's equipment are performed automatically by today's equipment. Another significant change is found in the equipment's operating speed. Today's equipment is much faster.

Regardless of the configuration of either the reprographics area or the mailroom, the administrative office manager, by designing effective operations, can make a significant contribution to organizational efficiency. Doing so will help the organization more readily achieve its profitability goals.

REVIEW QUESTIONS

1. What is a satellite reprographics center and why is it used?

2. What factors need to be considered in determining the layout of the reprographics center?

3. How might the cost of a reprographics center be controlled?

4. Which of the various types of copying processes appear to be the most efficient? Why?

5. What are the various categories of plain-paper copiers?

6. What factors should be considered in selecting copiers?

7. On what chemical principle is the offset process based?

8. What mechanical devices are used for transporting internal correspondence?

9. Explain the uses of the more commonly found equipment in a mailroom.

DISCUSSION QUESTIONS

1. The organization in which you work is studying the efficiency of its mailroom operations. You were appointed to chair the committee looking at layout. In designing layout recommendations for the proposed center, what factors need to be considered?

2. Several desktop copiers were placed in strategic positions in the company in which you are the administrative office manager. These are in addition to the high-volume copier located in the reprographics center. During the three months that these copiers have been in place, copier usage has increased an average of 11 percent each month, yet the volume of business operations has not increased significantly. The vice president of administration is concerned that the open copying privilege is being abused. He has asked you to develop a "control" system to reduce the opportunity for abuse. Outline your plan.

3. At the present time, reprographics in the small company in which you work is decentralized. Each department has a small desktop copier on which all of the unit's copying is completed. Various individuals have suggested that considerable time could be saved if a larger copier capable of performing multiple functions (collating and stapling, for example) were available. You have been asked by the company president to prepare a list of pros and cons for the two alternatives: centralized copying with no unit copiers available or decentralized copying using only the unit copiers. Prepare the list.

STUDENT PROJECTS AND ACTIVITIES

1. Interview the manager of mail services in an organization. Learn how the needs of the present operation were determined.

2. Obtain promotional brochures for two competing office copiers. Compare and contrast these copiers on the basis of the information contained in the brochures.

3. Going Online: Using the Internet, conduct an online search based on one of the concepts presented in this chapter or based on one of the chapter terms. Identify four or five things you learned from the material that you did not know prior to your online search.

Minicase

The Murphy Implement Company has had a 55 percent increase in its copying costs during the last two months. Approximately 25 percent of this increase can be attributed to company growth during the last 18 months. Another 15 percent can be attributed to increases in the costs of paper, copier supplies, and equipment rental.

1. What factors may be responsible for the remaining 15 percent increase in copying costs?

2. What suggestions do you have for controlling these costs?

Case

The Premier Insurance Company, which is headquartered in Kansas City, Missouri, is one of the largest insurance companies in the Midwest. At the present time, approximately 1,800 employees work in the headquarters building.

For several years now, the company has had a policy that all office equipment is to be purchased by bids. The competitive nature of the office equipment vendors in the Kansas City area is responsible for the company's present use of eight different brands of office equipment. The company presently has thirty-five copiers located throughout the premises. In most instances, the supplies and chemicals used by the eight brands of copiers are not interchangeable. Some brands of equipment require more maintenance than other brands, and some brands have higher repair costs.

You, as administrative office manager, are concerned that the bidding process may be creating some problems. This policy may result in lower purchase prices, and it may also be responsible for higher supply and maintenance charges.

1. Explain how you might determine whether or not the bidding process is more costly than a nonbidding process might be over the long run.

2. Outline your recommendation for solving this problem.

3. Explain how you will determine the effectiveness of your recommendation once it has been implemented.

*C*hapter 24

QUALITY AND QUANTITY CONTROL

*C*hapter *A*ims

After reading this chapter, you should be able to design an effective quality and quantity control program for an organization.

*C*hapter *O*utline

The Process of Control
Objectives of Control
Advantages of Control
Elements of Control
    Factors to Control
    Identification of Anticipated Results
    Measurement Devices
    Application of Corrective Measures
Quality Control
    Quality Control Techniques
    Total Quality Management (TQM)
Quantity Control
    Controlling Fluctuations
    Short-interval Scheduling
Work Scheduling
    Work Scheduling Devices
Implications for the Administrative Office
    Manager

*C*hapter *T*erms

Control limits
Critical path
Gantt Chart
ISO 9000 Certification
Normal distribution
Performance standards
PERT
Quality control
Quality standards
Quantity control
Quantity standards
Sampling
Schedule log
Short-interval scheduling
Spot checking
Statistical quality control
Total inspection
Total Quality Management (TQM)
Work chart
Work measurement
Work schedule calendar
Work scheduling
Zero defects

*A*s one of the five basic management functions, control is essential because it helps assure that actual operational results conform with desired or anticipated results. When the desired results are not attained, control facilitates the application of corrective measures.

In addition to a wide range of other responsibilities, the administrative office manager will find that control is an important management tool. The absence of control often results in the diminished effectiveness of many office activities, which frequently results in a negative effect on the quantity and quality of work. The long-term results of the lack of adequate control are seen in reduced output and higher production costs.

Administrative office managers generally have access to several types of control; this chapter covers two important types: **quality control** and **quantity control.** Two additional types of control—budgetary and cost control—are covered in Chapter 25.

For what is ISO Certification necessary?

Organizations that sell their products in countries that belong to the European Community are expected to have **ISO 9000 Certification** (International Organization for Standardization). This certification pertains to baseline quality management and quality assurance. The ISO 9000 Certification process typically involves the following steps: assessing the organization's quality systems and procedures, developing a quality assurance and policy manual, training employees, documenting work instructions, and auditing the quality system to assure compliance with the certification process. Although the administrative office manager may not be directly responsible for the ISO 9000 Certification process, he or she should be familiar with the organization's program.

Although not a component of quality or quantity control, **work measurement** is an equally important management responsibility. The presence of certain control measures helps assure the timely completion of projects. A discussion of work scheduling is also included in this chapter.

THE PROCESS OF CONTROL

Control, when used for quantity and quality evaluation, involves the following five-step process:

What steps are involved in the process of control?

Step 1: Define the parameters of the work being subjected to the control process.

Step 2: Determine actual results.

Step 3: Evaluate actual results.

Step 4: Compare actual results with expected results.

Step 5: Apply corrective measures when needed.

Because it results in the application of corrective measures, control is considered by some to have disciplinary or punitive overtones. Of the five functions of management, the control function is often viewed the most negatively. The administrative office manager frequently has to apply corrective measures that can have an adverse effect on employer-employee relations. For the individuals responsible for carrying out the control function, such personal qualities as tact, empathy, and helpfulness are important.

OBJECTIVES OF CONTROL

As one of the functions of management, control has several important objectives:

1. To increase the operating efficiency of the organization.
2. To assess the degree to which anticipated results and actual results conform.
3. To coordinate the various elements of a program or a task.
4. To increase the likelihood that the organization's objectives will be achieved.
5. To assist the office employees in performing their jobs more efficiently.
6. To maximize the organization's profits by decreasing the amount of work that has to be redone and by reducing the misuse of supplies and materials.

ADVANTAGES OF CONTROL

What advantages result from the use of control?

Among the distinct advantages of applying control to office operations are the following:

1. It helps maximize the profits of the organization.
2. It helps employees improve their productivity because they are aware of quantity and quality output requirements.
3. It provides a yardstick by which an organization can measure its operating efficiency.
4. It identifies the areas in which actual and anticipated results do not coincide, which facilitates the modification of various work processes.
5. It helps in the meeting of scheduled deadlines.

ELEMENTS OF CONTROL

The effectiveness of the control process cannot be maximized when certain elements are missing. These elements include factors to control, identification of anticipated results, measurement devices, and application of corrective measures.

Factors to Control

Before beginning the process of controlling an office operation, those responsible for the process must be made aware of which factors within the operation are to be controlled. Factors considered as being insignificant are eliminated from further consideration. Attempting to control insignificant factors typically wastes time and energy. On the other hand, inefficiency and a waste of resources will likely result if significant factors are not controlled.

The control factors within many office operations are the important documents or forms used in carrying out specific operations. In a purchasing system, for example, the purchase order is likely to be the critical factor to be controlled. By applying control measures to the purchase order, the actual results and the anticipated results of all the other components of the system will likely match one another.

Identification of Anticipated Results

Why must anticipated results be identified?

The absence of a clear identification of anticipated results often makes an attempt to compare actual and anticipated results impossible. In addition to identifying the anticipated results, their appropriateness should also be determined.

After the anticipated results have been identified and their appropriateness assured, the results must be communicated to the employees whose performance will be evaluated. Employees who are unaware of expected performance levels cannot be held accountable for their failure to reach the desired levels. A primary responsibility of managers and supervisors is communicating the anticipated results to subordinates.

Measurement Devices

Before the actual and anticipated results can be compared, the actual results will have to be measured. In some instances, measurement will involve determining quantity output. In this instance, the measurement device will likely be **performance standards,** such as those discussed in Chapter 15. In other instances, the measurement device may involve determining the degree of accuracy with which data are entered on a form.

In organizations that have installed Total Quality Management (TQM), the measurement process is likely to be different than it is in other types of organizations. In some instances, the measurement device focuses on how well the organization's customers believe they are being served. This information is collected by means of a customer survey.

What is a baseline goal?

Another difference in the measurement process between TQM-oriented and non-TQM-oriented organizations is in the establishment of baseline goals. An example of a baseline goal is the on-time delivery of a product or service a minimum of 95 percent of the time. By continually tracking the results of the baseline goals and making employees aware of the findings, they become motivated to strive for continual improvement. TQM also employs self-directed work teams that get individuals more diligently committed to effective performance. Because these teams are often considered a small "company within a company," commitment to effective performance is much greater. Coupling the team concept with employee empowerment—which gives workers the opportunity to make productivity-related suggestions and then to implement the worthwhile suggestions in their work teams—is also having a positive effect in many organizations.

Application of Corrective Measures

When actual results are less than anticipated results, corrective measures become necessary. Suppose, for example, that an office employee fails to produce at the anticipated or expected rate. The manager or supervisor who has the needed authority to take corrective action against the employee will then have to determine whether corrective measures should be applied to this situation. Without this authority, the manager's or supervisor's effectiveness will be greatly diminished.

In an organization that uses TQM and that has "empowered" its employees, the corrective action most likely will extensively involve the members of the various work teams rather than management alone in determining the needed corrective action. When employees are able to determine the nature of the corrective action that needs to be taken, they are less likely to feel they are being punished than when management alone determines the nature of the corrective action.

QUALITY CONTROL

Why is quality control used?

Organizations use quality control to increase their operating efficiency because employees sometimes fail to produce error-free work. Without some form of quality control, errors are likely to go unnoticed. Over time, this results in a negative impact on organizational profit. In addition, if management uses erroneous data, incorrect decisions will likely result, which can affect the well-being of the organization.

Quality and quantity control both use standards as a basis for evaluation. While **quality standards** involve evaluating the accuracy with which work is produced, **quantity standards** tend to be more quantifiable. For example, the organizational structure of a document affects its quality. If it deviates too far from the norm, the quality of the document is diminished. The fact that individuals have different perceptions about what constitutes an effective organizational structure makes quality evaluation somewhat subjective. Quantity standards, on the other hand, are more definitive and clear-cut. Either an employee's output equals or exceeds expected output or it doesn't.

A quality control program involves determining minimum standards of acceptability. Once the standards have been determined, the acceptability of the actual work can be compared with the expected standards. When a serious discrepancy exists, corrective measures may be necessary.

Quality Control Techniques

Several techniques have been developed for maintaining quality control. Among these are total inspection, spot checking, statistical quality control, and zero defects.

What quality control techniques are available?

Total Inspection. As a quality control technique, **total inspection** involves a complete and total inspection of each unit of work produced by each employee. This is done to determine whether minimum quality standards have been attained. If not, corrective measures of some type will likely be implemented.

For certain types of office work, total inspection is quite desirable, if not mandatory. The most common example of total inspection of office work is the proofreading of typed/keyboarded documents. Other examples of office work that frequently receive total inspection are the verification of important arithmetical calculations and the results of compiled statistical data.

Because of the nature of some types of office work, total inspection may not be necessary, especially when the work is of limited importance. In other instances, little opportunity exists for the presence of errors. An example is the filing of clients' correspondence. Although some of the correspondence may be misfiled, ensuring the accurate filing of documents probably does not warrant the total inspection of the files.

Spot Checking. The **spot checking** technique involves periodically checking the quality of an employee's work. The desirability of this technique is frequently challenged because it does not use statistical processes to determine how much, who, and when the checks are to be made. However, by adding the statistical dimension, which is a characteristic of statistical quality control, more valid results are likely to be found.

Statistical Quality Control. When total inspection of work is not desirable and spot checking is not sufficiently accurate, **statistical quality control** may be a satisfactory alternative. This technique uses a statistical sampling base that helps produce accurate and reliable results.

What are the elements of statistical quality control?

Several fundamental statistical elements are found in statistical quality control: **sampling, normal distribution,** and **control limits.** Sampling, which is based on the laws of probability, is used to determine what percentage of the total output has to be examined to be relatively certain that total output is as error-free as the sample. In other words, if proper statistical procedures are used, the quality of the sample should be comparable to the quality of the whole.

Statistical tables, which are available for determining appropriate sample size, take into consideration (1) the total number of units from which the sample is being drawn and (2) the minimum accuracy level that is required. If the total output consists of one hundred units and an accuracy level of 90 percent is acceptable, fewer samples will have to be studied than when an accuracy standard of 95 percent is required.

To illustrate the concept, assume that total output consists of one hundred units and that 96 percent accuracy is required. Under these circumstances, the statistical tables indicate that fifteen of the units should be randomly selected for inspection. If no errors are found during the inspection of the fifteen units, the assumption is then made that the one hundred units are also error free. But, according to the law of probability, if one error is found within the sample of fifteen units, seven of the one hundred units can be expected to contain errors. If errors are found in two of the fifteen samples, approximately fourteen of the one hundred units could be expected to contain errors.

What impact does normal distribution have on statistical quality control?

Normal distribution is another of the elements involved in statistical quality control. Normal distribution is based on the principle that randomly observed occurrences of a sufficient quantity tend to be distributed around the mean or average of all the occurrences. For purposes of illustration, assume that the average or mean number of errors made by file clerks is two errors per one hundred units of work. While some clerks will make more than two errors in filing one hundred units, others will make fewer than two errors per one hundred units. However, the majority will make two errors in filing one hundred units.

The number of errors per total output is important because this factor has a bearing on the number of errors or deviations expected to occur within a given number of observations. Deviation is the distance from the mean and is calculated by using the formula for standard deviation. In any normal distribution, 68.3 percent of the total will fall within one standard deviation above and below the mean of the distribution; 95.1 percent will fall within two standard deviations above and below the mean; and 99.7 percent will fall within three standard deviations above and below the mean.

In the foregoing example, the file clerks were found to make an average (mean) of two errors per one hundred units filed. When calculating the standard deviation, assume that a deviation of .53 is found. According to the normal distribution, 68.3 percent of the number of errors made by each file clerk will be within one standard deviation above and below the mean, thus ranging from 1.47 to 2.53 (2.0 − .53 and 2.0 + .53). Two standard deviations above and below the mean (from 0.94 to 3.06 errors) will encompass 95.1 percent of the number of errors made by each file clerk. Three standard deviations will encompass 99.7 percent of the errors. Therefore, all but .3 percent of the number of errors made by each file clerk will be between .41 and 3.59 errors per one hundred units filed. This is illustrated in Figure 24–1.

What is the function of control limits?

The third element of statistical quality control is the control limits. Determining at what point the errors are attributed to chance and at what point they are attributed to some identifiable cause requires the establishment of control limits. For instance, in the foregoing example, if the control limits are set two

Figure 24-1 Normal distribution

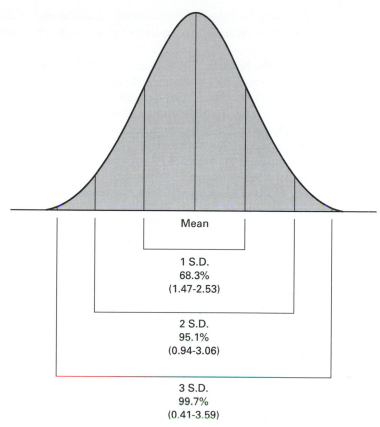

Mean

1 S.D.
68.3%
(1.47-2.53)

2 S.D.
95.1%
(0.94-3.06)

3 S.D.
99.7%
(0.41-3.59)

standard deviations above and below the mean, chance is the cause of errors in a situation that ranges from .94 to 3.06 errors per one hundred units. The chance nature of these errors may increase the difficulty of identifying their cause. On the other hand, some identifiable cause is responsible when employees have errors exceeding 3.06 per one hundred units. For example, the errors may be a result of poorly trained employees. Figure 24–2 illustrates the control limits for this particular example.

In Figure 24–2, with the exception of Sample 4, all samples fall within the control limits. Therefore, these errors are due to chance. Because the number of errors in Sample 4 exceeds the maximum for the upper control limit, some factor or factors other than chance are responsible. For example, one might

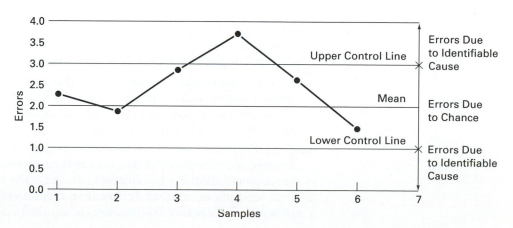

Figure 24-2 Control limits

speculate that the sample was taken at the end of the work day when employee fatigue contributed to an increase in their error rate.

Zero Defects. The fundamental characteristic of the **zero defects** technique is error prevention resulting from employees who do their work correctly the first time. Thus, zero defects involves more than identifying and correcting errors. It also involves motivating employees to do error-free work.

What are the characteristics of the zero defects technique?

When using the zero defects technique, employees make a pledge to management that they will support the concept by producing error-free work. They also make suggestions to management about ways to eliminate errors. Subsequently, their rewards are based on (1) the quality of the suggestions they submit, (2) the basis of the improvement they make, and (3) the extent of their error-free work.

In some instances, errors are attributable to management rather than to the employees themselves. If nothing is done to eliminate errors attributable to management, the effectiveness of the zero defects program cannot be fully realized.

Total Quality Management (TQM)

Total Quality Management (TQM) programs, which first got their hold in larger organizations, are now being installed in a number of smaller organizations. In fact, many larger manufacturing organizations today require that the suppliers from which they purchase parts have an effective quality program. Otherwise, the larger organizations will change suppliers rather than risk purchasing parts that have the potential for not meeting quality standards.

TQM is a more encompassing quality program than any other currently being used. It is concerned not only with the organization's products and/or services, but also with the delivery of the products and/or services and everything involved in getting them to the customer. Virtually every employee is involved. As a result, organizations that have implemented TQM programs are even concerned with how their telephones are answered or how a receptionist might greet a visitor.

What are the critical ingredients of TQM?

TQM programs have several critical ingredients, including the following:

1. *Customer satisfaction.* TQM has a primary focus on customer satisfaction; when customer satisfaction is lacking, regardless of the quality with which the organization's products are manufactured or its services are provided, increasing sales will be difficult. Two types of customers are found: external (the ones who purchase the products and/or services) and internal (an employee who does something with earlier-produced work). For example, a manager is a customer of a word processing specialist who produced the document the manager originated. Customer dissatisfaction either at the external or internal level has negative implications.

2. *Accurate statistical measurement.* TQM uses a variety of statistical techniques that measure every critical variable of the organization's operations. When the measuring process identifies problems, effort is immediately expended to eliminate the problems.

3. *Ongoing improvement of products and/or services.* Organizations have learned over the decades that satisfied customers are their best form of advertisement. Satisfied customers are generally repeat customers; dissatisfied customers frequently become customers of the competition. An organization's prime competition is regularly improving the quality of its

products and/or services; therefore, the organization also has to improve regularly the quality of its products and/or services.

4. *New employee relations.* TQM programs make extensive use of work teams and employee empowerment. Because TQM gives employees a greater stake in the organization's success, they have greater commitment to ensuring its success.

QUANTITY CONTROL

What provides a basis for developing quantity standards?

Quantity control, like quality control, uses standards that facilitate the comparison of anticipated and actual results. However, unless the standards are fairly accurate, the base for quantity control is not valid.

The data gathered during the work measurement processes are used as the basis for developing quantity standards. Several work measurement techniques and the setting of quantity standards are discussed in Chapter 15. Work measurement is designed to determine what constitutes a fair day's work for both the employer and the employee. Therefore, employees have some assurance that their anticipated output levels do not exceed what is reasonably expected, and the employers have some assurance employees are being paid for doing a reasonable amount of work.

In most organizations, the amount of work that needs to be done fluctuates from time to time. Occasionally, employees will have more work to do than they can be reasonably expected to complete. At other times, they will not have enough work to do. Therefore, management's responsibility is to develop ways to compensate for these fluctuations.

Because various techniques for measuring work and setting standards are covered in Chapter 15, these topics will not be repeated in this chapter. Included in this chapter is a discussion of several techniques that are used to control the inevitable fluctuation in the amount of work that has to be completed. In addition, the short-interval scheduling technique is presented. This technique is useful for monitoring how closely actual output levels conform with anticipated results. If a serious lack of conformity occurs, corrective measures may be appropriate.

Controlling Fluctuations

A considerable portion of the time spent by the manager or supervisor in controlling output involves determining the most effective way to handle workload fluctuations. Several techniques are available to handle these fluctuations.

When fluctuations result in too much work to be done in a given amount of time, one or more of the following techniques may be used:

How can fluctuations in excessive amounts of work be controlled?

1. *Employee overtime.* Many organizations use employee overtime as a way of controlling situations when too much work has to be done. If a situation can be remedied by a few hours of employee overtime, this method may result in significant advantages. On the other hand, if a large number of overtime hours will be required, another method of controlling fluctuations is recommended. This will help the organization avoid having to compensate employees at the rate of one and one-half times their regular pay rates.

   Rather than compensate employees for overtime hours, another possibility is to give them time off for the hours they previously worked overtime. If the employees take time off during slack times, the organization also has a satisfactory method for dealing with a situation of having too little work to be done.

2. *Temporary help.* Use of temporary help is another solution for controlling fluctuations when too much work has to be done. In many cities, temporary employment agencies can be used to obtain office help for one day or for several weeks. Temporary agencies are discussed in greater detail in Chapter 7.

3. *Part-time help.* When fluctuations occur regularly, part-time help may be the most desirable solution to handle work overloads. Hiring the same employees to work part time whenever the workload becomes excessive eliminates having to train them each time they are needed.

What is a floating work unit?

4. *Floating work unit.* Some organizations have developed a floating work unit as a solution to excessive workload conditions. Employees assigned to these units "float" to wherever they are needed in the organization. Unless these employees are fairly competent in many areas, they may find working under these circumstances somewhat dissatisfying.

5. *Cycle billing.* When this technique is used, one-twentieth of the customers' accounts are due each working day. Instead of having all the customers' payments due on one day, which makes staffing difficult and causes extreme fluctuations in workloads, the receipts are spread over a full month.

Following is a discussion of practices that may be used whenever too little work exists:

1. *Time off.* To compensate employees who work overtime, organizations sometimes allow them to take time off when an insufficient amount of work exists.

2. *Work backlog.* The nature of some work allows it to be postponed indefinitely. If this is possible, the work can be completed during slow times.

3. *Maintenance projects.* Some organizations have employees do maintenance projects when they do not have enough work to do. Examples of maintenance projects are reorganization of files, cleaning of files, review of work procedures, and the like.

Short-Interval Scheduling

As a control device, **short-interval scheduling** helps ensure the completion of a given amount of work in a given amount of time. It also provides the mechanism for determining whether or not the work is completed according to schedule. Short-interval scheduling enables managers or supervisors to determine whether or not output standards are being consistently maintained.

What are the characteristics of short-interval scheduling?

Short-interval scheduling is based on the following assumption: When employees are trying to attain production goals, they improve their chances of being successful by using short-range rather than long-range production goals. Employees are motivated to perform at higher levels because of the short-range nature of the goals and because of the frequent evaluation of their success in reaching predetermined goals.

The following illustrates how short-interval scheduling works. If an employee is expected to produce 400 units per eight-hour workday, his or her output could be determined at the end of the day. Unfortunately, the employee may not know until the end of the day whether his or her production goal has been achieved. With short-interval scheduling, the employee makes frequent checks throughout the day to determine how closely production rates conform with accepted standards. These checks are typically made each hour of the day.

In the foregoing illustration, the employee would have to produce an average of 50 units per hour to be successful in reaching the predetermined goal.

If, upon checking, the employee finds that 120 units were produced during the first three hours, he or she then knows that to reach the 400-unit goal, the 30-unit shortage (150 minus 120) will have to be made up during the day. When supervisors discover that employees are failing to meet their expected hourly production levels, corrective measures can be taken.

Before short-interval scheduling can be implemented, expected production levels must be determined. These levels, which are presented as work standards, identify the acceptable amount of time needed to produce one unit of output.

After the standards have been determined and the supervisor is aware of the employees' expected production levels, the work assignments can be made. A record is kept of how closely employees' actual results conform with expected results, using an assignment record such as the one illustrated in Figure 24–3. This information is also entered on the summary sheet, which is illustrated in Figure 24–4. After the work assignment is completed, the employee returns the assignment record, along with the completed work, to the supervisor who then compares actual results with anticipated or expected results.

The number recorded in the "expected" column parallel to each employee's name is the production level he or she is expected to achieve during a one-hour span. For example, M. Smith was expected to produce six units of output from 8 A.M. to 9 A.M. However, when he "reported in," the supervisor discovered that machine failure enabled him to produce only five units. Therefore, a "5" is entered in the "actual" column parallel to M. Smith's name. When an employee's actual performance fails to coincide with expected performance, an asterisk is entered in the appropriate place on the summary sheet.

What needs to be determined before short-interval scheduling can be implemented?

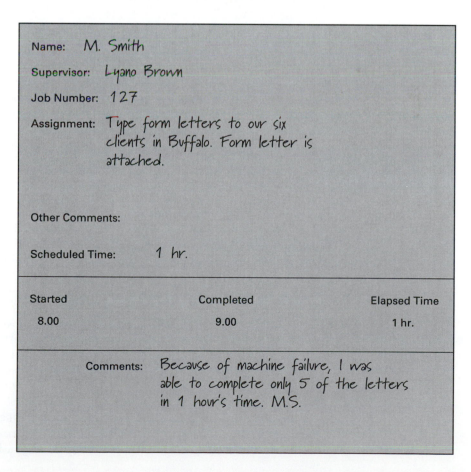

Figure 24-3 Assignment record

Figure 24-4 Summary sheet

Employee	Results	8-9	9-10	10-11	11-12	12-1	1-2	2-3	3-4	4-5
M. Smith	Expected	6	7	10	8	9	15	20	13	7
	Actual	5*	7	10	8	8*	15	21	13	7
M. Green	Expected	3	5	3	6	10	13	14	7	6
	Actual	4	5	3	7	11	12*	14	8	6

Department: Office Services

Supervisor: D. Brown

Today's Date: 11/15

By maintaining the summary sheet, the supervisor is readily able to determine at any point during the day whether an employee's productivity is ahead of, on, or behind schedule. When the output is consistently behind schedule, corrective measures may be appropriate.

WORK SCHEDULING

In this chapter, **work scheduling** is considered as a function of control. Without work scheduling, administrative office managers have little if any control over the completion time of a project. With work scheduling, greater control is possible, which helps ensure the successful completion of a given project.

Work Scheduling Devices

What work scheduling devices are available?

Several devices are available for use in scheduling work to be completed within a given amount of time. Some of the devices are rather simple and can be used for scheduling uncomplicated projects. On the other hand, some of the devices are rather sophisticated and are appropriately used in scheduling more complex projects.

Schedule Log. **Schedule logs** are frequently used to schedule office work. An example of a schedule log is illustrated in Figure 24–5. Although the schedule log is quite simple, other more complex logs could be developed for the

Figure 24-5
Schedule log

Name of Project: *Prepare proposal*   Completion Date: *11/19*

Project Supervisor: *Janice Otter*

Task	To be Completed by	Assigned to	Time Started	Time Finished
gather data	11/01	Bill Green	8:00	4:30
process data	11/07	Mary Smith	8:00 (11/2)	2:30 (11/6)
draft proposal	11/17	Bill Green	8:00 (11/7)	4:00 (11/15)
revise proposal	11/18	Bill Green	8:00 (11/18)	3:00 (11/18)
type proposal	11/19	Diane Brown	8:00 (11/19)	4:15 (11/19)

scheduling of a difficult or complex project. The schedule log is generally completed by the project supervisor who has good insight into the status of the project.

What is a work chart?

Work Chart. Illustrated in Figure 24–6 is the **work chart,** another of the simpler work scheduling devices. When using this chart, the project supervisor works backward from the completion date. For example, as Figure 24–6 shows, the project is to be completed by November 17. The work chart is developed to determine the starting time of the project and the days on which each sub-project must be started. The illustration, which deals with writing and submitting a report, indicates that for the project to be completed by the November 17 deadline, the data must be compiled by November 4, the report must be written by November 10, and so forth.

Work Schedule Calendar. Another of the simpler work scheduling devices is a **work schedule calendar,** such as the one illustrated in Figure 24–7. The calendar, which is a day-by-day schedule for a week's duration, lists jobs or projects that are to be started each day. Quite often the work schedule

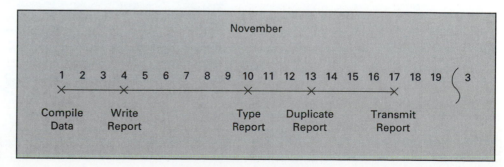

Figure 24-6 Work chart

Figure 24-7 Work
schedule calendar

Employee	Monday	Tuesday	Wednesday	Thursday	Friday
Sally B.	Type form letters Type invoices File correspondence				
Jane S	Type report ↓				
Diane	Type manuscript for Mr Jones Sort File cards				
Mary	On vacation				

calendar also provides a listing of the names of the employees. As jobs or projects are accepted by the work unit, the employee who is responsible for completing each project can be designated. When an employee completes one project, the next one can be started without the supervisor's having to make the assignment at that time.

Gantt Chart. Used as a work scheduling device, the **Gantt Chart** is more appropriate for longer, more complex projects than the work schedule calendar. The Gantt Chart and the work schedule calendar are similar because both identify the jobs or projects that are to be completed on any given day. Figure 24–8

For what is a Gantt Chart used?

Figure 24-8 Gantt
chart. Courtesy: Magna
Visual, Inc.

illustrates a Gantt Chart. Software programs are now available for use in developing computerized Gantt Charts.

The Gantt Chart, which was developed by Henry Gantt, an early management authority, provides a day-by-day list of the jobs that are to be completed, as well as the estimated completion time. Many noncomputerized Gantt Charts are now magnetized, which facilitates the movement of the tabs on which the various items are listed.

Although used for scheduling the work found in many offices, the Gantt Chart is especially useful in scheduling work projects involving the use of computer processing.

Program Evaluation Review Technique (PERT). This scheduling device was originally developed during the Polaris missile program and has been modified for use in scheduling complex projects. Because of its nature, **PERT** is most suitable for projects comprised of many parts or components. Its use in scheduling simple projects cannot be justified.

A PERT chart, which is illustrated in Figure 24–9, is developed to help schedule the component parts of the project. The various components and the estimated amount of time for completing each of them must be identified. The numbers within circles on the chart refer to the various components that comprise the total project. The network of lines indicates the various paths that may be followed in completing the project.

In preparing the PERT chart, a **critical path** must be determined. This path, which is also the longest route, consists of the components that must be

What are the characteristics of PERT charts?

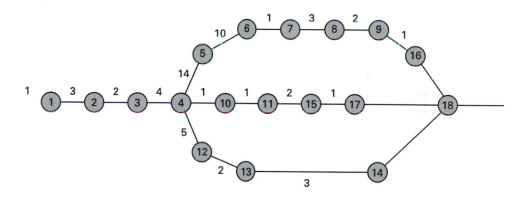

Legend:

1. Set convention date
2. Set convention location
3. Select convention chairman
4. Select convention facilities
5. Develop convention program
6. Select convention speakers
7. Set convention cost
8. Notify members of the convention program
9. Print program
10. Notify convention facility of desired setup of each meeting room

11. Select banquet menu
12. Determine recipient of outstanding member award
13. Prepare citation for outstanding member award
14. Determine honorarium for speakers
15. Arrange for registration booth
16. Make overnight lodging arrangements for members who desire to stay overnight
17. Arrange for transportation of members (from airport)
18. Await convention

Figure 24-9 PERT chart

What is a critical path?

completed before the project is finished. Each component or activity on the path must be completed on time and in the order in which the activities appear on the chart. A delay in completing a critical component will prevent finishing the project by the deadline. The noncritical components can be completed at any time during the course of the project with no adverse impact on its completion.

Figure 24–9 illustrates a PERT chart that outlines the various components involved in planning a convention. The critical path consists of components or activities 1, 2, 3, 4, 5, 6, 7, 8, 9, and 16. The paths consisting of activities 1, 2, 3, 4, 10, 11, 15, and 17, and 1, 2, 3, 4, 12, 13, and 14 are not critical. Therefore, the components represented by numbers 10, 11, 15, 17, and 12, 13, and 14 can be completed at any time prior to the opening of the convention. The components on the critical path, on the other hand, must be completed within the scheduled time if the convention is to be opened on time. The numbers above each line represent the estimated number of days needed to complete each component.

IMPLICATIONS FOR THE ADMINISTRATIVE OFFICE MANAGER

Administrative office managers have major responsibilities for quantity and quality control in the areas they manage. This responsibility results from the philosophy that prevails in most organizations whereby unit managers are responsible for quantity and quality control in their specific areas.

Regardless of how efficient and well managed the office area is, the results of certain operations do not always match desired results. The use of quantity and quality control helps ensure conformity of desired results with actual results.

One of the most effective ways for the efforts of administrative office managers to be noticed by top management is for the office function to provide the best quality service that circumstances will allow. Many administrative office managers have enhanced their promotability to higher level positions by establishing a credible quantity and quality control performance.

Although employees often affect the quantity and quality control performance of the office area, inefficient operating procedures and equipment also have a negative impact. The benefits of effective quantity and quality control performance are too great to overlook the implementation of a well-designed control program.

REVIEW QUESTIONS

1. Why is control needed in office situations?

2. What are the objectives of control?

3. What advantages result from implementing control procedures?

4. What is the evaluation basis for both quality and quantity control?

5. As a control technique, how do total inspection and spot checking differ from one another?

6. What steps are involved in developing a statistical quality control program?

7. How does a floating work unit help an organization control fluctuations in its work processes?

8. When used as work scheduling devices, how does the work chart differ from the work schedule calendar?

9. When PERT is used as a work scheduling device, how is the appropriate network chosen?

DISCUSSION QUESTIONS

1. The company in which you work is about to install a quantity and quality control program. At one of the preinstallation orientation meetings, several employees became rather vocal in expressing their opinions about the program. They indicated that they do not need this program to tell them that they should do more when they are already doing as much as they can. How can the apparent lack of employee support for the installation of a quantity and quality control program be reduced? Why should the resistance be reduced before the program is installed?

2. As the supervisor of seven employees, you are responsible for their level of productivity. Two of these employees who have consistently attained the expected level of quantity output in the past are now beginning to "slough off" to the extent that their output is below standard. When you mentioned this to them this morning, they indicated that two of their coworkers continually produce below standard and nothing happens to them, so why should they work any harder than anyone else? Outline what you plan to say to the two employees whose output level is becoming a problem.

3. In the department for which you are supervisor, the last week of each month becomes hectic because of additional work that must always be completed. For a time, the company used employee overtime in this department to get the work completed on time. Then management realized that obtaining employees from a temporary help agency during the fourth week of each month was more economical. Although the temporary employees are good workers, rarely are they assigned a second time to the company. As a consequence, you have to spend time training the new ones each time they appear. Your supervisor has asked for your input regarding this situation. What do you plan to tell her about the situation? What are your recommendations for improvement?

STUDENT PROJECTS AND ACTIVITIES

1. Interview an office employee whose output is measured using one of the quantity control techniques discussed in this chapter. Obtain the feelings of this employee regarding the technique.

2. Interview an administrative office manager who is responsible for the overall quantity and quality control in the organization in which he or she works. Try to determine what aspects of the control process create the greatest difficulties for the manager.

3. Going Online: Using the Internet, conduct an online search based on one of the concepts presented in this chapter or based on one of the chapter terms. Identify four or five things you learned from the material that you did not know prior to your online search.

Minicase

The Mitchell Company is the largest office supplies distributor in Colorado. At the present time, all of its accounts receivable billings are mailed out the last working day of the month. This means that a huge volume of payments is received between the 5th and 10th of each month. Employees who work in accounts receivable frequently have to put in several hours of overtime during this period each month. Management stresses the need to get these payments processed as quickly as possible because of cash flow.

1. What alternatives to the presently used billing system are available?

2. Which alternative do you recommend? Why?

Case

The Brandy Assurance Company is one of the most rapidly growing insurance companies in the Southwest. Much of its success is attributed to its excellent actuarial department.

At the present time, some departments are unable to get projects completed on time. This situation creates additional problems, especially when an overdue project impedes or slows progress on another project.

A few months ago, all department heads were asked to pay a little more attention to project completion dates. No appreciable difference has been noticed as yet. It is obvious that additional action will have to be taken.

1. What suggestions can you offer that will be helpful in assuring the timely completion of the project?
2. What scheduling devices may be appropriately used to help assure the completion of these projects?
3. Which scheduling device do you most prefer? Why?

Chapter 25

BUDGETARY AND COST CONTROL

Chapter Aims

After studying this chapter, you should be able to design an effective budgetary and cost control procedure for an organization.

Chapter Outline

Budgeting
- Purposes of Budgeting
- Advantages of Budgeting
- Limitations of Budgeting
- Prerequisites of Successful Budgeting
- Budget Preparation

Zero-Based Budgeting

Budgetary Control

Cost Control
- Techniques for Controlling Office Operating Costs
- Controlling Office Costs

Implications for the Administrative Office Manager

Chapter Terms

Budgetary control
Budgeting
Budget committee
Budget period
Budget revision
Cost analysis study
Cost breakdown technique
Cost control
Department budget
Direct salaries
Direct supplies
Fixed costs
Indirect salaries
Indirect supplies
Master budget
Moving review
Periodic review
Progressive review
Semivariable costs
Standard cost technique
Variable costs
Variance
Zero-based budgeting (ZBB)

*I*n addition to being responsible for quality and quantity control, the administrative office manager also has responsibility for budgetary and cost control. The absence of effective procedures or the use of ineffective procedures for controlling the budget or operational costs often results in increased costs of office operations. Therefore, effective cost control techniques need to be used.

BUDGETING

Budgeting is basically a planning process. It facilitates the preparation of a budget, which serves as the organization's financial blueprint. The budget identifies target numbers for such financial data as revenues, materials cost, operating expenditures, and so forth. The process of budgeting takes place at several levels within the organization. **Budgetary control,** which is discussed in the next section, is the process of regulating the operating budgets of the organization. Without budgetary control, the preparation and use of budgets is virtually wasted effort.

Purposes of Budgeting

Budgeting has a positive impact on the organization's profitability because the organization's operations are likely to be performed more efficiently. Budgeting also helps management maintain the cost effectiveness of the organization's operations. Unless operations are cost effective, the organization will not be able to maximize its profits. Budgeting also helps the organization better plan for the future.

Advantages of Budgeting

What are the advantages of budgeting?

The process of budgeting results in several significant advantages:

1. It requires adequate management consideration of the organization's policies.
2. It requires that department-level managers develop practices that facilitate the attainment of budgetary goals.
3. It requires that managers identify the resources necessary for accomplishing the organization's goals.
4. It helps management make accurate, timely decisions regarding various organizational operations.
5. It helps management determine which functions are not operating efficiently.
6. It helps management determine which functions are experiencing difficulty in achieving goals and objectives.

Limitations of Budgeting

Although budgeting results in some rather significant advantages for the organization, the administrative office manager also needs to be aware of its limitations:

What are the limitations of budgeting?

1. Because budgeting is based on estimates, the validity of the budget is to a large extent determined by the accuracy with which the estimates are made.

2. The operating effectiveness of an organization is clearly dependent upon how well management is able to motivate employees to operate within the budgeted allowances.

3. The effectiveness of the budget is to a large extent dependent upon the accuracy with which budget revisions are made.

Prerequisites for Successful Budgeting

What are the prerequisites of successful budgeting?

Successful budgeting does not simply happen. The absence of certain prerequisite conditions—proper organization, financial data, and commitment of top management—will likely result in wasted effort when undertaking the budgeting process. Although the presence of these conditions will not automatically ensure success in budgeting, their presence will improve budgeting efforts.

Proper Organization. Certain organizational characteristics must be present if the budgeting process is to be successful. These characteristics are (1) the proper grouping of tasks within functions, (2) definitive lines of authority and areas of responsibility, and (3) lines of communication. The absence of any of these characteristics may result in ineffective budgeting. For example, when a manager lacks necessary authority, he or she will not be able to take the necessary corrective action if the costs of various operations exceed the budgeted allowances. Furthermore, individuals who have not been assigned areas of responsibility cannot be held accountable when operations exceed the budgeted allowances.

Financial Data. The development of a budget requires the use of financial data. Unless these data are available, the basis for budget development does not exist. Types of financial data needed include (1) the number of units sold during the previous financial period, (2) the relationship between the units sold and the cost incurred in producing these units, and (3) emerging financial trends. Much of the financial data that are needed can be obtained from the financial records of the previous fiscal period.

Commitment of Top Management. Top management must be committed to the use of the budget as a control mechanism. Without such commitment, the budgeting efforts are likely to produce only minimal worthwhile results. Furthermore, without top management's commitment, lower management levels are unlikely to be committed to the attainment of the organization's budgetary goals.

Budget Preparation

Budget preparation consists of several distinct elements, including determination of the budget period, development of the budget, and revision of the budget.

Determining the Budget Period. The length of time covered by the office budget generally coincides with the organization's fiscal period. Therefore, if the organization's fiscal period begins in January of each year, so does its budget. The length of the **budget period** should be sufficiently long to compensate for any seasonal fluctuations.

Developing the Budget. The planning involved in developing a budget may consume considerable time. The use of employee participation in the planning process is advantageous.

How do departmental and master budgets differ?

The office budget, which is part of a larger budget, is classified as a **department budget.** The **master budget,** covering the entire organization, is a composite of the various departmental budgets.

Traditionally, after the organization's projected amount of income has been determined, a monetary sum is allocated to each of the departments. From this allocation, each department develops its operating budget. The departmental budgets are then consolidated into the organization's budget.

An alternative to the traditional budgeting process is zero-based budgeting (ZBB), which is discussed later in this chapter.

Figure 25–1 illustrates a portion of a departmental budget.

Before the actual work begins, responsibility for budget preparation needs to be assigned. In many larger organizations, overall responsibility is assigned to the organization's controller or treasurer. In others, responsibility may be assigned to the vice president who is concerned with the organization's financial affairs. In smaller organizations, the administrative office manager may have overall responsibility for preparaing the budget. Typically, the minimum responsibility the administrative office manager will have for budget preparation in any size of organization is the development of the budget for the office function.

What are the functions of the budget committee?

Many organizations now use a **budget committee** to provide input into the budget development process. At the organizational level, the budget committee, which is headed by the chief budget official, usually consists of department managers. In larger functional departments, a budget committee chaired by the department manager and consisting of the various supervisors in the department may also be used. In most cases, budget committees are advisory; therefore, their primary responsibility is to provide suggestions to the committee's chairperson.

While the chief financial officer is primarily responsible for the budget, several individuals likely will be involved in preparing it. The prevailing philosophy is that managers and supervisors who are responsible for various functional areas in the organization should have extensive involvement in preparing their department budgets. This results from the practice of making the department managers and supervisors responsible for organizing their units in a way that maximizes efficient use of organizational resources. Therefore, the budget is typically initiated by the chief budget officer who seeks assistance from other employees in the organization.

The president, chief executive officer, or chairman of the board frequently authorizes the chief budget officer to begin the development of a budget. This authorization is typically received in a letter or memo in which the president, CEO, or chairman may summarize the condition of the national economy, the projected outlook for the industry of which the organization is a part, and the anticipated organizational growth trends.

In most organizations, the office function generates no direct income; therefore, the office budget contains only expenses or costs. But before reasonable projections can be made for each type of expense or cost, an estimate of the

| | January | | February | | March | |
	Estimated	Actual	Estimated	Actual	Estimated	Actual
Salaries	$3,250	$3,140	$3,250	$3,250	$3,250	$3,300
Utilities	80	73	80	84	75	78
Telephone	120	150	120	110	120	125
Postage	50	73	50	75	50	80
Equipment	120	120	120	120	120	120
	3,620	3,556	3,620	3,639	3,615	3,703

Figure 25–1 Portion of departmental budget

cost of each unit of output produced by the office function during the budget period will have to be calculated. An estimate of the number of units of output projected for production by the office function during the budget period is also needed. These estimates are used to determine how to allocate the organization's financial resources to each type of expense or cost found within the office function.

What are some of the common types of expenses found in the office function?

The common types of expenses or costs found in the office function are the following:

1. Salaries and payroll.
2. Fringe benefits.
3. Equipment rental or purchase.
4. Equipment depreciation.
5. Furniture rental or purchase.
6. Furniture depreciation.
7. Telephone charges.
8. Materials and supplies.
9. Postage and mailing.
10. Utilities.
11. Rent.
12. Taxes.
13. Insurance.
14. Maintenance costs.
15. Training costs.

How do fixed, variable, and semivariable costs vary from one another?

Office costs or expenses can be divided into three groups: fixed costs, variable costs, and semivariable costs. **Fixed costs** are those that remain constant regardless of how many units are produced. Rent, insurance, and taxes are examples of fixed costs because they do not fluctuate in relation to the output levels.

Variable costs, on the other hand, vary proportionately in relation to the output levels. Examples of variable costs are materials or supplies. Except when discounts are offered for quantity buying, the cost of materials or supplies generally increases in direct proportion to the amount used. For example, two computer printers typically cost twice as much as one computer printer.

Semivariable costs increase as production increases, but not in direct proportion to production increases. An example of a semivariable cost is the rental of copy equipment, which is frequently based on the number of copies made during a given period. As the number of copies increases, the per-unit cost generally decreases. To illustrate, if 500 copies are made on a copier during a given time, the per-unit cost may be 4.8 cents. But if 750 copies are made during the same period, the per-unit cost may be 4.2 cents.

To facilitate budget preparation, certain guiding principles should be followed:

What principles should guide budget preparation?

1. *Employee participation in budget preparation is advantageous.* When employees are allowed to participate, they are given an opportunity to become directly involved in the fiscal affairs of the department in which they work. When given an opportunity to participate, they generally develop a feeling of greater commitment; and they are more likely to show greater concern for the budgetary allowances.

2. *The budget should reflect realistic estimates of operating costs.* In preparing budgets, some individuals believe the mark of a good manager is keeping operating costs at a low level. While this is theoretically desirable, the practical results of this operating philosophy are not always optimal. In some instances, the amounts budgeted for certain operating costs are so minimal that operating efficiency is actually impeded. The budget should reflect realistic estimates that take into consideration operating cost increases resulting from inflation, greater volumes of work, and the like.

3. *The budget must provide for unforeseen circumstances.* Because budgets are sometimes prepared as much as one year in advance, predicting the unforeseen circumstances that may have an adverse effect on the budget may be nearly impossible. For this reason, the budget must have built-in flexibility to compensate for these circumstances. For example, a contingency fund may be used for this purpose.

4. *The employees should feel committed to the budget.* Unless employees have committed themselves to use of the budget as a guide for certain of their actions, the budget may not be successful. A lack of commitment is likely to result in employees' being wasteful, their misusing organization facilities, and their failure to exert the amount of effort for which they are being paid.

Revising the Budget. Even though considerable effort may be involved in preparing a budget, a variety of uncontrolled circumstances may require periodic **budget revision.** For example, costs of materials may increase, which can have an impact on the organization's profit. In addition, operating costs may increase, which creates difficulties for the organization as it attempts to produce output at a constant level.

What techniques are used to revise budgets?

Among the various techniques used to revise budgets are periodic review, progressive review, and moving review. The review technique used depends on the policies of the organization, the organization's financial picture, and the emphasis the organization places on budget revision.

When **periodic review** is used, the budget is revised at predetermined times for the remainder of the year. Depending on the organization, the budget may be reviewed each month, every two months, or perhaps every quarter for the remainder of the year. Figure 25–2 illustrates periodic review.

What is the primary characteristic of progressive review?

The **progressive review** technique uses standard-length time spans of perhaps six months. Therefore, the progressive technique revises the budget at specified times and for a constant length of time. Figure 25–3 illustrates the progressive review technique.

When the **moving review** technique is used, the budget is revised each month; and as one month is completed, the same month in the next year is included. Therefore, when the moving review technique is used, the budget is

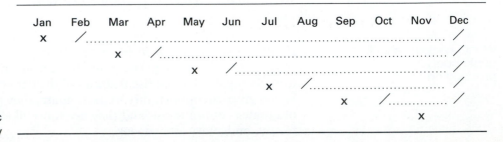

Figure 25-2 Periodic review

Figure 25-3 Progressive review

revised monthly, using the next twelve months in the process. The moving review technique is illustrated in Figure 25–4.

ZERO-BASED BUDGETING

What are the characteristics of zero-based budgeting?

As an alternative to traditional budget preparation, **zero-based budgeting (ZBB)** is being used by an increasing number of organizations and government units. According to its proponents, ZBB helps contain operating expenses.

Traditionally, annual budgets were prepared by increasing the current year's budget by a certain amount, usually a percentage. This practice makes two assumptions: (1) that all current expenditures are necessary and (2) that only the amount of budget increase needs to be substantiated. The traditional budgeting process may be erroneous because certain of the current year's expenses may not be justified. The continued use of an unjustified base in budget preparation perpetuates operating and cost ineffectiveness. Zero-based budgeting eliminates the "add-on" characteristic of traditional budgeting.

With zero-based budgeting, all programs and expenditures are reevaluated each budget period. This method requires that each department manager justify the department's existence each time a budget is prepared. When justification is not sufficient, reductions or even program elimination are possible.

Zero-based budgeting involves three steps:

What are the steps involved in zero-based budgeting?

1. Describing each discrete organizational activity in a decision package.
2. Evaluating and ranking these decision packages in terms of a cost-benefit analysis.
3. Allocating revenues on the basis of need.

Decision packages provide management with a mechanism for evaluating and comparing various organizational operations. They also identify and describe a functional activity or departmental structure. These packages enable management to evaluate and rank an activity against other activities that are competing for the same limited resources.

The preparation of the decision packages begins with a manager's analyzing in detail the status of the department's current operations and proposed operations. At this point, the manager considers alternatives that might be

Jan	Feb	Mar	Apr	May	Jun	Jul	Aug	Sep	Oct	Nov	Dec	Jan	Feb	Mar
x	/ .... /													
	x	/ .... /												
		x	/ .... /											

Figure 25-4 Moving review

available for performing these existing functions and perhaps the proposed functions. Once the alternatives have been evaluated, the manager selects the most appropriate course of action.

After the preliminary steps have been completed, the manager begins to analyze the function from a base of zero. While the most important service/ activity is selected and assigned a top-priority rating, the less important services/ activities are assigned decreased priority ratings.

The ranks of the various current and proposed functions prepared by each department manager are then forwarded to higher level managers who merge the various rankings. At this point, a determination can be made about which services/activities will be funded and which will not be funded because of their low-priority status. Only the justifiable services/activities are included in the budget, which helps eliminate waste of financial resources.

BUDGETARY CONTROL

After the budget has been prepared and approved, budgetary control becomes important. While the preparation process takes place once during the financial year, budgetary control is a continual process.

What use is made of budget reports?

The budget report is used frequently as a mechanism to coordinate, assess, and control various office operations. The detail needed in the budget report of the office function will be determined by the report's intended use. Because department reports are frequently consolidated to make a larger budget report, less detail will perhaps be needed than if such a consolidation does not take place.

A fundamental purpose of budgeting is the enhancement of the organization's profitability. In many instances, the organization's profit is improved because of the use of skillfully written, carefully prepared budget reports. Several types of reports might be prepared by the administrative office manager. Examples are summaries of actual and budgeted expenses; divisional or departmental summary cost reports; and daily or weekly labor reports comparing actual and standard worker hours.

When preparing budget reports, the following guidelines are suggested:

What guidelines are helpful in preparing budget reports?

1. *Exception situations should be pointed out.* Because managers and executives have an increasing number of job responsibilities, they have less time to devote to operations that are functioning smoothly and according to plan. Therefore, much of their time has to be devoted to operations that are not progressing according to plan. These operations are known as exception situations. Operations that exceed budgetary allowances should be identified in the budget report.

2. *When presenting figures in a report, a comparison base should be given.* Presenting figures without also presenting a base against which to compare the numbers renders the figures virtually useless. For example, to indicate in a report that the monthly telephone cost was $83.74 is meaningless. But to indicate that the budgeted amount was $70.00 or that the last month's bill was $67.29 provides a base against which comparisons can be made. The difference between the actual and projected costs of any budgeted item is known as a **variance.** Significant and/or ongoing variances will require managerial attention.

3. *Assist the reader by summarizing as much report information as possible.* The report writer can help the busy executive or manager by summarizing much of the information presented in the report. Generally, as reports are presented to higher management levels, fewer details and more summary information are desirable.

4. *When appropriate, reports should include interpretative information.* To assist the reader as much as possible, inclusion of interpretative information in the report may be quite useful. Perhaps the report writer is aware of the reasons why a particular expense exceeded the budgeted allowance. Unless the report reader is quite familiar with a particular situation, providing a valid explanation for the overrun may not be possible.

5. *Reports should be standardized as much as possible.* Preparing identical reports in the same format from one time to the next will help the reader. When reading a standardized format, the reader is able to recall more rapidly important facts or information regarding similar situations in earlier reports. Furthermore, standardizing the report format enables the reader to compare the information contained in one report with related information contained in other reports.

What are the common sections of budget reports?

Depending upon the nature of the budget report and its use, sections that may be included are (1) purpose of the report, (2) presentation of financial data, (3) summary, (4) conclusions, and (5) recommendations.

In some instances, the summary is presented first, followed by the recommendations and the three remaining sections. Consequently, if the report reader believes the first two sections contain a sufficient amount of information on which to make a decision, the remaining sections may not need to be read. If additional information is needed, however, it is available for the use of the report reader.

Increasingly, unit budget reports prepared on a monthly basis resemble the one illustrated in Figure 25–5. This type of report is an alternative to the narrative type discussed earlier. The variances are clearly identified and explained.

Department:	Office Services			For Month Ending		June 30, 20XX	
Expenses	Amount Budgeted	Actual	Over	Variance %	Under	%
01. Salaries	$6,500.00	$6,500.00				
02. Supplies	300.00	320.00	20.00	6.25		
03. Telephone	260.00	220.00			40.00	15.40
04. Xerox	280.00	340.00	60.00	17.65		
05. Postage	150.00	150.00				
06. Repairs	60.00	40.00	____	____	20.00	33.34
Totals	$7,550.00	$7,570.00	80.00		60.00	

Variances over or under allocation:

Expense	Percentage	Explanation
Supplies	+6.25	Significant increase in volume of work
Telephone	−15.40	Employees encouraged to correspond by mail or e-mail rather than make long-distance phone call
Xerox	+17.65	Significant increase in volume of work
Repairs	−33.34	Better equipment maintenance results in fewer breakdowns

Figure 25-5 Monthly budget report

COST CONTROL

What are the objectives of cost control?

In an office, **cost control** is concerned with the expenses incurred in performing various office operations. Cost control is also concerned with keeping expenditures as low as possible. A considerable amount of the administrative office manager's time will involve cost control activities.

The following list identifies several important objectives of cost control:

1. To develop standard costs for various office operations.
2. To develop within the employees a desire to be cost conscious.
3. To assist in the development of efficient operating procedures.
4. To allocate the costs of operations to the appropriate functions.
5. To identify inefficient operations.

Controlling the costs of some office operations is not warranted. For example, spending many dollars only to recommend that the cost of a particular operation be reduced by only a few cents is evidence of poor management. When identifying operations for which costs should be determined, the administrative office manager should take into consideration the following: (1) the volume of the operations, (2) the degree to which the operations are standardized, (3) the number of tasks involved in the operations, (4) the efficiency with which the operations are performed, and (5) the level of costs incurred in performing the operations.

The information used to determine operating costs can also be used to:

1. Identify how closely the costs of office operations conform with accepted operating costs.
2. Identify ways in which various operations are inefficient.
3. Help determine the type of new equipment needed when mechanizing office operations.
4. Help determine which work methods should be revamped or revised.
5. Identify which alternative office procedures are the most efficient in view of the costs involved.

Techniques for Controlling Office Operating Costs

What techniques are available for controlling office costs?

Several techniques are available for use in controlling the cost of office operations. While some of these techniques are rather simple to use, others are more complex, requiring certain prerequisite knowledge on the part of the administrative office manager.

Cost Breakdowns. An easy-to-use technique for controlling office costs is the **cost breakdown technique.** This technique involves determining what percentage of the total cost of an operation is classified as a salary or labor cost, a materials or supplies cost, and an overhead cost. The following percentages are generally regarded as being standard for most office operations:

- Salaries, including fringe benefits: 60–70 percent
- Supplies and/or services, including forms, postage, stationery, telephone, telegraph, and so on: 15–20 percent
- Overhead, including maintenance and depreciation of equipment, rent, utilities, taxes, and insurance: 15–20 percent

Some administrative office managers believe the salaries and supplies categories should be divided further into direct and indirect costs, as illustrated in the following:

How do direct salaries differ from indirect salaries?

- **Direct salaries:** The salaries paid to those individuals directly concerned with the production of office work. Examples include data-entry, keyboarding, word processing, and administrative assistants.
- **Indirect salaries:** The salaries paid to those individuals who help make the production of office work possible, although not directly involved in the production process. An example is the janitorial staff.
- **Direct supplies:** The actual supplies used in the production of office work. Examples include stationery and forms.
- **Indirect supplies:** The supplies used in producing office work that are not part of the work being produced. Example are magnetic disks and equipment depreciation.

To control office costs, the expenditures of actual operations are compared with standard cost breakdowns. If the actual costs exceed the projected cost breakdowns, the administrative office manager should make an attempt to determine the reasons for the excessive costs. After the reasons have been determined, the administrative office manager can develop a cost reduction plan.

Standard Costs. The **standard cost technique** for controlling office costs involves determining the unit cost of various office operations. As long as the operation can be broken down into the various component parts and the cost of each part can be determined, the unit cost of the operation can be determined.

The following example illustrates the use of the standard cost technique. Assume that the standard cost for processing claims in the health insurance industry is $2.56 per claim. In a particular insurance company, the financial data revealed that the processing of one hundred claims cost $310. Therefore, the unit cost incurred by the company was $3.10. Because this amount is significantly greater than the industry's standard cost, an investigation should be made to determine why the insurance company's cost exceeded the standard cost.

What information is provided by cost analysis studies?

Cost Analysis Studies. The last cost control technique to be discussed in this chapter is the **cost analysis study.** This type of study is used to compare the costs of a current period's operations with those of a prior period. For example, the office salaries for the current month might be compared with the office salaries for the same month a year ago. If the current figure is considerably higher than the previous figure, the reason for the increase should be determined.

Because the cost analysis study technique is greatly influenced by inflation and increases in operating costs, certain adjustments may have to be made when it is used during inflationary times. To have a comparable base, for example, the consumer price index (CPI) may be used to adjust the figures.

Taking Corrective Action. Control is necessary, especially when actual results fail to conform to anticipated results. Corrective action is necessary when the cost of an office operation exceeds an acceptable level.

The administrative office manager or office supervisors are responsible for undertaking the appropriate course of action when such action is necessary. Because many employees consider control to be a punitive measure, the individual responsible for taking the corrective action must use considerable discretion and judgment. Not all individuals respond in the same way to the corrective action.

The following is a composite of some of the reasons actual costs exceed anticipated costs:

1. Work procedures are not efficient.
2. Employees are not properly trained to perform their assigned tasks.
3. Equipment does not function properly.
4. Supplies are not the appropriate quality for the situation.
5. Employees are not cost conscious.
6. Employees lack motivation to perform at accepted levels.

Controlling Office Costs

An important element of cost control is determining whether actual costs exceed anticipated costs. When actual costs exceed anticipated costs, corrective action may be necessary. The most expedient way to control office costs may be to implement practices that prevent excessive costs. The following suggestions are offered:

Personnel Costs. Because personnel salaries account for the major portion of office costs, controlling personnel salaries provides greater flexibility than controlling costs in other areas.

How can personnel costs be controlled?

Personnel costs can be controlled in several ways. One suggestion is to make sure the number of personnel in each work unit is appropriate for the amount of work that needs to be done. If outside employees are needed because of a shortage of personnel in the organization, hiring additional full-time, permanent employees may be less expensive in the long run. Because turnover is likely to increase if employees believe their output expectations are too great, the cost of frequent selection, placement, and training of new employees may actually exceed the cost of hiring additional help.

Other suggestions include the following:

1. Hire employees who are qualified for the jobs they are expected to perform.
2. Train employees who are not qualified for the jobs they perform.
3. Determine which of the following alternatives results in the greatest cost savings to the organization when the amount of work to be done exceeds the number of personnel available: employee overtime, part-time employees, employees from temporary help agencies, or floating work units.
4. Inform employees of the output levels they are expected to maintain. Employees who are aware of expected output levels are more likely to reach their levels than those who are not.

Supplies and Materials Costs. Because most office work involves the use of supplies, forms, and materials, the cost of these items is another area of concern. One of the most significant ways to control these costs is to keep the wasting of supplies to a minimum. Waste occurs because employees are careless, make uncorrectable errors, or do not know how the supplies are to be used. In most instances, a desirable way to control waste of supplies is either to hire properly trained employees or to train existing employees.

How can supplies and materials costs be controlled?

Another way to control costs of supplies—more specifically the cost of forms—is to minimize the number of forms that are used. Before the use of a new form is approved, its need should be thoroughly justified.

Office costs can also be controlled to a certain extent by using equipment that accepts interchangeable supplies rather than requiring a particular brand of supplies. With the exception of copiers, most office equipment uses interchangeable supplies.

The cost of supplies can also be controlled by implementing an efficient inventory system. The absence of an effective inventory system may result in overstocking some supplies while understocking others. By reordering supplies before they are all consumed, the extra cost of rush orders can be kept to a minimum. Taking advantage of discounts on quantity buying will also help the organization control the cost of office supplies.

Equipment Costs. Because some office equipment is not as reliable as other equipment, maintenance costs increase. Before purchasing an expensive piece of equipment, the administrative office manager should investigate the dependability of several types of equipment. After a piece of equipment has been purchased, maintenance records should be kept. When a particular piece of equipment has a considerably higher than average maintenance record compared with other machines, its trade-off should be accelerated even if the equipment has not been used the specified number of years.

How can equipment costs be controlled?

Equipment costs can also be controlled by obtaining equipment appropriate for its intended use. Some office equipment is rather sophisticated; and if extra features are not needed for the efficient processing of present work, its purchase should be discouraged. If, however, the more sophisticated equipment may be needed in the future, its purchase is more justifiable.

Work Process Costs. Work processes are not always developed with the same degree of efficiency. Because some processes are inefficient, their modification should be considered. Some of the inefficiency of work processes can be identified by work measurement, work simplification, and systems and procedures analysis. Rather than controlling the costs of an inefficient work process, greater economy may result in first revising it.

In many work processes, any inefficiencies that are present are multiplied during each step of the process. Therefore, inefficient processes demand immediate attention.

How can work process costs be controlled?

In developing work processes designed to minimize costs, one should consider the following:

1. The cost of smooth-flowing work processes is less than the cost of erratic work processes.
2. Controlling the cost of work processes should focus on the greatest number of employees.
3. Work processes involving considerable backtracking and criss-crossing are more costly than processes in which the work flows in a straight line.

Overhead Costs. Because some overhead costs are variable—for example, lighting, air conditioning, and electricity—they can be controlled by making employees more conscious of their excessive use. As a result of increased energy consciousness among employees, specific programs designed to result in energy conservation are being developed. In many instances, all that is needed is an energy conservation awareness on the part of employees.

How can overhead costs be controlled?

Some organizations have brought about the conservation of energy by establishing contests in each department. The employees in the department who achieve the greatest net reduction in consumption over a specified period receive special recognition. In some instances, financial awards are presented to the employees in the winning unit.

IMPLICATIONS FOR THE ADMINISTRATIVE OFFICE MANAGER

Just as administrative office managers become noticed as a result of their performance in quantity and quality control efforts, they can also become noticed as a result of their performance and achievements in budgetary and cost control. For many years, top management focused only minimally on budgetary and cost control of the office function. This is no longer the case.

Nowadays, top management is well aware of the large percentage of organizational administrative costs that originate in the office area. By controlling these costs more effectively, the organization can increase its profitability.

Administrative office managers often have to make compromises between maximizing the efficiency of various office operations and allocating costs to these areas. For example, because managers have to operate within budgetary constraints, they are not always able to purchase equipment that will enable them to maximize the efficiency of the office function. Rather, a compromise approach is used in which they maximize efficiency as much as they can—given the resources with which they have to work.

REVIEW QUESTIONS

1. Why is budgeting important in budgetary control?

2. What are the advantages and limitations of budgeting?

3. Who is generally responsible for the preparation of the office budget?

4. What are the differences among fixed, variable, and semivariable costs?

5. Why is employee participation in budget preparation so useful?

6. Why must a budget provide for unforeseen circumstances?

7. What steps are involved in using the zero-based budgeting process?

8. Why should exception situations be pointed out in the budget report?

9. What advantages result from cost control?

10. As cost control techniques, how do cost breakdowns, standard costs, and cost analyses studies differ from one another?

DISCUSSION QUESTIONS

1. You are the administrative office manager in the company in which you work. Your superior, who was recently hired, asked that each unit manager for whom he is responsible be conservative in the expenditure of budgeted funds. He indicated that he likes to have his subordinates end the fiscal year with at least a 5 percent surplus in each budgeted item in their respective budgets because doing so "makes you and me look good to the higher ups." Discuss the implications of this situation.

2. When departments receive their budget allocations in the company in which you work, evidence suggests that managers who spend time "apple polishing" the vice president for finance receive higher allocations than those managers who do not. The managers who believe they are not treated fairly claim that this is a tactic used by top management to force them out of their positions. They believe that if top management makes life sufficiently miserable for these "nonsupportive managers," they will be forced to step down. Discuss the implications of using financial allocations as a way of rewarding or punishing managers.

3. Certain managers in the company in which you work are allowed to overspend their budgets. When this happens, their manager simply gives them unspent allocations from other managers' budgets. As a consequence, top management does not realize this is happening. Discuss the implications of this situation.

STUDENT PROJECTS AND ACTIVITIES

1. Interview a manager who has budgeting responsibilities as part of his or her position. Find out about the budget review process used by the manager.

2. Interview a manager in an organization that uses ZBB. What advantages and disadvantages does the manager see for the ZBB technique?

3. Going Online: Using the Internet, conduct an online search based on one of the concepts presented in this chapter or based on one of the chapter terms. Identify four or five things you learned from the material that you did not know prior to your online search.

Minicase

When she took office, one of the first actions of the new president of the Data Methods Corporation was to embark on a cost-cutting campaign. Costs in several areas were not well controlled during the presidency of her predecessor. As one of the department heads, the new president has asked you to provide the following information:

1. A list of suggestions for controlling the cost of office supplies.

2. A list of suggestions for controlling equipment and equipment maintenance costs.

Case

The Metropolitan Publishing Company, located in St. Louis, Missouri, is the publisher of the largest daily newspaper in the greater St. Louis area. The management of the organization has become quite concerned about rapidly increasing office costs.

One of the vice presidents recently undertook an informal study. He discovered that during certain times of the month, some employees are idle because of an insufficient amount of work. Some of the office supervisors he talked with also indicated that greater waste of office supplies seems to be occurring now than was the case earlier. An examination of energy consumption data also revealed that consumption has increased quite dramatically—and for no apparent reason.

The vice president who undertook the informal study has asked you, the administrative office manager, to prepare for him a proposal regarding the installation of a cost control program. Specifically, he has asked that the following information be included in the report:

1. Benefits that will result from the installation of a cost-control program.

2. Suggestions and guidelines that will facilitate the installation of such a program.

3. Suggestions for evaluating the effectiveness of the program once it becomes functional.

INDEX